Refo500 Academic Studies

Edited by
Herman J. Selderhuis

In co-operation with
Christopher B. Brown (Boston), Günter Frank (Bretten),
Bruce Gordon (New Haven), Barbara Mahlmann-Bauer (Bern),
Tarald Rasmussen (Oslo), Violet Soen (Leuven),
Zsombor Tóth (Budapest), Günther Wassilowsky (Frankfurt),
Siegrid Westphal (Osnabrück)

Volume 74

Kirk Summers / Scott M. Manetsch (eds.)

Theodore Beza at 500

New Perspectives on an Old Reformer

Vandenhoeck & Ruprecht

Bibliographic information published by the Deutsche Nationalbibliothek:
The Deutsche Nationalbibliothek lists this publication in the
Deutsche Nationalbibliografie; detailed bibliographic data available
online: https://dnb.de.

Typesetting: le-tex publishing services GmbH, Leipzig
Printed and bound: CPI buchbücher.de, Birkach
Printed in the EU

Vandenhoeck & Ruprecht Verlage | www.vandenhoeck-ruprecht-verlage.com

ISSN 2198-3089
ISBN 978-3-525-56041-9

To our mentors and dear colleagues
Douglas Kelly
John Woodbridge

Contents

Preface 9

Abbreviations 11

Kirk Summers, Scott Manetsch
Introduction: New Perspectives on an Old Reformer............................ 13

Part One: Theodore Beza's Place in History

Michael Bruening
Chapter 1: Before the *Histoire Ecclésiastique*. Theodore Beza's
Unknown Apologetic History of the Lausanne Pastors and Professors 57

Jeannine Olson
Chapter 2: Theodore Beza and Nicolas Des Gallars, Best of Friends? 77

Scott Manetsch
Chapter 3: Theodore Beza in England 97

Part Two: Theodore Beza and Biblical Interpretation

David Noe
Chapter 4: Suppress or Retain? Theodore Beza, Natural
Theology, and the Translation of Romans 1:18..................................... 139

Jennifer Powell McNutt
Chapter 5: From *Codex Bezae* to *La Bible*. Theodore Beza's
Biblical Scholarship and the French Geneva Bible of 1588..................... 157

Molly Buffington Lackey, Kirk Summers
Chapter 6: Beza Among the Lutherans. Acts 3:21 in the
Wittenberg *Catechism* (1571) and *Formula of Concord* (1580) 177

Part Three: Theodore Beza on Prophecy, Prodigies, and Predestination

Jon Balserak
Chapter 7: Theodore Beza on Prophets and Prophecy............................ 205

Eunjin Kim
Chapter 8: "The Leader of the Ancient Theologians". Beza's Use
of Augustine in His Predestination Doctrine....................................... 221

Kirk Summers
Chapter 9: Theodore Beza's Elegy on the Five Martyrs of Lyon.
Wonder and Consolation 241

Part Four: Theodore Beza and his Catholic Opponents

Theodore Van Raalte
Chapter 10: Compelling Each Other. Theodore Beza's Response
to John Hay as Part of Geneva's Anti-Jesuit Efforts 263

Jill Fehleison
Chapter 11: Nemeses to the End. Theodore Beza and His Last
Catholic Adversaries... 283

Part Five: Memories of Theodore Beza

Martin Klauber
Chapter 12: Michel Le Faucheur and Edme Aubertin.
Seventeenth-Century Memories of Theodore Beza's Eucharistic Polemics... 303

Max Engammare
Chapter 13: Theodore Beza, Collector of Paintings. Unexpected
Intellectual Commerce in the First Century of the Reformation.............. 317

Bibliography.. 341

Index 379

Notes on Contributors 391

Preface

The two editors of the present volume first met in Geneva in September 2005 while attending a colloquium there marking the 400th anniversary of Theodore Beza's death. The University of Geneva and the Institute of the History of the Reformation hosted the memorable gathering and Librairie Droz under the direction of Max Engammare (who contributes an essay to this volume) published the proceedings in 2007. Beza certainly received honors due his stature. Even so, we would seem remiss if we then allowed the occasion of the 500th anniversary of his birth to pass without receiving a similar observance. As 2019 approached, the editors began conversations about ways to pay homage to the influential reformer while at the same time highlighting the work of a new generation of scholars who are interrogating the life and work of the reformer from fresh perspectives. A valuable set of tools and conditions have emerged to aid their investigations, most notably the completion of the correspondence volumes begun by Alain Dufour in 1961, as well as a greater availability of archives and original source material online. Thus, the editors invited a group of gifted scholars from Asia, America, and Europe whose research focuses on Beza and his influence to submit papers to four panels, organized around certain broad themes, to be held at the Sixteenth Century Conference in St. Louis, Missouri in 2019. The H. Henry Meeter Center in Grand Rapids, MI, lent its *gravitas* to the event by sponsoring all four of these panels. The presenters further marked the occasion with a celebratory dinner one evening during the conference. Expanded versions of these papers now compose the contents of this volume. We hope that future generations will look back to 2019 and know that a group of scholars assembled for a weekend to remember the talents and convictions of an often-forgotten reformer who made such a significant impact on history.

As one would expect, we have many people to thank for the resulting publication. First, we are grateful to our contributors for their willingness to share their scholarship and for meeting the deadlines that allowed this project to move forward so quickly. They did so amid a devastating pandemic, the likes of which would have been so familiar to those living at Geneva and throughout Europe in the Early Modern period. We acknowledge too the excellent editorial work carried out by Bryan Just, a graduate assistant at Trinity Evangelical Divinity School in Deerfield, IL. Furthermore, we thank Thomas Carlton, a doctoral student in French at the University of Alabama, for kindly making the initial translation of Max Engammare's article for us, and to the University of Alabama's Department of Modern Languages and Classics for remunerating him for his services on our behalf. We are indebted to the encouragement and resources offered by Karin Maag, director of the Meeter Center, where many of the ideas in this volume first germinated and were brought to fruition; it was she who so graciously offered the sponsorship of the panels.

Finally, the editors recognize the many scholar-mentors in their own careers who modeled the dedication and academic acumen necessary to carrying out this project. We have chosen to single out two to whom to dedicate this volume, Dr. Douglas Kelly, who for many years taught theology at Reformed Theological Seminary and who guided some of Dr. Summers' first research on Beza, and Dr. John Woodbridge, a one-time mentor and now colleague of Dr. Manetsch, who just completed his fiftieth year on the faculty at Trinity Evangelical Divinity School. For these two colleagues and friends, along with the greater community of scholars who have touched and enriched our professional and personal lives over the years, we are profoundly grateful.

Abbreviations

AEG	Archives d'Etat de Genève
ANF	The Ante-Nicene Fathers
Archiv Tronchin	Archives Tronchin, Bibliothèque Publique et Universitaire, Geneva.
ARG	*Archiv für Reformationsgeschichte*
BC	*The Book of Concord*
BHR	*Bibliothèque d'Humanisme et Renaissance*
BSHPF	*Bulletin de la société de l'histoire du Protestantisme français*
CB	*Correspondance de Théodore de Bèze*
CO	*Ioannis Calvini opera omnia quae supersunt.*
CR	Corpus Reformatorum
CTJ	*Calvin Theological Journal*
CTS	Calvin Tract Society (Calvin's Commentaries)
Die Debatte	Die Debatte um die Wittenberger Abendmahlslehre und Christologie
HAAG	*La France protestante ou vies des protestants français*
Hist Ecclés	*Histoire Ecclésiastique des Église Réformées au royaume de France*
HZW	*Huldrych Zwingli Works*
JEMH	*Journal of Early Modern History*
Lefort, ed.	*Le Livre du recteur: Catalogue des Etudiants de l'Académie de Genève*
LW	Luther's Works
NPNF	Nicene and Post-Nicene Fathers
OER	*Oxford Encyclopedia of the Reformation*
PG	*Patrologiae Cursus Completus, Series Graeca*
PL	*Patrologiae Cursus Completus, Series Latina*
RE	*Real Encyklopädie für protestantische Theologie und Kirche*
RCP	*Registres de la Compagnie des Pasteurs de Genève.*
RHPR	*Revue d'Histoire et de Philosophie Religieuses*
RRR	*Reformation and Renaissance Review*
RTP	*Revue de Théologie et de Philosophie*
SCJ	*Sixteenth Century Journal*
WSFS	*Oeuvres de Saint François de Sales*
WTJ	*Westminster Theological Journal*

Kirk Summers, Scott Manetsch

Introduction: New Perspectives on an Old Reformer

The End Goal of Faith

Théodore de Bèze (or Theodore Beza) marked two birthdays in his life: the first on the 24th day of June, 1519, when his mother Marie Bourdelot and his father Pierre de Bèze welcomed him into this world in the cathedral town of Vézelay in Bourgogne; and a second that he identified as his spiritual birthday and "the beginning of all good things," when at the age of nine his uncle, who was overseeing his care, sent him to live and study in the home of Melchior Wolmar at Orléans.[1] Wolmar, a German immigrant who favored the new evangelical movement recently set in motion by Luther, immersed the young Theodore in a rigorous humanist curriculum and profoundly shaped his outlook on life. "Although I was a mere boy when you took me in," Beza recalls later, "and you had other, more advanced students of great hope to teach, what effort did you not put forth willingly for my formation?"[2] Under his German tutor, Beza learned both the new evangelical critique of Roman Catholicism and also the tools of the past: Hebrew, Greek, Latin, philosophy, ancient law and history. Wolmar instilled these in him until they became second nature. He learned Latin to the point that, as Alain Dufour observes, he could compose in the ancient tongue even more easily than his native French.[3]

It is natural for us, from our vantage point five hundred years later, to celebrate the first birthday and to honor the life of someone who had a significant impact on the sixteenth century. The occasion of the quincentennial of his birth (1519–2019) leads us to think in broad brush strokes of such a remarkable individual who put his stamp on so much: we remember Beza the theological polemicist, Beza the successor of Calvin, Beza the first rector of the Genevan Academy, and so on. None of these great achievements, however, should minimize in our minds the other way in which Beza reckoned time, beginning with his entrance into the residence of Wolmar and his slow spiritual awakening

---

1 Beza to Wolmar, 12 March 1560, in CB 3:45: "And therefore it happened that I arrived at your house on 5 December 1528, a day that I am in the habit of celebrating as none other than a second birthday, and rightfully so." Beza included these autobiographical details in a letter addressed to Wolmar that serves as the preface to his *Confessio Christianae fidei* (1560).
2 Beza to Wolmar, 12 March 1560, in CB 3:45.
3 DUFOUR, A. (2006), 12.

that began, by his own account, at age sixteen when there he read Heinrich Bullinger's *De origine erroris, in divorum ac simulachrorum cultu* (1529).[4] This was for him a pivotal moment, a starting point, one in which he began to prepare—though with fits and starts—for his life's calling as a pastor-teacher and to face the long and arduous process of personal sanctification.[5] The same Beza who so confidently defended the Reformed faith on an international stage, who for so long after Calvin's death bore the mantle of elder statesman in the cause, also carried a heavy inner burden for ministering to the Genevan flock and traveling his own path of obedience and renewal.

Beza tended to think of the Christian's experience as a journey. Throughout his many writings, especially the correspondence, the poems and emblems, the sermons that he preached, and his New Testament annotations, he characterizes this journey as one fraught with perils and temptations, requiring constant circumspection, resolute fortitude and endurance. He knew this from his own struggles. The man whom we know best through his most enduring accomplishments saw himself differently, as he anxiously fought with all his resources to finish the course and reach the final goal set before him. This perspective, his inward focus on his personal relationship with God, emerges starkly from a letter written to a wealthy Moravian baron Václav Morkovský the Elder of Zástřizl (1554–1600; hereafter Zastrisell the Elder) in September of 1597.[6] Though the letter never arrived at its destination, the aged Beza intended to relate news of the publication of his *Poemata varia*, the cost of which was borne by the Zastrisell family itself, and to communicate the difficulties created for Geneva and his own household by the ongoing war between France and Savoy. To these more mundane matters he adds the following solemn reminder of his personal spiritual journey, begun so long ago under the care of Wolmar:

> If you are wondering how I am faring and what I am doing, old age–but
> not any illness, by God's grace–prevents me from meeting my public
> responsibilities, so I keep myself at home, resting, consoling myself with
> prayers and private studies day and night, intent on just one goal, escaping
> a shipwreck of faith and hope to arrive finally at the longed-for harbor.[7]

---

4 On Beza's gradual conversion, see MEYLAN, H. (1976), and MANETSCH, S. (2006). Manetsch discusses the role of Bullinger's tract in Beza's disillusionment with Roman Catholicism on 42–43. For Beza's debt to the Zurich reformer, see Beza to Bullinger, 18 August 1568, in CB 119–123.

5 Meylan likens Beza's conversion to a "long hesitation of a Christian humanist." See MEYLAN, H. (1976).

6 Beza to Zastrisell the Elder, 26 August/5 September 1597, in CB 38:152–156.

7 Beza to Zastrisell the Elder, 26 August/5 September 1597, in CB 38:155.

Beza favors this harbor motif in his writings, as it spoke to him in optimistic terms of the end of the journey—the safety, the calm refuge of a port, the heavenly rest that awaits.[8] He worries much about shipwrecks too, though only in the metaphorical sense: the journey into the harbor is beset on all sides with perils. Writing later to the same Zastrisell the Elder and more aware than ever how quickly his health is failing, he describes the same state of mind: "intent on this one thing, that I not falter (*impingam*) in the harbor itself, as they say."[9] Serious illnesses constantly sent him to this mental picture. A protracted bout of bronchitis, for example, that incapacitated him for two whole months in 1580, made him assume that he was close to his life's goal. Thus, he confides to James Lawson (1538–1584), then Moderator of the Church of Scotland, that only God's grace keeps him from being overwhelmed by the tempests during his illness and faltering in the harbor itself (*in ipso portu impingam*).[10] He repeats the exact same sentiment to the tutor of Scotland's King James VI, Peter Young (1544–1628), a few months later.[11] This is the very same year in which Beza publishes an emblem in the edition of the *Icones* (dedicated to King James VI himself) that warns the godly not to approach their final destination undisciplined, recklessly, and at the mercy of fortune.[12] The accompanying woodcut, fittingly, depicts an out-of-control ship reaching the harbor with sails fully furled and beginning to sink. Later iterations of this emblem bear the revealing title "A Ship Faltering in the Harbor" (*impingens in portu*).

In the letter to Zastrisell the Elder cited above, Beza is concerned about a shipwreck *of faith and hope*. He uses a comparable phrase in the dedicatory letter of his paraphrases on Solomon's *Ecclesiastes* (1588), addressed to Jean Casimir, Count Palatine, and his nephew.[13] Beza considers the *Ecclesiastes* to

---

8 On the harbor motif, see the editors' comments at CB 41:33n.10. The motif appears frequently after Beza's sixtieth birthday (see Beza to Heinrich Möller, 21 August 1579, in CB 20:164 and n. 9 for Beza's application of it in the context of his own life's journey); it appears also in Beza to Rudolph Gwalther, 9 July 1580, in CB 21:171; Beza to Nicolas Rhediger, 21/31 December 1597, in CB 38:228; and Beza to Philippe Duplessis-Mornay, 4/14 July 1599, in CB 40:92. In writing to Crato von Krafftheim (13 March 1577, in CB 18:51), Beza speaks of the Lord as the helmsman who aims the ship for the port amid the tempests. Also in 1577 (ibid., 208), he describes himself as "wholly intent, by the kindness of God, on being transported through the midst of the tempests to the port." For *impingere* in the non-classical sense of "to stumble, to falter," cf. Beza's Latin translation of 1 Cor 8:9 (*impingendi causa*).

9 Beza to Zastrisell the Elder, 1/11 March 1600, 41:33. The editors note that he borrows the expression from Quintilian 4.1.61 and Augustine, *Enn. in Psalmum* 54.24. See also Beza to Paludius, 1/11 March 1600, in CB 41:41; and Beza to David Paraeus, 10/20 April 1660, in 41:46.

10 Beza to James Lawson, 16 March 1580, in CB 21:79.

11 Beza to Peter Young, 20 May 1580, in CB 21:127. Here the editors point to Augustine's *De vita beata* and *De cataclysmo* as the source of this image (see 128n.6).

12 Beza, *Icones*, Mm.iii[v].

13 Beza to Jean Casimir and his nephew, 15/25 August 1588, in CB 29:243–263 (appendix XI).

be a work that surpasses by far all the wisdom of the philosophers of antiquity. There is "no twist of the labyrinth of this mortal life, however winding," he says, "from which I feel this guide cannot extricate us." Human reason may resist these remedies for human affairs, but a mind that is open to them and not dependent on its own powers will avoid many a Scylla on the one side and many a Charybdis on the other. On these, people have frequently, not only faltered (*impegerunt*), but even made a shipwreck of piety and salvation. He concludes:

> In this work one does not hear Heraclitus uselessly weeping or Democritus mocking the wretched, nor someone blaspheming nature, or rather attacking God; no, one hears the Spirit, the one teacher of the truth, who seeks out the blind through all the byways of this world and takes them by the hand, leading them sweetly to the harbor of eternal happiness.[14]

In contrast to the Greek philosophers, Beza recognizes that human wisdom in and of itself fails to lead lost souls from the darkness to the harbor of eternal happiness. As a person tries to become clever in his own thoughts, apart from the revealed Word, he says in 1567 while referencing the heretical ideas of Valentino Gentile (c. 1520–1566), "they dash against the rock and make a shipwreck."[15] Thus in a later letter he warns his friend Pierre Loiseleur de Villiers (1530–1590) against panicking and relying on his own wits while traversing the vast sea of life's voyage: many an unfortunate sailor, he tells him, seized by ambition or desperation, or even a sudden ill-advised impulse, grabs the rudder of their own ship and consequently brings about their own ruin.[16]

In the letter to Zastrisell the Elder, Beza mentions two remedies he relies upon to safeguard his journey: he consoles himself by constant praying and by immersing himself in his studies. These are not mere platitudes. The reference to praying here is grounded in an important feature of Beza's spiritual life and piety, embodied in the "daily prayers" that Beza translated into Latin and sent to Zastrisell the Younger at the latter's request.[17] Since the young nephew of Zastrisell the Elder once lived in Beza's home while studying in Geneva, it seems likely that the young nobleman heard these prayers firsthand from Beza and admired them; there is also a likely connection to the somewhat mysterious book of household prayers published in London by John Barnes with the title

---

14 Beza to Jean Casimir and his nephew, 15/25 August 1588, in CB 29:259.

15 Preface to the Collection on Valentino Gentile, 5 August 1567, in CB 8:241 (ital. mine): "*impingens* scopulum *naufragium* faceret."

16 Beza to Pierre Loiseleur de Villiers, 23 July 1578, in CB 19:129.

17 MANETSCH, S. (2003), esp. 281. See also Beza to Zastrisell the Younger, 18/28 June 1597, CB 38:97 and n. 12.

Maister Beza's Houshold Prayers (1603, 1607, 1621).[18] The title page (1607) proclaims these prayers to be "for the consolation and perfection of a Christian life," and as such reflect Beza's fervent requests before God. Among the twenty-eight prayers included in the English version appears "A prayer to know God in Jesus Christ;" "A prayer for the well using of afflictions;" "A prayer to obtain the virtue of hope;" and "A prayer that we may not depart from the holy Church." In the latter, we hear a very familiar refrain from the deep wells of the reformer's soul:

> In only one thing, therefore, must my soul take comfort, that as Noah was preserved from the universal shipwreck in his wooden mansion by the promise that he kept in his heart, so that a thousand falling on his right hand, and a thousand on his left hand, he remained sound and safe under your wing, even so I hold myself assured against the assaults of sin, and in the midst of the woeful rocks of this world, yea, even in the straits of the grave, that you will always preserve from all calamities and miseries those who stand fast in the ark of your Church, grounded upon your Word in the gospel of reconciliation to the Lord Jesus, and depart in his faith.[19]

Beza prays for the same mercy once bestowed upon Noah. While the flood waters overwhelmed and *shipwrecked* his less-fortunate earthly compatriots, Noah remained protected in the ark with his family. Beza envisions the Christian life in the same way, as a journey in a boat through the flood of the deadly perils lurking beneath the waves and through the straits. For the Christian, the ark becomes the Church, and the solid ground on which it comes to rest the Word. "The Church," Beza remarks in his notes on 1 Timothy 3:15, "produces children of God and brings them up through the preaching of the Word and examples of truly good works." He continues: the chaotic world lacks this truth; to live outside the protective ark of the Church is to "inhabit a world of darkness, lies, error, deceit, superstitious fears, the spirit of confusion and bafflement, with corruption permeating everything."[20]

Beza also relies on prayer to steady his soul in the face of the storm buffeting and battering the Church. He is convinced that the Church is the safe haven from the universal shipwreck of the human race. Yet, Beza was keenly aware that the Church itself faced a relentless and direct assault from Satan and the

---

18 MANETSCH, S. (2003), 281.

19 BEZA, T., *Maister Beza's Houshold Prayers* (1603), F9^r-11^r (we have taken the liberty to modernize the orthography).

20 BEZA, T., *Iesu Christi Domini nostri Novum Testamentum* (1598a), pt. 2:351. The phrase *spirit of confusion* comes from Isaiah 19:14. In [Beza] to Dürnhoffer, 9 April 1577, in CB 18:81, Beza describes the enemies of the Huguenots in France as being "drunk with the spirit of confusion."

Figure 1   from *Les vrais pourtraits* (1581); Beza recognized that God's hand faithfully steadied
the Church while human frailty constantly destabilized it. Credit: Kirk Summers.

Antichrist, and that it is possible for individuals within the visible Church to
succumb to the onslaught, even if God always keeps afloat a remnant Church.
How will he and others endure the violence of their enemies without faltering?
He shares with Lorenz Dürnhoffer of Nuremberg (1532–1594)[21] his fear that if
tensions with Catholics and other confessional adversaries continue on pace
in various parts of Europe, that there will be "no street corner immune from
slaughter."[22] What a relief, he exclaims, that God has given this world as a place
to tarry for a time, as in an inn, but not to live permanently! Thus, he encourages
his friend: "Let us therefore appeal to God for either a timely departure from
here to Heaven, or the necessary constancy to finish the remainder of our course
successfully" (Figure 1).

Beza persistently appeals to God for the strength not to falter before arriving
safely in the harbor of his reward or not to stumble before reaching the goal

---

21 On Dürnhoffer and his favorable disposition toward the Calvinists, see Beza to Dürnhoffer, 9
    March 1570, in CB 11:80n.1; and CB 31:xxii.
22 Beza to Dürnhoffer, 3 May 1580, in CB 21:112.

(*meta*) of the course.[23] The remedy of prayer to which he constantly returns underscores the devotion of his heart and soul to the task of holding true to his faith. This intense piety and inner striving to "put to death the old man" remains an under-studied aspect of the reformer's story, but in every case it should be the starting-point to appreciate his life's work and accomplishments. His consuming passion to please and obey God, born from a spirit of gratitude and humility, expresses itself in myriad, complex ways. Whether Beza is sitting in the Consistory or writing a polemical treatise, whether he is attempting to influence international politics or exhorting the persecuted, one senses his fervent belief and devotion.

Of course, Beza could not have the influence on the world stage or in theological disputes or even as a leader among pastors at Geneva unless this fervency was matched in him by a remarkable intellectual rigor. Wolmar's tutelage together with other evangelical influences prepared him, not only to face the long journey of sanctification, but also for his calling as pastor, teacher and defender of the faith. He revealed in the letter to Zastrisell the Elder that he relied on prayer *and* study of the Word to steady his soul. In his retirement from public life, Beza devoted himself to the polishing of his fifth and final edition of the major annotations on the New Testament, which would appear the next year in 1598.[24] This scholarly work seems to have comforted him in many ways. While he only occasionally preached from the pulpit because of his physical frailty during these final years, he still had the mental capacity to serve the Church through translation and annotation, the influence of which on subsequent generations proved profound. With this, he retains the sense that he is fulfilling his calling to the end. He never characterizes his scholarly annotating, paraphrasing, translating, or poetry writing as burdensome, no more than he did his preaching; however, he did see the back-and-forth polemical exchanges as extremely tedious and perhaps unproductive. There was something about using his training and creativity to edify people directly that satisfied him.

But was Beza, then, not the austere polemicist as he is commonly depicted today? Is he not the one who systematized, dogmatized and gave Calvin's teach-

---

23 Johannes Crato (1519–1585) alludes to Beza's frequent use of this imagery in a letter written on 11 November 1582, in CB 23:201: "If I have written anything that misses the mark, please guide me back to the path. Often I remember that saying of yours: 'Those finishing the last stretch of life's race need more *spiritus*.'" The play is on *spiritus*: athletes need deeper breaths and more wind; Christians nearing the end of their life's journey need more support from the Spirit.

24 For Beza's immersion in this final edition of his major annotations in the year 1597 during his retirement (which began in 1595), see the editors' comments at CB 38:xv. On his editions of the New Testament, see KRANS, J. (2006), 202–206; GORDON, B./CAMERON, E. (2016), 187–216.

ing a Scholastic turn? Again, Beza despised the business of writing polemical treatises. In 1579, while writing to the Hebraist Heinrich Möller (1530–1589) about his forthcoming poetic renditions and paraphrases of the Psalms (a topic to which we will return later), an exasperated Beza sighs, "How I really prefer to spend my life consumed in readings and writings of this type rather than in writing doctrinal apologies!"[25] In the same year, he tells André Dudith that he will not waste time responding with yet another treatise to the Ubiquitarians, since he is more interested in Christian writings that console him about his coming death than anything Aristotelian.[26]

Even so, with reluctance, Beza continues to write these apologies, as irksome as they are, because he fears his opponents are not errant faithful, but calculating enemies of the true Church. Just three years later, in the dedicatory letter of the third volume of his *Tractationes theologicae* (1582), addressed to Walter Mildmay (1520–1589), Chancellor of the Exchequer for Queen Elizabeth, Beza warns that one of Satan's most shrewd deceits is to "dispatch his wolves to howl at the terrified flock," thus drawing away the pastors from their daily chores to defend dogma.[27] Beza recognizes that, while the pastors need to guard the truth, they do so against militant adversaries so tenacious in attacking it that they never cease to pour out their "scribblings" to confuse ordinary people. This sport of writing polemics, into which the pastors are drawn, plays right into Satan's schemes, and, he laments, "what was the outcome of those old disputes among philosophers is happening now: that too often among a great majority the truth imperceptibly descends into Academic skepticism and ends finally in open atheism." But there is something more that Satan's ploy achieves. Beza rails against the role that polemics play in transforming religion into a mere intellectual exercise, devoid of spiritual application on the level where people really live. He continues:

> Second–in Heavens name!–are we very far away now from introducing a kind of new Scholastic theology into the Church in place of a true theology that we should be proclaiming openly from the pulpit in the presence of all? Finally, how preposterous is it for us to seem willing to defend one side of this sacred city known as the Church–admittedly the most important side, but not the only one–while neglecting a breach by the enemy on the other side? This also is a very clever trick of Satan for which we should be on guard: we should not occupy ourselves with defending the dogmatic part of the Christian religion to the point that we not only do not show concern for the

---

25 Beza to Heinrich Möller, 25 March 1579, in CB 20:52. Möller, who studied under Melanchthon, taught Hebrew at Wittenberg from 1560–1574; he abandoned his post for his native Hamburg for fear of repercussions over his crypto-Calvinist leanings; see RE 13:269 and CB 13:40 n.5.
26 Beza to André Dudith, 2 June 1579, in CB 20:123.
27 Beza to Walter Mildmay, 15 March 1582, in CB 23:30.

practical part, which is the end goal of our faith, but go so far as to lose it altogether. This is the expected outcome for churches where the pastors have been thrown out and the pillars of the schools overturned: extravagance, drunkenness, usury, blasphemy, contempt for the divine Word receive no rebuke. Instead, it becomes the essence of piety to mock God and men with the marvels of an omni-majestic monster, to dissolve all hope of concord by incendiary speeches and writings, and finally to heap any and every kind of shameless lies, in front of the uneducated, on all those disagreeing with them.[28]

The editors of Beza's correspondence believe that by the phrase "new Scholastic theology" here Beza is alluding to the controversary caused by Pierre Ramus' (1515–1572) brief sojourn in Geneva in 1570 and the likelihood, in their view, that he "accused Beza of introducing a *Scholastic*, that is, Aristotelian educational program."[29] Should we imagine, however, that this controversy is still fresh on Beza's mind ten years after Ramus' death? Surely, Beza has new concerns and a different point to make to Mildmay.

The context of Beza's ruminations shows he worries that the legitimate defense of dogma could degenerate into Scholastic-type disputes that are excessively subtle and technical, thus detracting from the practical application of theology.[30] "Are we not very close to becoming Scholastic theologians again?" he asks, in essence. By far the majority of the treatises included in the third volume of the *Tractationes theologicae* reflect just such technical disputes with Lutherans on the presence of Christ in the Supper. Also, the phrase "omni-majestic monster," an allusion to the ubiquity controversy, suggests his current preoccupation. This endless dogmatic wrangling over finer and finer points, particularly with the Lutherans, is what is giving him pause, if not weighing down his spirit. In fact, he does not want to resort to Aristotelian subtleties. A quick perusal of his correspondence in the late 1570s and early 1580s reveals his growing angst over the creation and eventual publication of the Lutherans' *Formula of Concord* (1580). This is a doctrinal challenge that signals the further fracturing of the Church and portends persecution for Reformed-leaning Protestants in Germany. He feels the constant pull to refute its assertions with overwhelming

---

28 Beza to Walter Mildmay, 15 March 1582, in CB 23:30. Already in 1576 Wilhelm IV Landgraf von Hessen-Kassel advised Beza that too much "quibbling over things known only to God and inscrutable to human reason" will destroy the unity of the Church while doing nothing to strengthen the piety of its members (21 October 1576, in CB 17:203). On Beza and the balance of orthropraxy and orthodoxy in pastoral work, see MANETSCH, S. (2007).

29 Beza to Walter Mildmay, 15 March 1582, in CB 23:32–33n.5.

30 For Beza's concern for practical ministry over scholarly writing, see MANETSCH, S. (2012), 302.

precision.[31] It is noteworthy, however, that as early as 1578, Zurich antistes Rudolf Gwalther (1519–1586) conveys his appreciation for Beza's restraint in responding to the drafters of the Lutheran *Formula*, observing that he uses language that is "brief, clear, simple, yet weighty."[32] But at the same time, in a moment of startling frankness and contrast, Gwalther expresses his doubt that dogmatic theologian Girolamo Zanchi (1500–1576) can draft a common Reformed confession effective enough to counter the *Formula*.[33] Gwalther complains that Zanchi resorts to unnecessary ambiguity and ingenuity in his language, noting that he once proposed the impenetrable phrase, "The bread is the *essential* body of Christ, but not *essentially*." Such "intolerable" word-battles (λογομαχίαι) may be suited to the schools, Gwalther quips, but they are nonsensical to the faithful in the churches.[34] He much prefers Beza's more straightforward way of writing.

Gwalther's detection of a studied clarity in Beza's writing warrants our attention. For Beza, by his own account, orthodoxy remains fundamental to the Christian religion, but it does not exist for its own sake or as an academic exercise; it exists to support the restoration and renewal of God's people. The congregations in the churches need the pastor to translate dogma into practical

---

31 Indicative of the inner *pull* are Beza's comments about polemical writing to Rudolf Gwalther (5 October 1576, at CB 17:171): "Would that I were permitted to spend whole days in these tasks that are most proper to our calling [sc. as teacher], for my own consolation, at least, and since I am needed. But neither these times nor many other factors allow for it much, distracted as I am by various concerns, though still ones that are not foreign to the duties of our office. Still, I do what I can, and granted I am not doing as good a job as I should, I ask for help, and I pray that those who have an abundance of free time write these parts, now more necessary for us than before, seeing that much craftier adversaries have emerged as a result of our writings."

32 Gwalther to Beza, 26 March 1578, in CB 19:79. Gwalther is referring to Beza's work titled *Ad repetitas Jacobi Andreae et Nicolai Selnecceri calumnias responsio* (1578). This work of seventy-four pages does not directly concern the *Formula*, only a work of Selnecker that circulated in German and an oration of Andrea. On this see Beza's letter to Dürnhoffer, 25 March 1578, in CB 19:76–77.

33 Zanchi never accomplished this common Reformed synthesis, but did produce a confession laying out his theological positions that now exists in a modern critical edition: Zanchi, *De religione Christiana fides/Confession of Christian Religion*. Throughout much of 1578, Beza continued to call for someone to step forward to write a common confession, but to no avail (see Beza to Dürnhoffer, 20 May 1578, in CB 19:97), but he soon began to favor an idea, suggested to him by Dutch jurist Paul Knibbe, for a "harmony" of Reformed confessions (Beza to Gwalther, 27 May 1578, in CB 19:101–106).

34 Beza to Gwalther, 26 March 1578, in CB 19:79. Daniel Toussain later the same year complains to Beza, "I often advised him [Zanchi] that he should treat everything more briefly, clearly, and less scholastically, yet I did not insist as much as I wanted to." See Toussain to Beza, 14 September 1578, in CB 19:171. Beza himself tells Gwalther on 6 December 1578 that after reading some of it, he is not satisfied with the results of Zanchi's work (CB 19:190).

principles for living, which Beza identifies in the letter to Mildmay as the "end goal of our faith." In other words, the pastor's responsibility to the flock and even to other pastors lies ultimately in the work of encouragement, instruction, and correction. Beza felt this pragmatic calling in his own soul: "My larger annotations," Beza writes to Dürnhoffer with great satisfaction in April 1581, "are at press; I much more gladly put my effort on those than I do writing apologies and 'recooking cabbage.'"[35] The colorful reference to rehashed cabbage is borrowed from the Roman satirist Juvenal, who uses it as a metaphor for the repetitious drudgery of classroom lessons that suck the life from the schoolmaster, so to speak. Beza sees a parallel in the kind of apologies he is forced to write to defend one of the "walls" of the Church. The admission to Dürnhoffer is telling: while it is true that Beza left behind a conspicuous polemical corpus that earned him a reputation among some for being Aristotelian, Scholastic, and doctrinaire, we would be mistaken to think of this as his primary love rather than a rock of Sisyphus.[36] Beza devoted himself first and foremost to the standing of his flock and himself before God. A spiritual potency drives him more than an intellectual one. "Remember to pray for us here," Beza asks the same Dürnhoffer, referencing threats Geneva faced around the same time Gwalther wrote the aforementioned letter, "that we continue on in our current state of safety or else become a pleasing sacrifice to the Lord."[37] And it was only a year earlier that he confides to the same Dürnhoffer his willingness to win the martyr's palm while "relying on the Lord's goodness and kindness."[38] These simple words, so full of devotion and resolve to surrender to God's will even to death, reflect Beza's unbending commitment to live the Christian life to the very end.

Christian Humanism

The *shipwreck* figure that Beza employs with such frequency and his uneasiness with abstract doctrine exposes an underlying and underappreciated current of devoutness within his personality. Another current running deep in Beza's spirit accounts for much that is patently observable in his life's work: the humanistic learning that Wolmar imparted to him in those early years continues to inhabit his mental and moral reflexes throughout his life. Despite the criticism he directs to secular learning from time to time, with balance and caution he

---

35 Beza to Dürnhoffer, 25 April 1581, in CB 22:96.
36 DUFOUR, A. (2009), 39.
37 Beza to Dürnhoffer, 25 March 1578, in CB 19:76.
38 [Beza] to Dürnhoffer, 9 April 1577, in CB 18:80.

himself consistently embraces it. His German tutor formed and molded him through the study of antiquity, instilling in him its language, its best ideas and values, its rhetorical power and its storehouse of treasure. He taught him to engage it. Although first and foremost a religious reformer, Beza also embodies well the humanist ideal of the Renaissance. When his mind grows weary from the bitter theological debates and the battles with Satan, Beza seeks refuge in the measures and rhythms of poetry, in beautiful expressions and themes, and in clever turns of phrase that draw from and vie with the remnants of Greek and Latin literature. Beza in no way rejects the best attainments of the human spirit.

Beza's 1599 edition of poetry includes a poem written by Jean Jaquemot (1543–1615) that testifies to the complex interrelationship between piety and learning in Beza. Jaquemot was no passing acquaintance.[39] Son of a refugee from Bar-le-Duc, he served as Rector of the Genevan Academy from 1586–1591. He not only translated Beza's *Abraham Sacrifiant* into Latin and advised Beza on the publication of his 1597 edition of poems,[40] he imitated Beza's own output by writing tragedy, prayers and poems, even including some of the same stock characters in the latter, such as the fictional Zoilus.[41] In his *Lyrica* (1591), he addresses an acclamatory ode to Beza and rejoices when Beza approves his poetry; in another volume, he includes two tombeaux to Beza's wife.[42] But it is the poem appearing in Beza's 1599 volume that draws special attention here because it is directed to Beza's library.[43] Beza must have recognized it as an homage to a poem on his library that he himself originally published in his 1548 edition of poetry and reprised in later editions.[44] Beza's original speaks to the breadth of his humanist learning by describing in glowing terms the cherished books on his shelf. Here we find a nod to Livy, Ovid, Propertius, Plautus and Terence, and more on the Latin side; and Homer, Aristotle, Sophocles, among others on the Greek side. Although these texts point to an earlier period in his

---

39 On Jaquemot, see HAAG 4:39–40. Jaquemot left Geneva for a brief time to serve the church of Neuchâtel in 1591 (see Beza, in the name of the Pastors of Geneva, to the Classis of Neuchâtel, 8/18 July 1591, in CB 32:104). See also the letter from Beza and Jaquemot to the church at Neuchâtel, 14/24 October 1589, in CB 30:272 and n. 1.

40 Jean Jaquemot's translation of the *Abraham Sacrifiant* appears in the 1597 edition of Beza's poetry (283–343) and as an independent edition: *Abrahamus sacrificians: Traegaedia Gallice a Th. Beza iam olim edita, recens vero latine a Ioanne Iacomoto Barrensi conversa*. For his involvement in the publication of Beza's *Poemata varia* (1597), see CB 37:233n.13.

41 For the prayers comparable to Beza's *Houshold Prayers*, see JAQUEMOT, J., *Musae Neocomenses* (1597), 75–98.

42 JAQUEMOT, J., *Lyrica* (1591), 62–64; 110; *Variorum poematium liber* (1601), 155–156.

43 The poem appears in BEZA, T., *Poemata varia* (1597), at Aa3.

44 On the poem and its fortunes, see SUMMERS, K. (2001), 220–221 and 347–348; SUMMERS, K. (1991); and LUDWIG, W. (1997), 141–144.

life marked by more secular allegiances, Beza never abandoned them, as his frequent allusions to them throughout his writings testify.[45] Jaquemot's address, however, is not to the individual books in Beza's library, which by 1597 had grown considerably in number,[46] but to the Library itself, here personified, with the request that it make room to receive Jaquemot's own books of poetry. The poem succinctly and cleverly expresses the kind of interplay that took place in Beza's library between books as serious sources for the truth and books as a refuge from the things that trouble the mind. Jaquemot pens the following hendecasyllables to honor his mentor:

> *To the Library of the Most Reverend Doctor Theodore Beza*
> Learned Library of the great Beza–the nine sisters of Phoebus and Charm
> devoted to the chorus of the Muses admires nothing more genuine, nothing
> more eloquent, elegant, or erudite than him–would you please place a few
> books on your lowest shelves, if there is room? It is a small gift my daring
> Thalia now bids me dedicate to you. But do not hand them over to your
> master to read immediately; wait until you see him freed from heavy cares
> and seeking to break the long tedium of his serious Muse with honest diver-
> sion. Then and only then, faithful Patroness, please ask him to relax with our
> Muses. If he finds a bit of pleasure in reading them, they will not fear the
> rather insolent tongues of the crowd, nor will the drinking vessels of the stall
> that sells hot pepper be meagre.

The ending likely alludes to Horace, *Epistle* 2.1.269-70, where the Augustan lyricist dismisses his rivals' poems as worthy for the shops in the district where peppers are sold. Horace imagines that the shopkeepers could use the sheets of paper with their ephemeral poems to wrap up purchased spices for patrons. Zurich classicist and theologian Josias Simler (1530–1576) implies its currency as a literary reference when he appeals to it in an analogous context in a much earlier letter to Beza: if the Genevan theologian will reply to the Antitrinitarians, Simler says in essence, he will gladly send his own response to fishmongers and Horace's pepper shops.[47] Here, in contrast, Jaquemot hopes to celebrate in

---

45 For Beza's embrace of humanistic learning throughout his life, albeit with appropriate caveats, see SUMMERS, K. (2018b). Here in the poem addressed to his library, Jaquemot praises Beza for combining serious spiritual matters with more humane pursuits. Jaquemot himself in another poem praises the study of the ancients and advocates for an openness to reading pagan authors: JAQUEMOT, J., *Musae Neocomenses* (1597), 169–170.

46 On the sale of Beza's library toward the end of his life, see Georges Sigismond de Zastrisell to Beza, 1/11 March 1598, in CB 39:42–43, esp. n. 2 and 106–110.

47 See Simler to Beza, August 1568, in CB 9:132, with additions by the editors at CB 11:348. Simler, who is sending his work *De aeterno Dei Filio* as a gift to Beza, expresses his wish in the accompanying letter that Beza will write a tract against the anti-trinitarians: though he realizes Beza is occupied by the sad situation confronting the Reformed churches in France,

such a district with substantial draughts and toasts to Beza's approval.[48] The very elusiveness of the concluding pun underscores the easy transition that Jaquemot envisions within Beza's study. The reformer moves deftly between the *grave* Muse of theology, polemics, and academics, to the *relaxing* Muse of epigrammatic puns and pleasing lyrics. Jaquemot observes in Beza a marriage of passionate spirituality and deep classical learning, of humanism and a thirst for serving God. Beza wants to be correct in his doctrine, no doubt—he loathes inexactness and ambiguity—but he also stays grounded to his humanity through the ancient models. His library catered to both these facets of his personality.

Beza dreamed of a religious peace that would allow him to retire from his defense of the faith to literary pursuits in his library. He says so explicitly in a letter to his friend André Dudith (1533–1589).[49] When political changes compelled the Hungarian humanist and former Roman Catholic bishop of Pécs to retreat from public life to Moravia, Beza observed that he was enjoying the kind of leisure that Scipio Africanus once did, that is, withdrawn from service, not out of desire for inaction and self-indulgence, but because of the vicissitudes of fortune. Beza regrets that the world will lack the benefit of his public service, but adds on a more personal and self-reflecting level: "Still, when I consider you as an individual, I cannot but envy your solitude, in which I do not doubt but that you prove Cicero right when he says, 'Nothing is sweeter than leisure devoted to literature.'"[50] This is a forced leisure that allows for time to read, think, and write. Cicero certainly knew such extended periods of leisure on his country estates, reading literature and discussing philosophical ideas with a gathering of friends. For these two humanists of another era, such an ideal scenario smacked of paradise. In an earlier letter, Dudith requests that Beza send him some intellectually gifted person to keep him company,[51] and Beza responds that he would gladly oblige if only the troubles of the times permitted. Unfortunately, he says, these adversities have "turned almost all Gauls from refined citizens into soldiers, from cultivators of the Muses into savage warriors."

---

    still, if he should write it, Simler adds, "gladly I will see to it that these writings of mine are sent off to the fishmongers and, as Horace said, 'carried down to the district where they sell incense and perfumes and pepper.'"

48 Jacques Lect (1558–1611) expresses a similar sentiment when sending his own volume of poems to Beza: "I hope that then Apollo, who now scarcely offers me a few drops of water, will fill my goblets to the brim." See BEZA, T., *Poemata varia* (1599), 98r. Lect is referring to his *Poematum liber unus*.

49 Dudith left the Roman Catholic Church while on a mission to Poland, where he met and married a Reformed woman. On Dudith, see COSTIL, P. (1935); GÁBOR, A. (2009); and Christophe Thretius to Beza, 15 September 1567, in CB 8:170n.8.

50 Beza to Dudith, 15 December 1577, in CB 18:207.

51 Dudith to Beza, 10 September 1577, in CB 18:178–182.

This cultivation of the Muses for Beza here stands in as a shorthand for human beings living to their potential as human beings. God did not create human beings for conflict, but for interaction and the enjoyment of beauty. It is this shared appreciation for "leisure devoted to literature," surely, that led Beza to dedicate the 1569 edition of his poetry to Dudith.[52]

To judge by the frequent references made to ancient authors in later poems, Beza continues to add classical texts to his library throughout his life. He does so without apologies or disparagement; the constant assumption is that these writings can enrich his thought and in some ways even strengthen his piety. We can glean this from a poem that he composes in late 1578 or early 1579; it is a commendatory poem meant to accompany Jean de Serres' new edition of the works of Plato.[53] As is to be expected in such cases, Beza offers high praise for the scholarly editing and annotating of Serres, without whom, we are told with a considerable degree of hyperbole, the ancient philosopher would succumb to the ravages of time. More importantly, though, Beza also uses the opportunity to consider the proper Christian attitude to pagan wisdom by addressing Plato himself. For a pastor and theologian so keen on defining and defending orthodoxy within the Church, his accommodating stance to a system of thought not originating from Christianity comes as a surprise. The full poem reads as follows:

> If the fall of the human race left behind any trace of the divine in mortals—
> the fall that enveloped the mind's light in a blinding fog and made the will
> tumble so completely and miserably headlong into vice–even this residual
> element seems to have been swept off along with right reason. If someone
> should disagree that these were restored and embodied in you, great Plato,
> as though by divine agency, what would this person not deny with a bold
> face? And yet, what else is this intellectual light you provide except one akin
> to the moon's pale light that illumines the dark night? Thus, we marvel at the
> celestial gifts you preserved, and we can study them, appropriating and
> adapting them for our purposes. This we may do, provided the light that
> shines from Heaven above for us, the only light drawn from the bosom of
> the true God, alone governs us as we wander on the sea of the world. But
> how I would wish, immortal glory of wise men, that you bore the gifts of
> this heavenly light as well, for truly then you would deserve to be called a
> divine prophet! Still, since such wishes are futile, what remains but for me
> to thank you for this extraordinary gift? Now that the rust is finally rubbed
> away, rust that–alas!–so many introduced, as did the long passage of time,
> you finally shine beautifully from Serres' great skill and labor. For this

---

52 The text can be found at Beza to Dudith, 14 May 1569, in CB 10:88–100.

53 For the poem, see CB 19:226–227 (Note that line 13 should not end in a period but a semi-colon; and in line 24, *niteas* should be emended to *niteat*); and *Poemata varia* of 1599, 109ᵛ-110ʳ. For its original context: SERRES, J., *Platonis opera quae extant omnia* (1578), ***.vʳ.

reason, Plato, we owe you many things, but I must say we owe Plato himself to you, Serres.[54]

Serres has presented the text of Plato with exceptional skill; this is the basic premise of the tribute. More to our interests, though, the poem illustrates how certain themes wend their way through Beza's writing, crossing genres and making their appearance in diverse contexts. They are themes incubated and birthed from the principles, values and metaphors that populate the reformer's thinking. For us, this means that his worldview can and should be pulled together and examined from across his literary output. Each type of writing along with its circumstances or aim adds nuance to certain central, leading ideas.

Thus, in the poem for Serres we recognize a number of concepts familiar from elsewhere in Beza's writings. As we have noted before, for example, Beza imagines the Christian experience in terms of a maritime voyage. As with all travelers on the sea, the Christian needs guidance, though for this type of journey a divine helmsman is required, seeing that human wisdom does not suffice to reach the intended harbor safely. Calvin's doctrine of the noetic effects of the Fall—the notion that, in the fall of Adam and Eve, mankind's rational capabilities were severely damaged—is represented through imagery of light and fog.[55] The Fall, as the poem says, ruined the will completely, but in the case of the rational mind some dim light still shines, even if not always visible under the thick mist. In other words, by God's grace human beings can grope through that darkness and still stumble upon a measure of earthly truth. For the phrase "blinding fog," Beza uses the Latin *caligine caeca*. Notably, he pens this around the same time that he would have been composing a series of three emblems (published in 1580 with the *Icones*) teaching visually and poetically this very truth by way of the spatial positioning of the moon/earth/sun.[56]

---

54 *Poemata varia* of 1599, 109v–110r.

55 For Calvin on the noetic effects of the Fall, see HELM, P. (1998); HELM, P. (2004), esp. chapter 5 on the soul and its ability to reason rightly, and chapter 8 on natural theology (esp. 238–240); ADAMS, E. (2001); STEINMETZ, D. (1991); HOITENGA, D. (2003). See also the overviews by SCHREINER, S. (2009); and LANE, A. (2009). Also, SUMMERS, K. (2018b), esp. 141–144.

56 The emblems (by which we mean both poem and image) appear at BEZA, T., *Icones, id est verae imagines virorum … illustrium* (1580a), Pp.iii^r-Qq.iv^r. The connection between the poem praising Plato and the three emblems is betrayed through his echo of the fog metaphor with the Latin phrase *atra caligine*, that is, *dark fog*, or perhaps better, *obscuring fog*. The three emblems together form a single narrative. In the first, the moon stands opposite her brother the sun and reflects his light with her full face (here the Artemis/Apollo conceptions of the heavenly bodies predominate), just as the Church shines with full splendor when face-to-face with Christ. In the second emblem, however, the earth, representing human wisdom, intervenes between the sun and the moon, showing how the pure radiance of the Church can grow dark. Human

Human wisdom operates surrounded by a dark, almost impenetrable mist. But Beza, as other Christians embracing some of the humanist ideals, does not find the mind completely incapacitated to the extent the human will is. The ancients exercised remarkable insight, attaining to some degree of truth and beauty. This was a concession on the part of God, a virtue graciously extended so that human beings could retain a modicum of dignity while functioning and coexisting in the world. Thus, Beza can praise Plato for the "celestial gifts" he preserved, while signaling his readiness to engage the philosopher's ideas as worthy of study. He even talks of adapting and appropriating Plato's teaching. His careful choice of words is important, because they indicate his willingness to gain "common grace" insights from Plato, but not become a Platonist.[57] It is only in the context of Christ's work to redeem his people from the damage caused by the Fall that Plato can be truly useful. In other words, what Plato teaches must be adjusted in accord with the heavenly knowledge that only comes through renewal in Christ. He illumines the mind so that the faithful can understand more clearly everything in the world they see. Primarily, the redeemed understand that God has created everything for his own glory and that creation operates within his purpose and power. Still, the poem makes a remarkable assertion that reveals a deep appreciation for the human capacity to learn and know: if only Plato could have truly recognized the divine aspect in the nature of things, Beza regrets, he himself would not only be praising him for his earth-bound wisdom, he would be extolling him as a prophet of God! Such was Beza's appreciation for mankind's intellectual achievements.

Friends and Correspondents

We have so far given attention to several aspects of the Genevan reformer that add richness and depth to his character. We have observed in his most intro- spective moments a spiritual sensitivity and devoutness manifesting itself in surrendering to God's mercy. He contemplates his journey with all its hazards, the endurance needed for the race, the end goal, the harbor and the hoped-for

---

wisdom, in essence, envelopes the Church in a mist from which it is difficult to peer outward at the truth. The third emblem shows the moon positioned between the earth and the sun, revealing a dark face toward the earth itself while illumined on the opposite side by the bright sun. In this case, those on the earth cannot see the darkened moon and therefore imagine that it has disappeared, just as human wisdom imagines the martyrs of the true Church have vanished. The enemies of Christ do not realize that the martyrs now look upon his face up close and shine more brightly than they can imagine.

57 Calvin discusses the value of secular wisdom and common grace insights at *Institutes* II.ii.12–24 (CO 2:195–205). See also SUMMERS, K. (2018b), 142–143.

rest. Conspicuous too is an inner pastoral compass that regularly redirects his impulses from the defense of orthodoxy, seemingly interminable and increasingly academic, to what is immediately practical and useful for the flock. He is, certainly, attuned to the innate simplicity and more mundane concerns of the faithful. How should they live day to day? From where do they gain assurance in their faith? These kinds of questions lie far from the purview of abstract theological debates, yet they give shape and purpose to much of what Beza writes and does. We should not overlook his love of poetry and literature either. Before fleeing Paris to devote himself to the Protestant cause, Beza dreamed of living the life of a Latin poet. But more broadly speaking, he was true to his training under Melchior Wolmar in that he embraced all that ancient learning had to offer. Yet, even after abandoning this purely literary proclivity for a more celestial-oriented vocation, he did not completely turn his back on the ancient world. As a reformer, he continued to engage it as a way to think about the human potential as God originally intended it to be. In some ways, he thought, the Greeks and the Romans had pointed humanity back to its roots, even if feebly and inadequately so. They remain, in other words, a valid starting point for talking about the proper place for human beings in the universe. What does it mean to be a man or a woman perfectly integrated into God's creation? The ancients had at least recognized that human beings thrive best where there is harmony, order, beauty, righteousness and piety, even if they never realized them as they should.

Fortunately, Beza left behind a voluminous and varied correspondence, which we have relied on here to support various points in our characterization of him.[58] Without question, these are valuable historical documents that chronicle events—sometimes major, sometimes trivial—that would otherwise be lost to history. They function for the latter half of the sixteenth century much as Cicero's equally ample correspondence functions for the late Roman Republic, if one is alert to both the personal spin and misinformation that pervades the great orator's letters. This is not to say that Beza writes without his own Genevan and Reformed biases, but we do not see him fashioning the facts to enhance his own personal prestige as does Cicero, who often looks out first and foremost for his own standing, power and reputation. Even so, Beza mirrors Cicero in the range of friendships he maintains: some are cordial and practical in nature, others political, or existing primarily as part of a network for the sharing of international news. But just as Cicero has his Atticus, an intimate and trusted friend with whom he could share personal information or unguarded thoughts

---

58 The extant letters to and from Beza, dating from 1539 to 1605, number 2,792 in the published correspondence.

and emotions, so Beza has a close circle of correspondents with whom he rejoices, bemoans, regrets, empathizes and confides. At times he gives consolation or receives it in turn. It seems that it is here, in the correspondence with his most trusted friends, and not in Geneva itself, where Beza's own spiritual needs are ministered to the most. Given their less-guarded, more personal nature, these exchanges with trusted friends fill in missing lines and add touches of color to the portrait of our reformer.

Beza had one such friend in Heinrich Bullinger (1504–1575), antistes of the Zurich church after Zwingli and father-in-law of the future antistes Gwalther (mentioned above). Perhaps in the rich correspondence with Bullinger, more than that with any other, the density of Beza's personality, including his internal vulnerabilities and uncertainties, stands on full display.[59] In addition to sharing information and strategizing with Bullinger about the direction of the Reformed movement, Beza finds in him a confidant, mentor, spiritual encourager and steadying hand.[60] "I have always attributed to you paternal authority and I always will," Beza tells Bullinger in a mysteriously strained exchange of 1573.[61] The other letters that would shed light on the matter of contention are lost, but what is clear is that Beza is at pains to assure his old friend of his continuing respect and sincerity toward him. With so many depending on him for advice and guidance, Beza seems genuinely relieved to have someone who will question his actions and motives to keep him on the right path.

Several threads running throughout the letters illustrate this. In one remarkable exchange extending over several years, Bullinger can be seen constantly tempering, or attempting to temper, Beza's bitterness toward the controversial Parisian educator and rhetorician Pierre Ramus (1515–1572). Beza's longstanding hostility toward Ramus continues to seethe even after the latter met an untimely death during the general massacre of Huguenots in France that began on St Bartholomew's Day in August 1572. Writing to Beza a few months after the tragic event on 10 January 1573, Bullinger describes a work of suspected apostate Pierre Charpentier (1524–1574) that has come to his attention; in it, this thorn in the side of Protestant leaders attacks Beza personally and blames him and his followers for the bloodshed in France.[62] Bullinger notes that Charpentier seems to be claiming both Ramus and Francesco Porto (1511–1581),

---

59 For an overview of the correspondence between Bullinger and Beza, see CAMPI, E. (2007).

60 In the signature of a letter of 1554, Beza calls himself "a son born by you in the Lord." See Beza to Bullinger, 7 May [1554], in CB 1:128.

61 Beza to Bullinger, [October 1573], in CB 14:235.

62 Bullinger to Beza, 10 January 1573, in CB 14:2. The title of the work is *Lettre de Pierre Charpentier, Jurisconsulte, addressée à François Portes, Candiois, par laquelle il monstre que les persecutions des Eglises de France sont advenues, non par la faulte de ceux qui faisoient profession de la Religion, mais de ceux qui nourissoient les factions et conspirations qu'on appele la*

Professor of Greek at Geneva during this time, as partisans supporting his side in this particular argument, and so he advises Beza that a response is necessary.[63] Ramus is dead, however, and Bullinger submits that he was a better person than to approve of this sort of divisiveness and betrayal. In any case, the Zurich reformer believes Beza has carried on his vendetta against Ramus long enough and therefore includes this gentle rebuke: "I have gathered from your letters that you and Ramus did not see eye to eye on all matters. But now that he has died in martyrdom, I would prefer you not continue to express your aggravation with him. And seeing that there is enough aggravation all around us, I pray that the Lord protect his churches from evil."[64]

Bullinger's counsel is marked by varying degrees of understatement. His concession that in the past Beza and Ramus "did not see eye to eye on all matters" hardly reflects the plethora of disagreements and the level of enmity. As Ramus remained ostensibly Roman Catholic until 1569 (albeit for years suspected of Protestant leanings), certainly Beza had little cause to waste time on him before that date. Nonetheless, in two works published in 1543, Ramus famously vilified the supremacy of Aristotelian logic in the schools while promoting his own program to reform how students should think and analyze problems. He followed these with additional works disparaging the methodologies of several Classical thinkers. These attacks on traditional logic and time-honored texts without question long rankled Beza. Early in 1572, he writes to Bullinger that, when he was in Paris in 1543, he saw firsthand the sort of trouble Ramus' ideas could cause. He adds that already in 1562, during a return trip to France, he feared Ramus and his educational reform as potential sparks for discord among Protestants themselves.[65] Beza attempts to undermine Bullinger's rather positive opinion of Ramus by arousing fears of anarchy in the Church:

Cause. For a discussion of this work and relevant bibliography, see KINGDON, R. (1967), 112–113; MANETSCH, S. (2000b), 46–50.

63 Ironically, Ramus and Charpentier were bitter adversaries, famously quarreling before Parlement over the transfer of a royal professorship in the mid-1560s, and so it is clear that Charpentier is being disingenuous by appealing to him (see SKALNIK, J. [2002], 83–87). As for Porto, the editors of Beza's correspondence note that Charpentier's entire letter is "written under the assumption that Porto does not approve of Beza and the extremists, but should be counted with the party of moderates who respect the edicts and are friends with Charles IX, who treats them well." This association put Porto in an uncomfortable position and forced him to write a response. On his response, published in both Latin and French, see MANETSCH, S. (2000b), 50.

64 Bullinger to Beza, 10 January 1573, in CB 14:2.

65 Cf. Beza's tirade against Ramus as a fomenter of discord at Beza to [Joachim Camerarius], 1 July 1572, in CB 13:144–145 and n. 11.

I did not write about his erudition, nor his eloquence, but about the man's character, seeing that I first encountered it some thirty years ago. I saw with my own eyes at that time the controversies he stirred up in the Parisian Academy, what sorts of viewpoints he espoused in literary matters, and what and how many evils he inflicted by opening a school of the most outrageous ignorance. Therefore, when I was in France ten years ago and I came to understand that he in no way favors our side, already then I predicted— that I were a false prophet!—that the spirit of discord will enter into the French churches together with this man. Who imagines we could be on good terms with someone who thinks Aristotle a sophist, Cicero ignorant of how to teach rhetoric, Quintilian without learning, Galen and even Euclid illogical?[66]

Ramus' educational vision and methodologies were so repugnant to Beza that there was little room for compromise among them. Beza clung to Aristotelian logic as an orderly and precise system, and therefore a gift of God, while regarding Ramus' dialectics as untidy and imprecise, unsuited to the forming of young minds or the discussing of theology. While Ramus traveled through Germany and Switzerland after his conversion to Protestantism in 1569, hoping to size up possible safe landing spots for himself during religious turmoil in France, he found Geneva (not to mention many other cities) already wary of him. Beza and the rector of the Genevan Academy at the time, Jean le Gasgneux, objected when Ramus began to teach a public course on Cicero's *Catilianarian Speeches*, complaining to the Company of Pastors in May of 1570 that he was refusing to "change his method of teaching," being confident in his own methodology.[67] When Ramus inquired about a job at the Academy through a third party, Beza wrote directly to Ramus to refuse him.[68] He was emphatic that, not only did the school have no current vacancy, but also it was the resolve on the part of everyone there to follow the Aristotelian method in all things. Ramus was not the right fit.

In October 1570, Ramus returned to Paris after the restoration of peace there. Meanwhile, the Huguenot churches were taking advantage of the current climate to reorganize themselves into a more coherent, uniform body. Despite being a relative newcomer to the Protestant faith, Ramus used the opportunity to assert his views on the "priesthood of all believers" and to interfere with Beza's more centralized ecclesiastical vision.[69] As moderator of the pivotal French National

---

66 Beza to Bullinger, 14 January 1572, in CB 13:31. Beza employs the "false prophet" image frequently in this way; for example, Beza to Bullinger, 4 September [1553], in CB 1:113; and Beza to Crato, [30 November 1574], in CB 15:203.

67 RCP 3:26.

68 Beza to Ramus, 1 December 1570, in CB 11:295.

69 SKALNIK, J. (2002), 90.

Synod of La Rochelle (1571), Beza found himself battling the congregationalist views of Ramus and Jean Morély (ca. 1524–ca. 1594). His utter frustration with their opposition at such a crucial moment of unity manifests itself pointedly in the above-mentioned letter to Bullinger, the same one in which he boasts his prophetic awareness that Ramus would harm the church in the future. Beza trumpets how his prophecy was fulfilled at the synod and its aftermath: this "neophyte to Church order," he grumbles, now promotes chaos in the Church; Beza accuses him of pushing for a structure devoid of clerical leadership or hierarchical oversight.[70] Ramus' real purpose was probably less nefarious than Beza portrays it: guided by his own experiences in trying to obtain an education, Ramus sees value in involving more voices of the laity in decision-making and matters of excommunication and discipline. But Beza must have felt that Ramus was rejecting the Genevan model of ecclesiastical government and creating a divide between the Genevan model and that practiced by the French churches. There was also in Beza an innate suspicion of social climbers because of his own upbringing in the lower nobility.[71] For these reasons, it greatly relieved him to secure a letter of condemnation against Ramus and Morély at the French National Synod of Nîmes in May of 1572.[72] Beza undoubtedly understood that Morély represented a more extreme position regarding democratic governance in the churches than his supposed collaborator.[73] Ramus was only advocating for wider access to members of the congregation to the governing processes of the church, in "geometric proportion" to their education and standing.[74] Even so, for Beza there was value and economy in linking them together as a common opponent.

Bullinger is not so sure that this constitutes the best approach to the problem. For the sake of peace in the Church, he has been attempting to moderate Beza's vitriol against Ramus for more than a year. The fact is, Ramus made a positive impression on both Bullinger and Gwalther when he visited Zurich during

---

70 Beza to Bullinger, 14 January 1572, in CB 13:31.

71 Kingdon considers these prejudices of Beza in KINGDON, R. (1967), 18.

72 The details of how all these events unfolded and what actions Ramus took need not detain us here; it is enough to note that sharp conflict over matters of Church order and discipline (often termed *eutaxia* in Beza's letters) rocked the French churches and boiled Beza's blood. For the ecclesiastical dispute between Beza and Ramus, see CB 12 (1571) *passim*, and Bullinger to Beza, 11 February 1572, in CB 13:43 n.2. Besides these passages and editorial notes, I have relied on SKALNIK, J. (2002); BIETENHOLZ, P. (1971); MARUYAMA, T. (1978), 80–129; KINGDON, R. (1967), 37–137; and MANETSCH, S. (2000b), 39–50.

73 For an extensive treatment of Morély's proposal, see KINGDON, R. (1967), 43–96; also, SUMMERS, K. (2018a), 104–111.

74 On the importance of the word *geometric* in Ramus' thinking about Church government, see SKALNIK, J. (2002), 155–157.

his tour after his conversion.[75] In the immediate aftermath of the synod at La Rochelle in April 1571, whose Geneva-backed decisions Ramus and others found objectionable, Bullinger continually reminds his fellow reformer that Ramus is a sincere friend to Geneva. In December of that same year, for example, Bullinger sums up the Zurich position about the controversy among the French churches, saying he and his colleagues know nothing of Morély except what Beza tells them, while adding the following evaluation of Ramus:

> But Pierre Ramus, when he was visiting Zurich, conferred with us on all the major doctrines of our religion; indeed, he seemed far different than the way you depict him, unless he has undergone a complete transformation. Nor in his conversations did he say things that showed him to be hostile to the Genevan church and you; to the contrary, he showed himself a sincere friend of it.[76]

Bullinger is responding to a lengthy letter, written just weeks before, in which Beza defends the Genevan form of consistorial discipline and tries to thwart the efforts, as he sees it, of the "democrats" in France to drive a wedge between Zurich and Geneva.[77] There, Beza characterizes Ramus as "completely ignorant," someone who has never brought a Bible or a godly interpreter's book into his home." Instead of assenting to the decisions of the synod, or at most humbly dissenting, Beza claims he has ample evidence that Ramus "arrogantly, haughtily, and stubbornly cursed both the living and the dead and shredded the acts of the synods."[78] Furthermore, Beza echoes Bullinger's earlier assessment that Ramus and Morély are "learned and pious men" with a sneering and ironic "those good men of yours."[79]

---

75 KINGDON, R. (1967), 101; SKALNIK, J. (2002), 114–115. Skalnik cites an entry in Bullinger's diary dated 28 August 1569: "Professor Petrus Ramus of the famous University of Paris exhibited for my judgment some books he had written on the subject of religion and especially on the sacraments. They pleased me."

76 Bullinger to Beza, 4 December 1571, in CB 12:244.

77 Beza to Bullinger, 13 November 1571, in CB 12:220–221; cf. 228: "I beseech you earnestly and with my whole heart to be on constant guard against what they are intent on accomplishing, namely, to involve you in these quarrels and thereby alienate you from us; we will take care to do the same." KINGDON, R. (1967) transcribes the same letter in Appendix II, 209–215, with the relevant material on 212. According to Beza, Morély and his partisans act "as if those who refuse to establish disruptive and seditious democracy in the Church are introducing oligarchy or tyranny into it." Beza does write to Ramus directly on the matter around the same time (the precise date of this letter is unknown), as it appears in the *Epistolae theologicae* [1573] without date or addressee; on the likelihood that it was sent to Ramus, see Beza to [Ramus], 1571, in CB 12:253–257). MARUYAMA, T. (1978), 123–125, provides a brief analysis of it.

78 Beza to Bullinger, 13 November 1571, in CB 12:221.

79 For Bullinger's original statement, see his letter to Beza, 24 October 1571, in CB 12:207.

After the synod of Nîmes, the exchange concerning Ramus between the two reformers continues along the same lines. In response to Beza's rant about Ramus' assessment of Aristotle and other ancient authors, along with his own prophecy that Ramus would introduce discord into the churches, Bullinger gently rebukes Beza, urging him to treat Ramus with moderation by admonishing him in a friendly way and instructing him with kindness.[80] He adds a warning based on experience and knowledge of Church history:

> I cannot approve of the tactic of those who are too prone to engage in condemning and renouncing, especially in matters not related to the overthrow of the chief points and articles of our faith. I have always approved of moderation and always will, since I have learned from ecclesiastic history how many evils have befallen the Church because of the rash judgments of even the best men against those who could have been dealt with in moderation. These become frustrated by the harsh way in which their brothers treated them and afterwards become pernicious enemies of the Church.[81]

In essence, Bullinger wants to start with the assumption that Ramus' heart is in the right place. He urges Beza to take the same tack.

As noted, Beza secures his victory against his rivals when in May of 1572 the synod of Nîmes condemns Ramus and his partisans over the matter of discipline.[82] When Bullinger hears the decisions taken, he expresses to Beza in the strongest terms his regret that the two did not reconcile, stooping instead to calling each other names; he believes that if they do not resolve their differences in private soon, they will cause harm to many faithful.[83] Even so, Beza's frustration over the matter is not spent with the success of the synod, nor is he immediately swayed by Bullinger's admonition. The fact that Ramus

---

80 Bullinger is referring to the comments that Beza made about Ramus on 14 January 1572 (see CB 13:30–31). For Bullinger's response, see his letter to Beza, 11 February 1572, in CB 13:43.

81 Bullinger to Beza, 11 February 1572, in CB 13:43.

82 A letter from the Synod to the pastors of Zurich on 17 May 1572 (CB 13:267–272, annex 3) describes the censoring of Ramus, Morély, and their supporters in their absence (see 269).

83 Bullinger to Beza, 12 July 1572, in CB 13:166: "As for your private letters to me, I have not read them without sadness, because from them quickly I understood with what near implacable hostility the two of you carry on. He labels you a 'substantial' philosopher, and you call him a most vain trifler. Yet if this burst out into the public, these mutual hard feelings and anger toward those whom many people in France have a high regard will supply the longed-for weapons for our adversaries and will damage those in the Church who still have rather fragile consciences. Therefore, I would wish you settle your quarrels by a friendly and earnest conference, privately, whether in writings or in direct conversation, and, abstaining from the name-calling and abuse as befits brothers who are servants of the same Lord and confessors of the same faith, you forgive each other."

continues to agitate does not help the matter. Dufour calls attention to a letter written by Ramus to Gwalther in July of 1572 in which he defames Beza shortly before being murdered in the St Bartholomew's Day Massacre.[84] Despite the fact that Ramus did not attend the synod, he nonetheless accuses Beza of having read aloud a letter from Bullinger to the Synod in which allegedly the Zurich reformer adopts the Genevan positions on both the Eucharist and discipline. The implication is that Beza was trying to manipulate the synod through deceit. Gwalther naturally shares the letter with Bullinger, who himself quickly fires off a rebuttal to Ramus: "Doctor Beza, a man who has done well by the Church and a beloved brother, could not have read such letters of Bullinger, because he neither received nor had such letters. Nor is he so vain—I know this well enough—to concoct and read aloud in a gathering of brothers something that he did not receive from me." Bullinger informs Beza of this letter and his response to it, though notably not mentioning Ramus by name in the process.[85] Clearly, neither know that Ramus has already perished in the massacre.[86]

At some point before the beginning of 1573, however, both hear the news about Ramus' murder.[87] The passing touches Bullinger deeply and occasions the frank admonition to Beza on 10 January 1573 with which we began this account: "I would prefer that you not continue to express your aggravation with him." Bullinger explicitly interprets the death of Ramus as a martyrdom, indicating that despite the bad blood he engendered among colleagues at times, he is still to be included among the faithful. Thus, when writing to Beza a few weeks later and relaying his eagerness to see François Hotman's (1524–1590) retelling of the massacres in the *Narratio de furoribus Gallicis*, Bullinger reminds Beza—apparently under the assumption that Beza himself is contributing to the work—that Ramus deserves a place in the narrative: "Truly the most fitting thing for you to do is to honor the name of our friend Ramus who died for Christ."[88]

---

84 DUFOUR, A. (2009), 144. For the letter, see Ramus to Gwalther, 17 July 1572, in CB 13:276 (annex 5), and Bullinger's reply to Ramus, 10 August 1572, in CB 13:278–279 (appendix 5). Ramus died on 26 August.

85 Bullinger to [Beza], 9 September 1572, in CB 13:186.

86 See the editors' comment on this at CB 13:195n.10.

87 For a description of the assassination, see KINGDON, R. (1967), 111–112, and the bibliography cited on 112n.1.

88 Bullinger to Beza, 27 January 1573, in CB 14:21. The jurist Hotman escaped the massacre because he was away teaching at the University of Bourges when it occurred. He published his work under pseudonyms, at four presses in six different editions: one at Basel by Thomas Guarin, one at La Rochelle by Barthélemy Berton, and four at London by Henry Bynneman or William Williamson. In each case, false locations of publication were given. Bynneman also produced an English version in 1573 titled, *A true and plaine report of the furious outrages of Fraunce & the horrible and shameful slaughter of Chastillion the admirall*. On Hotman's pseudonym, see BIETENHOLZ, P. (1971), 351.

Bullinger's warning to Beza and reminders of his piety, so delicately expressed to a person of Beza's stature, nonetheless exhibit a palpable impatience with the unending denunciations. Bullinger attempts to pull Beza from the bitter path of vindictiveness. At the same time, Bullinger's words reveal a genuine brotherly affection for the Parisian scholar: Ramus proved himself a sincere follower of Christ while at Zurich and died for his faith. To his mind, Beza is unfairly treating him as an enemy of true religion.

Beza finds himself duly admonished. Just nine days after Bullinger writes his letter of 10 January, Beza replies with a contrite acknowledgement of Bullinger's reprimand:

> As for Pierre Ramus, although it is true that I disliked many things about him, and for good reason, nevertheless I have learned, by God's grace, to hate sins and failings, not people; and, even if I feel hatred toward the person, far be it from me to keep attacking a dead person, especially one who was cruelly butchered. To do so would not only be inhuman, but even impious.[89]

It is difficult to think of many correspondents or friends in 1573 who could elicit an admission on the part of Beza that he had strayed so grievously. Beza stands at the pinnacle of the French Reformed movement at this time, admired and respected by many for his intellect and gravitas. Even so, the refrain concerning Ramus that runs through several years of letters with Bullinger leading to this final exchange exposes to what extent Beza needed his network of correspondents to moderate and correct him. His far-flung friends in a variety of ways constantly serve to remind him of his humanity—"to do so would not only be inhuman"—and the kind of love that his faith demands—"but even impious." These words open a small window into the deep, internal tensions that tug and pull on him as the external and public work of ministry is carried on. Surely, without the letters we would be at a loss to assess the motivations and struggles of a spiritual leader caught between the now and the not-yet.

The number of stories that the letters tell and the range of topics on which they touch surpass our ability to catalog them here. Even the exchange concerning Ramus is but one narrative illustrating the deferential relationship between Beza and the Zurich reformer during the latter years of his life. For other examples of the same, we could also point to Beza's alteration of his *Epistolae theologicae* (1573) in the middle of the press run due to Bullinger's displeasure with one of the letters. In this unusual case, Beza replaced a letter written to the minister Pierre Dathenus on the subject of discipline with a less controversial

---

89 Beza to Bullinger, 19 January 1573, in CB 14:14.

one on Traducianism to an unknown recipient.[90] It saddened him to hear of Bullinger's disapproval of the initial version. Another letter from 1574 has Bullinger chiding Beza over his excessive complaints about kidney ailments: "I pity you, my brother Beza. If at fifty-five years of age you feel such discomfort because of your kidneys, how do you think it will be if you reach my age of seventy? I could not begin to tell you the pain and discomfort I have been experiencing over the past five years."[91] Clearly, Bullinger has no qualms about putting Beza in his place from time to time. But the conversations between these two are in no way limited to deference and admonishment. They take on many shapes and forms, exhibiting in every instance a remarkable interdependence, profound love, and shared sense of calling. Until Bullinger's passing in 1575, for example, Beza fretted often over the fellow reformer's health, but worried too for the health of the Reformed movement in his absence. In one letter, Beza assures his friend that he is lifting up prayers that God preserve him for the Church "in these tempestuous times," even if admittedly it is sweeter for Bullinger himself to complete the course of his life.[92] And when Bullinger's end is very near, Beza writes a touching note in which he conveys how mutually beneficial the frequent communication between them has been:

> Even though nothing pleases me more, my father, than when I write to you, and I have no doubt that letters from your friends bring joy in your time of suffering, nevertheless I have abstained for a while. Knowing how conscientious you are, I fear that any letter would make you feel the need to respond. But since people tell me that you receive respite from your torments from time to time, I return to the business of writing, but on the condition that you worry not in the least about writing me back. My hope is that what you desire to tell me (I especially want updates about your status), you will easily communicate through others to me; it will not be a problem for our dear brothers who are very devoted to me to take on this task for your sake and mine.[93]

These dear brothers, as the editors of the correspondence note, are without question Gwalther and Simler, other prominent Zurichers whom we have already met above. Along with Bullinger, they represent a crucial and truly unique part of Beza's correspondence: in moments of despair or sickness, when

---

90 For the two letters and the swap mid-printing, see Beza to [Dathenus], 6 February 1571, in CB 12:33–36 and Beza to [Anonymous], 1 April 1571, in CB 12:99–102; see also Beza to Christoph Hardesheim, 12 February 1574, in CB 15:36n.10.

91 Bullinger to Beza, 10 January 1574, in CB 15:8.

92 Beza to Bullinger, 5 October 1573, in CB 14:226–228.

93 Beza to Bullinger, 16 August 1575, in CB 16:154.

difficulties arise in the ministry or fears need to be allayed, this circle of distant friends forms a solid pillar of support for him.

Ministering through the Psalms

Throughout these same years when Beza complains of Ramus to Bullinger, defends Reformed doctrine against the Lutherans, agonizes over the effects of the Torgau Articles, and attempts to put his stamp on affairs in France—the major biographical material—Beza has also thrown himself into another labor of love: he is translating the Psalms into various kind of Latin verse for a book that he envisions. This is the kind of quiet activity that must have engaged Beza in his study on a snowy evening in Geneva. It is clear, if one follows the narrative about them throughout his letters, he finds in the Psalms profound inspiration. David's songs of praise and lament, his cries for aid and his words of consolation, become for Beza a spiritual refuge. His mind is filled constantly with their poetry and message.

In 1566, Beza first published Latin lyric compositions of six Psalms together with George Buchanan's renderings of all the Psalms into Latin verse.[94] He had already contributed more than a hundred French verse compositions to the Genevan Psalter published in 1562. The 1566 contributions, however, mark a new focus for Beza: the possibility of creating his own book of the Psalms turned into Latin verse. Although he has mostly finished the task by 1577, it would be 1579 before the first edition of his Psalms issues from the press, followed quickly by a second edition in 1580.[95] In the intervening years, from 1566 up to 1580, the correspondence tells the story of this earnest passion for David's songs, from the purposes envisioned for the renderings, the constant reworking and polishing of them, apprehensions about the quality of the publication and the sense of calling to the task. Here we can only scratch the surface of the entire

---

94 Not every edition of Buchanan's 1566 *Psalms* contains Beza's verses; on the three versions, see Beza to Buchanan, [12 April 1572], in CB 13:121–122 and n. 5. Beza thanks Buchanan for sending an edition of the poems and praises his renditions. The editors hypothesize that Beza had already seen the volume, as one would have to assume. The version that includes Beza's renderings bears the title, *Psalmorum Davidis paraphrasis poetica . . . eiusdem Davidis Psalmi aliquot a Th. B. V. versi*, and was published by Henri Étienne and his brother Robert at Geneva. See GARDY, F., 130–131. It is possible that Beza's poems were published without his knowledge (on this, see the editors' remarks at CB 18:141n.10.)

95 BEZA, T., *Psalmorum Davidis et aliorum prophetarum libri quinque; argumentis et Latina paraphrasi illustrati ac etiam carminum genere Latine expressi* (1579a) and BEZA, T., *Psalmorum sacrorum libri quinque, vario carminum genere Latine expressi, et argumentis, atque paraphrasis illustrati; secunda editio tum emendatior, tum actior quatuordecim canticis* (1580b).

narrative, but taken as a whole, it has as much bearing for our understanding of Beza as an individual person as well as leader of the Reformed faith as anything else that he accomplished.

We pick up the story in 1574 in the midst of the controversy over the Torgau Articles, a declaration of Lutheran orthodoxy born from the sacramentarian disputes in the previous years.[96] Beza writes to his friend Dürnhoffer his reaction to the news that in June several Crypto-Calvinist theologians succumbed to the pressures of imprisonment at Leipzig at the hands of Gnesio-Lutherans and signed the articles.[97] Probably Beza did not know at this juncture, as many never did, that the Saxon theologians only agreed to sign if they could qualify their submission in accord with Melanchthon's modified positions. This was information not revealed when their signatures were later broadcast and their positions misrepresented. Present among this illustrious group was Heinrich Möller (mentioned above), professor of Hebrew at Wittenberg, who was one of the several Philippists brought in by Gaspard Peucer (1525–1602).[98] In this same year of 1574, Möller published scholarly notes on the Psalms that Beza would utilize when composing his paraphrases and poems of them.[99] This incongruity alone must have added to Beza's distress. He tells Dürnhoffer that, while he is appalled by the audacity and impudence of the Gnesio-Lutherans to force this signing,

> it tortures me more that no one is found who thinks he must even die for the truth. Still, this deed deserves pity instead of censure; and I am convinced that the Lord has saved such great men so that they might at some time in the future bring back a more glorious victory against a lie. Therefore, may the Lord our God the Father of mercies restore them, suppress the spirit of error, open the princes' eyes, so that their zeal may accord with knowledge, lift up the fallen, strengthen those who are standing, and, lastly, punish those wicked and true Antichrists, as he will do in his own time.[100]

---

96 For the document, see DINGEL, I. (2008), 1103–1151; in the same volume, see Dingel's historical introduction, 3–15.

97 Beza to Dürnhoffer, 30 November 1574, in CB 15:199–200; background information on Beza's friends here is drawn from information provided by the editors in n. 1; also CB 15:159n.3–5. In response to this crisis, Beza wrote *Apologia modesta et Christiana ad Acta Conventus quindecim theologicorum Torgae nuper habiti.* See GARDY, F. (1960), 171.

98 Shortly after this incident, Möller returned to his hometown of Hamburg; see RE 13:269.

99 See Beza to Eric Mylaeus [Heinrich Möller], 12 May 1576, in CB 17:117n.5; also, Beza to Heinrich Möller, 21 August 1579, in CB 20:165, where Beza reiterates his dependency on Möller's interpretation and says that his published verses on them are as much Möller's as they are his. For Möller's work, see *Enarrationis Psalmorum Davidis.* It was Dürnhoffer himself who sent the commentaries to Beza in 1575, at which Beza exclaimed that the Psalms provide him so much consolation that he loves any works about them; the commentaries were reprinted at Geneva in 1591 (see Beza to Dürnhoffer, 7 October 1575, in CB 16:223–224 and n.6).

100 Beza to Dürnhoffer, 30 November 1574, in CB 15:199.

The Antichrists here are the Gnesio-Lutherans, who are currently persecuting their Reformed-leaning brethren in Germany. The anguish that this "indignity" causes Beza, mingled tenuously with the prayerful faith in God's plan, "wrung from him" a poetic rendition of Psalm 94, which he includes with the letter. He is confident that Dürnhoffer's literary sensibilities will be touched by it. This version of Psalm 94 is, in fact, the same one that eventually appears in the published editions of the Psalms.[101] Beza sees immediate application of the work in his study to the struggle before him. The correspondence and the poetry serve as an extension of Beza's ministerial counseling and consoling, carrying out the pastoral work he cannot do in person. When even this avenue is blocked, he can only offer pitiful laments to God: "Would that in some way I could restore those honorable brothers of ours with letters, at least. But, seeing that I cannot because of the cruelty of those Cyclopes, I accomplish by prayers and sighs what I am not permitted by voice or hand, and I hope that my groans will not be in vain."[102]

This exchange with Dürnhoffer suggests several things about the work on the Psalms. Beza, who seems already by this date to have made significant progress on his translations—the following year finds him working sequentially through the 70s and including the resulting poems with letters to friends—is also thinking about the *argumenta* that eventually are published with his Psalms. Edward Gosselin identifies these summaries as "Beza's commentary" on the Psalms, and he suspects from internal evidence that they were composed "late 1578 or early 1579."[103] Without addressing his evidence in detail, we only observe here that

---

101 See Beza to Dürnhoffer, 30 November 1574, in CB 15:199 and 201n.2. The editors there refer this to the wrong Psalm, however, misled by a typo in the text; the poem that Beza included with his letter would be the one on pages 359–361 of the 1580 edition, beginning, "Ultor Deus, Deus Ultor illa flammea | adverte terris lumina."

102 See Beza to Dürnhoffer, 30 November 1574, in CB 15:199. The *Cyclopes* are referred to because they were flesh-eaters and thus serve to mock the Gnesio-Lutheran doctrine of the real presence of Christ's body in the Supper.

103 GOSSELIN, E. (1976), 37–39. Already in August of 1576 Gwalther writes to Beza that he is "eagerly awaiting his Psalms," as if he has reason to expect their imminent publication (in CB 17:142), and in 1577, Beza tells André Dudith, "Opus Psalmorum absolvi, sed quotidie emendo," that is, "I have completed my work on the Psalms, but I am correcting them every day" (15 December 1577, in CB 18:208). Already a few months before this, he tells Peter Young that "they are now ready" (22 July 1577, in CB 18:138). It seems most plausible that Beza has already attached the *argumentum* to each poem. In a letter to Dudith in 1579, he states explicitly that he wrote the paraphrases for each Psalm in the previous months, but seems to imply that the *argumenta* already were attached to the verses; see Beza to Dudith, 2 June 1579, in CB 20:123. A poems-only version of the Latin Psalms was produced in January of 1579 "to make the volume cheaper for the more erudite readers who do not need the paraphrases and arguments," but this indicates nothing about the time frame in which they

Beza already assumes a particular interpretation of the Psalm when he sends it to Dürnhoffer. In other words, the poetic compositions are so dependent on and bound up with the overall meaning, indeed, they are attempting to express this meaning in the most powerful way possible, that it is difficult to envisage poem without summary. We can even imagine that Beza sketched out the commentaries in some rudimentary form before composing the poems themselves. In any case, we do not have to assume that Beza discovered meaning for the Psalms only as events unfolded in France in late 1578; in the letter to Dürnhoffer, Beza chooses this particular Psalm for this moment because of the meaning that it holds. Additionally, Beza relates Psalm 94 to the events at hand, as he will do with other Psalms for other correspondents in the coming years. The tragic events at Leipzig *inspire* his translation; to his mind, the experiences of David mirror the current ones being faced. The great Jewish king finds himself beset with enemies, crying out for God, and being racked by his own failings and faithlessness. Is not David's spiritual journey a microcosm of the journey of all Christians? And because the Psalms speak with relevance to the experiences of God's people, Beza adopts them as the cornerstone of his ministry: the encouragement and consolation, the sighs and laments, the contriteness, hope, and exaltation that he shares with others, all echo with the songs of David. The work of translating them into poetry both seals their message onto his soul and elevates their language to something transcendent and Spirit-filled. Beza treats poetry as a gift from God with a unique and sacred power to fill the faithful with his presence.

Throughout the year 1575, Beza continues to distribute his poetic compositions of the Psalms among various friends. In July, he sends a note of consolation to the Crypto-Calvinist Benedict Thalmann (d. 1577), who languishes, suffering in a prison at Ansbach in Bavaria at the hands of Gnesio-Lutherans.[104] Beza's words are strikingly beautiful in their encouragement, praising Thalmann for his constancy and reminding him it is a privilege to suffer for Christ while being conformed to his image. God will reward him, Beza assures him, and take out his vengeance on those who persecute him. To finish the race and reach the goal, he need only keep his eyes fixed on Christ and not the vicissitudes of this world. "Christians can die and even desire to do so," he concludes in the body of the letter, "but they cannot be conquered."[105] He then includes this touching postscript: "I have adjoined to this letter a paraphrase of the seventy-first Psalm, a token of my high regard for you: Fido tibi, quaeso, Deus, patere ut [. . .]" The

---

were written. For the text explaining why the volume appears without the added elements, see Beza to Henry Hastings, 16 May 1579, in CB 20:104.

104 Beza to Benedict Thalmann, 19 July 1575, in CB 16:127–132.

105 Beza to Benedict Thalmann, 19 July 1575, in CB 16:128.

full Latin poem that follows is the same as that appearing in the editions of the Psalms and is particularly apropos to Thalmann's predicament: "Through a thousand crosses, a thousand deaths, you lead me away into the bosom of a blessed life. You sink me down into a fierce and stormy abyss, only that from there I may be lifted on high."[106] As much as Thalmann must have appreciated the encouragement and wisdom of the letter itself, he must have discerned something even more comforting and divine in the exalted language of the poetry. Certainly, Beza believes that the poems will communicate to him on a different level than his own words can.

In several more instances in 1575, Beza attaches his translations or paraphrases of the Psalms to letters. Interestingly, on the same day on which he writes to Thalmann, he also writes to theologian Christoph Thretius in Poland to discuss politics and express his opinion about the imminent election of a king there.[107] The letter ends with well-wishes for Thretius and his circle in making their choice, along with an allusion to 2 Kings 6:17 and "the faithful legions of angels" supporting them. Here again Beza inserts a Psalm translation, this time the very next one, Psalm 72: "May the Lord on high direct the counsels of your people with his Holy Spirit, so that the one who will be your king will come close to the example described in the seventy-second Psalm I am sending to you and which I have put into Latin verse as best I could: "Tu regnaturum Regem tua iura doceto [. . .]," that is, "Teach your laws to the king who is about to rule [. . .]"

Beza choice of Psalm 72 suits the situation, but is its proximity to the Psalm used for Thalmann just a coincidence? In September of 1575, we find Beza writing to his friend, former Wittenberg scholar Esrom Rüdinger, about the same troubles in Saxony.[108] There he adds yet another Psalm, this time Psalm 74, with the following note (italics ours): "I send to you Psalm 74 in Latin measures, *translated by me several months ago or so*, which I persuaded myself will not displease you."[109] In the Psalm, David complains to God that he seems to have abandoned his people and allowed his enemies to trample the holy places. The time stamp is of special interest, especially when the sequential appearance of the poems throughout the letters is considered: together these suggest that Beza is prone to share his translations where applicable as he writes them. They minister to him and, he imagines with justification, will do the same for others.

---

106 Beza to Benedict Thalmann, 19 July 1575, in CB 16:129. Thalmann's response a few weeks later is equally moving: 26 August 1575, in CB 16:160–167.
107 Beza to Christoph Thretius, 19 July 1575, in CB 16:136–142.
108 Beza to Esrom Rüdinger, 7 September 1575, in CB 16:192–198. By this time, Rüdinger has left Saxony for Moravia.
109 Beza to Esrom Rüdinger, 7 September 1575, in CB 16:193.

The way that Beza uses the translations in uplifting friends highlight the spiritual purpose behind them. Beginning in 1577, several letters also reveal the more mundane side to producing the intended volume. Beza has prepared the volume by this time,[110] but remains in a quandary: Will he offend George Buchanan by duplicating his work? We recall that Buchanan published his poetic renditions of the Psalms in 1566, and that a few of Beza's own early efforts appeared in the Genevan edition, though without the latter's knowledge or approval.[111] Beza mulls over the dilemma to Peter Young in a July letter.[112] He writes:

> Greet our friend Buchanan with the utmost affection from us. You know, when he published his volume, he appears to have deterred all people of sane mind from pursuing this genre.[113] So, I was insane when I continued to work on this project, which now I have completed, and which is ready to go to press. But to what end am I "bringing owls to Athens," or setting myself up so you can deride me? And yet, if he would send his poems to me that I hear he has emended in several places, that is, rendered the best better, I would also dare, if it should not displease him, to publish mine together with his. In that way, as the moon is illumined by the rays of the sun, so I may gain something from the splendor of his light. But if by chance it happens rather that I am obscured by him and suffer an eclipse, I will, as Livy said, "console myself by the greatness of him who has blocked the light from shining on my name."[114]

Beza reiterates his concerns to Young in March of the next year, and with almost the same words, though with the added idea that the joint volume be dedicated to the young King of Scotland, James VI, whom both he and Buchanan serve as teachers.[115] A false rumor has alarmed Beza that his edition's publication may coincide with that of the renowned Buchanan and thus make him appear presumptuous or redundant. But a solution comes to mind: if Buchanan would allow their poems to be published jointly in the same volume, then there would be no more question of competition or impropriety. Beza tries to assure the elder poet (through Young) that in such a happy combination his own efforts

---

110 He never fully accepts that the work is "ready" for the press. In a letter late in the year, he tells Dudith that he has finished the volume but continues to emend it. See Beza to Dudith, 15 December 1577, in CB 18:208.

111 Beza to Peter Young, 22 July 1577, in CB 18:141n.10.

112 On Peter Young, see CB 13:122n.4.

113 Beza repeats this sentiment in the letter to Henry Hastings that served as the dedication to the published Psalms; see 16 May 1579, in CB 20:103.

114 Beza to Peter Young, 22 July 1577, in CB 18:138.

115 Beza to Peter Young, 5 March 1578, in CB 19:58.

will pale in comparison to those of himself. Buchanan, however, never produced such a work and never appears to have intended one. The rumor of a revised version may have originated from Strasbourg, where the printer Josias Rihel was planning to reissue the original.[116] No doubt merchants coming from there carried with them half-truths. And although in 1581, Jean le Preux published a volume at Morges containing both the translations of Beza and Buchanan, this was not the joint edition dedicated to the king as Beza envisioned it when writing to Young.[117] This was essentially Beza's 1580 volume with the poems of Buchanan inserted.

Once it was realized that Buchanan was not of a mind to publish a new edition of his Psalms, Beza considered himself freed to issue his own. Beza announces to André Dudith in early June of 1579 that the book of Psalms "by the urging of friends is published."[118] The book was many years in the making. Even so, all was not well. Beza was terribly distraught and even ashamed about the poor quality of the editing and the missed errors in the text, so much so that within two months of their publishing he was planning a second edition. On 25 August 1579 he writes to Dürnhoffer his flustered assessment:

> I sent to you previously a copy of my Psalter that was printed full of
> errors, which I assume you received. Soon a second edition will follow,
> better corrected, I hope, especially if you are not reluctant to share in
> writing and in detail your thoughts with me about this little work.
> Indeed, I am very disappointed with the verses. I hope the ones in the
> future will be neither displeasing nor completely useless.[119]

These comments indicate that two issues are bothering Beza: both the printing problems *and* an abundance of errors and even infelicities in the translation. On the very same day that he writes to Dürnhoffer, he also pens a letter to Nuremberg jurist Christopher Hardesheim (1523–1585) in which he again mentions the Psalms.[120] There he describes unequivocally the embarrassment he feels for the errors he himself overlooked as well as for the sloppy printing. Yet he shares a copy of the book with Hardesheim and indicates that he will

---

116 See the editors' conjecture at CB 19:59n.15.

117 BEZA, T./BUCHANAN, G., *Psalmorum sacrorum Davidis libri quinque duplici poetica metaphrasis, altera alteri e regione opposita vario carminum genere Latine expressi* (1581).

118 Beza to Dudith, 2 June 1579, in CB 20:123. The phrase "by the urging of friends" may seem disingenuous, since Beza was anxious for these poems to see the light of day, but he constantly tweaked them over the years and was never fully satisfied that they were perfect. For example, we observe this dissatisfaction in comments to Dürnhoffer as late as October 1578, in CB 19:188.

119 Beza to Dürnhoffer, 25 August 1579, in CB 20:167.

120 Beza to Hardesheim, 25 August 1579, in CB 20:171.

send one to fellow Nuremberger and humanist physician Joachim Camerarius the Younger (1534–1598), with the hope that the more emended, more polished second edition to follow will lend aid "for these most sad times."

Not surprisingly, though, Beza did not send a copy to either Young or Buchanan, as was the norm in this period when respected friends have a marked interest in the subject matter.[121] What he communicates to Young on the very next day after writing to Dürnhoffer and Hardesheim has a defeatist, despondent tone to it:

> As for my private affairs, I press on to life's end goal to the extent I can, but I fear that you will think that, not only have I become old, but also demented. Lo and behold, my sad little verses were finally published. Now, while I was hoping to shed light on the sacred psalms, I am afraid instead I have cast a shadow over them. But come on, let truly bad poets lose their mind. But Doctor Buchanan will be indebted to me to some degree because my faults will make clear the greatness of his poetic power even more so than before. So, even for this reason alone I would send several copies of my book, unless it were printed so sloppily that I am ashamed to offer it to any of my friends. I hope soon a more polished and corrected edition will follow.[122]

Beza follows here the well-established convention of ancient Latin poets to self-deprecate even while hoping for an enduring legacy. We can see that Beza yearns deeply to be a great poet; his inner satisfaction that he is fulfilling his God-given vocation is bound up with his ability to produce beautiful and technically-sound poetry. He has given nearly fifteen years to this one project and yet even now frets over its polish. He aspires to match the standard set by Buchanan. Additionally, these comments to Young show Beza worrying about his reputation; he thinks about how Buchanan and others in Scotland will evaluate the quality of his work. He finds reasons not to send this edition to them because a better one will soon follow. But as much as we may be struck by Beza's concern for the external and personal dynamics involved with the publication, we should also pay attention to what he says about his spiritual motivation: he believes that his poetry can serve the Church by shedding light

---

121 For Beza's reluctance to send the first edition to Scotland, see his letter to George Buchanan, 16 March 1580, in CB 21:84–85 and n. 5. That sending it would be the norm, cf. Beza's willingness to send it to Gwalther and others at Zurich, see Beza to Gwalther, 11 August 1579, in CB 20:153. Gwalther acknowledges receipt a few weeks later (28 August 1579, in CB 20:176). Though Beza probably hoped for a more enthusiastic reaction from Gwalther, the latter does remark in passing, "For this the whole Church owes you eternal gratitude." Later, Grynaeus of Basel asks Beza to please use a larger print in the next edition so that the text can be more useful in a public setting (24 October [1579], in CB 20:218).

122 Beza to Peter Young, 26 August 1579, in CB 20:172–173.

on the Psalms. This is a repeated theme running through all his correspondence about it. In the letter dedicating the work to Henry Hastings, Lord Huntington, he explains in more detail why the Psalms, so long an integral feature of the Church, merit more illumination: new attention to the Hebrew version, better linguistic scholarship, commenting that is more faithful to the original intent, all these open up an opportunity to rethink the meaning of the text.[123] In the poetry, therefore, he simply tries to reflect those advances in understanding of the precise meaning in a way that will inspire the flock. "Even if Buchanan obscures my light," he concludes his justification in the preface, "aside from the fact that I will be abundantly satisfied with what I have produced if my efforts prove useful for the Church, I will also take comfort in Vergil's phrase, 'You fall by the right hand of the great Aeneas.'"[124]

Perhaps to some extent these words reflect the conventional courtesies of the time. Still, Beza was accustomed to extolling Buchanan publicly too. In his dedication of the *Icones* (1580) to James VI of Scotland, for example, Beza alludes to the royal youth's education under Young and Buchanan, the latter of which he describes as "the parent of the finer liberal arts and especially poetry."[125] Beza must have been exceptionally pleased, therefore, to publish a new, emended edition of his Psalms in 1593 in which the poems of Buchanan are interwoven with his own, and which includes Buchanan's tragedies "Iephthes" and "Baptista."[126] Here, the staggering humanistic talents of two pious poets stand on equal footing, forever fused and submitted to the service of the Church. When in the next century noted Classical scholar Isaac Vossius read through his personal copy of the 1580 edition of Beza's *Psalms*—a text he may have inherited from his grandfather, Jan Vossius, a Reformed minister from the Netherlands who died in 1585—he inked into the margins notes about the Psalms as well as numerous alternative Latin verses. It is a testament to the longevity of a long-distance friendship born from a mutual appreciation for the healing power of poetry that almost all the marginalia are drawn from Buchanan (Figure 2).

---

123 The preface is available at CB 20:101–114; for this argument by Beza, see pp. 102–103.

124 Beza to Henry Hastings, 16 May 1579, in CB 20:103.

125 BEZA, T., *Icones* (1580a), iii[v].

126 BEZA, T., *Sacratiss. Psalmorum Davidis libri V; duplici poetica metaphrasi, altera alteri e regione opposita, vario genere carminum Latine expressi* (1593a). Beza nowhere mentions his involvement in the publication, but for such a "more emended" edition to be published without his approval is unthinkable.

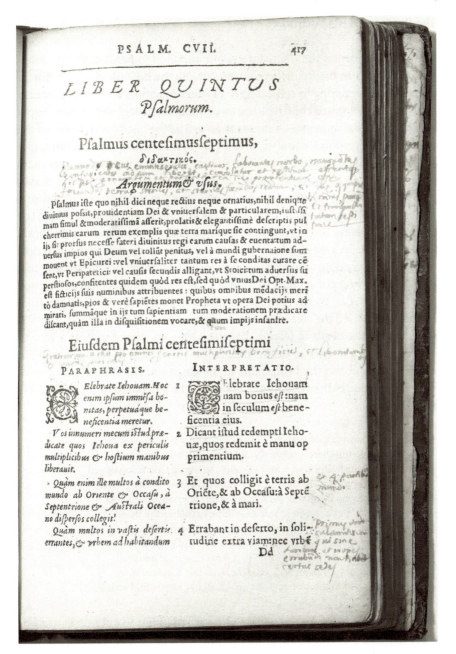

PSALM. CVII.   417

LIBER QUINTUS
Psalmorum.

Psalmus centesimusseptimus,

δισακτικός.

Argumentum & usus.

Psalmus iste quo nihil dici neque rectius neque ornatius, nihil deniqꝫ
diuinius possit, prouidentiam Dei & vniuersalem & particularem, iustissi-
mam simul &moderatissimã asserit,prolatis& elegantissimè descriptis pul-
cherrimis earum rerum exemplis quæ terra marique sic contingunt, vt in
ijs sit prorsus necesse fateri diuinitus regi earum causas & euentatum aduersus impios qui Deum vel tollũt penitus, vel à mundi gubernaione sum-
mouent vt Epicurei : vel vniuersaliter tantum res à se conditas curare cẽ-
sent,vt Peripatetici: vel causis secundis alligant,vt Stoici:tum aduersus su-
perstiosos,confitentes quidem quòd res est,sed quòd vnius Dei Opt.Max.
est ficticijs suis numinibus attribuentes : quibus omnibus mẽdacijs mer̃
tò damnatis,pios & verè sapiẽtes monet Propheta vt opera Dei potius ad-
mirari, summãque in ijs tum sapientiam tum moderationem prædicare
discant,quàm illa in disquisitionem vocare,& quam impijs insanire.

Eiusdem Psalmi centesimiseptimi

PARAPHRASIS.

Elebrate Iehouam. Hoc
enim ipsum immẽsa bo-
nitas, perpetuáque be-
neficentia meretur.

Vos innumeri mecum istud præ-
dicate quos Iehoua ex periculis
multiplicibus & hostium manibus
liberauit.

Quàm enim ille multos à condito
mundo ab Oriente & Occasu, à
Septentrione & Australi Ocea-
no dispersos collegit!

Quàm multos in vastis desertis
errantes,& vrbem ad habitandum

INTERPRETATIO.

1 Elebrate Iehouam
nam bonus est :nam
in seculum est bene-
ficentia eius.

2 Dicant istud redempti Ieho-
uæ,quos redemit è manu op-
primentium.

3 Et quos colligit è terris ab
Oriẽte,& ab Occasu:à Septẽ-
trione,& à mari.

4 Errabant in deserto, in soli-
tudine extra viam:nec vrbẽ
                    Dd

The Pastor and His Vocation

The correspondence, to be sure, draws our attention to Beza's role as an international leader in the Reformed movement. He teaches, advises and informs as needed, intervening to some degree or other in almost all the disturbances affecting the Reformed churches. His theological, exegetical and literary output exerts additional influence over events as well as the hearts and minds of the pious. The correspondence also reveals his inner struggles and anxieties, that is, his personal race to the finish line. But even these sentiments do not seem to be primary in Beza: we recall in the letter to Zastrisell the Elder a persistent sadness in the reformer over the feebleness keeping him from his pastoral duties. Even at the sanctuary of his desk, as he completes revisions on the last edition of his New Testament annotations, Beza's mind remains on his flock. This is because he embraced, not only the ecclesiastical office of teacher, now tasked with defending and explaining important doctrinal points, but also that of pastor, now responsible as well for a local congregation most concerned about the everyday, concrete problems of uncertainty, loss, sin and despair.[127]

Beza considered the role of minister a holy and God-given calling. In 1572, shortly after the death of Jeanne d'Albret, Queen of Navarre, Beza wrote to her son and heir, Henri, to exhort him to remain faithful to his upbringing in the faith and protect the Protestants in his kingdom. His characterization of ministers indicates the enormous importance he attributed to the calling. He writes,

> It is of the utmost importance that you never contempt or grow weary
> of preaching in the churches; you should not only offer your ears to
> pastors giving instruction in sound doctrine, to whom God has assigned
> the office of preaching the divine Word, and concerning whom Christ
> said, "The one who hears you, hears me; the one who repudiates you,
> repudiates me;" but also you should be willing to listen to all those
> who with godly sermons try to exhort you to piety and steer you
> away from transgressions. Certainly, to hear the Lord's Word does
> not mean simply offering your ear to it; it must penetrate into the
> secret recesses of your heart and settle there, so that it guides your
> eyes and ears and in this way rule all your thoughts, words, and actions.[128]

Beza does not shrink back from bidding even a king to submit himself to ministers who are faithfully expounding and applying the double-edged sword of the Word. God has appointed them to shepherd his people, from the most

---

127 See, e.g., Beza's comments to Gwalther, 5 October 1576, in CB 17:171.
128 Beza to Henri, King of Navarre, 10 July 1572, in CB 13:161.

exalted to the humblest, through the transitions of life and along the path of sanctification.

It would be inaccurate to imagine Beza living a life cloistered from the mundane concerns of the people of Geneva. This was not the case. The rigors and demands of Beza's ministry at Geneva were great and time-consuming. Indeed, he considered these local responsibilities so much a priority of his calling that he sometimes recruited others to defend doctrines in writing lest he neglect them. This ministry involved more than just preaching; it was fraught with a seeming unending string of daily chores. Husbands and wives quarreled and became alienated from one another; merchants broke contracts or accused others of wrongdoings; parishioners skipped church services to enjoy leisure activity; some people clung to Roman Catholic practices deemed superstitious. These sorts of interpersonal conflicts and signs of indifference or obstinacy had to be addressed and resolved on an individual basis by Beza and the other pastors. Beza and his colleagues also carried out the regular functions of their office, performing baptisms, leading worship, educating the flock in basic doctrines and preparing for the administration of the Supper.[129] Furthermore, during the plagues of 1571 and 1578, all the pastors took turns visiting the plague hospital at enormous personal risk, even rejecting attempts by the city's leaders to interfere; the responsibility and need to minister to the afflicted overrode such practical concerns.[130] Illnesses of many kinds, even when the plague subsided, always added constant demands on the pastors' time, as the sick required spiritual comfort and families consolation. Beza likewise climbed the scaffold as required to proclaim the gospel one last time to prisoners facing execution, praying over them as the noose was placed around their neck.[131]

This was an exhausting calling, even in the best of times. Writing to Flemish theologian Thomas Van Til, then at Heidelberg, Beza provides a summary of the situation at Geneva and his current occupations:

> We are all doing well by the mercy of God, still enjoying the usual peace.
> I am now lecturing in the school about the ceremonial law arranged according
> to topic. As for my preaching, I have almost worked through the Epistle to
> the Hebrews, mixing in sermons on Jeremiah's Lamentations, a subject quite
> suited to these most miserable times. Pray to the Lord for me, a wretched
> sinner, that the responsibility, which he himself placed on me, I be able to
> sustain steadfastly to the end.[132]

---

129 On the daily responsibilities of the pastors in Geneva, see the summary by MANETSCH, S. (2012), 255–256. Also, see WRIGHT, S. (2007).

130 MANETSCH, S. (2013), 287–289.

131 MANETSCH, S. (2013), 284.

132 Beza to Thomas Van Til, 25 August 1573, in CB 14:190.

A quarter century later, the pastoral burden was no less heavy. In a letter to a friend in Breslau in 1589, the seventy-year-old reformer concluded with these words: "Remember to pray more and more for your friend Beza as he looks down the final stretch of his course. Although I am worn out, the Lord has never before given me a heavier load to carry."[133]

It appears that Beza's pastoral instincts developed during the course of his long career. Over time, the brash young humanist who once delighted in stinging satires and theological sparring matches matured into a seasoned gospel minister and humanist who recognized that the care of souls involved spiritual sensitivity and practical wisdom as well as theological precision. Beza's sermon series on the Song of Songs and on the death and resurrection of Jesus Christ, which appeared in print for the first time in the late 1580s and early 1590s, are especially rich in such pastoral reflection.[134] In these sermons, Beza frequently reminds his congregation that Christian ministers must "teach, exhort, and console their flocks by the living Word [of God]."[135] As such, the ministry of the Word requires a lifetime of careful study. But this must never distract the pastor from his sheep. Beza notes:

> It is a very holy and necessary desire for a preacher to be diligent and careful in study so that he has something to feed his sheep. But if he throws himself so much into it that, while he is studying, Satan devours one of his sheep, then he cannot be called a true pastor. A true pastor not only attends to the reading of Scripture [...] but also guards his flock.[136]

The Genevan reformer insists that a true pastor must have a personal knowledge of his people. He must remember them by name and pray for them. He must be attentive to their needs and proactive in caring for them personally. Indeed, "pastors must run after lost sheep, bandaging up the one with a broken leg, strengthening the one that is sick. [...] In sum, the pastor must consider his sheep dearer to him than his own life, following the example of the Good Shepherd."[137] Changing the metaphor, Beza elsewhere compares the faithful pastor to a spiritual doctor who prescribes the right medication to his patients. The Christian minister needs "not only to discern the illness, but also the situation and disposition of the patient, looking for the best medicine to prescribe, preaching the Law to the hardened, and the gospel of grace to those despairing.

---

133 Beza to Jacob Monau, 14/24 December 1589, in CB 30:312.
134 See MANETSCH, S. (2007), 241–256.
135 BEZA, T., *Sermons sur l'histoire de la passion* (1592b), 319–320.
136 BEZA, T., *Sermons sur le Cantique of Cantiques* (1586b), 48–49.
137 BEZA, T., *Sermons sur l'histoire de la resurrection* (1593b), 567.

In brief, let us always condemn the sin, but try to save the sinner."[138] What becomes clear, then, is that for Beza, pastoral ministry involves applying God's Word to people in every stage of life, from cradle to grave. Pastoral ministry takes place when babies are baptized, when children are catechized, when the liturgy is read aloud, when the people of God are nourished at the Lord's Table, when the congregation attends to the sermon, when recalcitrant sinners are disciplined, when the sick and dying are consoled at bedside.

To be sure, the ministry of the Word usually involves face-to-face encounters. But for Beza, it can also take place in a carefully written letter, brimming with theological insight, deep concern and unwavering Christian confidence. This is illustrated in Beza's memorable epistolary exchange with the Polish humanist Johannes Crato von Krafftheim, a personal physician to the Habsburg emperors.[139] Crato first made contact with Beza in the mid-1570s, and over the course of the next decade the two men wrote occasional letters, reporting news from their respective corners of the world, discussing mutual friends and comparing good books. As Crato's health began to decline, their correspondence began to probe the darker, more difficult aspects of the human condition. What are God's purposes in human suffering and affliction? How can we be confident that we are God's elect children? Where does one find courage in the face of death and the grave? Beza's pastoral sensitivities are on full-display throughout this poignant interchange, as he encourages his friend to find confidence in God's promises and sturdy hope in Christ's glorious resurrection. Paraphrasing Paul's words in 1 Timothy 2:12—"If we suffer with Christ we will also reign with him"—Beza exhorts his friend: "I admit that righteous people suffer, but through suffering they will win the victory and obtain the eternal weight of glory that cannot be compared to the suffering of this present age."[140] On another occasion, the reformer reminded his colleague: "It is the Lord's custom to raise all the way to the heavens those people he has first brought down to hell. [...] Therefore, come on! Let us continue to fight strongly until we receive from him the prize for our struggle."[141] In the midst of Crato's despondency and death-struggle, Theodore Beza once again holds up for his friend the image of the Christian life as a perilous sea voyage that finds its happy conclusion in a safe harbor. In one of his final letters to Crato, Beza writes: "May God, our most merciful Savior strengthen us more and more by his Spirit so that, after weathering so many fierce storms and having sailed into that harbor of true tranquility, we might celebrate eternal triumph with him who has secured our

---

138 BEZA, T. *Sermons sur l'histoire de la resurrection* (1593b), 129–130.
139 See MANETSCH, S. (2012), 293–294.
140 Beza to Crato, 15 January 1583, in CB 24:9.
141 Beza to Crato, 30 October 1583, in CB 24:284.

victory."[142] Triumph, tranquility, eternal security—for Beza, these constitute the glorious inheritance that awaits God's people as they navigate the tragedies and troubles of their earthly journey.

Conclusion

Theodore Beza arrived at the end of his earthly life and reached his own safe harbor on 23 October 1605, as the bells of St. Pierre summoned the people of Geneva to the eight o'clock sermon.[143] The next day, the city magistrates posted a notice to the doors of the Genevan Academy that read: "Like sailors arriving in port, so is the entrance into another life of those whose death is precious in the eyes of the Lord. Yesterday, a great light in the Church was extinguished."[144] Beza himself could not have crafted a more fitting eulogy.

Over the course of eighty-six years, Theodore Beza left a sizeable imprint on Europe's churches and society as a cultured humanist, a gifted poet, a top-flight biblical scholar, a Reformed theologian, a formidable polemicist, a talented preacher and a conscientious pastor. Through his extensive correspondence, Beza maintained relationships with a vast network of friends and colleagues, stretching from Scotland to Transylvania, that included powerful princes and magistrates, and the most influential Protestant theologians and church leaders of his generation. More than Calvin's epigone, Theodore Beza was recognized by his contemporaries as the leader of the French Reformed movement and one of Europe's most influential (and controversial) scholars and public intellectuals. On the 500th anniversary of Theodore Beza's birth, it is appropriate that scholars of a new generation reconsider the legacy of this Genevan minister and, in so doing, provide new perspectives on an old reformer.

---

142 Beza to Crato, 15 January 1583, in CB 24:15.
143 See GEISENDORF, P.-F. (1967), 424–429.
144 BORGEAUD, C. (1900), 1:313.

Part One: Theodore Beza's Place in History

Michael Bruening

Chapter 1: Before the *Histoire Ecclésiastique*

Theodore Beza's Unknown Apologetic History of the Lausanne Pastors and Professors

Although Theodore Beza's *Histoire Ecclésiastique des Eglises Réformées au royaume de France* is his best known historical work,[1] an untitled, almost completely unknown work, still in manuscript form and written well before the *Histoire Ecclésiastique*, represents Beza's first major piece of historical writing. In this text, composed entirely in Latin, Beza presents an apology on behalf of the pastors and professors of Lausanne following their expulsion from the city in 1559 by the Bernese. He does so by relating the history of the conflicts over ecclesiastical discipline between the Bernese and the church of Lausanne where, from 1549 to 1558, he served as professor of Greek. As he would do later in the *Histoire Ecclésiastique*, Beza includes full transcriptions (or translations) of letters and other primary source documents from the period, including many that remain unpublished, the most notable of which is a short treatise, or *libellus*, on ecclesiastical discipline written by Pierre Viret in 1558 that has long been considered lost. This manuscript by Beza, therefore, both contains much previously unknown historical evidence about the Reformation era in Lausanne and sheds light on Beza's early historical method, which he would develop later with the production of the famous *Histoire Ecclésiastique*.

1.1 The Manuscripts

Two manuscripts at the Bibliothèque de Genève contain portions of this text, namely volumes 7 and 64 of the Archives Tronchin manuscript collection.[2] One reason for the text's relative anonymity is the somewhat misleading description

---

1 [BEZA, T.], *Histoire Ecclésiastique* (1883–1889). For many years, Beza's authorship of the work was in doubt, but the editors of the CB have established Beza's role as author and lead editor. See CB 21 (1580), vii-xiii. It remains true, however, that Beza drew on accounts sent to him from various churches in France, as well as on previously published histories, such as those by Régnier de La Planche, Pierre de La Place, and Henri de Condé. On the *Histoire Ecclésiastique* see also CARBONNIER-BURKARD, M. (2007), 145–161.

2 Archiv Tronchin, 7 and 64.

of the volumes provided by Frédéric Gardy in his catalogue of the Archives Tronchin manuscripts. Gardy notes that volume 64 is an

> Apologetic memoir of the Lausanne chapter and Viret and an account of their discussions with the magistrates of Bern from 1538 to 1558. [...] It is accompanied by the partial original of the text in Theodore Beza's hand, which allows us to attribute the paternity of this writing to him. [...] Many of the copies are Latin translations of documents whose French originals are found in volume 6.[3]

The Gardy catalogue goes on to indicate that volume 7 is "another, more complete contemporary copy of this memoir."[4] These descriptions—and especially the note that these were mostly Latin translations of the French originals—suggest that one is unlikely to find much new or original in these volumes. In fact, the manuscripts contain both narrative sections and many additional documents that are not present in volume 6 of the Archives Tronchin and that remain unpublished to this day.

Credit for the discovery of this text should go to Henri Meylan, who used a section of it to relate the story of Jean Davion, a critic of Calvin's doctrine of predestination who is mentioned a couple of times in Beza's correspondence.[5] In 1959, Meylan described the volume as "the great memoir compiled in the name of the Lausanne chapter after the catastrophe of January 1559. [...] This *pro domo* apology apparently was meant to be published at the time; no doubt due to issues of opportunity, it was abandoned, and this important document remains in manuscript form."[6] In a later, 1978 article, Meylan notes that "the great apologetic memoir compiled by Theodore Beza at the end of the 1558–1559 crisis has never been either published or used."[7] As an editor of the early volumes of the *Correspondance de Bèze*, Meylan also used the manuscript to clarify the story of Beza's departure from Lausanne in 1558.[8] Despite its discovery by Meylan, however, the volume has had almost no impact on scholarship on Beza or Lausanne, nor have its contents ever been examined in detail.[9]

---

3 GARDY, F. (1946), 28–29.
4 GARDY, F. (1946), 29.
5 MEYLAN, H. (1959), 177–181.
6 MEYLAN, H. (1959), 179.
7 MEYLAN, H. (1978), 15–23. In a footnote to this article, he describes the volume as follows: "Ce mémoire latin, qui a été rédigé par Bèze pour justifier ses collègues de la Classe des pasteurs de Lausanne—la minute des premiers folios est de sa main—nous est parvenu dans deux copies contemporaines, revues par Bèze lui-même, dans les vol. 7 et 64 des Archives Tronchin .... L'oeuvre est inachevée, s'interrompant au milieu de décembre 1558, alors que la sentence de déposition est du 20 janvier 1559." Ibid., 15n.4.
8 CB 2 (1556–1558), 267–269, appendix 14, which cites only Archiv Tronchin, vol. 7.
9 I was unaware of it in all my previous works on Viret and the Reformation in the Pays de Vaud. Karine Crousaz does not mention it in her monograph on the Lausanne Academy. Paul-F.

Between the two manuscript volumes, there are three partial versions of the same text. In chronological order of production, they are, first, the initial draft in Beza's hand at the beginning of volume 64 (fols. 1r-12v), second, a full, early draft in volume 7 (entire manuscript), and third, the final draft in volume 64 (fols. 13r-end, 243v). The order of the drafts can be illustrated by looking at one example of the same text in all three versions. In the text in Beza's hand, we read the phrase, "ut per nos fierent eorum malorum certiores quae ab ipsis unis sanari possunt ac debent, ex ~~iis ipsis~~ nostris scriptis."[10] The text in volume 7 has exactly the same phrase, omitting "iis ipsis," which Beza had crossed out in the initial draft.[11] Finally, the final draft in volume 64 reads, "ut per nos fierent eorum malorum certiores quae ab ipsis unis sanari ~~possunt ac debent~~ **potuerunt**, ex nostris scriptis."[12] Thus, one can easily trace the editing process, with Beza first making corrections to his own text, then the text in volume 7 incorporating those changes, and finally the text in volume 64 reproducing the text in volume 7, but with additional changes in Beza's hand.

Looking first at the draft in Beza's hand, we see this version is only partial, containing twelve folio leaves, with a narrative that breaks off in the midst of the pastors' quarrels with André Zébédée and Jerome Bolsec (d. c. 1584). This version is the least neatly written of the three, and it contains many textual corrections and insertions, reinforcing the conclusion that it served as the initial draft. Beza composed his narrative in Latin, but he interspersed indications in French where letters and others documents were to be inserted.[13] His notations indicate that he had labelled the original documents and letters he wanted to include in his text. So here we get a glimpse into Beza's working method and how he organized the primary documents for insertion into the larger text. One suspects he did much the same thing with the reams of documents he needed to put together for the *Histoire Ecclésiastique*.

The volume 7 copy then seems to have been produced as a full draft of the text and includes the text of the inserted documents. Gardy designated the

---

Geisendorf and Alain Dufour make no reference to it in their biographies of Beza. Catherine Santschi does not mention it in her article on Beza and the Bernese. And Gardy does not include it in his bibliography of Beza's works. BRUENING, M. (2005); Ibid. (2012); CROUSAZ, K. (2012); GEISENDORF, P.-F. (1949); DUFOUR, A. (2006); SANTSCHI, C. (1960), 113–130; GARDY, F. (1960).

10 Archiv Tronchin 64:5v.

11 Archiv Tronchin 7:3v.

12 Archiv Tronchin 64:16v.

13 E.g., " per id tempus scripsimus in quibus ista quoque erant comprehensa. Lettres à Messieurs cottées G. […] Addidimus igitur et nos literas tum ad amplissimum senatum tum ad fratres ac symmystas Bernensis Ecclesiae minstros, quarum hoc est exemplar. Lettres à Messieurs cottées H. […] Lettres aux ministres, cottées J." Archiv Tronchin 64:10v.

volume 7 copy as "more complete," for its text continues past the point where the final draft in volume 64 ends abruptly. The last page of volume 64 breaks off mid-sentence in a letter from the Lausanne pastors to their counterparts in Bern in late 1558. Fortunately, the draft in volume 7 continues the text past this point. Unfortunately, the continuation in volume 7 is also incomplete. It stops in the middle of a letter from the Bern city council to the Lausanne pastors, just before Viret's expulsion from Lausanne. Despite Gardy's claim that volume 7 is "more complete," however, one must note that it is missing many of the pages that form the middle of volume 64. The text that runs from folio 137r to 187r in volume 64 is missing entirely from volume 7.[14]

Volume 64 contains what was likely the final draft of the text. It contains a clear, highly legible copy of the text. The text of this copy ends, as noted above, mid-sentence on folio 243v.[15] With more than 200 folio leaves, we have here a document of more than four hundred pages, filled with letters and documents from the period, as well as interspersed narrative from Beza. In the midst of this version in the copyist's hand, we also find descriptions of the included documents and occasional textual corrections in Beza's hand. Thus, Beza clearly read and edited this copy, demonstrating that it is, in fact, a contemporary copy produced under his supervision.

1.2 The Manuscripts' Contents

Beza's manuscript contains a mixture of narrative and letters and other documents from the period, reproduced or translated into Latin. Sixty-two documents form, by far, the majority of the text. Of these, three have been published

---

14 The bottom of vol. 7, 54v contains the text, "Quis nescit synodum illam primam Hierosolymis actam summas utilitates Ecclesiae attulisse, ut puritas doctrinae conservaretur, et gentium" followed by "mores impuri" as the bottom indicator of the first words that should appear on the next page. This is a portion of a letter from the Lausanne chapter to the Bern pastors dated 18 August 1557, and corresponds to vol. 64, fol. 137r. The top of the next page in vol. 7, fol. 55r, begins, "prophanationem quotidie oculis nostris cernimus," which is from a letter from the Lausanne chapter to the Bern council before Easter 1558, and corresponds to vol. 64, fol. 187r.

15 Fols. 20–49, however, seem never to have existed. The numbers are missing, but the text proceeds smoothly midsentence, without break or interruption, from fol. 19v to fol. 50r.

by Herminjard,[16] fourteen are in the *Calvini Opera*,[17] seventeen are in *Epistolae Petri Vireti*,[18] and three are in other publications.[19] That leaves twenty-five documents in the manuscript that remain unpublished. These are listed in Table 1. Most of these documents are letters between the Lausanne pastors or chapter, and the Bern city council or pastors.[20]

Table 1   Unpublished documents in the manuscripts

Vol. 64 foliation	Vol. 7 foliation	Title by Beza or general description if no title given
50r-51v	6v-7v	Response made by the Lausanne pastors in person to the Bern council in January 1543 on the controversy over ecclesiastical goods
51r-52v	7v-8r	Response made by the Lausanne pastors to the Bern council in January 1543, the day after the response above
53r-54v	9r-10r	Excerpta ex articulis qui nomina omnium classium novae Bernensis provinciae propositi sunt in synodo Bernae habita mense Martio anno 1549
70v-73r	19v-21r	Particula responsi Lausannensis classis ad superiora edicta [concerning predestination, ca. February 1555]
74v-76r	21v-22v	Literae eiusdem Lausannensis Classis, ad Bernensis Ecclesiae ministros, super eodem negotio [i.e., the "calumnies" of André Zébédée and Jean Lange]
76r	22v	Responsum Bernensis Senatus ad superiores literas
83r-87r	26v-29r	Literae Lausannensis classis ad Bernenses ministros super eodem negotio [i.e., Bern's anti-Calvinist decree of 3 April 1555], 24 April [1555]

---

16 1.) Articuli exhibiti totius classis Lausannensis nomine in synodo Lausannae habita 4. April. 1538 (Archiv Tronchin 64:16v-17v ; ibid. 7:4r-v), HERMINJARD, A. (1866–1897), 4:410–413 ; 2.) Lausanne chapter to Bern council, 1 November 1542 (Archiv Tronchin 64:17v-19v; ibid. 7:5r-6r), HERMINJARD, A. (1866–1897), 8:171–176, no. 1174; 3.) Bern council to Lausanne chapter, 2 January 1543 (Archiv Tronchin 64:19v-50r; ibid. 7:6v), HERMINJARD, A. (1866–1897), 8:238, no. 1194, French original.

17 CO vol. 13–17, nos. 1284, 1285, 2020, 2021, 2046, 2096, 2127, 2097, 2115, 2117, 2176, 2195, 2878, 2979.

18 *Epistolae Vireti*, nos. 134, appx. nos. 1, 2, 4, 5, 6, 10, 14, 15, 16, 17, 18, 19, 20, 21, 22.

19 MEYLAN, H. (1956), 105–106, Lausanne chapter to the Bern council, [summer 1557]; BRUENING, M. (2006), 21–50; BARNAUD, J. (1911b), 113–116.

20 Technically, this was the *classe* of Lausanne, which included the pastors of all the churches along the northeastern shore of Lake Geneva and into the Four Mandated Territories southeast of the lake. In the past I have used the untranslated French word *classe* in my published works. In German, the Bernese used *Kapitel*, and I am now using the standard English translation of *Kapitel*, i.e., *chapter* for the French *classe*.

Vol. 64 foliation	Vol. 7 foliation	Title by Beza or general description if no title given
92v-94v	31r-32r	Articuli in quibus ministri classis Lausaniensis suppliciter orant Principes Bernenses ac dominos suos, ut malis Ecclesiae prospiciant et consulant [early 1553]
95r-99v	32r-34r	Alii articuli complectentes disciplinam Lausanne perturbatam et confusam cum in Consistorio, tum etiam in caeteris omnibus, quae ad reformationem principum nostrorum pertinent [early 1553]
99v	34v	Responsum ampliss Senatus. Bernensis ad superiores querelas, 15 April 1553
99v-102r	34v-35v	Responsum Lausannensis classis ad superiores literas [after 15 April 1553]
102r-112v	36r-41r	Scriptum Lausannensis classis super ecclesiastica disciplina [1553]
112v-121v	41r-46v	Aliud eiusdem classis scriptum in eodem negotio: Quae ministri classis Lausannensis desiderent in illa quae hodie habentur consisteriorum forma et constitutione [1553]
121v-124v	46v-48r	Articuli Lausannensis classis super eodem negotio ecclesiasticae disciplinae ad ampliss. Senatum Bernensem missi [1553-1555?]
130r-133r	51r-53r	Articuli de disciplina symmystis nostris Bernensibus ministris missi [1553-1555?]
133v-136v	53r-54v	Aliae Lausannensis classis literae ad ampliss. Senatum Bernensem pro instaurandis Ecclesiarum ruinis [1555-1557?]
142v-185r	n/a	P. Vireti Libellus de disciplina Bernensi Senatui exhibitus [March 1558]
185r-188r	55r-v (partial)	Consuli Senatuique Bernensi salutem in Christo [from Lausanne chapter, ca. April 1558]
188v-190r	56r-57r	Lausanne chapter to Bern council [22 May 1558]
236v-237r	87r	Bern council's response to the Lausanne pastors in Bern, 15 Aug. 1558
238r-243r	88r-91v	Lausanne pastors to Bern council, 31 October 1558
243r-v (partial)	91v-93v	Lausanne pastors to Bern pastors, [31 October 1558]
n/a	93v-96v	Viret to the Bern council, 6 November 1558
n/a	98r-100r	Viret to the Bern council, 27 November 1558
n/a	100r-v	Lausanne chapter to the Bern council, [ca. 27 November 1558]

In general, this material covers most of the key conflicts among the pastors of the Pays de Vaud in the 1540s and 1550s, notably those over ecclesiastical goods, predestination and especially ecclesiastical discipline.[21] This unpublished material helps to fill gaps in our knowledge of this period. Several of these documents are referred to in other published sources from the period, which currently contain footnotes bemoaning the reference to "an apparently lost letter."[22] Among the unpublished material, perhaps the most notable texts that appear in this manuscript are the articles proposed at the Synod of Bern (1549),[23] the series of texts from 1553 on ecclesiastical discipline,[24] and Viret's *libellus* from 1558.[25]

The 1549 Synod of Bern was the only synod held in the Pays de Vaud between the Synod of Lausanne (1538) and Viret's expulsion from Lausanne in 1559.[26] A few extant letters refer to the synod,[27] but the text Beza reproduces here is one of the only texts to survive from the synod, and it reveals that Viret and his colleagues—Beza would not join them until later that year as professor of Greek—were interested in more than the divisive dispute over the Eucharist and the power of the ministry. The text has sections on the election of ministers, paupers, discipline and the sacraments.

The six texts from 1553 on discipline reveal a push from the Lausanne chapter at that time that has gone almost entirely unnoticed in the scholarship.[28] The later 1558 debates over discipline are, of course, well known, but the texts in this manuscript reveal that Lausanne pastors were drafting substantial proposals

---

21 On these conflicts, see BRUENING, M. (2005), ch. 7; CROUSAZ, K. (2012), 91–114; VUILLEUMIER, H. (1927–1933), 1:627–666.

22 See, e.g., *Epistolae Vireti* 519n.4, 7, appendix 22, 4 December 1558, which refers to two letters from Viret, dated 6 and 27 November 1558, both of which I indicated are "apparently lost," but which both appear in the Archiv Tronchin manuscript.

23 Archiv Tronchin 64:53r-54v, with the following subheadings: *De ministrorum electionibus, De Pauperibus, De populi disciplina et statu doctrinae ratione,* and *De sacramentis.*

24 Archiv Tronchin 64:92v-121v.

25 Archiv Tronchin 64:142v-185r.

26 On the 1549 Synod of Bern, see VUILLEUMIER, H. (1927–1933), 1:295–297. On the 1538 Synod of Lausanne, see BRUENING M./CROUSAZ, K. (2011), 89–126.

27 See, esp., Johannes Haller to Calvin, 29 April 1549, in CO 13:240–244, no. 1178.

28 I do not refer to it in *Calvinism's First Battleground.* Vuilleumier only briefly mentions some (uncited) complaints by the Lausanne pastors in late 1552 (VUILLEUMIER, H. [1927–1933], 1:661). Jean Barnaud refers to a letter from Bern pastor Johannes Haller, in which he mentions the Lausanne pastors' complaints (BARNAUD, J. [1911a], 441–442). One of the unpublished texts in the Archiv Tronchin is likely that referred to by Haller, which the editors of the *Calvini Opera* could not find, in a letter to Bullinger: "Nulli tamen vehementius hoc urserunt quam Lausannenses, sicut hoc ex scripto ipsorum, cuius apographum tibi mitto, colligere potes, quod nobis communi consensu exhibuerunt." See 6 September 1553, CO 14:609n.3, no. 1789.

on discipline well before then. The six documents from 1553 constitute twenty-nine folio leaves and outline both the rationale for implementing more rigorous discipline and suggestions for how to do so. They also contain interesting tidbits about local religious practice. For example, the pastors complain that fathers in the region frequently refrained from attending the baptisms of their children because they believed that their presence at the baptism created a bond of affinity that required them to abstain from their wives afterwards.[29]

The most important previously unpublished document in this manuscript collection, however, is the *libellus* by Viret on ecclesiastical discipline from March 1558. Scholars have long known that Viret wrote this work, for he refers to it in his letters to Calvin from the period.[30] To this point, however, everyone has either ignored the work or deemed it lost.[31] Here, the document appears in full, contains seventy-four titled sections, and takes up more than forty folio leaves. The table of contents of the work are found in Table 2 below:

---

29 "Accidit autem in his regionibus tertius error quod superstitione quadam stulta existimant patres si liberorum Baptismo interessent, contrahi vinculum affinitatis, quo cogantur ab uxoribus postea abstinere, quem errorem fovet haec patrum absentia in Baptismo." Archiv Tronchin 64:109v.

30 Viret refers to the *libellus* in a few letters to Calvin in March 1558: 1.) "Cupiebam tuam audire sententiam de scripto et opusculo quod senatui nostro exhibuimus, quod nobis esset vice apologiae apud eos qui consilia nostra calumniarentur." 19 March 1558, in CO 17:104, no. 2836; 2.) "Bernam missus est libellus. Exspectamus durum responsum, ac nos ad abitionem paramus." 23 March 1558, in CO 17:113, no. 2840; 3.) "Antequam vocaremur ad senatum, audita est lectio nostri libelli in compendium a Zerkinte redacti et in linguam germanicam versi, iussu senatus. Zerkintae placuit nostra sententia, quam se bona fide interpretatum contestatus est, nullo praetermisso capite, cuius summam non sit complexus, quantum res ipsa postulare videbatur. Vidimus translationem, quae satis multas continebat chartas." 4 April [1558], in CO 17:126, no. 2845.

31 Louis Vulliemin thought he was publishing portions of Viret's *libellus* in his edition of Abraham Ruchat's *Histoire de la Réformation de la Suisse*, for he dated the text to March 1558. But the excerpts he published actually came from the project on discipline that the Lausanne chapter drew up in June 1558. On this error, see BRUENING, M. (2006), 24. Viret's biographer, Jean Barnaud, refers only to the letters and Lausanne council registers in which the *libellus* is mentioned and says nothing about the text itself. BARNAUD, J. (1911a), 448–450. Neither Vulleumier nor Crousaz mentions it.

Table 2   Contents of Viret's *Libellus*

Vol. 64 Foliation	Section Titles
142v	Summaria quaedam et leviter informata descriptio provisionis eius, quae certis Ecclesiae morbis adhibenda est
147v	De officio Pastorum Ecclesiasticorum in administratione verbi divini
148r	De usu et administratione sacramentorum et quibus ea comissa est
148v	Quibus administrari aut negari debeant sacramenta
149r	De profanatione sacramentorum aliarumque rerum sacrarum, deque interdicto, quod ea de re a Christo est interpositum
149v	De atrocitate peccati quod admittitur in profanatione sacramentorum deque ministrorum in eiusmodi rebus officio
149v	De disciplina a Domino instituta in Ecclesia, ad praecavendam rerum sacrarum profanationem quae alioqui in Ecclesia posset accidere
150v	Qua attentione et cura observandum sit, universae Ecclesiae verbone divino obtemperetur, an repugnetur et quibuscum hominibus ei res potissimum sit
150v	De praecipua Ministrorum in hac parte cura
151r	De subsidio quod reliqua Ecclesiae membra ministris hac in re debent, deque periculo participandi aliena peccata, et quo pacto id accidere possit
151v	De religionis et doctrinae Christianae confessione ac professione, quae ab unoquoque exigenda est in Ecclesia, deque rationibus et viis ad id efficiendum a Deo praescriptis, permulta mala et incommoda fugiendi gratia
152r	De exemplis et testimoniis indicantibus quam parvi fiat doctrina Evangelii ac prope pro nihilo ducatur, unde iudicari potest, num religionis ac fidei professio, quae ab unoquoque fit in externa communione sacramentorum satis idonea ac legitima sit ipsa per se nullo alio testimonio addito
153r	De iis qui neque ad sacram concionem omnium communem neque ad catechismum ad rudes idiotarum animos religionis cognitione informandos inprimis comparatum, neque ad communionem Sacramentorum unquam accedunt
153r	De iis, qui tum dictis, tum factis et audacia in tuendis suis erroribus aperta indicant, ac prae se ferunt, se Christianae doctrinae veritati adversari
153v	De iis qui manifesto Papismum tuentur, quibusque nihil certi omnimo est in religione
154r	De stupida quorundam ignorantia, in praecipuis religionis capitibus, deque iis qui se magis ἀθεούς et Epicureos, quam Christianos suis ipsi sermonibus et vitae instituto declarant
154v	De iis qui sacrarum literarum veritatem in dubitationem vocant, omnes religiones probando

Vol. 64 Foliation	Section Titles
155r	De iis qui quanvis Papisticam doctrinam improbent, tamen puritate doctrinae cum veris Evangelii Ministris non consentiunt, quin etiam illis maledicunt atque obtrectant
155r	De exigua audientium frequentia in sacris concionibus, tum profestis tum Dominicis diebus, prae hominum ingenti multitudine, qui in singulis Ecclesiis reperiri possint
156r	De confusione quae interdum nonnullis in locis existet, propter ingentem hominum multitudinem, qui omnes concionem percipere non possunt
156v	De publica sacrarum concionum et sacramentorum contemptione, quae apparet in multis etiam eorum qui nonnunquam intersunt
157v	De prava iuventutis institutione, et quam valde plerique negligant curare suos liberos vera religione erudiendos, ac de periculo, quod eam ob rem impendet Ecclesia
158r	De iis, qui passim vagantur per rura, per sylvas et montes
158v	De advenis, et eorum diversis generibus ac primum de iis, qui non religionis causa in hanc regionem se conferunt
159r	De Senatusconsulto, quod a Principibus factum est de peregrinorum coniugiis, quantoque attentior cura et diligentia eorum causa adhibenda sit in administratione Sacramentorum
159v	De advenis, qui Evangelii nomen ementiuntur
159v	De causis eorum peccatorum quae supra commemorata sunt
160r	De incommodis inde manantibus, quod melior disciplina non est constituta, neque ante provisum est, ut omnes in religionis cognitione probe edocti essent, deque periculo irae divinae, tum in magistratus, tum in Ministros, totamque Ecclesiam impendentis
160v	De animadversione in eos etiam adhibenda, qui, cum Evangelica reformatione glorientur, dedecoris et offensionis plenam vitam agunt
161r	Quid Paulus hac de re scripserit, atque instituerit
161r	Num Christiani, qui Evangelicae religionis instauratione gloriantur in Sacramentorum communione ferre possint eos, qui nullo inhonesto coetu ferri possint
161v	De disciplina quam Papistae atque Ethnici in sua religione semper habuerunt: quod quidem iis magno probro est, qui Evangelii nomine gloriantur
162r	Sit ne consentaneum legitimam verae Ecclesiae disciplinam abrogare, quia Papistae ea abusi fuerint
162v	Quanto maiore diligentia cautio adhiberi soleat, ne civiles, quam ne Ecclesiastici conventus ulla ignominia afficiantur
163r	De disciplina Ecclesiastica, quae olim in populo Israëlitico fuit, ac deinceps rursum instaurata et confirmata in Ecclesia Christiana ab ipso Iesu Christo
163v	De solicitudine, atque anxietate, qua veri Ministri ac precones Evangelii, ubi administrandorum sacramentorum tempus adventat, afficiuntur propter summam dissolutionem et perturbationem rerum, quae amplius ab iis tolerari non debet

Vol. 64 Folia-tion	Section Titles
163v	Num culpa et negligentia, quae ante hac in re extitit debeat unumquem-que ad remedium adhibendum potius incitare, quam ad pergendum sicuti fieri coeptum est
164r	Num absurdum id videri debeat, cum de religione agitur, quod nullo pacto videtur absurdum, in agnoscenda rerum mancupi authoritate, quam vulgo recognitionem possessionum vocant
165r	De scandalo et offensione, quae accidere potest in Ecclesia, si min-istri sacramentorum administrationem denegent, et quis eius rei culpam sustinere debeat.
165v	Quam sit necessarium in Ecclesia, bene constitutam esse aliquam exam-inandae doctrinae formam, ut unusquisque, quid de doctrina sentiat tes-tifecetur
165v	Quid Deus edixerit atque imperarit de legis suae promulgatione eiusque studio atque iuventutis institutione
166r	De professione, quae requirebatur in Ecclesia Israëlitica, deque circunci-sione et argumento quo infantium circuncisio nitebatur
166v	De convenientia Ecclesiae Christianae, et Israëliticae, in Baptismi et cir-cumcisionis ratione, et foederis a Deo nobiscum facti, quod quidem fun-damentum est omnium sacramentorum
167r	De Catechismis veteris Ecclesiae et eorum usu
167r	De praecipuo fundamento Baptismi infantium, quamque vim in eo habeat foederis divini ratio
167r	De infantibus qui ad Baptismum recipiendi sint, et a quibus ad eum accip-iendum illos offerri conveniat
167v	De iis qui suos liberos ad Baptismum offerendos tradunt pueris, aut ado-lescentulis, qui per aetatem id munus quod suscipiunt praestare non possint, deque patribus qui suorum liberorum baptismo non adsunt
168r	De iis qui suos liberos ad baptismum Papistarum manibus offerunt, alio-rumve qui mala doctrina imbuti sunt, aut flagitiosa vita inquinati
168v	De iis qui ad reliqua Ecclesiae Israëliticae sacramenta admittebantur, deque iis, qui illius ordinis exemplo ad coenam recipiendi sunt, ac de re-bus quae ab illis requirendae sunt
169r	Cur pueri ad sacram Coenam non admittantur, sicuti ad baptismum, deque Catechismo eorum causa instituto
169v	Num pueri aetatis tantum ratione a Coena excludantur
169v	Num pueris ex annorum numero, an ex progressu quem in Dei notitia fe-cerint, praefiniendum sit ad Coenam adeundi tempus
170r	Sit ne iustior ratio adulteriores ad Coenam admittendi, quam pueros, si illi non magis quam hi eius sacramenti compotes sint atque etiam minus
170v	Sit ne unusquisque conscientiae suae arbitrio relinquendus, cum agitur de Coena ac nihil praeterea inquirendum

Vol. 64 Foliation	Section Titles
171r	Num Ecclesia et eius Ministri omne iudicium permittere, debeant eorum conscientiae, qui ipsi coniuncti sunt indignitatis suae, quod ad Coenam attinet
171r	Quo numero habendi sunt Papistae in vera Ecclesia
171v	De sententia in quam accipiendum est illud Pauli de privata sui probatione, antequam ad Coenae communionem adeatur, quosque homines potissimum eo loco Paulus alloquatur
172r	Quam sit necessarium ab iis fidei confessionem exigi, qui a vera religione aberrarunt, si quando in Ecclesiam redire rursumque in eam recipi velint
173r	De exemplis piorum Iudicum, Regum, Principumque populi Israëlitici, quae pertinent ab probandum officium publicae confessionis ab universo populo exigendae
173r	De exemplo Ezechiale, in quo sanctificavit populum, quo melius paratus esset ad sacramentum agni Paschalis
173v	Quam sit necessarium his temporibus, ut saltem semel cognosci possint, qui religionis Christianae instaurationem vere acceperint atque approbarint, necne, deque peccato quod usque adhuc admissum est in hac parte
174v	Quanto magis conveniat, Principes ac Magistratus rerum ad gloriam Dei pertinentium, salutemque populorum, qui illorum ditioni commissi sunt, quam rerum caducarum esse studiosos
175r	De exemplo in Ezechiae persona, magistratibus et Principibus, Christianis ad imitandum proposito
175v	Num Ministri Ecclesiae, minorem curam diligentiamque in rebus spiritualibus (quae cum illorum munere coniunctae sunt) quam politici Magistratus in temporariis et fluxis rebus adhibere soleant
175v	Quantopere necesse sit modum et rationem aliquam in Ecclesia institui, qua dignosci possint veri Christiani a falsis, et fideles ab infidelibus tollendae confusionis gratia
176r	Quantopere necessarium sit disciplinam a Iesu Christo institutam de correctione vitiorum, ex quibus Ecclesia offensionem aliquam excipere potest, restitui in veram germanamque formam, si velimus integram in Ecclesia reformationem habere
176v	De rationibus, quibus patet Ecclesiam neque recte administrari, neque ulla regula recte constitui posse, nisi ea disciplina atque norma, quae a Christo ipsi Ecclesiae tradita est
177r	Num Ecclesiae quibus praesunt Christiani Magistratus, carere facile possint hac disciplinae forma
177v	De distinguenda administratione civili ab Ecclesiastica
178r	Num Ministri tuto in aliena conscientia acquiescere possint, in iis rebus quae ipsorum munus attingunt
178r	Num decreta et edicta Principum per se satis mederi possint iis incommodis quae supra commemorata sunt
178v	Quid peccetur in ratione exequendi Principum decreta

Vol. 64 Foliation	Section Titles
178v	Num si Magistratus officio suo desint Ministri debeant ipsi suum
179r	De iis, quae desiderantur in Synedriis ut nunc sunt constituta, inque iis legibus quae ibi sequendae sunt
179v	De confusione politicae et Ecclesiasticae administrationis, itemque officii magistratuum ac ministrorum, quae est in Synedriis deque finibus Censurae ac disciplinae Ecclesiasticae
180v	Quid sit ex communionis finibus exterminare vel Ecclesia movere
180v	De differentia politicarum animadversionum et Ecclesiasticarum, quamque necessarium sit eos cum Ecclesia restitui in gratiam qui eam offenderunt, si ad sacramenta admitti velint
181r	Quanto ludibrio ac despicatus Synedria esse soleant iis qui illuc vocantur in ius, deque exigua emendatione quam prae se ferunt
181v	De vitio, quod est in eligendis Ascriptoribus sive assessoribus Synedriorum, deque viatoribus atque apparitoribus illorum
182v	Quam sit difficile potentiores nonnullos castigare Ecclesiastici consessus opera quantoque ludibrio ipsa Synedria esse soleant etiam iis, qui per illa aliquo modo castigantur
182v	De flagitiis et sceleribus quae a nonnullis admissa sunt Apparitoribus, cum fideliter suo munere fungi debuissent
183r	Num ministri possint salva fide administrare Sacramenta in iis Ecclesiis, quae vitiis non medentur, quibus illi contaminari possint
183v	Num Ministri Ecclesiae quicquam postulent amplius quam quod ipsorum munus ferat, cum petunt, ut verae disciplinae in ea sit locus ex Domini praescripto atque instituto
183v	Num administratio disciplinae Ecclesiasticae quicquam officiat, aut deroget muneri atque authoritati Magistratuum
184r	Num quid Ministri postulent praeter ea quibus ipsorum summi Principes libenter se submiserunt
184v	Quam libenter se submissuri sunt Ministri iudicio Ecclesiae Domini et eorum omnium qui ipsis afferent verbi Domini testimonium

Thus, we have with this manuscript not only a previously unknown apologetic history by Beza but also, within it, a complete, previously lost work by Viret. Clearly, future studies of the conflicts over ecclesiastical discipline in the Pays de Vaud will need to consider this important text by Viret, for it constituted the initial push in 1558 by the Lausanne pastors and professors for more rigorous discipline in the Vaud, an effort that would ultimately result in their expulsion from Bern's territories.

In addition to the many unpublished documents in the manuscript, it also contains twenty-five documents that have previously been published in French but are presented here in Latin. Examining these texts closely could shed light on Beza's practices and principles of translation from French into Latin.

Moreover, the manuscript's silences speak almost as loudly as its contents. Most striking in this regard is the almost total absence of material regarding disputes over the interpretation of the Eucharist. Throughout the 1540s, there were almost constant quarrels over the sacrament between the Zwinglian and Calvinist or Bucerian factions in both Bern and the Pays de Vaud.[32] Beza discusses the chief Zwinglian proponent in the Vaud, André Zébédée, but almost entirely in association with the Bolsec affair on predestination. We noted above the unpublished articles from the 1549 Synod of Bern, but the articles presented in the manuscript make no mention of the bitter quarrels between Viret and Zébédée over the Eucharist and power of the ministry that prompted the convocation of the synod in the first place. The one other text that survives from the time of the synod is Viret's *Confessio de ministerio verbi et sacramentorum*,[33] which Beza chose not to reproduce. His decision to omit material regarding the Eucharist provides an important clue regarding the purpose and intended audience of his history.

1.3   Intended Audience, Purpose, and Date of the Manuscript

The omission of material on the Eucharist suggests that Beza's intended audience included those who would have been annoyed or offended by rehashing these old debates. Moreover, since he produced the text in Latin—in contrast to the French of the *Histoire Ecclésiastique*—it seems that he was writing chiefly for an international Reformed audience, and especially those in German-speaking Switzerland. The Eucharistic controversies in Switzerland had bitterly divided the Zwinglian and Calvinist factions in the 1540s, but the 1549 *Consensus Tigurinus* had largely resolved them. Had Beza been writing a text aimed chiefly at fellow Calvinists, he may well have included discussion of the earlier Eucharistic debates. His avoidance of them here suggests that he did not wish to open old wounds but to deal directly with the most recent clashes, namely the disputes over ecclesiastical discipline that had led to the expulsion of Viret and his colleagues from Lausanne.

The introduction of the text sheds greater light on Beza's motivations for writing it. The first thing to note is that Beza writes almost entirely in the first person plural, which indicates that he is writing on behalf of all of the pastors

---

32   See BRUENING, M. (2005), 176–199; HUNDESHAGEN, K. (1842).
33   CO 7:727–732.

and professors of Lausanne. Moreover, the text makes it clear that their recent expulsion from the city is what prompted the drafting of this apology:

> Since we foresaw what would happen but could in no way stop it, it was not enough for Satan to expel us from our churches (for we prefer to attribute this misfortune to Satan than to any mortal), but also to bury the best cause with many false calumnies. At stake is not so much our cause as that of all the churches. In order to explain the controversy that led to this wretched dissipation, we believed it was our duty to explain each one of the reasons not only of our actions but also of our judgments.[34]

The Lausanne ministers encountered much criticism following their expulsion. After an initial sentence of banishment following Viret's delay of the 1558 Christmas Eucharist, the Bernese gave him and his colleagues several chances to submit to Bern's church ordinances and avoid banishment. But the Lausanne pastors and professors stood firm in their demands for greater ecclesiastical discipline.[35] Some Swiss theologians believed they had effectively deserted the Lausanne church.[36] Beza explains further in the introduction that he and his colleagues have produced this account in order to demonstrate the righteousness of their cause, the rationale behind their efforts of more than twenty years and their treatment by the Bern council.[37]

---

34 "Quoniam autem quod futurum quidem prospeximus, sed impedire nullo modo potuimus, non satis fuit Satanae nos ex nostris Ecclesiis expulisse (maluimus enim haec mala Satanae quam cuiquam mortalium tribuere) nisi porro etiam optimam causam multis falsis calumniis obrueret: et non tam nostra quam omnium Ecclesiarum interest, ut semel explicetur haec controversia quae causam miserae huic dissipationi praebuit, existimavimus nostri esse officii singulas non tantum actionum, sed etiam consiliorum nostrorum rationes sigillatim explicare." Archiv Tronchin 64:13r-v.

35 See BARNAUD, J. (1911a), 471–475.

36 E.g., Peter Martyr Vermigli wrote to Viret in January, "Attamen illud extremum esse arbitror, et ne dixerim nullo modo, vix tamen attingendum, ut ecclesiam in qua es deseras." 18 January 1559, in CO 17:416, no. 3001. Johannes Haller in Bern noted to Bullinger a month later, "Nam cum ab illis [the Lausanne pastors] qui 24 die examinati sunt intellexissent, quae cum ipsis acta essent omnia, de novo quasi conspirarunt iterum ad non consentiendum, sed ad exsilium potius eligendum." 28 February 1559, in CO 17:460–461, no. 3022. Soon afterwards, Bullinger added his own plea to Viret to return to his "deserted" church: "Nunc vero cum intelligam, abs te illam [ecclesiam] esse desertam, oro pietatem tuam, colendissime mi domine et frater, et quidem per Dominum Iesum, ut ad eandem redire non dedigneris." 3 March 1559, in CO 17:470, no. 3025.

37 "Ipsam vero narrationem ita distribuemus, ut primo loco paucis explicemus quam iustis ac necessariis causis adducti simus ad ea postulanda remedia quae prorsus necessaria esse iudicavimus: Deinde quam rationem in ista postulatione per annos plus minus viginti tenuerimus: Postremo quomodo in nostra expulsione nobiscum sit actum: ac nos vicissim cum amplissimo senatu egerimus." Archiv Tronchin 64:13v.

In so doing, we hope in the future that everyone will understand that we undertook these efforts neither rashly, lightly, nor ambitiously. Even now we do not repent of them. Nor did we strive vainly, nor persevere in our opinion stubbornly or seditiously, as some maintain. Finally, we did not desert the churches but were ejected from them, ripped away from the people who for the most part were praying to ward off our exile.[38]

Thus, the apologetic nature of the text, on behalf of all the expelled ministers and professors of Lausanne is clear from the text's introduction.

This apologetic emphasis in the wake of their expulsion makes Beza's authorship somewhat puzzling, for Beza had left Lausanne in November 1558, three months before his former colleagues were expelled. Thus, Beza was drafting an apology on behalf of the colleagues he had left behind. Of course, many of these individuals then came to Geneva and were once again working alongside him in a new city. Beza's efforts to assist his fellow Lausanne pastors and professors suggest a couple of paradoxical conclusions. First, the criticism of Viret and his colleagues for abandoning their posts may have rubbed off onto Beza as well. He had left Lausanne only a month and a half before Viret's initial sentence of banishment, and some in the region may have been lumping him in with the other Lausanne pastors and professors. This could help to explain why Beza inserted a section in the narrative on his own, earlier departure from Lausanne, in an attempt to distance himself from his former colleagues.[39] At the same time, he must have felt a strong sense of commeraderie with his Lausanne colleagues, or he would not have undertaken the task of writing the apology in the first place. As he noted to Viret shortly before the latter's arrival in Geneva, "The Lord knows I am certainly a partner in your grief."[40] Thus, Beza was at the same time distancing himself from his Lausanne colleagues and defending their cause.

As for the date of the text, it was likely written in the first half of 1559. Internal evidence from the text reveals that Beza was still working on it in late May 1559, for the section on his move from Lausanne to Geneva refers to François Bérauld's appointment to the Geneva Acacdemy as professor of Greek on 22

---

38 "Ita vero futurum speramus ut omnes intelligant nos neque temere aut leviter aut ambitiose ista consilia coepisse quorum ne nunc quidem nos poenitere potest: neque de nihilo laborasse: neque pertinaciter aut seditiose, ut nonnulli dictitant, in sententia perseverasse: Denique non esse a nobis desertas Ecclesias, sed nos ex Ecclesiis eiectos fuisse, et maxima ex parte deprecantibus exilium nostrum populis ereptos." Archiv Tronchin 64:13v-14r.

39 Printed in CB 2:268–69, appendix 14; Archiv Tronchin 64:237r-238r.

40 "Et sane sum tuorum dolorum particeps, ut novit Dominus." Beza to Viret, [February 1559], in CB 3:14.

May 1559.[41] External evidence about the text is sadly lacking. Both Beza's and Viret's correspondence in early 1559 is relatively minimal and contains no hint of the preparation of such a text. From January through August 1559, only one letter written by Beza survives, namely the one to Viret cited above. There is one possible reference to the work in one of Calvin's letters from the time. On 2 March 1559, Calvin wrote to Peter Martyr Vermigli, "I will not write to you about how atrociously the Bernese raged against and blasted our brothers. It is better if the whole story is explained to you, which I trust will happen soon."[42] It is impossible to say, however, whether this is an oblique reference to Beza's text or simply a wish that someone might explain the situation to Vermigli more fully.

By the summer of 1559, Beza's correspondence with Bullinger and the other German-speaking Reformed pastors seems to have normalized. This may well explain why the text was never finished. My hypothesis is that the text was produced to address a severe crisis in the winter and spring of 1559 that had been prompted by the expulsion of Viret and his colleagues whose effects spilled over onto Beza as well, but as the crisis abated in the summer of 1559, the perceived need to publish or circulate the apology faded with it.[43] By that time, circulating such a work may well have been seen as an attempt to reopen old wounds that had recently healed. Thus, Beza's work remained unfinished and unpublished.

1.4   The Lausanne History and the *Histoire Ecclésiastique*

Beza's text, as we have noted, had a clear apologetic intent, namely to justify the actions of the Lausanne pastors and professors in advocating for Calvinist ecclesiastical discipline and in choosing exile over submission to the Bernese. He pursues this goal almost entirely through historical narrative and the collection of historical documents. Thus, we can examine the manuscript to discover

---

41 "Itaque multis modis quaesito illi successore et tandem post quintum mensem, misera dissipata Lausannensi academia, reperto Francisco Beraldo, in Collegium Ministrorum vicesimo et altero die Maii anno 1559 est allectus." Archiv Tronchin 64:269,in CB 2:269, appendix 14.

42 "Quam atrociter saevierint Bernates ac fulminaverint in fratres nostros, quia non sine ingenti horrore audio, tibi non scribam. Et praestat integram historiam vobis explicari, quod brevi fore confido." Calvin to Vermigli, 2 March 1559, in CO 17:469, no 3024.

43 In a panel at the Sixteenth Century Studies Conference in 2019 (St. Louis), Karin Maag made the important point that the city councils of the period carefully guarded their documents and correspondence, and so the Bernese likely would not have been pleased to see their letters circulated in published form. She suggests that Beza's text may always have been intended for manuscript circulation rather than publication.

elements of Beza's early historical method, some of which he developed later in the *Histoire Ecclésiastique*. First and foremost, we note the inclusion of entire primary source documents in both works. Beza incorporates the full, unedited texts of letters and other documents in his story. Detailed analysis of the copies of documents in the Lausanne text and their relation to the originals still needs to be done, but initial investigations suggest that the texts match closely. Although Beza carefully selected *which* documents to include—omitting, for example, texts on the Eucharistic debates in the Vaud—once he decided to include a document, he included it in its entirety. Behind this decision seems to have been a humanist faith that the sources can and should speak for themselves. Just as one needed to go *ad fontes* to the full sources of classical antiquity and the early church to learn their true stories, so also with recent history, one must examine the entire document—and not just carefully made selections—to gain a true account of events.

Second, one function of both historical texts was to help construct an identity of the true church. Marianne Carbonnier-Burkard notes,

> With his *Histoire Ecclésiastique*, Beza proposed a third text [in addition to the French Confession of Faith and the Discipline], which also includes the first two, at the heart of a great origin story. Assembling the scattered histories into the common 'body of history,' at the same time national and multi-centered, one can suppose that the author intended to provide the Reformed churches, which were themselves scattered or even divided, with a common memory, a common image, and a specific collective identity.[44]

The manuscript in the Archives Tronchin likewise presents the Lausanne pastors and professors as united behind a common cause for more than twenty years. Beza himself was not even present in Lausanne during the first eleven years addressed in his text, but his narrative is not interested in addressing the arrivals and departures of individual pastors and professors in the city. Instead, he gives them a common identity and purpose. These are the "true" Reformed pastors and professors of the Suisse romande. He clearly distinguishes them from other individuals outside the core group, such as Zébédée, Bolsec, and Sebastian Castellio, all of whom he portrays negatively.[45] Writing this apology, therefore, perhaps helped Beza realize the power of writing history to create a common story and identity, the need for which was even stronger in the far-flung kingdom of France than it had been in the Pays de Vaud.

Finally, both texts have an apologetic nature. It is perhaps more overt in the Lausanne text, but in both cases, the identity Beza crafts was that of the "true church" in opposition to a hostile magistrate. In both, he seeks to show that

---

44 CARBONNIER-BURKARD, M. (2007), 160–161.
45 See, e.g., Beza's narrative in the Archiv Tronchin 64:60r-63r.

disobedience offered to the magistrate stemmed not from sedition or disloyalty but from a desire to follow the "pure Word of God." French Protestants could not obey the king in all cases because the French crown was still in thrall to the "false church of the Antichrist." The Lausanne pastors could not obey the Bern city council because it repeatedly sought over twenty years to suppress the "God-given duties" of the pastors and consistories. In this sense, the manuscript is a precursor to not just the *Histoire ecclésiastique* but also Beza's *Right of Magistrates*,[46] in which he argues for the right to resist a tyrannical government.

1.5 Conclusion

Beza's apologetic history of the Lausanne pastors and professors has lain unknown in manuscript form for too long. He produced the text at a time of crisis in the Swiss church. Had it been published, it may even have exacerbated existing divisions, for it lays blame for the crisis squarely in the hands of the Bernese. Beza's decision not to publish—although we must concede that the decision may not have been Beza's alone—represents a fork in the road of his career. He could have published the text, given up on the German-speaking Swiss and followed his former Lausanne colleagues into France. Instead, he kept the text in manuscript form, remained in Geneva, and repaired relations with the Swiss, especially Heinrich Bullinger. At the same time, the decision not to publish could well have alienated his former Lausanne colleagues. One of the puzzles of the years following Viret's move to France in 1561 is the almost total absence of correspondence between the formerly close colleagues, Beza and Viret. Several guesses have been offered to explain this absence, from class differences to competition for the role of Calvin's successor to a quarrel over lodging in Geneva to Viret's possible support for Jean Morély.[47] The episode around the text considered here suggests yet another possible reason: Perhaps Viret saw the apology Beza was preparing as his best chance to free himself from blame for the expulsion of the Lausanne pastors and professors. Viret may, therefore, have viewed the decision not to publish or circulate it as a betrayal by Beza of their earlier alliance. Perhaps Viret thought Beza was no longer the "partner in his grief" that he had claimed to be. Of course, the absence of

---

46 BEZA, T., *Du droit des magistrats* (1970).

47 Robert Linder and Heiko A. Oberman suggest that the grooming of Beza as Calvin's successor annoyed Viret. Linder also points to the class difference between the commoner Viret and the nobleman Beza. LINDER, R. (1964), 40–41 and n.88; OBERMAN, H. (1998), 57–58. I have suggested that Viret effectively "stole" Beza's house in Geneva after he moved there. BRUENING, M. (2008), 190–191. Philippe Denis suggests that Viret may have been too close to Beza's nemesis Jean Morély. DENIS, P. (1992), 402–403.

external evidence about the manuscript places this possible explanation firmly in the realm of speculation. Whatever role Beza's manuscript played in the matter, after the expulsion from Lausanne, Viret turned his back on the Swiss, living out the remainder of his career in France and Béarn, while Beza repaired his relations with the Swiss, continuing to strive to work together with them.

Regardless of the circumstances around the failure to circulate the manuscript at the time, its contents and its very existence deserve to be better known. Anyone researching Beza, Viret, the Reformation in the Vaud, the Lausanne Academy, or related topics should be aware of this text. The previously unpublished documents, Viret's *libellus* on discipline, and Beza's narrative provide a wealth of information that has thus far gone almost completely unanalyzed. Beza's decision to start his text twenty years earlier demonstrates his keen sense of the value of history in forging identity and collective memory, along with what we might today call "spinning" a story with an unhappy ending to his own advantage. Alain Dufour subtitled his biography of Beza "Poet and Theologian," which is, of course, perfectly appropriate. But the reformer's work on the ecclesiatical histories of France and Lausanne demand that we acknowledge "Beza, Historian" as well.

Jeannine Olson

Chapter 2: Theodore Beza and Nicolas Des Gallars, Best of Friends?[1]

How did a handful of people in refuge from their homeland, France, newly installed in a strange city, Geneva, accomplish so much in advancing the Reformation across Europe and the British Isles? Why did adjusting to their new environment not sap all their energies as it does for so many who live outside their comfort zone, estranged from familiar surroundings? Were the reformers not in culture shock? Were they not homesick?

One might say that the reformers of Geneva were able to accomplish so much because of their common goal of advancing the Reformation of the Church. You might say that it could be that, despite personal difficulties, they were emboldened by their focus on the spread of the reform, but I say, that was not enough. Could they have done what they did without friends? Above all, were they not sustained in times of hardship by their bonds of fellowship?

Take for example, the case of two friends, Theodore Beza and Nicolas Des Gallars. These two men had a great deal going for them to establish a friendship. They were both French. We think they were about the same age: Beza was born on 24 June 1519 in Vézelay, "to parent's of Burgundy's minor nobility."[2]

We do not know when Nicolas Des Gallars was born. We do not have his baptismal record. We do know that he came from a parlementary family of Paris and that he seems to have claim to a noble title and that he lived in Paris or the region around Paris, but we do not know his age. The vital statistics of Paris were burned in uprisings that occurred at the end of the Franco-Prussian War and the transition to the Third Republic. Nevertheless, Des Gallars' life trajectory would seem to place him at about the same age as Beza. That is the estimate of Henri Bordier and of Eugène and Émile Haag, editors of *France Protestante*.[3] That Des Gallars was born in about 1520 was also the estimate of E. Doumergue in his seven volume work, *Jean Calvin, Les hommes et les choses de son temps*.[4]

---

1 I would like to thank Rhode Island College Faculty Research Committee and the Alumni Association for financial support for this article.
2 MANETSCH, S. (2000b), 10, 347.
3 "Nous parait être né à Paris vers l'année 1520." (It appears to us that he was born at Paris about the year 1520.) "Des Gallars (Nicolas) seigneur de Saules," in HAAG, 5:298.
4 DOUMERGUE, É. (1899–1917), 3:597.

But is being of the same age and having a noble title enough for people to become friends? What more does it take to build a friendship? Consider three ingredients in friendship, simply 1.) having something in common, 2.) spending time together, and 3.) keeping in touch when apart. Let's apply these three criteria to Beza and Des Gallars from their early education in the 1530s to 1581, the year of Des Gallars' death.

2.1   A Common Background

Beza and Des Gallars were both educated men. Beza, at the age of nine or ten, began tutelage with the great Hellenist Melchior Wolmar (1497–1560) at Orléans and Bourges. (John Calvin had also studied with Wolmar.) Beza's study under Wolmar ended when Wolmar retreated to Germany for safety from royal persecution after the Affair of the Placards (17 October 1534) against the Catholic Mass, posters that were affixed in several places in France, including the King's bedroom door at Amboise.[5] Beza continued his education in the humanities and in law at the University of Orléans.[6]

We have no sure record of Des Gallars education, but he came from a family that educated its sons. He was an excellent Latinist, as evidenced by the fact that John Calvin gave Des Gallars tracts written in French for Des Gallars to translate into Latin, the first of which was Calvin's small tract concerning the Lord's Supper.[7] Des Gallars also edited several of Calvin's works and composed Calvin's first commentary on Isaiah from listening to Calvin's sermons and lectures on Isaiah. Émile Doumergue credited Des Gallars with being one of three in the Genevan Company of Pastors who was a doctor of law: "Jean Calvin, Nicolas Des Gallars, and Mathieu de Geneston."[8]

The study of law was characteristic of other early reformers of the Reformed Reformation, including Beza and Laurent de Normandie (c. 1510–1569), a great publisher of Geneva.[9] They studied civil law, including Roman law, in provincial

---

5 OER 3:279.

6 MANETSCH, S. (2000b), 10–11.

7 "Libellus meus de Coena in latinam linguam versus est a collega nostro Parisino." (My book on the Supper has been translated into Latin by our Parisian colleague.) CALVIN, J., *Petit traicté de la sainte Cene de nostre Seigneur Jesus Christ* (1541).

8 "Les trois juriconsultes, ou avocats officiels du Conseil, auraient été les trois ministres docteurs en droit, Jean Calvin, Nicolas des Gallars et Mathieu de Geneston." (The three legal consultants or official lawyers of the Council [of Geneva] had to have been the three ministers, doctors in law, Jean Calvin, Nicolas Des Gallars, and Matthieu de Geneston.) DOUMERGUE, É. (1899–1917), 3:469.

9 OLSON, J. (2018), 33–55.

universities, for in Paris only canon law was offered. Provincial universities influenced their religious formation.

We do not know in which provincial university Des Gallars studied. The University of Orléans is an obvious choice because of the influence that the humanist teaching at the University of Orléans had on reformers who studied there: Calvin, Beza and Laurent de Normandie. In December 1559, Orléans professor and parlementarian Anne de Bourg, sympathetic to the Reformed, was burned at the stake.[10]

If Nicolas Des Gallars studied at Orléans, he might have overlapped with Beza. Unfortunately, archives in Orléans are scant. They do not have University of Orléans sixteenth-century enrollment records. At the onset of World War II, the center of Orléans, including the archive, was bombed. A fire burned documents and two archivists died.

2.2 Emigrants from France

Another common element among Des Gallars, Beza, and other reformers, including Laurent de Normandie, is that they, like Calvin, left France. They left at different times and for similar but unique reasons: Calvin left early, fleeing first from Paris because of his association with Nicolas Cop (1501–1540), a medical doctor from Basel who was appointed rector of the University of Paris and whose inaugural address on 1 November 1533 alarmed the authorities.[11] Calvin was implicated. He moved south from Paris, and then on to Basel, which became his home base until the summer of 1536, when Guillaume Farel (1489–1565) recruited Calvin for the reform in Geneva.[12]

As for Nicolas Des Gallars, he arrived in Geneva eight years later, in 1544 or before, shortly after he had completed his formal education. Perhaps he was still being educated. He became a Genevan pastor and member of the Venerable Pastors of Geneva on 4 August 1544.[13] Four years later, perhaps

---

10 MANETSCH, S. (2000b), 18.

11 OER 1:335.

12 MONTER, E.W. (1967), 13–15, 29, 56.

13 "Noble Nycolas des Gallars de Paris [. . .] quil a pleu a Dieu inspire de servyr a Dieu aux ministere et annoncement de son sainct evangille: et ayans etendu la relacion de M. Calvin et de M. de Geneston lesqueulx les trouvent fort capables: et sur ce ordonne quil soyent admys aut ministere pour servyr tant en la ville que aux terres." (Noble Nicolas Des Gallars of Paris [. . .] who it pleased God to inspire to serve God in the ministry and the proclamation of his holy gospel; and having heard the report of Monsieur Calvin and of Monsieur Geneston, who find them very capable; and on this, it is ordained that they should be admitted to the ministry in order to serve in the city as well as in the countryside.) The *Annales Calviniani*, in CO 21:341, quoting the Registre du Conseil (hereafter Reg. Conseil), 310v.

fearing persecution, Laurent de Normandie, the mayor of Calvin's hometown, Noyon, France, arrived in Geneva with his wife and several children towards the end of October 1548.[14] At about the same time as de Normandie's immigration, Beza arrived in Geneva with Claudine Denosse, on 23 or 24 October 1548, after a serious illness deepened Beza's commitment to the reform.[15]

Between October 1548 and October 1549, Beza and Des Gallars overlapped in Geneva for about a year. In November 1549, Beza was appointed to the chair of Greek at the Academy at Lausanne on Lake Geneva (Lac Léman).[16] The Genevan Academy was not yet founded. In those days, Geneva to Lausanne was not a daily commute. Beza would not return to live in Geneva until October 1558.[17]

The reasons for Nicolas Des Gallars to settle in Geneva are less clear than for Beza; perhaps the pull of the reform and contacts with Calvin, but family reasons also might have motivated Des Gallars to stay away from home. Nicolas Des Gallars' father, Richard, died. By 1547 his mother remarried Nicolas Thibault, *procureur au Parlement* (procurator to the Parlement). Des Gallars appeared uncomfortable with his stepfather. He borrowed a horse from the hospital[18] to make a trip to Paris with Guillaume Budé in August 1547 to see Des Gallars' mother and to bring back his sister, whom Nicolas considered not well-treated by Thibault. His sister did not accompany Nicolas when he returned to Geneva at the end of September 1547.[19]

Given Des Gallars' questionable relationship with his stepfather, could Calvin have been a substitute for Nicolas Des Gallars' deceased father? Nicolas could even have been living in Calvin's household. A letter from Calvin to Farel of 13 December 1544 could be read to imply that Nicolas Des Gallars, still a bachelor, was living along with John Calvin in the household of Antoine Calvin, John's brother. Calvin's letter to Farel ended with this comment: "Everyone sends heartfelt greetings: colleagues, our family, and *that of* Nicolas, which grew in size recently thanks to a baby daughter of my brother."[20] Or, perhaps the "Nicolas" to whom John Calvin referred in this passage was someone else?

---

14 From 1546 to the first-half of 1548, Laurent de Normandie had been mayor of Noyon, Calvin's hometown. LEFRANC, A. (1888), 135. For context, see OLSON, J. (2017), 66.

15 Beza to Melchior Wolmar, Geneva, 12 March 1560, in CB 3:47. See also MANETSCH, S. (2000b), 12–13.

16 MANETSCH, S. (2000b), 13–14.

17 MANETSCH, S. (2000b), 347.

18 *Annales Calviniani* in CO 21:352, based on Reg. Conseil, 92.

19 Calvin to Pierre Viret, 25 August 1547, in CO 12:582; DOUMERGUE, É (1899–1917), 3:598.

20 "Omnes nostri reverenter te salutant. Collegae, familia nostra, et Nicolai, quae aucta est nuper fratres mei filiola" (Calvin to Farel, in CO 11:804). That Nicolas was living in the household of John and Antoine Calvin could be possible. Nicolas Des Gallars was young, single, and useful to Calvin for Des Gallars' translations from French into Latin. Genevans often rented rooms

Whether Nicolas Des Gallars was living in the same household or not, he and Calvin were in close proximity. Geneva was a small city.

2.3 Early Contact: 1557–1561

From Lausanne, Beza maintained contact with Genevan reformers and educated Des Gallars' son. Nicolas had married noble Gabrielle Morones in 1545. In a letter to Viret of 8 or 9 June 1545, Calvin stated Des Gallars' nuptials were to take place in Geneva Sunday at twelve noon.[21] By 27 November 1557, when Beza commented on Des Gallars' son, the boy could have been eleven.[22] The letter's last sentence reveals Beza's positive view of Nicolas Des Gallars:

> Concerning the son of our friend Gallasius, what that talkative person has told you is mere gossip. You know Prevotius well enough. If Rendonus, who is the boy's teacher in the second class, errs in anything, it would be that he is too kind. At home I found out that Prevotius has beaten him from time to time, though within reason,

---

to immigrants and refugees because of limited living space within the city walls in Geneva during the sixteenth century. Nicolai in the Latin appears to be genitive singular, referring to his family, but Des Gallars' mother, stepfather, and sisters were living in Paris not Geneva. Could Nicolai in the Latin refer to the family of Antoine and John Calvin that Nicolas was being included in while he lived with them? (Irena Backus confirmed this understanding of the Latin sentence. Interview, Geneva, Switzerland, June 2009.) But the Nicolas to whom John Calvin referred could have been someone else entirely, for several lines above, Calvin referred to Nicolas Des Gallars as "our Parisian" rather than as Nicolas: "Libellus meus de Coena in latinam linguam versus est a collega nostro Parisino." (My book about the Supper has been translated into the Latin language by our Parisian colleague.), ibid., 804. As for Antoine Calvin's baby daughter, babies born in Calvin's Geneva were baptized so soon after birth that even their mothers did not attend the baptismal services, but scholars cannot check this baby girl's name in the baptismal records of Geneva because they do not begin in earnest this early. (Baptismal records serve as birth certificates in early modern Europe.) The records of babies who do not live very long, just like stillborn babies, are often not available to posterity, especially when there are no baptismal records being kept.

21 "Sin minus: fac tamen ut ad Nicolai *Galasii* nuptiae te sistas, quae futurae sunt die dominico, hinc ad 12. Diem [. . .] Genevae, 4. Nonas Iunias." Calvin to Pierre Viret, 9 June 1545, in CO 12:87–88.

22 This is perhaps the oldest of Nicolas Des Gallars' children. Calvin said in a letter to Viret of September 1549 that Nicolas was rich in children. Calvin to Viret, 4 September 1549, in CO 13:376–377: "Quanquam monachi perperam iudicant, qui collegas meas faciunt percuniosos. Nam qui solus censeri dives potest, tribus aut quatuor est obaeratus. Copum dico. Abel [Poppin] et Gallasius liberis sunt divites. Borgoinus et Raymondus binas habent filias, praeterea nihil." The clause "Abel et Gallasius liberis sunt divites" was mistranslated in 377n.7, as Abel and Gallasius being "rich in books." However, "liberis" refers to children. Books would be "libri(s)" according to Irena Backus. Interview, Geneva, June 2009.

and he assures me that this has had excellent results. For although [the young man] was previously somewhat petulant and highly given to lying, he is much improved after light punishment. At this point I have decided to keep an eye on him myself as though he were my own. For I owe this to his father for his kindness and excellence of character [piety].[23]

Could Des Gallars' son have been adversely affected by the absence of his father? Nicolas Des Gallars was in France in the fall of 1557. The Genevan Company of Pastors selected him on 12 July 1557 in response to the request made by the Paris church for a pastor from the Genevan church. Des Gallars left for Paris on 16 August.[24] He arrived in time for a gathering of Reformed Christians on 4 September 1557, in a home on the *rue de St. Jacques.* The gathering was broken up. Some participants escaped, some were jailed, some put to death. Paris was unsafe for Reformed Christians. Henry II, King of France, had continued the policy of persecution of Francis I, his father. Des Gallars wrote on 7 September 1557 that he was known too well in Paris to remain there.[25] Nine days later, Calvin suggested that Des Gallars not leave Paris immediately.[26] Des Gallars wrote again on 27 November 1557.[27] Jean Macard left Geneva on 1 January 1558 to replace Des Gallars.[28] (The Genevan Company of Pastors recalled Macard to Geneva on 15 September 1558 and then sent François de Moreil to Paris as his replacement.)[29] Des Gallars served as a pastor in Geneva again until 1560, overlapping with Beza, who relocated to Geneva in October 1558 to serve as a city pastor.[30] Thus Beza and Des Gallars would have seen each other several times a week as members of the Company of Pastors. Beza also lectured in Greek literature. In June 1559, Calvin selected Beza to be theology professor

23 "De Galasii nostri filio vanum est quod illa loquacula apud vos sparsit. Prevotium satis nosti. Rendonus, quo praeceptore utitur puer in secunda classe, si qua in re, certe in nimia lentitate peccat. Domi comperi illum semel atque iterum vapulasse, sed intra modum, idque ut mihi affirmavit Praevotius, non sine magno fructu. Nam quum antea esset quodammodo petulans, et ad mentiendum valde pronus, levi castigatione multum profecit. Ego vero perinde illum curare constitui ac si meus esset. Hoc enim paternae benevolentiae ac pietati debeo." Beza to Calvin, 14 November 1557, in CB 2:127; Beza to Calvin, in CO 16:702.

24 RCP 2:78.

25 DOUMERGUE, É. (1899–1917), 3:600, citing Des Gallars to the Genevan Ministers, 7 September 1557, in CO 16:602–603.

26 DOUMERGUE, É. (1899–1917), 3:600, citing Calvin to Des Gallars, 16 September 1557, in CO 16:628.

27 Des Gallars to Calvin, 27 November 1557, in CO 16:712–713.

28 RCP 2:80.

29 RCP 2:82.

30 MANETSCH, S. (2000b), 347.

and first rector of the newly founded Genevan Academy.[31] From October 1558 to the spring of 1560, Beza and Des Gallars were together in Geneva again.

Less than two and a half years after Des Gallars returned from Paris, the Genevan city council agreed, on 26 April 1560, to a proposal of Calvin, Viret and Des Gallars for Des Gallars to fill the request for a pastor from the newly restored French Reformed church in London, known as the Stranger Church.[32] Nicolas left his family behind in their Genevan home near the *Collège*. In June, Calvin wrote Des Gallars that his son, Amos, had been gravely ill. His wife, also sick, was recovering.[33]

Soon thereafter, in July 1560, Beza left Geneva to visit the Court of Navarre in Nérac for three months.[34] In Geneva, the house where Gabrielle and the children were living was designated for Beza and his family. Gabrielle objected to being moved out. She wrote her husband. She spoke with Calvin, who supported Beza's moving to the house she was living in. She spoke to Beza, whose response was "open and frank," according to Calvin.[35] Calvin wrote that if the Genevan Company of Pastors were to definitively designate Des Gallars for London, the house in Geneva was Beza's. Gabrielle Morones and the children were to be relocated but not before winter. "Let us not suddenly become inflamed by these feminine ineptitudes [or 'nonsense']," stated Calvin.[36]

Des Gallars responded on 14 October 1560 that he could not afford to bring his wife to London. His situation was uncertain. He wanted to return to Geneva if Calvin and his colleagues agreed.[37] Calvin proposed to the city council on 11 November 1560, however, that Beza live where "Monsieur de Saul" had lived.[38]

About the same time, Calvin responded negatively to Des Gallars' desire to return to Geneva: "Has he forgotten what has been decided? His successor has just been named." Calvin added that Gabrielle "had complained bitterly that for three months she was paid only a fourth of what was due to her [. . .] although she is paid fully [as much] as the others."[39] (This comment is proof

31 MANETSCH, S. (2000b), 17. See also NICOLLIER, B. (2007), 41–54.
32 *Annales Calviniani*, 731, based on Reg. Conseil, 32v.
33 Calvin to Des Gallars, [June 1560], in CO 18:117.
34 MANETSCH, S. (2000b), 19–20, 347.
35 "Ouverte et franche." French translation by DOUMERGUE, É. (1899–1917), 3:601 of Calvin's letter to Des Gallars, 12 October 1560, in CO 18:212–214.
36 "Ne pas nous laisser enflammer tout à coup par ces inepties féminines." French translation by DOUMERGUE, É. (1899–1917) of Calvin's letter to Des Gallars, 12 October 1560, in CO 18:212–214. "Ineptie" can be translated into English as "nonsense." FRENCH DICTIONARY, s.v. "ineptie."
37 Des Gallars to Calvin, 14 October 1560, in CO 18:219–221.
38 *Annales Calviniani*, in CO 21:738, based on Reg. Conseil, 98v.
39 "A-t-il oublié ce qui a été décidé? On vient de nommer son successeur. [...] Ta femme [...] s'est plainte amèrement qu'on lui a payé ici, trois mois, le quart du traitement, tandis qu'on le

that in Geneva families of absent missionary pastors, and perhaps colporteurs, had financial support.)

2.4 Colloquy of Poissy (1561)

Des Gallars' family had been separated almost a year when the Stranger Church of London sent a deacon to bring his family to England. Gabrielle Morones and four small children appeared before the Genevan Council on 3 April 1561 to thank them before leaving for London.[40] The reunion of the family did not last long. Gaspard de Coligny invited Des Gallars and Beza to represent the Reformed cause in France at the Colloquy of Poissy to take place near Paris in September 1561. By 17 August 1561, eight Huguenot pastors conducted by Nicolas Des Gallars had been received at the French Court.[41]

The Queen mother, Catherine de Medici, and her chancellor, Michel de l'Hôpital, hoped that Catholic prelates and Reformed pastors could reconcile their differences. Reconciliation did not happen. It was too late. Positions had hardened.[42] Moreover, there was no good reason for the Catholics to agree with the Protestants, especially over the nature of the bread and the wine in the Lord's Supper (the Cêne or the Eucharist). For their part, the Reformed party was not about to agree on a compromise formula presented by the Cardinal of Lorraine. The Reformed thought it was the *Confession of Augsburg*, a Lutheran confession unacceptable to Calvin and Reformed leaders at this point.[43] When the Cardinal brandished a "*texte Wurtembergeois*," the Reformed delegates would not agree to it and interpreted these offers as an attempt to embarrass them with the Germans.[44]

Although the Colloquy of Poissy failed to reconcile Catholics and Reformed leaders, both Beza and Des Gallars played key roles and worked closely together. At the end of September 1561, after the larger assembly had dissolved, Beza and Des Gallars were asked to become part of "the Petit Colloquy," a smaller group of Catholic prelates and Reformed pastors who continued to attempt to resolve differences. Catherine de Medici asked Beza and Des Gallars to meet with two Catholic prelates whom she considered moderate to compose a formula of agreement on the Lord's Supper, which they did, but when their work was

---

paie intégralement à d'autres absents." Translation by DOUMERGUE, É. (1899–1917), 3:602 of Calvin to Des Gallars, November 1560, in CO 18:242–243.

40 *Annales Calviniani*, in CO 21:746, based on Reg. Conseil, 169v.
41 GEISENDORF, P.-F. (1967), 133.
42 For a study of the evolution of Beza's position on the Lord's Supper see RAITT, J. (1972).
43 Beza to Calvin, 30 August [1561], in CB 3:143–144.
44 Beza to Calvin, 27 September [1561], in CB 3:161.

shown to the larger Reformed delegation, Peter Martyr Vermigli (1498–1565) resisted strenuously. The Assembly of the Catholic clergy of France also rejected it.[45] The attempt at compromise failed.[46]

After all attempts at reconciliation were exhausted, a small group of Reformed participants—Beza, Des Gallars and Vermigli—stayed on at Court, exerting influence, especially on Catherine de Medici, regent for her minor son, King Charles IX. Beza kept Calvin informed since Gaspard de Coligny had not invited Calvin to the Colloquy. Between 22 August and 30 December 1561, Beza wrote no fewer than eighteen letters to Calvin, half of which contained references to Des Gallars.[47]

Calvin's letter of 17 September 1561 to Beza mentioned that the church of Poitiers wanted Des Gallars,[48] but Beza's letter to Peter Martyr Vermigli of 14 December 1561 stated Des Gallars returned to England[49] where Des Gallars' personal account of the Colloquy was published, written in Latin but published in English: *A true report of all the doynges at the Assembly concernying matters of religion lately holden at Poyssy in Fraunce . . . .*[50] Beza stayed on in France and participated in the January Colloquy of St Germain with Catholic prelates over the use of images in worship.[51]

---

45 Alain Dufour has published the compromise document in his biography of Theodore Beza. See DUFOUR, A. (2006), 84–85.

46 OLSON, J. (2009), 227–238; OLSON, J. (2007), 664–683.

47 Beza's extant letters to Calvin in 1561 are as follows: 1.) 22 August 1561, in CB 3:132–133, mention of Des Gallars at p. 132; 2.) 25 August [1561], in CB 3:134–139; 3.) 30 August [1561], in CB 3:143–145, mention of Des Gallars at p. 144, 145n.18; 4.) 12 September [1561], in CB 3:151–153; 5.) 27 September [1561], in CB 3:161–172; mention of Des Gallars in the notes, 170n.31; 6.) 4 October [1561], in CB 3:181–18, mention of Des Gallars at pp. 181 and 182; 7.) 5 October [1561], in CB 3:185–186; 8.) 21–23 October [1561], in CB 3:194–198, mention of Des Gallars at pp. 194 and 195; 9.) 24 October 1561, in CB 3:199–200, mention of Des Gallars at p. 199; 10.) 30 October [1561], in CB 3:201–204, mention of Des Gallars, p. 201; 11.) 4 November [1561], in CB 3:205–207, mention of Des Gallars at p. 206; 12.) 9 November [1561], in CB 3:213–215; 13.) 25 November [1561], in CB 3:225–229, mention of Des Gallars at pp. 226, 228n11; 14.) 29 November [1561], in CB 3:232–234; 15.) 11 and 12 December [1561], in CB 3:235–238; 16.) 16 December [1561], in CB 3:242–243, mention of Des Gallars at p. 243n.9; 17.) 22 December [1561], in CB 3:244–248; 18.) 30 December [1561], in CB 3:251–254.

48 Calvin to Beza, 17 September [1561], in CB 3:154.

49 Beza to Peter Martyr Vermigli, 14 December 1561, in CB 3:239, 240n,6.

50 The subtitle indicates that this work was translated from Latin into English by "J.D." (1561?).

51 MANETSCH, S. (2000b), 22–23.

2.5   First War of Religion (1562–1563)

The efforts of the Reformed pastors who remained at court in France after the Colloquy of Poissy were not wasted. The Crown issued a January Edict (1562), a step forward in the Huguenot struggle for recognition. The Edict allowed Reformed worship outside city walls and permitted Reformed synods (with royal officers present).[52]

However useful their presence at the French Court, Beza was rector of the Genevan *Collège*. His absence was felt. Nevertheless, the Genevan city council continued to pay him. On 28 November 1519, Beza wrote *Monsieurs de Genève* (the city council), thanking them for continuing his salary despite his absence,[53] but by March 1562 the patience of the Genevan city council had worn thin. The Genevan magistrates wrote Beza on 9 March 1562, requesting that he be in Geneva by the beginning of May, "which is the time, as you know, to put order in the school."[54] "The scholarly year [at the *collège*] began the day after promotions, for which the date had been fixed at [. . .] 1 May,"[55] but the first War of Religion intervened. Beza would only comply with the request to return to Geneva a year later, in May 1563.[56]

Despite limited toleration by the Crown, feelings against the Reformed churches were too strong among the populace and some of the nobility to maintain peace. Warfare broke out in France in April 1562. Des Gallars' return to London as pastor to the French-speaking Reformed congregation meant he was in England rather than Poitiers during the First French War of Religion (April 1562 - March 1563). Beza was less fortunate. He was deeply involved, serving as chaplain and advisor to the first prince of the blood, Louis de Condé.[57] Beza raised money and troops and even marched at the head of Condé's army but "neither fought nor fled," quipped Scott Manetsch.[58] After the war was over, Beza returned to Geneva, arriving less than two months before Des Gallars returned from England.

---

52 MANETSCH, S. (2000b), 23.
53 Beza to Magistrates of Geneva, 28 November [1561], in CB 3:231.
54 "Qui est le temps, comme vous sçavez, de mettre ordre à l'escole." Magistrates of Geneva to Beza, 9 March 1562, in CB 4:70.
55 "L'année scolaire commençait le lendemain des promotions, dont la date avait été fixée [. . .] au 1er mai." BORGEAUD, C. (1900), 54.
56 MANETSCH, S. (2000b), 347.
57 MANETSCH, S. (2000b), 347.
58 MANETSCH, S. (2000b), 24–25.

2.6 Between London, Geneva, and France: 1563–1566

In England Des Gallars' wife and some of his children had died, apparently sometime between a letter of Des Gallars to Calvin on 7 March, 1563[59] and his departure from England in June. Patrick Collinson, British historian of the Elizabethan Puritan movement, suggested Des Gallars' family could have succumbed to the Bubonic Plague in London in 1563.[60] Nicolas survived but considered himself unwell and blamed the English climate. Bishop of London, Edmund Grindal, concurred with Des Gallars' diagnosis in a 19 June 1563 letter to Calvin: "Our climate, it seems, does not agree with his constitution, and has greatly injured his health [. . .] so that him whom we now send back as an invalid, there would be reason to fear, if he remained among us another winter, that we should not send back at all."[61] Bishop Grindal gave this letter to Des Gallars to deliver to Calvin.

The *Annales Calviniani* stated Des Gallars had returned to Geneva by Saturday, 3 July 1563.[62] The *Annales* also indicated that on 30 July 1563 Des Gallars appeared before the city council of Geneva and offered his services.[63] The council seemed inclined to accept his offer. It looked as if Beza and Des Gallars would be together in Geneva again, but on 2 August 1563, Calvin "reported that he [Des Gallars] needed nothing and that it was necessary that he go to France."[64] Nevertheless, on 3 September Des Gallars received six "*escus pistoletz*" because he "had served these past days in the ministry."[65]

Des Gallars had the option of going either to Nîmes, where Gaspard de Coligny wanted him to go, or to Orléans, which Calvin preferred. Des Gallars wrote Calvin on 17 September 1563 from Châtillon that he had decided to go to Orléans, the center of the Reformed cause during the First War of Religion.[66] He would stay there almost five years from 1563–1568, as pastor and teacher.[67] By the mid-1560s French churches no longer depended only on academies outside France to train pastors. Reformed education in Orléans was so successful that

---

59 PETER, R./ROTT, J. (1972), 81–89.

60 Personal Interview of author with Patrick Collinson, London, England, April 2001.

61 ROBINSON, H. (ed.) (1845), 96.

62 "Juillet, Samedi 3, Des Gallars est de retour à Genève." (Saturday 3 July, Des Gallars has returned to Geneva). *Annales Calviniani*, in CO 21:805.

63 *Annales Calviniani*, in CO 21:805–806.

64 Calvin "a raporte quil navoit besoin de rien et quil fauldra quil alle en France." *Annales Calviniani*, in CO 21:806.

65 Des Gallars "qui a servy ces iours passez au ministere." *Annales Calviniani*, in CO 21:808, based on Reg. Conseil, 99.

66 Des Gallars to Calvin, 17 September 1563, in CO 20:157–158.

67 OLSON, J. (2012), 344–357.

the editors of Beza's correspondence stated: "The new Academy of Orléans was as solicited as that of Geneva for furnishing pastors."[68]

2.7 The Morély Affair (1566–1567)

From Orléans we have our largest number of letters from Des Gallars to Beza within a six month period because of the attempt to dislodge Jean Morély as tutor to Henri of Navarre, future King of Navarre (1572) and King of France (after 1589).[69] Des Gallars felt Morély's "democratic" ideas for the Reformed church were "dangerous," especially because members of the French nobility defended Morély. Des Gallars perceived a threat: "There was, of course, the greatest danger that the Church would be split."[70]

The case against Morély was built in Orléans because of the discovery there of a cache of letters from Morély to an Orléans pastor, Hugues Sureau, called Du Rosier. Morély's Latin letters criticized Beza, Des Gallars and the Genevan church as overbearing and tyrannical. This elicited nine letters from Des Gallars to Beza between 12 August 1566 and 21 January 1567[71] and two letters from Des Gallars to the Company of Pastors of Geneva. (The first of the two letters, from July 1566, did not concern the Morély Affair.)[72]

Des Gallars tried to convince members of the Company of Pastors of Orléans as to the seriousness of the threat Morély was to the Church. We do not have Beza's letters to Des Gallars in response, according to editors of the Beza correspondence,[73] but on 25 September 1566 Beza wrote a scathing letter on behalf of the Genevan Company of Pastors to the pastors of Orléans. Du Rosier had already recruited Monsieur Baron, another Orléans' pastor, to support

---

68 "La nouvelle Académie d'Orléans était aussi sollicitée que celle de Genève de fournir des pasteurs." Des Gallars to Beza, 12 August 1566, in CB 7:197n.2.

69 For an analysis of the letters of Des Gallars in 1566 and the Morély Affair see OLSON, J. (2016), 409–421.

70 "Periculum certe maximum fuit ne scinderetur Ecclesia." Des Gallars to Beza, 21 January [1567], in CB 8:47–48. Thanks to Mary Preus for translations from Latin.

71 These letters from Des Gallars are as follows: 1.) 12 August 1566, in CB 7:195–197; 2.) 16 August 1566 (if Des Gallars' date of 17 September is wrong) in CB 7:200–201; 3.) 1 September 1566, in CB 7:216–217; 4.) 2 September 1566, in CB 7:218–219; 5.) 10 September 1566, in CB 7:229–230. (The editors of Beza's correspondence list this letter's origin as Geneva. The letter's text reads "d'Orléans, ce Xe de septembre, 1566.") 6.) 30 September 1566, in CB 7:241–243; 7.) [24 October 1566], in CB 7:256–258; 8.) 20 December 1566, in CB 7:290–292; 9.) 21 January [1567], in CB 8:47–48. Des Gallars wrote all nine of these letters from Orléans.

72 Des Gallars to the Company of Pastors, 14 July 1566, in RCP 3:211–212; Des Gallars to the Company of Pastors, 24 October 1566, in CB 7:313–315.

73 Des Gallars to Beza, 21 January 1567, in CB 8:48n.1.

Morély.[74] Beza addressed Du Rosier and Baron: "If we thought that you would not have moved along in step with your brothers, we would never have sent you. [...] You not only ignore the authority of the legitimate synods [...] if each one would desire to follow his opinion as you do yours, where would be the Church of the Savior."[75] Then Beza made two points to the Orléans Company of Pastors:

> The first is that you conjoin with us in order to lead our two brothers in the path from which they were diverted. [...] The second point is that you be better united and conjoined in a same spirit, having always before your eyes the doctrine and the discipline through which you have been engendered, nourished, and so happily maintained until the age where you are. Guard you well from all spirit of pride and of fickleness from which proceed the divisions and finally the ruin of the churches! [...] Have neither your eyes nor your feet apart, but perceive and make your way with a common accord with the rest of your brothers, according to the course of our vocation, until we will arrive at this true repose to which even we have charge to lead and attract those who are committed to us.[76]

The Hebrew Professor at Orléans, Matthieu Béroald, translated Morély's letters into French for the elders and deacons of the Orléans consistory. Des Gallars persuaded them to send Béroald and the defamatory letters to the Court of Navarre. Béroald met with Jeanne d'Albret on 17 November 1566 and again 23 November. This second meeting included Gaspard de Coligny and Odet de Châtillon.[77] Morély's letters turned these 'Princes of the Religion' against Morély and persuaded Jeanne d'Albret to dismiss Morély as tutor to Henri,[78]

---

74 Le Maçon, Seigneur de la Fontaine to Beza, 4 August 1566, in CB 7:190–192.

75 "Si nous n'eussions estimé que vous deussiez [...] cheminer d'un pied avec vos freres et les nostres, nous ne vous eussions jamais envoyés. [...] Vous n'ignorez quelle est l'authorité des synodes legitimes [...] si chascun vouloit suivre son advis comme vous faites le vostre, où seroit l'Eglise du Seigneur?" Beza in the Name of the Company of Pastors to the Church of Orléans, [25 septembre 1566], in CB 7:309.

76 "Le premier à ce que vous vous conjoingnez avec nous pour amener nos deux freres susdicts au chemin duquel ils se sont detraques. [...] Le second poinct est pour vous [...] soyés mieux unis et conjoincts en un mesme esprit, ayans tousjours devant les yeulx et la doctrine et la discipline par lesquelles vous avez esté engendrez, nourris et si heureusement entretenus jusques en l'aage où vous estes, vous gardans bien de tout esprit d'orgueil et de legereté dont procedent les divisions et enfin les ruines des Eglises. [...] N'avoit point d'yeux ny de pieds à part, mais de veoir et cheminer d'un commun accord avec le reste de voz freres, selon le cours de nostre vocation, jusques à ce que nous soyons arrivez à ce vray repos auquel mesme nous avons charge d'amener et attirer ceulz qui nous sont commis." Beza in the Name of the Company of Pastors to the Church of Orléans, [25 September 1566], in CB 7:310–311.

77 M. Beroald, "Rapport de Mattieu Béroald sur son intervention contre Morély auprès de Jeanne d'Albret en novembre 1566," in DENIS, P./ROTT, J. (1993), 296–312.

78 Pierre Hesperien to Beza, 26 and 27 November 1566, in CB 7:272–274.

but perhaps not as quickly as the letter to Beza from Jean d'Albret's pastor, Pierre Hesperien, implied.[79]

Meanwhile, Des Gallars was not satisfied with what he considered the Orléans consistory's lax sanctions of Du Rosier, minimizing the affair, reducing it to a matter of personal injuries. He complained to Beza on 21 January [1567], and added he had not heard from Beza for three months. Others had not written since October. Could not Beza get someone else to write so Des Gallars would know Beza's state of mind?

> I am unable to divine the reason for such a long-lasting silence on your part. For three whole months and more I have not received any letters from you or your associates. Nor has any sense of your judgment [regarding my letters] been reported back to me; others have written nothing to me since October. Therefore I beg you over and over to free me from this anxiety. I am not ignorant of how many matters are pressing on you, but you could get someone else to write and inform me of your state of mind, and let me know whether my letters to you (I have written several) have been received.[80]

The message on the back of the letter had a friendly tone: "To the faithful servant of Christ, D. Theodore Beza, Pastor of the Geneva Church, most esteemed friend and brother at Geneva."[81]

Beza and Des Gallars addressed each other in letters as "brother" but Calvin as "father," although Calvin was only ten years older. There were other signs of friendship and perhaps socializing between Beza and Des Gallars. Des Gallars had remarried. His letter to Beza on 30 September 1566 states, "My wife salutes you and yours."[82] There are no additional surviving letters between Beza and Des Gallars in either 1567 or 1568. In October 1568 Des Gallars was back in Geneva.

---

79 Pierre Hesperien to Beza, 26 and 27 November 1566, in CB 7:273.

80 "S. Quae causa sit tam diuturni silentii vestri ego suspicare nequeo. Totos enim tres menses et eo plus et tuis et vestratium omnium literis careo. A te mihi ex quo convaluisti nullae redditae sunt, alii nihil scripserunt ab initio Octobris. Ego igitur ut me hac solicitudine liberes, etiam atque etiam rogo. Non ignoro quam multa te negocia urgeant; verum potes efficere ut al[ter]ius cujuspiam literis certior reddar de statu vestro, et an literae tibi meae, quas plures cripsi, redditae sint." Des Gallars to Beza, 21 January [1567], in CB 8:47.

81 "Fideli Christi servo, D. Theodore Bezae Genevensis Ecclesiae pastori, fratri et amico plurimum observando Genevae." Des Gallars to Beza, 21 January [1567], in CB 8:48.

82 "My femme vous salue at la vostre." Des Gallars to Beza, 30 September 1566, in CB 7:242.

2.8 Colleagues in Geneva (1568–1571)

Between the Second and Third Wars of Religion, in the summer of 1568, Orléans was a dangerous place. Des Gallars fled for his life on 6 September 1568 to the estate of Renée of France.[83] War broke out (fall 1568 - 8 August 1570). A royal edict demanded Reformed pastors leave France within fifteen days. Des Gallars fled to Geneva, arriving on 11 October 1568.[84]

In Geneva, Beza encouraged Des Gallars to engage in teaching and preaching and to edit the church fathers, of which Des Gallars' edition of Irenaeus, *Adversus haereses*, was the product. Theodore Beza encouraged his colleague not to remain inactive in his chagrin, but to second him in his teaching and preaching. He also gave Des Gallars the task of editing the fathers of the church and to render them more accessible to the reader; at the same time Beza counseled him to rectify the errors that these texts could contain, accompanying them with a commentary.[85]

During the years 1568–1571 when Des Gallars was in Geneva, he may have also worked on the *Histoire ecclésiastique des Eglises reformees au Royaume de France*. Alain Dufour attributes the *Histoire ecclésiastique* to Beza, but Dufour also said that Beza might have confided in Des Gallars' work relative to the *Histoire ecclésiastique*.[86] The contribution of Des Gallars to the *Histoire ecclésiastique* has been obscured because of missing documents from the archives. These documents existed in the nineteenth century at a time when archivists would allow readers to borrow manuscripts from the archives as if they were books.[87]

Paul-F. Geisendorf's position on the authorship of the *Histoire ecclésiastique* was that although Beza had reunited the materials, the question of authorship has little importance because so many people contributed the information that he assembled.[88] Geisendorf's statement should be nuanced with Alain Dufour's revelation that in the 1890s Geisendorf became engaged in disagreements over

---

83 RODOCANACHI, E. (1896), 443–465.

84 For proof of dates see OLSON, J. (2015), 573–604.

85 "Théodore de Bèze l'a encouragé à ne pas rester inactif dans son chagrin, mais à le seconder dans son enseignement et la prédication. Il lui a en aultre donné pour tâche d'éditer les Pères de l'Eglise et de les rendre plus accessible au lecteur; de même il lui a conseillé de rectifier les erreurs que ces textes pourraient contenir en les accompagnant d'un commentaire." Des Gallars to Edmund Grindal, 31 January [1569 or 1570]. Letter preface to *Divi Irenaei Graeci scriptoris . . .* [Geneva], 1570. Found in CB 10:267, annex 3.

86 DUFOUR, A. (2006), 186, 263.

87 DUFOUR, A. (2006), 185.

88 GEISENDORF, P.-F. (1967), 344–345.

the authorship of the *Histoire ecclésiastique* because the archivist, Théophile Dufour (Alain's direct ancestor), had taken an opposing position.[89]

Besides his literary efforts, Des Gallars served as a city pastor and was paid by the city council but was not part of the Company of Pastors of Geneva. He put down roots. He began to pay the city for a habitation on the *rue des chanoines*.[90] Through the city council, he attempted to become a fully-recognized member of the Genevan Company of Pastors, 26 September 1570. Messieurs of the city council notified the pastors that they "desired to retain him for the service of this church to which he was originally attached."[91] Four months later, after a request in writing from the city council, Beza reported to Messieurs on 11 January 1571 that there was a question to which church Des Gallars "belonged" that should be settled at a general synod.[92] Des Gallars maintained that there was no longer a Reformed church in Orléans.

Meanwhile the Genevan pastors reported to the city council on 22 January 1571 that they had received a request from the Church of Frankfort for a "minister of quality." They had decided to send Des Gallars,[93] but on 8 February 1571 Des Gallars reported to Messieurs he had received letters from Gaspard de Coligny, as had Beza, begging them to attend a national Synod of the French Reformed churches in La Rochelle in April 1571.[94] Des Gallars left for the Synod before Beza, who left on 10 March and arrived in La Rochelle on 29 March. The Synod opened three days later. Beza moderated the Synod. Des Gallars was secretary.[95]

2.9 Des Gallars' Final Years (1571–1581)

At the conclusion of the National Synod at La Rochelle, Beza returned to Geneva; Des Gallars started on his way there, but Jeanne d'Albret stopped Des Gallars in route, persuading him to replace Pierre Viret, recently deceased, in Béarn, the most Reformed of Jeanne's territories. Under Jeanne d'Albret, Des Gallars served as a pastor in Pau and shepherded Ecclesiastical Ordinances through

---

89 DUFOUR, A. (2006), 86–87.
90 AEG, Finances M, fols. 7v, 22, 36v.
91 "Messieurs desirent de le retenir pour le service de ceste eglise, à laquelle il est premierement astreint." AEG, Reg. Conseil 65 (1570), fol. 147v [image 164]. The registers of the early modern city council of Geneva are available online on the home page of the Archives d'Etat de Genève. The number of the image does not necessarily conform to the number of the page or folio.
92 AEG, Reg. Conseil. 66 (1571–1572), fol. 4-4v [images 8–9].
93 AEG, Reg. Conseil 66 (1571–1572), fol. 11 [image 15].
94 AEG, Reg. Conseil 66 (1571–1572), fol. 24 [image 28].
95 GEISENDORF, P.-F. (1967), 302.

the confirmation process of the Synod of the Reformed Church of Béarn. He then became a professor and was put in charge of the Reformed Academy in Lescar, today a suburb of Pau.

Des Gallars married for the third time in March 1572, less than a year after he arrived in Pau. He acquired a stepdaughter through his wife, Françoise de Contades (or de Candau).[96] At least two of his own children lived with him or nearby. Nicolas died in August 1581. His son, Daniel, was executor of his father's will.[97]

2.10   Conclusion

Were Beza and Des Gallars best friends? Perhaps at one point, but the epistolary evidence suggests Beza confided more consistently in Heinrich Bullinger, who was also a friend of Des Gallars. Bullinger and Des Gallars corresponded. Bullinger took care of one of Des Gallars' sons in exchange for Des Gallars taking care of a child for whom Bullinger was responsible. Yet, on at least one occasion, when Beza wanted to confide in someone, Beza confided in Bullinger. Beza feared for his life after the St Bartholomew's Day massacre (24 August 1572). In a 1 September 1572 letter to Bullinger, Beza wrote, "My father [. . .] This is perhaps the last letter I will ever write to you. [. . .] Assassins are seeking to kill me, and I contemplate death more than life."[98]

Beza might have confided also in his everyday companions. Who were they? With regard to Calvin, a nineteenth-century historian, Jules Bonnet, in multiple editions of his *Récits du seizième siècles*, suggested Calvin's daily companions were Galeazzo Caracciolo, Laurent de Normandie, Nicolas Des Gallars, *les Budé*, and Colladon.[99] In a similar vein, Alain Dufour commented that Calvin was a great organizer and listed as those who worked around Calvin as *les Budé, les Estienne*, Charles de Jonvillers, Nicolas Des Gallars, and Laurent de

---

96 "7 mars 1572, Contrat de mariage entre Nicolas Des Gallars, ministre, and Françoise de Contades," fols. 274v-275v, Archives Départmentales des Pyrénées-Atlantique. Menaud de Lexia, notaire de Pau, Registre E. 2001, 1570–1573; The family name of Françoise is "de Contades" in her marriage contract but "de Candau" in other documents. DUFAU, A./JAURGAIN, J. (1976).

97 For a fuller description of Des Gallars in the Kingdom of Navarre, see OLSON, J. (2019); OLSON, J. (2001), 75–79. In 2001, I had not yet discovered the fact that Des Gallars had remarried. Thus Françoise was not his second but his third wife, and I have adjusted the date of their marriage from 1573 to 1572 after discussions with Professor Pierre Charyere about the date of the New Year in Pau.

98 Beza to Bullinger, 1 September 1572, in CB 13:179; English translation MANETSCH, S. (2000b) 34.

99 BONNET, J. (1870, 1885).

Normandie, as well as many others whom he did not name. On a more personal level, Dufour cited as Calvin's most intimate friends Pierre Viret, Guillaume Farel, and Theodore Beza. "They do not cease to consult each other on each subject."[100]

Although Des Gallars and Beza did not seem to be "best friends," they were certainly good friends and were in frequent contact. There are examples of their continuing work together and of Beza defending Des Gallars.[101] Des Gallars presided at the French Reformed National Synod (1572) in Nîmes, where Beza asked the synod to allow Des Gallars to remain in Béarn, for he was sorely needed.[102] In a letter to Bullinger from March 1574, Beza indicated that Des Gallars and the churches of Béarn were doing well.[103] However, Des Gallars was not mentioned by Beza in his extant correspondence after 1574, and there are no surviving letters between them in the last decade of Des Gallars' life.[104]

Beza and Des Gallars overlapped in Geneva less than a decade. They worked closely at the Colloquy of Poissy, at synods of the Reformed church of France, and over the Morély affair. Their letters reveal they were good friends. How is it then that there could have been no correspondence between them from 1571 to Des Gallars' death in 1581? Were their letters lost or simply not written? How could this have happened in such a friendship? There are several possible reasons for the lack of letters in the last decade of Des Gallars' life. Letters could have been lost or not have reached their destinations. After all, the editors of the Beza correspondence point out that we do not have letters of Beza to Des Gallars during the Morély affair.[105] Nevertheless, many, perhaps most, of Beza's letters have survived, and there are no letters between Des Gallars and Beza contained in the Beza *Correspondance* during the last ten years of Des Gallars' life.

During the final decade of Des Gallars' life, I have found no surviving letters from him to anyone. It is hard to believe that such an ardent correspondent as

---

100 "Ils ne cessent de s'écrire et de consulter sur chaque sujet." DUFOUR, A. (2006), 40–41. The question of who Beza's most intimate friends were still needs to be explored.
101 Beza to Cassiodore de Reina, 9 March 1572, in CB 13:73, 76.
102 RCP 3:74, 74n.6; "Remerciements du Synode de Nîmes aux Syndics et Conseils de Genève," 18 mai 1572, in CB 13:273–274.
103 Beza to [Bullinger], 28 March 1574, in CB 15:58–59, 61.
104 After 1574, Des Gallars is several times referenced in Beza's published correspondence. At CB 17:81n.12, the editors note that Calvin published his *Pro G. Farello adversus Petri Caroli calumnias, defensio* (1545) under Des Gallars' name. The last mention of Des Gallars in Beza's published correspondence is in the introduction to volume 21, where the editors suggest that during Des Gallars' sojourn in Geneva from 1568–1571, when Beza encouraged Des Gallars' exegetical work, Beza "perhaps confided to him some work relative to the *Histoire ecclésiastique* (or its continuation)." See CB 21:xi.
105 See the footnote to Des Gallars to Beza, 21 January 1567, in CB 8:48n.1.

Des Gallars did not write any letters for ten years, especially since he apparently maintained contact with Geneva. At one point when he was serving in the Kingdom of Navarre, he asked permission to make a trip to Geneva. Also, Des Gallars remembered Geneva in his will. He willed money to the *Bourse française* of Geneva, a fund for poor French refugees to Geneva founded in the late 1540s by French immigrants and refugees to Geneva, including John Calvin.[106]

There were always more letters written by Des Gallars to Beza than Beza to Des Gallars. At one point during the Morély affair, Des Gallars had even chided Beza for not writing for months and not having someone else write so that Des Gallars would at least be kept abreast of what was going on and that his letters had been received.[107]

Sometimes Des Gallars appears to have written letters out of frustration or exasperation. We have no letters from Des Gallars to Beza as long as Calvin was alive. When Des Gallars wrote to Calvin, he addressed him as father. After Calvin died, Beza became moderator of the Company of Pastors of Geneva, and Des Gallars wrote to him, addressing Beza as brother. When Beza wrote, he often was writing on behalf of the Company of Pastors of Geneva.

Another factor to consider in the absence of letters from Des Gallars during the last decade of his life is strictly hypothetical: Could he have been less frustrated in the Kingdom of Navarre and therefore less in need of reaching out to friends who lived at a distance? It is difficult to measure the health of other people's marriages, especially if they have been dead over four hundred years, but perhaps Des Gallars' third marriage was a good one. He married soon after he arrived in Pau, within a year. His third wife was a widow of an important man in Jeanne d'Albret's government. She appeared to be of a social standing and financial level appropriate for a man of Des Gallars' education and Parisian family background. Both partners had children. Des Gallars' wife, Françoise, had a daughter. Notarial documents reveal that Des Gallars assumed the role of a father to her in marriage negotiations and possibly also in other ways. Likewise, Nicolas Des Gallars had some of his own children with him. His son, Daniel, seemed to enter fully into the life of the Kingdom of Navarre and perhaps lived with or near his father. Daniel was the executor of his father's will. Nicolas Des Gallars also had a daughter who lived near him. He had married her to an officer in the government in Pau.

In the last ten years of his life, Nicolas Des Gallars seemed to be relieved of the financial worries of earlier in his life, which could have been a great relief to him. Jeanne d'Albret gave him considerable responsibility in the Reformed churches. He received the treatment or salary of his predecessor, Pierre Viret.

---

106 OLSON, J. (1989).
107 Des Gallars to Beza, 21 January [1567], in CB 8:47.

After Jeanne died and he had become a professor at the Academy at Lescar (suburban Pau, today), he was in charge. As such, he was paid more than the other professors. Finally, in his will, Nicolas Des Gallars was able to bequeath money and property.[108]

Nevertheless, one should write to good friends despite the pressure of lack of time to do everything one would like to do. It happens to many, however, that they become so preoccupied with the task at hand and too busy to write or to call friends. It happens to us. Letters and e-mails are not written; phone calls are not made even to people we consider good friends. It might have happened to Beza and Des Gallars. Are we busier than Beza and Des Gallars who were actively expanding the Reformed Church in its first generations? I do not think so.

---

108 OLSON, J. (2020).

Chapter 3: Theodore Beza in England

Shortly after Queen Mary acceded to the English throne in 1553, Theodore Beza (1519–1605) wrote an urgent letter to Heinrich Bullinger (1504–1575), his colleague in Zurich, demanding information about the deteriorating religious situation in England: "Is there anything certain from England?" he writes. "I am filled with dread when I think about these things. [...] If you have any news about Elizabeth, please share it with us!"[1] Theodore Beza's intense concern for England's unfolding religious crisis marked the beginning of five decades of engagement with the English church and her leaders. Though the Genevan reformer never visited England in person, his role in the development of English Protestantism as an author, theological advisor, and religious provocateur was not insignificant. Beza corresponded with powerful English bishops and noblemen and noblewomen; he maintained crucial ties with Puritan leaders; he curried the favor of Queen Elizabeth (1533–1603)—all in an effort to further England's Reformation and foster political and religious cooperation within the larger world of Reformed Protestantism.

Several historians have recognized the significant role that Theodore Beza played in England's religious establishment during the second half of the sixteenth century. Scholars of Elizabethan England such as Patrick Collinson and Peter Lake have argued that Beza's sustained criticisms of English church rituals, his strident attacks on episcopal church government, and his advocacy of presbyterian polity both inspired and emboldened Puritan nonconformists from the 1560s on.[2] According to Collinson, Beza was the primary "inspiration of the presbyterians."[3] Other scholars such as Marvin Anderson and C.M. Dent have called attention to the sizeable number of Beza's theological and exegetical writings that were translated and printed in England during the period, many finding their way into the private libraries of English churchmen.[4] Finally, Beza's biographers have touched lightly on the reformer's role in the English Vestments Controversy of the 1560s and his dispute with Adrian Saravia and Matthew Sutcliffe thirty years later.[5] None of this scholarship, however, pro-

---

1 Beza to Heinrich Bullinger, 7 May [1554], in CB 1:128.
2 COLLINSON, P. (1990); LAKE, P. (2004).
3 COLLINSON, P. (1990), 121.
4 ANDERSON, M. (1987), 171–185; DENT, C.M. (1983), 95–102.
5 GEISENDORF, P.-F. (1967), 291–292, 385–386; DUFOUR, A. (2006), 227–231; MARUYAMA, T. (1978), 174–184.

vides a detailed, synthetic study of Beza's relationship to the English church that is sensitive to the goals and changing strategies of the reformer and his historical context. This essay will describe the important role that Beza played in England's religious controversies by tracking his contact with and influence among Puritan leaders, his changing attitude toward Queen Elizabeth, and his strategic engagement with English church authorities during the second half of the sixteenth century. It will be shown that, although Beza was not successful in influencing Queen Elizabeth's religious policy as desired, he did play a significant role in shaping the Puritan theological program and advocating for political support for Geneva and the Reformed churches of France. Five stages can be discerned in Beza's engagement with the island nation.

3.1   Stage One: First Contacts (1553–1564)

During the twelve-year interval from 1553 to 1564, Theodore Beza became increasingly attentive to the religious crisis in England and began to establish strategic contacts with key political and religious leaders in the kingdom. The first reference to England in Beza's extant correspondence appears in the summer of 1553, when the reformer, as a recent convert to the Reformed faith, was teaching Greek at the Academy of Lausanne. In late August, couriers raced through Switzerland bearing the news that King Edward VI had died and his half-sister Mary Tudor (1516–1558) was posturing to seize the English throne. In a letter dated 25 August, Beza reported this disturbing news to his friend Bullinger in Zurich, expressing his darkest fears that the Catholic queen would stop at nothing to crush the gospel and destroy the "still fragile" Protestant church in England.[6] By return post, Bullinger expressed grave concerns for the safety of Protestant leaders in England who now faced the queen's wrath: "Where is our [Peter] Martyr?" he writes. "Where is Johannes à Lasco? Where is our John Hooper? Where is our Thomas Cranmer? [...] Where are innumerable other good men? Oh Lord, have mercy on them!"[7] Over the next twelve months, Beza's correspondence is filled with anguished reports and false rumors received from England. John Dudley, the Duke of Northumberland (c. 1504–1553), who had staged a failed coup d'état against Mary, was convicted of treason and executed—but not before he made a spectacular abjuration of the Protestant faith. Queen Mary—whom Beza calls that "English Jezebel"—was welcoming Catholic bishops and priests back to her realm, even as she was preparing to

---

6   Beza to Bullinger, 25 August [1553], in CB 1:107.
7   Bullinger to Beza, 30 August 1553, in CB 1:111.

slaughter Protestant "heroes" who refused to submit to her wicked decrees.[8] And what of the godly princess Elizabeth? Rumors were circulating that she had been charged with high treason and was languishing in a prison cell, soon to face the executioner. Beza reports that he was unable to contemplate the terrible fate that awaited this "very resolute" princess without shedding tears.[9] Many of the reformer's letters during these dark months were punctuated with urgent prayers filled with fear and faith: "You see these things, O Lord. Look upon your afflicted church and relieve the hardships of your people on account of your name!"[10]

In the midst of the crisis, Theodore Beza wrote an anonymous treatise in defense of the English Reformation and her first martyrs, entitled *Response a la confession du feu duc Iean de Northumberlande* (1554).[11] In this brief work, Beza responded to the published abjuration and confession of the Duke of Northumberland, which had appeared in print the previous year.[12] In his confession delivered shortly before his execution on 22 August 1553, Northumberland had accused English Protestants of being sectarians and heretics who taught novelties and false doctrines that undermined the one universal Catholic faith.[13] Beza answered each of these accusations in turn, while impugning the Duke for his pride, ambition, greed, and hypocrisy.[14] At the same time, the reformer reminded his readers of a larger truth: God, in his providence, builds up the Church and brings glory to his name through the suffering of his beloved people.[15] In the final pages of his *Response*, Beza described the heroic death of an English courtier named Sir Thomas Parmer [sc. Palmer], who was executed by decapitation several minutes after Northumberland's death.[16] In the moments before his execution, Palmer announced to the crowd that, while in prison, he came to understand the depth of his sin as well as the bounty of God's grace offered in the gospel. Having given a true Christian confession, he died joyfully,

---

8 Beza to Bullinger, 4 September [1553], in CB 1:113–114; Beza to Bullinger, 29 March [1554], in CB 1:123–124; Beza to Guillaume Farel, 24 April [1554], in CB 1:125–126.

9 Beza to Guillaume Farel, 24 April [1554], in CB 1:125–126; Beza to Bullinger, 11 August [1554], in CB 1:133.

10 Beza to Farel, 24 April [1554], in CB 1:125–126.

11 [BEZA, T.], *Response a la confession du feu duc Iean de Northumberland* (1554). Beza acknowledges authorship of this work in a comment made to the queen mother Catherine de Medici during the Colloquy of Poissy. For more on Beza's *Response*, see the facsimile edition of CHAUBARD, A.H. (1959).

12 [ANONYMOUS], *The saying of John late Duke of Northumberland upon the scaffolde* (1553).

13 BEZA, T., *Response a la confession* (1554), 11, 20.

14 BEZA, T., *Response a la confession* (1554), 6, 12–15.

15 BEZA, T., *Response a la confession* (1554), 3–4.

16 The account of Sir Thomas Palmer's confession and execution is later found in John Fox's famous martyrology. See FOX, J. (1830), 249–250.

as a Protestant. For Beza, the contrast could not have been clearer: "I say to you, when one watches two men die—one of whom is trembling and so troubled that he doesn't know what he is saying; and the other with a peaceful heart that invokes God and confesses the certainty of his faith without flinching—which of these two men should we resolve to follow?"[17]

Scholars of the English Reformation estimate that around 290 Protestants were executed for heresy during Mary's reign, and another 800 fled to the continent, where they established refugee churches in cities such as Emden, Frankfurt, Strasbourg, Zurich and Geneva.[18] It appears that Theodore Beza had only limited contact with these Marian exiles during his tenure in Lausanne,[19] although in 1556 the English refugee William Whittingham (c. 1524–1579) did translate Beza's *Tabula Praedestinationis* (1555) into English.[20] After Beza relocated to Geneva in December 1558 to serve as pastor and rector of the Academy, the reformer began to have extensive and regular contact with English church leaders. According to best estimates, the English exile community in Geneva from 1555–1560 numbered 186 men, women, and children, in 113 households—a modest company whose number included such Protestant luminaries as Sir William Stafford (c. 1500–1556), John Knox (1513–1572), John Bodley, Perceval Wiburn (c. 1533–c. 1606), Christopher Goodman (1520–1604), William Whittingham, Thomas Sampson (c. 1517–1589), Laurence Humphrey (c. 1527–1590) and Miles Coverdale (1488–1568).[21] Many of these churchmen belonged to the more radical wing of English Protestantism, uncompromising in their commitment to Reformed worship, church discipline and presbyterian church government. In the decade that followed, a significant number of these Genevan exiles returned home and became the "intellectual leaders of English Puritanism."[22] The presence of Knox and Goodman in Calvin's city had an additional—indeed, a disastrous—impact on Geneva's relationship with England and her church going forward. In 1558, Genevan print shops published incendiary political treatises by Christopher Goodman and John Knox that defended

---

17 BEZA, T., *Response a la confession* (1554), 35.
18 See DICKENS, A.G. (1976), 266–267; GARRETT, C. (1966), 32; and BARTLETT, K., "Marian Exiles," in OER 3:8–10.
19 In November 1553, Calvin sent refugees Francis and Henry Knollys to Lausanne to meet Beza. See Chaubard's preface to BEZA, T., *Response a la confession*, 18. English exiles Sir Anthony Cooke; Sir Francis Russell; Michael Lok; and Thomas Sampson are also known to have visited Lausanne and met Beza during his years in Lausanne. See CB 6:136–138; 24:191–193; 42:121–122. See also MARTIN, C. (1915), 73.
20 MARTIN, C. (1915), 52. See GARDY, F. (1960), 147–152.
21 See MARTIN, C. (1915); DANNER, D. (1999).
22 COLLINSON, P. (1990), 45–46, 48–49.

popular resistance to ungodly monarchs and raised questions about the legiti-macy of female rulers.[23] Intended as ammunition against Mary's regime, the books saw the light of day just as Elizabeth was coming to the English throne. Despite Calvin's best efforts to distance himself from these radical treatises, and despite his claims of noninvolvement in the whole affair,[24] Queen Elizabeth was furious and never forgave Calvin or Geneva for the slight. As we will see, Theodore Beza will spend the next forty years attempting to repair the political and religious damage resulting from what Bruce Gordon has aptly called "the worst mistiming of the European Reformation."[25]

It comes as a surprise that the most consequential events in English church history between 1555 and 1559—the executions of Hugh Latimer (c. 1485–1555), Nicholas Ridley (c. 1502–1555) and Thomas Cranmer (1489–1556); the death of Queen Mary; and the accession of Queen Eliza-beth—are not reported in Beza's extant correspondence during this period.[26] Whether this lacuna was due to the vagaries of time and transmission, or the incessant demands that Beza faced in these years is impossible to know. During this pivotal period Theodore Beza emerged as Calvin's loyal disciple, a respected churchman, a capable Reformed theologian, and a leading figure in French Protestantism. Beza's growing stature among the Reformed churches was reflected in his appointment as chaplain to the house of Navarre during the summer of 1560, and in his role as head of the Reformed delegation that defended the Protestant religion before the French royal family at the Colloquy of Poissy in the fall of 1561.[27]

It was at Poissy that Beza came to the full attention of the English court. In regular dispatches sent back to London, the English ambassador to France, Sir Nicholas Throckmorton (1515–1571), kept Queen Elizabeth and her advisors

23 KNOX, J., *First Blast of the Trumpet Against the Monsterous Regiment of Women* (1558); GOODMAN, C., *How Superior Powers Oght to be Obeyd of their Subjects* (1558). See GORDON, B. (2009), 263–266.

24 In a letter to Sir William Cecil, First Baron Burghley, written several years later, Calvin insisted that he had no prior knowledge of Knox's controversial work before it was published. Further, Calvin stated that he first learned of the Queen's displeasure from Sir Antony Cook (Cecil's father-in-law), who had communicated it through Theodore Beza. Calvin to Sir William Cecil, after 29 January 1559, in *The Zurich Letters*, 2nd series (1845), 35.

25 GORDON, B. (2009), 263.

26 Beza did report and interpret these historical events in his later writings. In the *Icones* (1580a), for example, Beza provided a brief summary of Protestant martyrdoms during Mary's reign, focusing particular attention on the celebrated deaths of Archbishop Thomas Cranmer, Bishop Hugh Latimer, and Bishop John Hooper. These three church leaders are also memorialized with a brief poem celebrating their achievements and memory. See BEZA, T., *Les Vrais Portraits des Hommes Illustrés* (1986), 190–203.

27 See NUGENT, D. (1970); MANETSCH, S. (2000b), 20–22.

apprised of the daily proceedings of the colloquy. Throckmorton and Beza had direct contact with one another; on several occasions the ambassador requested that the reformer supply him with manuscript copies of his public speeches, which were then sent on to England for translation and publication.[28] In all, three of Beza's speeches were translated and printed in English during this period[29]—at least one of these speeches was hand-delivered to the Queen herself.[30]

The Colloquy of Poissy failed to breach the confessional divide between French Protestants and Catholics. In the spring of 1562, France descended into a bloody civil war, the first of eight armed conflicts that afflicted the kingdom over the next thirty-six years. As the fighting ensued, Beza remained in France to serve as the private chaplain, advisor and fund-raiser for the Huguenot commander Louis de Bourbon, the prince of Condé (1530–1569). During these dramatic months Beza was in regular contact with the English ambassador Throckmorton and received letters from other prominent members of Elizabeth's government, including England's Secretary of State, Sir William Cecil (1520–1598).[31] In April 1562, Throckmorton sent a letter to Elizabeth informing her that Beza—whom he described as "the principal minister of the Reformed churches"—had communicated his greetings to the queen and was sending to her through a third party a copy of his recently published Genevan Psalter.[32] In late September, the Huguenot commander Prince Condé and the Admiral Gaspard de Coligny (1519–1572) negotiated with Elizabeth the Treaty of Hampton Court in which the queen promised to supply them 6,000 troops and 20,000 pounds in return for English occupation of the French ports at Dieppe and Le Havre.[33] Coligny appointed Theodore Beza as one of his three

---

28 See Nicholas Throckmorton to Queen Elizabeth, 20 September 1561, in *Calendar of State Papers, Foreign Series, 1560–1561* (1966), 4:313–314. See also ibid., 4:281, 360, 372, 550. Beza mentions contact with Throckmorton in a letter to Calvin, dated 27 September [1561]. See CB 3:166.

29 See BEZA, T., *An Oration made by Master Theodore de Beze* (1561); BEZA, T., *Ane answere made the fourth day [sic 24th] of septembre … by Maister Theodore de Besza* (1562a); BEZA, T., *The second Oration of Master Theodore de Beze* [1562b]. For more editions of these works, see GARDY, F. (1960), 85–102.

30 Thomas Randolph to Cecil, 17 October 1561, in *Calendar of State Papers, Foreign Series* (1966), 4:72. The summary of Randolph's letter reads: "Presented to her [the Queen] the oration of Theodore Beza which he received from Throckmorton, it is now in hand to be translated."

31 In a letter to Cecil dated 16 March 1563, Beza acknowledged the receipt of several letters from the Secretary. See CB 4:135–136.

32 Throckmorton to Queen Elizabeth, 24 April 1562, in *Calendar of State Papers, Foreign Series, 1560–1561* (1966), 4:622.

33 Beza to Calvin, 1 September [1562], in CB 4:102–103. For more on these events, see HOLT, M. (1995), 56.

deputies responsible for collecting the English funds and transferring them to the Protestant commanders.[34] When the promised English money had still not been received five months later, an exasperated Beza announced plans to cross the English Channel to expedite the receipt of these funds. "I think that I will go over to England within a few days," Beza informed Calvin in early March 1563.[35] As it turned out, this trip proved unnecessary when the civil war abruptly ended several weeks later, after the Catholic Duke Francis de Guise (1519–1563) died of wounds inflicted by a Protestant assassin named Poltrot de Méré. In the war's immediate aftermath, English dispatches to London continued to report on Beza's activities. Several English informants reported Catholic rumors that implicated Beza in the assassination of the Duke of Guise. Another letter addressed to the queen described a Protestant communion service in the city of Orléans, attended by Condé and Coligny, where Theodore Beza preached and distributed the sacrament to between 5,000 and 6,000 men and women.[36]

Through the events of 1561–1563, Beza had gained international prominence among the Reformed churches and had made first contact with important members of England's government. In an effort to strengthen these bonds of goodwill, Beza dedicated the second edition of his *Annotationes* on the New Testament to Queen Elizabeth in December 1564.[37] In the dedicatory epistle, the reformer praised Elizabeth's outstanding gifts, her exceptional virtue, her natural clemency, her unwavering commitment to the true worship of God.[38] Beza remembered the happy reign and untimely death of her half-brother, King Edward—who was "a Josiah of our time." He also recalled the many martyrs who had suffered at the hands of Queen Mary, and the courageous exiles who had found refuge in the city of Geneva. Beza extolled Elizabeth as God's chosen instrument to restore peace and pure religion to her kingdom, and thanked her for the military support she had given to the Huguenots during the First War of Religion. In the middle of this panegyric, Beza included these words of advice to the queen:

> But to you, O queen, [...] has been given in its fullness the profession of the pure and sincere doctrine of the gospel, so that if [...] you were also to add the full restoration

34 Throckmorton to Cecil, 26 February 1563, in *Calendar of State Papers, Foreign Series, 1562–1563* (1966), 6:161, 170.

35 Beza to Calvin, 5 March [1563], in CB 4:132–133. Beza had announced his intentions to visit England already in a letter to Calvin on 31 January 1563. See CB 4:125.

36 Sir Thomas Smith to Queen Elizabeth, 31 March 1563, *Calendar of State Papers, Foreign Series, 1561–1563* (1966), 6:251. This event is described by GEISENDORF, P.-F. (1967), 222–223.

37 Beza, *Iesu Christi D. N. Novum testamentum ... Th. Bezae annotationes* (1565b).

38 For this entire epistle, see Beza to Queen Elizabeth, in CB 5:165–171, supplemented with CB 2:225–229.

of church discipline, I do not see what more either England could ask of you, or your majesty could confer on your kingdom—unless perhaps God would soon see to it that so illustrious and worthy a virgin queen might get married to a king, so that you, O happy queen, after you have enjoyed a very long life, might leave behind for your people a successor to your kingdom who displays these same maternal virtues.[39]

What Beza meant by a "full restoration of discipline" is not clear, although he was likely advocating for a program where ecclesiastical discipline would be maintained by consistories of ministers and elders. In any event, the reformer's advice to Queen Elizabeth proved to be a serious miscalculation on two fronts: First, Elizabeth and her bishops did not take kindly to the suggestion that English church polity and doctrine were in any way deficient and in need of a Genevan-style correction. Second, Beza's expressed hopes for a husband for the virgin queen no doubt rankled Elizabeth, who had not forgotten Geneva's role in the publication of Knox's diatribe *Against the Monsterous Regiment of Women*.[40] Between 1553 and 1564, Beza had gone from being a spectator to an active participant in England's religious crisis. However, as time would tell, his influence would not be welcomed by Elizabeth or most of her bishops.

3.2 Stage Two: The Vestments Controversy (1565–1571)

Beza's assessment of Elizabeth and the English Church became more critical during the so-called Vestments Controversy and its immediate aftermath. During the decade of the 1560s, an especially intense variety of Protestantism appeared in England that objected to various aspects of Elizabeth's religious settlement and lobbied for a thoroughgoing reformation of the English Church. This religious movement—labeled as 'Puritan' by its detractors—was resolutely Reformed, stridently anti-Catholic, and oftentimes nonconformist in its engagement with Elizabeth's state church.[41] A number of the leaders of this nascent Puritan movement had been part of the exile community in Geneva and were acquainted with Beza. In January of 1565, Queen Elizabeth sharply rebuked the Archbishop of Canterbury, Matthew Parker (1504–1575), for turning a blind eye to bishops and parish priests who did not conform to the Church of England's liturgy or refused to follow prescribed ceremonies. Although a

---

39 Beza to Queen Elizabeth, 19 December 1564, in CB 5:167.

40 Beginning with the third edition of Beza's *Annotationes* (1582b), the reference to a royal husband was discretely removed.

41 For the difficulties of defining the terms "Puritan" and "Puritanism," see COFFEY, J./LIM, P. (2008), 1–7; COLLINSON, P. (1990), 21–28. Collinson famously describes the English Puritans as the "hotter sort of protestants" (ibid., 27).

number of practices were in dispute—including the sign of the cross at baptism, the practice of exchanging rings at weddings, the use of the organ and kneeling when receiving the Lord's Supper—special concern was given to the liturgical vestments required of the clergy. After months of wrangling, Parker finally published a series of *Advertisements* in March 1566 which required all English churchmen to wear the white surplice in their churches; those who refused to conform were to be dismissed from office by their bishops.[42] A significant number of Puritan ministers, who viewed the surplice as "popish apparel" and "Roman rags," refused to comply with this mandate and within several weeks, thirty-seven of them were removed from their parishes.[43] As Collinson notes, the Vestments Controversy raised important questions regarding the state's involvement in defining and enforcing religious practices deemed indifferent (*adiaphora*). The controversy also illustrated that Elizabeth's doctrine of royal supremacy might well clash with the efforts of reform-minded ministers to effect renewal in the English church.[44]

Beza was horrified by these developments, and confided growing frustration to his friend Bullinger. In one letter, he bemoaned the "miserable condition" of the church in England. "There are very few pastors," he writes, "and the greater part of the hirelings are uneducated. There is no concern for godly behavior. There is no church discipline."[45] In another letter, Beza railed against Elizabeth and her "abominable" bishops. Events now made it clear that "the papacy was never abolished in that country, but rather transferred to the sovereign."[46] The problems of the English church, Beza now recognized, extended beyond the neglect of church discipline to the very structure of its episcopal government. In late June 1566, Beza sent Bullinger a copy of Parker's *Advertisements*, again complaining of the abuses and disorder of the English church. But what could be done? When Beza dedicated his *Annotationes* on the New Testament to Elizabeth in 1564, he was hopeful of winning the queen's goodwill and support. But the fact that the queen never acknowledged receipt of this gift now left Beza convinced that Elizabeth continued to harbor resentment toward the Genevan ministers for the inflammatory treatises of Goodman and Knox. In a letter to Bullinger, Beza explained the reasons for the royal snub this way:

> The reason for her dislike is two-fold: one, because we are accounted too severe and precise, which is very displeasing to those who fear reproof; the other is, because formerly, though without our knowledge, during the lifetime of queen Mary two books

---

42 For the Vestments Controversy, see COLLINSON, P. (1990), 69–83; CRAIG, J. (2008), 37–39.
43 CRAIG, J. (2008), 38.
44 COLLINSON, P. (1990), 71, 74.
45 Beza to Bullinger, 6 November 1565, in CB 6:196–197.
46 Beza to Bullinger, 3 September [1566], in *The Zurich Letters*, 2nd series, 128, 129.

were published here in the English language, one by master Knox against the government of women, the other by master Goodman on the rights of the magistrate. As soon as we learned the contents of each, we were very displeased, and their sale was forbidden in consequence; but she notwithstanding cherishes the opinion she has taken into her head.[47]

Beza feared that, given his unpopularity in Elizabeth's circle, any intervention in the Vestments Controversy would do more harm than good.[48] Nevertheless, in late June 1566 the Genevan reformer overcame his caution, and wrote a long letter to the moderate Bishop of London, Edmund Grindal (c. 1519–1583), expressing his concerns.[49]

Given the importance of this letter, it is necessary that we summarize it in some detail.[50] Beza began his letter to Grindal by defending the Genevan church from accusations that it was overly severe and restrictive in matters of religion. Geneva's doctrine and church discipline were drawn from the pure fountain of the Word of God, he insisted.[51] So too, Beza urged Grindal to encourage Elizabeth to adopt the recently published Second Helvetic Confession (1564)—such an action would display the doctrinal unity shared by the Reformed churches of England, France, and Switzerland, and would refute the accusations of their opponents that the Reformed were divided against each other. After these preliminary concerns, Beza next turned to the pressing matter at hand: whether or not churches should prescribe extra-biblical ceremonies deemed "indifferent." Beza admitted that he had received reports that faithful gospel ministers in England had recently been deposed from office by their bishops for no other reason than refusing to wear prescribed clerical garments as well as rejecting other "superstitions" such as signing with the cross and kneeling during the communion service. Moreover, it was reported that the queen and her bishops claimed absolute authority to impose such ceremonies on the church.[52] Proceeding cautiously at first, the reformer admitted that there were two general points of view

---

47 Beza to Bullinger, 3 September [1566], in CB 7:224.

48 Beza to Bullinger, 19 June 1566, in CB 7:141–143. In this letter, Beza again complains that Elizabeth had never thanked him for his gift of the *Annotationes*.

49 Beza first established contact with Grindal in 1565 when he sent to him a copy of the second edition of his *Annotationes*. Grindal responded warmly to this letter, praising Beza as the worthy successor of John Calvin and enclosing a gift of five angelots of gold. See Edmund Grindal to Beza [20 April 1565], in CB 6:139.

50 This letter is found in CB 7:154–166. An English translation of this letter is found as an appendix to FIELD, J./WILCOX, T., *An Admonition to Parliament* (1572). The *Admonition* is available in FRERE, W./DOUGLAS, E. (ed.) (1954), 43–55. See below for more information on this important document.

51 Beza to Grindal, 27 June 1566, in CB 7:155. English translation, 45.

52 Beza to Grindal, 27 June 1566, in CB 7:155–156. English translation, 45.

among Protestants. Some Protestants believed that the doctrine and practice of the apostolic church should be normative. Other Protestant churches saw value in retaining ancient ceremonies and customs that, although post-apostolic in origin, were profitable and necessary for the sake of unity. Beza argued that both viewpoints were deficient. For, in the case of the apostles, though their doctrine was impeccable, their missionary context had forced them to retain temporarily certain Jewish practices and ceremonies that detracted from the simplicity and purity of the gospel.[53] Consequently, Beza argued, Christians living after the age of the apostles should seek to abolish all Jewish and pagan ceremonies not prescribed by Scripture so that "Christ might henceforth be displayed unclothed and walking in the clear light, no longer darkened with any figures or shadows."[54]

Having rejected the first viewpoint, Beza turned his attention to refuting the second. In the centuries after the apostolic era, ceremonies and traditions had "horribly disfigured all parts of Christian doctrine," he believed.[55] Consider baptism: Catholics—and now many Protestants—had debased the sacrament with a myriad of trifles such as exorcisms, burning candles, salt, baptismal gowns, and godparents. The same was true of the Lord's Supper, where Christ's once-for-all sacrifice for sinners was obscured or even forgotten amidst a theatrical display of marble altars, ornate garments, golden chalices, chanting choirs, and mandatory genuflections.[56] This was not reformation, Beza believed, but de-formation (*deformatio*).[57] But what of the argument that many of these ancient ceremonies and practices were *adiaphora*—indifferent matters? Beza responded that indifferent customs and ceremonies habitually metastasized into superstitions that obscured the gospel and violated the teaching of Scripture. Hence, any practice "not grounded upon the authority of God's Word, or upon any example of the Apostles" must be rejected.[58]

Beza's attack on religious ceremonies was a *tour de force*. But the reformer's most controversial and dangerous grievance was yet to come. In the final paragraphs of his letter to Grindal, Beza rebuked the English bishops for a variety

---

53 Beza to Grindal, 27 June 1566, in CB 7:156. English translation, 45–46. It is likely that Beza has in mind such "Jewish" rites as circumcision and love feasts.

54 Beza to Grindal, 27 June 1566, in CB 7:157. English translation, 48.

55 Beza to Grindal, 27 June 1566, in CB 7:157. English translation, 48.

56 Beza to Grindal, 27 June 1566, in CB 7:157–160. English translation, 48–53.

57 Beza to Grindal, 27 June 1566, in CB 7:157. English translation, 48.

58 Beza to Grindal, 27 June 1566, in CB 7:158. English translation, 50. Kirk Summers has recently demonstrated that Beza's stated aversion to unbiblical ceremonies is also depicted in Beza's epigram on True Religion that appears in the front matter of his *Confessio Christianae fidei* (1560). Summers notes: "True Religion, as Beza would have it, invites the faithful to hear God, understand the Gospel, and know Christ as their redeemer and brother without theatrics, unnecessary pomp, or artificial mediation." See SUMMERS, K. (2020), 349.

of "very filthy abuses," and then took aim at episcopal government, and by extension, the doctrine of royal supremacy itself. The reformer stated that he saw no biblical warrant for either the civil magistrate or the bishops to establish new rites or ceremonies or abrogate the old without the judgment and consent of an assembly of elders.[59] With this one statement, he hinted at his presbyterian convictions and challenged the whole structure of Elizabeth's Protestant church. Beza's words would not be forgotten, either by his friends or foes. Finally, since Edmund Grindal in his office as Bishop of London had jurisdiction over the French stranger church in London, Beza concluded his letter by asking Grindal to continue to show favor toward this refugee congregation.[60] By way of summary, then, Beza's long missive to Grindal clearly illustrates three separate objectives: to promote the unity of the Reformed churches in Europe, to spur the English church on to further reformation, and to protect the fragile French refugee congregation in London.

In the meantime, Puritan leaders in England were making preparations to send a delegation to Switzerland to request support. In late August 1566, a recently deposed minister named Perceval Wiburn appeared on Beza's doorstep, bearing a letter from Puritan leaders Miles Coverdale, Laurence Humphrey and Thomas Sampson.[61] All four men had once taken refuge in Geneva during the Marian exile, and now again sought Geneva's help in the present English crisis. The letter described the unhappy condition of the English church, the decline of pure doctrine, and the recent depositions of nonconformist ministers. Echoing Beza's earlier sentiments, the Puritans argued that doctrine and practice should be drawn from Scripture, not human traditions, and that liturgical garments should not be numbered among the "indifferent things" imposed by bishops. Instead, "the clergy should be distinguished from the people by their doctrine, not their garments; their behavior, not their dress; their purity of mind, not their adornment of persons."[62] The letter concluded with three requests of Geneva's ministers and their friends: First, the Puritans asked for advice as to whether their ministers should submit to the bishops' commands to wear the surplice, or should they desert their posts for conscience sake? Second, they requested that Beza and his colleagues write a treatise on the nature of ceremonies and

---

59 Beza to Grindal, 27 June 1566, in CB 7:161. English translation, 54.
60 Beza to Grindal, 27 June 1566, in CB 7:161. English translation, 55. For more on the French refugee congregation of London, see SCHICKLER, F. DE (1892), and PETTEGREE, A. (1986).
61 Coverdale, Humphrey and Sampson to Farel, Viret and Beza, July 1566, in CB 7:340–343. An English translation of this letter is found in the *Zurich Letters*, second series, 121–124. The Englishmen were apparently unaware that Farel had been dead for over a year and Viret had departed for France five years earlier. See ibid., note 2.
62 CB 7:341 (annex 7). This is a loose quotation drawn from a letter of the fifth-century Pope Celestine I to the Province of Vienne and Narbonaise. See ibid., 343n.6.

indifferent things. And, third, the Puritan leaders asked the Genevans to send letters of support to the English bishops, urging them "not to persecute Joseph on account of a garment; nor to tear apart the church with schism for so slight a cause."[63]

After consulting with Beza and the Company of Pastors, Wiburn went on to Zurich in early September 1566 to solicit Bullinger's support. Wiburn carried with him a letter written by Beza, addressed to Bullinger, in which the Genevan reformer gave his strongest support to the Puritan cause.[64] Beza admitted that some of the more extreme Puritan leaders were "rather hard to please," yet he agreed with their many grievances against Elizabeth's church and enumerated them in detail. Beza indicated that, underlying these grievances, were crucial structural problems in the English church, including the queen's supreme authority in religious matters, the power of the bishops, and the absence of presbyterial oversight of church discipline.[65] Yet Beza acknowledged that it would be strategically unwise for him and the Genevans to intervene directly in the controversy, given Elizabeth's continued hostility toward them. "I am not unaware of the suspicion I have long labored under by people who hardly know me," Beza lamented.[66] Instead, he encouraged Bullinger and the Zurich ministers to write to the English bishops directly, and, if necessary, to send their colleague Rudolf Gwalther (1519–1586) to England in an effort to pacify the controversy. In addition to enumerating these grievances, Beza also offered at length his judgment on the troubling question of whether Puritan ministers should leave their pastoral posts for the sake of conscience. Beza advised a middle course: Puritan ministers must remain at their posts and not abandon their congregations; but at the same time, they should not obey commands regarding liturgical vestments and ceremonies that violated their consciences. The ministers must respectfully protest the bishops' ungodly commands and hope that Parliament might soon intervene on their behalf. But if that did not happen, Beza counseled, the ministers should be prepared to suffer the cross.[67]

It took nearly fifteen months before Beza and the Company of Pastors finally responded to the questions raised by the Puritan delegation.[68] The ministers

63 Coverdale, Humphrey and Sampson to Farel, Viret and Beza, July 1566, in CB 7:341.
64 See Beza to Bullinger, 3 September 1566, in CB 7:222–228. An English translation of this letter is available in the *Zurich Letters*, series 2, 127–136.
65 Beza to Bullinger, 3 September 1566, in CB 7:223. English translation, 129. In a letter to Bullinger on 29 July 1567, Beza noted: "But if the situation [of the English church] is as I hear it to be […] where did such a Babylon ever exist?" See CB 8:152.
66 Beza to Bullinger, 3 September 1566, in CB 7:226. English translations, 135.
67 Beza to Bullinger, 3 September 1566, CB 7:225–226. English translation, 153–155.
68 This letter appears in BEZA, T., *Epistolarum Theologicarum … Liber Unus* (1573b), 103–113; hereafter *Epistolae Theologicae*. A summary of this letter is provided in RCP 3:234.

began by challenging the exalted authority of England's bishops. A legitimate call to ministry and the right to preach must be based, not on episcopal authority, but on the decision of a group of elders (*presbyterii*), whose duty it is to examine the doctrine and morals of ministerial candidates, and then present them to their parishes for approval. Presbyterian assemblies should also have jurisdiction over pastoral supervision and be responsible for excommunication.[69] Beza and his colleagues devoted the rest of their letter to enumerating church practices in England that they found particularly objectionable, including liturgical vestments, formal psalmody, baptisms performed by midwives, the sign of the cross and kneeling during the Lord's Supper—all of which smacked of superstition and threatened to reintroduce Catholic idolatry to the kingdom. At the same time, Beza and his colleagues advised their English counterparts not to abandon their ministries on account of the Vestments Controversy, nor should ordinary believers withdraw from worship services because of the clothing worn by their pastors.[70] The Genevans concluded their letter by celebrating the many martyrs that had once helped restore the Christian religion in England, and then warning their Puritan colleagues that England risked invoking God's wrath and losing the light of the gospel if she did not repent.[71]

The Vestments Controversy of 1565–1567 further strengthened bonds of trust and mutual support between Beza and Puritan leaders, even as it intensified the reformer's suspicions of Elizabeth and her religious settlement. Whereas Bullinger was more cautious—warning Beza not to believe every report that he heard, and especially not to trust Puritan extremists such as Thomas Sampson[72]—Beza remained resolute in his view that the English church was facing a terrible crisis and needed significant reformation. Writing to a colleague in Bern in February of 1567, Beza bemoaned the fact that in England, "the misery of the churches increases; many of the bishops there are far worse than many of the bishops in the papacy."[73] From Beza's perspective, the Church of England was a Reformed church that, in its Thirty Nine Articles, shared confessional unity with other Reformed churches in Switzerland, France, Flanders, and Scotland.[74] And yet, he feared that the royal supremacy, episcopal hierarchy and the neglect of church discipline would inevitably undermine the doctrinal purity of the English church. "I cannot disguise the fact from you," Beza informed Bullinger, "that I strongly disapprove of that episcopal domination, from which

---

69 Beza, *Epistolae Theologicae*, 104, 111.
70 Beza, *Epistolae Theologicae*, 107.
71 Beza, *Epistolae Theologicae*, 111.
72 Bullinger voiced his distrust of the Puritan Thomas Sampson in several letters to Beza, dated 31 March 1567 and 11 April 1567. See CB 8:97–101, 111.
73 Beza to Berchtold Haller, 4 February 1567, in CB 8:57–58.
74 See Beza to André Dudith, 18 June 1570, in CB 11:172.

I anticipate no other outcome than for the future of true religion to become much worse than it was in previous times."[75] For Beza, pure doctrine, biblical church government and church discipline remained inseparable.

During the next five years, the Genevan reformer continued to monitor the religious situation in England and sought to strengthen ties with Puritan colleagues. In addition to exchanging letters with Puritan leaders such as Sampson and John Gilpin, Beza also received frequent updates on the English situation from Jean Cousin (the Reformed minister of the French refugee church in London), who was in regular contact with Puritan leaders.[76] On at least one occasion, Beza concluded a letter by requesting that Cousin pass his greetings on to the Puritan leaders "Thomas Cartwright, Perceval Wiburn, Thomas Sampson, William Whittingham, and John Gilpin."[77] These relationships were further strengthened in 1570, when a small group of nonconformist churchmen that included Cartwright (1535–1605), Walter Travers (1548–1635), and the Scottish theologian Andrew Melville (1545–1622) came to Geneva to study with Beza. Cartwright, who had been a professor of theology at Cambridge University before his dismissal, was assigned a temporary teaching post at the Genevan Academy, and was even permitted to attend sessions of Geneva's consistory.[78] Beza praised Cartwright as a "good and well-educated man"; indeed, "the sun does not see a more learned man."[79] When Cartwright returned to England in 1572, Beza sent a glowing recommendation of him to the English Chancellor of the Exchequer, Sir Walter Mildmay (1523–1589).[80]

Beza's reputation among the Puritans during the 1560s and early 1570s is also indicated by the popularity of his theological work *Confession de la foy Chrestienne* (1559), which appeared in seven English editions between 1563 and 1585. In the preface to this English work, the Puritan translator described Beza as "a precious pearl sent amongst us from God in this our troublesome age" and praised the reformer "for his singular godly learning, knowledge, and conversation."[81] In the book itself, Beza numbered church discipline as one of the three marks of a true church, asserted the equality of the ministerial office

---

75 Beza to Bullinger, 3 May [1567], in CB 8:119.

76 Beza to Cousin, 3 August 1572, in CB 13:170.

77 Beza to Cousin, 3 August 1572, in CB 13:170.

78 RCP 3:49, 50. For Cartwright in England, see also COLLINSON, P. (1990), 110–111.

79 Beza to Bullinger, 19 September 1571, in CB 12:188; *The Zurich Letters*, 2nd edition, 479n.3.

80 Though this letter of recommendation is lost, Sir Walter Mildmay makes reference to it in his letter to Beza dated 10 April 1572, in CB 13:116–117n. 4.

81 BEZA, T., *A briefe and pithie Summe of Christian faith* (1589a), A2r-v. See GARDY, F. (1960), 60–80.

and argued that episcopal hierarchy was a form of tyranny that prevented the reformation of the church.[82]

Beza's attitude toward Elizabeth and her bishops remained cautious during this period. Reports that Elizabeth's church continued to persecute nonconformist churchmen intensified Beza's mistrust of the queen. Moreover, rumors that Elizabeth was negotiating a royal marriage to the Catholic Archduke of Austria raised fears that England was on the precipice of returning to the Catholic religion.[83] And yet, at the same time, Catholic plots to depose Elizabeth and place her half-sister Mary Stuart (1542–1587) on the English throne—and, toward that end, the papal bull of Pope Pius V in 1570 that declared the English throne vacant and Elizabeth excommunicate—gave Beza some hope that the resolute English queen would remain in the Protestant fold. Additionally, by 1570, Beza had become convinced that the Roman Catholic Church was orchestrating a universal conspiracy against England and the other Protestant states with the goal of imposing the Tridentine Decrees on all of Europe by political subversion and military force.[84] Finally, the fact that Elizabeth was willing to provide Condé and Coligny with weapons and money during France's second civil war from 1567–1568 signaled that the queen remained an important—if somewhat, mercurial—ally.[85] Though Beza recognized that direct appeals to Elizabeth would probably not succeed, he did maintain contact with several members of the queen's inner circle whom he judged to be sympathetic to the Puritan cause, including the moderate Bishop Grindal, Sir Walter Mildmay, and Sir William Cecil. Beza dedicated the first volume of his *Tractationes theologicae* (1570) to Mildmay as an expression of gratitude for a gift of 400 pounds that the chancellor had given to Geneva in support of religious refugees from France.[86] Though the Vestments Controversy alerted Beza to the dangers of England's episcopal church government and raised suspicions about the English queen, nevertheless, Beza remained cautious in his criticisms of Elizabeth given her strategic support for Reformed churches in Geneva and France, and the refugee church in London. As will become clear, Beza's evaluation of Elizabeth and the English church remained closely linked to his concern for the Reformed churches on the continent.

---

82 BEZA, T., *A briefe and pithie Summe of Christian faith* (1589a), 93[r-v].

83 These rumors are found throughout Beza's correspondence from 1567 to 1570. See, for example, Beza to Bullinger, 24 February 1568, in CB 9:29.

84 Beza often speaks of this universal plot in his correspondence. See, for example, Beza to Bullinger, 7 February 1570, in CB 11:41. For more on this, see MANETSCH, S. (2000b), 149. A similar concern was expressed by Sir Henry Norris in his letter to William Cecil, dated 2 January 1570. See *Calendar of State Papers, Foreign Series, 1560–74* (1966), 9:164–165.

85 See Beza to Bullinger, 8 December 1568, in CB 9:200–202, and n. 6.

86 Beza to Walter Mildmay, 27 February 1570, in CB 11:67.

3.3 Stage Three: The Admonition Controversy (1572–1581)

Through most of the decade of the 1560s, Beza was hesitant to intervene in England's religious crisis. Given the suspicions of the queen, he did not want to do anything that would turn Elizabeth against the Reformed churches in France or further alienate her from her Puritan subjects.[87] During the years 1572 to 1581, however, Beza's campaign against England's episcopal order entered a new phase as his theological writings gained wider currency in the kingdom and as he became more outspoken in his support of presbyterian church order and Geneva-style discipline. Edwyn Sandys (1519–1588), who replaced Grindal as Bishop of London in 1570, no doubt expressed the opinion of many of his colleagues when he accused Beza of being "the first inventor" and the "author" of this "new form" of church government, and after him, Thomas Cartwright.[88] Three episodes were especially important in enhancing Beza's prominence in England: the controversy surrounding the publication of the *Admonition to the Parliament* (1572); the publication of Beza's *Epistolae Theologicae* (1573); and the appearance of Beza's *De Triplici Episcopatu* (c. 1576).

The *Admonition to the Parliament* has been called "the first open manifesto of the puritan party."[89] The anonymous authors of this treatise were two London ministers, John Field (1548–1588) and Thomas Wilcox (c. 1549–1608), who wrote the inflammatory booklet in June of 1572 in an effort to enlist popular opinion and marshal parliamentary action against the decision made the previous year by the royal commissioners to require all clergymen to subscribe to the Prayer Book and other religious articles. Significantly, Field and Wilcox affixed two letters of support to their treatise, one of which was a translation of Beza's programmatic letter to Bishop Grindal written six years earlier. Immediately following Beza's letter, Field and Wilcox concluded their treatise with this provocative poem:

England repent, Bishops relent
returne while you haue space,
Time is at hand, by truth to stand,
if you haue any grace.
Joyne now in one, that Christ alone,
by scepter of his Word:
May beare the stroke: lest you prouoke
his heauy hand and sword.[90]

---

87 See, for example, Beza to Bullinger, 3 May [1567], in CB 8:119.

88 Edwyn Sandys to Rudolph Gwalther, 9 August 1574, in *The Zurich Letters*, 2nd edition, 478–479.

89 FRERE, W./DOUGLAS, E. (ed.) (1954), xi.

90 FIELD, J./WILCOX, T., *Admonition* (1572), in FRERE, W./DOUGLAS, E. (ed.) (1954), 55.

Though Field and Wilcox were quickly identified, arrested and imprisoned, the *Admonition* created a sensation and was reprinted multiple times, soon combined with Thomas Cartwright's longer treatise titled *A Second Admonition to Parliament*. The popular reception of these works is indicated by Bishop Sandys complaint in 1574 that London "will never be quiet until these authors of sedition who are now esteemed as gods, as Field, Wilcox, Cartwright [...] be far removed from the city."[91] Taken together, the treatises of Field and Wilcox—along with Beza's appended letter—contained a devastating indictment of both the religious practices and episcopal structure of the English church as well as a clarion call for the "restitution of true religion and reformation of God's church."[92] With Scripture as their stated norm, the authors identified in exquisite detail dozens of "stinking abominations" and "popish remnants" that were found in the Prayer Book, including private and emergency baptisms, prescribed prayers, the reading of homilies, kneeling during communion, plural benefices, wearing the surplice and cope, Lenten fasts, saints days, wedding rings, prayers for the dead, and the abuse of excommunication. All of these practices, it was argued, had been drawn out of the "popish dunghill" of the Catholic Mass.[93] In addition to their criticisms of the Prayer Book and its subscription, Field, Wilcox and Cartwright also called for fundamental reforms in church polity according to their presbyterian convictions, giving priority to church discipline, regular preaching, the equality of the ministry, the cessation of episcopal hierarchy, and the positive role of synodical oversight. From Cartwright's perspective, the Reformed churches in Geneva and France offered the best contemporary examples of churches Reformed according to the pure Word of God.[94] Even if Theodore Beza was mentioned by name only a handful of times in these treatises, his influence loomed large in the Puritans' theological proposals.[95]

The publication of the *Admonition* by Field and Wilcox, along with Cartwright's *Second Admonition*, sparked a battle of books that raged for the next three years. Walter Travers added his voice to this controversy by publishing a detailed defense of presbyterian government titled *An Explication of Church Discipline* in 1574.[96] As the struggle unfolded, Cartwright and John Whitgift (c. 1530–1604), the Professor of Divinity at Cambridge University,

---

91 Sandys to Lords Burghley and Leicester, 5 August 1573, in FRERE, W./DOUGLAS, E. (ed.) (1954), xxiii.
92 FIELD, J./WILCOX, T., *Admonition* (1572), in FRERE, W./DOUGLAS, E. (ed.) (1954), 8.
93 FIELD, J./WILCOX, T., *Admonition* (1572), in FRERE, W./DOUGLAS, E. (ed.) (1954), 21.
94 Cartwright, *A Second Admonition*, in FRERE, W./DOUGLAS, E. (ed.) (1954), 94.
95 For references to Beza in these treatises, see FRERE W./DOUGLAS, E. (ed.) (1954), 33, 82.
96 See COLLINSON, P. (1990), 107–108.

emerged as the principle antagonists.[97] In their interchange, the two apologists frequently cited the writings of Theodore Beza and debated their significance. This is clearly seen in Whitgift's magisterial work, *The Defence of the Answer to the Admonition, Against the Reply of Thomas Cartwright*, originally published in 1574.[98] In this book of more than 800 folio pages, Whitgift attempted to blunt Cartwright's arguments by demonstrating that the Puritan leader had misquoted or misunderstood the theological writings of major continental reformers, including Peter Martyr Vermigli (1499–1562), Martin Bucer (1491–1551), John Calvin and Beza.[99] Drawing from a variety of Beza's theological and exegetical works, Whitgift went toe-to-toe with Cartwright, arguing that Beza's ecclesiology was flexible and more generous than Cartwright asserted, given that the Genevan reformer recognized that church practices and structures needed to be adapted "according to the diversity of time, place, and persons."[100] Thus, contrary to Cartwright's assertions, Beza did not mandate a single rule for electing ministers, nor did he universally condemn such practices as diaconal preaching, private baptisms or distinguishing rank among Christian ministers.[101] Moreover, Whitgift insisted that Beza's many harsh statements against bishops and church abuse should be read as a critique of the corrupt papal church, not as criticisms of the English church which is "now Reformed" and "under a Christian prince that professes the gospel."[102] But what of Beza's letter to Bishop Grindal from 1566? Whitgift responded that Cartwright and other Puritans had misinformed the Genevan reformer; certainly Beza would have responded differently had he received a more accurate description of the controversy![103] Whitgift was forced to admit, of course, that Beza shared Cartwright's critical assessment of such practices as priests wearing the surplice, signing the cross at baptism, singing the Gospels in the liturgy and bishops possessing multiple benefices. But what did that matter? For, as Whitgift noted stiffly, "our faith and church depends neither upon M. Beza, nor any other man; neither do they look for any such prerogative."[104]

John Whitgift's *Defence* was a masterful attempt to refute and isolate radical Puritans such as Field, Wilcox, Cartwright and Travers by distinguishing their

---

97 For more on this controversy, see COLLINSON, P. (1990), 118–121 and NEW, J. (1986), 203–211.
98 WHITGIFT, J., *Works* (1851–1854).
99 This approach of appealing to the theology of the continental reformers *against* the Puritans became a common feature of Anglican apologetics. See KRUMM, J. (1962), 137–140.
100 WHITGIFT, J., *Works* (1851–1854), 1:253–254.
101 WHITGIFT, J., *Works* (1851–1854), 2:266; 3:62–65, 548.
102 WHITGIFT, J., *Works* (1851–1854), 3:541–543.
103 WHITGIFT, J., *Works* (1851–1854), 2:278.
104 WHITGIFT, J., *Works*, vol. 3:277–278.

views from Beza and other continental reformers. Whitgift's attempt to rehabilitate Beza's ecclesiological position fell short, however, in light of the publication of Beza's *Epistolae Theologicae* (1573), a work that gave far wider currency to the reformer's controversial views.[105] The *Epistolae Theologicae* contained eighty-four of Beza's letters, several of which presented his doctrine in a programmatic fashion. Included in this collection was a letter to John Knox in which Beza condemned the "pseudo-bishops" of Scotland and accused them of introducing Epicureanism into the kingdom.[106] In another letter, sent to the Dutch refugee church of London in 1568, Beza and the Company of Pastors defended at great length the practice of church discipline and Christian freedom in indifferent matters.[107] More provocative still, the *Epistolae Theologicae* included Beza's letter to Bishop Grindal from 1566, the Company of Pastors' missive to the Puritan delegation of 1567, and (most recently) Beza's epistle to the High Lord Treasurer, William Cecil, Lord Burghley. In this latter epistle to Cecil, we see Beza taking a more proactive approach to England's religious controversy. Beza begins his letter by admitting ambivalence in writing Cecil. "Whether it is wise or unwise, I cannot restrain myself," he writes.[108] Beza recognized that some people would accuse him of being audacious to interfere in the affairs of the English church—what motivates him is only his intense desire to see the English church established according to the Word of God.[109] Beza emphasized that he approved the doctrine and faith of the English church without reservation. The problem was the absence of discipline, without which "neither churches, nor states, nor even families are able to survive for long."[110] For this reason, Satan is eager to destroy church discipline as well as right doctrine. Beza chose not to rehearse the many Catholic practices that continued to infect the English liturgy, although he offered to itemize these evils should Cecil request it. Rather, Beza called on Cecil to encourage Queen Elizabeth to seek out Puritan leaders who might work alongside the bishops to introduce proper discipline to the kingdom.[111] Although Beza did not mention these Puritan leaders by name, it is likely that his friends Thomas Cartwright and Walter Travers were chief among them.

The third important episode that signaled Beza's more aggressive stance against episcopal government was the appearance of his *De Triplici Episcopatu*

---

105   For the publication history of Beza's *Epistolae Theologicae,* see GARDY, F. (1960), 160–161.

106   Beza to John Knox, 12 April 1572, in *Epistolae Theologicae* (1573b), 344. See also CB 13:119.

107   The Genevan Company of Pastors to the Dutch Refugee Church in England, 25 June 1568, *Epistolae Theologicae,* 149–167.

108   Beza to [Cecil], 7 July 1572, in CB 13:157.

109   Beza to [Cecil], 7 July 1572, in CB 13:157.

110   Beza to [Cecil], 7 July 1572, in CB 13:158.

111   Beza to [Cecil], 7 July 1572, CB 13:158.

(c. 1576). The treatise circulated in manuscript form for around nine years before being translated into English and published in 1585 under the title of *The judgment of a most reverend and learned man from beyond the seas concerning a threefold order of bishops*.[112] Here one finds Beza's most detailed defense of presbyterian church government to date. The *De Triplici Episcopatu* consisted of two sections.[113] In the first part, Beza described and evaluated three different kinds of episcopal office: what he calls the biblical office; the human office; and the satanic office. In the second part of the treatise, Beza responded at length to six questions addressed to him by the Grand Chancellor of Scotland, John Lyon, Eighth Lord Glamis (c. 1544–1578), in a letter from April 1575. In part one, Beza examined the historical development of episcopal government. In the New Testament, he argued, the apostles used the terms "elder" and "bishop" interchangeably to describe those office holders responsible for overseeing the souls of God's people through the ministry of the Word and prayer. No elder (or bishop) had preeminence over his colleagues. This is the only legitimate "episcopal" office, Beza believed. After the apostolic age, a "human office" of bishop

---

112 For the Latin and original English versions of this text, see NIJENHUIS, W. (1972), 130–187. Nijenhuis incorrectly states that his book was first published in English translation in 1580, rather than 1585. Though published anonymously, Beza was recognized widely as the author of this text.

113 Scholars continue to debate whether both sections, or only the second section, of this document came from Beza's pen. The editors of Beza's *Correspondance* have argued recently that only the second part of this treatise—the detailed response to the questions of John Lyon, Lord Glamis—originated with Beza. They conjecture that part one was written by an unknown author, was attached to Beza's response to Glamis, and was published as a unified, anonymous work. The editors base their argument on what they see as the more radical content of part one, and this statement that Beza makes in a letter to John Whitgift in 1592: "Quae nunc quidem, quasi trajecto mari, ad nos usque, et quidem ad me privatim, quasi harum turbarum vel autorem vel fautorem redundant." See CB 33:170–171n.6. See also ibid., xiv-xv. Following Nijenhuis, I think it more likely that both parts of this treatise were written by Beza for the following reasons: 1.) Whereas part one discusses the threefold order of bishops in detail, part two only makes passing reference to the satanic and human offices of bishop. The fact that both the original English and Latin titles of this manuscript make reference to the "threefold order of bishop" suggests that part one was included in the original manuscript. 2.) In 1584, Beza's friends Jean Castol and Andrew Melville encouraged him to publish a manuscript which they name as *De Triplici Episcopatu*. This title only makes sense if the manuscript included part one, which describes the three-fold episcopal system. 3.) When *The judgment of a most reverend and learned man from beyond the seas* was first published in 1585, it included both parts one and two. 4.) John Whitgift and Adrian Saravia both ascribed authorship of this entire publication to Theodore Beza. 5.) The first Latin version of this treatise, published by Saravia (with his refutation) in 1611, included both sections one and two of this document. 6.) Although section one contains a sharp attack on both the human and satanic offices of bishop, section two is equally "radical" in that it applies the author's biblical and theological conclusions to the specific case of the Scottish church.

was gradually introduced, where certain ministers were elevated above their colleagues and given preeminence and authority over the church and her assemblies. This human form of episcopacy—which Beza appears to identify with the polity of the Scottish church—was illegitimate and should be abandoned because it is "not founded on the Word of God, but on custom."[114] During the Catholic Middle Ages, the episcopal office degenerated further, as bishops cut themselves off from the elder assemblies; wrested control over clerical elections, depositions, and excommunications; and became dissipated by temporal power and worldly pomp. Beza asserted that such a "satanic oligarchy" and "tyranny" had soon paved the way for the emergence of the papal Antichrist, predicted in Scripture.[115] This "satanic office" of bishop had destroyed the Christian church and continued to threaten the Christian kingdoms of Europe. From Beza's perspective both the human and satanic offices of bishop needed to be "eradicated root and branch" for the Church to flourish.[116]

In the second section of *De Triplici Episcopatu*, Beza addressed the Chancellor's six questions regarding the legitimacy of bishops in the Scottish church, the authority of the monarch in religious affairs, the nature and application of excommunication and the appropriate use of church property. Here Beza threw his unqualified support behind a presbyterian system of church government that affirmed the equality of the ministry, placed local leadership in the hands of ministers and elders together, and recognized the authority of representative assemblies at the provincial and national levels to maintain right doctrine, church order and godly discipline. In this part of his treatise, Beza's advice to Glamis was practical and direct. The Scottish king James VI (1567–1625) must abolish the office of bishop in his kingdom or, if he chooses, allow this office to terminate once the installed bishops were deceased. Bishops must no longer be permitted to sit in the Estates General. Beza argued that the king should take leadership to convene the first national assembly of ministers and elders in the Scottish church. Thereafter, regional synods should meet regularly every six months, while national synods should be convened only in cases where right doctrine or church government were in dispute.[117] Beza also recommended that a presiding officer should be chosen by each synod to ensure the good order of the assembly. He insisted, however, that this officer must not be given superior rank or preeminence; his authority was one of order, limited to the duration of the assembly.[118] Finally, the Genevan reformer emphasized that

---

114 Beza, *De Triplici Episcopatu*, in NIJENHUIS, W. (1972), 149.
115 Beza, *De Triplici Episcopatu*, in NIJENHUIS, W. (1972), 159.
116 Beza, *De Triplici Episcopatu*, in NIJENHUIS, W. (1972), 163.
117 Beza, *De Triplici Episcopatu*, in NIJENJUIS, W. (1972), 173.
118 Beza, *De Triplici Episcopatu*, in NIJENHUIS, W. (1972), 165.

these presbyterian assemblies were not to infringe on the temporal authority of the king; nor could they make laws regarding matters of conscience or based on ancient customs. As for excommunication, it must be reserved only for people guilty of egregious sins who did not demonstrate earnest repentance. Though addressed to a Scottish nobleman, Beza's *De Triplici Episcopatu* presented a direct challenge to the English church as well. For, if Scotland's moderate presbyterianism, formulated in the *First Book of Discipline* (1560), did not satisfy the Genevan reformer, what could be said of England's overtly episcopal system?[119] Though the English translation of this work was published anonymously, the paternity of *De Triplici Episcopatu* was known by members of the French refugee community in London. By the early 1590s the English translation of this treatise caused a major uproar in England that further alienated Beza from England's bishops.

As we have seen, during the period from 1572 to 1581, Theodore Beza's criticism of the English church and his support for presbyterian church government gained wider currency throughout England, thanks in large part to the *Admonition* Controversy, the publication of his *Epistolae Theologicae* and the circulation of a manuscript version of his *De Triplici Episcopatu*. In these years, no fewer than seven of Beza's theological and exegetical writings appeared in English translation, including his *Tabula Praedestinationis* (1555), his *Confession de la foi chrétienne* (1559), his *Vie de Calvin* (1564), his *Quaestiones et responsiones* (parts one and two; 1570, 1576), his *Petit catéchisme* (1575), and his treatise *De peste* (1579). The fact that Puritan writers were the translators of many of these titles, and that several of these works were dedicated to Puritan noblemen, further indicates the extent to which the Genevan reformer had emerged as a major theological resource and authority for nonconformist churchmen in the kingdom.[120]

In addition to writing books, Beza supported the Puritan cause by maintaining friendly relations with prominent English noblemen and noble women who were considered allies of the Puritans. In 1579, Beza dedicated his *Psalmorum Davidis ... Paraphrasi* to Henry Hastings the Earl of Huntingdon; during that same year Beza welcomed two of Hasting's nephews into his home when they came to study at the Genevan Academy. Two years later, Beza also provided lodging for Anthony Bacon, the son of the deceased Nicolas Bacon (one-time

---

119 For the *First Book of Discipline*, and the emergence of Scottish Presbyterianism, see HART, D. (2013), 52–54; GRAHAM, F., Presbyterianism, in OER 3:338–341; and KIRK, J., Scottish Books of Discipline, in OER 4:31–33.

120 Arthur Golding, for example, dedicated Beza's first *Book of Questions and Answers* (1572) to the Earl of Huntingdon, Henry Hastings in 1572, for the purpose that "the children of light may learn from it how to withstand the adder's brood of the Romish Antichrist." See CROSS, C. (1966), 25.

Guard of the Seal of England) and the nephew of William Cecil, Lord Burghley.[121] In a friendly letter thanking Beza for his warm hospitality, Anthony's mother Ann Bacon (1528–1610) extolled the reformer, noting that he was famous in England on account of his zeal for the house of God.[122] In response, Beza dedicated his *Chrestiennes meditations* (1581) to Madame Bacon in hopes that the book would provide her godly consolation as she experienced widowhood. To solidify further the support of this powerful noble family, Beza donated two precious documents, one an ancient copy of the Pentateuch, the other a sixth-century manuscript of the Gospels and Acts, to the Puritan stronghold Cambridge University—an institution and its library that William Cecil supervised.[123] Although Cambridge University was slow in acknowledging these remarkable gifts—leaving Beza frustrated and fearful—the school did finally communicate its gratitude. In this letter, a member of the university senate named Anthony Wingfield reported that Beza's theology nourished the pastors at Cambridge daily. Indeed, next to Scripture, "there exists no writer from any period of time that we prefer more than you and that memorable man John Calvin."[124]

3.4 Stage Four: Elizabeth Ascends (1575–1589)

Theodore Beza's attitude toward Queen Elizabeth and her kingdom continued to be cautious during the mid-1570s and early 1580s. When the reformer compared the Scottish King James VI to the English queen Elizabeth, James invariably won out.[125] Positive religious reforms in Scotland only accentuated the unfavorable condition of the English church and her leaders. The reformer was especially critical of the queen's continued efforts to negotiate nuptials with a Catholic prince, this time François, duke of Anjou (1555–1584), the brother of the French king, whom Beza likened to a serpent. How "wretched and unhappy" such an alliance would be for a kingdom filled with "so many godly people," Beza fretted.[126] But even so, there were other factors that inclined Beza to have a more positive assessment of Elizabeth and her island kingdom. For one, Elizabeth remained resolute in her Protestant allegiance,

---

121 Ann Bacon to Beza, 18 May 1581, in CB 22:51.

122 Ann Bacon to Beza, 24 July 1581, in CB 22:130.

123 See Beza to Cecil, 6 December 1581, in CB 22:191–192; and Beza to the Academy of Cambridge, 6 December 1581, in CB 22:245–246.

124 Academy of Cambridge to Beza, 18 May 1582, in CB 23:246.

125 See Beza to Bullinger, 16 August 1575, in CB 16:155.

126 Beza to Gwalther, 17 September 1581, in CB 22:176. See also Beza's comments to Dürnhoffer, 23 June 1574, in CB 15:113.

despite assassination plots and (what Beza feared to be) an international Tridentine conspiracy against the Protestant states of Europe. On the high seas, English warships continued to attack and plunder Spanish galleons returning from the New World weighted with gold.[127] So too, Elizabeth and wealthy English patrons provided financial support for French refugees seeking asylum in Geneva following the St Bartholomew's Day massacres of 1572.[128] Despite Beza's regular complaints about England's bishops, he had not changed his overall assessment that, at least in its confessional documents, the English church remained a member of the family of Reformed churches—even if the English church was the only Reformed Church in Europe that did not practice church discipline.[129] This basic conviction was illustrated in 1581 when Beza and a group of Reformed ministers published the *Harmonia confessionum fidei* in response to the attacks of the Lutheran *Book of Concord* (1580). The *Harmonia* contained a catalogue of the Augsburg Confession (*variata* edition) and ten Reformed confessions—including the Thirty Nine Articles—that demonstrated their doctrinal agreement point by point.[130] From Beza' perspective, the English church was not an apostate church. Rather, it was a Reformed church badly in need of additional reforming. Unfortunately, Elizabeth and her bishops were impeding rather than promoting such a reformation.

During the 1580s, Theodore Beza's attitude toward Elizabeth underwent a significant change. There appears to have been a number of reasons for this. For one, much to Beza's relief, the queen finally broke off marriage negotiations with the Duke of Anjou in 1582. So too, the English admiral Sir Francis Drake staged several spectacular raids against the Spanish fleet during the years leading up to the defeat of the Invincible Spanish Armada in 1588. But it was probably the financial support that Elizabeth and several of her councilors provided Geneva during the city's protracted conflict with the Catholic Duke of Savoy that was most important in changing Beza's opinion of the queen.

In 1582, the Duke of Savoy, Charles-Emmanuel (1562–1630), blockaded Geneva in hopes of capturing the city and reimposing the Catholic religion. Beza believed this attack was the first stage in the long-awaited Tridentine conspiracy against the Protestant cities and states of Europe.[131] Geneva was forced to hire

---

127 See, for example, Beza to Gwalther, 2 December 1580, in CB 21:253.
128 In a letter to Christophe Hardesheim (12 February 1574), Beza reports that the Company of Pastors had received donations from England to support the exiles of St. Bartholomew's Day. See CB 15:37n.11.
129 See, for example, Beza to Constantine Fabricius, 20/30 May 1592, in CB 33:84.
130 See HIGMAN, F. (1995), 243–262.
131 See, for example, Beza to Sir Francis Walsingham, [10] October 1582, in CB 23:197; also MANETSCH, S. (2000b), 120–121.

at great expense 1,200 mercenaries to repulse the Savoyard threat.[132] In order to alleviate this sizeable war debt, Theodore Beza encouraged Geneva's magistrates in late September to send an ambassador to solicit financial assistance from Queen Elizabeth and her court.[133] Subsequently, a city councilor named Jean Malliet was dispatched to England in October, carrying a packet of letters that included several from Beza addressed to his English contacts, including the pastor of the French refugee church in London, Robert Le Maçon, sire of La Fontaine (c. 1534–1611); the Lord High Treasurer William Cecil; and the Secretary of State, Francis Walsingham (c. 1532–1590).[134] Beza also wrote to his friend the Puritan leader Walter Travers, requesting his prayer and support. Geneva's situation was so perilous that "tossed as it were in the sea of a great debt, we have great cause to fear shipwreck from it."[135] Beza's letter to William Cecil is most interesting, in that his request for financial assistance was couched in a defense of Geneva and her long-standing relationship with England. Beza reminded Cecil of the many exiles that had found refuge in Geneva during the reign of Mary. Contrary to the accusations of some, Geneva had never served as a haven for religious subversives. Indeed, the Genevans had condemned and tried to suppress the controversial books written by Knox and Goodman when they first appeared in 1558. Moreover, Beza asserted, England and Geneva shared the same religious confession. Though minor differences regarding ceremonies and rites existed between the two churches, these only pertained to indifferent matters (*adiaphora*).[136] In the end, Malliet's embassy to England was a clear success. Though the ambassador was never granted a formal audience with the queen, she did allow Malliet to solicit funds from churches in and around London, and several members of her Privy Council made sizeable contributions as well. When Malliet returned to Geneva in 1583, he brought with him promises for 5,730 pounds sterling to meet Geneva's war debt.[137]

But the crisis with Savoy was far from over. From 1586 to 1587, the Savoyard army returned and once again blockaded Geneva from land and lake in an attempt to starve the city into submission. As the price of wheat tripled, and

---

132 MONTER, W.E. (1967), 198–199.

133 The *Registres* of the City Council make clear that this English embassy was Beza's idea. See CB 23:186n.1.

134 See Beza to La Fontaine, 10 October 1582, in CB 23:183–186; Beza to Cecil, 10 October 1582, in CB 23:189–192; Beza to Walsingham, [10] October 1582, in CB 23:197–199.

135 Beza to Walter Travers, [10] October 1582, in CB 23:193–196. Illustrating the warmth of their relationship, Beza stated that he thought of Travers and Thomas Cartwright daily, and continued to savor their friendship. Ibid., 193.

136 Beza to Cecil, 10 October 1582, in CB 23:190.

137 See CB 23:187n.10. According to Monter, 5,730 pounds sterling represented one-third of Geneva's annual revenue during this period. See MONTER, W.E. (1967), 199.

as starvation threatened peasants in Geneva's countryside, Beza once again looked to England and Queen Elizabeth for political and financial support.[138] In several letters to members of the queen's Privy Council, Beza argued that in the face of the unfolding Tridentine conspiracy, the security of Reformed states such as England and Geneva was inextricably intertwined. Indeed, the defense of Geneva was "of vital importance for the safety of all the Christian churches now presently assailed, and particularly for the benefit of the affairs of her most serene Majesty."[139]

England's generous response to Geneva's financial need contributed to Beza's more favorable opinion of Elizabeth. In 1584, when the reformer learned that Elizabeth had narrowly escaped a Jesuit assassination plot, he commented to his friend Johann Jakob Grynaeus (1540–1617) in Basel: "If only the Lord might continue to preserve the queen of England. If anything happened to her—humanly speaking—nothing would be more miserable for that kingdom!"[140] Two years later, in a letter to William Cecil, Beza assured the Lord High Treasurer that he was praying for the members of the royal court, and "especially for her most serene Majesty, the Queen, who is not only the defender of so many godly people, but also the defender of those people most undeservedly oppressed." Beza went on to praise Elizabeth's exceptional zeal "for the propagation of the gospel" and to pray that God would "continue to equip and amplify her with every exceptional gift by his Holy Spirit."[141] In another letter to Cecil, Beza extolled Elizabeth's extraordinary kindness for her generous support of Geneva in the city's hour of need.[142] The following year, when Beza learned of the English naval victory in the Spanish port of Cadiz, the reformer compared Sir Francis Drake to David fighting Goliath, and then requested prayers that God would protect "that most worthy heroine" Elizabeth.[143]

It was in late 1588, several months after England's extraordinary defeat of the Invincible Spanish Armada, that Beza unleashed the full measure of his eloquence in a Latin poem of thirty-four stanzas celebrating England's victory and extolling the virtues of the English queen. Beza praised Elizabeth's wisdom and humility, her virtue and piety, her courage and devotion to prayer. She was a queen who "loved to follow the teachings of Christ." Surely, England was "three-times happy and more […] to be governed by such a brilliant princess!"[144] In

---

138 Beza to Cecil, 27 September 1586, in CB 27:180–181.

139 Beza to William Davison, 22 December 1586, in CB 27:215.

140 Beza to Grynaeus, 11 February 1584, in CB 25:30.

141 Beza to Cecil, 17 May 1586, in CB 27:90.

142 Beza to Cecil, 27 September 1586, in CB 27:180.

143 Beza to Johann Stumpf, 6/16 June 1587, in CB 28:81.

144 See Beza's "Triumphalis ad Elizabetham, Angliae Reginam, de Clade Hispanicae Classis," in CB 29:284–289. A French translation of this poem appears at ibid., 289–293.

addition to this longer poem, Beza also wrote and published in 1589 a shorter Latin poem dedicated to Elizabeth to celebrate the victory of the previous year. The final stanzas of this poem read:

> O noble Queen of all the world, the only true delight,
> go forward still to rule for God, ambition laid aside.
> Go forward still for Christ his flock, in bounty to provide,
> that thou may England govern long, long England thee enjoy.
> As well as love unto the good, as to the bad annoy.[145]

By the time Beza published these verses, Geneva was once again in a desperate war of survival against a superior Savoyard force that lasted for the next four years. Tired and discouraged, Beza longed for a peaceful death: "We are now encircled on every side," he wrote in September 1589. "If only the Lord would grant to me what he once gave to Augustine, when Hippo was besieged by barbarians."[146] Nevertheless, the reformer, who was entering his eighth decade of life, picked up his pen to solicit once again financial and political assistance from his English allies. Over the next two years, Beza and his colleague Antoine de Chandieu (1534–1591) wrote letters to Queen Elizabeth, the French stranger church in London, William Cecil and the Archbishop of Canterbury John Whitgift requesting help. The Genevans also sent an ambassador named Jacques Lect (1560–1611) to England, who received permission from the queen to make a collection on behalf of the besieged city. In all, Lect raised more than 5,000 écus for Geneva.[147] During these dramatic months, Elizabeth was also providing critical support for the Huguenot war effort in France. In April 1590, Beza received the report that the Virgin Queen had loaned Henry of Navarre 20,000 pounds, and also provided 4,000 men to protect Dieppe from Leaguer armies.[148]

As part of his campaign to marshal Elizabeth's support, Beza also dedicated his Latin *Commentary on Job* (1589) to Queen Elizabeth. In the dedicatory preface, the reformer remembered the many ways that God had providentially protected Elizabeth throughout the course of her life: from the wrath of Queen Mary, from would-be assassins and now from the mighty Spanish Armada. Beza also remembered with gratitude how this compassionate and faithful

---

145 This Latin poem, entitled "Ad Serenissimam Elizabetham Angliae Reginam," is found in CB 29:292–293. It was published as a separate piece in 1589. See GARDY, F. (1960), 201. I have modernized the sixteenth-century English translation of this poem.

146 Beza to Grynaeus, 13/23 September 1589, in CB 30:257. For more on Geneva's protracted conflict against Savoy during this period, see MONTER, E.W. (1967), 201–205.

147 For more on Lect's embassy to the royal court, see GAUTIER, J.-A. (1903), 6:38–87; CRAMER, L. (1958), 191.

148 Nicholas de Harlay de Sancy to Beza and Chandieu, 20/30 April 1590, in CB 31:106.

princess had welcomed poor refugees to her shores and how she had generously supported Geneva eight years earlier when it faced pestilence, famine and war.[149] Now, once again, the enemy is "hard at our gates, scarcely allowing us to breath."[150] In the final pages of the preface, Beza discussed the background of the book of Job, its various translations, and its timely message regarding divine providence. The letter was signed "From Geneva, besieged by the Duke of Savoy, 12 of August 1589. To your royal majesty, from your most devoted servant, Theodore Beza."[151] Over the course of the previous decade, Beza had laid aside his criticisms and reservations regarding the English queen. He now recognized that Geneva's future survival was in large part tied to the generosity of the courageous and pious Virgin Queen Elizabeth.

3.5   Stage Five: The Revenge of the Bishops (1590–1605)

During the final fifteen years of his life, as Theodore Beza grew weak and tired, he frequently expressed his longing to retire to the quiet of his books, especially to his beloved *Annotationes* and *Poemata*, and forget the incessant theological disputes that swirled around him. But such was not to be the case. Beginning in 1589, Beza was drawn almost unwittingly into an explosive controversy concerning ecclesiastical polity and discipline that was in large part fueled by his written judgments of the previous thirty years. The Archbishop of Canterbury, John Whitgift, was quick to seize the opportunity to attack Beza's position in an effort to diminish his influence in England and crush the Puritan movement.

When John Whitgift was elevated to primate of the English church in October 1583, Beza immediately recognized the danger. As vice-chancellor at Cambridge, Whitgift had expelled Thomas Cartwright from his professor's chair in 1570. Thereafter, Whitgift had become a chief apologist for Elizabeth's religious settlement and an intractable opponent of the Puritans, as illustrated in his crucial role in the *Admonition* Controversy.[152] Now, as Archbishop of Canterbury, Whitgift lost no time in resuming his attack against the Puritans by requiring all clergy within the Church of England to subscribe to the royal supremacy, the Prayer Book, and the Thirty-Nine Articles and affirm that each was consistent with Scripture.[153] Watching from Geneva, Beza expressed his darkest fears that the archbishop would strengthen the tyranny of England's

---

149 BEZA, T., *Iob* (1589b), A.2.v.
150 BEZA, T., *Iob*, (1589b), A.2.v.
151 BEZA, T. *Iob*, (1589b), A.5.v.
152 See COLLINSON, P. (1990), 124, 132–139.
153 KNAPPEN, M. (1966), 265–267.

bishops, further erode the discipline of the church, and even disband the French refugee congregation in London.[154] Beza wondered if the "Roman Hydra," once slain with the "sword of the Lord," was coming back to life in England.[155] Clearly, Whitgift was made out of very different stuff than his predecessor Edmund Grindal—"that excellent and wisest of men."[156] But despite these depressing developments, Beza still held out hope: "The Lord will preserve [his people] in such great storms, as he always did, and will no doubt do all the way to the end."[157]

Two years after Whitgift's appointment, Beza's letter to the Scottish Lord Glamis—which had heretofore circulated in manuscript form under the title *De Triplici Episcopatu*—was published in English translation as *The judgment of a most reverend and learned man from beyond the seas* (1585). Historians are uncertain whether Beza officially approved its translation and publication, although several of his friends encouraged him to do so.[158] Moreover, scholars continue to debate whether both parts, or only the second part, of the treatise were written by Beza himself.[159] Whatever the case, the fact that the radical Puritan John Field translated the work is of great significance. In 1585, Field and other Puritan extremists began to construct a presbyterian system of synods and assemblies within the existing episcopal structure of the Church of England. Shortly thereafter, in 1586 or 1587, Walter Travers completed in manuscript form a Book of Discipline—which closely resembled Geneva's *Form of Prayers*—to which Puritan ministers would voluntarily subscribe.[160] Without dismantling the episcopal structure of the English church, nonconformists leaders such as Field and Travers were seeking to create a Puritan "church within a church"—and doing so, with the apparent support of a "most learned man from beyond the seas," that is, Theodore Beza. The broad diffusion of Beza's *De Triplici Episcopatu* pulled the Genevan reformer into the center of England's religious controversy and triggered a flurry of books that left him and Geneva's church exposed to the wrath of the Archbishop of Canterbury. The three most important books in this controversy were written by Thomas

---

154 See Beza to Grynaeus, 8/18 June 1584, in CB 25:114; Beza to Gwalther, 11 August 1584, in CB 25:197; Beza to Grynaeus, 27 August/6 September, 1584, in CB 25:231.

155 Beza to La Fontaine, 1 July 1584, in CB 25:166.

156 Beza to Gwalther, 11/21 August 1584, in CB 25:197.

157 Beza to Grynaeus, 27 August/6 September 1584, in CB 25:231.

158 See Castol to Beza, 26 August/5 September 1584, in CB 25:213; Andrew Melville to Beza, 26 August 1584, in CB 25:221.

159 For this debate, see note 113 above.

160 See COLLINSON, P. (1990), 291–302, 333–382; KNAPPEN, M. (1966), 283–292.

Erastus (1524–1583), Adrian Saravia (c. 1532–1613) and Matthew Sutcliffe (c. 1550–1629).[161]

The first book, Thomas Erastus's *Explicatio gravissimae quaestionis* (1589), appeared as if from the grave.[162] Erastus had once been a physician in Heidelberg who, in the late 1560s, had locked horns with the Reformed minister Caspar Olevianus over questions related to church polity and discipline. In 1569, Erastus wrote seventy-five *Theses* that rejected presbyterian discipline as oligarchic and tyrannical, arguing instead that Scripture gave civil magistrates jurisdiction over the church and the practice of excommunication. Though Bullinger approved of Erastus's *Theses*, Beza strenuously disagreed and composed a long manuscript in which he defended the church's jurisdiction over the spiritual realm, including the practice of church discipline and excommunication. Erastus quickly responded to Beza with his own *Confirmatio*. Thanks to the intervention of Bullinger, this minor theological squabble was pacified in 1570 and the two men agreed on account of friendship to bury the controversy and refrain from publishing their attacks.[163] And so the matter remained nearly forgotten for two decades. In 1589, six years after Erastus died, the physician's widow and her new husband came to England and promptly published Erastus's *Theses* and *Confirmatio* under the title *Explicatio gravissimae quaestionis*. When Beza first heard of this development, he was shocked and feared that Erastus's attack on presbyterian doctrine would cause turmoil in Reformed churches throughout Europe and give an opening to the Jesuits. The fact that Erastus's book was reported to have been published with the support of the bishop of London and that it was being distributed throughout England only heightened his concern.[164] But what should be done? After polling his friends, Beza decided not to write a new treatise against Erastus, but to publish his original response to the Heidelberg physician. This work, with a new preface, was published both in Geneva and London in 1590 under the title *Tractatus pius et moderatus de Excommunicatione*.[165]

---

161 For Beza's use of this image of a three-headed monster, see Beza to Sibrand Lubert, 20/30 August 1592, CB 33:122–123. For other episodes in the Anglican offensive against Geneva, see KRUMM, J. (1962), 129–144.

162 For this controversy, see GUNNOE, C. (2010), 163–260; GEISENDORF, P.-F. (1967), 228–231; BAKER, J.W., Erastianism, in OER 2:59–61; and especially MARUYAMA, T. (1978), 112–22.

163 See, for example, Beza to Bullinger, 27 August 1570, in CB 11:261.

164 Beza to Grynaeus, 8/18 December 1589, in CB 30:306–307. The bishop of London during this period was John Aylmer. J. Wayne Baker indicates that Archbishop Whitgift was instrumental in the printing of Erastus's book as well. See OER 2:60.

165 See GARDY, 204. For the preface to this work, see Beza to the Christian Reader, 1/11 March 1590, in CB 31:40–63.

Soon after Erastus's book appeared, a second publication attacking presbyterianism ricocheted through England, this one written by a Dutch-Calvinist turned Anglican by the name of Adrian Saravia.[166] Saravia's book, entitled *De diversis ministrorum Evangelii gradibus* (1590), was dedicated to the Archbishop of Canterbury Whitgift, the English Chancellor Christopher Hatton and William Cecil. Whitgift was Saravia's patron who once received the Dutchman as a guest in his household.[167] In the preface to this work Saravia acknowledged that Roman Catholic bishops had abused their power and corrupted Christ's church. But the presbyterian reaction was equally dangerous in that it degraded the biblical office of bishop, which in turn undermined Christian unity and the well-being of the church.[168] The problem was not with the order of bishops per se, but the abuse of episcopal power. In the pages that followed, Saravia provided a careful defense of the episcopal office, arguing that Scripture and early church fathers recognized degrees of power, authority, and dignity in the Christian ministry. God himself had ordained that there be a superior order of bishops and an inferior order of priests within the church. In the penultimate chapter of the work, Saravia applied his analysis directly to the Puritans and the English church:

> In the present day, some people in this country attack with great bitterness clerical garments, caps, ornaments, music, organs, and certain other rites of the Anglican church, contending that they are profane and ungodly because they are used in the Church of Rome. And they say the same thing about bishops and archbishops, their possessions, and the rank which they enjoy in this Christian state. But unless these things can be proved contrary to the Word of God, I maintain that it is not a sufficient reason for their abolition to assert that Antichrist was their author and inventor.[169]

Given its learned style and moderate tone, Saravia's book was considered especially dangerous. Jean Castol (c. 1554–c. 1600), one of the pastors of the French exile church in London, begged Beza to respond to it, noting that Saravia's evil doctrine was "spreading everywhere" and threatened to divide the English church from the Reformed churches in France.[170] Dutifully, Beza penned a

---

166 For more on this controversy, see MARUYAMA, T. (1978), 179–194. See also NIJENHUIS, W. (1980), 110–160.

167 SARAVIA, A., *De Diversis Ministrorum Evangelii Gradibus* (1591), 3. An English translation appeared in 1592. For a more recent edition of this English version, see SARAVIA, A., *A Treatise on the Different Degrees of the Christian Priesthood* (1840).

168 SARAVIA, A., *De Diversis Ministrorum Evangelii Gradibus* (1591), 10; English translation, 9–10.

169 SARAVIA, A., *De Diversis Ministrorum Evangelii Gradibus* (1591), 98–99. English translation, 254–255.

170 Castol to Beza, 12/22 August 1591, in CB 32:125–126.

response to Saravia that appeared two years later under the title *Ad Tracta-tionem de Ministrorum Evangelii Gradibus ab H. Saravia ... Responsio* (1592).[171] Here Beza provided a chapter-by-chapter refutation of Saravia's work, restating and defending the view that Scripture nowhere permits degrees of hierarchy among Christian ministers. Beza also restated his conception of the threefold episcopacy—the divine episcopacy, the human episcopacy, and the satanic episcopacy.[172] Only the divine episcopacy had apostolic origin, reflected in a presbyterian-synodical system where ministers served alongside each other as equals, and where presiding officers were elected for a limited time to ensure good order.

The third book directed against Beza and the Puritans was written by an Englishman named Matthew Sutcliffe, Dean of Exeter. Sutcliffe's work, entitled *De Presbyterio eiusque nova in Ecclesia Christiana politeia* (1591), revisited Erastus's *Theses* and attacked the English translation of Beza's *De Triplici Episcopatu* in order to discredit the practice of church discipline in general. Considering Sutcliffe a heckler and a buffoon, and wearied by the unending conflict, Beza chose not to respond to Sutcliffe's attack.[173] To a friend in Germany, Beza described the deplorable condition of the English church this way:

> The German Erastus posthumously, the Flemish Saravia, and the Englishman Sutcliffe are not of the same view, but they join together to fight against the truth. The one wants to abolish all church discipline; the other desires the domination of the bishops; and the third places all jurisdiction only in the civil magistrates.

Certainly, "this is a three-headed monster."[174] The appearance of these three books, along with the publication of many other pro-episcopal pamphlets and books during the early 1590s, hastened the end of radical presbyterian experiments by Field and Travers and marked a strategic setback for the English Puritan movement.[175]

At the same time that Beza was battling the books of Erastus and Saravia, the Genevan reformer was also engaged in a tense epistolary exchange with the Archbishop of Canterbury, John Whitgift. The Archbishop had first written to

---

171 BEZA, T. *Ad Tractationem de Ministrorum Evangelii Gradibus ab H. Saravia .... Responsio* (1592a). See GARDY, ,F. (1960), 209. For a description of this work, see MARUYAMA, T. (1978), 184–193.

172 BEZA, T., *Ad Tractationem de Ministrorum Evangelii Gradibus ab H. Saravia .... Responsio* (1592a), 177.

173 Beza to Ludwig Sayn-Wittgenstein, 23 August/2 September 1592, in CB 33:129n.7.

174 Beza to Ludwig Sayn-Wittgenstein, 23 August/2 September 1592, in CB 33:130.

175 KNAPPEN, M. (1966), 295–300.

Beza and his colleague Antoine de Chandieu in the summer of 1590 to report that he had met with Geneva's emissary Jacques Lect and was doing all he could to raise funds for the city in its desperate struggle with Savoy.[176] The overall tone of this first letter was friendly, although at one point Whitgift asked the Genevans to show the same honor to the English church that they gave to other Reformed churches.[177] Before Beza had a chance to answer Whitgift's letter, he received an alarming report from Jean Castol in London.[178] Castol warned Beza that his *Tractatus pius et moderatus* against Erastus, together with Saravia's treatise, were being circulated by associates of Whitgift and the Chancellor Hatten in order to discredit the church government and discipline espoused by the Puritans and practiced by the exile churches in London. Castol feared that the Bishop of London might seize this opportunity to expel the foreign refugee churches from the kingdom. Moreover, Castol reported that Whitgift had begun to pressure Puritan churchmen to subscribe to articles regarding ceremonies and the primacy of bishops; many Puritan ministers, he feared, would soon be deposed from their offices and imprisoned. All of this, then, required that Beza proceed with great caution as he interacted with Archbishop Whitgift. Castol noted: "I judge that it is expedient for the glory of God and the peace of the churches that you maintain [Whitgift's] friendship without giving him any reason to abuse us. For I fear that under the pretext of your authority he might damage still further those who desire reformation."[179] Castol recognized far too well that words written by Beza in far-off Geneva could easily jeopardize the cause of reform in England.

Taking Castol's warnings to heart, Beza wrote a long and deferential letter to Whitgift nine months later. In this letter, Beza thanked the Archbishop for his generous financial support of Geneva. He then assured the English primate that the Genevan church was in no way attempting to force its model of government and discipline on England or any other Reformed church. The reformer noted: "Although I confess that we think that this discipline which we observe is in complete agreement with the Word of God and conforms to the purest example of the early Church," nevertheless, God has not given Geneva "authority over any other church. Far be it that we should be so arrogant!"[180] As long as Reformed churches agreed on essential points of doctrine, Beza asserted, they might well differ on points of *adiaphora* related to antiquity, customs, and the unique circumstances of places, times and persons.[181] At the same time, the Genevan

---

176 Whitgift to Beza, 21/31 July 1590, in CB 31:168–169.
177 Whitgift to Beza, 21/31 July 1590, in CB 31:169.
178 Castol to Beza, 22 July/1 August 1590, in CB 31:170–177.
179 Castol to Beza, 22 July/1 August 1590, in CB 31:173.
180 Beza to Whitgift, 8/18 March 1591, in CB 32:53–54.
181 Beza to Whitgift, 8/18 March 1591, in CB 32:54.

reformer expressed hope that Reformed churches in various corners of Europe might convene a general synod to settle "according to the Word of God and the pure canons of the ancient church" various controversies regarding ecclesiastical government. Beza concluded this irenic letter by praising the "most majestic and dignified" Elizabeth, a queen "celebrated by the memory of all generations," who was "nurse" of the English church and the "Protectress" of the foreign exile churches.[182] Though Beza's letter to Whitgift was tactical and prudent, it was also disingenuous, given the reformer's unqualified statements made earlier regarding the essential nature of presbyterian government and church discipline in a well-ordered church. The Archbishop would soon capitalize on these inconsistencies.

John Whitgift's reply to Beza's letter is no longer extant, but the defensive tone of Beza's response in 1592 suggests that the Archbishop's letter was more critical than the previous one. Once again, Beza insisted that the English and Genevan churches shared the same religious confession; they disagreed only on matters related to external ceremonies.[183] Unfortunately, wicked men had tried to exaggerate these differences by blaming him and his Genevan colleagues for spreading controversy and troubles in England and beyond. Beza insisted that he was neither "the author nor instigator" of England's religious problems.[184] Instead, it was calumniators such as Sutcliffe, Saravia and (from the grave) Erastus who were stoking the fires of controversy in books that alleged that Beza and the Genevans wished to abolish all bishops and impose their ecclesiastical organization on all the Reformed churches, thereby unleashing "democratic confusion" upon the world.[185] Though Beza did not implicate Whitgift directly, he was clearly frustrated that the Archbishop had granted permission for these books to be published in England in the first place.[186] In the next part of the letter, Beza rehearsed his view of the three-fold episcopacy laid out in his treatise against Saravia and in his book *De Triplici Episcopatu*. Drawing from the writings of Jerome, Augustine, and Ambrose, Beza argued that the "human episcopacy" that emerged in the early church—which was now replicated in the Church of England—was the product of human invention rather than of divine origin.[187] Finally, in an effort to be conciliatory, Beza informed the Archbishop

---

182 Beza to Whitgift, 8/18 March 1591, in CB 32:55.
183 Beza to Whitgift, 1592, in CB 33:170.
184 Beza to Whitgift, 1592, in CB 33:170.
185 Beza to Whitgift, 1592, in CB 33:171–172. In addition to these three authors, Beza also criti-
     cized the unknown author of the *Querimonia Ecclesiae*, and Jean Gau de Frégeville, the author
     of *Palma christiana, seu Speculum veri status ecclesiastici* (1593). See ibid., 171–172n.9–10.
186 Beza to Whitgift, 1592, in CB 33:172n.11. In this regard, see also Beza to Whitgift, 8/18
     March 1591, in CB 32:54.
187 Beza to Whitgift, 1592, in CB 33:173.

that if his writings had offended anyone, he was prepared to give an explanation for his theological position.[188]

Whitgift accepted Beza's challenge. In a long and painfully candid letter from January 1594, the Archbishop countered Beza's claims of innocence, enumerating the many ways that the reformer had sowed discord and unrest in the English kingdom over the previous thirty years. Whitgift began his letter by deflecting Beza's complaint that the archbishop was culpable for not prohibiting the publication of so many scurrilous books and pamphlets against Geneva. Whitgift never had such power over London's print shops, and only wished he could convince Reformed controversialists to attack Roman Catholics rather than fellow Protestants.[189] Next, Whitgift addressed Beza's central complaint that he and the Genevans were being blamed for religious disturbances in England and falsely accused of trying to abolish episcopal government and impose foreign discipline on the English Church. Here Whitgift was blunt and direct. Since the beginning of Geneva's Reformation, Reformed leaders such as Calvin, Lambert Daneau (1535–1590), Chandieu and Zacharias Ursinus (1534–1583) had propagated the teaching that Geneva's polity and brand of discipline was the only true form of church government established by Christ. This uncompromising attitude had enflamed Puritan discontent in England for many years and emboldened them against Elizabeth's religious establishment and her bishops.[190] To prove that Beza was especially blameworthy in this regard, Whitgift proceeded to identify specific passages from the reformer's writings over the previous three decades in which he had rejected episcopal government and defended presbyterian polity and discipline. Here Whitgift listed Beza's dedicatory preface to Queen Elizabeth in the *Annotationes* (1564), Beza's *Confession de la foi chrétienne* (1559), Beza's letter to Bishop Grindal (1566) as well as several other letters published in the reformer's *Epistolae Theologicae*. Indeed, "even before these letters were published, copies of all of them were dispersed here among us and came into the hands of many [disaffected] people."[191] Beza even had the temerity to write a letter to the royal counselor, William Cecil, urging him to support the Puritan cause.[192] Beza's campaign against English church doctrine had created so much suspicion among the Puritans that they began to attack "first the vestments and ceremonies," of the church, "then the liturgy, and

---

188 Beza to Whitgift, 1592, in CB 33:174. Beza attached to the letter his poem "Triumphal Ode to Queen Elizabeth" as an expression of his goodwill.

189 Whitgift to Beza, 16/26 January 1594, in CB 35:7. An English translation of Whitgift's letter is found in STRYPE, J. (1718), 4:406–408 [sic 412].

190 Whitgift to Beza, 16/26 January 1594, in CB 35:8; STRYPE, J. (1718), 4:407.

191 Whitgift to Beza, 16/26 January 1594, in CB 35:11; STRYPE, J. (1718), 4:407.

192 Whitgift to Beza, 16/26 January 1594, in CB 35:11; STRYPE, J. (1718), 4:407.

finally the whole basis of church government practiced" in England.[193] Whitgift emphasized, moreover, that Beza's interference in England was not simply a thing of the past. For, recently, the reformer published his *De Triplici Episcopatu* in which he described the episcopal system in England as a "satanical tyranny" threatening to destroy the church. Almost immediately, this dangerous writing was "flying through the hands of many people, set[ting] a new torch to the flame that was before almost quenched."[194] Given all this evidence, how could Beza now complain that he was being falsely accused of fomenting discord in the kingdom? "Dear brother," Whitgift wrote,

> what is this if it is not to force Genevan discipline on all the churches, and to wish to abolish all bishops (at least those whom we would call bishops)? If you commit all ecclesiastical affairs to the whole church, what is this but to allow the church to be governed by the mob (*ochlokratia*), or at least by the common people (*democratia*)?[195]

For these reasons, then, Beza had no reason to complain about the publication of the books of Saravia and Sutcliffe, who were simply defending the episcopal system in England, which was a "divine institution," attested to by the apostles and early church fathers.[196] In the final paragraphs of Whitgift's long letter, the archbishop offered a brief historical and biblical defense for the order of bishops. He also expressed regret that Beza had never visited England to see the Church of England first-hand—if he had done so, he would have had a very different view of the situation than that disseminated by a few disgruntled persons.[197]

Whitgift's strongly-worded letter exposed the contradictions present in Beza's theological position with respect to the English church. On the one hand, in his correspondence with English bishops and magnates such as William Cecil, Beza regularly argued that the Reformed churches of England and Geneva were in perfect accord as to their doctrine; what separated them were only indifferent matters of rites and ceremonies. Given their doctrinal unity, Beza insisted, Geneva had no desire to enforce its particular brand of church polity and discipline on the English church. At the same time, in a number of his private letters, and especially in his (anonymous) *De Triplici Episcopatu*, Beza offered a far more critical assessment of Elizabeth's religious settlement. In these writings he vilified the English bishops, attacked the "popish" ceremonies in the English

---

193 Whitgift to Beza, 16/26 January 1594, in CB 35:12; STRYPE, J. (1718), 4:408.
194 Whitgift to Beza, 16/26 January 1594, in CB 35:12; STRYPE, J. (1718). 4:405 [sic 409].
195 Whitgift to Beza, 16/26 January 1594, in CB 35:13; STRYPE, J. (1718), 4:405 [sic 409].
196 Whitgift to Beza, 16/26 January 1594, in CB 35:16; STRYPE, J. (1718), 4:406 [sic 410].
197 Whitgift to Beza, 16/26 January 1594, in CB 35:18; STRYPE, J. (1718), 408 [sic 412].

church and called for structural reforms patterned after presbyterian assemblies found in Scotland and France. The most likely explanation for Beza's duplicity on this matter is found in his competing political and religious concerns. Though he shared the Puritans' commitment to England's further reformation, he also recognized that Elizabeth and her bishops were crucial allies for Reformed churches in Geneva and France, especially in the face of what he believed to be an unfolding Tridentine conspiracy against the Protestant states. Beza's position cannot be described as *Realpolitique*—he certainly did hold strong convictions regarding the necessity of godly church polity and discipline. But the need for political and financial support—and the vulnerability of the French exile congregation in London—all required pragmatic dissimulation and strategic silence.

It does not appear that Beza responded to Whitgift's letter; nor did he answer Adrian Saravia's subsequent attacks against him.[198] Beza informed colleagues in London that his decision to remain silent was not borne of self-protection, but of prudence "as long as the time of the power of these shadows lasts."[199] In addition, the weakness of old age was no doubt taking its toll. And yet, at the same time, the Geneva reformer found strength to remain in contact with friends and key allies in England. In 1595 he sent copies of his recently published *Saincts cantiques recueillis tant du Vieil que du Nouveau Testament* to the noblewoman Ann Bacon, to her son Edward, and to the son of Lord Francis Hastings.[200] Three years later, Beza rededicated the final edition of his *Annotationes* to Queen Elizabeth. This dedicatory epistle contained a number of important revisions from the original epistle written thirty-two years earlier: Beza no longer expressed his hopes that the virgin queen would find a husband. He praised Elizabeth's illustrious leadership, under which England had remained safe and prosperous. He thanked Elizabeth for the many times she had assisted Geneva over the years. Truly, she had become "the protectress of the Reformed churches in the whole world."[201] Beza concluded his letter with more verses of commendation and praise:

> That you might govern England long, and you England long enjoy.
> Bring blessing to the good, but the wicked to destroy.
> Happy are you, O Britain, when she reigns long o'er your land,
> Permitting the virgin queen to lead you ever by the hand.[202]

---

198 Archbishop Whitgift appears to have written Beza at least one additional time. In this letter (dated c. 1594) Whitgift provided an exposé of the history and structure of the English church that focused special attention on the episcopal courts that were responsible for moral discipline and local clergymen responsible for regular preaching. See CB 35:175–195.

199 Beza to La Fontaine and Castol, 27 August/6 September 1595, in CB 36:88.

200 Beza to La Fontaine and Castol, 27 August/6 September 1595, in CB 36:87.

201 Beza to Queen Elizabeth, 1/11 August 1598, in CB 39:132–133.

202 Beza to Queen Elizabeth, 1/11 August 1598, in CB 39:134.

Theodore Beza's final letter to Queen Elizabeth was dated from January 1603, a month after Savoy had attacked and nearly captured Geneva on the night of the Escalade (11–12 December 1602). It was now reported that the Duke of Savoy was recruiting mercenaries from Spain and Italy in order to wage a war of extermination against the city. In these dire straits, Beza and the Company of Pastors appealed one last time to the queen's "Christian charity and accustomed generosity."[203] Three months later the Virgin Queen of England was dead.

3.6 Conclusion

For over fifty years, Theodore Beza was a keen observer and an active participant in England's religious controversies. As we have seen, the Genevan reformer maintained extensive contact with many of the key figures of the English Reformation, including the bishops Edmund Grindal and John Whitgift as well as nonconformist leaders such as Percival Wiburn, Thomas Sampson, John Gilpin, Thomas Cartwright and William Travers. These English churchmen variously appropriated or attacked Beza's theological vision for Reformed churches in England and beyond. Beza's critique of the theology and polity of Elizabeth's established church became more nuanced and more expansive with time. In the early 1560s, Beza's primary concern was with the lack of discipline, corrupt bishops, and "papal" ceremonies in the English church. As a result of the Vestments Controversy in the mid-1560s, the reformer became convinced that more foundational problems were at stake, namely the royal supremacy and the hierarchical structure of the English Church. Hence, by the mid-1570s, Beza began to advocate more forcefully for structural reforms that placed governance of the church, including the authority for church discipline and clerical appointment, in the hands of presbyterian assemblies and synods. From Beza's perspective, the only form of "bishop" that was divine—and thus legitimate—was a Christian minister chosen by his colleagues to preside temporarily over a presbyterian assembly consisting of elder and clerical delegates.

Despite what he saw as the serious flaws in Elizabeth's religious establishment, Theodore Beza remained convinced that England's church was a legitimate member of the family of Reformed churches, even if it was the only one that did not practice biblical discipline. As we have noted, the intensity of Beza's critique depended on the background of his correspondent and the context of his writing: when he corresponded with bishops like John Whitgift or royal counselors like William Cecil, he was quick to highlight the doctrinal fidelity of the English church, and to describe any weaknesses as *adiaphora*. Beza was

---

203 Beza and Antoine de La Faye to Queen Elizabeth, 17/27 January 1603, in CB 43:6–7.

far more critical in his assessment when writing to nonconformist leaders or in treatises such as *De Triplici Episcopatu*. Though clearly Janus-faced, Beza's varied assessment illustrates the fact that the reformer's concern extended beyond the doctrinal purity of the English church. In the face of (what Beza perceived as) an international Catholic conspiracy against the Protestant states of Europe, the Genevan reformer recognized Elizabeth and her church as crucial allies for preserving Reformed Protestantism in France and Geneva. The survival of the French refugee congregation in London was also a concern. Thus, over the course of these decades, Beza undertook a protracted campaign to win the queen's favor as well as the support of key members of her government. Elizabeth's financial and military support of Huguenot leaders such as Condé, Coligny and Henry of Navarre, and the assistance she provided Geneva in its struggle against the Duke of Savoy proved crucial in building Beza's trust in her. Hence, by the 1580s, Beza had become an enthusiastic supporter of Queen Elizabeth, whom he extolled as a Christian heroine and moral exemplar. Even if he did not succeed in achieving the "further reformation" of the English church according to a presbyterian model, Beza's extensive efforts did help unify Reformed churches in England, France, and Geneva as they faced a resurgent Catholic threat. To a significant degree, then, Theodore Beza—this "troubler" of England—proved to be a key player in promoting an international movement of Reformed churches.

Part Two: Theodore Beza and Biblical Interpretation

David Noe

Chapter 4: Suppress or Retain? Theodore Beza, Natural Theology, and the Translation of Romans 1:18

In 1598, Theodore Beza completed the final version of his *Annotationes In Novum Testamentum*. This culmination of 42 years' worth of labor and five significant editions reflected a number of changes in style and emphasis as the author refined his translation of the Greek text into Latin and significantly augmented the continuous commentary that accompanied the text. Yet there is one pivotal verse whose translation Beza materially altered only once: Romans 1:18. Thus in the 1556 edition Beza translates his Greek text[1] as follows:

> Palam est enim ira Dei e caelo adversus omnem impietatem & iniustitiam hominum, ut qui veritatem iniuste detineant.[2]

> God's wrath is openly revealed from heaven against all the ungodliness and unrighteousness of men because they hold onto the truth unrighteously.

The 1565 edition, the first to feature in a three-column format the Greek text, Beza's own Latin construal, and then the Vulgate, introduces a minor variation in translation by the transposition of the conjunction *enim* from the third to second position in the clause.[3] Thereafter the text remained unchanged until 1598. In the *Annotationes Maiores* of 1598 Beza decided to replace the initial adverb *palam* and *est* with *Patet enim*, leaving the reading as follows:

> Patet enim ira Dei e caelo adversus omnem impietatem & iniustitiam hominum, ut qui veritatem iniuste detineant.[4]

---

1 The Greek text has only one recorded variant, the insertion of the article τοῦ before θεοῦ in ar vg[d] sa and Ambst. The attestation for this verse is very secure and thus Beza's text is identical to Nestle-Aland 28: Ἀποκαλύπτεται γὰρ ὀργὴ θεοῦ ἀπ᾽ οὐρανοῦ ἐπὶ πᾶσαν ἀσέβειαν καὶ ἀδικίαν ἀνθρώπων τῶν τὴν ἀλήθειαν ἐν ἀδικίᾳ κατεχόντων.

2 BEZA, T., *Novum Domini Nostris Iesu Christi Testamentum* (1556), 174.

3 "Palam enim est ira Dei e caelo adversus omnem impietatem & iniustitiam hominum, ut qui veritatem iniuste detineant." In BEZA, T., *Novum Domini Nostris Iesu Christi Testamentum* (1556), 136f.

4 BEZA, T., *Iesu Christi Domini nostri Novum Testamentum … annotationes* (1598a).

What did not change, however, in any of the editions was his use of the subjunctive *detineant* to represent the Greek participle κατεχόντων. This was a very careful rejection of the indicative *detinent* that Jerome employs in the Vulgate. Desiderius Erasmus followed the Vulgate reading both in his 1516 translation and in the fifth and final edition of 1535.[5] Calvin on the other hand, in his 1540 commentary on this passage follows the Vulgate for the first part of the verse but in imitation of the Greek rather conservatively employs a participial form for κατεχόντων, namely "continentium: Revelatur enim ira Dei e caelo, super omnem impietatem et injustitiam hominum, veritatem Dei injuste continentium."[6] The verb on which this form is built, *continēre*, is itself a cognate of the *detinēre* of Jerome, Erasmus and Beza.

This choice on Calvin's part is significant in light of the vexing ethical and noetic issues latent in the theology of verse 18. Put simply, do the unbelievers addressed in Romans 1 truly know God as he is and "retain/hold onto" that knowledge, whether in a condition of injustice or by means of injustice? This is what one might call the ethical interpretation that prior to the twentieth century dominated the history of the verse's exegesis. Or do they, on a noetic reading, "suppress/repress" the true knowledge of God (yet in some culpable fashion) so as to, in effect, not know him at all?[7] At least two important implications arise from how one answers this question. First, as we will see, there is an obvious and direct effect on the translation of the verse. Second, the view one may properly take of natural theology is affected, as the most common version of the noetic reading rules out a robust natural theology while the ethical interpretation clearly reinforces it.

In light of these considerations, this chapter will seek to demonstrate the following: First, that Beza's Latin translation of τῶν κατεχόντων as *detineant* is the most accurate of the major sixteenth-century translators/interpreters. Second, that Beza's translation reinforces a robust natural theology by best

---

5 "Manifestat enim ira dei de caelo, adversus omnem impietatem et iniusticiam hominum qui veritatem in iniusticia detinent." In ERASMUS, D., *Novum Instrumentum Omne* (1516). "Palam fit enim ira Dei de coelo adversus omnem impietatem & iustitiam hominum, qui veritatem in iniustitia detinent." In ERASMUS, D., *Novum Testamentum Iam Quintum Accuratissima Cura Recognitum Omne* (1535).

6 Calvin explains as follows: "'Holds it in check' means 'to suppress' or 'obscure.' Consequently, they are convicted of a kind of theft. Where I have translated 'unjustly' Paul has 'in injustice.' This Hebrew expression has a similar meaning but I have tried hard to be lucid." (*Eam continere, est supprimere seu obscurare, unde veluti furti subarguuntur. Ubi vertimus iniuste, habet Paulus, In iniustitia: quae hebraica phrasis idem valet, sed nos studuimus perspicuitati.*) CALVIN, J., *In Omnes Pauli Apostoli Epistolas ... Commentarii* (1557), 7–8.

7 Clearly the ethical and noetic interpretations are related and one wants to avoid any false dichotomy. My contention is that they are distinct.

demonstrating the accuracy of the ethical interpretation. Third, that the majority of English translations until the twentieth century, in part due to Beza's influence, are in keeping with the meaning conveyed by *detineant*. Fourth, that the most common twentieth-century translation of κατεχόντων, "suppress," is an unfortunate revival of Calvin's compromised, noetic interpretation. And fifth, the translation "suppress" was likely occasioned by the influence of Sigmund Freud and helped by Karl Barth's antagonism toward natural theology.

We begin then with Beza's first explanation for his departure from Jerome and Erasmus, given in the 1556 edition.

> The phrase τῶν [...] κατεχόντων I construe as "because they hold onto," though the Vulgate and Erasmus have "the persons who hold onto." But the subject matter itself demands that the article [τῶν] not be taken distinctively [διακριτικῶς] but causally [αἰτιολογικῶς]. This is a usage that I have often noted in other contexts. For Paul is stating the reason why he said that all men are rendered liable to God's judgment, both the wicked [*impios*] and the unrighteous [*iniustos*], namely because they hold onto the truth unjustly [...] Paul describes whatever light remains in the human being like this: it is not such that by its guidance they may return to God's favor (this is the work of Christ only, who is the true light, way, and truth). Instead, it is the seed [*semen*] of knowledge of God for worshiping him and of some determination between what is just and unjust, so that by their own judgment they are convicted of wickedness toward God and toward men. From this has arisen the Law of nature against which Paul measures human life, and openly proves all men and individual ones guilty. I have rendered ἐν ἀδικία "unrighteously." This is a Hebraism, בחמס [*bechames*], which the Vulgate and Erasmus have translated literally "in unrighteousness." Now injustice is defined as not rendering to each what he is due.[8] Therefore, because the truth teaches us to worship one God as omnipotent and eternal and to harm no one, and toward this point in some way truth itself longs to break out, men act unjustly because they do not worship the true divinity correctly, nor do they stop harming one another and even themselves. And so they push down [*reprimunt*] the truth as it struggles within them that it may not exert its power. Consequently, the word "unrighteousness" in this passage has a broader meaning than in the previous clause.[9]

This explanation clarifies many aspects of Beza's understanding of natural law, the retention of natural knowledge of God and the extent of God's condemning anger for unbelief. First, he rejects the indicative *detinent* of the Vulgate and Erasmus on the grounds that they wrongly interpret τῶν [...] κατεχόντων, διακριτικῶς, i.e. "distinctively." In other words, the interpretation that the indicative in the relative clause *qui* [...] *detinent* suggests that God is not angry against men indiscriminately. For the indicative clearly limits the extent of application. We could thus translate Jerome and Erasmus as "God's anger is

---

8 For this classical definition of injustice, see CICERO, *De Natura Deorum*, 3.38.

9 BEZA, T., *Novum Domini Nostris Iesu Christi Testamentum* (1556), 175.

revealed against the unrighteousness and injustice of those particular men," i.e. not all of them, "who retain the truth in unrighteousness." Beza's use of *utqui* and the subjunctive, what he calls the αἰτιολογικῶς or "causal" reading of the article τῶν, renders the expression causal. Some Latin grammarians designate this an "explicit causal" clause.[10] If Beza's causal reading is correct, as I maintain, it rules out the possibility that Jerome, Erasmus and other interpreters understood the verse properly. This is because it makes the fact that human beings have the truth the essential and necessary reason for their condemnation and not an accident.

Second, we notice that Beza carefully limits both the extent and effect of the natural knowledge of God. On his interpretation of Paul, there is true knowledge—he describes it as "light" (*quidquid lucis*) and "seed" (*semen*)—and this entails knowledge of God for the purpose of worshiping him and some distinction (*discrimen aliquid*) between right and wrong. There are two immediate implications of this interpretation: First, the condemnation of those who are not in Christ is a self-condemnation because of the internal light or seed. In some sense God does not need to condemn them, his decree of judgment comes after they already have been self-convicted. His judgment ratifies what they have already determined concerning themselves. Second, this internal light and seed is the origin of natural law and is the standard against which God measures human morality. Here, Beza does not distinguish between Jew and Gentile in his interpretation of Romans 1:18, though obviously he does elsewhere. Finally, when explaining how this knowledge is treated by unbelievers Beza uses the verb *reprimunt*, which I have construed as "push down." Its object is *veritatem*, and Beza modifies this with *luctantem*, "struggling" or "wrestling."

Beza did not substantially alter this commentary through subsequent editions, although he did add an important caveat in 1598.

> If anyone should prefer to take the article τῶν distinctively [διακριτικῶς], i.e. not in a general sense concerning the whole human race conceived of as outside of Christ, I would reply that this injustice ought to be understood as referring to the Greeks alone and in light of their violation of natural law. For the apostle begins to deal with the Jews separately in 2:17.[11]

In other words, he here provides an alternative interpretation for the article which would lend some credence to the Vulgate or Erasmian indicative *detinent*, provided the extent of application is suitably defined. If one wants to take the

---

10 This usage is attested in classical authors (Plautus and Terence, inter alios) and it is likely Beza adapted it from Pliny the Younger. See CHALFANT, M. (1921), 72. Charles E. Bennett suggests they be called "stipulative subjunctives." See BENNETT, C. (1900), 223–250.

11 BEZA, T., *Iesu Christi Domini nostri Novum Testamentum … annotationes* (1598a), 8.

article as introducing a distinction Beza will not object, so long as they realize that Paul according to the larger argument of Romans (i.e., as seen in chapter 2) intends ἀνθρώπων as comprehensive.

We next must examine the meaning of the Greek verb κατέχω to demonstrate the accuracy of Beza's construal not merely with respect to his predecessors but in an absolute sense. We will then look at three representative contemporaries—Wolfgang Musculus, Peter Martyr Vermigli and Caspar Olevianus—before turning to Calvin's idiosyncratic understanding of the passage as presented by David Steinmetz.

We consult three categories of sources for the meaning of κατέχω, though of course there is much overlap: Classical, Koine, and Patristic. The authoritative Greek-English Lexicon of Liddell, Scott and Jones cites the earliest instances of this word as *Iliad* 11 and 15, wherein κατέχω means restraining by force someone who is unwilling.[12] Note here the strongly ethical component. As is so often the case with the history of Greek words, the original note sounded by Homer continues to echo throughout the life of this lexeme. Similarly, in Herodotus 6.129, it bears the meaning of "check" or "bridle." The distributive notion inherent in the prefix κατά makes itself felt in Plato's *Phaedrus* 254a, where it shows the meaning of "restraining oneself." It is interesting to realize that most of the classical uses with a direct object have a sense of violence. But, on the other hand, with a genitive complement (Aristotle, Philemon, Stobaeus, Appian) it bears the notion of "gain possession of," "be master of," "control." As we will see, these latter meanings construed with a genitive—which the Greek text of Rom 1:18 does not contain—are more in line with various twentieth-century mistranslations. κατέχω can mean likewise "to have one in their power" with reference to persons, but II.9.a. and b. cite Plato's *Philebus* 26c and *Meno* 72d, as well as a fragment of Epicurus, to provide what is arguably the best way for us to understand our phrase in 1:18: "master, understand"; "keep in mind, remember." We reach this conclusion by process of elimination, inasmuch as the other meanings for this verb bear objects that are too semantically disparate from the object of the participle, namely τὴν ἀλήθειαν, to be plausible.

The second group of lexica consulted are those specific to the New Testament, namely Grimm-Thayer and the so-called BDAG. These are valuable primarily because they include all New Testament and Septuagint occurrences of the word. Thayer divides the word's meaning into two broad categories, "to hold back, detain, retain," and as the equivalent to the Latin *obtinēre*, "to get possession of, take" or "to possess."[13] A form of the verb occurs in Matt 21:38, as well as Luke

12 εἴ με βίῃ ἀέκοντα καθέξει Il. 15.186. All citations in this section are from LIDDELL, H./SCOTT, R. (ed.) (1968), 926.
13 THAYER, J. (ed.) (1889), 339–340.

14:9 under the second meaning according to Thayer. Paul uses forms of this verb in 1 Cor 7:30 (κατέχοντες), 15:2 (κατέχετε), 2 Cor 6:10 (κατέχοντες), and 2 Thess 2:6 (τὸ κατέχον). In each of these instances except the last, where it is a substantive, the majority of English interpreters have construed κατέχω with the connotation of simple possession. Thus, although Thayer himself suggests that Rom 1:18 be construed as "restrain, hinder (the course or progress of)," the clear consensus of Pauline passages suggests Thayer's second meaning. As I will argue, this is not a meaning well-represented by the most popular twentieth-century translation "suppress." To summarize these findings, we cite the more recent efforts of Bauer, Denker, Arndt and Gingrich:

> 1. a. hold back, hold up – α. hold back, hinder, prevent from going away β. Hold down, suppress τί someth., prevent from going away γ. restrain, check b. α. keep in one's memory β. hold fast, retain faithfully γ. keep in one's possession, possess.[14]

The third group, the Patristic references provided by Lampe, do not depart much from classical sources.[15] For example, he cites the mental meaning of "hold fast to a truth" from *Const. ap. Ath. Apol. Sec.* 68. But of course it is impossible to know whether this was not in turn influenced by the Pauline passage in question. Chrysostom's *Homily* 59.2 on Matthew gives the meaning "keep a commandment," which is noteworthy only because like the Pauline passage it takes as its object an abstract noun. Diognetus, as referenced by Lampe, provides us with the notion of "hold in" or "down," i.e. "control."

To summarize our findings thus far: Classical, Koine, and Patristic sources show clearly that meanings of κατέχω with an abstract noun as object like the one in Romans 1:18 cannot readily bear the sense of influence or suppress, what I take to be a noetic interpretation. Instead, with the exception of the substantive use in 2 Thess 2:6, each falls into the broad semantic category of simple possession, with varying degrees of ethical shading from "holding illegitimately" to "holding back from some external, intended purpose foreign to the agent."

Returning then to Beza, we find that both in his choice of the subjunctive *detineant* as well as his careful elucidation of the overwhelmingly ethical component of τῶν [...] κατεχόντων, he has hit the mark. This really should be no surprise, inasmuch as the adverbial, prepositional modifier within the attributive phrase, i.e. ἐν ἀδικίᾳ, can bear precisely and only this meaning. In addition, this was the majority interpretation—with the exception of Calvin—until the

---

14 ARNDT, W./GINGRICH, F.W. (1952), 432.
15 All citations in this section are from LAMPE, G. (1961), 731.

twentieth century. This is despite the poor translation of the participle as indicative by both Jerome and Erasmus. Beza's edit of the Latin text here provides an important corrective.

What about his contemporaries? Taken chronologically, we look first at Wolfgang Musculus (1497–1563). In the 1555 edition of his commentary on Romans we read:

And Paul's treatment of this argument extends all the way to the end of the chapter.

1. He sets out the sin and impiety of idolaters as the source of the other crimes by which the truth is held back [*detinebatur*] in unrighteousness.
2. Next, he proclaims God's justice and anger.
3. He appends a list of vices as a review, and by these very faults the entire generation of the unrighteous during that time [*isto tempore*] became guilty.
4. He shows that these unrighteous men are without excuse, inasmuch as they are abandoning [*deliquerint*] the truth contrary to knowledge [*contra cognitionem*].[16]

We see that Musculus is very much in agreement with Beza in broad terms, though he follows without correction the Vulgate and in his third point seems to limit the extent of guilt to a certain age, *isto tempore*. Beza, on the other hand, is emphatic by his causal interpretation of the article that it is the most comprehensive condemnation possible. In his fourth point, Musculus stresses the ethical element clearly.

The Italian reformer Peter Martyr Vermigli (1498–1562) in the posthumous 1568 edition of his commentary on Romans also follows the Vulgate text without correction and writes:

They had acquired enough truth by which to understand how they were supposed to behave toward God and their neighbors. Nevertheless, they held onto [*detinuerunt*] this truth "in unrighteousness." The Hebrews had behaved the same way with regard to the truth God revealed to them through the Law. And so, because the Hebrews were punished as severely as the ones mentioned in this passage, what should men who are Christian by profession hope for, when they hold on to such great light of the gospel without fruit? Surely they shall become very wicked. And the very subject matter teaches us that those who boast of Christ and yet live shamefully surpass all other people, no matter how debauched they are, in their depravity and shamefulness. The truth is in a certain way held captive among those who understand it and do not express it in their life and behavior. The truth is moreover defeated and tightly bound by chains of all manner of lust. These lusts, arising in a cloud from all the lower parts of our soul, cast a pall over the

---

16 MUSCULUS, W., *In Epistolam Apostoli Pauli ad Romanos, Commentarii* (1550), 29–30.

mind and enclose in a gloomy prison the truth that has been acknowledged. God kindles it in our minds but it is shockingly darkened over by our lusts.[17]

Unlike Musculus, Vermigli seems careful not to limit the ethical element to a given generation and in this he aligns with Beza. Vermigli also stresses the ethical element perhaps more than any other Protestant Reformer and describes the truth as "held captive" [*vincitur*] and "bound with chains" [*constringitur cupiditatum malarum cathenis*]. Other metaphors that Vermgli uses are those of darkening [*mentem offuscant*] and imprisonment [*veritatem agnitam concludunt*].

Our third example is Caspar Olevianus (1536–1587). In 1579 he uses Beza's translation of 1565 (no doubt because Beza wrote the preface to Olevianus' work) and adds this commentary:

> Paul begins here to discuss the reason that we are saved by faith in the gospel alone. For he shows that apart from a knowledge of the gospel all men stand condemned, in keeping with the adequate division we have previously described. Whoever wants to stand before God must be righteous, either by his own righteousness—that is, the righteousness of his own strength, a righteousness that the Law of God whether written or unwritten requires from us by the mere right of creation. Or he must do so by an alien righteousness, that is, God's, that has been imputed to the one who believes. But there is not anyone righteous by his own righteousness. Paul goes on to prove this minor proposition, and again employs a division. He summons the whole world, i.e. individual men, before God's tribunal and treats them as criminals. Moreover, he divides the world into these two groups Gentiles and Jews, that is, those who have only the law of nature and those who have the written law or Decalogue. First, he demonstrates the minor proposition in the case of the Gentiles, and next with the Jews. He shows, moreover, from their punishments and from the cause, namely their wickedness, that the Gentiles do not possess righteousness in themselves. God punishes their wickedness from heaven by throwing them over to a reprobate understanding: therefore they are not righteous. [...] This is the sum of the argument against the Gentiles (for demonstrating the minor proposition): the knowledge of God has been revealed to them and nevertheless they do not worship him. They oppress the obvious truth, and so they are wicked and deserve God's anger from heaven. This is because God is immutably righteous. Although this proposition is known by nature, the missing portion is that it must be understood.[18]

It is no surprise that Olevianus follows Beza so closely, and this indeed is a testimony to the success of the latter's interpretation and translation of the passage in question. In addition, Olevianus' colleague in Heidelberg, Zacharias Ursinus, was himself a student of Vermigli, and perhaps this also influenced the

---

17 VERMIGLI, P.M., *In Epistolam S. Pauli Apostoli Ad Romanos ... Tertia Editio* (1568), 29.

18 OLEVIANUS, C., *In Epistolam D. Pauli Apostoli ad Romans Notae, ex Gasparis Oleviani Concionibus Excerptae, & a Theodoro Beza editae* (1579), 30–31.

ethical element that we see so prominent in Olevianus' treatment. In fact, he uses the very same phrase as Vermigli to describe this clear knowledge of God, *agnitam veritatem*, but reverses the order (it is thus impossible to tell whether this was an instance of borrowing or a coincidence). In sum, each of the three theologians is consonant with Beza's interpretation of the verse, but only the last provides a consistent Latin translation that accords with their understanding, i.e. Beza's own.

We now turn to the seminal article by David Steinmetz concerning Calvin and the natural knowledge of God. This will set the stage for demonstrating that although Beza's understanding was followed by English translators and commentators from his time through the nineteenth century, a decisive turn was made in the twentieth century. This turn arguably repeats Calvin's error, and does so, I suggest, under the twin influences of Barthian theology and Freudian psychology. In his 1995 monograph *Calvin in Context*, Steinmetz identifies the conflict between Karl Barth and Emil Brunner as highlighting Calvin's understanding of Romans 1 and natural knowledge of God:

Against Brunner's reading of Calvin, Barth argued that Calvin constantly pointed to the Bible as the true source of the knowledge of God.

> The possibility of a real knowledge by natural man of the true God, derived from creation, is, according to Calvin, a possibility in principle, but not in fact, not a possibility to be realized by us. One might call it an objective possibility, created by God, but not a subjective possibility, open to man. Between what is possible in principle and what is possible in fact there inexorably lies the fall. Hence this possibility can only be discussed hypothetically: *si integer stetisset* Adam (Inst., I, ii, I). (Emil Brunner and Karl Barth, *Natural Theology*, trans. Peter Fraenkel (London: Geoffrey Bles, 1946), p. 37.
> Because the human race has fallen into sin, the content of its natural knowledge of God is nothing more than idolatry and superstition. Therefore, the revelation of God in nature, whatever its original purpose may have been, serves only to render fallen human beings inexcusable and to justify the wrath of God against them. As Barth understands Calvin, there is no knowledge of God the creator apart from the knowledge of God the redeemer.[19]

Is Barth's understanding of Calvin correct? Steinmetz answers with a barely qualified yes:

> What is striking, however, is the singularity of Calvin's reading of Paul. In the judgment of Calvin's contemporaries, Paul does not stress an acute noetic impairment because of sin or distinguish sharply between what is revealed in nature and what is perceived by fallen human reason. The thrust of Paul's argument, indeed, runs in the opposite direction. The point that Paul makes is not how little the Gentiles knew, but, considering the

---

19 STEINMETZ, D. (1995), 28–32.

circumstances, how much they did know and how little use they made of it. By stressing the damage human reason has incurred through sin, Calvin makes the argument for the moral responsibility of the pagans all the more difficult to sustain. Other Protestant theologians, of whom Melanchthon may be taken as representative, tend to argue that God is revealed in nature, that this revelation, however limited and inadequate, is nevertheless perceived by fallen human beings, who, precisely because of their sinfulness, proceed to suppress, distort, deny, ignore, forget, and abuse what they know. Calvin argues, rather, that God is revealed in nature, that this revelation is misperceived by fallen human beings, who, precisely because of their sinful and culpable misperception, proceed to suppress, distort, deny, and abuse the true knowledge of God offered to them through the natural order. Calvin avoids the difficulties he has placed in his own path by arguing that human blindness is culpable; but it is an argument which, in the form Calvin presents it, is not embraced by Denis, Melanchthon, Bullinger, or Bucer.[20]

I take Steinmetz's reading of Calvin, his idiosyncrasy on this point, as accurate. And, in addition to the long list of supporting names that Steinmetz cites, we have the results of our own investigation of Musculus, Vermigli, and Olevianus.

If then the sixteenth century is nearly unanimous with respect to the ethical element of Rom 1:18, what effect has this had on translation and interpretation of this verse, and what is the current state of the question? To begin with, every major English translation that could be identified between Beza's time and the twentieth century opted for the ethical interpretation of τῶν [...] κατεχόντων as plainly reflected by the translation.[21] This should be no surprise, for as Irena Backus has documented, Beza's influence on the text of the English Bible was enormous.[22] However, sometime around the beginning of the twentieth century, a new word entered English translations to describe the idea of the participial phrase τῶν τὴν ἀλήθειαν ἐν ἀδικίᾳ κατεχόντων in Rom 1:18, namely "suppress." Although it has not been possible yet to identify the first occurrence of the English word "suppress," a viable candidate is the Modern American Bible (1902), translated by Frank Schell Ballentine. He construes the phrase

---

20 Steinmetz continues, citing Swiss Reformed, Lutheran, and Roman Catholic interpreters: "These four commentators are joined in their dissent by Desiderius Erasmus, Faber Stapulensis, Martin Luther, Huldrych Zwingli, Johannes Oecolampadius, Erasmus Sarcerius, André Knopken, Johannes Bugenhagen, Thomas de Vio (Cajetan), Johannes Lonicer, Jean de Gagney, Jacopo Sadoleto, Ambrosius Catherinus Politus, Marino Grimani, Johannes Arboreus, Claude Guilliaud, Konrad Pelikan, Alexander Alesius, Wolfgang Musculus, Johannes Brenz, Peter Martyr Vermigli, Domingo de Soto, and André Hyperius." STEINMETZ, D. (1995), 31.

21 These include the Geneva Bible (1599), "withhold"; King James Version (1611), "hold"; Authorized Standard Version (1901), "hinder"; Young's Literal Translation (1862), "holding down." This is not to suggest that there were not noetic interpretations of the phrase in question during this time period. The more than 290 estimated English translations since 1653 were not all individually canvassed.

22 BACKUS, I. (1980).

in question as "unrighteously suppress the truth."[23] At that time, however, the ethical interpretation still had wide acceptance, even in translations that were attempting to shed archaisms and give new and modern construals.[24]

But as the century progressed, "suppress" became not only more popular but eventually ubiquitous. The list of translations that opt for "suppress" is very long, including Revised Standard Version (1946), New American Standard Bible (1960), Amplified Bible (1965, "suppress and stifle"), New American Bible Revised Edition (1970), New International Version (1978), New King James Version (1979), New Revised Standard Version (1989), Holman Christian Standard Bible (1999), English Standard Version (2001), Modern English Version (2014) and Christian Standard Bible (2017).

There are two comments especially worth making here. First, translators of the letter into English are as susceptible to the winds of popular influence as any others, and so it is not unreasonable to conclude that once the RSV of 1946 had used the noetic "suppress" for τῶν [...] κατεχόντων in place of the ethical interpretation others quickly followed suit. Second, the adoption of this interpretation by the NKJV is especially noteworthy, as it represents a significant change from the much more modest—and accurate—"hold" of the English version on which it was based. And unlike changes in pronouns and suffixes (e.g. "you" for "thou," and the updating of archaic language), substituting the word "suppress" in the NKJV for "hold" in the KJV offers no clear advantage in terms of contemporization.[25] Indeed, the only change in verse 18 from the

---

23 Modern American Bible (1902). For another early instance of "suppress" see Weymouth New Testament (1903), which renders this verse "who through iniquity suppress the truth." A translation that arguably veers toward the noetic but does not use the word "suppress" is The Twentieth Century New Testament (1900), which renders the passage "who by their wicked lives are stifling the truth."

24 Translation of the New Testament from the Original Greek (1902): "hold the truth in un-righteousness"; Holy Bible in Modern English (1902): "pervert the true into the false"; The New Testament Revised and Translated (1904), "hinder the truth in unrighteousness"; The Holy Bible: Containing the Old and New Testaments (1912), "hold back the truth in un-righteousness"; Rotherham's Emphasized Bible (1872), "hold down"; The Corrected English New Testament (1904), "in unrighteousness hinder the truth." Perhaps the most popular new translation and most influential was the American Standard Version (1901), a KJV revision that reads "hinder the truth in unrighteousness."

25 Perhaps we should also note in passing that the ethical interpretation continued to survive in the twentieth and into the twenty-first centuries, but ironically did so mostly in versions and paraphrases that were free to the point of inaccuracy: Philips New Testament (1958), "render truth dumb and inoperative"; Living Bible (1971), "push away the truth from them"; New Century Version (1987), "by their own evil lives they hide the truth"; The Message (2002), "as people try to put a shroud over truth." Another irony is that a Bible translation intended mostly for Roman Catholic readers, the New Jerusalem Bible (1985), comes very close to Beza's understanding: "in their injustice hold back the truth."

KJV to NKJV is the substitution of "suppress"[26] for "hold." This clearly indicates a change in theological category and not merely an updating of unfamiliar wording.[27]

What explains this sudden and rapidly dominant shift from an ethical understanding of the verse to an noetics one, i.e. from "hold onto something that is clearly and fully known and renders one culpable," to "suppress in such a way as not to be clearly and fully known," with questions of culpability suspended or rendered incoherent? Given the nature of shifts of this sort it would be impossible—without interviewing the translators directly and asking them what influenced their word choice (if they themselves have not suppressed that knowledge)—to do more than speculate. Nevertheless, the phenomenon would seem to require some explanation, and a very promising candidate is at hand. The ideas of the Austrian father of pscyhoanalysis, Sigmund Freud, began gaining widespread popularity in the English-speaking world at the turn of the century. By the time Freud visited America in 1909 for a series of lectures, he already had many Anglophone readers. Indeed, as Howard Kaye writes, "In the United States [Freud's] ideas quickly won professional and popular acclaim—they were the stuff of articles in women's magazines by 1915."[28] Popular and professional knowledge of what Freud actually taught vary considerably, but an idea central to much of his teaching is that of suppression, i.e. that one may push down an unhappy memory (especially sexual trauma) so as effectively not to know any longer of its existence. As Freud states:

> we shall say that the dream affords proof that the *suppressed material continues to exist even in the normal person and remains capable of psychic activity.* Dreams are one of the manifestations of the suppressed material.[29]

It is important to note that Freud's own view of suppression does not, so far as I have been able to discern, discuss matters of propositional knowledge nor the question of God's existence. Indeed, Freud limits repression and suppression (which are not identical but sometimes interchanged) primarily to wishes, not propositions, and explicitly says that he is not dealing in a "historic sense—that such wishes have once existed and subsequently been destroyed." He then

---

26 Footnoted with "hold down."

27 In the preface to the NKJV the editors indicate as much: "Where new translation has been necessary in the New King James Version, the most complete representation of the original has been rendered by considering the history of usage and etymology of words in their contexts."

28 KAYE, H. (1993), 120.

29 FREUD, S. (1938), 539. Emphases added.

compares this to "'sub-pression', or pushing under."[30] But the picture is not so clear after all, for as Simon Boag explains the popularity of Freud's notion of "suppression" carries with it significant noetic freight not tied to sexual trauma and wish-fulfillment:

> As Freud notes, "there are mental things in a man which he knows without knowing that he knows" (Freud, 1916–17, p. 101), and although some maintain that in knowing something one is "conscious" of knowing it […] the problem with this position is that it leads to an infinite regress of knowing: If I know that I know, then I should also know that I know that I know, and so on, *ad infinitum*. […] Like anything else, however, we remain ignorant of our own knowing unless we direct our attention to it. […] The possibility of knowing many things without necessarily knowing that we know them leads further to the simple demonstrable point that at any given moment *the vast majority of our beliefs (etc.) are unknown.*[31]

This Freudian sense of repression/suppression of beliefs comes remarkably close to the way that very many twentieth- and twenty-first century commentators—unlike their forebears—have chosen to identify a noetic element in Rom 1:18 at the expense of the ethical norm based on natural theology. In other words, I contend that they are in danger of repeating the error of Calvin that Steinmetz identified. We turn now to those commentators.[32]

---

30 FREUD, S. (1938), 288. At other times, however, he does seem to link explicitly the notion of suppression to propositional knowledge. "The tendency to overlook something because it is wearisome, or the reflection that the concerned thought does not really belong to the intended matter, seems to play the same role as motives for the reflection of a thought (which later depends for expression on the disturbance of another), as the moral condemnation of a rebellious emotional feeling or as the origin of absolutely unconscious trains of thought and insight into the general nature of the condition of faulty and chance actions cannot be gained in this way" (ibid., 176).

31 AMERICAN PSYCHOLOGICAL ASSOCIATION (2010), 27.2, 170. Emphases added. See also SZABADOS, B. (1982), 691–707. Szabados makes clear that the Freudian notion has gained currency as a more broad noetic category: "Both 'repression' and 'suppression' are said to involve removing mental content from awareness. However, repression is generally said to be unconscious, whereas suppression is said to be conscious. The meanings of the terms 'unconscious' and 'conscious', though, are open to a variety of interpretations and so the validity of this distinction is uncertain" (ibid., 707).

32 For a criticism of Freud more broadly, see WEBSTER, R. (1995): "Largely because Freud's concept of the unconscious appeared to embrace many of those irrational or demonic aspects of human nature which had been implicitly repudiated by Protestant rationalism it possessed very considerable psychological resonance. If Freud had himself grasped the nature of his achievement it might well have been genuinely illuminating. […] Instead of recognizing the traditional basis of his psychology, he genuinely believed he was making a new scientific discovery. […] What was novel in Freud's theories was that, instead of simply accepting the ancient intuitive insight that some aspects of the self were less accessible to the conscious mind than others, he put forward the idea that there was a mental entity whose specific function was

A sampling of the major English commentaries on Romans 1 from the twentieth and early twenty-first centuries allows us to divide opinion into three categories: 1.) those in which the ethical interpretation (à la Beza, Vermigli, etc.) dominates; 2.) those in which the noetic interpretation dominates (Calvin qua Steinmetz, Barth, and nearly all twentieth-century translations); 3.) those that are mixed or, I would, say confused. In the first category we hold the comments of Grant Osborne as representative:

> The major point is that sinful people "suppress the truth in their wickedness." They know the truth about God (v. 19) and deliberately ignore it. The verb "suppress" means to hinder something by hiding or removing it from sight. The truths of God are buried under an avalanche of rationalization. People surmise that their sinful behavior cannot be all that bad if they can engage in it over and over and get away with it. Nothing could be further from the truth![33]

Though Osborne chooses to translate using the word "suppress," he nevertheless clearly believes that it is a rational process of deliberate, conscious activity in which people are engaged when they ignore God's truth. Dmitri Royster similarly opts for a word laden with Freudian baggage but nevertheless hews to a strongly ethical (and traditional) interpretation:

> "Hold," translating the Greek verb *katēcho* in the last clause of the verse ("who hold the truth in unrighteousness"), could be misleading, since the sense here is clearly more like "to hold back" or "suppress." Is it possible that some men have perceived the truth but have willfully behaved contrariwise?[34]

Royster also unfortunately conflates "hold back" with "suppress" though, in my view, he gets the meaning right otherwise.

Those who belong to the second category, the noetic interpretation, are clearly in the majority. The criteria of selection for belonging to this group was first use of the word "suppress." But because this could be construed as circular, the second criterion was the absence or rejection of an overtly ethical interpretation ("retain," etc.) and/or the explicit mention of lack of knowledge, i.e. suppression in the broadly Freudian sense. Representative of this group is Douglas Moo:

> to harbor our hidden thoughts, memories, and impulses. He called this hypothetical entity 'the Unconscious' and treated it as an autonomous region of the mind 'with its own wishful impulses, its own mode of expression and its peculiar mechanisms which are not in force elsewhere.' He simultaneously claimed that certain mental states became unconscious because they were 'repressed,' that these repressed mental states might have pathological consequences and that the resulting illness could be cured by making conscious what had been unconscious" (245).

33 OSBORNE, G. (2017), 39.
34 ROYSTER, D. (2008), 37.

The verb κατέχω here probably means "suppress." While the verb can mean "possess" or "retain" (I Cor. 7.30; 11.2, 15.2; 2 Cor. 6.10; I Thess. 5.21), and Lightfoot, e.g., argues for this meaning here, the qualification ἐν ἀδικίᾳ favors the meaning "suppress" or "hinder" (BDAG; cf. 2 Thess. 2.6, 7; Phlm. 13). Cranfield gives the verb a conative force—"attempts to suppress"[35]—in order to preserve the concept of the "inherent futility of sin." But although it might be true that all sin is *ultimately* futile, in that it can never dethrone God or deflect from his purposes, the truth does not in fact accomplish what God intends for it when it is not obeyed and lived by. In that sense, people do "hinder" the truth, and this is the point that Paul is demonstrating in the following verses.[36]

Moo's commitment here to the noetic meaning makes his interpretation of the passage quite strained. The truth in this case does in fact accomplish what God intends for it because it serves to condemn those who reject it. Nor does he attempt an explanation of ἐν ἀδικίᾳ but only says without argument that it favors the meaning "suppress."[37]

The third category are those interpretations that mix and confuse the ethical and noetic. Thus Craig S. Keener:

Whereas some philosophers believed that true knowledge would lead to right living Paul believes that knowledge merely increases moral responsibility ("without excuse," 1:20; cf. 2:1, 15). God revealed enough for Gentiles to be damned, though people who know the Scriptures are more damned than those who have only nature and conscience (2:14-18). God revealed the truth about God within people (1:19), and internal knowledge based on being made in God's image (Gen. 1:26-27). More generally, God revealed his power and divinity, as well as benevolence in providing creation, so those who fail to recognize his

---

35 Moo rightly rejects here the conative force, which would uphold the ethical interpretation that is the verse's true meaning, but on the wrong grounds. The present participle does not bear a conative meaning. But once one has committed to the "suppression" language, i.e. knows but does not know, then such strained and ungrammatical interpretations become necessary to maintain coherence. It would have been better for Moo to reject the conative notion Cranfield suggests (participles are NOT verbs after all) and simply translate with older editions as "hold" or "retain."

36 MOO, D. (1996), 103n.52.

37 In note 51 on the same page Moo makes an unsatisfactory attempt in that direction, again suggesting "suppress": "ἐν ἀδικίᾳ ('in unrighteousness') may be adverbial ('they suppress the truth unrighteously') (Godet) but is more likely to be instrumental: 'through unrighteousness [e.g. unrighteous acts] they suppress the truth' (e.g. Murray). p. 103." Another commentary in the same vein is that of RHYS, H. (1961): "Obviously the Greek verb KATECHO here cannot bear its alternative meaning of *hold fast*. Irreligion and immorality, as has already been made clear, bring upon themselves judgment in the nature of God's moral government of the universe" (24). They do indeed "hold fast," and stating otherwise is rejection of the ethical interpretation. All are unable to let go of the truth of God, but do so ἐν ἀδικίᾳ, disobediently or wickedly.

power and character, worshiping their idols or human conceptions, are without excuse (1:20).[38]

As is typical of this category, what Keener gives with one hand, "God revealed enough for Gentiles to be damned,"[39] he takes back with the other, "those who fail to recognize his power and character [...] are without excuse." How is this possible, since the same Scriptures teach that God does not condemn the innocent?[40] Surely some recognition of God's power and character is necessary for moral guilt, and is what God is revealing for the damnation of the Gentiles.

In the end, it is the nature of a paper like this that full persuasion may be impossible. To review: we have seen Beza's careful exegesis of Rom 1:18 and its correction of both the Vulgate and Erasmus. We argued for the strong ethical/natural theology interpretation from the Greek text, and explained how it dominated the sixteenth century and influenced all subsequent English translations until the twentieth century. In addition, we noted Calvin's surprising vacillation on the question of ethics versus epistemology in that verse, as teased out in Steinmetz's seminal article. And last, we showed that the seismic shift in translation of the participial phrase τῶν τὴν ἀλήθειαν ἐν ἀδικίᾳ κατεχόντων likely indicated a change in understanding, and that this was reflected in numerous commentaries contemporary with this new translation.

It may only be a coincidence that this stark change coincided with the popularity of Freud's notion that there is a part of us, comprised of sexual desires and trauma, wishes, etc. that are expressed in dreams, and that this could include as well beliefs that we hold but do not know that we hold. While it is conceivable that one could as a Freudian[41] hold that genuine moral culpability arises from

---

38 KEENER, C. (2009), 32.

39 Note the rejection of Beza's aetiological interpretation of the article.

40 Prov 17:15, Ex 23:17. Douglas Moo also affirms the ethical interpretation but does so while using "suppress" and muddying the waters in other ways. See MOO, D. (1996), 102–103. For another example of a mixed or confused interpretation, see HOEKSEMA, H. (2002): "Do they not know? Yes, the apostle says, in the third description he gives of the world; they hold down the truth in unrighteousness. This is an ethical principle. This is the dominating principle in the life of natural man: he holds down the truth in unrighteousness. Not *a* truth. Men seek after truth, as, for example, the truth that two times two is four. But *the* truth they hold down in unrighteousness. What is the truth? The truth is God. [...] When it comes to the truth of God, men hold this truth down; they suppress it in nrighteousness. What does this mean? It means that men want to live in unrighteousness. They love unrighteousness, and hate righteousness" (20–21). Hoeksema strongly asserts the ethical principal, but seems to limit true knowledge to matters not having to do with God. Thus he lapses into suppression language.

41 Even a "weak" one, who has inaccurately imbibed only popular notions of Freud's elaborate teaching on suppression/repression.

such "unknown knowledge," it strains credulity to see how.[42] Thus adoption of the word "suppress" is at odds with Beza's interpretation, with the Greek text itself, and the majority of interpretations and translations up to the twentieth century.

In conclusion, I would like to offer a modest proposal for what I hold is the most accurate translation of Romans 1:18 in the hopes that something like it will eventually dislodge the ambiguous (and vitiated) "suppress," with all its noetically dubious baggage: "God's wrath is openly revealed from heaven against all the ungodliness and wickedness of men because they hold onto the truth unrighteously."[43]

---

42 It is no surprise that Brunner, as Barth's foil, summarizes this point well: "The denial of such a 'general revelation' preceding the historical revelation of grace in Jesus Christ can appeal neither to Paul nor to the Bible at large. It contradicts the fact of responsibility. If man did not know God, how could he be responsible? But he is responsible, for he knows about God on the strength of the divine self-revelation. The apostle does not speak of the past, now buried, possibility but of something actually present; for it is true of everyone that he is inexcusable in his godlessness. It is true of every godless man that he does not give the honour to the God who made himself known to him, but obscures the divine revelation by the productions of his own undisciplined imagination and arbitrariness. ... It is his selfishness, however, which prevents this knowledge from becoming practically effective. He does not want to submit and has no intention of being grateful." BRUNNER, E. (1959), 18–19.

43 Space does not permit a defense of this translation, particularly the adverbial prepositional phrase—is it instrumental or truly locative?—ἐν ἀδικίᾳ.

Jennifer Powell McNutt

Chapter 5: From *Codex Bezae* to *La Bible*

Theodore Beza's Biblical Scholarship and the French Geneva Bible of 1588

In 1961, Robert Kingdon published a review of the first volume of the correspondence of Theodore Beza.[1] There he called for consideration of the lesser-known reformers, beyond the great founders of the churches, who collaborated, aided and furthered the work of reform. Kingdon wrote, "Luther and Calvin themselves would have been the first to deny that their churches were one-man organizations."[2] A decade later, David Steinmetz would describe them as the "Reformers in the Wings"[3] because the story of the Reformation could not be told without them though they were not the primary figures of the drama. Like Kingdon, Steinmetz also identified Beza among this group. Since that time, studies on Beza have slowly advanced, though Beza's contribution to the story of the Reformation has often been tethered to John Calvin's life and ministry, and there is good reason for that.

It is widely recognized that when Beza joined the effort to reform the church, he developed a fierce loyalty for his colleague, mentor and father-figure, John Calvin.[4] Their educational formation from Paris to Orléans (with the same Greek teacher, Melchior Wolmar) culminating with a degree in law was a journey they shared. Both were Frenchmen driven to Geneva in exile. Leadership in Geneva as professor, rector and pastor prepared Beza to step into Calvin's role as Moderator of the Company of Pastors at Calvin's death in 1564. By the end of Calvin's life, Beza was loathe to leave his side, and no one would nurture, protect and advocate for the good remembrance of the Genevan reformer better than Beza. Just months after Calvin's death, Beza published Calvin's commentary on

---

1 KINGDON, R. (1961), 415–522.
2 KINGDON, R. (1961), 415. Kingdon believed that enabling more accessibility to primary sources would help Beza's scholarship to advance.
3 See chapter on Theodore Beza in STEINMETZ, D. (2001).
4 Bruce Gordon notes the different types of relationships that Calvin fostered within his closest network and describes Beza as "the son," in GORDON, B. (2009). Machiel A. van den Berg depicts the dynamic with Calvin as "spiritual father," in VAN DEN BERG, M. (2006), 239. See also Daniel Ménager's analysis in MÉNAGER, D. (1983), 231–255.

Joshua posthumously[5] along with *La vie de Calvin*.[6] It was a sensitive endeavor at that cultural moment to write an account that could finesse the line between historical remembrance and hagiography, and Beza denied any intention on his part to promote an alternative cult of the saints in his effort to recognize—as he described it—Calvin's extraordinary "learning" and "piety" in a "simple narrative".[7]

In these ways and more, Beza's close relationship with Calvin helped to preserve Beza's inclusion in the Reformation story. Yet, drawing Beza out from Calvin's towering, historiographical shadow has not been straightforward. His *Tabula Praedestinationis* has certainly not helped historical memory to see beyond his affirmation of the doctrine of predestination, although scholarship has argued persuasively for a misinterpretation.[8] In 1961, after reflecting on Beza's polemical attitudes and his emphasis on predestination, Kingdon described Beza as "not entirely a man of hatred."[9] Moreover, when Beza is not inconspicuously present as the supporter of Calvin in historiography, he is overbearingly present as the great distorter of Calvin's legacy.[10] Though the latter concern has been thoroughly addressed by Richard Muller's work, historiography tends to depict Beza's theology as "stagnant, speculative, or scholastic."[11]

Part of the challenge faced when assessing Beza is that he is a third generation reformer, who has too often been treated as a fringe figure of the second wave.[12] Beza was a contemporary and co-worker of Calvin's, but he was also the inheritor of his ministry right as the Reformation landscape was dramatically shifting in post-Tridentine Europe. Beza's ability to preserve Calvin's reputation and further his legacy did not preclude him from the necessity of

---

5 CALVIN, J., *Commentaires de M. Iehan Calvin, sur le livre de Josué. Avec une preface de Theodore de Besze, contenant en brief l'histoire de la vie et mort d'iceluy* (1564). See MÉNAGER, D. (1983), 231–255.

6 Nicolas Colladon and Antoine Teissier contributed to the revision, expansion and translation of the account. According to Irena Backus, Beza's first edition was not apologetically motivated. BACKUS, I. (2013), xxii. For a history of Calvin's remembrance, see MCNUTT, J. (2020), 383–392.

7 BEZA, T. (2009), xxi. See also the collection in CO 21.

8 See Richard Muller's chapter, "The Use and Abuse of a Document: Beza's Tabula Praedestinationis, the Bolsec Controversy, and the Origins of Reformed Orthodoxy" in TRUMAN, C./CLARK, R.S. (ed.) (1999), 33–61; MULLER, R. (2005), 184–210, esp. 198.

9 KINGDON, R. (1961), 421. Kingdon described the Table of Predestination as "a visual aid with a vengeance" (ibid., 420).

10 For the "Calvin vs. the Calvinists" debate, see HALL, B. (1967), 19–37; BELL, C. (1983), 535–540.

11 Scott Manetsch summarizes the historiographical tenor surrounding Beza in this way, in MANETSCH, S. (2013), ix.

12 Steinmetz notes the importance of Beza's generation, in STEINMETZ, D. (2001), 114.

navigating the realities of increased confessional entrenchment in Europe and, with that, political complexity. It is one of the reasons why the many dimensions of Beza—pastoral, scholarly and political—and of his work are not easily disentangled, particularly after the St. Bartholomew's Day Massacre in 1572. In 2000, Manetsch's landmark book on Beza made significant headway for anglophone scholarship by presenting Beza on his own terms and as his own man within the web of Geneva and France's Reformation after Calvin's time.[13] Marking the 500th anniversary of Beza's birth in 2019 has become another key opportunity for bringing attention to the significance of his life and contributions.

This chapter will offer an overview of Beza as biblical scholar with attention to his relationship with *Codex Bezae* and his advancement of the French Geneva Bible of 1588. This analysis understands Beza's work in biblical scholarship as an outworking of his training as a humanist scholar as well as a manifestation of his dedication to church reform and to the advancement of Calvin's legacy.[14] In the end, Beza's contributions to the field of biblical scholarship proved geographically far-reaching and enduring well beyond the church of Geneva for centuries.

5.1 A Life of Biblical Scholarship

In October 1548, after battling sickness and a troubled conscience, Beza fled Paris for Geneva in search of evangelical refuge. Correspondence from March 1560 provides an account of his difficult decision: "I broke every chain, collected my possessions, and abandoned my native country, my kinsmen, and my friends in order to follow Christ. Accompanied by my wife, I went to Geneva in voluntary exile."[15] The decade of his departure was a period of escalating persecutions against Protestants in France, and Beza's relocation reflects the "brain drain" to Geneva that transpired along with other prominent sympathizers including Jean Crespin and Laurent de Normandie.[16] Beza well knew that his departure risked the loss of scholarly prestige and financial solvency, and thus, he viewed his exile through the life of the Old Testament Patriarch, Abraham. Manetsch explains, "As the patriarch Abraham had once offered his son Isaac on the altar in obedience to God, so he had sacrificed his ambitions

---

13 MANETSCH, S. (2000b). Manetsch argues that Beza continued to be significantly involved in the French crisis from 1572 to 1598 (ibid., 7).

14 Gordon writes, "Like Bucer, Bullinger and Calvin, Beza asserted unequivocally that biblical exegesis was primarily to serve the life of the church." See GORDON, B. (2016), 474.

15 Cited and translated in MANETSCH, S. (2000b), 12. They arrived in Geneva on October 23 or 24.

16 MONTER, E.W. (1999), 114.

for literary glory on the altar of the evangelical faith."[17] The biblical story was so formative for Beza that he composed the biblical drama, *Abraham Sacrifiant* (1551), which enjoyed at least 11 editions in his lifetime.[18] In the end, Beza's literary ambitions found an outlet in the biblical reform of the church.

Beza's decision to leave France behind proved a windfall for the leadership of the evangelical cause because of the educational training that he brought with him as well as his family pedigree. By November 1549, he was appointed to the chair of Greek at the Academy of Lausanne at the recommendation of Pierre Viret and John Calvin and by the decision of the magistrates of Bern. In March 1559, Beza was named Professor of Theology and the first Rector of Geneva's newly founded academy.[19] According to his oration, the work of the Academy was not mere pedagogy but educational formation dedicated to God's glory, and so began the Academy's role in equipping and sending the pastors of the French Reformation.[20] By the time of Calvin's passing in May 1564, it had become the largest Protestant academy in francophone Europe.[21] After the loss of Calvin that year, the Company of Pastors were persuaded by Beza to alter election procedure in order to institute an annual election for moderator, but this ended up ensuring Beza's own election sixteen times over the next sixteen years.[22] Beza, thus, juggled immense multifaceted responsibilities of teaching, pastoral ministry, and academic and religious leadership (with political dimensions). Remarkably, none of these responsibilities prevented him from engaging in the elite world of biblical scholarship that had been carved out by Erasmus' *Novum instrumentum omne* (1516), the first published Greek New Testament,[23] and the first critical edition of the Greek New Testament (1550)—*Novum Testamentum Graece*—by Robert Étienne (Stephanus).[24]

---

17 MANETSCH, S. (2000), 13.

18 PELIKAN, J. (1996), 172.

19 MANETSCH, S. (2000), 17.

20 REID, W.S. (1992), 3:246. For an English translation of the oration, see "Address at the Solemn Opening of the Academy in Geneva," in KINGDON, R. (1974), 175–179.

21 According to Charles Borgeaud's research on *L'Université de Genève* as cited by MANETSCH, S. (2000), 18n.29.

22 MANETSCH, S. (2013), 63.

23 The title was revised in the 1519 edition to *Novum Testamentum*. In fact, Cardinal Ximénes' (Francisco Jiménez de Cisneros) Complutensian Polyglot was the first printed Greek New Testament from 1514–1517 before its publication in 1522. For more details on polyglot critical editions, see HAMILTON, A. (2016), 140–143.

24 For more on Étienne, see ARMSTRONG, E. (1954).

5.1.1 Beza's Season with *Codex Bezae*

The work of the Renaissance humanist was as much about philology and hermeneutics of ancient languages as it was about the recovery of the ancient manuscripts themselves, and Beza's work reflects those trends as he sought the reform of the church. Translation, exegesis and the textual witness of Scripture occupied his scholarship, and he was aided in this work by owning two uncials of the earliest surviving biblical manuscripts known today as *Codex Claromontanus* (D^P)[25] and *Codex Bezae* (Codex D).[26] This section will consider the codex that would bear his name.

Codex Bezae is valued by textual critics of the New Testament because it is a bilingual codex written in Greek and Latin scripts in two columns by a single hand, which is a rarity.[27] At 406 leaves, it is incomplete, and the original length of the manuscript as well as its origins are contested. Nevertheless, most of Matthew, John, Mark and Acts are included as well as all of Luke.[28] A scholarly consensus dates the text to c. 400 before the alienation of the languages sets in regionally.[29] The manuscript travelled likely from Eastern origins (perhaps Berytus) to Lyon as indicated by clues from later supplementary leaves[30] and due to the city's "important role in the conservation of ancient texts during the early medieval period."[31] The codex was brought to the Council of Trent to contribute to a revision project of the Latin Vulgate led by Guglielmo Sirleto.[32] Importantly, *Codex Bezae* was then referenced in the critical apparatus of Stephanus' Greek New Testament (1550) according to the Greek letter *beta*. A decade later, the codex made its way to Geneva and into the hands of Beza.

---

25 Likely loaned to Beza by Pierre Pithou based on Beza's correspondence. See KRANS, J. (2006), 209.

26 A facsimile is available through the University of Cambridge where the original is still housed: http://cudl.lib.cam.ac.uk/view/MS-NN-00002-00041/1.

27 PARKER, D.C. (1992), 7. The scribe "used the same letter forms for Greek and Latin characters of similar appearance." See PARKER, D.C. (2009), 104.

28 The order of the text is as follows: Matthew, John, Luke, Mark, and Acts. Parker notes the inclusion of 3 John as well.

29 Parker argues for Latin-speaking Christians in Berytus around the year 400. See PARKER, D.C. (2009), 281. SCRIVENER, F. (ed.) (2015), vii. For a summary of the scholarship, see AUWERS, J.-M. (1995), 405–412.

30 The formation of the question mark and the use of blue ink for the colophon to Mark are indicators of its location in Lyon. See PARKER, D.C. (2009), 105.

31 PARKER, D.C. (1992), 282–283.

32 MANDELBROTE, S. (2016), 96. Other codices used for comparative analysis included *Codex Amiatinus* and *Codex Vaticanus*. In fact, the Council of Trent did not demand a revision of the Vulgate by the central administration of the Church though it was much discussed at the time. See GORDON B./CAMERON, E. (2016), 210.

According to Beza, the codex was located at the monastery of St. Irenaeus in Lyon when,[33] during the French Wars of Religion in 1562, the city was sacked by François de Beaumont, baron des Adrets (1513–1587).[34] Although Beza did not visit Lyon himself, he had close connections with the pastors there, and the influx of Lyonnaise refugees to Geneva after the First War of Religion including printers and booksellers has served as a plausible explanation for how the text moved into his possession.[35] The arrival of Protestant refugees from all over Europe had turned Geneva into a veritable hub for Bible translation, scholarship and publication. Critical to that developing reputation was Stephanus' arrival in Geneva from Paris in November 1550 after the Chambre Ardente banned his biblical editions.[36] Stephanus had made his name as a printer by printing editions of the Bible from 1532 during the reign of King Francis I. A few years later, he was honored as King's Printer in Greek, Hebrew and Latin. In addition to being named Royal Typographer, he was known as a biblical scholar in his own right and considered today to be the founder of Latin and French lexicography due to his critical edition of the entire Latin Bible as well as his *Thesaurus Linguae latinae* and accompanying bilingual dictionaries. One of his most enduring legacies was the versification of the Bible published for the first time in Geneva in 1551 and still used today. It was significant that Stephanus came to Geneva, and that he began working with Beza.

Before *Codex Bezae* came into Beza's possession, he had already begun contributing to the scholarship of the Bible with attention to French, Latin and Greek translations. He was first drawn into the task at the invitation of John Calvin to help collaborate, along with Louis Budé, in the revision of the French Geneva Bible of 1551.[37] In 1556/1557, Stephanus published Beza's first Latin New Testament translation paired with Stephanus' Vulgate. Over the next forty years and over the course of five editions (1556/7, 1565, 1582, 1588/9, 1598), Beza honed his work by adding the Greek text and his annotations (or exegetical

---

33 Beza to the Academy of Cambridge, 6 December 1581, in CB 22:245.

34 For an overview, see KNECHT, R. (2014). Confirmation of date and place are found in CB 22:ix, 247n.1

35 Parker writes, "It seems more charitable to ascribe the codex's removal to Geneva to the love of books of one of these than, like Scrivener, to the spoliations of a looter." PARKER, D.C. (1992), 283.

36 The timing is based upon a letter from John Calvin to Guillaume Farel, 10 November 1550, in which he indicated Étienne's arrival in Geneva. See CO 13:657; ARMSTRONG, E. (1954), 215.

37 Budé worked on the Psalms and Beza worked on the Apocrypha. An account is given in the preface titled, "Si je voulois icy…": *La Bible* (Genève: Jehan Crespin, M.D.LI.). See CHAMBERS, B. (1983), #150.B1551cre(1). Importantly, this was also the year that Sebastian Castellio published the first edition of his Latin Bible. See GUGGISBERG, H. (2003). Beza was highly critical of Castellio's translation, and he published these polemics in *Defensiones et Reprehensiones* (1563).

notes) of scripture passages, which were also expanded and revised. The 1565 edition, published by Henri Étienne, was significant for including Beza's revised Latin translation with copious *Annotationes*, the Greek and the Vulgate. The final edition was published in Geneva, coinciding with the year of the Edict of Nantes in 1598, and dedicated to Queen Elizabeth I. Beza's New Testament proved to be one of the most important Protestant translations of the New Testament for his time and beyond.[38] Attention to Beza's treatment of *Codex Bezae* through that process gives insight into the practices and limitations of the flourishing world of biblical scholarship at the time.

Codex Bezae was no mere collector's item to Beza, but a challenging piece of the puzzle. The primary challenge faced in discerning Beza's process of engaging with ancient manuscripts was that he lacked a clear and consistent system for identifying and evaluating textual variation.[39] Without a complete collation of the manuscript, tracing his usage of the texts behind the text has not been straightforward.[40] In 1980, Irena Backus' early work evaluated Beza's engagement with Codex D in order to explore Beza's influence on the English New Testament, which revealed the links as well as the limitations of Beza's textual scholarship by modern standards.[41] More recently, Jan Krans' work has illuminated in detail Beza's process of translation and evaluation over the course of all five of his New Testament editions. This careful study has revealed Beza's priority for his Latin translation with less editorial concern directed at the Greek.[42] In the end, Beza tended to favor the harmonization of the text and the protection of Scripture's authority theologically.[43] Nevertheless, there is consensus that Beza incorporated the witness of *Codex Bezae* in the third edition of his New Testament in 1582.[44] The annotations of 1565 also indicate that he evaluated

---

38 See KRANS, J. (2006). With gratitude to Jon Balserak for bringing my attention to this excellent work.

39 See KRANS, J. (2006), 232.

40 Krans concludes that the 1565 edition is not actually a critical edition but a commentary and companion volume to Stephanus' 1550 edition. See KRANS, J. (2006), 217. The process is further confounded by the fact that Beza likely did not recognize Stephanus *beta* symbol as a reference to the codex he had in his possession (ibid., 227–228). Stephanus was selective himself in what he noted so that selectivity further narrowed the textual conversation for the next phase of scholars (ibid., 231, 241).

41 BACKUS, I. (1980), 6–7.

42 Krans sees significance in the fact that the first edition does not include the Greek text. See KRANS, J. (2006), 204. The Greek is included in order to communicate the validity of the Latin translation (ibid., 205). Beza accepts Stephanus' version of the Greek and "does not see himself as the editor of the Greek text" (ibid., 218).

43 KRANS, J. (2006), 301–302, 305.

44 Beza claims to have done this in his letter to the University of Cambridge, see Beza to the Academy of Cambridge, 6 December 1581, in CB 22:245–246; GORDON, B. (2016), 474.

and noted the witness of the codex even when the translation of the text was not immediately updated.[45] The codex seems to have served as a conversation partner, providing confirmation and a sounding board for evaluating variation. He compared the codex to Stephanus' collation and the Complutensian Polyglot as well as the Syriac and Arabic witnesses in matters of textual variation thanks to key editions published by Immanuel Tremellius (1510–1580) and Franciscus Junius the elder (1545–1602).[46] Sometimes the codex's witness transformed the Greek and sometimes it transformed the Latin.[47] It had a place in the process and the product even if limited.

Beza owned *Codex Bezae* from 1562–1581. He used its witness to shape the annotations and the text of the New Testament, and then he passed it on. Parting with the codex was not a sign of disregard, but a custom of the time. As Mandelbrote has written, "Greek manuscripts [...] were extensively copied, traded, looted and exchanged in the sixteenth and seventeenth centuries."[48] In this case, Beza presented the codex as a gift to the University of Cambridge library as a way to enhance their collection and honor the relationship he was fostering with William Cecil, Lord Burghley and Chancellor of the University of Cambridge then.[49] Beza had been in correspondence with Cecil since 1563, and they became even more connected when Cecil's nephew, Anthony Bacon, studied at Geneva from February to November 1581.[50] It has also been inferred that with his gift Beza sought to encourage greater acceptance of Puritan students.[51] On 6 December 1581, Beza sent a letter addressed directly to Cecil where Beza offered his respect, his desire to enhance the prestige of Cambridge's library and his friendship.[52] His letter offered an additional gift of a two-volume

---

Parker highlights that Beza used the codex for the first edition of his Greek New Testament. See PARKER, D.C. (2009), 105. Scrivener claims that Beza made occasional reference to *Codex Bezae* in several editions of his Greek New Testament. See SCRIVENER, F. (2015), x. Epp points out that Beza "made little use" of either of the codices he owned in the 1565 edition of his Latin New Testament as well as the many editions and printings thereafter. See EPP, E. (2016), 116. Krans points to Backus on this point. See KRANS, J. (2006), 234.

45 KRANS, J. (2006), 301–302.
46 Backus' work notes these facets of Beza's work. See also KRANS, J. (2006), 208–222.
47 KRANS, J. (2006), 236–237 (citing Backus).
48 MANDELBROTE, S. (2016), 93.
49 As a result, the text received the additional name of *Codex Cantabrigiensis*.
50 Ann Bacon to Beza, 18 May 1581, in CB 22:109n.2. Anthony Bacon (1558–1601) is noted in the *Livre du recteur* of the Academy. Bacon's travel schedule would not have permitted him to be the one to carry the codex to England. See ibid., 110n.4.
51 This understanding of events is cited in CB 22:xviii, 248n.7. Beza's friendship with the Puritan Thomas Cartwright is noted by the edition. Not long before, Geneva had been drawn into the controversy between Puritans and Cambridge during the Cartwright affair in the 1570s.
52 Beza to William Cecil, Lord Burghley, 6 December 1581, in CB 22:191–192.

Pentateuch Hexaglot, which had been printed in Constantinople (1546–1547) with translations in Hebrew, Arabic, Persian, Greek, Spanish and Aramaic.[53]

Beza's second letter written that day was directed to the university and offers a fascinating glimpse into his thought process.[54] The letter first described the state of the codex in rather bleak terms: incomplete, insufficiently preserved, and inappropriately marked on. Beza rightly noticed the amount of variations evident in comparison to the accepted versions of the time. He, therefore, described the codex as "not very correctly copied," but he also suggested that the faculty may know better than he of its value. Beza raised particular concern with the variations he saw with Luke in terms of the choice of words rather than meaning. Consequently, he suggested that the codex be stored rather than published to avoid controversy. The recommendation gives an account of how unsettling textual variation could be, particularly without a system for understanding the relationship between ancient texts. Nevertheless, Beza was also complimentary when claiming that the codex did not advance heresy and even that many of the readings were worthy of attention because they conformed to teachings of the Greek and Latin fathers as well as the old Latin Vulgate. Beza's recommendation that the text be preserved for posterity and further study before distribution through print captured his commitment to both scholarly advancement and pastoral concern for the church. On 18 May 1582, Anthony Wingfield, the vice-chancellor at Cambridge, thanked Beza for his gifts with profuse appreciation.[55] Wingfield indicated the highest regard for the theology of Calvin and Beza as the two most preferred theologians of their time, and noted how their names and theology fill the conversations and the sermons of their context. Beza's desire to strengthen a close bond between Geneva and Cambridge appeared to have been a success.

At every step, Beza's relationship with the codex provides a window into his world of biblical scholarship. As a proponent and practitioner of the Renaissance humanist method employed for the sake of church reform, he received the text and used it even though his linguistic focus differed from Stephanus' attention to the Greek.[56] In the emerging field of text criticism, Beza's treatment of codices reflected common tendencies and assumptions practiced among the scholarly circles of his network. Beza's relinquishment of *Codex Bezae* is a mark of the highest scholarly gift at the time and of the limitations of biblical scholarship to

---

53 The text was owned by Cambridge's library from 1583–1588 and then returned to Geneva in 1703 by way of Professor Louis Tronchin. See CB 22:xviii–xix. The text has a complex formation history. See ibid., 192n3.

54 Beza to the Academy of Cambridge, 6 December 1581, in CB 22:245–246.

55 Beza to the Academy of Cambridge, 6 December 1581, in CB 22:245–246.

56 Krans points to the mistakes made by Stephanus though he created a critical edition.

understand the authority of texts in light of textual variation. In the end, *Codex Bezae* was undervalued by its ownership through the eighteenth century and overlooked in favor of lesser authorities for generations.[57] According to Epp, this was based upon a shared but faulty premise that a single recension was recoverable from the fourth century.[58] It was this premise that hampered ancient manuscripts from being printed—as evidenced by Beza's own hand—until the late eighteenth and mid-nineteenth centuries before facsimiles became commonplace.[59]

The leaps and bounds that took place in the field of textual criticism in later centuries may stand to correct the past, nevertheless, the root of such discovery is still found in the flourishing of biblical scholarship during the Renaissance and Reformation. In that context, Beza's contributions to the translation of the New Testament were treated by Protestants as some of the best scholarship of their day. The Marian Exiles looked to Beza's translations and annotations for shaping the Geneva Bible (1560).[60] Immanuel Tremellius' 1569 polyglot, also printed by Henri Étienne, contained the Greek and Syriac texts of the New Testament as well as Beza's Latin translation.[61] The English King James Version (1611) is an often-cited example for showing the impact of Beza's work since that translation relied extensively on Beza's 1588–1589 and 1598 editions.[62] Most noteworthy is Beza's link to the *textus receptus* in 1633. Krans writes, "His Greek text was not contested but faithfully reprinted; through the Elzevir editions it was elevated to the status of 'received text.'"[63] Beza's biblical scholarship was considered so significant at the time that it was even used without his permission and without recognition of his contribution.[64]

---

57 Epp writes, "the few Greek manuscripts that can be identified as actually used for these early editions from Erasmus to Elzevier stem from the twelfth century or so, while the much earlier manuscripts known at the time, Codices D and D^p, were little used because their differing readings seemed to depart too dangerously from the 'received text.'" See EPP, E. (2016), 117.

58 See BEDIER, J. (1928), 161–196. The "Recensionist" Method had not yet been developed (Karl Lachmannian, 1793–1851), and so Beza and those that came after him were not looking for how texts belonged to the same textual families (or *stemma codicum*) in order to determine the point of origin.

59 EPP, E. (2016), 119. The text became available to a broader readership with Frederick Scrivener's edition and publication in 1864.

60 KRANS, J. (2006), 197.

61 KRANS, J. (2006), 208; AUSTIN, K. (2007).

62 EPP, E. (2016), 117.

63 KRANS, J. (2006), 197.

64 Nicolas Barbier pirated Beza's 1557 Latin Bible from Robert Étienne, and then he may have translated Beza's corrections from Latin into French. Armstrong includes council records and letters relating to pirating committed by Barbier. See ARMSTRONG, E. (1954), 275–288. Chambers speculates that the anonymous reviser of the Old Testament could have been

Beza's work in biblical scholarship was never disconnected from his calling to the leadership of the church. In fact, Beza's concern for the Latin Bible was a sign of his concern for the church and the training of pastors.[65] And so, biblical scholarship was by no means an end to itself. As a pastor and an exiled Frenchman, Beza's attention to matters of text and philology were instrumental in his contribution to the advancement of the reform of the French-speaking churches especially. The project of the French vernacular Bible was for Geneva and his brethren beyond. This conviction is no better seen than in his contribution to the 1588 French Geneva Bible, which would shape French Bibles in francophone Europe for centuries.

5.1.2   Beza and the 1588 French Geneva Bible

Beza's commitment to biblical scholarship for the church extended beyond the translation of the Latin New Testament. He was also instrumental in shaping the French Bible as well.[66] The two languages had different purposes and functions and, therefore, can reveal important priorities at work in Beza's scholarship. Because Latin was the shared language of biblical scholarship that transcended vernacular communities, Beza's Latin New Testament aided in the formation and support of Protestant clergy beyond the francophone world. Meanwhile, since the vernacular tongue was now the language of Protestant worship according to region and community, contributing to the French Bible provided Beza with the opportunity to shape the worship life of francophone Europe beyond Geneva. Therefore, Beza's biblical scholarship in Latin and French reflect a two-pronged commitment to clerical training, on the one hand, and the worship life of the church and for common believers, on the other hand. This dual activity is what enabled Beza's biblical scholarship to have such a far-reaching and multifaceted impact.

Beza's work on the French Bible began at Calvin's invitation, a dynamic that often shaped Beza's life. Collaboration with Calvin on the revised translation of the French New Testament in 1560 was treated as a landmark moment at the time for vernacular Scripture.[67] To mark the occasion and significance of their

---

Theodore Beza in Nicolas Barbier and Thomas Courteau's *La Bible* (1559). See CHAMBERS, B. (1983), #253, B1559bar-cou.

65 GORDON, B./CAMERON E. (2016), 202–203.

66 For an overview of the history of Geneva's French Bibles, see ENGAMMARE, M. (1997), 177–189.

67 *La Bible* (Geneve: Robert Étienne). See CHAMBERS, B. (1983), #261, B1560est. Beza first became involved with the French Bible project by revising the translation of the Apocrypha in *La Bible* (Genève: Jehan Crespin, M.D.LI.). See CHAMBERS, B. (1983), #150, B1551cre(1).

contribution, a new preface to the New Testament was added titled, "A tous fideles Chrestiens."[68] The preface highlighted Beza's entrée to the project as value added given the imperfections of Calvin's previous work despite his best efforts and consultation of the Greek.[69] With analysis, it becomes clear that the purpose of this rhetoric was not to critique Calvin and elevate Beza but to emphasize the importance of their collaboration and willingness to confer with the approval of the Company of Pastors. With a harshness not seen in other Geneva prefaces, Calvin and Beza singled out Sebastian Castellio[70] for publishing an independent translation, which the preface describes as advancing Satan's work of filling the market with misleading translations. The emerging era of Confessionalization rears its head in so far as it is no longer the absence or prohibition of Scripture that fuels Protestant vernacular translation projects but the prospect of a world awash with unfaithful vernacular Scripture that demands revised translations. The text declares,

> For there is nothing more essential than to have a right and firm knowledge of the doctrine of salvation equipped with the means to resist every heresy and falsity by having the text of Holy Scripture faithfully translated since the sin of men has introduced to the world such a diversity of language.[71]

In this way, the preface highlights Beza's collaboration with Calvin over the French New Testament revision as a step toward overturning the consequences of sin due to no less than the Tower of Babel. This was a French New Testament that could not be missed, and a scramble for printing rights ensued. Geneva's Council determined that Henri Étienne would have exclusive privileges to the Old Testament, but all plaintiffs would have the right to print Calvin and Beza's New Testament.

By 1565, the year after Calvin's death, Geneva's French Bibles were published in every francophone publication center in Europe including Lyons and Paris. The Calvin-Beza revision of the New Testament was treated as the definitive

---

68 There is some question about the authorship and dating of the preface, which is dated 10 October 1559, though Robert Étienne died on 7 September 1559. The publication of the Bible was carried out by his son, Henri Étienne. It is included in other editions of the Bible including Robert Étienne's *Le Nouveau Testament* (1560) and François Étienne's publication of *Le Nouueau Testament* (1568).

69 It is customary for Bible prefaces to vaguely compliment and critique previous translations as in need of updating. Calvin was forthcoming about the limits of his translations and his desire for further revision. See his preface, "Si je vouloi icy," which appeared for the first time in *La Bible* (Genève: Jehan Girard, 1546). See CHAMBERS, B. (1983), #128, B1546gir.

70 *La Bible Nouvellement Translatée* (Basel: Jehan Hervage, M.D.LV.). See CHAMBERS, B. (1983), #202, B1555chat.

71 *La Bible* (Geneve: Robert Étienne). See CHAMBERS, B. (1983), #261, B1560est.

version until 1588. Nevertheless, even Calvin expressed the desire for further revision of his New Testament at the March censures just two months before his death in 1564. According to Beza's account, Calvin "felt that the Lord had given him a short respite, and taking a French New Testament into his hands, he read some passages from the notes which are appended to it, and asked the opinion of the brethren respecting them, because he had undertaken to get them corrected."[72] That process began soon after with Beza's leadership.

As early as 1569, a complete revision of the entire French Bible began with and under Beza's role as moderator.[73] Significant focus was directed toward revising the Old Testament since it had not been pursued in 1560. For that reason, Corneille Bonaventure Bertram, Professor of Oriental Languages (i.e., Hebrew) at Geneva's Academy, was a key leader in the effort along with Charles Perrot, Jean Jaquemot and Jean-Baptiste Rotan.[74] Beza and Bertram led the effort and developed their translation from the critical work of Tremellius, Junius and Beza.[75] On 1/11 March 1588, Beza and Rotan presented the revision of the French Geneva Bible to the Small Council with great expectation after several years delay. With printings in three different sizing formats (folio, quarto, octavo) of more than ten thousand copies,[76] Geneva's Company of Pastors intended to provide Scripture for every stratum of francophone Europe. Beza's efforts to advance the new translation involved dispatching copies to influential figures including Ludwig Wittgenstein and to the Frankfurt Book Fair to promote the reach and sale of the Bible.[77]

The 1588 French Geneva Bible emerged during an uncertain time for the Huguenot church after 1572 and before 1598. Beza's settlement in the city of Geneva in 1558 had occurred at a point when the consolidation of Calvin's leadership was stable and as the Huguenot cause was riding the wave of growth and expansion in France. The death of two, consecutive persecuting kings—Henry II due to an injured eye and Francis II due to an infected ear—empowered the movement forward with a sense of God's providential blessing and favor. The triumphant tenor of Beza's poetic tribute is notable: "Ye crafty, foolish, dull-eared kings, to you; These awful warnings cry, Or now prepare your evil deed to rue, Or in your blindness die."[78] Even in the midst of civil war, expec-

---

72 Beza, "Life of John Calvin" (2009), lxxxiv.
73 ENGAMMARE, M. (1997), 183.
74 ENGAMMARE, M. (1997), 184.
75 ENGAMMARE, M. (1997), 184, 188.
76 Engammare compares these numbers with the publication of other French Bibles to show the magnitude of the endeavor. See ENGAMMARE, M. (1997).
77 Beza sent a copy to Ludwig von Sayn-Wittgenstein on 12/22 March 1588, in CB 29:48–51. On that same day, Beza also sent a copy to Constantin Fabricius (ibid., 44–45).
78 CO 28:270–272. For a translation, see DUKE, A. (1992), 81.

tations were high as the National Synod of La Rochelle met in 1571 as Beza presided. However, the death of Queen Jeanne of Navarre followed by the St. Bartholomew's Day Massacre were profoundly devastating for the Huguenot cause. At this juncture, Beza faced a dramatically different religious and political landscape for advancing reform, and his work to preserve the Protestant church of France included the advancement of the vernacular Bible. With the victories of the Duke of Guise against Swiss Protestant forces creating turmoil for the future of the city in October and November 1587, Beza nevertheless prepared for the launch of the 1588 Bible despite "the severity of these fearful times."[79] The 1588 French Geneva version became the standard French text for Geneva and French Reformed churches until David Martin's revision in 1699–1707 and Jean-Frédéric Osterwald's Bible of 1744. On the part of Geneva's Company, no significant changes were made to the 1588 text until the Napoleonic era in 1805.[80]

Beza played a prominent role in shaping the 1588 French Geneva Bible at every level of the project. Importantly, he wrote a new preface to the Bible, "A tous vrais amateurs de la verité Dieu,"[81] that was ordered before Calvin's preface.[82] Beza's prefatory remarks were so important to framing the 1588 translation that even the smaller formats included them though Calvin's preface tended to be removed due to size. The goal of Beza's preface was to emphasize the necessity of the vernacular Bible project as well as frame the significance of the 1588 French Geneva Bible. Whereas Calvin's prefaces had reflected the concerns of the first and second generations over a lack of access to Scripture, Beza's preface revealed third generation concerns over those disengaged from the value of Scripture and its wisdom. At nearly seventy-years old, Beza's tone strikes a note of frustration with the current generation, perhaps in reflection of all the sacrifices that had been made in order to promote access to Scripture.[83]

---

79 Beza to Constantin Fabricius, 24 January/3 February 1588, in CB 29:7–11.

80 Engammare writes "le Bibles genevoises on peu ou prou influencé toute la production biblique en française au XVIe siècle." See ENGAMMARE, M. (1997), 187.

81 Theodore Beza's "A tous vrais amateurs de la vérité de Dieu," *La Bible Qvi est Tovte la Saincte Escritvre dv Vieil & du Nouueau Testament* (Geneve: [Jeremie des Planches], M.D.LXXXVIII). See CHAMBERS, B. (1983), #515, B1588geneve(fol). The translation of this document is my own.

82 Beza's preface received feedback and approval from Geneva's Company of Pastors. Calvin wrote several different prefaces for the French Bible including "Christ est le fin de la Loy" (also known as "Dieu le Createur") as included here, which was first published for the 1535 Olivetan Bible.

83 Beza emphasized the way in which turning one's back on Scripture could lead to immoral living, which would become a prominent theological and pastoral focus for Geneva's seventeenth- and eighteenth-century generations, particularly in response to the Enlightenment. See MCNUTT, J. (2014), chapters 4–5.

He described groups as idle in some cases and ignorant in others for not rightly seeking the treasure of Scripture to understand the purpose of one's life: "Their eyes, instead of being enlightened by the light that shines there, are blinded, and instead of being changed and amended their affections are strengthened and worsened."[84] The preface urged believers not to neglect Scripture for their formation. In his own words, Beza's goal was nothing short of inspiring an appetite for eating from "this incorruptible meat" of Scripture for those who had tasted and those who had not.[85]

Beza's pastoral message is complemented by his perspective as a biblical scholar and educator. This is evident in Beza's emphasis upon the conservation of the Bible in Greek and Hebrew as well as its translation into Aramaic, Syriac, Ethiopic and Latin. The Bible's preservation in diverse languages was a marvel to Beza of God's faithfulness to the church over the centuries despite the devastations of the world and the intentions of Satan.[86] Beza treated the rediscovery of the two original languages of Scripture as a God-ordained transformation for the church[87] that opened the door to the wisdom of Hebrew scholars and the ancient Latin and Greek fathers. Meanwhile, this diversity of language was an indication of the nature of Scripture as God's speech to all people: "The one who speaks here is Eternal, the Living God, Father, Son and Holy Spirit, and who must be not only heard but also adored with all reverence."[88] Beza took care to emphasize that every single person was intended to "hear" God's speech no matter their nationality, condition, sex or age.[89] With this point, Beza stressed the inclusion of women and children, and he cited a litany of support from Chrysostom to Jerome and Justinian to Charlemagne.[90] Beza elevated the example of the Church of Ethiopia, the Greek Church and the Churches of the

---

84　These tendencies did not surprise Beza, who also alluded to Jesus' teaching in Matt. 7:13–14 regarding the narrow path that leads to salvation.

85　BEZA, T., "A tous vrais amateurs," fol. 2. Beza also recognized that some sheep were without a shepherd in his time and other sheep were prevented from the true pasture. In this regard, Beza echoed Calvin's 1546 preface.

86　BEZA, T., "A tous vrais amateurs," fols. 1-2.

87　BEZA, T., "A tous vrais amateurs," fol. 4.

88　Beza wrote, "Celui qui parle ici, c'est l'Eternel, le Dieu vivant, Pere, Fils, & S. Esprit, & qui doit estre non seulement escouté, mais aussi adoré en toute reuerence." BEZA, T., « A tous vrais amateurs, » fol. 2.

89　It is noteworthy that Beza emphasized hearing over reading, and he explained that this happens in the worship context through the preaching of the Word and the administration of the sacraments.

90　Chrysostom was also cited by Thomas Cranmer's preface to the second edition of the Great Bible (1540). That introduction continued in the first edition of the Bishop's Bible (1568). See PELIKAN, J. (1996), 144.

Levant as precedent for the emulation of using one's spoken language for Scripture.[91] For him, Scripture must be in a language that is understandable because it leads to a proper understanding of oneself and the impact of sin.[92] When Scripture is heard in a language that is understood entrance into the mystical union with Jesus Christ through faith is available. Since Christ is "the sole and unique remedy" for sin and the assured hope for eternal life,[93] a vernacular rendering of Scripture is crucial. For these reasons and more, Beza taught that Scripture must be shared in a language that can be understood,[94] which means that the task of the church to provide Scripture had not yet been accomplished even though the transmission of Scripture is not a new command. In this, Beza's work as biblical scholar and pastor of the church reveals a united purpose.

5.1.3 The Genevan Psalter

Beza's prefatory remarks were intended to shape the reader's experience of the 1588 French Geneva Bible from the first moments of opening the Bible, but his impact did not stop there. Beza's hand was also evident in the development of the French Psalter frequently published with or bound to French Bibles during the early modern period. In this task, Beza combined biblical scholarship with his abilities as a poet to extend the practice of singing French verse in the worshipping life of the church.[95] As with so many of the defining features of Geneva's Reformation, John Calvin first led the way toward replacing the Gregorian plainsong of the medieval church by following in the footsteps of Martin Luther and Martin Bucer's Strasbourg. The first Geneva Psalter was published in 1542. With Clement Marot's arrival in Geneva, Calvin relinquished this work, and a newly expanded collection of 49 Psalms was published in 1543 before Marot's untimely death in 1544.[96] The first revision of the New Testament to carry Calvin's name included verses from Clement Marot and Étienne de la Fontaine before Beza took up the task of completing the project of Marot from

---

91 BEZA, T., "A tous vrais amateurs," fols. 3-4.
92 Beza's understanding of the impact of sin reflects Calvin's teachings in the *Institutes* on Law and Gospel.
93 BEZA, T., "A tous vrais amateurs," fol. 2 : "le seul & vnique remede."
94 Beza provided a robust biblical argument for vernacular Scripture by pointing to evidence from Scripture including Abraham's use of common languages to Paul's teachings in 1 Cor. 14. See BEZA, T., "A tous vrais amateurs," fol. 3.
95 Beza's published poetry includes the collection *Juvenalia* as well as a French versification of *Abraham Sacrifiant*.
96 Fifty psalms were ready by 1546, and eighty-nine psalms were prepared for the 1551 publication.

his arrival in 1548. In 1551, a new publication of the Psalms was issued with 34 new Psalms turned into verse by Beza. The collection was titled, *Pseaumes octantetrois* (83 Psalms), and Beza's treatment of Psalms 16 and 47 were singled out for particular appreciation. The complete edition of the Genevan Psalter was realized with publication in 1562 for a print run of between thirty- and fifty-thousand copies.[97] The Psalter was introduced by Beza with a preface, also in French verse, titled, "A L'Eglise de nostre Seigneur Jesus Christ."[98] Through Beza's abilities and attentions to the task, the French Psalter came to define the worship life of the Reformed churches to this day.[99]

From the paratextual material, to the translation, to the Psalter and more, Beza played a significant role in forming one of the most influential French Bibles in history. Indeed, if success breeds contempt, then the 1647 New Testament by the Roman Catholic Doctors of Louvain (particularly François Veron, Doctor of Theology), bears witness in its polemics to the influence of the 1588 translation. This was not a Bible that could be ignored.

5.2   The Flourishing of Beza's Biblical Scholarship

Beza's contribution to the life and ministry of Geneva and the Reformed tradition were manifold, but one important way in which Beza stands out from the shadow of Calvin is in the global impact of his biblical scholarship. In some cases that legacy is readily apparent. Seventeenth-century polyglot Bibles, for example, visibly promoted the importance of Beza's biblical scholarship. In 1628, Jean de Tournes printed a three column New Testament with French, Greek, and Latin, which was then reissued the following year.[100] The Latin translation was Beza's while the French came from the 1588 French Geneva Bible, though it lacked the arguments, chapter summaries and marginal notes. Two of the

---

97 Scholars are less certain about the composers involved in the final publication. Mathias Greiter was certainly involved in the 1539 publication in Strasbourg. Some identify Guillaume Franc, Huguenot from Rouen, who became a music master at Geneva in 1541 and then cantor of St. Pierre in 1543, as the primary or solo author of melodies published in 1542–1543.

98 Beza's epistle appears in a 1553 edition of the Psalter, titled *Octantetrois Pseaumes de David mis en rime Françoise*. See PIDOUX, P. (1962), 61–64.

99 The paratextual elements of the French Bible were hugely significant for shaping readers and churches scattered throughout Europe. One of the reasons that Beza was so hostile toward Castellio's translation was due to the fact that his treatise *On Heretics* was attached to his translation of the Bible. See BEZA, T., *Life of Calvin* (1564), lxvi. Beza does not mince words in his conversation about it, and he responds to Castellio in order to assist Calvin, who was at the time writing his commentary on Genesis.

100 *Nouum D.N. Iesu Christi Testamentvm* (Genevæ: Ioannem de Tovrnes, M.D.CXXVIII). See CHAMBERS, B. (1983), #1145. N1628tou.

translations presented were the result of Beza's hand and being passed down for the next generation to consult. At the same time, Beza's impact has not always been so visible.

Each Bible possesses a complex family lineage that plays a role in the formation and appearance of its parts whether one is evaluating the translation or the material culture of the Bible. Family resemblances can appear due to a shared fount, and this is what Beza's biblical scholarship provided, namely, a fount for a variety of vernacular Bible families worldwide. Beza's links to the British Isles are more well-known. For example, Beza's Latin translation (1556) and marginal notes informed William Whittingham's Geneva New Testament (1557) and then the Geneva Bible (1560).[101] Additionally, Densil Morgan's research on early modern Wales has shown that,[102] while the Prayer Book was translated directly from Thomas Cranmer's English version, Beza's Greek-Latin New Testament served as the basis for the translation of the Welsh Bible.[103] Furthermore, across the Atlantic, Beza was valued by the Pilgrims of North America. Perry Miller once declared, "If we were to measure by the number of times a writer is cited and the degrees of familiarity shown with his works, Beza exerted more influence than Calvin."[104] David Lupher's work highlights William Bradford's interest in Beza's Latin New Testament as a key source for the translation of the Geneva Bible with added notes in the margins of excerpts from Beza's smaller annotations.[105] Bradford arrived on the continent via the Mayflower, assisted in writing the Mayflower Compact, and served as governor for thirty years. Beza's reach also extended to the first Romanian edition of the New Testament, which was published in Transylvania in 1648. According to the work of Emanuel Conțac of the University of Bucharest[106] the Romanian version was based upon Theodore Beza's Greek-Latin New Testament, and the publication of this New Testament had a significant impact on the Transylvanian Reformation. Finally, the Portuguese New Testament, *O Novo Testamento*, provides another example of the influence of Beza's biblical scholarship. João Ferreira d'Almeida based his translation on Beza's Latin New Testament, and published his work in Amsterdam in 1681.[107] Again and again, Beza's biblical scholarship shows influence behind the scenes in the formation of a wide variety of vernacular translations.

---

101 PELIKAN, J. (1996), 146; KRANS, J. (2006), 197, 205n.31. See also Backus's research.
102 MORGAN, D. (2017), 71.
103 See JONES, G. (1967), 56–61. Morgan cites THOMAS, I. (1976), 151–205.
104 MILLER, P. (1954), 93.
105 See LUPHER, A.D. (2017). With gratitude to Kirk Summers for pointing this out to me.
106 See CONȚAC, E. (2017).
107 PELIKAN, J. (1996), 157. D'Almeida relied upon Beza because he did not yet know the Greek language.

A global impact is further evident in relation to Beza's translation of the Psalter into French.[108] In 1554, an Italian translation of 20 Psalms was printed by Jean Crespin and developed from there.[109] In 1556, a Pyrenees translation in Gascon (a dialect of Occitan) was translated by Pey de Garros and published at Toulouse with a dedication to Queen Jeanne of Navarre.[110] In 1566, Pieter Datheen translated Beza's Psalter into Dutch, which was adopted by several synods of the United Provinces and used until 1773. The spread of Dutch colonies led to the expansion of the Psalter into Portuguese (1703), Malay (1735) and Tamil (1755). In 1573, a German translation was completed by Ambrosius Lobwasser and published in a bi-lingual edition with the original French text and dedicated to Frederick the Elector of the Palatinate (1587). That edition then became the basis for a Polish translation by Matthias Rybinski (1605), a Spanish translation (1606), and a Hungarian version by Albert Molnar (1607) with reprints through the nineteenth century in Czech and Turkish. The ripples of Beza's work are surely too numerous to track.

5.3   Conclusion

In conclusion, the importance of Beza's biblical scholarship is not always easy to trace given that his work was focused on providing resources for the expansion of vernacular translations through his Greek-Latin New Testament. Translation may hide the originator, but the fingerprint is Beza's, and by looking at his contribution this way, the interconnections are extraordinary. Whether Beza was advancing resources relating to the original languages and manuscripts or shaping the French Bible and Psalter, the flourishing of Beza's scholarship, it appears, bore fruit that promoted a legacy with a global reach. Time spent in the work of advancing biblical scholarship was time spent for the purpose of expanding the ministry and reform of the church.

---

108 This account is based on the anonymous publication of Geneva's Bibliothèque publique et universitaire (1986).

109 This is believed to be the work of Count Massimiliano Celso Martinengo, who pastored the Italian Church in Geneva from 1552. A new translation was published in 1560, but the first complete Italian translation was published by DeTournes in Geneva in 1603 with a dedication to Queen Elizabeth in England.

110 This was translated into the language of Béarn by Arnaud de Salette a few years later in 1583 and dedicated to her son, Henri IV of France.

Chapter 6: Beza Among the Lutherans

Acts 3:21 in the Wittenberg *Catechism* (1571) and *Formula of Concord* (1580)

Theodore Beza's translation of the account of Christ's ascension in Acts 3:21 played a vital role in the Lutheran Crypto-Calvinist affair of the 1570s. When the Crypto-Calvinists adopted Beza's translation of Acts 3:21 in their 1571 *Catechism*,[1] the die was cast: Beza's version of the passage, in contrast to Martin Luther's in his 1522 *Neue Testament Deutsch*,[2] understood Christ as physically contained in the heavens in his ascension—and thus *not* present in his body in the Eucharist. This signaled to the Gnesio-Lutherans (those Lutherans who remained "true" to Martin Luther's explicit doctrinal expressions, as opposed to those who were leaning in a Genevan direction) that the professors at Wittenberg were not remaining faithful to Martin Luther's view of the Supper, namely, that a straightforward reading of the words of institution in the Gospels[3] reveals that Christ is physically present in his Supper. In response to this alarming shift, Nicholas Selnecker (1530–1592) and Martin Chemnitz (1522–1586) instigated debate with Beza to expose the Crypto-Calvinists in the Lutheran church, simultaneously drawing Beza himself into the midst of Lutheran confessionalization.

Theodore Beza is rarely considered from the Lutheran lens. Yet, Beza loomed large in the controversy and debate that ultimately resulted in one of the central documents produced for the Lutheran church: The *Formula* of Concord.[4] Beza's translation of Acts 3:21, as appropriated by certain Wittenberg theologians, set into motion events that contributed to the *Formula*'s creation in ways that heretofore have not been fully appreciated. A series of ensuing debates between Beza and Gnesio-Lutherans over the precise rendering of Acts 3:21 served as

---

1 See esp. *Catechesis continens explicationem simplicem et brevem*, 72. Also, Zacharias Ursinus in the Palatinate espoused a more Reformed view on Christ's ascension in *Catechismus, oder christlicher Underricht* (1563), 35; he later expounded on this more fully in his commentary, for which see URSINUS, Z., *The Commentary* (1852), 244.

2 We have utilized Luther's 1522 New Testament throughout this work: *Das Neue Testament Deutzsch*, 1522.

3 Matt 26:26-28; Mark 14:22-24; Luke 22:19-20; see also 1 Cor 11:23-25.

4 *Concordia: Christliche widerholete einmütige Bekentnüs nachbenanter Churfürsten* (1580). All citations of the *Formula* or other Lutheran confessional documents, unless otherwise stated, are from BC (2000).

a touchstone in the divergent doctrinal development of both parties. These discordant Christological and Eucharistic views find their fullest polemical expression in seven uncompromising published letters exchanged between Selnecker, Chemnitz and Beza in the early 1570s. Because each side was forced to clarify, defend and calcify their positions on the issues surrounding the text of Acts 3:21, issues that touched on the matter of Christ's presence in the Supper, Beza himself unwittingly became an important catalyst for Lutheran unity. The Gnesio-Lutherans deemed it crucial to distinguish their Eucharistic doctrines unequivocally from those of the Reformed to prevent a dilution of Luther's original teaching. Thus, in an episode that caught the Genevan reformer completely by surprise and exhausted much of his energy in the 1570s, an episode born from a disagreement over the translation of a single verse, Beza left a permanent mark on the confessional development of the Lutheran churches. The present contribution aims to unravel the complex story of this dispute while demonstrating how and why Beza and his interpretation of Acts 3:21 impacted the *Formula*.

6.1 The Historical Context

Before discussing Beza's place within the Lutheran debate, we must first briefly review the events preceding this controversy. Luther's understanding of the real presence of Christ in the Eucharist came under attack from theologians such as Huldrych Zwingli (1484–1531) and Kaspar Schwenckfeld (1589–1561), who denounced Luther's doctrines as contradictory, irrational and unbiblical on the grounds that the ascended Christ could not be in two (let alone manifold!) places simultaneously. Luther confronted his dissenters in his 1528 work *Vom Abendmahl Christi, Bekenntnis*, in which he vigorously defends the Real Presence.[5] Luther's argument here centers on God's omnipotence, even over the laws of nature.[6] Luther brushes aside the issue of the ascension as a red herring.[7] In October of the next year, Luther and Philipp Melanchthon (1497–1560) met with Zwingli and Johannes Oecolampadius (1482–1531) at the Marburg Colloquy in an attempt to draft a joint declaration of faith. Throughout the debate, Oecolampadius and Zwingli invoked Christ's ascension to the right hand of God to refute Luther's belief in Christ's physical presence in the Lord's

---

5 *Confession Concerning Christ's Supper* (1528), in LW 37:161–372.
6 LW 37:223.
7 LW 37:195.

Supper. Luther still held firm to a literal reading of Scripture and insisted on God's utter transcendence to explain the apparent contradiction.[8]

In the years following the Marburg Colloquy, Melanchthon increasingly vacillated on doctrinal details regarding the Lord's Supper. Melanchthon made alterations in the wording of the Eucharistic language in the original Augsburg Confession for the 1540 *Variata* (the altered Augsburg Confession), changes that confused many Lutheran pastors and theologians, but at the same time resulted in a more irenic document that John Calvin himself could sign.[9] Melanchthon's lack of clarity instead led to confusion and factions following his death in 1560. A group of professors at Wittenberg, the so-called "Philippist" party, preferred Melanchthon's broader interpretation to Luther's exclusionary view of the Supper; whereas Luther worked to distinguish between his views and the views of other Protestants, Melanchthon hoped to reconcile Lutheran and Reformed ideas about the Eucharist.[10] Among these Wittenbergers were Christoph Pezel (1539–1604) and Caspar Peucer (1525–1602), whose 1571 *Catechism* adopted a Reformed—or at least a Reformed-friendly—understanding of the Eucharist.

Due to its treatment of the Eucharist, Christology and the ascension, the 1571 *Catechism* catapulted the Wittenbergers into the confessional party's crosshairs. So controversial were the *Catechism*'s contents that it was never published in German, only Latin.[11] The Wittenbergers were first attacked because they wrote that the Lord's Supper was the "communication of the body and blood of Jesus."[12] This is significantly broader than Luther's Small Catechism, which states simply that "[The Lord's Supper] is the true body and blood of our Lord Jesus Christ, under the bread and wine, for us Christians to eat and to drink, instituted by Christ Himself."[13] Marginalia in later editions of the Wittenberg *Catechism* would note that Chemnitz and others condemned this stance as too ambiguous, but the Wittenbergers fired back that this was the explanation given in Melanchthon's *Examen ordinandorum*.[14]

A yet greater controversy hid within the pages of this catechism, namely, the treatment of the ascension in the article on the Apostles' Creed. In the section on the Apostles' Creed, the *Catechism* states that Christ is located in heaven, his body physical and circumscribable. The authors cite Acts 3:21 in Beza's version

---

8 *The Marburg Colloquy and the Marburg Articles* (1529), in LW 38:29, 32.

9 BENTE, G. (2005), 468. For the altered language in the so-called *Variata*, see *Confessio fidei exhibita invictiss. Imp. Carolo V* (1540), 9[r].

10 KOLB, R. (2012), 236.

11 DINGEL, I. (ed.) (2008), *Die Debatte um die Wittenberger Abendmahlslehre und Christologie*, 81. Hereafter abbreviated as *Die Debatte*.

12 *Wittenberger Katechismus* in *Die Debatte*, 278.

13 *Small Catechism* 1–2, "The Lord's Supper," in BC (2000).

14 *Wittenberger Katechismus* in *Die Debatte*, 278.

in defense of this stance: "it is fitting that Christ be held by heaven until the time of the restitution of all things" (*Opportet Christum coelo capi vsque ad tempora restitutionis omnium*).[15] The Wittenbergers rationalized this choice because Melanchthon himself had lectured on Colossians 3:1-2 and Christ's physical ascension into heaven, which they also reference in the *Catechism*.[16] The Wittenbergers, however, moved far beyond Melanchthon's ambiguity. This thrust Beza among the Lutherans: by borrowing a translation and hermeneutic from the most prominent living Reformed theologian, the Wittenberg Party shocked the confessional wing into immediate action.

So shocking was this nebulous language that members of the Wittenberg Party began to align themselves with conservatives who saw themselves as faithful to Luther's teaching. Jakob Andreae (1528–1590) left the Wittenbergers in 1570 for the conservative wing and eventually helped assemble the *Book of Concord*.[17] Nicholas Selnecker (1532–1592) likewise found himself at odds with the Philippists due to their stance on the Lord's Supper in the early 1570s, in part due to the influence of Martin Chemnitz.[18] Though Chemnitz was deeply troubled by the Philippist developments, he was uncomfortable publicly addressing the faults of the late Melanchthon, his old teacher and friend.[19] Others did not have these same reservations. A group of theologians at the University of Jena released a treatise titled *Warnung Vor dem vnreinen vnd Sacramentirischen Cateschismo etlicher zu Wittenberg* condemning Beza and his translation for his "false understanding of the Sacrament."[20] In a sermon published at Tübingen in 1573, Andreae accused the "new theologians at Wittenberg" of "pointing their ears in a Zwinglian direction."[21] He compares the theological drift of the Wittenberg faculty to Nestorius, Arius and Mohammed.[22] Selnecker and Chemnitz took this debate a step further, addressing Beza directly in a series of polemical treatises, which we discuss at length below.[23]

In April 1574, the electoral prince of Saxony requested a meeting to address the Wittenberg theologians suspected of harboring Calvinist leanings. The commission met in May of that year and produced the Torgau Articles.[24]

---

15 *Wittenberger Katechismus* in *Die Debatte*, 204.
16 *Wittenberger Katechismus* in *Die Debatte*, 204. For more on Melanchthon's treatment of this issue, see WENGERT, T. (2012), 209–235.
17 ANDREAE, J., *Six Sermons on the Way to Lutheran Unity* (1977), 39.
18 PREUS II (1994), 172–173.
19 PREUS II (1994), 170–171.
20 WIGAND, J. (1570), in *Die Debatte*, 347.
21 ANDREAE, J., *Six Sermons on the Way to Lutheran Unity* (1977), 108.
22 ANDREAE, J., *Six Sermons on the Way to Lutheran Unity* (1977), 118.
23 An early condemnation of Beza's influence appears in CHEMNITZ M./MÖRLIN, J., *Treuhertzige Warnung* (1571). For the text and mention of Beza, see *Die Debatte*, 300.
24 On this, see the introductory note to the *Torgauer Artikel* (1574), in *Die Debatte*, 1093.

The authors condemn Beza's understanding of the nature of the ascended and glorified Christ with relation to the Lord's Supper. They condemn Beza and his *Consorten* as childish, *schwermerisch* Sacramentarians and his teachings as blasphemy against Scripture and faith.[25] The Torgau Articles would eventually be revised into the *Formula of Concord*, in which Beza's name makes several appearances. It is intriguing that the Gnesio-Lutherans focused their ire most directly on Theodore Beza himself, instead of any of the Lutheran theologians who were utilizing his work. Because of this (perhaps misdirected) anger, Beza found himself at the center of one of the debates that would help solidify the Lutheran faith as separate and unique from the other Protestant church bodies.

6.2 Beza's Controversial Translation of Acts 3:21

In 1561 Martin Chemnitz produced a work titled *Repetitio sanae doctrinae* that set forth what became for many an authoritative expression of Lutheran doctrine on the Eucharist.[26] The work addresses such controversial matters as the ubiquity of Christ's body and the meaning of the phrase "seated at the right hand" in the creed. Even so, nowhere in its pages does Chemnitz mention Beza's translation of Acts 3:21 or recognize it as a potential problem for the Lutheran teaching on Christ's presence in the elements. The 1570 revised edition of this same work, however, indicates that in the intervening years something changed. Here Chemnitz includes several pages directly rebutting Beza's translation, calling it a "clear perversion" (though without ever mentioning Beza's name) and arguing forcefully for the validity of Luther's translation.[27] Given that the date subscribed to the work's preface indicates the year 1569, we can assume that already somewhere in the late 1560s the Philippists were beginning to appeal to Beza's translation of Acts 3:21 in theological disputes and doctrinal instruction.[28] This new trend to a strictly spiritual view of the Eucharist among some Lutherans culminated, in the early days of 1571, in the publication of the aforementioned catechism at Wittenberg that contained Reformed language, supported, in part, by Beza's translation of Acts 3:21.

---

25 *Torgauer Artikel* (1574), in *Die Debatte*, 1133–1134.
26 CHEMNITZ, M., *Repetitio sanae doctrinae de vera praesentia* (1561).
27 CHEMNITZ, M., *Fundamenta sanae doctrinae de vera et substantiali praesentia* (1570), Aaaa3^v-4^v. This falls within the broader discussion of Christ's ascension into Heaven, his sitting at the right hand of the Father, and his return for the Last Judgment. See also J.A.O. Preus II's translation of the 1590 edition of this work: CHEMNITZ, M., *The Lord's Supper* (1979), 217–218.
28 See the discussion in KOLB, R. (2012); also, MAGER, I. (1993), 130–134.

Censures of this new doctrinal standard came from many quarters, but most notably from Nicholas Selnecker at Leipzig, who was otherwise irenic toward the Reformed and hoping for unity among the German churches.[29] He took it upon himself to engage with the Wittenbergers over the major issues surrounding Christ's presence in the Supper and sparred with them in several disputations both before and after the publication, with both sides publishing their arguments in a series of tracts in Latin and German.[30] Even then, Selnecker merely saw himself as advising his Lutheran brethren of an error. When Beza accused Selnecker of defecting from his fellow Wittenbergers, Selnecker insisted that he was on good terms with the professors at Wittenberg: he blamed Beza himself for duping a small group of his friends to insert the controversial translation of Acts 3:21 to alter Lutheran doctrine and identified Beza's friend Esrom Rüdinger (1523–1590) as the sole author of the *Disputatio grammatica*, where the Acts interpretation was defended.[31] At the same time, this conflict motivated Selnecker to consult the source of the interpretation, that is, Beza's annotated translations of the New Testament, to understand why his Latin version differed from that of Luther's German.[32] He explicitly says this in the introductory remarks of his *De verbis Actorum 3*: he "has seen some writings scattered about" that rely on Beza's "impious" translation of Acts 3:21 as a proof text.[33] This treatise is meant as a refutation of Beza's "version" and "gloss."[34] Martin Chemnitz joined him in these efforts with new works

---

29 See esp. the claims in SELNECKER, N., *Ad D. Theodori Bezae calumnias* (1571a), A3ᵛ: "Laboravimus hactenus his in Ecclesiis omnibus viribus."

30 In 1570, Selnecker published *Exegema collationis*, from which it is evident that the interpretation of Acts 3:21 had not yet come to the fore. When the Wittenbergers responded with RÜDINGER, E., *Disputatio grammatical* (1571) the next year, the correct translation of Acts 3:21 had become a major point of contention. See also [THEOLOGICAL FACULTY OF WITTENBERG], *Christliche Fragstück* (1571).

31 SELNECKER, N., *Responsio vera et Christiana* (1572), A8ʳ, B1ᵛ, B2ʳ, G4ᵛ. On Rüdinger's interest in Beza's "explications" of the New Testament, see Esrom Rüdinger to Beza, 17 October [1566], in CB 11:341–343.

32 SELENECKER N., *Ad calumnias* (1571a), 34–35, accuses Beza of twisting the meaning of an earlier statement by himself that seems to suggest he has been upset about Beza's translation since it appeared. Selnecker says explicitly that he only now (in 1570 or 1571) consulted Beza's translation, even though he knew the doctrine itself was disturbing the Church. Even at this late date, Selnecker seems to have relied on Beza's 1556 first edition (although a second edition of 1565 was also in print at this point). Beza himself identifies this as the edition that Selnecker consulted in his *Ad Nicolai Selnecceri et Theologorum Ienensium calumnias* (1571), 17.

33 SELNECKER, N., *De verbis Actorum 3* (1571b), A1ᵛ-A2ʳ. For a modern edition of the text, see *Die Debatte*, 304–317.

34 SELNECKER, N., *De verbis Actorum 3* (1571b), A6ᵛ; but note in his *Exegema collationis* (1570) he does not mention Acts 3:21, though he addresses various issues surrounding the doctrines of the communication of idioms and Christ's human nature.

expanding on the arguments already begun in the *Fundamenta* (1570) and naming Beza directly.[35] It was in the ensuing debate with Beza himself that the Lutheran and Reformed positions on Acts 3:21 realized their fullest expression.

Before we can understand the Lutheran stance, we should first review the basic position that Beza sets forth in his annotations. Beza was aiming to remove the ambiguity exhibited by previous Latin translations of the first part of verse 21, renderings that reflected an inherent vagueness in the Greek text: ὃν δεῖ οὐρανὸν μὲν δέξασθαι ἄχρι χρόνων ἀποκαταστάσεως πάντων. The text presents a puzzle: one could take the initial relative pronoun, with its antecedant *Jesus Christ* in the previous verse, to be the subject of the verb, or, equally, οὐρανὸν (Heaven) could serve as the subject; in either case the remaining noun serves as the object. In other words, either Christ is acting upon Heaven, or Heaven is acting upon Christ; the Greek text is not clear. The Vulgate avoided controversy by retaining the ambiguity of the original: "quem oportet quidem caelum suscipere usque in tempora restitutionis omnium."[36] Erasmus follows the Vulgate in his own translation, only substituting *accipere* for *suscipere*.[37] But Luther was not so cautious. In his German translation, he made the definitive choice for his readers, one that supported his understanding of the real presence of Christ's body in the elements of the Supper. He makes Peter proclaim that Jesus Christ triumphantly accepted or took possession of Heaven, implying that in doing so he was coming into the full extent of his majesty, honor and power.[38] Luther saw no indication in Peter's words that Heaven was accepting, holding or possessing the physical body of Christ. Both Selnecker and Chemnitz, as will be seen shortly, repeatedly turn to this *exaltation* or *genus maiesticum* argument.

While Luther's translation is grammatically possible, Beza saw the matter differently. In both the 1556 and 1565 editions of his *Annotationes*, he turned the active verb of the Greek into a passive in Latin, making *Heaven* the agent of the verb: "quem oportet quidem caelo capi usque ad tempora restitutionis

35 CHEMNITZ, M., *Bedencken der Theologen zu Braunschweigk* (1571a) is also leveled against the Wittenberg *Catechism*; Bii^{r-v} contains the discussion of Acts 3:21 and names Beza directly. See also CHEMNITZ, M., *Widerholte Christliche Gemeine Confession* (1571b), where he again references Acts 3:21 beginning on Pi^{r}-ii^{r}.

36 Beza's various editions of the *Annotationes* (1556, 1565, 1582, 1589, 1598) report *recipere* for *suscipere*. Selnecker, in his *De verbis Actorum 3* (1571b), A2^{v}, knows the reading *suscipere*, but places *recipere* in parenthesis after it.

37 ERASMUS, D., *Novum Testamentum omne* (1522), 1:251.

38 SELNECKER, N., *De verbis Actorum 3* (1571b), A3r, reports Luther's translation of the passage in question as "welcher mus den himel einnemen bis auff die zeit da erwiderbracht werde alles." The relative pronoun representing Christ is in the nominative, while *Heaven* is in the accusative, receiving the action of the verb *einnemen*.

omnium."[39] Thus, Beza has Peter say that Christ was received and held *by* Heaven, meaning that Christ's physical body ascended and remains in a fixed locale. His annotation on the verb *capi* draws out more fully the implications of his translation (underlining shows the additions of the 1565 ed.):

> That is, *contained by Heaven*; to explain: among the Hebrews (as we said elsewhere) often the consequence is understood from the use of a single word, as when ἐξελθεῖν stands for *venire*, and many similar examples which we have noted at their own places. We used the passive voice instead of the active to avoid ambiguity. It is valuable that there exist in the Church of God this clear testimony against those who, instead of our having to ascend by faith into the heavens to have union with our head, not only believe that we must evoke the body of Christ from heaven as some sort of Jupiter Elicius, but also with great stubbornness defend it; or they think he still dwells on earth.[40]

Beza alludes to Jupiter Elicius, the Jupiter called down by the ancient Roman king Numa with a magic spell in order to receive revelations.[41] He sees the Lutheran view of the Real Presence in the Supper as a superstitious manipulation of a weak Christ, who is treated like the object of a magic incantation. Beza creates a stark duality: the Lutheran Real Presence is pagan, while its rejection is Christian. Beza here follows Calvin in stressing the spiritual nature of the Supper. When celebrants of the Supper partake of the consecrated bread and wine, which serve as signs of a spiritual reality, but without undergoing transformation, the Holy Spirit by his power nourishes believers with the body and blood of the ascended Christ, thereby infusing them with life and strengthening their mystical union with him. The Greek words may be ambiguous, Beza admits in later editions of his annotations, but the reality of what happens is not: "Clearly, Peter is talking about the physical flesh of Christ and his physical ascension from the physical earth into the physical heavens."[42]

6.3 Selnecker's Objections to Beza's Translation

For the Gnesio-Lutheran case in support of the conservative view, we will examine Selnecker's direct rebuttal of Beza's translation and *allegatio* (a reference to Beza's annotations) in the *De verbis Actorum 3* (mentioned above), collating its

---

39 There is some question whether Beza was aware that Castellio had come to the same translation a few years before him. See the discussion of the matter at BEZA, T., *Modesta et Christiana defensio* (1572), 40–41.
40 BEZA, T., *Iesu Christi D.N. Novum testamentum* (1565b), 2:18.
41 See OVID, *Fasti*, 3:275–328.
42 BEZA, T., *Testamentum Novum* (1589c), 1:444.

arguments against Selnecker's series of rebuttals to Beza's responses. The fifteen pages of the *De verbis Actorum 3* contain the nucleus of the argument that both singles out Beza's version and interpretation of Acts 3:21 as a major flash-point of contention, dangerous to the Church for its implications, and models for Gnesio-Lutherans how they can organize their material. All subsequent arguments from Gnesio-Lutherans are developed within these broad parameters, though often with much more precision and vigor, and with the occasional innovation. These are the same arguments too that color the assertions made in the *Formula* of 1580, and as such reveal much of the thinking behind them.

Selnecker begins the *De verbis Actorum 3* by citing the Greek text of Peter's sermon there and citing three translations, all of which follow the original closely in its ambiguity: the Vulgate (or "Jerome," as he calls it), Erasmus and the Syriac. As a kind of trump card, he ends with Luther's German rendering, a translation that he calls "the most skillful and especially clear."[43] From the unanimity of these translations he draws the following conclusion:

> Therefore, these words (*quem oportet coelum accipere*) have never been
> understood in the true Church to be about anything except the exaltation
> of the human nature in Christ, or his sitting at the right hand of the Father,
> as learned antiquity and the consensus of all sound-minded people attest.
> This *sitting* does not reference a locating or fixing at a specific place in
> heaven or the heavens, rather, it indicates that all authority is being given to
> the glorified and exalted human nature in Christ.[44]

Selnecker's points here do not lack a degree of irony. His primary refutation is that a consensus on Acts 3:21 exists that prohibits any innovation on the part of Beza[45]—an argument once used against Luther's entire reforming program by Eck, Cajetan and other Roman Catholic theologians. All the reformers faced this charge, and Beza himself tried to turn the argument of novelty back on Selnecker and Luther.[46] The reference to the Syriac translation, both in Selnecker and Beza, underscores the recent weight and authority attributed to it in Protestant circles.[47] Scholars were treating it as the oldest of the translations, one based on manuscripts no longer extant and one closely in tune with the language

---

43 SELNECKER, N., *De verbis Actorum 3* (1571b), A2^v-A3^r. Selnecker has an almost *ipse dixit* reverence for Luther, something that Beza picks up on for his polemics against him; see SELNECKER, N., *Ad Theod. Bezae tergiversationem* (1573), C5^r and F3^{r-v}, where Selnecker complains that Beza calls him an "ape of Luther."

44 SELNECKER, N., *De verbis Actorum 3* (1571b), A3^r.

45 See also SELNECKER, N., *Responsio vera et Christiana* (1572), G4^r and M8^r.

46 Selnecker mentions Beza's ridiculing at SELNECKER, N., *Ad D. Theodori Bezae calumnias* (1571a), C1^r.

47 BEZA, T., *Modesta et Christiana defensio* (1572), 67, calls it "very learned and very old."

and thinking of the Scriptures. If support could be mounted from the Syriac translation, an argument would have secure footing. Selnecker says in his *Ad calumnias* that he would not object to Beza's *capi* if by it he meant the same as the Syriac *kibel* and the *accipere* or *recipere* of the other Latin translations, that is, *to receive* or *to accept*.[48] In his view, Peter is saying that Christ received his dominion over all things when he ascended into the heavens. The fact that the Syriac has its verb in the plural, a clear indication that the heavens are doing the act of receiving, only shows that the heavens are joyfully receiving Christ as their Lord, not containing or holding him.[49]

Selnecker also introduces the *sessio-qua-exaltatio* argument, namely, the assertion that God seated his Son at his right hand only in the sense that he glorified and exalted him.[50] As suggested above, this will become a central argument in his and his colleagues' works, though they find themselves applying figurative language in this instance but not allowing for it in the words of the Supper's institution. Selnecker's immediate aim is to underscore that a *consensus* on Acts 3:21 exists and marshal several church fathers to support his strictly figurative reading of what it means for Christ to sit at the right hand of God. Augustine, he says, rejects the notion that this is a definite place for a body to go to physically. For him, the phrase indicates a transformation of Christ's human nature to equal status with the majesty, glory and honor of God. He finds similar statements in John of Damascus, Chrysostom and others. Hebrews 7:26 (*excelsior coelis factus est*) is adduced as further proof that no place contains the body of Christ: the passage must refer to the exaltation of Christ's crucified and buried body, Selnecker observes, because his coeternal divinity was already exalted.[51]

Selnecker agrees that Christ corporally left the earth, but for him that does not mean it is contained or held locally by the heavens. Christ, as God, can be where he wishes and he can fulfill the promise that he made in the words of the Supper's institution. This is a constant refrain in Selnecker. He writes,

> It does not follow that Christ ascended with his body into the Heavens, is contained there in a fixed place, as if in a vessel, or kept and detained in a cell, in such a way that he is not able to be bodily elsewhere in his own kind of celestial way, a way that is unknown to us, hyperphysical, preternatural, and paradoxical to physical properties (for all articles of faith are paradoxical to human reason, Sapient 5, Matt 11, 1 Cor 1), where he wishes it to be, clearly,

---

48 SELNECKER, N., *Ad D. Theodori Bezae calumnias* (1571a), A7ᵛ.

49 SELNECKER, N., *Ad D. Theodori Bezae calumnias* (1571a), B3ᵛ.

50 For Selnecker's views on what it means for Christ to have a glorified body, see SELNECKER, N., *Ad Theod. Bezae tergiversationem* (1573), C3v.

51 SELNECKER, N., *De verbis Actorum 3* (1571b), A3ᵛ-A4ʳ.

as in the Table, in which he said and promised that he would be present bodily with his own flesh and blood in the words of his last Testament.[52]

The phrase *where he wishes to be* is key. Beza and the so-called Sacramentarians were fond of accusing the Gnesio-Lutherans, and especially Johannes Brenz, of ubiquitarianism, the idea that Christ's body is everywhere in everything, even stones and grass. Selnecker considers this a monstrous and abusive exaggeration, defaming the memory of the pious Johannes Brenz (1499–1570) and creating a distraction from the real arguments.[53] Christ's ascension into the heavens, he goes on to say, implies the inscrutable and immeasurable exaltation of Christ's human nature, while the phrase *sitting at the Father's right hand* indicates the assumption of all power and dominion. If he is so exalted, who can deny that he can be in two places at once? Christ is God, and God holds all physical rules in his hands; his power surpasses human limitations.[54] It would be futile, therefore, to try to explain the exact nature of the presence of Christ's body and blood in the elements; instead, we simply believe the words of Christ without recourse to reason.[55] Somehow inexplicable to mere human beings, we can eat the bread, with Christ present there, without eating his flesh;[56] Christ can be bodily in the elements without ceasing to be truly human in his essential properties. If God so wills this paradox, then it will happen. Beza and his "sacramentarian" followers fail at this very point, Selnecker argues: as μυστηριομαχοί, that is, *fighters against mysteries*, their doctrines are dangerous, full of hidden poison, even blasphemous.[57] "If you continue," he exclaims with patent frustration in his third apology, "to counter us with fancies of physics and philosophy, with

52 SELNECKER, N., *Ad D. Theodori Bezae calumnias* (1571a), C3ʳ; see also SELNECKER, N., *Responsio vera et Christiana* (1572), B8ᵛ, D1ʳ, H5ʳ, and M1ᵛ.
53 SELNECKER, N., *Ad D. Theodori Bezae calumnias* (1571a), C6ᵛ-C7ʳ; SELNECKER, N., *Responsio vera et Christiana* (1572), D4ᵛ.
54 SELNECKER, N., *Ad D. Theodori Bezae calumnias* (1571a), C3ʳ-C4ʳ; SELNECKER, N., *Responsio vera et Christiana* (1572), D3ʳ⁻ᵛ; SELNECKER, N., *Ad Theod. Bezae tergiversationem* (1573), B5ᵛ-6ᵛ.
55 SELNECKER , N., *Responsio vera et Christiana* (1572), D5ʳ⁻ᵛ.
56 Selnecker states: "We flee, curse, and detest the Capernaitic and carnal imaginations concerning eating, digesting, and absorbing into the body. We trust Christ, who said, 'Take, eat, this is my body which is given for you.' We rest upon these words, and are satisfied with them. We check all absurdities, nor do we dispute further. He himself said it, he himself did it. The Lord's Word is power, the Lord's Word surpasses all others. And the body of Christ is not diminished, nor assimilated through digestion, but is a body and remains a body, but is taken in us according to the words of the Testament, in a way that the testifier himself, Jesus Christ, knows." SELNECKER, N., *Responsio vera et Christiana* (1572), F3ʳ.
57 SELNECKER, N., *Ad D.Theodori Bezae calumnias* (1571a), B8ʳ; SELNECKER, N., *Ad Theod. Bezae tergiversationem* (1573), B7ʳ⁻ᵛ and D3ʳ⁻ᵛ, where Selnecker says he does not want to quibble over the prepositions *in*, *sub* and *cum* in regard to such a great mystery.

Aristotelian principles and the like, drawn from the pits of human reason, which you place above the words of Christ, then go away and leave alone our churches, hearing this one axiom of Christ: 'Heaven and earth will pass away, but my words will never perish.'"[58]

Selnecker anticipates an objection that faults him for confusing properties of the divine and human natures.[59] He insists in his third apology: "We do not deny the veracity of Christ's body, and, speaking in strictly physical terms, that it has the characteristics and essential properties of a real body."[60] Some point out, however, that when Christ's body was on earth, it was not in heaven, since the flesh is not everywhere as the divine nature is; otherwise, what does it mean for Christ to come again, if he is with us in body already on earth as in his divinity? Selnecker agrees that the body retains its essential properties, but admits an exception: the body of Christ has some *hyperphysical* qualities already alluded to in Scripture.[61] In other words, the Scriptures record Christ performing miracles with his body (walking on water, resurrecting from a sealed tomb, walking through walls in the presence of his disciples, etc.) that show his body is not bound by normal physical laws.[62] The divinity, in a sense, has endowed the human side of Christ with powers that surpass human understanding, but "without violation of the human nature and its properties."[63] In its essential nature, Christ's humanity is human and limited, and "nothing more must be attributed to it than what and how much physical realities admit;"[64] but inasmuch as he is conjoined with the divine, he is more. God can grant that power to anyone, and indeed does when the apostles heal the sick and so on. Luther made this same claim years before at the Colloquy of Marburg (1529) with his usual forceful rhetoric. At issue here, really, is whether Christ's body is bound by place, given that it is conjoined with divinity, or whether we want to limit God in any way. Thus, to Zwingli's assertion that Christ's body is finite and therefore must be in a certain place, Luther retorts:

---

58 SELNECKER, N., *Ad Theod. Bezae tergiversationem* (1573), B4^r-B5^v.

59 SELNECKER, N., *De verbis Actorum 3* (1571b), A5^{r-v}.

60 SELNECKER, N., *Ad Theod. Bezae tergiversationem* (1573), C4^r.

61 SELNECKER, N., *De verbis Actorum 3* (1571b), A5^v.

62 The phrase Selnecker uses at *Ad D. Theodori Bezae calumnias* (1571a), C4^r to describe Christ's miracle-working power is "praeter rerum seriem et contra corporis physici proprietates." In SELNECKER, N., *Responsio vera et Christiana* (1572), E5^v, he distinguishes between the Lutheran view of miracles (God can do whatever he wants whenever he wants) to the "Calvinist" view that miracles are a special dispensation by God to spread the gospel in its initial stages. At SELNECKER, N., *Ad Theod. Bezae tergiversationem* (1573), C6^v-7^r, Selnecker asks if Beza admits that Christ's body accomplished many feats that are inexplicable, why does he not do so in reference to the Supper?

63 SELNECKER, N., *Ad D. Theodori Bezae calumnias* (1571a), C4^r.

64 SELNECKER, N., *Ad Theod. Bezae tergiversationem* (1573), A8^v.

I have said that it can be in a place and not in a place. God can even arrange
my body so that it is not in a place. In this text there is no room for mathematics.
"Place" is a mathematical consideration. The sophists have held that one body
can be in many places; he does not want to deny this. Who am I to measure the
power of God? The driving force of the universe is not in one place.[65]

Luther, therefore, maintains that accepting Christ's words of institution literally
as spoken is a matter of faith and not subject to scientific scrutiny. Along these
lines, Selnecker cites with approval the catechism used at Meißen and its rejection of the reading of any figurative language in the institution of the Supper.[66]
We have no reason to suspect that Christ expressed himself in anything but
simple and unembellished terms in such a solemn and important moment.

Selnecker believes that the aggregate of these arguments show conclusively
that Beza's "perversion" is diametrically opposed to the analogy of faith and
rightly rejected.[67] None of the Fathers, he exclaims in the *Ad calumnias*, dared
to assert with Beza, Peter Martyr Vermigli (1499–1562) and their *suffraganei*
that Christ's body is limited physically and cannot be present anywhere now
but in the Heavens, even if he so wishes.[68] He concludes his *De verbis Actorum*
3 with five final points that he believes will please anyone who loves the truth:
1) Beza pretends that the text is ambiguous then changes the natural word
   order to make his translation work out;
2) The majesty and pure truth of Scriptures does not allow for such clever
   linguistic tricks, as if we are reading the leaves recording the Sibyl's responses
   at Delphi;
3) Beza converts an active verb to a passive one merely to support a precon-
   ceived doctrine that has no parallel in the Scriptures: Christ's human nature
   is glorified, not contained;
4) No person of sound mind accepts this translation, not even the Zurichers;
5) The sole purpose of this novel translation is to undermine Lutheran doctrines of the Table.[69]

In short, Selnecker's rebuttal of Beza's translation relies on the authority of
key theologians, the consensus of translations, syntactical arguments, proof
texts, the analogy of faith and the doctrine of the communication of idioms.
He criticizes Beza for "having a philosophical and restless brain," relying too

---

65 *Marburg Colloquy* in LW 38:32.
66 SELNECKER, N., *De verbis Actorum 3* (1571b), A6[v].
67 SELNECKER, N., *De verbis Actorum 3* (1571b), A6[v].
68 SELNECKER, N., *De D. Theodori Bezae calumnias* (1571a), D2[r]. He mentions Vermigli again
    at SELNECKER, N., *Responsio vera et Christiana* (1572), D2[r].
69 SELNECKER, N., *De verbis Actorum 3* (1571b), A7[r-v].

much on science and refusing to "shut the eyes of reason."[70] Christ's truth is more powerful than reason.[71] "Basing our argument on the Word of God," he concludes in the *Ad calumnias*, "we are of the view that Christ can be bodily present wherever, however, and whenever he wishes, because all things are possible for God, as Augustine put it, and he can do anything he pleases with his body and yet it remains a body."[72]

Selnecker's last response to Beza repeats the same arguments as in the *De verbis Actorum 3* and the two subsequent responses to Beza. A consistent argument runs throughout all the treatises. Here, however, one can feel a heightened sense of urgency amid the emotional currents and intense invective. Selnecker describes Beza as the "most impudent antistes of the sacramentarians, not afraid to spew forth the most disgusting blasphemies."[73] Selnecker appeals to the magistrates and princes to intervene, because, in his view, Beza almost singlehandedly is sowing discord among the churches of Germany. While not calling for violence or cruelty, he asks his princes as "guardians of the truth" to do their duty and check this dissemination of the sacramentarian madness across the region.[74] Among the "blasphemies" of Beza that especially irk Selnecker is one to which we have not given much attention yet but which must have seemed to him especially divisive: Beza charges that "the oral eating of the true body of Christ in the Table is cannibalism and a fiction of the Devil." Beza found numerous clever epithets to drive this point home effectively: man-eating Cyclopes, Thyestes, God-devourers and so forth.[75] Selnecker questions how Beza can paint such an image of fellow Christians. However baffling the mystery, he says, none of the early church fathers deny the real eating and drinking of Christ's flesh and blood. Selnecker compares Beza to pagans and followers of Mohammed who charge Christians with "eating their God and devouring the body and blood of him" and setting tables of human flesh. Selnecker urges Beza to cease the name-calling and to trust the words of Christ in the institution. Christ, he says, is in the heavens both in a physical way, because his body is real, and in a hyperphysical way, seated at the right hand of the Father and possessing all power, though we cannot comprehend how. We cannot name

---

70 SELNECKER, N., *Responsio vera et Christiana* (1572), I7^r-I8^r, L3^v.

71 SELNECKER, N., *Ad Theod. Bezae tergiversationem* (1573), D5^r.

72 SELNECKER, N., *Ad Theodori Bezae calumnias* (1571a), D3^r.

73 SELNECKER, N., *Ad Theod. Bezae tergiversationem* (1573), A4^r.

74 SELNECKER, N., *Ad Theod. Bezae tergiversationem* (1573), A3^r. Beza felt no shame about the term "sacramentarian;" at BEZA, T., *Modesta et Christiana defensio* (1572), 38 he writes, "You adorn us with that beautiful name *sacramentarians*."

75 SELNECKER, N., *Ad Theod. Bezae tergiversationem* (1573), D2^{r-v} and F1^v.

the place where Christ is, because Scripture only tells us that he went to the heavens to sit at the right hand of the Father.[76]

6.4   Beza's Responses to Selnecker's Objections

Beza held all of Selnecker's objections in low regard. In 1574, he writes to Lorenz Dürnhoffer the following:

> I finally put my hands on Selnecker's response, which is, unless I am mistaken, the most inept of all. I hear also that a certain other person published something against me, but whose author is Chemnitz, a work which I have not yet been able to see. And, to be sure, I think we make a mistake in some way when we waste time refuting this nonsense that has been conclusively disproved a hundred thousand times. I hope that in the future their efforts against men of exceptional learning will turn out to be an embarrassment for themselves and they will seek to learn from those who otherwise would have never thought to enquire into these matters. May the Lord be present for his own and break off the attacks of the wicked.[77]

When Beza says "most inept of all" here in reference to Selnecker's response, he means that this latest treatise of Selnecker, namely, the 1573 *Ad Theod. Bezae tergiversationem*, defends the Gnesio-Lutheran case less convincingly than even the previous ones.[78] Beza has obviously tired of the repetitive nature of the arguments at this point; he tells Dürnhoffer that he considers this endless exchange to be fruitless. He had already responded to Selnecker's 1571 *De verbis Actorum 3* with the *Ad calumnias brevis et necessaria responsio* later the same year. When Selnecker responded to this, Beza followed up again with his *Modesta et Christiana defensio* in 1572. Yet another retort by Selnecker, also in 1572, led Beza to publish the *Apologia tertia* in 1573. One imagines that if Beza responded to the latest volley from Selnecker, he would set the stage for still more exchanges. He remained silent this time, at least until 1577 when the *Formula of Concord* was created.

Beza really had nothing left to say anyway. Throughout the series of treatises, he defends his original notes on Acts 3:21 simply by expanding on them and offering additional proofs. Furthermore, he attempts to dismantle any and all objections raised by Selnecker, sprinkling rhetorically-charged invective

---

76 SELNECKER, N., *Ad Theod. Bezae tergiversationem* (1573), G3ᵛ.

77 Beza to Dürnhoffer, 14 May 1574, in CB 15:92–93.

78 This is significant, because in his second treatise, *Modesta et Christiana defensio* (1572), 47–48, Beza instructs Selnecker on how to form arguments; later in the same treatise (p. 60) he calls him "not at all refined or sharp."

throughout to discredit his opponent's learning. The arguments themselves can be reduced to a few key points, which, for the sake of space, we will sketch out here briefly by drawing upon all the works.

Beza organizes his response to Selnecker's criticisms around the latter's charge that his translation of Acts 3:21 (*quem oportet coelo capi*) is both *false* and *impious*. The first charge looks to the translation itself; Selnecker thinks that Beza has failed to understand the syntax and the meaning of the words. In short, the Gnesio-Lutherans reject Beza's use of *capi* to translate the Greek δέξασθαι (though both sides agree that Paul used it as an equivalent of δέχεσθαι). Not only do they find it repulsive to translate an active verb with a passive one, and, more importantly, thereby to make Christ the recipient of the action, they reject *capi* as an equivalent rendering.[79] The latter charge of impiety has to do with the doctrinal implications of the translation. How should we comprehend Christ's bodily ascension vis-à-vis the assertions found elsewhere in the New Testament that he is sitting at the right hand of the Father? What does it mean for Christ to have a glorified body? And, how does his ascension fit with his promise that he will be present in body and blood during the Eucharist?

Beza's grammatical refutation is quite linguistically technical and need not be rehashed here in all its details. A few points do stand out, however. Beza argues that the word δέχεσθαι corresponds most closely to the Latin *recipere*, as the Old Latin version has it, but less so with *accipere*, as Erasmus and the Gnesio-Lutherans (by following Luther's choice of *einnemen*) have it.[80] The latter, he says, best translates the Greek word λαμβάνειν. But *recipere* (to receive) never means *accipere* (to accept) even if sometimes *accipere* can stand for *recipere*: one can "accept letters" or "accept a guest into one's home." Yet, Beza asks, what would be indicated by the phrase, "it is necessary that Christ accept Heaven *until* (ἄχρι) the restoration of all things"?[81] How does the momentary act of accepting (or even receiving) fit with the future restoration? And if the reception of Heaven equates with the sitting at the right hand of the Father, is this only consummated when all things are restored and Christ comes again? It is true, he says, that sometimes the phrase *until* or *up to* does not imply the end of what preceded it. He offers two examples: Joseph is said not to have known Mary *until* she gave birth, and Christ promises to be with us *up to* the end of the age. In neither case is it suggested that the former state does not continue after

---

79 It rankled Beza that the Gnesio-Lutherans worried about the active-passive issue, or that they disputed him about the precise meaning of the Greek verb; see BEZA, T., *Modesta et Christiana defensio*, (1572), 48–49; BEZA, T., *Apologia tertia* (1573a), 4ᵛ-6ʳ.

80 BEZA, T., *Apologia tertia* (1573a), 5v; Beza also argues that δέχεσθαι stands for χωρεῖν, if one has in view the consequence of receiving along with the action of receiving.

81 Beza saw the ἄχρι argument as decisively supporting his interpretation; on this see BEZA, T., *Modesta et Christiana defensio* (1572), 52; BEZA, T., *Apologia tertia* (1573a), 5ʳ.

the goal is reached. But in this case, Beza continues, clearly Peter is saying that Christ's dwelling in Heaven will not be ended, but interrupted by his descent back to earth, just as the angel told the disciples at the ascension.

These facts lead Beza to set aside those words and to choose instead the Latin word *capere*, which translates the basic sense of δέχεσθαι, *to receive*, together with its extended sense, *to hold* or *to contain*. This phenomenon, whereby the consequence is understood from the antecedent action (in this case, in order to hold a thing one must first receive or admit it) is common in the Hebrew language (Peter would have used a form of *kib(b)el* in his native tongue, he argues, as the Syriac version shows) and is best reflected in Greek by δέχεσθαι and in Latin with *capere*.[82] Among the many proof texts he provides, one is particularly strong: Plato, while discussing the erection of tombs at *Laws* 12, employs the word δέχεσθαι, a passage which Cicero in his *De legibus* translates as follows: "Nor for a larger block of stone to be erected or placed on the grave than that needed to contain (*capi*) the inscription praising the dead." Beza also can point to Cicero's statement at Philippics 2:114 that "they have obtained the kind of glory which heaven scarcely seems capable of containing (*caelo capi*)." Thus, Beza concludes: "From all these examples, I wish there to be one outcome, that my translation of the word δέχεσθαι is not false, whether the force of the word or the use of the Hebrew, Greek, or Latin language is in view, and that I was right to change the translation of others."

Next, Beza faces the objections that he turned the active of the Greek into a passive. Beza scoffs at the attempts of his detractors to suggest that he does not know the sentence is active. "Who imposed this law on translators," he exclaims, "so that it is not allowed to turn something written in the active into a passive?"[83] We noted above that he eventually ended any debate about the matter by turning to the active in his 1582 edition of the New Testament, while at the same time making it clear that the Heavens themselves were engaged in the action of the verb. Beza sees this as a distraction from the real issue, however. He challenges Selnecker: "Come now, of the writers of antiquity, no, even from the writers of recent memory who came before Luther, let him show one who interprets these words to mean Christ took possession of Heaven instead of that Christ according to his flesh was received into Heaven and there, though enjoying the highest glory, is contained in a space that is suitable to a spiritual but indeed true and natural body."[84] Beza will spend most of his treatises attempting to prove that he has history on his side in this interpretation.

---

82 Cf. BEZA, T., *Modesta et Christiana defensio* (1572), 61–62.
83 BEZA, T., *Ad Nicolai Selnecceri et Theologorum Ienensium calumnias* (1571), 12.
84 BEZA, T., *Ad Nicolai Selnecceri et Theologorum Ienensium calumnias* (1571), 13–14.

Both Selnecker and Beza appeal to the Syriac rendering of this passage as a kind of trump card in favor of their own cases. This is understandable. The reformers held the Syriac version to be the oldest and closest to the original language used by the apostles.[85] Selnecker first mentions the Syriac translation in the *De verbis*,[86] but Beza corrects what he deems to be his misunderstanding of the original and Tremellius' translation of it, which, he says, did not anticipate the Lutheran reading and so was not precise enough. He is confirmed in this in later years by the Tremellius-Junius edition of the Bible, which includes the Latin translation of the Syriac in columns next to that of Beza. There, to Tremellius' translation of Acts 3:21, "Quem oportet caelos excipere," Junius adds this note in support of the Reformed position: "The Syriac has the unambigious rendering, *quem oportet caeli ut capiant*," that is, "whom it is necessary that the Heavens hold." His use of *capiant* is a recognition of Beza's arguments that *excipere* does not fully reflect the meaning of the Greek verb.

To address the charge of "impiety" that Selnecker leveled against him, Beza takes up the questions of the nature of Christ's ascension, the precise import of the phrase *sitting at the right hand of the Father*, the communication of idioms in the hypostatic union and the glorification of Christ's body. He deals one by one with the citations from the church fathers that Selnecker marshaled to bolster his argument.[87] Mostly, he rejects Selnecker's contention in each case that the passage cited precludes Christ's body, albeit exalted and glorified, from being contained in a specific place.[88] Moreover, he turns Selnecker's own words from the *Propositiones* (1570) against him, demonstrating that Selnecker accepts traditional doctrines that belie his own arguments. He points to Proposition XXXI, for example, where the following assertion is made:

> Proper to the divine nature alone are omnipotence, eternity, infinity, and omnipresence; proper to the human nature are its beginning in time, finiteness,

---

85 See, e.g., his comments at BEZA, T., *Ad Nicolai Selnecceri et Theologorum Ienensium calumnias* (1571), 22.

86 See SELNECKER, N., *De verbis Actorum 3* (1571b), A2ᵛ-3ʳ; also, SELNECKER, N., *Ad Theod. Bezae tergiversationem* (1573), C2ᵛ.

87 Cf. Beza's assertion about this at BEZA, T., *Modesta et Christiana defensio* (1572), 43: "But I, responding to you and citing that passage of Vigilius, in which expressly he testifies that the flesh, because it is now contained in Heaven and in a place, is by no means on the earth; this is the catholic faith which the apostles handed down, the martyrs confirmed, and the faithful everywhere now guard. I said what I still say, that they cannot be considered orthodox or martyrs or faithful pastors who deny that the flesh of Christ is not received into Heaven, that is, in such a way contained and held there that it is nowhere in the earth, since it is in the Heavens."

88 For example, Beza refutes Selnecker's citation from Chrysostom in this way at BEZA, T., *Ad Nicolai Selnecceri et Theologorum Ienensium calumnias* (1571), 31–32, 63–64.

and circumscription. Seeing that these are essential properties of human nature, they are never cast away. But there are other things in the human nature which the *Logos* took upon himself, which are rightly attributed to the body not yet glorified, such as hunger, thirst, injury, death, and other qualities of human weakness; these have ceased to exist after glorification. Still, human nature is not lost, and it is not according to itself made infinite or omnipotent, nor are the idioms of the divine nature poured out or transferred into it.[89]

While it is true that Selnecker only contributed to the book, Beza observes that his name is printed on the title page.[90] "If you really feel this way," Beza asks him pointedly, "How do you reconcile these statements with what you wrote against me? Have you become a new man?"[91]

6.5 From Chemnitz's Letter to the *Formula*

Martin Chemnitz—the "Second Martin" of the Lutherans—was the conflict-averse but staunchly conservative superintendent of Braunschweig.[92] In 1573, the Acts 3:21 issue had grown so controversial that he jumped into the fray. As mentioned above, Chemnitz alluded to the topic of Eucharistic Christology in other works, such as the *Fundamenta*. He also addresses the argument that Christ in his body cannot really be in the Supper following the ascension in *De Duabus Naturis in Christo*.[93] However, in neither of these texts does Chemnitz discuss the Acts 3:21 issue *per se*; his 1573 letter represents the first time Chemnitz addresses the problem of Acts 3:21 extensively.[94]

---

89 BEZA, T., *Ad Nicolai Selnecceri et Theologorum Ienensium calumnias* (1571), 68. While Beza has kept the essence of the original, his citation is not completely accurate. For a modern edition of the original, see *Die Debatte*, 38.

90 See the reproduction of the title page at *Die Debatte*, 16.

91 BEZA, T., *Ad Nicolai Selnecceri et Theologorum Ienensium calumnias* (1571), 69.

92 PREUS II (1994), 14–15, 337. Preus's biography of Chemnitz is the only such book-length treatment and provides a good overview of the theologian's work, writings, and personal life.

93 CHEMNITZ, M., *De Duabus Naturis in Christo* (1578). For a modern English version, see CHEMNITZ, M., *The Two Natures of Christ* (1971) or the reprint in vol. 6 of CHEMNITZ, M., *Works* (2008).

94 Chemnitz is aware of the issue in earlier works; see, e.g., CHEMNITZ, M., *Wideholte Christliche Gemeine Confession* (1571b), Bi[r] and Pi[r]-ii[r]. Also, in a letter to Landgrave Guillaume IV of Hesse (CB 12 [1571], 60–81), Beza details his objections to Chemnitz (starting on p. 78) on the hypostatic union and communication of idioms, and ties those discussions to Acts 3:21 (starting on p. 80). See also p. 166, where Beza mentions the defense of the Wittenbergers against Selnecker (referring to either the *Disputatio grammatica* or the *Frägstuck christliches*, both of 1571).

As mentioned above, Beza knew that Martin Chemnitz had written a letter against him and his Acts 3:21 translation, although he had not read it.[95] A brief overview of the letter's complicated history is in order before a discussion of its contents. Originally published in 1573,[96] the printer falsely attributed it to Georg Stamke or Stammich (Gregorius Stammichius), the first Lutheran senior pastor of Lüneburg.[97] Polycarp Leyser was the first to correct the error in his 1591–1592 edition of *Loci Theologici*, Chemnitz's commentary on Melanchthon's *Loci Communes*. Leyser included a brief letter to the reader before the letter, explaining that he added the letter and other writings to the section on the Lord's Supper because Chemnitz had died before finishing it, and wished to include more than the sparse commentary Chemnitz had written in his last days. He also mentions the falsely attributed edition and explains that it was common knowledge that Chemnitz had written the work.[98] Leyser's collection was reprinted in 1594[99] and 1610.[100] Chemnitz's letter has, to the authors' knowledge, not been included in any modern German critical editions or English translations.[101]

The letter, written to the pastor Timothy Kirchner regarding Beza's Third Apology, is divided into seven chapters, the third of which is most relevant to this article: "On the Locus of Peter of Acts 3: *oportet Christum caelum accipere*."[102] Chemnitz begins by saying that this "abnormality [...] should not be buried in silence," and complains that debates of this nature have been going on for nearly fifty years, saying that "the Sacramentarians have vigorously argued that Christ was taken—contained, caught, and confined—bodily by heaven into one certain location. He neither wishes nor is able to be elsewhere until the end of time." This kind of argumentation leads them to abandon the Words of Institution, because they are unable to understand them in their "simple, proper, native, and Scriptural meaning."[103] For Chemnitz, Beza's debate is merely a new angle on the old Sacramentarian argument against the Lord's Supper. Chemnitz goes on to accuse Beza of hubris, stating that not even Calvin nor the Zwinglians went as far as he has.[104] He also condemns the Wittenberg Party for their involvement

---

95 Beza to Dürnhoffer, 14 May 1574, in CB 15:92–93.
96 CHEMNITZ, M., *Epistola* (1573).
97 BERTRAM, J./MÜLLER, S. (1719), 209.
98 "Candido Lectori S." in CHEMNITZ, M., *Epistola* (1591–1592), 187^r.
99 CHEMNITZ, M., *Locorum Theologicorum* (1599).
100 CHEMNITZ, M., *Loci* (1610).
101 This letter is notably absent from Concordia Publishing House's *Chemnitz's Works*. The editors note in the preface that they did not include these sections in their translation, although the reasons why are not entirely clear. See CHEMNITZ, M., *Works* (2009), vol. 8.
102 CHEMNITZ, M., *Epistola* (1591–1592), 187^v–223^r.
103 CHEMNITZ, M., *Epistola* (1591–1592), 195^v.
104 CHEMNITZ, M., *Epistola* (1591–1592), 195^v–196^r.

in this controversy with their *Catechism*, also discussed above.[105] He dismisses them with a hint of Luther-like irritation, somewhat unusual for the theologian otherwise known for his patience and avoidance of controversy. The heart of his accusation is that they are "twist[ing] certain testimonies in Scripture to fit their opinion."[106] The doctrine of a fixed Christ in a locative Heaven reflects a faulty exegetical approach that disregards not only other clearer texts, but also the context of Acts 3:21 itself. Chemnitz sees Beza's translation as both an attack on a key doctrine of the church, and on the sanctity of Scripture itself.

In addition to arguing that Beza's translation is based on his judgment and not on the original text, Chemnitz goes on to argue that his translation is faulty because it does not make sense within the immediate context of Acts 3:21. Chemnitz argues that, when Peter is speaking to the Jews, his sermon is on the "reign, glory, power and dominion of Christ" in order to prove to them that Jesus was the Messiah, which they were, at that moment, rejecting and ridiculing. Since even the believing do not experience this power "with the senses," Peter is attempting to prove the power of Christ by discussing his ascension to power and might:

> The heavens are said to be God, not because God is enclosed in heaven [...] but because glory, power, and dominion itself is divine and heavenly, not following the reason of this world [...] Therefore Peter wished to explain and describe the glory, power, and dominion, to which Christ was exalted through the ascension with respect to His humanity, with the word of heaven.[107]

Here, Chemnitz implies that Beza's translation is illogical due to its context; a discussion of Christ's physical location in heaven would not engender converts from among the Jews, whereas proof of Jesus' divinity through the ascension to the right-hand of God would. Chemnitz believed Beza's translation would have lacked rhetorical logic in that situation, another reason to translate Acts 3:21 as highlighting Christ's glorified humanity.

Chemnitz frequently refers to Beza's translation as "inverted" and even "perverted," complaining that Beza ignores "the natural, proper, simple, and genuine order" of the words in their original Greek, which he believes testify to his active translation.[108] He goes so far as to pit Beza against the Holy Spirit:

---

105 CHEMNITZ, M., *Epistola* (1591–1592), 196[r–v].
106 CHEMNITZ, M., *Epistola* (1591–1592), 195[v].
107 CHEMNITZ, M., *Epistola* (1591–1592), 196[v]–197[r].
108 CHEMNITZ, M., *Epistola* (1591–1592), 199[v]; see also 195[v]–196[r].

> Because the Holy Spirit is with the true words in the Scriptures, as they were handed down and put down, they ought to be observed with great reverence and the translator ought not to substitute his logical consequence or paraphrase in translating, but faithfully translate the text of the Scripture itself, as by the Holy Spirit. Therefore the pious are rightfully attacking this inverted and perverted text, while Beza roars against it in vain. For it interests the Church that the text of Scripture be retained safe and uncorrupted just as it was passed down and handed down by the Holy Spirit.[109]

Chemnitz closes the third chapter of this letter authoritatively: "Therefore Beza has destroyed himself, insofar as he thinks himself able to force and impose his interpretation and sense of this sermon of Peter on the universal church, indeed even the whole world as though it were canonical and catholic."[110] Beza is no longer merely a rival theologian or heterodox teacher: he is an enemy of the church and of the truth.

Chemnitz did not end his critique of Beza in this letter, however. In 1577, Chemnitz, along with Kirchner, Selnecker, Andreae and others, presented the *Formula of Concord*, a new summary of the Lutheran faith intended to put to rest the squabbles between the Crypto-Calvinists and Gnesio-Lutherans, published as the conclusion of the *Book of Concord* in 1580. This specific issue is addressed in the *Formula* of Concord, in the seventh article of the Solid Declaration, mentioning Beza by name: the original German singles Beza out as the chief Sacramentarian fanatic ("die Sakramentschwärmer [Theodorus Beza]")[111] for flouting Christ, St Paul, and the whole church. They include a (supposed) quote from Beza deriding the Real Presence that they deem so offensive and blasphemous as to leave it untranslated both in German and even in modern English translations.[112] The authors of the *Formula* include Beza's translation to reject it as blasphemy against the Holy Spirit:

> Likewise, when it is taught that because of His ascension into heaven Christ is so enclosed and circumscribed with his body in a definite place in heaven that with the same [His body] He cannot or will not be truly present with us in the Supper, which is celebrated according to the institution of Christ upon earth, but that He is as far and remote from it as heaven and earth are from one another, as some Sacramentarians have willfully and wickedly falsified the text, Acts 3, 21: *oportet Christum coelum accipere*, that is, *Christ must occupy heaven*, for the confirmation

---

109 CHEMNITZ, M., *Epistola* (1591–1592), 199ᵛ.
110 CHEMNITZ, M., *Epistola* (1591–1592), 200ᵛ.
111 *Formula of Concord*, Solid Declaration 7:67, in *Concordia Triglotta* (1921), 996.
112 *Formula of Concord*, Solid Declaration 7:67, in *Concordia Triglotta* (1921), 996.

of their error, and instead thereof have rendered it: *oportet Christum coelo capi*, that is, Christ must be received or be circumscribed and enclosed by heaven or in heaven, in such a manner that in His human nature He can or will in no way be with us upon earth.[113]

The *Formula of Concord* was meant as a document around which Lutherans would rally and unite, especially against the encroachment of Crypto-Calvinist influences. The authors chose to include Beza's Acts 3:21 translation and interpretation in order to further delineate the Lutheran view of the Lord's Supper—and of Christ—from other church bodies' understandings.

When both Lutherans and non-Lutherans reacted critically to the *Book of Concord*, Chemnitz again joined Kirchner and others in 1583 to write *Apologia, order Verantwortung deß Christlichen Concordienbuchs*. In a section on the Person of Christ, they reiterate their rejection of Beza's translation of Acts 3:21, the "corruptelam des Spruchs Act. 3." The authors contend that Beza's passive translation of the Greek, in contrast to the traditional Lutheran active translation with "eynnemmen," is false and erroneous ("falsche und irrige"), accusing Beza of tampering ("verfälschen") with the text. Acts 3:21 is not about the mere location of Christ's physical body, the authors of the *Book of Concord* maintain, but rather describes his sovereignty over heaven and earth; Beza's argument to the contrary is, to them, stunningly impudent.[114] Their refutation of Beza and by implication those Crypto-Calvinists who were using his version of the text is definitive: an enclosed, circumscribable Christ absent from the Supper is not the Christ of the Lutheran church.

---

113 *Formula of Concord*, Solid Declaration 7:119, in *Concordia Triglotta* (1921), 1013. Current English translations obscure the original understood meaning of the two translations of the Acts passage. Here, "occupy" likely carries a military sense, as opposed to a strictly locative one. The 1851 English translation perhaps captures it better than modern ones, which reads: "Some sacramentarians, for the confirmation of their error, have willfully perverted this text, Acts 3, 21: *Oportet Christum coelum accipere*; that is, *It behooved Christ to receive the heaven* ; and instead of this faithful translation, they have replaced these words: *Oportet Christum coelo capi*; that is, *It behooved Christ to be received by* or *into the heaven*, or *to be circumscribed and contained in heaven*, so that he neither can nor will be with us on earth in any manner with his human nature. See *Formula of Concord*, Solid Declaration 7:119, in *The Christian Book of Concord* (1851), 596.

114 CHEMNITZ, M., *Apologia, order Verantwortung deß Christlichen Concordienbuchs* (1583), 53[r].

6.6 Conclusion

In the sections of the *Formula of Concord* (1580) touching on the Eucharist, the authors twice reference Beza and his translation of Acts 3:21. We have argued here that, in doing so, they intentionally are evoking a decade of conflict surrounding Reformed teachings on the nature of Christ's physical presence in the Supper and those espoused by Luther. This conflict had its genesis in various Wittenberg public disputations that occurred at the beginning of the decade that coincided roughly with the appearance of the Wittenberg *Catechism* in 1571. Bolstered by ambiguity in the formulations of Melanchthon concerning the Supper, the composers of the *Catechism* adopted language that looked more to Geneva than had previously been seen in Lutheran documents. Significantly, they cite Beza's translation of Acts 3:21—noticeably bypassing Luther's counter-version—as a proof text for their position. Conservative Lutherans, who became known as Gnesio-Lutherans, pushed back, accusing the new Crypto-Calvinists of deceitfully altering fundamental teachings of Luther. This backlash in turn led directly to the creation of the Torgau Articles of 1574 and the persecution of the Crypto-Calvinists. Sharp lines were being drawn between Reformed and Lutheran. Through it all, the Gnesio-Lutherans blamed the trouble on the influence of Beza, while often citing his translation of Acts 3:21 with all its implications as the spark that ignited the fire. Along with the two explicit references in the *Formula*, in fact, much of the Eucharistic doctrine set forth there has Beza in view: he had clarified the Genevan position over the last decade with unprecedented precision. He showed the creators of the *Formula* exactly where and how they needed to press their arguments. In the process, they came to understand plainly and unmistakably what it means to be Lutheran as opposed to being Reformed.

Nothing in the record indicates that Beza was actively attempting to foment a rebellion among Lutheran ranks when he translated the passage in Acts as he did in 1556. His first contact with Esrom Rüdinger, a key figure in the whole affair and an important correspondent, did not even occur until the latter sent Beza a letter of recommendation in July 1568.[115] He simply came to the same conclusion about Acts 3:21 as Castellio did a few years before him, that *the heavens receive and hold Christ*, not that *Christ received the heavens*. Nevertheless, his translation did serve as a fulcrum for the position that the Wittenbergers were championing, and in the process of rebuking their fellow Lutherans, the Jena theologians, Selnecker and Chemnitz all censured Beza himself. This exposed a rift between Geneva and Lutherans not seen before. In speaking of them, Beza's language takes on a dark tone. Writing to Dürnhoffer

---

115 Rüdinger to Beza, 13 July 1568, in CB 9:103.

in 1576, for example, Beza gives news of the activities of the Gnesio-Lutherans with an embittered allusion to Revelation 13: "As for the 'new popes,' surely they will heal the wound of the Beast if they can; therefore, they will perish with the Beast."[116] To Landgrave Guillaume IV of Hesse, Beza bemoans a small number of Lutheran "pseudo-theologians" who are "working to tear up the foundations of Christianity and revert to rancid heretical blasphemies."[117] And again to Dürnhoffer he calls them "ἀλάστορες illi," that is, "those monsters."[118]

Even so, opportunities for compromise did present themselves. Earlier in the same year that Beza complains to the Landgrave of a few Gnesio-Lutherans who are tearing up the foundations of the Church, he pleads with the same Landgrave not to abandon the persecuted French churches since, as he puts it, at issue between Reformed and Lutherans is but a disagreement on a few minor formulations concerning the Eucharist: "On the major points of doctrine, we agree."[119] He notes unhappily that the Jesuits are taking advantage of the current dissension among Protestants.[120] This is a noteworthy opening to compromise: it would seem that a common enemy could unite them more than subtle differences divide them. Just how subtle they were is hinted at in Beza's treatise, *Modesta et Christiana defensio*. There Beza distills the difference between Selnecker and himself to the single question of circumscription of the physical body of Christ: to his mind, Selnecker is not just denying that the body of Christ is held in Heaven such that it can be nowhere else.[121] This would not have led him to accuse Beza of creating an impious translation, seeing that the dispute would be about the doctrinal implications rather than the wording of the text itself. Instead, Beza notes, Selnecker is denying that any such localization of Christ's body can be in accord with Christ's power. In other words, Selnecker and the Gnesio-Lutherans do not believe that Christ in his physical form as a man ascended to a particular place because, as king of Heaven, he cannot be contained by it. This position stands at odds with Beza's translation. Ironically, the specificity of both Luther's and Beza's translations of Acts 3:21 prevented the unity that seemed possible in 1540 when Calvin signed the modified Augsburg Confession.

---

116 Beza to Dürnhoffer, 20 September 1576, in CB 17:161. For the attribution "new pope," or "new papacy," which derives from a title of a work by Daniel Toussain, see 106n.6 in the same volume.

117 Beza to Landgrave Guillaume IV of Hesse, 15 December 1577, in CB 18:211.

118 Beza to Dürnhoffer, 3 May 1580, in CB 21:112.

119 Beza to Landgrave Guillaume IV of Hesse, 25 March 1577, in CB 18:60.

120 On this, see the editors' discussion at CB 18:63, n. 12.

121 BEZA, T., *Modesta et Christiana defensio* (1572), 71–72.

Part Three: Theodore Beza on Prophecy, Prodigies, and Predestination

Jon Balserak

Chapter 7: Theodore Beza on Prophets and Prophecy

On 19 August 1564, Theodore Beza described the scene following Jean Calvin's death a few months earlier: "The following night and the day after as well, there was much weeping in the city. For the body of the city mourned the prophet of the Lord."[1] This was not the only time Beza referred to Calvin as a prophet. In his *vita Calvini*, Beza wrote: "Calvin in the dedication of his Lectures on the prophet Daniel to the French churches declares, in a prophetic voice, that tempestuous and severe trials were hanging over their heads."[2]

Study of prophets and prophecy in the Medieval and Reformation eras is hardly new. A myriad number of people—Birgitta of Sweden,[3] Joachim of Fiore,[4] Girolamo Savanarola,[5] Jan Hus,[6] Martin Luther,[7] Ulrich Zwingli,[8] Heinrich Bullinger,[9] Theodore Bibliander,[10] John Calvin,[11] Argula von Grumbach,[12] Katharina Schütz Zell,[13] John Knox,[14] late-medieval women,[15] the Marian exiles[16]—have either been identified as people who believed themselves to be prophets or have had their views on prophecy examined. For example, in 2012 I published an essay examining Peter Martyr Vermigli's understanding of

---

1 CO 21:45–46.
2 CO 21:91. Beza left Lausanne for Geneva in November 1558; see "Le départ de Bèze et son remplacement" in CB 2, annex 14. Thus, he was with Calvin for a little less than ten years, though he knew Calvin as early as 1547. In February 1559, Beza tried to encourage Pierre Viret to come back to Geneva and join them in their work. On Beza's life and ministry, particularly his ministry to France, see MANETSCH, S. (2000b).
3 FOGELQUIST, I. (1993).
4 REEVES, M. (1969); MCGINN, B. (1985).
5 HERZIG, T. (2008).
6 OBERMAN, H. (1999), 135–167; HABERKERN, P. (2016).
7 PREUSS, H. (1933); KOLB, R. (1999); OBERMAN, H. (1999), 135–167.
8 BÜSSER, F. (1950); OPITZ, P. (2007), 2:493–513; OPITZ, P. (2017).
9 PETERSON, R. (1991), 245–260; BOLLIGER, D. (2004), 159–177; TIMMERMAN, D. (2015).
10 GORDON, B. (2012), 107–141.
11 GANOCZY, A. (1966); ENGAMMARE, M. (1998), 88–107; BALSERAK, J. (2014a).
12 MATHESON, P. (1995); PAK, G.S. (2012), 151–169.
13 MCKEE, E.A. (1998).
14 DAWSON, J. (2015).
15 VOADEN, R. (1999).
16 DAWSON, J. (1994), 75–91.

prophecy in which I demonstrated that, though Vermigli did not see himself as a prophet, he did believe that the Swiss reformer Ulrich Zwingli was one.[17]

In this present essay, I will not claim that Theodore Beza thought himself to be a prophet—because I do not think he did. Instead, I will examine his thinking on prophecy. At this point someone may lodge the objection: was it not the case that in the early modern period prophesying was essentially the same as preaching? If so, then all of the people mentioned above would have considered themselves to be prophets in the sense that they were preachers of the gospel, but nothing more. This is, of course, true. And so we have works like William Perkins' *The Art of Prophesying* (1607) which is about preaching. Hence its full title is: *The arte of prophecying, or, A treatise concerning the sacred and onely true manner and methode of preaching.* In point of fact, Sujin Pak has recently claimed something not entirely dissimilar from this. In a sophisticated and thoughtful analysis of the development of prophecy during the sixteenth century, she argues that the rise of Anabaptism in the 1520s and the tendency exhibited by Anabaptists and other Radicals to claim a prophetic calling despite lack of education, particularly education in the languages (what Pak identifies as a kind of "prophethood of all believers" doctrine) moved second generation reformers to adapt and soften their use of, and claims to, the prophetic mantle.[18]

But that is not what Beza meant when he called Calvin "the prophet of the Lord" in the quote with which this essay began. Beza did not simply mean that Calvin was a preacher. Rather, Beza believed that Calvin had received a special calling from God—a calling distinct from the general calling to preach the gospel. Or, perhaps we should not prejudge the case. So, instead, let us ask this question: did Beza mean to indicate that Calvin possessed a special prophetic calling from God? Or, to state the question generally: did Beza identify such a category, that is, did Beza discuss prophecy so as to identify a category in which the prophet is understood as an individual raised up by God during particular periods of decline in the church's life with the special and authoritative calling to restore the church? That is what I will address below, but let me first introduce the topic.

7.1 Prophecy from Antiquity to Early Modernity: Revelation, Interpretation, Questions

Prophecy has been a part of the Christian church since its inception. The presence of biblical passages like 1 Corinthians 12:10 and Romans 12:6 guarantee

---

17 BALSERAK, J. (2012), 148–172.
18 PAK, G.S. (2018).

this.[19] Theologians and church leaders from the earliest centuries of the Christian era explored the nature of prophecy, oftentimes arriving at different views as to its character. Some, like Cassiodorus, identified prophecy as "divine revelation." He states this in the preface to his *Expositio Psalmorum*.[20] A similar note is struck in Augustine's *Super Genesim ad Litteram*[21] and Gregory the Great's homilies on Ezekiel.[22]

Others, however, identified prophecy with interpretation, specifically the interpretation of Scripture. Ambrosiaster, for example, states: "Prophets, however, are those who explain the Scriptures."[23] Some in discussing this emphasized exploration of the scriptural mysteries and so in this way aligned themselves more closely to those who saw prophecy as revelation. Others emphasized the idea of proclamation and practical application (see, for instance, Bruno,[24] Rabanus,[25] Lanfranc,[26] Strabo,[27] Haymo,[28] Pseudo-Jerome,[29] Thomas Aquinas in his *Expositio in Epistolam Romanos*[30] and William of St Thierry).[31] In doing so, they move away from the idea that a prophet received revelation and towards the notion that a prophet is an interpreter and preacher of the Scripture. Early modern examples of this would be François Lambert of Avignon's commentaries on prophecy (1526) and Hosea (1525),[32] or, for that matter, works by Guilielmus

---

19 Both of these passages refer to prophecy: "To one there is given through the Spirit a message of wisdom, […] to another miraculous powers, to another prophecy." (1 Cor 12:8-10); "We have different gifts, according to the grace given to each of us. If your gift is prophesying, then prophesy in accordance with your faith." (Rom 12:6). Both passages quoted from the NIV.

20 PL 70:12.

21 PL 34:458–461.

22 GREGORY THE GREAT, *Homélies sur Ézéchiel* (1986), 50–64. For more on the medieval period, see ALPHANDERY, P. (1932), 334–359.

23 AMROSIASTER, *Divi Ambrosii episcope Mediolanensis omnia* (1516), fol. 208.

24 PL 153:192.

25 PL 112:116.

26 PL 150:199.

27 PL 114:542.

28 PL 117:580.

29 PL 30:788.

30 AQUINAS, T., *Sancti Thomae Aquinatis doctoris angelici, Opera Omnia* (1852–1873), 13, 123.

31 PL 180:673.

32 LAMBERT, F., *Commentarii de Prophetia* (1526); *Praefatio in Primum Duodecim Prophetarum, nempe, Oseam* (1525), 8r.

Estius,[33] Johann Bugenhagen,[34] Konrad Pelikan,[35] Johannes Brenz,[36] Rudolf Gwalther,[37] Caspar Olevianus[38] and Erasmus.[39] The same, broadly speaking, can be seen in Oecolampadius's commentary on Romans 12:6.[40] In fact, Oecolampadius there focuses more on the congregational aspects of prophesying, viewing the text as encouragement for the congregation and as something that presumably could be done by any member.

But this is merely the tip of the iceberg. Innumerable questions were asked: Does prophecy have to be understood as either revelation or interpretation? Could it not be both? In regards to revelation, should we understand it to be revelation of the future or can it relate to the past or the present? Is prophecy mediated or unmediated? Can it err? What is the difference between a prophetic spirit and demon possession? What is the difference between the prophetic spirit and madness? Are there different grades of prophecy? Do prophets still exist today and, if so, how do they differ from the biblical prophets? Who was the greatest prophet and why? All of these, and many other, questions were addressed. So, to give one example, Gregory the Great is extremely clear on the timeless nature of prophecy: "Prophecy has three tenses; the past, of course; the present and the future."[41] Similar thoughts abound in other church fathers, including Theodoret,[42] Lanfranc of Bec,[43] Peter Lombard[44] and Aquinas.[45] Thus, within the Christian tradition, theologians routinely raised and discussed a variety of questions as they treated the locus of prophecy.

In relation to our exploration of Beza's thinking, we are going to find that his understanding of a divinely-ordained category of prophet concerns interpreta-

---

33 ESTIUS, G., *Estius in Omnes Canonicas Apostolorum Epistolas* (1841), 1, 369.
34 BUGENHAGEN, J., *Annotationes Ioan. Bugenhagii Pomerani in X. epistolas Pauli, scilicet, ad Ephesios, … Hebraeos* (1524), 13r.
35 PELIKAN, K., *In omnes apostolicas epistolas, Pauli, Petri, Iacobi, Ioannis et Iudae D. Chuonradi Pellicani* (1539), 250.
36 BRENZ, J., *In Epistolam, quam apostolus Paulus ad Romanos scripsit, commentariorum libri tres* (1588), 723.
37 GWALTHER, R., *In D. Pauli apostoli epistolam ad Romanos homiliae* (1566), 169r-v; *In Epistolam D. Pauli Apostoli ad Corinthios Priorem* (1590), 270r.
38 OLEVIANUS, C., *In epistolam D. Pauli Apostoli ad Romanos notae, ex Gasparis Oleviani concionibus excerptae, & a Theodoro Beza editae* (1579), 614.
39 ERASMUS, D., *Ecclesiastes: sive de ratione concionandi* (1535).
40 OECOLAMPADIUS, J., *In Epistolam B. Pauli Apost. ad Rhomanos Adnotationes a Ioanne Oecolampadio Basileae praelectae, & denuo recognitae* (1526).
41 GREGORY THE GREAT, *Homélies sur Ézéchiel* (1986), 56.
42 PG 80:861.
43 PL 181:958–959.
44 PL 191:1659.
45 AQUINAS, T., *Summa Theologiae* (2006), II-II q171 a3.

tion of Scripture. But we need to comment on a crucial quality associated with this.

7.2 Prophecy and Authority

The question of the relationship of prophets to authority has been a perennial concern within the Christian tradition. This arguably took on increasing importance beginning in the late Medieval period. That this should be the case is easy to see.

If one considers the New Testament prophets mentioned in 1 Corinthians, one has to acknowledge that they represented a potential threat in that they claimed the right to speak on God's behalf in the midst of the congregation, and so Paul set down guidelines for how their work ought to be understood and treated so as to avoid conflict. These guidelines were not always followed, as the rise of the Anabaptists in the 1520s illustrates. One cannot help but be amused by the portion of Wolfgang Capito's 1526 letter to Nicolaus Prugner in which he says that "Today our weaver shouted at Matthew in the cathedral."[46] The Matthew he has in mind is his colleague Matthew Zell, who was preaching at the time. Zell had read a passage from Deuteronomy 28 and commented on the repercussions of disobedience, and the weaver, Hans Wolff, "barked": "You are disobedient to the Holy Spirit. What you say goes against him and is a lie. In his name I command you to withdraw and permit me to say what the Spirit wishes to say."[47]

The relationship between prophets and authority is arguably more awkward and pugnacious in regards to the Old Testament prophets. It may come as little surprise, then, that many who arose in the Medieval and Early Modern eras with the idea of reforming the church and civil realm aligned themselves in various ways with Old Testament prophets. Ulrich Zwingli and John Knox comes to mind.[48]

John Calvin also aligned himself with prophets like Jeremiah—or so Rodolphe Peter has argued.[49] In fact, Peter was not the only modern scholar to argue this. Many other examples might be cited.

Beginning in the mid-twentieth century, Peter, Richard Stauffer and Alexandre Ganoczy began exploring Calvin's prophetic self-awareness. Joining their

---

46 CAPITO, W., The Correspondence of Wolfgang Capito (2009), 2:204. For more on this incident, see BALSERAK, J. (2014b), 17–32.

47 CAPITO, W., The Correspondence of Wolfgang Capito (2009), 2:204.

48 DAWSON, J. (1994), 75–91; ibid. (2015), 33–34; OPITZ, P. (2017).

49 PETER, R. (1971), xiv–xvi.

ranks later in the century were Olivier Millet, Bernard Cottret and Max Enga-marre, who also argued that Calvin believed himself a prophet.[50] Denis Crouzet, Bruce Gordon, Jon Balserak and Jean-Luc Mouton added further nuance to scholarly understandings of this subject in the twenty-first century. Thus, by 2009, Gordon could write in a matter-of-fact manner: "The 1557 preface to the psalms commentary was written by a man who regarded himself as a prophet of the Church."[51]

Among the material discovered by these scholars which led them to draw this conclusion was the following. Discoveries were made concerning several encounters Calvin had. Already mentioned is Calvin's encounter with Farel recorded in the 1557 Psalms preface, concerning which Ganoczy wrote in 1966. "The context of this passage is clearly prophetic." Ganoczy listed Isaiah 5:25, 9:12, 17, 21, Jeremiah 15:6, Psalm 55:1 and 138:7 as possible sources for Calvin's language and mindset.[52] Additionally, Calvin's allusion in one of his letters to Louis du Tillet was found to provide another glimpse into Calvin's mind. It concerned a meeting he had about the possibility of Calvin returning to Geneva (which he did in 1541). In this letter, Calvin compares himself to the prophet Jonah: "the most moderate among them threatens that the Lord would find me out, as he did Jonah."[53] Millet examined the epigraphs on the title-pages of Calvin's anti-Nicodemite treatises (*Petit traicté* and *Excuse à Messieurs les Nicodémites*). In Calvin's *Excuse*, which was written as a vehement rebuke against evangelicals in France who (in Calvin's judgment) refused to suffer for the gospel and were engaged in idolatry and sinful duplicity, the epigraph Calvin chose for the title-page was Amos 5:10: "They have hated the one who delivers rebuke in the gate, and they loathed the one who speaks what is right."[54] Millet's inference seems justified: Calvin's thinking was that his (Nicodemite) opponents hated him in the same way the opponents of other prophets (such as Amos's) hated him. Turning to oral communications, Engammare and Balserak cited examples from Calvin's sermons and *praelectiones*, respectively. When Calvin preached on Daniel 5, he declared:

> For if one preaches in this city that God's vengeance will be felt, that people
> do not wish to receive what we announce in the name of God, and that it is in
> his name that we have spoken, that there is a prophet, they will ridicule all that.[55]

---

50 COTTRET, R. (1995), 205, 268, *et passim*; I will cite the others later in this paragraph.

51 GORDON, B. (2009), 34.

52 GANOCZY, A. (1966), 305; BALSERAK, J. (2014a), 94.

53 Calvin to Du Tillet, 20 October 1538, in CO 10b:269–272.

54 GILMONT, F./PETER, R. (1991–2000), 3:82/7. Discussed by MILLET, O. (2011), 86–87.

55 CO 41:335, as cited in ENGAMMARE, M. (1998), 95.

Engammare also cited from an Ezekiel sermon:

> There are some who say: "There's Calvin who makes himself a prophet, when
> he says that one will know that there is a prophet among us. He's talking about
> himself." Is he a prophet? Well, since it is the doctrine of God that I am announcing,
> I have to use this language.[56]

The prophetic authority in view here is nicely illustrated by these last two citations. It was *not* the authority to reveal new doctrinal truths, but rather the
authority of God speaking through a spokesman who knew unequivocally he
had been raised up to turn the church away from error, particularly idolatry.
Calvin explains in his preface to his lectures on Isaiah and his preface to his lectures on Hosea (and the Minor Prophets) that God raised up the Old Testament
prophets at a time when the priests had failed.[57] Hosea, Isaiah, Jeremiah and the
other Jewish prophets were raised up to rightly interpret and apply the law to
the people of God, correcting the priests' errors. The prophets spoke with such
force and purity that to disagree with them was to disagree with God. Calvin,
Zwingli and others implied that this was now the authority with which they
themselves spoke. God had raised them up and given them authority to steer the
church away from Romanist idolatry towards the truth. They spoke God's word
purely, adding nothing human to their interpretations. So complete was the
acceptance of this calling by the prophets themselves that they lost themselves,
as it were, in their vocation—what Denis Crouzet refers to, concerning Calvin,
as being "absent à soi" (absent to himself).[58]

7.3 Interpreting the Rise of the Prophet

Given the late-medieval rise in tensions between prophets and the authorities,
it is arguably not surprising that theologians around this time began to turn
their attention to interpreting these tensions. Accordingly, we discover increasingly sophisticated interpretations of the momentous work that God was doing
through his prophets in the Reformation. We will have a look at this briefly
now.[59]

Ulrich Zwingli, for instance, produces an inchoate, but perceptive, discussion
of his times in his treatise *Der Hirt* where he notes that just as the Spartans
had their ephors, the Romans their tribunes and German cities their chief

---

56 STAUFFER, R. (1965), as cited in ENGAMMARE, M. (1998), 95.
57 CO 36:20, 42:198.
58 CROUZET, D. (2000), 9.
59 For my initial foray into this subject, see BALSERAK, J. (2017), 123–136.

guildmasters, so God has his shepherds or prophets.[60] "God always sends his prophets in time to warn the sinful world, as Jeremiah 25 and 29 point out."[61] Likewise, Philip Melanchthon identifies Luther as a prophet and, interpreting the times, explains that prophets are singularly gifted for the renewal of doctrine "as Augustine was in his age and Luther is in ours."[62] In both these examples, the basic ideas are present: that 1.) God raises up prophets during particular periods of redemptive history; 2.) these are times when renewal is needed; 3.) those whom God raises up are specially gifted to do this work; and 4.) this gift and authority came directly from God and ordinarily stands at odds with the established church. These writings were produced quite early. Zwingli's *Der Hirt*, for instance, was first published in 1524.

If we move into the 1540s and 1550s, we find Peter Martyr Vermigli speaking in a more prolix manner. His analysis of prophecy was historical in its approach. He asserts with respect to prophecy that there is a discrimination of times (*discrimina temporum*). There were prophets such as "Abraham, Noah, Enoch and Adam" before the law; prophets during the time of the law, "such as Moses and others"; and prophets during the apostolic era, "such as the prophecies of many holy men during the time of the primitive church."[63] Vermigli employed this historical framing in his assessment of the role of the prophet in redemptive history. And what we find, for example, in his treatment of 1 Samuel, is Vermligi explaining: "If the ordinary ministry at any time does not fulfill their duty, God raises up prophets extraordinarily (*extra ordinem*) in order to restore things to order."[64]

The paradigm Vermigli sets out helps explain his thinking about his own Reformation era. So, he states elsewhere, "in my judgment, it ought not to be denied that there are still prophets in the church"—though precisely who he had in mind he does not say.[65] But it is obvious he does not mean "everyone who preaches the gospel," because if that were his meaning, it would be bizarre for him to assert it in the way he does. Such historical framing is also found in the

---

60 Zwingli aligns shepherds with pastors, bishops, people's priest, prophet, evangelist or preacher (see ZW 3:13; HZW 2:86).

61 ZWINGLI, U., *Der Hirt*, in ZW 3:36, HZW 2:102.

62 CR 15:1133–1134.

63 VERMIGLI, P., *In duos libros Samuelis prophetae qui uulgo priores libros Regum appellantur ... Commentarii* (1567), 112r.

64 VERMIGLI, P., *In duos libros Samuelis prophetae ... Commentarii doctissimi* (1567), 113r.

65 VERMIGLI, P., *In Primum librum Mosis ... commentarii* (1579a), 81r.

thinking (on prophecy) of other reformers like Martin Bucer[66] and Wolfgang Musculus.[67]

Turning to Calvin, whose lectures and commentaries also appeared in the 1540s through early 1560s, we find that he also adopted a historical approach to the treatment of the prophets. In fact, Calvin and Vermigli employ the same language. When lecturing on Jeremiah 32, Calvin explained that "when through either laziness or ignorance, the priests failed in the performing of their office, God raised up prophets in their place."[68] Calvin made a similar remark in comments on Amos 7:10-13[69] and comments on Micah 3:11-12. Calvin also made the same comments in his introductions to the prophetic books, as I noted earlier. On the Micah 3 passage, Calvin adds that due to the corruption of the priests, "it became necessary that prophets should be raised up as it were extraordinarily (*quasi extra ordinem*).[70] In his sermons on Deuteronomy 18, Calvin made particular reference to his own day and to the authority prophets possess in every era. In the process, Calvin declared that the blueprint which God had adopted (which was set out, by Calvin, in comments on Jeremiah 32 and elsewhere, noted above) continued throughout the church's history up to the present day. Calvin insisted that what Moses says in Deuteronomy 18, concerning the promise of a prophet was not meant merely for Moses and the old covenant administration but "extends to us also."[71] In this context, he made an explicit distinction between an ordinary preacher of the faith and prophets who know the languages and can dispute for the truth with certainty. It was the latter who God raises up when the church has fallen into error and who are given the authority, directly from God himself, to correct and make necessary changes to the church, her doctrine and practice. Thus, he declared, "there will always be prophets."[72]

---

66 BUCER, M., *Epistola D. Pauli ad Ephesios* (1527), 84v-85r; ibid., *Enarrationes perpetuae in Sacra Quatuor Evangelia* (1530), 113v-115v.

67 MUSCULUS, W., *In Epistolas Apostoli Pauli ad Galatas, et Ephesios Commentarii* (1569), 106.

68 CO 39:28.

69 CO 43:131–132.

70 CO 43:333–334.

71 CO 27:527.

72 CO 27:499. Note, in particular, Calvin's sermon on Deut 18:9-15, preached on Wednesday, 27 November 1555. On this, see BALSERAK, J. (2010), 85–112. There is an issue concerning the explicit statements Calvin made about the existence and permanence of prophets in the church and a slightly broader issue concerning his views on ordinary and extraordinary offices in the church. These issues exhibit a complexity that occludes detailed coverage in a short essay like this one that is focused on Beza, not Calvin. For more on these questions and, in particular, a more careful adjudication of the apparently conflicting statements Calvin made on this topics, see BALSERAK, J. (2014a).

7.4 Theodore Beza

Where does Theodore Beza fit into the development we have briefly mapped out? As we shall see, he produces a similarly historical reading of the prophets. He discusses prophets in *Sermons sur l'histoire de la passion* (1592), *Annotationes majores in Novum ... Testamentum* (1594), and elsewhere. He also discusses sixteenth-century reformers and his understanding of them in texts like *Response aux cinq premiere et principals demandes de F. Iean Hay, Moine Iesuite aux ministers Escossois* (1586). Much like Calvin, he did not devote a separate locus to the subject of prophecy—the way Vermigli and others did. But that said, he did treat the topic. In fact, his treatment of it is as substantial as Calvin's discussions, or perhaps more so.

Let us set his thought into a fuller theological context as we begin to examine it. Beza believes that the church is born of the Word of God. This is true of the church ever since it came into being.[73] The Word of God gave birth to the church as mother to daughter.[74] This, of course, is fundamentally different from the Roman Catholic understanding, which believed the opposite. The debate between the reformers and their Roman Catholic opponents frequently centered on the famous words of Augustine's from his *Contra epistolam Manichaei quam vocant fundamenti*, where he said: "For my part, I should not believe the gospel except as moved by the authority of the catholic church."[75] The simple Roman reading of this was that the church preceded everything else, and in particular, it preceded production of the New Testament writings, for which reason it has authority over the New Testament and its interpretation. We see this argument in a myriad of Catholic sources.[76] By contrast, Beza insists that the Word of God is the "incorruptible seed" from which the church grew and grows still.[77]

Fundamental here for Beza is John 10:27, "My sheep hear my voice, and I know them, and they follow me." For an earlier generation, New Testament passages such as this one had prompted reflections on prophecy that focused on the congregation as I mentioned above briefly with respect to Oecolampadius,[78]

---

73 BEZA, T., *De veris et visibilis ecclesiae catholicae notis, tractatio* (1579b), 54.

74 Of course, Beza could have adopted such a belief from numerous sources, including Calvin; see CO 7: 612–613.

75 "Ego vero Evangelio non crederem, nisi me catholicae Ecclesiae commoveret auctoritas." PL 42:176.

76 See, for example, BIEL, G., *Defensiorem Obedientiae Apostolicae et alia Documenta* (1968), 74–75; COCHLAEUS, J., *De Auctoritate Ecclesiae et Scripturae* (1524), 1, 7.

77 BEZA, T., *De veris, et visibilibus ecclesiae catholicae notis, tractatio* (1579b), 54, as cited in MARUYAMA, T. (1978), 217.

78 See also WA 11:408–416; ZELL, M., *Christeliche Verantwortung* (1523); BUCER, M., *Das ym selbs niemant, sondern anderen leben soll, und wie der mensch dahyn kummen moeg* (1523). For more on this, see PAK, G.S. (2018), 35–63.

but Beza was not a part of that generation. Nonetheless, Jesus' words from John 10 still served a role for him, but that role had to do more with the part it plays in identifying the true church as the body which listens and follows the true Shepherd.

Given this focus on the priority of the Scriptures, it will come as no surprise to see that Beza is conscious of canonical and text-critical issues[79] and is sufficiently concerned with, and condemns, the Anabaptists and others Radicals who sometimes claimed the ability to speak through the direct inspiration of the Holy Spirit apart from the Scriptures. To Beza, these groups—the Anabaptists and other radical sects—are heretics, as could easily be seen by their rejection of infant baptism and their anti-Trinitarianism.[80] Beza, thus, labored to ensure that the understanding of the closing of the canon is made clear.[81]

God appointed ministers to care for God's church through the preaching of the sacred Scriptures. The preaching of God's Word is not for anyone and everyone within the church to handle.[82] Beza's understanding of this ministry exhibits nuance and care, but is not provocative or especially original. God calls pastors (pastor-doctors), deacons and elders to ministry roles in the church.[83] These are found under the heading or under the category of ordinary vocations. Prophets, apostles and evangelists fall under the category of extraordinary vocations on which we will have more to say momentarily.

In God's providence, the church has been allowed to fall into corruption. The Western Church had descended from piety to such a desperate condition that it no longer possessed true doctrine nor did it exhibit true ecclesiastical government.[84] Again Beza, though clear and sophisticated in his thinking here, is not provocative. Likely adopting ideas from Calvin *inter alios*, Beza spoke of the church in different ways and from different perspectives.[85] The church is mother, school, body of God's elect and such like.[86] In terms of identifying the church, Beza argued that the two standard marks set out by Protestant and evangelical theologians—namely Word and Sacrament—are, indeed, the marks

79 KRANS, J. (2006).

80 BEZA, T., *Sermons sur l'histoire de la passion … de nostre Seigneur Iesus Christ* (1592b), 211, 217. Beza's concerns on the church do not reflect the kind of intense concern over schism (and the charge of schism hurled at evangelicals by the Roman Catholics) that one finds in the writings of Calvin; see BALSERAK, J. (2011), 19–64.

81 BEZA, T., *Sermons sur l'histoire de la resurrection de nostre Seigneur Iesus Christ* (1593b), 406.

82 BEZA, T., *De veris et visibilibus ecclesiae catholicae notis, tractatio* (1579b), 85.

83 BEZA, T., *Confession de la foy chrestienne* (1560), sections v, xxiv, xxv, xxvi.

84 BEZA, T., *Confession de la foy chrestienne* (1560), sections v, xvii.

85 MARUYAMA, T. (1978), 197–211.

86 BEZA, T., *Sermons sur l'histoire de la resurrection de nostre Seigneur Iesus Christ* (1593b), 400.

for which one ought to look.[87] Beza did occasionally, famously or infamously (depending on one's point of view), add the third mark of discipline to his discussion of the *notae ecclesiae*, yet, as Maruyama has rightly argued, Beza focused the greatest attention and significance to the first mark of the right preaching of the Word of God.[88]

As Beza plotted the history of the church from its inception to the present day and sought to explain the disappearance of these marks and the decline of the Roman Catholic church, we find him again following lines already etched and made visible by Calvin and others. In the Old Testament era, the church of God gradually fell into spiritual decline, though it still retained the divine promise.[89] God raised up Moses and Aaron, and also the Judges. There was a division between the false church and the remnant which emerged, with God raising up prophets for the purpose of caring for his remnant church. With the advent of the New Testament era and the establishment of the New Testament church at Pentecost, there was a great restoration of piety. Beza viewed the ancient Christian church era as a kind of golden age.[90] But with the eventual rise of the papacy, the ecclesiastical order came to be destroyed as the Antichrist took over and exerted greater authority.

Beza's understanding of the Protestant Reformation exhibits similar lines of analysis. Through it, God has restored God's church. The links we find between Beza and the others, particularly Calvin, concerning how God did this are clear and unsurprising. "The Reformers are above all the ones who restore the original apostolic doctrine and build the church upon the apostolic foundation."[91] Beza identifies Jan Hus and John Wyclif in this capacity—that is to say, as prophets whom the Lord had raised up extraordinarily.[92] Beza is, in fact, profoundly conscious of the work God has been doing in his day, and this work is a manifestation of God's great power and love for God's church.[93] Through the Reformation, right order has been re-established in the church as well as correct doctrine.[94]

---

87 BEZA, T., *De haereticis a civili Magistratu puniendis* (1554), 214; *Sermons sur les trois premiers chapitres du cantique des Cantiques* (1586b), xi, 1, 220.

88 BEZA, T., *Sermons sur les trois premiers chapitres du cantique des Cantiques* (1586b), 36, 488; MARUYAMA, T. (1978), 209–210.

89 Calvin discusses this at length in his *Institutes of the Christian Religion*, IV.ii-iv (CO 2:767–798).

90 BEZA, T., *Sermons sur les trois premiers chapitres du cantique des Cantiques* (1586b), xxx, 1, 624–626.

91 MARUYAMA, T. (1978), 220.

92 BEZA, T., *De veris et visibilibus ecclesiae catholicae notis, tractatio* (1579b), 79.

93 BEZA, T., *De veris et visibilibus ecclesiae catholicae notis, tractatio* (1579b), 87–90.

94 BEZA, T., *Sermons sur l'histoire de la resurrection de nostre Seigneur Iesus Christ* (1593b), 390.

Beza's comments on the instruments that God employed include discussion of prophets, as I have already suggested. Beza frequently identifies others agents of reform, including pastors and doctors[95] and magistrates.[96] At the same time, Beza sometimes also points to the role of prophetic agents in reformation along the lines argued by Calvin and Vermigli. Hence, in a sermon he preached on Mark 14:60-61 (and the parallels from the other synoptic Gospels), Beza sets out the same principle, illustrated by identifying the divine protocol when reforming the Old Testament church by raising up prophets: "Foreseeing that not all the priests would be like Aaron or Phineas [...] the Lord extraordinarily raised up those who are called prophets, on the promise that he had made in Deut. 18:15."[97] The reference to Deuteronomy 18 suggests a possible link with Calvin, though of course we cannot be certain of this.[98]

So we find these kinds of statements in Beza's writings—just as we did in the other reformers considered earlier. But we also find more. In Beza's thought on this theme, or cluster of related-themes, one finds some interesting development, which may perhaps be due to his distance from the early days of the Reformation coupled with his extensive biblical and theological knowledge. Whatever the source of it, we find the following. When responding in 1592 to Adrianus Saravia's defense of episcopacy *De diversis gradibus ministrorum Evangelii* (1590), Beza takes up the subject of ordinary and extraordinary vocations specifically. Saravia had argued that the work of reforming the corrupt church belonged to the ordinary ministry. Against this, Beza argues that just as God raised up the prophets extraordinarily to reform the Old Testament people of God, so "in the post-Apostolic Church" he raised up extraordinary reformers to do this work[99]; that reform "is primarily the responsibility of the extraordinary vocations."[100]

Likewise in Beza's *Response aux cinq premiere et principals demandes de F. Iean Hay*, we find the same. Hay, a Jesuit, had challenged the authority of Protestant doctrine. How, he queried, was it justified for individuals to establish churches and such like, apparently usurping for themselves the authority which God had given to his church and placed within the care of the offices and governance of the church? The work of answering Hay on this point prompted "Beza to a detailed explanation of ordinary and extraordinary callings"[101] in an

---

95 BEZA, T., *Iesu Christi D.N. Novum testamentum* (1565b), 2:239f.

96 BEZA, T., *Confession de la foy chrestienne* (1559a), v, xvi.

97 BEZA, T., *Sermons sur l'histoire de la passion ... de nostre Seigneur Iesus Christ* (1592b), 327.

98 See BALSERAK, J. (2010), 85–112.

99 BEZA, T., *Ad tractationem de ministrorum Evangelii gradibus ... Theodore Bezae responsio* (1592b), 15, 17–19.

100 MARUYAMA, T. (1978), 188.

101 SUMMERS, K. (2018a), 311.

effort to justify the nature of the authority of men like Martin Luther, Matthew Zell, Martin Bucer, Ulrich Zwingli, Johannes Oecolampadius, Peter Martyr Vermigli and many others.[102] Beza's response included an explanation effectively identical to those we have seen above. Beza explained that the calling of men was identical to "the vocation of so many Prophets who were set up in opposition to the Priests." They were "not called by any ministry of men (*& non appellés par aucun ministere des hommes*), nor by the law of the succession of Levites." They could, Beza explained, never have acquired "the gift of prophecy [...] by ordinary means (*par moyen ordinaire*)." Their calling, then, was a "pure and immediate vocation of God." Beza then cites 1 Kings 19:16, which recounts the extraordinary anointing of Elisha.[103]

Not only does this explanation reflect what was seen from Zwingli, Vermigli, Calvin and others as regard God's plan to always raise up prophets to correct the church, but it also exhibits the same understanding of authority. These prophets' authority was an authority direct from God, one which enabled Zwingli, Bucer and others to speak and act with the authority of God, such that they could not be legitimately challenged by pope, bishop or king. Their divinely-appointed duty was to correct the erring church of their day, and to redirect it back to truth. To challenge them was to challenge God. This helpfully returns us to the question with which this chapter began, which we will return to again shortly.

The idea of Luther, Zwingli, Oecolampadius or anyone else being raised up by God and possessing prophetic authority may well make one wonder about the kind of authority these figures actually possessed and whether Beza believed that their authority was such that their writings (those of Bucer or Calvin, for instance) ought to be added to the canon. Nor was this only an issue associated with Beza's understanding of prophecy, but also with any number of Protestant and evangelical theologians: Zwingli, Bullinger, Vermigli, Calvin, John Knox and others. They all seem to have believed that God raised up special individuals such as Martin Luther and imbued them with divine authority. Given this fact, though, none of these reformers suggested that that individual's writings ought to have equal authority with canonical Scripture. For Beza and other Protestant colleagues, the canon is closed and the books of the Old and New Testament alone have highest authority within the Church.

---

102 Beza does not mention Calvin in this list. I suspect, as several scholars have noted, that Beza was wary in his debates with Roman Catholics (and Lutherans too) not to appear to hold Calvin in unduly high regard.

103 BEZA, T., *Response aux cinq premiere et principals demandes de F. Iean Hay* (1586a), 14; I am grateful to Kirk Summers for this reference.

7.5   Conclusion

And so we return to Beza's reference to Calvin as "the prophet of the Lord." I would argue that it is clear, in fact crystal-clear now, that Beza meant to communicate something quite profound when he spoke of Calvin in this way. First, I would contend that his identifying of Calvin here is intended to identify him as a prophet in this special sense—that is, as an individual raised up by God at a time of spiritual decline, when the ordinary priestly ministry had failed in its duty, for the purpose of restoring the church.

Second, I would argue that Beza used this language because he—like many of his Protesant contemporaries—had developed a theological understanding of the extraordinary vocation of the prophet raised up by God to restore the church and was simply identifying Calvin as one who legitimately fits into this category.

Third, it seems that Beza's formulation of prophet, appearing almost thirty years after the deaths of Vermigli and Calvin, helps clarify quite significantly the concept of prophet-reformer that was first introduced during the Reformation by thinkers like Ulrich Zwingli.

Theodore Beza, of course, was not the only person who identified Calvin in this way. Antoine Fumée, a contemporary and friend of Calvin, referred to him as a prophet in an undated letter to the reformer,[104] as does Jean Morély, writing in his *Traicté de la discipline & police chrestienne*.[105] Nor does this seem surprising, given that we have identified in the theological work of a variety of sixteenth-century church leaders a recognition that God plays an active role in redemptive history by raising up authoritative interpreters who are tasked with "righting the ship" of the church.

---

104 MILLET, O. (1998), 65. In an undated letter, Antoine Fumée calls Calvin "the great prophet of our age (*plus grand prophète de notre époque*)."

105 MORELY, J., *Traicté de la discipline & police chrestienne* (1562), 257.

Eunjin Kim

Chapter 8: "The Leader of the Ancient Theologians"

Beza's Use of Augustine in His Predestination Doctrine

The fact that the Protestant reformers appealed to the authority of the church fathers is now an agreed observation among sixteenth-century scholars.[1] Against their opponents, it was a common practice for the reformers to cite the writings of the Fathers not only to explain, articulate, and support their arguments but also to accuse and label their enemies with heresies from the early church. For example, claiming Augustine to be on their side of the argument was one way of indicating that they were on the right side of church history while their opponents were not. As such, identifying their views with the church fathers was not only a matter of explaining and defending their faith, but at the same time a means to criticize the wrong theologies of others. The sheer number of references to the Fathers embedded in their writings is an easy indicator of the important place that the patristics occupied in their thoughts. Furthermore, the sixteenth century was a peak time in the development of patristic scholarship. The humanistic endeavor to return to original sources allowed for increased access to patristic sources. David C. Steinmetz and Robert Kolb write, "the humanists changed the theological situation at the end of the middle ages by providing reliably edited editions of the complete, or at least more nearly complete, works of patristic writers."[2] The growing interest in original languages and sources provided theologians of the sixteenth century with new ammunition to fight their enemies in polemical battles.

The practice of using the church fathers, however, had deeper implications for the issues of tradition and authority. One of the main changes that the Protestant Reformation brought to sixteenth-century thinking was a different perception of authority. The reformers emphasized the authority of the Scripture over that of tradition, but they did not seek to abandon or exclude the use of ancient authorities. In fact, as Steinmetz and Kolb pointed out, the reformers read the Fathers as their allies and members of the same family.[3] The reformers'

---

1 See GRANE, L./SCHINDLER, A./WRIEDT, M. (ed.) (1993); STEINMETZ, D. (ed.) (1999); FRANK, G./LEINKAUF, T./WRIEDT, M. (ed.) (2006); BACKUS, I. (ed.) (2001).
2 STEINMETZ, D. and KOLB, R., "Introduction," in STEINMETZ, D. (ed.) (1999), 9.
3 STEINMETZ, D. and KOLB, R., "Introduction," in STEINMETZ, D. (ed.) (1999), 11.

contribution was not in rejecting the tradition but in redefining the relationship between the authority of Scripture and tradition.

Two other factors to be considered are the issues of genre and selectiveness. Certain genres of writings called for more frequent references to the Fathers than others. For obvious reasons, it was more likely for a polemical tract to be saturated with patristic references than other less polemically driven writings. But this did not mean that genres such as sermons or catechetical materials did not contain references to patristic texts. Different genres were written for different purposes and audiences, which required a different kind of use of the Fathers, thus sometimes as a means of encouraging and edifying believers.[4] There was also the question of selectiveness. Each reformer had his own standard or context that determined the value of each patristic source. For example, while Erasmus favored Jerome for his contribution to biblical text and translation, Luther, for whom the doctrine of justification was crucial, considered Augustine to be the "shining light" of the church.[5] In Calvin's case, he preferred Augustine for his doctrine of grace, but when it came to reading the Scriptures, he appreciated Chrysostom's exegesis for his literal interpretation.[6] Thus, there was no single normative rule for using the Fathers. Rather, the confessional context and the goal of the genres governed the choices that reformers would make in selecting which Fathers to use, and when, and which Fathers to leave out.[7]

Overall, these considerations paint a complex and fascinating picture of the sixteenth-century use of the church fathers. Primarily over the last two decades, many scholars have focused on this aspect of the Reformation. The number of books and articles focusing on either one reformer or a theological debate on the use of the Fathers has multiplied, including, for example, Peter Fraenkel's study of Philipp Melanchthon and Anthony Lane's work on John Calvin.[8] There have also been several edited volumes of collected essays which have further stimulated research in this field of study.[9] The best comprehensive study is probably Irena Backus' work entitled *The Reception of the Church Fathers in the West* (2001). This volume introduced the history of patristic scholarship covering a one-thousand year period from the Carolingians to the Benedictines

---

4 STEINMETZ, D. and KOLB, R., "Introduction," in STEINMETZ, D. (ed.) (1999), 14.
5 SCHULZE, M. (2001), 573–579.
6 KREIJKES-VAN ESCH, J. (2018), 260–263.
7 For a study on the formation of confessional identity in the Reformation, see BACKUS, I. (ed.) (2003).
8 FRAENKEL, P. (1961); LANE, A. (1999). See also THOMPSON, N. (2005); CHUNG-KIM (2011).
9 GRANE, L./SCHINLDER, A./WRIEDT, M. (ed) (1993); STEINMETZ, D. (ed.) (1999).

of the Congregation of St. Maur.[10] These large volumes of collected essays have opened up opportunities for further research in the field. However, the essays cover such a broad timeframe, diverse locations and a variety of topics that unifying themes that provide definitive insight into the use of patristic sources in the Reformation remain unidentified. As part of this ongoing discussion, my chapter seeks to contribute to our understanding of Theodore Beza's use of the Fathers.

In this brief essay, I will explore Beza's use of the Fathers in his formation of theological thought, particularly by examining his use of Augustine in the doctrine of predestination as a test case.[11] There has been much discussion on Beza's doctrine of predestination, but not from the approach of analyzing his use of Augustine.[12] As Christian history makes clear, Augustine was a seminal figure whose polemics against Pelagius fundamentally set the tone for future generations in predestinarian conversations. Beza himself acknowledged the importance of Augustine in his *Ad Acta Colloquii Montisbelgardensis* (1588) stating that Augustine is "easily the leader of the ancient theologians who treats this question thoroughly against the Pelagians."[13] Through this study, I hope to place Beza and his use of the Fathers in the larger framework of his theological program and also within the context of patristic scholarship of the sixteenth century.

The investigation will divide into two sections. The first part of this essay will explore Beza's knowledge of the church fathers, looking at Beza's education and his general attitude towards the use of patristic sources. With this background in place, the second section will seek to analyze some of Beza's main predestinarian writings from the perspective of how he uses Augustine in constructing his arguments, taking into consideration the different genres and historical context. Special attention will be payed to how genres shape the way that Beza uses the Fathers. This essay will build upon the arguments made by previous studies that patristic texts provided sources of authority for the Protestant reformers in defending their catholicity, and further demonstrate Beza's approach to the

---

10 BACKUS, I. (ed.) (2001).

11 For studies on Beza's doctrine of predestination, see BRAY, J. (1975); HOLTROP, P. (1993); BEEKE, J. (2003), 69–84; BEEKE, J. (2017); MULLER, R. (1993), 33–61.

12 There have been a number of studies on Beza and the church fathers. See FRAENKEL, P. (1979), 63–81; and MALLINSON, J. (2000), 36–101.

13 BEZA, T., *Ad acta Colloquii Montisbelgardensis Tubingae Edita, Theodori Bezae Responsionis, Pars Altera* (1588), 180: "Istis autem agedum subiiciamus etiam duorum scriptorium gravissima testimonia, Augustinus videlicet veterum Theologorum facile principis, a quo adversus Pelagianos pertractata est multis libris & locis haec questio, & Thomae, scholasticorum omnium doctissimi."

use of the Fathers within the broader perspective of the sixteenth-century understanding of tradition and authority.

8.1   Beza's Instruction in the Church Fathers

In 1528, when Beza was nine, he was placed under the tutelage of Melchior Wolmar, one of the most talented humanists of his day.[14] Under Wolmar's teaching, Beza inherited the humanistic program which consisted of studying rhetoric, grammar and moral philosophy through reading Latin and Greek literature.[15] He excelled in languages and thoroughly invested himself in reading ancient authors like Cicero, Catullus, Pliny, Varro, Ovid and Quintilian to name a few.[16] His knowledge of these ancient orators and philosophers was so extensive that he wrote in his autobiographical letter to Wolmar that there was "no celebrated Greek or Latin writer of whom I did not get a taste in the seven years which I spent with you."[17] The fact that his first published work was a collection of poetry in which he tried to imitate the styles of Catullus and Ovid revealed his love for these ancient sources.

From his early years, Beza's imagination had been so gripped by this humanist ideal that his aspiration for ancient and classical sources never faded from his life. Even after his conversion experience in 1548, he continued to regard the *studia humanitatis* as serving a useful purpose for his Protestant cause. Kirk Summers claimed that the humanistic training that Beza received became a tool for his work in the Academy of Geneva as an interpreter of the Scriptures.[18] From the many references to ancient Greek and Latin authors in Beza's published writings and private correspondence, it is clear that Beza was an expert in classic literature and an advocate of the humanistic program throughout his adult life.

For the purpose of this essay, then, a question arises. How much did this humanistic training include the readings of the church fathers? Did Beza's love for and use of classical sources throughout his career include patristic sources? Certainly, the humanistic preoccupation with classical literature also included early Christian writings. Backus explains that "many of the fifteenth-

---

14 For biographies on Beza, see BAIRD, H. (1899); GEISENDORF, P.-F. (1949); RAITT, J. (ed.) (1981), 89–104; STEINMETZ, D. (1971), 162–171.

15 KRISTELLER, P. (1979), 22.

16 Beza writes in his poem *Ad bibliothecam*: "Salvete, incolumnes mei libelli / Meae deliciae, meae salutes, / Salve, mi Cicero, Catulle, salve, / Salve, mi Maro, Pliniusque uterque, / Mi Cato, Columella, Varro, Livi, / Salve, mi quoque Plaute, tu Terenti, / Et tu salve Ovidi, Fabi, Properti." Cited in SUMMERS, K. (1991), 195–197. See also MANETSCH, S. (2000b), 400n.3.

17 Beza to Melchior Wolmar, 12 March 1560, in CB 3:45.

18 SUMMERS, K. (1991), 193–207.

and sixteenth-century translations and editions of the Fathers were the work of classical scholars and not of 'trained' theologians."[19] In the sixteenth century, one did not have to be a theologian to read and study the patristic tradition. The *studia humanitatis* entailed studying the original biblical languages of Hebrew and Greek and searching for the right interpretation of Scripture, which naturally included the effort to examine patristic sources in new ways spurred on by the invention of the printing press. Thus, part of Beza's education would have included reading the collections of patristic texts that were passed down from the medieval era, such as the *Glossa Ordinaria*, *Decree of Gratian*, and the *Sentences* of Peter Lombard, along with new critical editions and translations of patristic authors published in the sixteenth century.

Furthermore, one must not overlook Wolmar's significance in Beza's spiritual formation. During his years with Wolmar he had been introduced to the study of Scriptures and Christian resources of his contemporaries, one of which was Heinrich Bullinger's work *De origine erroris, in divorum ac simulachrorum cultu* (1529).[20] As Beza later recalled in a letter to Bullinger, it was when he was reading this book that the Lord opened his eyes for the first time.[21] But what follows is particularly interesting for our purpose. He writes that "the Lord opened my eyes, particularly when I came upon that section where you refuted the commentaries of Jerome."[22] This remark is significant because it implies Beza had some familiarity with the writings of Jerome. He does not explain in detail, but Beza confesses that it was at this point that he came to see the truth in clarity. This moment of realization could not have been possible if he had not known of Jerome and of his writings. This incident demonstrates that under Wolmar's tutelage, Beza was taught to study the Scriptures, part of which required reading commentaries and exegetical works of the early church fathers.

While there is no clear evidence on Beza's attitude towards the church fathers before his conversion, it is not difficult to notice that his predilection for classical studies naturally translated into his study of the patristic tradition. Even in the early years as a reformer, Beza made extensive use of patristic sources. The writings of Augustine made up a large part of his argument in his *Tabula Praedestinationis* (1555). The first edition of his *Annotationes in Novum Testamentum* (1556) included numerous references to early church theologians

---

19 BACKUS, I. (1991), 291.

20 MANETSCH, S. (2006), 42.

21 Beza to Bullinger, 18 August 1568, in CB 9:121.

22 Beza to Bullinger, 18 August 1568, in CB 9:121: "Quod enim hodie Christum agnosco, […] l[ege]rem, aperuit tum mihi Dominus oculos ea praesertim parte que Hieronymi commenta refutas, ut in lucem veritatis intuerer."

like Origen, Ambrose, Jerome, Chrysostom and Augustine. This shows that already at this developing stage as a reformer, Beza had an extensive knowledge of patristic sources from which he did not hesitate to draw his arguments. The writings of the Fathers provided a solid source for Beza's formulation of theological doctrines.

This practice, however, was not unique to Beza. His contemporaries, such as Melanchthon, Huldrych Zwingli, Martin Bucer, Peter Martyr Vermigli and Calvin had their own approaches to using the ancient sources, including the church fathers. In a fascinating exchange of letters between Calvin and Beza, they allude to their differences on this issue. Dated 18 February 1562, shortly after Calvin heard news about the Colloquy of Poissy, he wrote to Beza expressing his concern about Beza's use of the ancient sources. Calvin wrote, "That method of yours has always displeased me, as half of your arguments consist in the testimony of the ancients."[23] To this, Beza responded assuring Calvin that his method was not very different from that of Calvin's:

Now, as I hope, you have recognized from my last letter what was the issue of our colloquy. We have not inconsiderately, trust me, placed side-by-side the testimony of the ancients with the clear Word of God. For otherwise we would never have been listened to, and all would have declared us to have abandoned our task. Always, however, an exception had been added that their authority is valid in no other way than *if it should consent to the Word of God.* Nor at the one and same space of time have we defined the antiquity, because, as you have known, abuses were being brought in little by little, just as we have always testified.[24]

---

23 Calvin to Beza, 18 February 1562, in CB 4:49: "Semper mihi displicuit vestra illa ratio, ut dimidia pars causae in Antiquitatis testimonio consistat." Here, it is not clear whom Calvin had in mind when referring to "the ancients," whether it was the pagan authors or the church fathers or both. Since this letter was written in the aftermath of the Colloquy of Poissy, it seems most natural to think that Calvin was showing concern for how Beza used "the ancients" in his arguments at the Colloquy. Interestingly, however, Beza's orations from the Colloquy reveal that Beza did not use pagan authors but relied on the church fathers to support his views. Thus, when understood in the context of the Colloquy, "the ancients" seems to be suggestive of the church fathers. But then, this makes one wonder why Calvin used the word "the ancients" (*antiquitatis*) instead of "the fathers" (*patres*). Whether Calvin is referring to another writing or work by Beza, it is hard to tell from this letter. Although this question will remain unanswered, I think it is reasonable to understand "the ancients" in this context as referring to all ancient sources in general, which can include pagan and/or patristic sources of Latin and Greek authors.

24 Beza to Calvin, 4 March 1562, in CB 4:67–68: "S. Jam, ut spero, cognovisti ex postremis literis meis quis fuerit nostrae colloquutionis exitus. Quod antiquitatis testimonia cum expresso Dei verbo conjunximus, non est a nobis, mihi crede, temere factum; nam alioqui nunquam fuissemus auditi, et omnes judicassent nos tergiversari; semper autem addita fuit exceptio, non aliter valituram illorum authoritatem quam *si cum Dei verbo consentiret.* Neque uno et

This short exchange between Calvin and Beza demonstrates that their practice of using the ancients was a deliberate exercise. Reformers selected carefully which ancient texts to use, at which point, and at what frequency. As Beza mentioned, it was not done in an "inconsiderate" way. To answer Calvin's concern about his excessive use of the ancient sources, Beza justifies his action in two ways. First, he claims that he used the testimonies of antiquity only when they conformed to the Word of God. Scripture was the norm by which all other authorities were to be judged.[25] He makes it clear that Scripture has the superior authority over all other sources. Secondly, Beza points out that there are those who misuse or distort ancient texts. Because of this, he did not define the boundaries, but rather tried to use them according to their proper sense. He was not interested in creating a set of ancient sources appropriate for his polemical agenda, which would then limit his use of them. If the sources consented to the Scripture and were proper to the context, Beza did not feel the pressure to restrict which ancient authorities to use in the process of constructing his arguments. Beza's extensive use of the ancients and the Fathers did not refer to an indiscriminate use, but rather a selective use, in relation to the authority of the Scripture.

Beza's attitude towards using the Fathers was also evident in his response to Jesuit John Hay, in which he refuted the Catholic accusations of the Reformed on five different topics. One recurring criticism of the Reformed was that they refuse all interpretations of the ancient fathers.[26] To this accusation, Beza explained that "on the contrary, we receive indifferently the writings of all the Doctors of the Church, without distinction of old or new." He further indicated that the reformers recognize and listen to the ancient writers, whether Greek or Latin, with reverence.[27] Beza then suggested there are two conditions for using the Fathers: first, their interpretations must confirm with the Scripture and articles of the faith as received by the Church, and second, each exegete should have the freedom to choose between the various interpretations of the Fathers

---

eodem temporis spatio antiquitatem definivimus, quoniam abusus, ut nosti, paulatim inventi sunt, sicut semper sumus testati." [Italics mine]

25 This is evident in many of Beza's writings. For example, see BEZA, T., *Sermons sur l'histoire de la resurrection de nostre Seigneur Jesus Christ* (1593b) 240–272. An English translation is provided in WRIGHT, S. (2006), 243–258.

26 BEZA, T., *Response aux Cinq Premieres et Principales Demandes de F. Jean Hay* (1586a), 105: "Tiercement, vous autres avez accoustume de no reprocher fur ce mesme propos, que nous allegons la seule Parolle escrite, en refesant toutes interpretations des Peres anciens, voire mesme de toute l'Eglise: choie trescalomniuesement forgee."

27 BEZA, T., *Response aux Cinq Premieres et Principales Demandes de F. Jean Hay* (1586a), 106: "Car au contraire nous recevons indifferemment les escrits de tous Docteurs de l'Eglise, sans distinction de vieux ou de nouveaux, [...] Nous recognoissons aussi & escoutons avec reverence entre les anciens, ceux que Dieu a fait reluire entre tous les autres, foyent Grecs ou Latins."

that he considers to be most appropriate to the Scriptural passage in question.[28] Here, again, there is a similar theme that runs through Beza's approach to using the church fathers. If the patristic texts conformed to the Scripture, Beza did not limit or define the use of them.

With his vast knowledge of the Fathers, Beza enjoyed the freedom of choosing between different patristic texts that would serve his arguments depending on the context of each of his writings. Mallinson provides a helpful tabulation of the names and the frequency of each Church Father that Beza used in his *Tractationes Theologicae* and his *Annotationes Majores*. To take the *Annotationes* as an example, Mallinson counted that Beza cites Augustine 265 times, Cicero 197 times, Tertullian 192 times, Chrysostom 176 times, and Jerome 175 times.[29] From these numbers, one can conclude that the patristic tradition was a significant source for the content of Beza's writings in formulating theological doctrines and exegetical arguments. Hence, when Vermigli donated books to the Academy of Geneva, most of which were patristic writings, Beza welcomed them and found them "useful."[30]

Of these early church fathers, Augustine was one of Beza's favorites. Especially when discussing predestination, Beza thought Augustine to be "the leader of the ancient theologians."[31] During Beza's lifetime, Augustine's vast literary corpus was reprinted multiple times, with almost five hundred editions published.[32] From the inventory of books of the Genevan Academy, it can be observed that Beza had at his disposal the ten-volume version of Augustine donated by Vermigli,[33] a six-volume edition of the complete works of Augustine (printed in Paris) and a separate copy of Augustine's *De Civitate Dei*.[34] This list does

---

28 BEZA, T., *Response aux Cinq Premieres et Principales Demandes de F. Jean Hay* (1586a), 106: "Mais c'est avec deux conditions que les Peres mesmes ont apposees: assavoir premierement entant que leurs expositions se trouvent confermees par la conference des passages de l'Escriture, & par la convenance avec les articles de nostre foy, receus de toute l'Eglise. [...] Secondement, pourveu que sans temerite ni presumption de foy mesmes, & retenans tousiours la convenance avec les articles de la foy, il foit libre a chacun lecteur de choisir entre les diverses interpretations celle qu'il estime la plus convenable au passage dont il est question."

29 MALLINSON, J. (2003), 40–41.

30 GANOCZY, A. (1969), 22: "Le fait que Théodore de Bèze a trouvé 'utile' de garder tous ces livres de Vermigli est également à retenir."

31 BEZA, T., *Ad acta Colloquii Montisbelgardensis Tubingae Edita, Theodori Bezae Responsionis, Pars Altera* (1588), 180: "Istis autem agedum subiiciamus etiam duorum scriptorum gravissima testimonia, Augustin. videlicet veterum Theologorum facile principis, a quo adversus Pelagianos pertractata est multis libris & locis haec questio, & Thomae, scholasticorum omnium doctissimi."

32 VISSER, A. (2011), 5.

33 GANOCZY, A. (1969), 22.

34 BACKUS, I. (1980), 9.

not mean that Beza would have read them all, but it gives an indication of how Augustine's writings were received in Geneva and at the Academy, where Beza taught and exercised leadership.

8.2 Beza's Use of Augustine in the Formation of the Predestinarian Doctrine

Based on Beza's principles towards using patristic texts, this section will investigate his use of Augustine in the formation of his predestinarian thought. Although the whole of Beza's literary corpus will form the general background for the following analysis, this section will pay particular attention to a few of his letters and four of his writings that are most instructive for understanding his use of Augustine in the doctrine of predestination. Careful attention will be made to the historical context and the genre of each of these writings.

8.2.1 Beza's Letters During the Bolsec Controversy (1551–1555)

Beza's doctrine of predestination developed during his teaching years at Lausanne through the controversies surrounding Jerome Bolsec (c. 1524–1584) in Geneva. Four letters written during this period, two addressed to Bullinger and two addressed to Calvin, illustrate the maturing process of his thought.[35] In an early letter to Bullinger, dated 29 October 1551, one sees Beza's parallelistic structure between election and reprobation. Since God does not elect based on foreseen belief, it could not be that God reprobates based on foreseen unbelief. For this parallelism to work, Beza understood that logically God must first elect individuals and then ordain the fall as a means of executing his decrees. A developed expression of this thought is present in the fourth letter to Calvin, written on 29 July 1555, in which more thorough distinctions and articulations are made. Here, Beza wrestles with the question of God's purpose in election and reprobation. It is in this context that Augustine makes his first appearance in Beza's discussion of predestination. Interestingly, however, Augustine is not used in a positive way. Rather, Beza disagrees to read with Augustine "the potter's clay" of Romans 9 as referring to an "entire human race corrupted in Adam."[36] With Augustine's rendering, one would have to take the fall as ante-

---

35 Beza to Bullinger, 29 October [1551], in CB 1:71–73; Beza to Bullinger, 12 January [1562], in CB 1:76–80; Beza to Calvin, 21 January 1552, in CB 1:81–84; Beza to Calvin, 29 July [1555], in CB 1:169–173. For a helpful study and English translations of these letters, see HOLTROP, P. (1993); and THOMAS, G. (2000), 7–28.

36 Beza to Calvin, 29 July [1555], in CB 1:170: "et certe videbimur in eam sententiam inclinare si cum Augustino per massam figuli totum genus hominum in Adamo corruptum intelligamus, quum hac ratione corruptio in mente Dei propositum eligendi et reprobandi antecedat."

ceding God's plan to elect and reprobate . Beza comments, "But I see nothing of that sort in Paul (Romans 9)."[37] He argues that the "lump of clay" of Romans 9 refers to "the human race not yet created."[38] From this, he concludes that the primary cause of God's decree is the will of God, which is superior to all other secondary causes.

As this letter illustrates, Beza did not hesitate to disagree with Augustine and use him in a critical sense. The use of Augustine in this context does not have a significant place, since even if his reference to Augustine was removed from the letter, the same message would still have been conveyed to Calvin. But what this reveals is that Beza and his contemporaries frequently interacted and wrestled with the writings of Augustine, whether it was for consent or disagreement.

8.2.2 Doctrinal and Polemical Writings (1555–1588)

Beza's polemical context required that he use Augustine in different ways. In his doctrinal and polemical writings, Augustine assumed a more authoritative role as an orthodox Church Father who spoke on the issue of predestination. The *Summa Totius Christianismi*, better known as the *Tabula Praedestinationis* (1555), was published as Beza's ideas expressed in previous letters were further developed.[39] Bolsec had been banished from Geneva in December of 1552, but having relocated in Bern, he was still making trouble for Calvin and Beza.[40] Even worse, in the aftermath of the Bolsec controversy, the Bernese magistrates had banned preaching on predestination in territories under their control, to which Lausanne belonged.[41] After wrestling with this theological topic for several years, Beza wrote the *Tabula* to construct a positive exposition of the predestination doctrine and also to respond to the Bernese prohibition against preaching the doctrine. As Muller rightly pointed out, Beza published this work with the intent of showing that the doctrine of predestination is "a source of consolation and strength" against the claims of Bolsec that "the doctrine was not based on a simple reading of Scripture and was a monstrous distortion of the gospel."[42]

---

37 Beza to Calvin, 29 July [1555], in CB 1:170: "At ego nihil tale in Paulo (Rom. 9) animadverto."
38 Beza to Calvin, 29 July [1555], in CB 1:170: "massae puto comparari a Paulo genus humanum nondum conditum."
39 BEZA, T., *Summa totius christianismi, sive descriptio et distributio causarum salutis electorum and exitii reproborum, ex sacris literis collecta* (1555); also in *Tractationes theologicae*, 3 vols. (1570–82), 1:170–205. Subsequent references will come from the *Tractationes*.
40 In the spring of 1555, Calvin and several colleagues from Geneva were still responding to Bolsec's accusations that Calvin was a heretic. See MULLER, R., (1999), 36–38.
41 MULLER, R. (1999), 39.
42 MULLER, R. (1999), 35.

What approach, then, does Beza take to respond to Bolsec's claims and convince his readers that predestination is a biblical and a preachable doctrine? Interestingly, Beza begins chapter one with quotes from Augustine's *On the Gift of Perseverance*, as if he wants Augustine to speak on the matter on his behalf. All citations speak to the usefulness of preaching predestination against common objections, which sets the tone for the whole treatise. As Beza concludes this chapter, he claims Augustine's thought to be "that most excellent man's opinion," but qualifies any further discussion of the doctrine by two conditions.[43] The first is that it must be discussed according to the Word of God, and the second that it must be expounded "skillfully" and for "edification."[44] Unlike the previously cited letter to Calvin where Beza's citation of Augustine did not add much to his argument, in this treatise, Beza presents Augustine as an authoritative figure who speaks on this matter.

Beza's use of Augustine here serves three functions. First, Augustine was an undeniable intellectual authority.[45] According to Diarmaid MacCulloch, it was "a new statement of Augustine's ideas on salvation" that set the Reformation on its explosive course.[46] Claiming Augustine to be on their side would have been an appealing idea for any western Christian theologian of the sixteenth century. Secondly, Beza's use of Augustine was driven by his historical context in which Bolsec had pitted Calvin and the Genevan ministers' predestinarian view against that of Augustine.[47] In fact, a court record dated 21 October 1551 reports that Bolsec had identified Augustine's views to be in line with his own. In response, the Genevan ministers derided him for his "stupid ignorance" and corrected him by citing numerous passages from Augustine's own writings.[48] Thus, as an extension of this debate, Beza cited Augustine as a way of refuting Bolsec's remarks. The third function of Beza's use of Augustine must be placed in a broader historical perspective. The controversy between Calvin and Bolsec was not just a debate between two people with different opinions concerning predestination, but it was a debate between two traditions, one representing the Augustinian monergism and the other following a strand of late medieval

---

43 Beza, *Summa Totius Christianismi,*(1555), I:171: "Haec est excellentissimi illius hominis sententia, quae tamen duas conditiones ponit.

44 BEZA, T., *Summa Totius Christianismi,*(1555), I:171: "Una est, si ex verbi Dei praescripto de his differatur: altera, si hoc ipsum quod Scriptura de his rebus explicat, dextre & in aedificationem exponatur."

45 Jaroslav Pelikan once stated that the study of the Western Christianity is "a series of footnotes to Augustine." See PELIKAN, J. (1971), 1:330.

46 MACCULLOCH, D. (2003), 110.

47 HOLTROP, P. (1993), 1:55. See also, RCP 2:81: "Puis qu'on faisait croire à st Augustine qu'il estoit de ceste opinion, ce qui estoit faulx, comme il monstreroit."

48 HOLTROP, P. (1993), 2:435–437.

synergism. Muller notes that "the controversy between Calvin and Bolsec was not, therefore, an epochal conflict" but "it was one heard over and over during the era of the Reformation."[49] Citing Augustine in this context allowed Beza to make the claim that he was in the line of the Augustinian tradition, whereas Bolsec and other opposing parties were not.[50] By claiming Augustine to be on his side, the burden of proving orthodoxy would have been transferred to those who were accusing Calvin's doctrine of predestination as heretical. As such, the patristic sources were at times used as a standard for judging between the true and the false traditions.

The *De Praedestinationis Doctrina* (1582) came at a much later stage of Beza's life, but still demonstrated a similar use of Augustine, that is, as an authority against polemical opponents. Originally Beza's lecture on Romans 9, *De Praedestinationis Doctrina* was published as a polemical treatise in 1582 during a time when theological controversies threatened Beza and his church from all sides.[51] Compared to the *Tabula* of 1555, the argument of *De Praedestinationis Doctrina* was structured with more refined distinctions and definitions. Bray called this the "scholastic" and "rationalistic tendencies" of Beza, who desired to justify Romans 9 for "his own peculiar, non-biblical theories,"[52] but other scholars have noted that the *Doctrina* demonstrated his depth and precision, along with the pastoral applications which he related to the life of a believer.[53] As for comparisons on his use of patristic sources, Augustine's writings take on an authoritative role similar to the *Tabula*. Throughout the treatise, lengthy quotations of Augustine appear in support of Beza's arguments. For example, as Beza explains that God's will is always just and never evil, he cites a long passage from Augustine's *Enchridion to Laurentius*. Numerous times, phrases such as "by the testimony of Augustine," "Augustine writes," "Augustine says," "Augustine states" or "Augustine refutes" appear, sometimes with direct quotation or sometimes with Beza's paraphrases, carrying an authoritative voice on the matter as the one who confirms Beza's position as the correct one.[54]

A similar pattern can be observed in *Ad Acta Colloquii Montisbelgardensis* (1588). In 1585, the colloquy was convened to resolve the issue of French refugees who wanted to take communion in Montbéliard according to their

---

49 MULLER, R. (1999), 42.

50 Muller identifies Bolsec's terminology of the predestined elect and the foreknown reprobate as following the synergistic theology present in Gabriel Biel and Johann Eck. See MULLER, R. (1999), 44. See also OBERMAN, H. (1967), 187–191, 194–195.

51 MANETSCH, S. (2000b), 138n.78.

52 BRAY, J. (1971), 118–119.

53 See BLACKETER., R. (2013), 121–141; and BEEKE, J. (2017), 188.

54 See for example BEZA, T., *De Praedestinationis Doctrina* (1582c), 4–5, 26–27, 30–31, 43–44.

confession using a French liturgy.[55] Jakob Andreae was the spokesperson for the Lutheran side, while Beza represented the Reformed position on behalf of the French refugee community. It was clear from the outset that this religious colloquy would only cause more theological division. Among the many theological points in dispute, André argued that God did not decree anyone to perish, to which Beza countered that since nothing happens outside of God's knowledge and will, God must have decreed some to be elect and others to be reprobate.[56] This work, more than Beza's other writings, contained the most number of references to Augustine. Beza employed the Father to delineate his views on particular grace,[57] God's willing,[58] definition of election,[59] God's secret will,[60] sinful man,[61] and so on. In fact, Beza sometimes simply delegated a few paragraphs to Augustine to speak with his own words, calling them "the most important testimony."[62] No doubt, in Beza's mind, Augustine was the most reliable person of the church fathers who spoke on this issue and gave him support from an authoritative source alongside the witness of the Scriptures.

In sum, the consistent theological theme that pervaded Beza's doctrinal writings was that predestination includes God's decrees of both election and reprobation, although the cause of damnation was within the damned not God, in order to reveal his glory through justice and mercy. Beza's use of Augustine was hardly surprising given his authoritative place in the tradition of the church, and because Beza's opponents were claiming Augustine to be on their sides. In such a polemical context, Beza's use of Augustine reflects two interesting characteristics. First, he tends not to refute Augustine. He knew of the places where he did not agree with Augustine, which in other writings he would simply note, but in debates, he chose to be silent on the disagreements, but magnify

---

55 RAITT, J. (1993), 8–10.
56 BEZA, T., *Ad Acta Colloquii Montisbelgardensis tubingae edita, Theodori Bezae Responsionis, Pars Altera* (1588), 8–11. For the English translation, see HOLTROP, P. (1982).
57 BEZA, T., *Ad Acta Colloquii Montisbelgardensis tubingae edita, Theodori Bezae Responsionis, Pars Altera* (1588), 149.
58 BEZA, T., *Ad Acta Colloquii Montisbelgardensis tubingae edita, Theodori Bezae Responsionis, Pars Altera* (1588), 153.
59 BEZA, T., *Ad Acta Colloquii Montisbelgardensis tubingae edita, Theodori Bezae Responsionis, Pars Altera* (1588), 157.
60 BEZA, T., *Ad Acta Colloquii Montisbelgardensis tubingae edita, Theodori Bezae Responsionis, Pars Altera* (1588), 163.
61 BEZA, T., *Ad Acta Colloquii Montisbelgardensis tubingae edita, Theodori Bezae Responsionis, Pars Altera* (1588), 168.
62 BEZA, T., *Ad Acta Colloquii Montisbelgardensis tubingae edita, Theodori Bezae Responsionis, Pars Altera* (1588), 155–156, 158–159, 162–164, 167–168, 180–181. "Istis autem agedum subiiciamus etiam duorum scriptorium gravissima testimonia, Augustin videlicet veterum Theologorum facile principis, a quo adversus Pelagianos pertractata est multis libris" (180).

the agreements. Thus, adverbs such as "rightly," "correctly" and "beautifully" are often used with Augustine's statements. This connects to the second point, that Beza's use of Augustine was based on a careful selection. Beza's writings indicate that he preferred to cite from Augustine's *City of God, Against Julian, On the Predestination of the Saints,* and *Enchridion to Laurentius.* Acknowledging Augustine as an authority who spoke on the matter, Beza appropriated his writings side by side with Scripture.

8.2.3 *Annotationes in Novum Testamentum* (1556, 1565, 1582, 1589, 1598)

Beza's predestinarian thought was expressed not only in his doctrinal or polemical writings, as previously discussed, but also in his exegetical writings. Of his exegetical works, especially worth noting is his *Annotationes*, which had earned him great fame as a biblical scholar among his contemporaries. Scott M. Manetsch commented that this writing became "the gold standard of Reformed biblical scholarship in the late sixteenth century."[63] Analyzing this work is significant for this article's purpose because on one hand, it will demonstrate Beza's use of Augustine in his exegetical writing, and on the other hand, the multiple editions of the *Annotationes* allow the opportunity to trace the developments between them. Since it would be impossible to analyze every section of the *Annotationes* in which Beza discusses predestination, the text to be examined here will be Romans 9, a classical text for explaining this doctrine.

In Beza's exegesis of Romans 9, Augustine is mentioned a total of one or three or five times depending on the edition. From just one reference to Augustine in the first edition of 1556, Beza adds two more to the second edition of 1565, and then two more in his later three editions. The one use in the first edition, which appears in subsequent editions, occurs in his annotations of Romans 9:22. Concerning the word "carry through" (*pertulit*), Beza notes that Augustine preferred to use the word "carrying" (*adferendi*). This rendering, according to Beza, makes it seem that God is the one who produces vessels of wrath and leads them to punishment. Beza says that such ideas were clearly refuted for a long time and disapproves of Augustine's translation.[64] Surprisingly, the only reference to Augustine in this first edition is a negative one. Beza had published his *Tabula* in 1555, a year before his first edition of the annotations, which indicates that by the time Beza was writing this work, he would have been fully aware and supportive of citing Augustine as a patristic authority, especially

---

63 MANETSCH, S. (2014), 32.
64 All five annotations on Romans 9:22: "*Pertulit*: Augustinus tamen uti maluit verbo Adferendi: quasi dicatur Deus vasa irae producere, vel in lucem edere, vel ad poena suis gradibus ac paulatim adducere. Sed haec plane sunt longius petita, nec satis apposite dicuntur."

when the topic in discussion concerned predestination. But unlike the *Tabula*, in which Beza began with Augustine, his *Annotationes* of 1556 refers to Augustine only once, and that with disagreement. This may be suggestive of the role that genre played in how church fathers were used. Moreover, it is interesting to note that while there was a minimal role attached to Augustine in the 1556 edition, there was a much greater emphasis on the philological contribution of Erasmus. As Beza revises and produces further editions, reliance on Erasmus remained but to a lesser degree, whereas references to Augustine increased.

From the second edition and onward, Beza mentions Augustine in two additional places. First, Beza employs Augustine's rendering of certain words as either sufficient or insufficient. For example, when referring to the word "worship" (*cultus*) in Romans 9:4, he comments that the Vulgate used the word "compliance" (*obsequium*), at which point he indicates that Augustine also used this rendering several times.[65] Here, Beza does not use Augustine as an authoritative figure, but simply presents him as one of the many biblical exegetes of the past. Augustine offers one philological option among many. The five editions also share a reference to Augustine concerning Romans 9:11, in which Paul states that God had already predestined the ends of Esau and Jacob, though they were not yet born and had done nothing either good or bad. Beza is certain that this verse excludes the idea of God electing and reprobating based on foreseen faith and unbelief:

> Therefore all consideration of persons or works is removed no less in the decree of eternal reprobation than in election, although these two are opposed, and the Apostle speaks about the rejection of Esau in no other way than about the election of Jacob, just as it is clear from verse 18. But if anyone accepts the Apostle's saying as follows, that in fact God decreed to elect or reject persons before they are good or evil, rather truly before they exist, since His decree is from eternity: but nevertheless that (God decreed) to elect on that account, seeing that He foresees the faith and the good works of the elect, and to decide reprobation on that account, seeing that He foreknows the incredulity and the evil works of the reprobate: I respond, the futility of this saying would be understood not only from many others, but also especially most manifest from the following objection.[66]

---

65 BEZA, T., *Annotationes* (1565b), on Romans 9:4, 188 (Book 2): "*Cultus.* Vulgata, *Obsequium*, ut etiam Augustinus aliquoties hunc locum citat." See also idem, *Annotationes* (1582b), 55 (Book 2); idem, *Annotationes* (1589c), 59 (Book 2); and idem, *Annotationes* (1598a), 63 (Book 2).

66 BEZA, T., *Annotationes* (1565, 1582, 1589, 1598) on Romans 9:11: "Ergo non minus in aeterno reprobationis decreto removetur omnis consideratio personarum vel operum quam in electione, quum haec duo opposita sint, & de Esau rejecto non aliter loquatur Apostolus quam de Jacobo electo, sicut apparet ex vers. 18. Quod siquis excipiat, sic loqui Apostolum quoniam reipsa constituit Deus homines eligere vel reiicere antequam boni vel mali sint, imo etiam antequam sint, quum eius propositum sit ab aeterno: sed tamen idcirco eligere (electioni destinare) quoniam praevideret eligendorum fidem & bona opera, & id circo reprobationi

The argument that Beza began to formulate during the Bolsec controversy that foreseen faith or unbelief cannot be the basis of God's decree is consistent in his explanations of Paul's words. There can be absolutely no human work on which God's decree depends. In fact, Beza makes it clear that God's decree comes logically before creation and the fall. After this statement, Beza writes, "About this issue let us listen to Augustine himself, lest anyone thinks we speak out of our sense,"[67] calling him "almost the only reliable attacker of Pelagianism."[68] Then, he cites a passage from Augustine's *Enchridion to Laurentius*, chapter 98, where Augustine denies the idea of foreseen faith and unbelief.[69] This could have ended Beza's argument, but interestingly, he goes on to report that this same Augustine has written in other places an opposite view, defining foreseen faith as the cause of election. This statement seems to diminish Augustine's authority. But immediately Beza adds that in the *Retractions*, Augustine corrected himself that he would not have written these things, if he had understood "faith as much as good works to be the gift of God."[70] It is worth asking why Beza reports Augustine's divergent claims, and then resorts to his retractions, instead of simply pointing to Augustine's retractions in the first place. This example demonstrates Beza's view on human authority, that is, he was fully aware that human interpreters make errors and change their views over time; they do not possess an absolute authority as does Scripture. Despite the errors, however, Beza redeems Augustine's status as an authoritative and reliable church father by complimenting his coming to the right conclusion.

In his third to fifth editions, Beza fortifies his argument with two more references to Augustine that were absent from the earlier versions. The first case is seen in Beza's comments on Romans 9:16. In the context of explaining that election depends solely on the mercy of God, Beza adds that those who allow a small room for thinking that our will can work towards election when associated with the mercy of God are hallucinating. Then, he writes that Augustine held this

---

decernere, quoniam praescit reprobandorum incredulitatem & mala opera: respondeo, huius dicti futilitatem cum ex aliis multis, tum vero maxime ex sequenti objectione manifestissme intelligi."

67 BEZA, T., *Annotationes* (1565, 1582, 1589) on Romans 9:11: "Qua de re audiamus ipsum Augustinum, nequis nos existimet ex nostro sensu loqui."

68 The expression "the only certain attacker of Pelagianism" only appears in the 1598 edition of the *Annotationes*: "qua de re audient salute isti Augustinum unicum paene illum Pelagianismi certum oppugnatorem."

69 This passage from Augustine is found in the *Enchiridion* in NPNF 3:268.

70 BEZA, T., *Annotationes* (1565, 1582, 1589, 1598) on Romans 9:11: "post ea lib. Retract. I. cap. I. "Illa," inquit, "non scripsissem, si fidem, non minus, quam bona opera, esse Dei dona intellexissem."

view in some places, but excellently corrected himself in the *Retractions*.[71] In addition, when commenting on Romans 9:18, Beza explains that God hardens whomever he wills not by implanting any new malice nor by force, but by "sinking the already corrupt more and more, then by effectually surrendering them to the lust of their own hearts and even to Satan," which, he says, Augustine abundantly demonstrated against Julian.[72] In both instances Beza commends Augustine for holding the correct view, although in the first case it was his later view in the *Retractions* that was the correct one.

The extended sections on Augustine certainly add detail to Beza's annotations, but they do not add or change Beza's original content in any way. What then is the purpose of inserting references to Augustine here? First, Beza adds authority to his position. Affirming R. Ward Holder's point, "the quoting of authorities demonstrated that one stood in the stream of tradition and had not fallen into heresy."[73] Such a method was a common strategy for defending one's orthodoxy in the sixteenth century. Second, by inserting Augustine to his argument, Beza adds sources of textual evidence. Backus argues that Beza's annotations basically followed the Erasmian model, although he was much more critical of the patristic sources than Erasmus. This is evident in his references to Augustine correcting himself in the *Retractions*.[74] Whatever his reasons, it can be concluded with Mallinson that "the course of Beza's exegetical career witnessed an increased use of the Fathers for philological and contextual insights."[75]

8.3 Conclusion

In short, Beza had an extensive knowledge of the Fathers, knowledge which he began to accumulate in his early years as a student under Wolmar. His attitude towards the Fathers was generally positive, respecting them as human authorities, but he consistently used them in accordance with the Scripture.

---

71 BEZA, T., *Annotationes* (1582, 1589, 1598) on Romans 9:16: "Quam autem hallucinentur qui supplent particulam solum, quasi non excludat nostrum voluntatem & opera Paulus, sed illa neget sufficere nisi cum Dei misericordia conjungantur, quod etiam aliquando Augustinus existimavit, ipsemet Augustinus seipsum corrigens egregie demonstrate lib. I. Retract. Cap. 23."

72 BEZA, T., *Annotationes* (1582, 1589, 1598) on Romans 9:18: "Reipsa igitur Deus quos vult indurat: non quidem novam aliquam malitiam eis ingenerando sicut in electis novas vires efficit quum eos immutat: nec etiam cogendo, quum nemo nisi volens peccet: sed primum quidem iam corruptos magis ac magis deferendo, deinde eos cupiditatibus cordium suorum, & Satanae quoque, tanquam justissimus judex, efficaciter tradendo, ut copiose adversos Julianum demonstrat Augustinus, libr. 5. Cap. 3."

73 HOLDER, R.W. (2009), 222.

74 BACKUS, I. (1980), 8.

75 MALLINSON, J. (2000), 46.

They served as solid sources of references for constructing his theology, as it can be observed in many of his writings. When it came to the formation of his predestinarian thought, the same rules applied, but its practice varied between different contexts and genres. In polemical contexts, Augustine assumed the more authoritative role as representing the orthodox tradition. Sometimes, Beza would simply use citations from Augustine as if his words themselves carried a weight of their own. In these settings, Beza preferred to keep Augustine's errors in silence if possible. In the exegetical writings, however, Augustine's writings still carried theological authority, but it was more his philological contribution that Beza found useful. Following the Erasmian model, Beza's *Annotationes* made extensive use of the Fathers, less than Erasmus but more than Calvin. However, as we have seen, Beza did not hesitate to point to errors in Augustine's translation and theology. Of course, one cannot argue that these seemingly varied use of patristic sources between the polemical and the exegetical writings were standard rules for Beza. But these patterns and tendencies indicate how genre can shape the way that patristic sources were used in varying historical contexts.

How, then, does Beza's use of the Fathers relate to the larger scheme of his theology? The answer can be found in Beza's understanding of orthodox and catholic tradition of the Church. In his *Confessio christianae fidei* (1560) he describes the nature of the church as such:

> Since the kingdom of Jesus Christ is perpetual, it is necessary that few always exist, who recognize him as their king. Thus, from the beginning of the world, there was always some Church, that is, assembly and multitude of men chosen by God, who recognized and worshipped the true God according to his Word, truly, in one Jesus Christ apprehended by faith, as we have abundantly shown.[76]

This statement demonstrates that by the necessity of who Christ is, there has always been God's people gathered in the form of a Church since the beginning of the world. The catholic church, according to Beza, is a congregation that preaches the gospel and that God has called from all places, all times and all nations.[77] Thus, Beza concludes that there can only be one church because "there is but one God, one faith, and one Mediator Jesus Christ."[78] This sense

---

76 BEZA, T., *Confessio christianae fidei* (1560), 142: "Praeterea quum perpetuum sit Jesu Christi regnum, necesse est aliquos semper existere, qui eum pro Rege agnoscant. Itaque ab initio mundi aliqua semper fuit Ecclesia, idest, coetus & multitudo hominum à Deo selectorum, qui verum Deum agnoverunt & coluerent ex ipsius verbo, nempe, in uno Jesu Christo per fidem apprehenso, sicut copiose suo loco ostendimus."

77 BEZA, T., *Confessio christianae fidei* (1560), 143–144.

78 BEZA, T., *Confessio christianae fidei* (1560), 143: "Quum unus sit Deus, una fides, unus Dei & hominum mediator Jesus Christus."

of the one catholic church was what drove Beza to see the orthodox Fathers as authorities, for they had faithfully proclaimed the gospel. Thus, Beza firmly believed that his theology was in line with the catholicity of the church and its tradition, defending the truth against enemies of his day, as the Fathers did in their own times.

Chapter 9: Theodore Beza's Elegy on the Five Martyrs of Lyon

Wonder and Consolation

The editions of Beza's poetry from 1569 onward contain an elegy bearing the poignant title "About the Five Martyrs of Christ, Steadfast to the End, Burned at Lyon Sixteen Days before the Calends of June, 1553."[1] The elegy recounts the tragic story of five theology students from the Lausanne Academy who were arrested in Lyon on the first of May 1552 while returning to their home country of France.[2] At the time, Beza held the Professorship in Greek at the Lausanne Academy and thus knew them well; one of the students had even served as a secretary to Beza.[3] In a letter dated 15 May 1552, Beza reports to Bullinger their arrests, describing them as "young men of singular piety" who were responding to a call to ministry from scattered Protestant churches in southwest France.[4] He commends them to Bullinger's prayers because "only God can protect those deprived of all human help."[5]

Trouble began for the five when they departed from Geneva after a brief detour there and set out on the road to Lyon. On the way, they met a man who pretended to befriend them, eventually winning their trust and inviting them to dinner at his home. Once there, he callously betrayed them to the Catholic authorities. The students languished in a prison cell at Lyon for a year, suffering interrogation, humiliation and maltreatment, until they met their gruesome end by being burned at the stake on 16 May 1553. During the long imprisonment, the boys carried on a substantial correspondence, writing to friends and family in their

---

1 BEZA, T., *Poematum edition secunda* (1569), 81–83; BEZA, T., *Poemata varia* (1597), 72–73; BEZA, T., *Poemata varia* (1599), 29v-30v. All translations from Latin are my own.

2 Crespin provides the following names of the martyrs: Martial Alba, from Montauban in Quercy, the oldest of the five; Pierre Escrivain of Boulogne in Gascogne; Bernard Seguin, of the Reole in Basadois; Charles Favre, of Blanzac in Angoulmois; Pierre Naviheres, of Limoges. They were imprisoned in Lyon on the first day of May 1552. The story and relevant correspondence of the students appeared in Crespin's martyrologies (most notably, 1554, 1582, 1619), but were published as a separate volume: Crespin, *Ces cinq escoliers*. See also ALBA, M. (1854), 7:905–907.

3 VUILLEUMIER, H. (1927–33), 1:435n.2.

4 Beza to Bullinger, 15 May [1552], in CB 1:89. Beza reports only four students to Bullinger, but later corrects himself in the elegy to match Crespin's version. On the confusion over why the five former students were entering France (to propagate the Reformed movement, to convert their parents, etc.), see the discussion in CROUSAZ K. (2012), 292–293.

5 Beza to Bullinger, 15 May [1552], in CB 1:89.

hometowns, even receiving letters of encouragement from Calvin and Viret. After their deaths, this pathetic documentation of their ordeal came into the hands of Jean Crespin and inspired him to collect similar material for his well-known book of martyrologies. The Lyon executions occupy a considerable position in this work. For his part, Beza responds by writing the above-mentioned elegy, rehearsing the final scene of their death in such a way as to assuage his own sorrow and encourage other faithful who face persecution. The poem features familiar consolatory themes to which Beza turns often in his long career when ministering to the downtrodden. It also contains a surprising thaumatological element, an allusion to a natural wonder or marvel not reported in the other sources and to which our modern sensibilities may not be well-attuned or sympathetic. We may suppose that the description of a strange and preternatural event functions merely as a poetic device lending visual and emotive coloring. For Beza, however, the wonder has a key role to play in the narrative, one which is not imaginary or incidental—this would undercut the whole aim of the poem—but genuine and intentional, essential for interpreting the events as they unfold.

How do we account for his receptiveness to wonder? As a man of his time, Beza accepted the possibility that nature, as governed by divine providence, could deviate from its prescribed norms and act extraordinarily for a specific reason. This credulity in regard to wonder extends beyond his poetry to his entire ministry. In this essay, I will argue that the recording of the preternatural event in the tale of the five martyrs of Lyon highlights a little-noticed aspect of Beza's thought that he shares with many contemporaries, namely, that in certain cases, wonders and marvels are reliable harbingers of the divine will.

9.1 The Elegy of the Five Martyrs

Beza never mentions when he wrote the elegy on the five martyrs. The intensity of emotion that appears to have swept over him in the immediate aftermath of the event surely inspired these verses. And while the elegy corresponds in many ways to Crespin's account, it differs in several details. The first appearance of the poem in print, however, is not until 1569, when Beza published the second edition of his poetry. There we find the version of the poem that runs through all later editions, which I translate as follows:

> Wondrous events I will tell (be attentive, young and old),
> I will sing of things worthy to be read for many generations to come.
> You have heard of the very noble name of Lyon,
> walls they say that were built under the auspices of Plancus;
> here where the sluggish Saône with its peaceful stream
> adds waters to the churning waves of the rushing Rhône;

a city long known for its riches (alas! how hard it is
for the rich to be pious!);
and so, a city once renowned for its rare gifts,
has earned a reputation more for its impiety.
I have no need to describe the unspeakable deeds of its fathers;
it suffices to recount one crime in place of the many.
Here recently a single flame—ah me!—devoured five sheep
plucked from the blessed flock of Christ.
Piety saw this and groaned, and hoary Faith is said
to have uttered something of this sort:
"Have mercy, cruel flames—what have I done
to deserve this?—have mercy! Look at this pyre;
our dear children are burning on it!"
The flame was moved (a marvel to tell!) and seemed
to show that this crime displeased it.
When the mob, crueler than the fires, stoked
the reluctant fires to hasten on the work begun,
the flame bursts upward and swiftly feeds on their holy
limbs, trying to lighten the punishment by being quick.
Amid the flames (Trust me, what I say is true—so
may the kindly spirits of Heaven support me),
their burning breasts heaved forth Christ alone,
and their faltering tongues still proclaimed Christ;
when the Father from on high pitied his dear children
who were stripped of their flesh,
he calls to himself with this voice:
"You, o souls, true offspring of Heaven, whom
the flame guides and reveals the path to Heaven,
come! happily enter your kingdom, happily
encircle me on either side."
Thus he spoke, and with gladness he placed them
in the lofty abode, where the whole fabric
of the vast universe spreads itself.
From here they laugh at the tyrants who rebel against
Christ's kingdom,
from here they laugh at the threats and violence
of the Roman wolf,
from here they spy the flame raging against their vitals,
until the fuel is exhausted and subsides.
Now the flame dies out, scant smoke remains in the air,
when the Father from his lofty citadel speaks thus:
"Do you see these ashes? These are the seeds of our kingdom;
I produce many a Phoenix from such flames.
Do you see this smoke?
So the raging cruelty of the world, whatever it does,
will be nothing but smoke."[6]

---

6 For the poem, see note 1 above.

Here, in describing the travails of the Lyon martyrs, Beza exhibits his remarkable literary and pastoral talents. The two rivers that frame the area, one peaceful, one churning, lead the reader to consider the internal contradiction of the city itself, paradoxically blessed in resources but marred by unspeakable crimes. The use of anaphora, *from here* (Latin *hinc*) repeated three times to introduce phrases once the martyrs reach Heaven, emphasizes the finality of their journey, the attainment of their reward, and the distance from their tormentors. These devices and more add force to the message of consolation. For Beza, the students' story should remind the persecuted of the path they follow, a rugged path of sanctification leading ultimately to Heaven. Ironically, the very flames meant to consume them, as God himself proclaims from his celestial throne, light their path and show the way. They themselves find the strength for the journey by remaining fixated on their savior: even amid the fires, the pain and the scorn, their lips continuously proclaim the name of Christ. They can also shrug off, even mock, the attacks of their enemies, whose torments are ineffective and unfelt as they ascend to claim their heavenly prize. The persecuted can be assured that God will always intervene on behalf of his own to bring them home, as he does here. Nor should the faithful fear their suffering is in vain or that the onslaught of the enemies forever reduces the true Church to ashes. God's people have a resilience that no fire can quash. Try as they may, the tormentors of the Church engage in a futile exercise; just as the Phoenix spontaneously bursts into flames but is born anew from the ashes, so from the charred bodies of the martyrs arise new champions of the faith, new pastors and new followers of Christ.

Beza favored this Phoenix image in his various writings as a means for consoling God's people in dark times. For example, among his *Emblemata*, where several images with their accompanying poems aim to uplift the hearts of the faithful in dark hours of persecution, we find one emblem titled "The Phoenix among the Flames," with a woodcut depicting a Phoenix amid the flames. The poem underneath it provides the explanation:

> If what they say is true, death itself regenerates the Phoenix,
> making one and the same pyre both life and death to this bird.
> Go on, executioners, burn the holy bodies of the saints:
> The fire gives birth to those whom you wish to destroy.[7]

Beza doubts the myth itself—note the *if what they say is true*—but he does have confidence in the resurrection of the saints. Not only do the persecuted

---

7 BEZA, T., *Icones* (1580a), Ll.ii[r]; BEZA, T., *Poemata varia* (1597), 229; BEZA, T., *Poemata varia* (1599), 115[r].

themselves find victory amid the ashes, as they die for Christ and are transported to eternal happiness, the Church itself is resurrected from its martyrs. The enemies of the Church will always fail to extinguish it with their cruel fires; such executions inspire more adherents of the truth to follow. Similarly, we also read in the *Icones* that Peter Martyr Vermigli, Italian convert to Protestantism, emerged like the Phoenix from the ashes of the reforming Savonarola.[8]

The elegy of the five martyrs of Lyon, therefore, offers a message of comfort to Protestants everywhere, but perhaps especially those swept up in the conflicts within France. It reassures the faithful that the persecution they endure sculpts and refines them in their journey of sanctification, that God never abandons his people even when times seem dark, and that the enemies of the Church will eventually receive their just punishment. If we think about these elements of the consolation, however, we can see that the narrative must operate on two levels: First, Beza represents the five students as paradigms of fidelity and endurance. They did not falter at the bitter end, even amid the torturous flames, but finished the course while holding tightly to their trust in Christ. Jean Crespin relates that the students were singing psalms and calling out encouragement to one another. Second, and more difficult to portray, is what happens on the divine plane. Crespin has nothing to report in this regard, but Beza wants his readers, who may face such trials themselves, to recognize God's presence in the students' ordeal, to know that God is watching and will not fail to keep his promises. The very first word of the elegy—*mira*, in Latin, which I have rendered with *wondrous events*—invites readers to ponder a natural world and creation that interacts with and even reflects the supernatural realm and the creator. It also evokes the martyrdom of another, more famous Christian from earlier days, viz. Polycarp, whose death also involved a prodigious fire: after the executioner lit the flame, says his anonymous chronicler, "a great flame flashed forth, and we, to whom it was given to see, beheld a marvel."[9] History, in a way, repeats itself. Wonders again occur, some of them exhibited by the students themselves as they suffered while remaining faithful, but one especially that points heavenward and confirms God's involvement in the unfolding events. This is *a marvel to tell*, a well-known Vergilian phrase that signals divine intervention in nature. In Beza's story, the fire reacts to Faith and Piety by doing something both extraordinary and unnatural. At first it holds back its fury and resists to burn the young men, but when the executioners stoke the tinder below, it bursts into a consuming flame to finish the job quickly and mercifully. Those who are observing this astonishing episode, unless blinded by their own rebellion and obstinacy, cannot fail to see God at work in this tragedy.

---

8 BEZA, T., *Icones* (1580a), P.ii[r].
9 For the translation, see BETTENSON H./MAUNDER, C. (2011), 12.

We should not dismiss this wonder in the story for several reasons: first, Beza's thought and writings do accommodate the existence of wonders, both before and after he embraced the reform; second, a fascination with wonders and their meaning forms a part of the cultural and mental milieu of this period; and third, wonders occupy a place, even if a limited one, in the theology of the reformers. All these factors account for the presence of a wonder in the elegy on the five martyrs and can guide our understanding of its function. Therefore, in the sections that follow, we will briefly examine these three contextual elements in turn.

9.2 Beza's Sense of Wonder

Toward the end of 1539, a youthful (and not-yet Reformed) Beza composed an epigram to mark the anticipated entrance of Charles V into Paris on 1 January 1540, the Kalends of January.[10] This momentous occasion was tied to a treaty struck at Nice in 1538 between the emperor and the king of France, Francis I, settling a long-standing conflict between the two. In this poem, included in the first edition of his poetry (1548), Beza heralds the appearance of two suns in the skies over Paris that he believed related to the new alliance. He describes the event as follows:

> Recently, France, as you spied the twin suns,
> you marveled (*mirata es*) that there were two.
> But now learn to marvel (*mirari*) more at the blessings
> you see the twin stars are promising to you.
> One sun is Francis, the other is Charles; surely
> the stars are shining favorably on them.
> And if the treaty struck unites them in harmony,
> you will never have to fear an eclipse.

At this crucial moment when peace is being confirmed and a friendship forged, the French observe a wondrous prodigy over Paris. Twice in the poem Beza uses the verb *mirari* (*to marvel*) to underscore the extraordinary nature of the phenomenon. *Mirari*, of course, is a cognate of the same word with which the elegy on the five martyrs begins, *mira* (*wondrous* or *marvelous events*), and to some extent shows how they are related. Beza's epigram describes what is known as a parhelion (mock sun), that is, the appearance of a mirror image or luminous ring opposite the sun caused by the interplay of light and ice within

---

10 For a discussion of this poem, see SUMMERS, K. (2001), 211, 331–333. The poem appears in BEZA, T., *Poemata* (1548), 58.

the upper-atmosphere. This scientific explanation was not known yet in the sixteenth century.

We know from a note in Beza's hand in his own copy of the 1597 *Poemata varia* that university authorities recited the poem to Charles at his arrival.[11] In the later editions of Beza's poetry, however, a modified version takes the place of the original. Now the title states explicitly that the poem was "offered to Charles V himself when he was entering Paris on the Kalends of January 1540." In this later version, the twin suns appear after a long period of rain—Francis I and Charles V had been engaged in conflict off and on since 1521—and there is no mention of the eclipse. Why there is a discrepancy and which version was really read is not known, but what is most interesting is that in both cases—the one published before Beza's conversion, the other well after—wonder is at play. Even in the second version, we are told that the crowd marvels (*miratur vulgus*) while recognizing the obvious message being conveyed by the unusual weather. The rains cease, the clouds clear away and the twin suns appear, all portending a new period of peace. Recall that, in the first version, the parhelion has the power to stave off another wonder of the heavens, the casting of a shadow of darkness on the earth through an eclipse.

These poems allow us to draw a couple of conclusions. First, Beza assumes that the natural world is in some sense watching the drama of the human race unfold and reacting to the most pivotal moments in spectacular ways. How this is possible and why nature is being personified will be addressed in the theology section below. Suffice it to say here that wonders in nature were taken to reflect, even comment on human activity as they speak for the creator. Second, Beza held this belief consistently throughout his entire life. The first version of the epigram is one of the earliest writings that we have from him, composed in 1539 when he was only twenty years old. The second version appears still in the 1599 edition of Beza's poetry, the last edition published in his lifetime.[12] In this sixty-year span, nothing alters this conviction that nature itself rejoiced in the concord between the two sovereigns and demonstrated its approval by producing a wonder.

Poetry, of course, speaks a transcendent language that can accommodate the supernatural. Even so, Beza's fascination with wonders extends beyond poetry and into his everyday experience. Several times throughout his correspondence we observe him reporting wonders to his friends and venturing an interpretation. He operates on the assumption that all creation watches and participates in the drama of redemptive history. As God is drawing out a remnant for himself

---

11 AUBERT, F./BROUSSARD, J./MEYLAN, H. (1953), 164–191, 257–294; see esp. 183.
12 BEZA, T., *Poemata varia* (1599), 76ᵛ.

from a wicked world, the process involved is so difficult and traumatic that it reverberates throughout the natural order.

A few examples will suffice to demonstrate the point. In late March 1574, less than two years after the St Bartholomew's Day massacre in France, Beza writes to Bullinger with news of the fortunes of the persecuted Huguenots, something he does frequently.[13] He describes the civil chaos, the various injustices, the attempts to broker peace, the status of scattered pastors and churches. The Catholics themselves know they have gone too far, he says, and fostered a dangerous tyranny that they regret. Such a lamentable state of affairs even prompted a negative reaction in nature. He observes:

> On the twentieth of this month in the evening it rained blood. No one noticed it, however, until two days later when they saw the merchants' papers and wares all bloodied; these had been transferred into the shops after the fierce storm arose during the night and were only brought out again on Monday morning. Thus, God shouts, Heaven weeps, the earth is indignant, and the sea bellows, convinced that soon it will be strewn with great fleets. Only human beings are not warned; just the opposite, they are perfectly willing to mock God himself when he thunders.[14]

Reports of blood rain extend back to Homer's *Iliad* and is a phenomenon known to the Romans and in Europe after the fall of Rome.[15] Beza follows the norm when he attributes the unusual event to divine anger at humankind's obstinance and rebellion. God created the world to serve humankind in an orderly and beneficial way, but when humankind itself introduces chaos, the natural world cannot stay within its bounds or fail to reflect the creator's displeasure. In the same year, when the greatly despised Cardinal of Lorraine died, it was widely reported that a hurricane-like wind blew across France. Beza hints at this several times to friends in the months to come while doing his due diligence to ascertain if the rumors are true. But writing in March of 1575 to Gabriel Schlüsselberger, Beza writes a scathing mock epitaph for the cardinal, adding also that at the instant of his passing a southwind began to wreak havoc, both in Avignon, where the cardinal died, and throughout much of France.[16] It was so furious, he says, that it "knocked down several steeples, houses, and forests; they refer

---

13 Beza to Bullinger, 28 March 1574, in CB 15:58–62.

14 Beza to Bullinger, 28 March 1574, in CB 15:59. The editors note the passage bears resemblance to Job 26:10ff and Hag 2:7. See also MANETSCH, S. (2000b), 53.

15 These almost always portend some sort of disaster; for the passages and a discussion see TATLOCK, J. (1914), 442–447.

16 Beza to G. Schlüsselberger, 27 March 1575, in CB 16:46–51. See also Beza to Bullinger, 1 January 1575, in CB 16:1; and Beza to Dürnhoffer, 8 January 1575, in CB 16:4.

to it as the cardinal wind."[17] In other words, nature itself found the cardinal repulsive and so expressed its disdain in a violent wind.

Earthquakes also caused much consternation and anxiety about divine displeasure. An earthquake on 1 March 1584, followed soon thereafter by an avalanche on 4 March that destroyed much of the town of Yvorne, prompted the Genevans to proclaim a fast accompanied by special prayers.[18] In a letter dated the tenth of that month, Beza describes the quaking to Rudolf Gwalther as being brief but strong.[19] He also sends to Gwalther a list of "the foreboding predictions [*praesagia*] that people are inventing for themselves." Thus, he implies that instantly a fear spread through the people there that God intends to express his wrath and they began speculating how it would manifest itself. A few days later Gwalther expresses his approval of the fasting, noting that earthquakes do indeed teach lessons and that the end of the world is obviously near.[20] For his part, Beza does not at all disagree, but he proposes a nuanced interpretation of the event: "I think I am right if I say the earth is not big enough to sustain people's crimes, and that it is reproaching humanity for its hardness."[21] He adds that God means to wake up the Genevans with those rumblings lest they experience the full brunt of his just wrath. He later tells Laurenz Dürnhoffer that the prayers and fasting at Geneva were aimed at averting the kind of disaster that struck Yvorne, where sixty-nine homes were destroyed and one-hundred and twenty-two people died.[22] In his view, these pious actions, the prayers and fasting, helped turn the anger of God as manifest in nature into kindness for the repentant Genevans, seeing that soon after they uncovered a traitor in their midst.[23]

Beza fully embraced the idea that God directly caused earthquakes in order to send messages. To attempt what once the Roman poet Lucretius did, namely, to introduce scientific explanations for these types of phenomena, often engendered charges of atheism. Thus, when another earthquake occurs in early January 1593, Beza does not entertain a range of possible natural explanations at all. His anxiety and singular focus is quickly revealed in a comment to Johann Jakob Grynaeus, antistes of Basel, when he confesses that the trembling terrified many and prays by God's grace that it not be a harbinger of some catastrophe.[24]

---

17 Beza to G. Schlüsselberger, 27 March 1575, in CB 16:48.

18 RCP 5:30; Beza to Gwalther, 10 March 1584, in CB 25:45n.4.

19 Beza to Gwalther, 10 March 1584, in CB 25:44–46.

20 Gwalther to Beza, 13 April 1584, in CB 25:87.

21 Beza to Gwalther, 10 March 1584, in CB 25:45.

22 Beza to Dürnhoffer, 3 May 1584, in CB 25:91.

23 For the details of this attempt on the part of François de Gatagurel to betray the city of Geneva to the enemy, see Beza to Dürnhoffer, 7 April 1584, in CB 25:1n. 2.

24 Beza to Grynaeus, 6/16 January 1593, in CB 34:64.

And it was not merely earthquakes that caused alarm. In a postscript of a letter to Johannes Crato von Crafftheim in 1582, Beza remarks that several strange phenomena and prodigies were causing the people of Geneva, as well as himself, to wonder what God was communicating.[25] He writes with trepidation,

> We have seen many prodigies here, specifically, the sky ablaze with a blood-red glow on the sixth of March around 9 o'clock between the West and the North; two parhelion orbs going around the sun, one extremely large and milky white and splitting the middle of the sun's body, the other like a rainbow moving on the perimeter. This happened on Quasi-modo Sunday, from about ten o'clock until noon. And lastly, we saw a comet producing a curved palm branch. What these things portend, the Lord will reveal in his own time. Would that we are sufficiently focused on his coming, compared with those who act as in the days of Noah.

Here, Beza is not inclined to take the parhelia as a positive indication of God's favor, especially when viewed in the context of the other signs. The strange events are difficult to read, but he assumes in the very least they are a call to repentance and a reminder to ready oneself for the coming Day of Judgment.

9.3   The Enchanted World of the Sixteenth Century

Theodore Beza's decision to include the reporting of a wonder in the story of the five martyrs has little to do with the genre in which he was writing and more to do with a frame of reference and mindset that he shared with most in his day. Beza and many of his contemporaries were inclined to interpret prodigies and marvels as examples of divine intervention and communication, often confirming their own reading of current events. This mode of thinking was pervasive, not just among the uneducated or Roman Catholics who may have been predisposed to it, but likewise within Reformed and Lutheran circles, including Beza's own correspondents.[26] Examples abound. In lamenting to Beza the cruel fate of their friend François de la Noue, whom the Spanish had

---

25 Beza to Crato, 5 July 1582, in CB 23:100–101.

26 For an overview of this kind of thinking, especially as it relates to comets, see MOSLEY, A. (2014). An early, illustrated (by Lucas Cranach) example of wonder literature among the Lutherans is Melanchthon and Luther's description of the popish ass and monk calf in *Von dem PapstEsel zu Rom vnd Münchkalbs zu Freyburg*. Luther considered the monk calf an indicator of the corruption of monasticism. On this, see the discussion in SOERGEL, P. (2012), 48–52. The Luther/Melanchthon treatise was republished several times, including at the press of Jean Crespin in 1557. For the prevalence of wonder literature and broadsheets in Germany besides the aforementioned treatment of Soergel, see SCRIBNER, R. (1981), 125–127, 131, 184; and BARNES, R. (2015).

imprisoned and been mistreating for years, Rudolf Gwalther takes comfort in several prodigies that portend God's coming retribution. "Among these," he asserts with no compunction and referring to an event reported from Geneva itself, "it seems to me a very good omen when you [sc. the people of Geneva] saw the new moon set resplendent in its whole orb." In other words, what should have been just a sliver of a moon became a full moon as it reached the horizon. He adds, "The moon is a type of the Church, which receives its own light of righteousness from Christ alone; therefore, he will illumine it by his grace when the world around threatens us with darkness."[27] The same Gwalther, writing in 1578, attributes an unexplained fire that destroyed an armament of the Duke of Bavaria at Munich to God's retribution. God was displeased because, a month earlier, the Duke had sent the Jesuits to go house to house in the city to look for banned books and to publicly burn them. "Surely, God was avenging the harm done to his own," he remarks.[28] In 1583, Jean Chassanion, pastor at Metz, relates to Beza that during the night "several credible and God-fearing people there saw a strange and prodigious thing."[29] He proceeds to describe an unusual combination of light and clouds that rose up from the horizon in the distance "like smoke and fire from a cannon."[30] This strange phenomenon continued to dance and whistle in the middle of the sky for much of the night, lighting it up so brightly that it hurt the eyes of those who had come out to see it, sending them terrified back to their homes. He reports that a few hours before daylight, the whole fireworks display dissipated into a fog. Chassanion ties these strange events to the new religious order instituted by Henri III at Paris, whose odd processions and flagellations Gwalther had already interpreted as a sign of coming punishment to the rulers in France.

These personal reports and interpretations of wonders and prodigies among Beza's correspondents run counter to the thesis of Max Weber and others that Protestants, especially those in the Reformed tradition, contributed to the disenchantment (*Entzauberung*) of the world, that is, the undoing of its magical, supernatural quality.[31] To the contrary, concomitant with the growth of

---

27 Gwalther to Beza, 15 April [1583], in CB 24:103.
28 Gwalther to Beza, 13 August 1578, in CB 19:141.
29 Jean Chassanion to Beza, 10/20 October 1583, in CB 24:270.
30 Jean Chassanion to Beza, 10/20 October 1583, in CB 24:270–271.
31 WEBER, M. (1989), 105, 149; LASSMAN, P./VELODY I./MARTINS H. (1989), 13–14. TAY-
   LOR, C. (2007), 77, saddles the Reformation with the label "engine of disenchantment" and
   blames Calvin for the "immense energy behind the denial of the sacred." His arguments are
   insightful, but even if it is true that certain Protestant groups stressed God's righteousness
   and process of sanctification over ritual, it is overly simplistic to conclude that they themselves rationalized the world and expelled the mystery (p. 81). The story of wonders in the
   Reformation also adds balance to Brad Gregory's assertion that Protestants "implied univocal

Protestantism in the mid-sixteenth century came a sudden surge in the printing of works and collections devoted to marvels, many of which were Protestant in origin.[32] Konrad Wolffhart (1518–1561), who adopted the humanist name Lycosthenes, produced important examples of this genre during the 1550s, a period that one scholar dubs "The Golden Age of Prodigies."[33] Lycosthenes was the nephew of Protestant theologian Konrad Pelikan and married to the sister of Basel printer Johannes Oporinus. In 1552 he published at Basel the first separate edition of a book of marvels by the fourth-century author Julius Obsequens, which included, also for the first time, illustrations of the marvels in the form of eighty-four woodcuts.[34] Obsequens' work covers the period at Rome from 249 to 12 BC and draws most of its material from Livy. Since the work survived only in fragmentary form, Lycosthenes used Livy, Dionysus of Halicarnassus, Eutropus and Orosus to fill in the lacunae. The woodcut on the title page suggests the range of topics included in the book: strange animals, abnormal humans, unusual weather events and astronomical marvels. Because of the success of the book, Lycosthenes followed it up with his own collection of wonders, the *Chronicle of Prodigies and Omens*, published at Basel in 1557.[35] As the title suggests, Lycosthenes traces the story of marvels chronologically from the serpent talking to Eve in the Garden up to 1557 itself. Well-known Protestants contributed entries or otherwise assisted, among whom we find the names Heinrich Bullinger and Caspar Peucer (1525–1602). Peucer was a

---

metaphysical assumptions in ways that probably did contribute to an eventual conception of a disenchanted natural world." See GREGORY, B. (2012b), 41. Gregory does not assign blame for the disenchantment of the world to Protestants per se, but believes they "opened the path that would lead through deism to Weberian disenchantment and modern atheism" (p. 41; cf. 46–47). See also Gregory's defense of his own work in GREGORY, B. (2012a), 939: "Once all natural events were in principle explicable with reference to natural causes, there was no 'room' for a univocally conceived (in contrast to a transcendent) God (43, 51–53, 54–56)."

32 This surge is one moment in an unbroken tradition extending all the way back to Homer and Hesiod, where wonders are reported and interpreted, and to the compiling of stories beginning with Callimachus of Cyrene and culminating in Phlegon of Tralles and Julius Obsequens in ancient times. For the history of the tradition, see the following: PARK K./DASTON, L. (1981), 20–54; PHLEGON OF TRALLES (1996, 2019); CÉARD, J. (1996); CRISPINI, F. (1983), 387–408; DIXON, S. (1999), 403–418; BEARDEN, E. (2019), esp. 180 and bibliography there; WILSON, E. (1993), 65–67 (describes the editions of Lycosthenes); BATES, A. (2005), esp. 67ff; BITBOL-HESPÉRIÈS, A. (2006), 47–62; HALL, D. (1990), 71–116. There is also the related tradition of making expiation for prodigies, in which regard the Romans seem the most adept; on this see MACBAIN, B. (1982).

33 CÉARD, J. (1996), 159.

34 OBSEQUENS, J., *Prodigiorum liber* (1552). This work was republished at Geneva at the press of Jean II de Tournes in 1589.

35 WOLFFHART, K. (LYCOSTHENES), *Prodigiorum ac ostentorum chronicon* (1557). Some of the material is repeated in BATMAN, S., *The Doome Warning All Men to the Judgment* (1581).

professor of Wittenberg who corresponded with Beza and was later counted among the Crypto-Calvinists. He produced his own work about divine signs in 1553.[36] Lycosthenes' massive work contains some fifteen-hundred woodcuts (some repeated), including depictions of meteor showers, conjoined twins, monsters, comets and buildings toppled by earthquakes.

In his "Greeting to the Fair Reader" at the beginning of the *Chronicle*, Lycosthenes explains how the material should be read.[37] He warns the reader not to deem every prodigy important, as the superstitious do, seeing that many marvels have a natural explanation. Types of signs that consistently portend events, however, should be heeded and scrutinized with a "fit and pious mind." In other words, "true prodigies" are reliable signs of divine anger and vengeance or at least of God's providence.[38] These types of prodigies will be followed quickly by momentous events. For example, an entry for 1479 describes a beam-like object traversing the sky, pointed at one end and marked by dots along its side and a sickle.[39] Lycosthenes ties this prodigy to three events occurring later the same year, all of them detrimental to God-fearing people: the Turks laid waste to the whole of Carinthia; the Teutonic Knights prepared war against the Poles; and in Hungary, the Treaty of Olomouc was concluded, leading to the harsh treatment of Hussite forces. In 1546, a strange stalk of winter-wheat found in the field of a widow near Basel portended the death of Martin Luther.[40]

With his edition of Obsequens, Lycosthenes includes a work of one of Beza's friends and correspondents, Joachim Camerarius the Elder (1500–1574). The book bears the title *De ostentis* (*On Signs*) and includes an endorsement by Philipp Melanchthon in the form of a preface addressed to astrologer Luca Gaurico (1476–1558).[41] Camerarius begins the work by describing the pervasive rebelliousness of the human race and impending punishment from the hand of God.[42] He notes:

> Discerning people have presaged this punishment for a long time now. It is indicated by many prodigies of diverse kinds, which our age sees in vast quantities. The frequency of these prodigies has caused the wonder and novelty of them to be shaken off. Why talk about the loathsome offspring? Why the terrors of an unknown cause, the screeching

---

36 PEUCER, C., *Commentarius de praecipuis divinationum generibus* (1553).

37 WOLFFHART, K. (LYCOSTHENES), *Prodigiorum ac ostentorum chronicon* (1557), vi[r].

38 WOLFFHART, K. (LYCOSTHENES), *Prodigiorum ac ostentorum chronicon* (1557), 629: "I am not going to say whether this is a prodigy or not; everyone can judge for themselves."

39 WOLLFHART, K. (LYCOSTHENES), *Prodigiorum ac ostentorum chronicon* (1557), 494.

40 WOLLFHART, K. (LYCOSTHENES), *Prodigiorum ac ostentorum chronicon* (1557), vi[v] and 594.

41 CAMERARIUS THE ELDER, J., *Norica sive de ostentis libri duo* (1532). On Melanchthon's interest in the work, see KUSUKAWA, S. (1995), 134–135. See also MOSLEY, A. (2014), 298.

42 OBSEQUENS, J., *Prodigiorum liber* (1552), 242.

and clanging of arms, the shouts, the sounds of something crashing to the ground? Let us look to heavenly signs. We have seen eclipses double, we have observed strange faces in the air and in the clouds, flaming swords, crosses, spears.[43]

Camerarius believes that the crown of all the prodigies are comets, a view held by many in his day.[44] These are sent out as a final warning, "like a voice bursting forth and shouting, 'Divine judgment is here in our house.'"[45] Later in the work he asserts that "no doubt anything in the heavens that is unusual portends some huge misfortune, but comets always herald unhappiness and gloom."[46] He is echoed in this by another friend of Beza, fellow Genevan pastor and scholar Simon Goulart, who in his own work on wonders describes comets as "oftentimes forerunners and trumpets of the wonderful judgments of the Lord."[47] He follows this assertion with verses from Huguenot Guillaume du Bartas' *La Sepmaine*, where the poet urges France to treat such strange signs in the heavens as a call to repentance.[48]

In another work, written in the form of a letter and published in 1561 in London, Camerarius describes a strange, fiery red light that blazed and moved across the sky so widely that it was seen across a wide swath of Europe.[49] This letter is made especially important by the interpretation of the event that Camerarius ventures, an interpretation that has bearing on our thinking about Beza's poem on the martyrs. Camerarius reads utter doom in this prodigy: its rarity makes it more foreboding, its red color points to war and bloodshed, its appearance at night indicates that people are not prepared, and so on. In general, the prodigy portends persecution for Christians because they are slipping in their faithfulness and discipline. But Camerarius also finds good news in the prodigy, because ultimately the true servants of God hear the message and devote themselves to prayer, good works and repentance.[50] The phenomenon's

---

43 OBSEQUENS, J., *Prodigiorum liber* (1552), 242–243.

44 This is clear from the overview of MOSLEY, A. (2014), 282–325.

45 OBSEQUENS, J., *Prodigiorum liber* (1552), 243.

46 OBSEQUENS, J., *Prodigiorum liber* (1552), 268.

47 "Nous disons seulement que souventfois les cometes semblent estre comme les avant coureurs et trompettes de ces merveilleux iugemens du Souverain." For the first edition of this work: GOULART, S., *Histoires admirables et memorables de nostre temps* (1600–1601); I have used the 1618 edition, quoting from p. 84v; see also GOULART, S., *Admirable and Memorable Histories Containing the Wonders of Our Times* (1607), 130. On the context of the *Histoires*, see POT, O. (2013), 11–12.

48 The verses cited by Goulart appear at DU BARTAS, G., *Le Sepmaine ou Creation du monde* (1588), 2:152, lines 821–827.

49 CAMERARIUS THE ELDER, J., *The History of Strange Wonders* (1561).

50 He makes this point also at CAMERARIUS THE ELDER, J., *De eorum qui Cometae appellantur* (1558), 17–21.

disappearance at daybreak suggests that God's Word will dispel the calamity; the short endurance of it gives hope that the persecution will not last long; its appearance around Christmas day indicates that grace will follow the event. Everyone else, including those who carry out the persecution, will face God's ultimate wrath and punishment while the faithful will reap a reward. But why would God allow his Church to suffer so? Because, Camerarius says, blood and the cross bring more profit to the Church than ease and leisure.

9.4 The Theology of Wonders

While most prodigies observed are forebodings of terrible things to come, ultimately God sends calamity and persecution for the benefit of his people and to the guilt and detriment of the unrepentant. This is the common Protestant approach to wonders and marvels: they serve as prophets to rebuke the enemies of the Church and to steer it back to the right path. Thus, many who write on comets during this period urge their readers to respond to these prodigies by confessing their sins and devoting themselves to prayer to mitigate the impending punishment.[51] In the case of the five martyrs of Lyon, we perceive the same mixture of dread and victory, of bearing the cross or the refinement of fire, but also the attainment of the prize. The important lesson for all Christians is that God is exercising his providential care. He is watching over his people and intervening in the progress of the redemptive story, both to refine his own and to destroy the wicked. Beza narrates the account of the strange behavior of the fire in the execution of the five students at Lyon because he sees in it the working of a loving God.

Do the Scriptures support this interpretation of wonders? Why should the Christian look for evidence of God's providence in nature's deviation from its rules and patterns? Lycosthenes himself justifies his collection of prodigies, signs and wonders by pointing to Psalms 9 and 105 in his "Greeting to the Reader."[52] In the ninth Psalm, David sings that he will declare God's wonders everywhere, and in the hundreth and fifth Psalm, he urges the pious to do the same: "Remember the marvels of God, what prodigies he wrought and the judgments of his mouth." Christians should want to become familiar with wonders. But why is this? In summarizing the subject matter of this latter Psalm in his own work, Beza maintains that, in the very act of remembering and

---

51 MOSLEY, A. (2014) enumerates such statements in the work of Abraham Rockenbach (p. 296), Joachim Camerarius the Elder (p. 298), Antoine Mizauld and Paul Eber (p. 303), Benedikt Aretius (p. 305), Thomas Erastus (p. 318), and Thaddeus Hagecius (p. 319).

52 WOLLFHART, K. (LYCOSTHENES), *Prodigiorum et ostentorum chronicon* (1557), A7.

recounting what wondrous things God has accomplished for his chosen people, the pious are confirmed in their faith in God's covenant. God's marvelous works testify to his power and show that he intends to bless his own.[53] He explains this in greater detail in his annotations on Hebrews 2:4, where the epistle writer urges the reader to heed the gospel as confirmed through "signs, prodigies, and various works of power."[54] Beza elucidates the nuances of all these terms applied to the witnesses of the gospel: "they are called *signs* in the sense that they are visible images of true doctrines; *prodigies*, because they present something new and unaccustomed; and *powers*, seeing that they represent an extraordinary example of divine potency." Signs and wonders herald the preeminence of the crucified Christ, he goes on to say, manifestly declaring that "not only is he not dead, but even rules in the Heavens, as was foretold; and not just for his own sake, but for ours too." The unexpected or unusual expressions of God's authority reveal his direct involvement in human affairs and increase his people's confidence that he will accomplish his promises. Beza sums up this idea succinctly in his notes on Romans 15:19, remarking that prodigies have the power to upset the minds of the people, but insofar as they derive from the Spirit of God, they create faith in the elect.[55] In essence, wonders comfort believers because, when read with self-validating confidence, they demonstrate God's support for their side.[56] Along these lines, while referencing the eclipse of 21 July 1590, Beza expresses to a friend the hope that "it foretells the destruction of the papacy and its Hispano-Gallic co-conspirators."[57] Typically, partisans assume that prodigies are endorsements for their side.

Conversely, wonders also "upset the minds of the people" by conveying God's strong repulsion for wickedness. We recall that after Pentecost, Jews from foreign lands dwelling in Jerusalem were perplexed by the apostles' ability to speak their native languages. Peter explains to them that this is a sign of the last days and quotes to them from the prophet Joel, who foretold of wonders and signs on heaven and earth. The sun will be turned to darkness, he says, the moon to blood, and so on. Beza's annotations on the passage associate the prophecy primarily to the Jewish people who were listening to the sermon: the destruction of the stubborn contemnors of the gospel is close at hand, as Jesus foretold in Matthew 24. But Beza identifies a principle that extends beyond

---

53 BEZA, T., *Psalmarum sacrorum libri quinque* (1580b), 399.
54 BEZA, T., *Testamentum Novum* (1589c), 2:363.
55 BEZA, T., *Testamentum Novum* (1589c), 2:91. At 2 Thess 2:9 (ibid., 2:316), Beza accepts that the impious can produce apparent wonders that deceive in order to help them establish false doctrine. For a wonder to be of the Spirit of God, it must only confirm existing doctrine and revelation.
56 On this, see FRIEDMAN, J. (1993), 41–56.
57 Beza to Grynaeus, 21/31 July 1590, in CB 31:166.

the immediate fulfillment of the prophecy signaled by the wonders. He writes: "The same calamity that once crushed Jerusalem, will crush the whole world guilty of the same ungoverned obstinacy."[58] That is to say, signs often precede destruction and thus strike fear in everyone. And everyone is to some degree a sinner. Even so, the pious will respond to these heralds of God's punishment with repentance, while the impious will respond with more obstinacy. John Calvin stresses this dual nature of prodigies repeatedly in his commentary on the Joel passage alluded to by Peter (Joel 2:1–11): when tokens of God's impending judgment appear, the people should admit their guilt and flee to his mercy; and, "as soon as he shows signs of his wrath, we ought to anticipate his judgment. When God then warns us of his displeasure, we ought instantly to solicit pardon."[59] The wicked never do this.

Also noteworthy is the application of Romans 8:22 to the interpretation of prodigious phenomena. While addressing the earthquake of March 1584 to Johannes Crato, Beza alludes to Romans 8:22, that creation groans with us awaiting our redeemer, adding, "not even the earth can bear us any longer."[60] The wonder of an earthquake, therefore, is one of the ways that the earth expresses its distress over its involvement with the corruption of humankind. In his annotation on Romans 8:21, Beza remarks that creation's groaning and hoping for restoration should also "greatly confirm the sons of God, so that they should constantly expect that day."[61] Therefore, the wonders instill hope in the faithful that one day there will no longer be need for groaning; Paul calls it the "groaning of labor," Beza notes, to signify the joyous outcome that follows the intense pain.[62] Believers can rejoice that they are provided the chance to put off the old man and suffer for Christ, thus becoming co-heirs with him.

It should be stressed that prodigies point to God's providence. Calvin's treatise warning against the practice of false or "judicial" astrology, for example, acknowledges that changes in the heavens influence natural processes on earth, even bodily ones, but they do not decide the fortunes of human beings.[63] Twins

---

58 BEZA, T., *Testamentum Novum* (1589c), 1:436 (on Acts 2:19); cf. ibid., 1:113 (on Matt 24:29).

59 CTS XX:46.

60 Beza to Crato, 7 April 1584, in CB 25:70.

61 BEZA, T., *Testamentum Novum* (1589c), 2:55.

62 BEZA, T., *Testamentum Novum* (1589c), 2:55. Cf. the discussion of miraculous events in the Bible and the groaning of creation by Peter Martyr Vermigli in VERMIGLI, P., *On Original Sin* (2019), 109–112. The text translated is drawn from Vermigli's commentary on Rom 8:20, VERMIGLI, P., *In epistolam S. Pauli Apostoli ad Romanos* (1559), 501–508.

63 For this treatise, I have used the translation of POTTER, M. (1983), 157–189. See also CÉARD, J. (1996), 129–131; PROBES, C. (1974–1975), 24–33; JORINK, E. (2010), esp. 123. For the text of Calvin's work, see CALVIN, J., *Advertissement contre l'astrologie qu'on appellee iudiciaire, et autres curiositéz qui regnent aujourd'huy au monde* (1549), CO 7:409–542; and Millet's edition, CALVIN, J. (1985).

emerge from the womb under the same horoscope but with differing natures. Unusual births should turn our attention to the overarching, dominant providence of God, who changes natures through his Spirit and works all things according to his purpose; the constellations or other inferior causes have no such power. The stars cannot engender good or evil within us. Instead, extraordinary signs proclaiming the anger of God should drive us all to examine our consciences and root out the rebellion within us. To the objection raised by the astrologers that Jesus foretold that heavenly signs will announce his final return, Calvin retorts, "If it is a question of the last day which will bring the completion of all things, we must say that there will be visible signs, which will serve as much to warn the faithful as to render unbelievers inexcusable."[64]

9.5 Conclusion

While the five students awaited their unhappy martyrdom at the stake, Beza records that something marvelous happened: the fire that would consume them first resisted the executioner's demands, then, under fervent stoking, hastened its work to spare the students a long ordeal of suffering. We have argued here that in the context of the reformer's thought and interactions, as well as the broader intellectual climate in which he lived, this detail about the fire holds special meaning: the wonder serves to remind readers of the real power operating behind the tragic events.[65] God providentially guides the redemptive story, refining and conforming his people to the image of his Son so that they can claim their inheritance while preparing destruction and punishment for the wicked. It would be inaccurate to claim that Beza and his fellow Protestants stripped the world of enchantment; rather, they formulated a reliable way of reading wonders, seeing them as a confirmation of the truths already taught in Scripture.

In a letter written to Heidelberg theologian Caspar Olevianus (1536–1587) in December 1572, Beza ends with a provocative request:

> If you have any astrologers there, advise them that there appears here a star of never-before-seen magnitude and incredibly bright light; it is where the milky way comes near-

---

64 POTTER, M. (1983), 181.

65 Thus, in commenting on miracles at Gal 3:5 (BEZA, T., *Testamentum Novum* [1589], 2:225), Beza stresses that, as creator and architect of the universe, "God alone can make changes to the order of the universe." What may appear to be miracles wrought by people or angels are really evidence of God working in them to bear witness to himself or answer prayers.

est the polar star around the constellation Cassiopea, I believe. I want to know what they themselves think it means, though I have learned to rely on the maker of the stars alone.[66]

After the tragic events in France on St Bartholomew's Day, Beza hopes for omens that will signal God's intention to keep his promises, and suspects this strange star, a comet, as he interprets it, reiterates the message of God's faithfulness amid persecution.[67] To mark the wonder, he composed a poem that he contributed to the *Epicedia* published in 1573 to honor Admiral Gaspard de Coligny, whose murder signaled the beginning of the massacre of French Huguenots.[68] He reprised it, with minor alterations, for a collection of his poetry published in 1576. The poem in its original version reads as follows:

What portends the new comet, dreadful without a tail,[69]
whose radiant splendor shines with a clear and unsullied fire?
The God of gods knows, and he will show what it foretells in
his own time.
But if human minds can learn anything beforehand, it is
not forbidden for me to enquire into such signs.
This is that light that once led the Magi first from the East
to the small town of David, and which shone on the child
as he was being born.
Behold, the same star has returned to announce that

---

66 Beza to [Caspar Olevianus], 2 December 1572, in CB 13:227.

67 In 1598, Beza's former student Raphaël Egli reminds his teacher that the latter once associated the new star with the death of the Admiral Gaspard de Coligny (see Egli to Beza, 6/16 November 1598, in CB 39:203). Egli is distraught, because now, some twenty-five years later, Beza is censuring the so-called fish prophecies as described in Egli's new book *Prophetia halieutica*, published at Zurich. The story is that some fish were caught in the North Sea in 1587 with prophetic writing on them about the end times (for the details, see CB 39:197n.1). Beza apparently rejects the notion that God would send a new revelation (his censure of Egli's book is lost but can be reconstructed through Egli's response), though Egli counters that these only reiterate prophecies already found in Daniel and the Apocalypse of John. Interestingly, Egli also objects that after the St Bartholomew's Day massacre, Beza communicated to Egli another sign of the Admiral's death: "Why is it allowed not to condemn that fingered turnip taking on the shape of a hand, before the Admiral's assassination, but I am not permitted to wonder at the prodigious letters on the fish?"

68 [Anonymous], *Epicedia illustri heroi Caspari Colignio Colignii Comiti* (1573), C1r-v. See also the poem on the same comet titled "In novam stellam" at ibid., B3v (the authorship is indicated only by the initials "P.S.M.").

69 Not a comet at all, this is really a "new star" (Supernova 1572), as first explained by BRAHE, T. (1573). Marcello Squarcialupi (1538–1592) mocks Beza (though without naming him,) for his poem that associates this phenomenon with the Bethlehem star in his "De cometa in universum atque in illo qui anno 1577, visus est," which is published in *De cometis dissertationes novae*, together with works by Beza's friends Simon Grynaeus and Andre Dudith, and his adversary Thomas Erastus.

God has returned and is at hand. So, applaud this, o happy
throng of the pious. But you, covered in the blood of innocents, fear it.

In a later version of the poem, Beza altered the last line to make his point more explicit, writing, "But you, Herod, covered in blood, fear it."[70] For Beza, omens of this sort are always two-sided, containing both threats and consolation, as do the Scriptures: the star announces that God has come to save his people, though before the final victory, a period of trial and persecution "under the cross" can be expected; conversely, the persecutors and unrepentant should dread the sign, because it portends their ultimate doom.

---

70 BEZA, T., *Poemata* (1576), 171.

Part Four: Theodore Beza and his Catholic Opponents

Theodore Van Raalte

Chapter 10: Compelling Each Other

Theodore Beza's Response to John Hay as Part of Geneva's Anti-Jesuit Efforts

During the 1580s Genevan printers turned out significant anti-Jesuit literature—most with the approval of the city council, but some without it.[1] Theodore Beza's letters show that he excused himself from writing such anti-Jesuit works; motivated other Reformed theologians, such as Antoine de Chandieu (c. 1534–1591) and Jean de Serres (c. 1540–1598), to do so instead; and, when they had done so, recommended and sent their works to his correspondents.[2] Already in 1580 Beza was excusing himself due to his age and ill health, and when the Jesuit Luca Pinelli visited Geneva that year, Beza told him that he did not like writing many books.[3] In October 1583 Beza even claimed in a letter to his fellow theologian Johann Jakob Grynaeus (1540–1617) in Basel that by his own outcries he had raised up Chandieu to oppose the Jesuits. He wrote,

> As to our Sadeele [Antoine de Chandieu], I have the same view as you. However, he would to this point have remained obscure had I not compelled him [to write] almost by my outcries. He is presently away to look after his domestic affairs, having departed for his castle [in France], but not without books [. . .] and I recognize God's hand at work that by my encouragement he [Chandieu] chose for himself those adversaries.[4]

Nevertheless, in 1586 Beza published his own anonymous response to parts of a challenge first written in English by the Scottish-born Jesuit John Hay (1546–1607) and published in Paris in 1580.[5] Hay, or likely his translator,

---

1 Printing in Geneva without the city council's approval risked fines, jail time and confiscation or destruction of the printed materials.
2 Two examples are: Beza to André Dudith, 8 March 1580, in CB 21:60, cf. xiv; Beza to Dudith, 2 July 1583, in CB 24:197–199.
3 See MANETSCH, S. (2000b), 135–137; MARTIN, A.L. (1988), 86. Beza to Dudith, 2 June 1579, in CB 20:122–125; Beza to Grynaeus, 29 November 1580, in CB 21:234–237.
4 Beza to Grynaeus, 25 October 1583, in CB 24:281–283. In the nineteenth century, August Bernus suggested that the adversaries in Beza's mind were Lutheran ubiquitarians, but more recently the editors of Beza's correspondence wonder whether Jesuits may be in view. I am convinced of the latter view. Chandieu at that time had just published some formidable work against Torres and the Polish Jesuits, but nothing against the Ubiquitarians. Grynaeus was also in the process of overseeing some anti-Jesuit disputations published at Basel in 1583 and 1584.
5 HAY, J., *Certaine Demandes Concerning the Christian Religion and Discipline, Proposed to The Ministers of The New Pretended Kirk of Scotland* (1580). The Scottish English original of Hay's

expanded the work in a French translation published in Lyon 1583, adding a greater focus upon Calvin and Geneva.[6] This work was then translated into German and published in Fribourg in 1585.[7]

Beza's publication in 1586 is titled *Response to the first five and most important demands of Father John Hay, Jesuit Monk, addressed to the Scottish ministers.*[8] In this work, Beza particularly engaged Hay's challenges regarding the lawful ordination of Reformed ministers, but also regarding Scripture, tradition and the church. His reply was modest, for he responded only to the first thirty-seven of Hay's 206 questions, as Hay notes in his rebuttal to Beza in 1588.[9] Beza's task was not easy, for Hay had raised serious questions. Consider the following sample taken from Hay's 206 questions:

> I demand that the ministers of Scotland show me that the confession of faith used in the English congregation in Geneva has ever been recognized by any Christian nation since the time of the apostles.[10]

> [I demand] that they tell me whether the gospel of Jesus Christ was ever preached in the Kingdom of Scotland before the time of Paul Methuen and of Mr. John Knox or not, and whether their ancestors who had not been of the Calvinistic religion, were damned forever to the fire of hell.[11]

> If no one may add or take away from the Scriptures [...] why do you sing in your assemblies the Psalms of David that Marot and Beza have spoiled, corrupted, added to, and changed as it seemed good to them, to fit their rhyme?[12]

---

work of 1580 contains 166 questions. Hay's first name appears in the sources as either Iohne, Iean, or Ian. I have chosen to use John.

6 HAY, J., *Demandes faictes aux Ministres d'Ecosse: Touchant la religion Chrestienne* (1583). The French translation contains 206 questions, not only adding to the number of "demands," but also citing many more Reformation sources and exposing disagreements between these sources. Maruyama attributes the additions to Coyssard, the translator. See MARUYAMA, T. (1978), 137–138.

7 HAY, J., *Flagstuck des christlichen Glaubens, an die neuwe sectische Predigkandten* (1585). The German was translated from the French.

8 [BEZA, T.], *Response aux cinq premieres et principales demandes de F. Iean Hay, Moine Jesuite aux Ministres Escossois* (1586a). Beza grouped the thirty-seven questions he answered, fitting them under five headings, which he called "the five principal points" (a1v). Beza's anonymity will be discussed later in this chapter.

9 HAY, J., *L'Antimoine, aux responses que Th. de Beze faict a trente sept demandes de deux cents et six, proposees aux Ministres d'Escosse* (1588). Hay draws attention to this aspect of his title also at a6v.

10 HAY, J., *Demandes faictes aux ministres* (1583), a6r.

11 HAY, J., *Demandes faictes aux ministres* (1583), a6v.

12 HAY, J., *Demandes faictes aux ministres* (1583), b2r.

Where is it written that there are only four evangelists and that the Gospel of St Matthew, with that of the other three, ought to be received, and not that of the Apostle of St Thomas? And what authority moves you to approve one writing as canonical and to reject the other as apocryphal?[13]

The present essay raises two questions: first, why did Beza publish a response to Hay at all? There are a number of reasons—as we will see, even pressing reasons—why Genevan theologians needed to reply to the Jesuits. But as noted, usually Beza relied on Chandieu and Serres for this. Why then did Beza, uncharacteristically, address the Jesuit challenge? Second, having undertaken a response, why did Beza compose one rather modest in size and argument, and why did he wait until 1586 to write it? Answering these two questions will require a close examination of the historical circumstances of Geneva as a focus of Jesuit counter-Reformation efforts, and, correspondingly, as a center of anti-Jesuit publication, particularly in the 1580s. Some of the reasons why Beza needed to publish the response at all will turn out to function also as reasons why he could and probably even had to publish a rather modest response. For reasons of space, this essay will not delve into the contents and arguments of Beza's tract.

10.1   Why did Beza respond to Hay?

The argument I will advance includes seven reasons why Beza did not have the luxury of remaining silent. First, Geneva had been in the sights of the Jesuits from the very day in 1540 that this new religious order received papal sanction. Second, in the following decades, Jesuit communities arose in several key places around Geneva and could not be ignored. Third—and tied to the formation of the Jesuit community (and college) in Tournon—Beza's own personal experiences going back to 1561 at the Colloquy of Poissy underlined the need to counter Jesuit power. Fourth, Beza was the foremost theologian in Geneva at the time and needed to show leadership, not to keep Geneva committed to Reformed views—that was hardly in question—but to maintain Geneva's place as a leading intellectual center of the Reformed churches. Fifth, the pressure on Beza was actually intense, for in 1586 Geneva was suffering under a Savoyard blockade. Not only did the city's grain prices soar, but all professors, save Beza and Antoine de la Faye (1549–1615), were dismissed from Geneva's Academy for lack of city funds to pay their salaries. Regarding the blockade, it should be kept in mind that from the start of Geneva's reform in the 1530s its political

---

13 HAY, J., *Demandes faictes aux ministres* (1583), b3r.

freedom and its adoption of reform had been closely tied, and in 1586 the designs of Charles Emmanuel, Duke of Savoy, clearly were not just to gain control of the city, but also to change its faith. Sixth, even Beza's colleague Antoine de Chandieu, who did not normally depend upon a city salary because of his independent wealth, had been summoned away in summer 1585 by Henri de Navarre to serve him as chaplain in what has often been called the last of the Wars of Religion. But Chandieu also surprised Beza in 1586, and this surprise may be key to the Beza's manuscript being published, as I will suggest.

While the first four reasons would support all of Geneva's anti-Jesuit efforts, the fifth and sixth factors, along with a seventh, were probably the triggers that led Beza himself to carve out time for a reply to Hay. This seventh factor was the publication of a German translation of Hay's *Demandes*, published in Fribourg in 1585. The leaders of Zurich responded by summoning three fellow evangelical cities to a conference in Aarau in 1585, the outcome of which was to be a letter of remonstrance towards Fribourg. They also wanted the French evangelical cantons to respond to Hay's book, and this request put Beza under some pressure.

10.2 *Doctrinae Iesuiticae* (1580–1589)

Several of the factors just mentioned gave rise to other anti-Jesuit works in Geneva in the 1580s. In particular, the larger window of Genevan anti-Jesuit publishing includes a set of six volumes of collected anti-Jesuit treatises published clandestinely in Geneva between 1580 and 1589 and titled *The Chief Heads of Jesuit Teachings*.[14] According to the title page of each volume, they were published in La Rochelle by a certain Theophilus Regius, or Théophile le Roy. I have previously demonstrated that this publisher's name was fictitious and that the place of La Rochelle was false, since all of these volumes were published in Geneva.[15] The first volume came from the presses of Antoine Chuppin in Geneva in 1580; then, in 1584, Eustace Vignon's printing firm in Geneva republished and augmented volume one, so that the length of the volume grew

---

14 CHEMNITZ, M. et al., *Doctrinae Iesuitarum praecipua capita, A doctis quibusdam Theologis (quorum libri sequente pagina continentur) retexta, solidis rationibus testimoniisque sacrarum Scripturarum & Doctorum veteris Ecclesiae confutata* (1580). I will refrain from supplying the full bibliographic information for each of the subsequent volumes, except to note that with volume 2 the title changes slightly from *Iesuitarum* to *Iesuiticae*, and is maintained with that change for the rest of the volumes. Thus I refer to the volumes as *Doctrinae Iesuiticae*.

15 VAN RAALTE, T. (2012), 569–591. The national library of France has adopted these findings in its information about Théophile le Roy, imprimeur. See https://data.bnf.fr/en/17728190/theophile_le_roy/. Accessed 16 Oct 2019.

to about 1000 pages. Between 1585 and 1588 Vignon added five more volumes of similar size, and in 1589 Jacob Stoer reprinted the expanded 1584 edition of volume one. These volumes contain mostly re-published anti-Jesuit works by Reformed authors as well as some by Lutheran authors. The later volumes also contain previously unpublished anti-Jesuit tracts, some supplied serially to the publisher.

It seems, then, that the pseudonym Theophilus Regius represents the patron of the series, someone who convinced three different printing firms in Geneva to print these works without the usual approval of city council, and whose rather roughly-cut fleuron adorns the title page of each of the six volumes. The detective work necessary to determine the identity behind Theophilus Regius has in large part been completed, and I hope to publish this in due time. In my opinion, it was not Beza.

10.3   The Brevity of Beza's Reply

At the same time, given Beza's prominent place in Geneva's religious life in the 1580s, it hardly seems possible that he was not aware that the *Doctrinae Iesuiticae* volumes were being published in Geneva. I suggest that at this point the reasons for writing his response to Hay and for keeping it brief come together. One must keep in mind that the general perception was that the six large volumes of the *Doctrinae Iesuiticae* had been published in La Rochelle. In light of this, Geneva as an intellectual center of anti-Jesuit writings appeared to be far behind La Rochelle. Thus, Beza needed to show some leadership. At the same time, he must have known about the massive contribution that these clandestine volumes were making to the Genevans' anti-Jesuits efforts, and thus could allow his own contribution to be modest. Whatever the case, he probably did not have time or energy for a more robust reply.

As to the brevity of Beza's reply, we need to know also—odd as this may seem to us in the twenty-first century—that Beza himself regarded his published sermons on the Song of Songs as at least as great an anti-Jesuit weapon as his reply to John Hay. In addition, two of Beza's colleagues in Nîmes, Jean de Serres and Jacques Pineton de Chambrun, were already engaged in written disputations with Hay. Finally, not only did Beza not desire to engage in such polemical writing at his age, he also was burdened with trying to keep Geneva's Academy running by himself. Thus, he had no time. I will now unpack in greater detail the seven reasons why Beza chose to respond to John Hay when he did in 1586.

10.4 Jesuit attention upon Geneva

To contextualize the entire anti-Jesuit movement in Geneva one must go all the way back to the earliest papal approval of the Society of Jesus. Whereas the followers of Ignatius of Loyola had begun to form a society before 1540, the official papal endorsement of the Society of Jesus occurred on 27 September 1540.[16] One of the signatories to the papal bull was Pierre de la Baume. Baume had been Geneva's prince-bishop who had once considered himself the sole sovereign of the city. Although Geneva was the place of his episcopal seat, Baume had never favored Geneva as his place of residence and had in various ways alienated the city council and the populace. After he left for good on 14 July 1533, Baume eventually was appointed to be a cardinal.[17] The eighteenth-century Genevan curate Jean-Antoine Besson, who wrote a lengthy history of the Diocese of Geneva and surrounding areas, describes Baume's further work as follows:

> Cardinal Baume having afterward gone to Rome, was one of the prelates who signed the bull of Paul III for the foundation of the new institution of Ignatius of Loyola, who was thereby designated to be its perpetual General. As this society was obliged by a fourth vow to ongoing missions for the conversion of infidels and heretics, Pierre de la Baume presented to Father Ignatius [the idea] that he could not begin this mission better than by the conversion of Geneva: he should send in effect the two men of the order who came from Savoy [bordering Geneva], namely, Father Montmar and Father Salvedro, to attempt, if they would be permitted, to preach in Geneva. If not, they could at least, by making the mission to the surrounding areas, hinder those from Geneva from carrying out the plan that they had formed to spread their religion. Of these two missionaries, one died in Annecy a little after he had arrived there, and the other died afterward during the plague.[18]

Whether Ignatius had foreseen or desired a counter-Reformation emphasis for his new religious order, the moment of commissioning included this, with a particular focus on Geneva: two of the ten men in the new Society were designated to bring Geneva back into the Roman fold.[19] Cardinal Baume, like Cardinal Jacob Sadoleto, probably thought at this time that the dismissal of Guillaume Farel, Elie Courauld, and Calvin from their preaching positions in

---

16 GRENDLER, P. (2017), 7.

17 BESSON, J.-A. (1759), 63–64.

18 BESSON, J.-A. (1759), 65. Translations in this chapter are my own.

19 Various authors make the point that, from Ignatius's point of view, the establishment of his society was not especially about countering heresy, but about reaching Muslims, especially in Jerusalem. However, none of the authors I will cite make mention of Baume. Thus, see WRIGHT, J. (2005), 22–25; DONNELLY, J. (ed.) (2006), 131; MARTIN, A.L. (1988), 88–89.

the city in 1538 had opened the way for Geneva to return to Rome.[20] In fact, the city council maintained the Reformed confession and continued to employ as preachers Henri de la Mare, Jacques Bernard and soon after, Pierre Viret; the problem with Farel, Courauld and Calvin was that they would not follow the demands of the city council to administer the Lord's Supper unless the city council would require all citizens to swear to uphold the new confession of faith.[21]

Beza was not likely thinking of the events of 1540 when he published his treatise in 1586, but these events did inform the collective memory of Geneva in terms of its relation to the Jesuits—their own former bishop had incited the very first Jesuits against them and had thought that if Geneva itself was not accessible, at least Jesuit mission in the surrounding areas should occur.

In 1559 the magistrates of Annecy, just forty-two kilometers from Geneva's walled city, were so greatly impressed with the Jesuit Louis Coudret (1523–1572) that they offered management of their local school to the Jesuits. This arrangement did not ultimately work out.[22] But by 1565 the Jesuits did establish themselves in Tournon and Chambéry, both about eighty-five kilometers south of Geneva. They also made great gains in the Calvinistic community of Lyon, about 150 kilometers southwest of Geneva. Shortly thereafter, they established communities in the Swiss city of Fribourg about 150 kilometers northeast of Geneva, and in Lucerne, another 100 kilometers beyond Fribourg. If one begins in Tournon, draws a line west to Lyon, then a line northeast to Fribourg, and then returns to Tournon by a straight line, one will have formed a scalene triangle around Geneva. While the Jesuits of Tournon, Chambéry and Lyon were more concerned with Geneva than were those of Fribourg and Lucerne, Beza's correspondence suggests that Geneva's leaders were concerned about the presence of all of these Jesuit communities.

10.5   Jesuit success at the Colloquy of Poissy and at Tournon

Beza's own memory of the Jesuits would certainly have included events at the famous Colloquy of Poissy in 1561, where Beza was the chief spokeman for the Reformed side, along with Peter Martyr Vermigli (1499–1562), while the pope had sent the Jesuit Superior General Diego Laínez, together with Jean

20 Cardinal Sadeleto's letter to the Genevans, in which he tried to woo them back to the Roman Catholic Church, was dated 18 March 1539, at Carpentas. Calvin's reply was dated 1 September 1539, at Basel.
21 SPEELMAN, H. (2014), 75–92, 96–97, 103.
22 MARTIN, A.L. (1988), 10–11, 50.

Polanco, to ensure that Roman interests were clearly and pressingly presented.[23] One of the results of the Colloquy of Poissy was a resolution of the assembled clergy of France in favor of the Jesuits, as follows. On 15 September 1561 the decision was taken in "the Assembly of the Gallican Church, held in Poissy by the command of the King in the great Refectory of the Venerable Religious Men of said Poissy, with the signs and seals of most Reverend Cardinal of Tournon," etc., that the assembly "had received and receives, had approved and approves, the said Society and Company in the form of a Society and College, and not of any newly-instituted religion."[24] This decision represented an important step forward in France for the Jesuits because, though royal edicts had been published in their favor prior to this, clerical opposition to the Society of Jesus had continued. Now the Gallican clergy, albeit with many caveats and limitations, was for the first time receiving and approving the Jesuits as a society acceptable to the church's leadership.[25]

The person of the Cardinal of Tournon—a man obviously close to the Pope—may have represented one of the strongest supporters of the Jesuits, for the cardinal was the famous François de Tournon (1489–1562), who played a prominent role influencing the French monarchy and the Estates General against tolerating the Protestants. Two years earlier the cardinal had turned over the fledgling Collège de Tournon, just eighty-five kilometers south of Geneva, to the Jesuits, and this had been confirmed by a decision of the parlement of Toulouse on 14 February 1561.[26] The Jesuits considered the decision made at Poissy on 15 September to include the clergy's endorsement of their college in Tournon.[27] During Beza's lifetime the Jesuits began to call their college in Tournon a university, but critics would always maintain that they were not permitted to call it such, nor to award university degrees.[28] Starting in

---

23 NUGENT, D. (1974), 118, 154. After the colloquy, Beza's attention was taken up, not by the Jesuit participants, but by Claude de Sainctes, who immediately wrote a tract against Beza and Calvin, and who in turn was answered by both Beza and Chandieu, in separate rebuttals.

24 [GAZAIGNES, J.] (1764–1765), 1:15–16.

25 Nugent reports that the pope was very encouraged by the performance of Laínez at the Colloquy of Poissy, and summed up his thoughts a couple of months later in a letter to Philip II, "Among all the religious orders [. . .] the Society of Jesus deserves to be embraced with special love by the Holy See." NUGENT, D. (1974), 188–189. The important place of Poissy in the history of the Jesuits is highlighted in BANGERT, W. (1972), 67–78.

26 The Cardinal of Tournon had apparently discovered that this school was being infiltrated by Huguenots and sought to overcome this by giving it to the Jesuits. BANGERT, W. (1972), 65.

27 [GAZAIGNES, J.] (1764–1765), 2:724–725, 835.

28 [GAZAIGNES, J.] (1764–1765), 2:835–837. Compare the title pages of John Hay's responses to Jacques Pineton and to Beza, printed in Tournon in 1586 and 1588 respectively: Hay maintained that he was, "*professeur ordinaire en Theologie, en l'Université de Tournon*," and his printer presented himself as "*Claude Michel, imprimeur de l'Université*."

1581, John Hay taught theology at the Jesuit college in Tournon. Pierre de la Baume's heart would have been warmed had he lived to see these events.

John Hay dedicated the French translation of his *Demandes* to Madame Claude de la Tour of Turenne, a Countess of Tournon by marriage, who, according to one source, had endured sieges of Tournon by the Huguenots in 1567 and 1570.[29] Madame Claude's husband, named Just, was blood brother of François, Cardinal of Tournon. Jesuit successes at Tournon, then, cannot have escaped Beza's attention.

Beza's experience with Jesuits at Poissy was also pertinent in his treatise against Hay that is under discussion here, for Beza himself recalled Poissy in his response. Whereas Hay had simply written that the confession of faith of the English congregation in Geneva contained "Calvinistic teaching," Beza added that this confession "contains summarily the teaching of Calvin, *as well as what Beza advanced at Poissy.*"[30] It is not clear why Beza added these words; perhaps he wished to show that the confession of the English exiles was more universal than Hay allowed, for Hay's point was that it was new and previously unknown.

10.6   The Jesuit Presence Around Geneva: Lyon (1565)

In the early 1560s a priest judged by later Jesuits as "among the first four or five great Jesuit preachers of all time," Émond Auger (1530–1591), was just beginning his career. William Bangert later described Auger as the one who "brought back Calvinists to the Church by the thousands [. . .] such as nearly two thousand in Lyon alone."[31] In May 1562 Auger was in Valence, where he was captured and sentenced to death. He had ascended the scaffold where he was to be hung and there gave an eloquent speech about salvation and peace. The listening Huguenot clergy were impressed and commissioned one of their own to petition the executioner for a stay in order that they might seek to convert Auger. Although the early eighteenth-century Jesuit biographer does not name the minister who was appointed, Pierre Viret's biographers name Viret as the minister chosen to try to convert Auger.[32]

Ironically, only a little over a year later, Auger, the "Chrysostom of France," was utilizing his rhetoric in a contest for the hearts of Lyon's citizens over against the irenic eloquence of his rescuer, Pierre Viret. Viret was himself considered

---

29 DU FRESNOY, N. (1775), 168. See also http://siefar.org/dictionnaire/fr/Claude_de_La_Tour_d%27Auvergne/Hilarion_de_Coste, accessed 29 November 2019.

30 BEZA, T., *Response aux demandes de Hay* (1586a), a2r.

31 BANGERT, W. (1972), 66.

32 Compare DORIGNY, J. (1716), 71 with SHEATS, R. (2012), 223.

the prince of preachers by the Reformed. Viret had been in Lyon from June 1562, shortly after the Huguenots had captured it. His task was to build up the young church. A year later, however, when the Peace of Amboise allowed Roman Catholics to return, Auger led the re-establishment of the Roman church in Lyon. Viret sought a public disputation with the Jesuits Auger and Antonio Possevino (1533–1611), who had since joined Auger, but his disputants refused unless the king would authorize it. Viret then resorted to disputing by writing.[33] However, by the fall of 1565, Auger had succeeded in having Viret banished from Lyon. Given the long and warm relations of Viret with Geneva, the Jesuit success against him would not have been forgotten.

Most pertinent to our study was the remark Possevino made in a letter to the Duke of Savoy on 10 March 1562 about the strategic importance of Lyon *vis à vis* the Savoy. Possevino stated that "in establishing the [Jesuit] order in this city, we will establish it in all your territories."[34]

10.6.1 The Collège at Chambéry (founded 1565)

The same charismatic young Jesuit, Antonio Possevino, also joined the Duke of Savoy in keeping his sights on Geneva. This suited the Duke Emanuele Filiberto well, for his family had once enjoyed power over Geneva and he himself continued to try to retake the city—all the way up to the night of the Escalade in December 1602.[35]

Possevino discussed with the Duke the idea of founding a Jesuit college in Chambéry, the capital of Savoy and of Piedmont-Savoy, close to Tournon, about eight-five kilometers south of Geneva. Grendler states, "Possivino argued that a college in Chambéry, so close to heretical Geneva, would yield great fruit. General Diego Laínez offered to establish a college in Chambéry if the duke would provide adequate financial support. [...] Agreement was reached October 1564, and a group of Jesuits arrived in August 1565."[36] Until 1577, the running of this school was difficult, since the Duke did not provide the promised funds and the Jesuits could only afford rented space in a Franciscan monastery, an arrangement that included its share of disagreements between the two orders. A large bequest, however, allowed the Jesuits to erect their own college building in 1577.[37]

---

33 For a contextual analysis of Viret's writing during his stay in Lyon, see CAMILLOCCI, D. (2014), 349–367.

34 CAMILLOCCI, D. (2014), 352.

35 For a brief description of the political structures of Piedmont–Savoy in relation to the Jesuit efforts to establish Jesuit professors at the University of Turin, see GRENDLER, P. (2017), 1, 101–114.

36 GRENDLER, P. (2017), 260–261; cf. 96–97.

37 GRENDLER, P. (2017), 261.

The Jesuits embraced education as their unique role, taking over existing schools and starting new ones. To be clear, a Jesuit college was not the same as a school. Grendler explains,

> A Jesuit college was an established community of Jesuits in a town. A college had a building in which the Jesuits lived, a church that they owned or was set aside for their exclusive use, and sufficient continuing financial support, preferably an endowment. Almost all colleges had a school (in another building) which offered free Latin education to boys and men who met the academic requirements. Although scholars often use "college" and "school" synonymously, they were not the same. Some of the Jesuits in a college carried on non-teaching ministries, including preaching, hearing confessions, ministering to the sick, and catechizing.[38]

As we have seen, the Jesuits in Tournon desired that their school be granted the status of university. The Jesuits pursued this same goal for their school at Chambéry in the seventeenth century. However, Bishop Étienne Le Camus, in a protracted conflict with the Jesuits and their royal patroness, succeeded in preventing the establishment of this university.[39] Nevertheless, when Beza wrote his tract in 1586, the Jesuit college of Chambéry had been established.

10.6.2   Fribourg and Lucerne

Northeast of Geneva, the Swiss cantons of Fribourg and Lucerne had never adopted the Protestant Reformation. Each of these cities had a community of Jesuits, which Beza and his correspondents in Zurich—the *antistes* Heinrich Bullinger (1504–1575), Rudolf Gwalther (1519–1586), Ludwig Lavater (1527–1586) and Johannes Stumpf (1500–1578)—as well as Johann Jakob Grynaeus (1540–1617) in Basel, kept a close eye on during these decades. For instance, on 2 November 1583 Gwalther expressed concern to Beza that they not provoke the Jesuits in these two cities.[40] Discussions about the Jesuits in Beza's correspondence were usually about these local situations, and, if not, he was typically meeting requests to help more distant Reformed communities deal with Jesuit opposition, which he did by sending copies of anti-Jesuit works by Chandieu and Serres.[41]

The French translation of Hay's work was published in 1583 as an expanded version of the original Scottish English of 1580, to which Beza had not responded. This translation had seen two editions in 1583 and another in 1584,

---

38 GRENDLER, P. (2017), 9.
39 GRENDLER, P. (2017), 261–281.
40 Gwalther to Beza, 2 November 1583, in CB 24:292–296. For other examples of discussions between these correspondents about the Jesuits, see CB 23:24–28; 25:55; 26:29.
41 Beza to Grynaeus, 29 November 1580, in CB 21:235.

suggesting that it was well-received.[42] In 1585, the French work was translated into German and published as the first book out of the newly-established presses of the Jesuits in Fribourg. Beza's correspondent from Zurich wrote to Beza on 5 September 1585 that the Jesuits intended to set up a press in Lucerne as well.

The next day, at the instigation of the city of Bern, a meeting of representatives of Bern, Zurich, Basel and Schaffhausen occurred. The minutes state that Bern had notified the others of "a little book titled 'Questions about the Holy Christian Faith to the New Sectarian Preachers,' which was published in the new press in Fribourg in Nechtland, and full of insults against the true Christian religion."[43] At this conference, the delegates decided to draft a common letter to Fribourg, asking the Fribourg authorities to stop the printing and destroy the already printed copies. The delegates did not really expect that Fribourg would comply, and thus they also authorized the theologians of their cities to refute Hay's work, including the provision that whatever the French theologians might write should be translated into German.[44] As far as I know, Beza's work was not translated into German, but there is no question that the evangelical cities felt the need to counter Hay's book.

10.7 Anti-Jesuit Publications from Geneva's Presses (1580–1585)

What I would like to do now is set forth a list of anti-Jesuit publications coming from Genevan presses between 1580 and 1585. A few of these were published in Morges, close to Geneva, and some appeared in Nîmes, but most were from Geneva. I will group some of the treatises together, and will separately note which ones were in French. Those for which the language is not mentioned were all printed in Latin.

First on the list would be the publications of Antoine de Chandieu against the Spanish Jesuit Francisco Torres (c. 1509–1584). Chandieu was teaching at the Reformed academy in Lausanne and would later teach in Geneva. His debate with Torres began in 1577,[45] with four treatises of Chandieu published between 1580 and 1583.[46] These were elaborate treatises replete with full syllogisms.

---

42 PETTEGREE, A./WALSBY, M./WILKINSON, A. (ed.) (2007), 2:7 (entries 24953–24955).

43 KRÜTLI, J. (1861), 886–887.

44 KRÜTLI, J. (1861), 886–887.

45 Antonio Sadeele [CHANDIEU, A.], *Sophismata F. Turriani Monachi ex eorum sodalitate qui sacrosancto Iesu nomine ad suae sectae inscriptionem abutuntur: Collecta ex eius libro De Ecclesia, & Ordinationibus Ministrorum Ecclesiae, adversus capita disputationis Lipsica* (1577).

46 A. Sadeele [CHANDIEU, A.], *Ad repetita F. Turriani Monachi Iesuitae sophismata de Ecclesia et ordinationibus Ministrorum ecclesiae, Responsio* (1580b); *Responsionis ad repetita F. Turriani … pars altera* (1581); A. Sadeele [CHANDIEU, A.], *Centum flosculi Turrianicae disputationis*

Another key work of Chandieu, titled, *A Theological and Scholastic Treatise on the Word of God over against Human Traditions* (1580), included mention of the Jesuits in its opening letter to the French pastors.[47] The year 1580 was also when the first volume of the *Doctrinae Iesuiticae*, purported to be published in La Rochelle, was printed in Geneva.[48]

In second place would be another lengthy interchange between two interlocutors, namely Jean de Serres, professor at the Reformed Academy of Nîmes, and John Hay, the Scottish-born Jesuit. In four rounds during the years 1582 through 1588 these two men engaged in lengthy debate, cast in careful scholastic form. This debate began when the Jesuits of Tournon posted theses for disputation on the door of the Academy of Nîmes.[49]

Third, in 1583, Chandieu published an analysis and refutation of some Polish Jesuits.[50] On the other side, sometime in the same year, Hay's *Demandes* were published in French translation, and in 1584 both Laurent Arthur Faunt, a Polish Jesuit, and Francisco Torres, the Spanish Jesuit already mentioned, published attacks on Chandieu. At this time, the Hungarian theologian Petrus Lascovius (d. 1587) was working in Geneva and published a learned anti-Jesuit treatise of about 600 pages, full of quotations and references.[51]

---

ex utroque eius libro decerpti, et in Iesuitarum gratiam collecti (1581a); CHANDIEU, A. *Index Elenktikos repetitionum & Tautologi Turriani ex Tertio eius libro quem dibiblon inscripsit, collectus* (1583). These works can also be found in Antonio Sadeele [CHANDIEU, A.], *Opera Theologica* (1592). See also the discussion in VAN RAALTE, T. (2018), 71–74.

47 "Huiusmodi sunt imprimis Pseudonymi (sic enim illos Monachos appello, qui sacrosanctum Iesu nomen perperam, nec sine blasphemia, suae sectae inscribunt)." Antonio Sadeele [CHANDIEU, A.], *Locus de Verbo Dei scripto, adversus humanas traditions, theologicae et scholastic tractatus* (1580a), a3v.

48 See note 14 of this essay.

49 For the ongoing polemics between Jean de Serres and John Hay, see the bibliography of HAAG (1859), 9:264–265. The Haag brothers do not mention that some of the works of Serres against Hay were also published in the *Doctrinae Iesuiticae*. See [SERRES, J.], *Academiae Nemausensis brevis et modesta responsio, Ad Professorum Tournoniorum, societatis, ut aiunt, Iesu assertiones, quas Theologicas & Philosophicas appellant*, in CHEMNITZ, M., et al., *Doctrinae Iesuitarum praecipua capita* (1584), 1:503–642; [SERRES, J.], *Academiae Nemausensis expostulatio de Iesuitarum Turnoniorum bis cocta (ut ipsi disertè aiunt) Crambe*, in *Doctrinae Iesuitarum* (1584), 1:643–673; SERRES, J., *Quartus anti-Iesuitae, sive, Pro Verbo Dei scripto et vere Catholica Ecclesia*, in *Doctrinae Iesuitarum* (1586), 4:a2r-400; SERRES, J., *Quarti anti-Iesuitae, sive de vera verae Ecclesiae autoritate, adversus Ioannis Hayi monachi-Iesuitae commenta et convicia, Responsionis posterior pars*, in *Doctrinae Iesuitarum* (1586), 6:1–540.

50 A. Sadeele [CHANDIEU, A.], *Posnaniensium assertionum de Christi in terries Ecclesia, quaenam & penes quos existat: propositarum in Collegio Posnaniensi, à Monachis novae Societatis, Quam illi Societatem Iesu, non sine blasphemia nominant, nisi forte unius Iudae Iscariotae posteri, ac haeredes haberi velint, Analysis et Refutatio* (1583).

51 The letter to the reader of this text was dated October 1583. For this text, see LASCOVIUS, P., *Theorematum de puro et expresso Dei verbo, tam scriptis quam viva voce traditio, et pari*

Fourth, the hitherto unnoticed *Doctrinae Iesuiticae* came out as an expanded edition of volume one and then proceeded, between 1584 and 1588, to appear as six volumes of collected anti-Jesuit treatises, about 1000 pages each. These volumes represent an enormous undertaking. An editorial hand is evident in many places, and at least five major new works, never published elsewhere before this, were embedded among the other reprinted treatises. Volumes 2 and 3 appeared in 1585, volumes 4 and 5 in 1586, and volume 6 in 1588.

Fifth, in 1584, Jacques Pineton de Chambrun (1515–1601), Reformed pastor in Nîmes, published a reply to John Hay in French.[52] Of Hay's 206 questions, he treated the questions 131 to 150, all of which were accusations of Hay against Calvin, charging him with blasphemy. Chambrun's work, and a translation of one of Serres' works into French, were the only French-language publications of all the works just mentioned; the rest were in Latin.[53] The year 1585 appears to have included the publication of two volumes of the *Doctrinae Iesuiticae*.

10.8 Factors that Prompted Beza's reply to Hay

In the midst of so many other publications, why did Beza add his own? On 15 April 1586, at Beza's request, the city council granted Jean le Preux permission to print Beza's reply to Hay.[54] We do not know exactly how soon after 15 April the work was under the press. Permission may have been requested before the writing was completed, since Beza was both the author and the proof-reader of the manuscripts.

It is likely that the most immediate reasons that prompted Beza to write against Hay were the urgings of the conference of evangelical cantons held in Aarau, the impact of the Treaty of Nemours which was painfully evident to him, the absence—and then the sudden reappearance—of Chandieu, and the precarious and fragile situation in Geneva due to the Savoyard blockade.

We have already noted the German translation of Hay's *Demandes* that was printed in Fribourg and the Protestant response at the Diet of Aarau on 6 September 1585. The magistrates and clergy urged rebuttals against the Jesuits.

---

utriusque authoritate nuper in gymnasio Claudio Jesuipolitano in Transylvania a novis Societatis Judae monachis (1584).

52 CHAMBRUN, J.P., *L'esprit et conscience jésuitique* [1584].

53 Jean de Serres' French work was titled *Le premier antijesuite de Jan de Serres, ou la reponce de l'académie de Nismes: Second antijesuite ou l'exposition et plainte de l'Academie de Nismes contre les vieux choux rebouillis* (1584).

54 Beza to Christian Amport, 4 August 1586, in CB 27:129n.4. See also MANETSCH, S. (2000b), 130n.53.

On 18 November 1585 Abraham Musculus rejoiced that Beza was undertaking a reply to Hay.[55]

Another trigger event that would have made Beza more resolute against the Jesuits was the so-called Treaty of Nemours, which became law on 18 July 1585 and required all Huguenot pastors to leave France within one month, gave all other Huguenots six months to depart and thus essentially outlawed all Protestantism in France. By January 1586 the results were very evident in Geneva, as the population of refugees once again increased dramatically.[56]

As civil war ensued in France, four prominent Reformed ministers, including Geneva's Antoine de Chandieu, were summoned to serve Henri de Navarre as chaplains and lead his troops in worship, while Jesuits accompanied the ultra-Catholic Duke of Guise Henri I and asserted influence upon King Henri III.[57] Chandieu left Geneva sometime in September 1585 to serve his three-month rotation sometime shortly thereafter. He returned to Geneva briefly on 13 April 1586, possibly on his way to Germany on a mission for Henri de Navarre.[58]

On the one hand Henri III had the Jesuit Émond Auger as his confessor, and the Jesuit provincial of France, Claude Matthieu, as a close confidant.[59] The Duke of Guise kept Jesuits close to himself much of the time. On the other hand, Chandieu helped Henri de Navarre build his war chest and worked with ciphers as part of Navarre's intelligence team.[60] This shows that Reformed opposition to the Jesuits was not merely because of religious concerns. Politics played an important role as well.

On 9 March 1586 Beza told Grynaeus that the French king Henri III had completely given himself over to his Jesuit confessor, Émond Auger.[61] But if Beza was working on his reply to Hay, it would have to wait while he participated in the Colloquy of Montbéliard from 14–27 March 1586, debating the Lutheran Jakob Andreae on the doctrines of the Lord's Supper, Christology, baptism, religious art and predestination. These theological disputations were published in the years that followed.[62] Shortly after Beza returned from Montbéliard, the Savoyard blockade of Geneva intensified greatly, as Beza's letters report in the

---

55 Abraham Musculus to Beza, 18 November 1585, in CB 26:210–212.

56 MANETSCH, S. (2000b), 150.

57 VAN RAALTE, T. (2018), 57–58; MARTIN, A.L. (1973), 208–229.

58 Duplessis-Mornay to Beza, March 1587, in CB 28:13n.2.

59 MARTIN, A.L. (1973), 75–80.

60 VAN RAALTE, T. (2018), 58.

61 Beza to Grynaeus, 9 March 1586, in CB 27:29. See also CB 27: 5, 97 ff. where Beza speaks of Henri III self-flagellating and coming completely under the control of Jesuits and Capuchins.

62 See RAITT, J. (1993). This debate was recently published in English translation. See ANDREAE, J. (2017).

spring of 1586.[63] At the beginning of this intensification Beza's work against Hay saw the light of day.

Antoine de Chandieu arrived in Geneva for a brief visit on 13 April 1586—two days before Beza requested permission from the magistrates to publish his response to John Hay. I think it likely that Chandieu stimulated Beza to publish this work. It is quite possible that Chandieu reported news from abroad about the Jesuits that increased Beza's concern; or, perhaps, he mentioned how extensive was the influence of Hay's treatise, or how necessary a reply was to prevent French-speaking evangelicals from leaving the Reformed churches.[64] It is also possible that Beza wished to write a more detailed reply to Hay but either had grown tired of doing so or, more likely, had no time, and that Chandieu then almost compelled Beza to publish the reply, in the same way that Beza had compelled Chandieu to write against the Jesuits three years earlier.[65] Whatever the reasons that prompted Beza's published response, it is quite remarkable that the permission to print was requested two days after Chandieu had arrived back in town. This fits the picture that Beza himself had of Chandieu, as the one whom God had raised up to oppose the Jesuits. In 1588, Jean de Serres would even call Chandieu the "terror of the Jesuits."[66]

10.9 Beza's Response to Hay, its Anonymity and Style

Beza's work against John Hay was published without an author's name, which was rather uncharacteristic of him. Probably, Beza believed himself to be writing on behalf of the Reformed churches, or, at least, at the request of the cities represented at the Conference of Aarau. The absence of his name did not at all secure his anonymity, however, for the Genevan printer Jean le Preux's name was displayed prominently on the title page. Further, Beza defends Calvin repeatedly in the treatise, and responds to questions that involve Geneva, Calvin and the French Reformed Churches. Finally, when Beza mentions himself or his own writings, he does not sound very distant.[67] Certainly, his interlocutor John Hay recognized immediately the author of this anonymous work, for his reply of over 300 pages, which was finished in September 1587, was addressed

63 Beza to Grynaeus, 26 April 1586, in CB 27:67; Beza to Dürnhoffer, 3 May 1586, in CB 27:85; Beza to Grynaeus, 20 June 1586, in CB 27:98.

64 See MANETSCH, S. (2000b), 162–167.

65 See note 4 of this chapter.

66 SERRES, J., *Quarti anti-Iesuitae, sive de vera verae Ecclesiae auctoritate, adversus Ioannis Hayi monachi-Iesuitae commenta & conuicia, Responsionis posterior pars*, in *Doctrinae Iesuiticae Praecipua Capita* (1586), 6:336.

67 BEZA, T., *Response aux demandes de Haye* (1586a), 3, 11, 29–30, 48, 49.

to Beza.[68] It appears clear that Beza made a conscious decision to omit his name as author, not to hide his identity, but because he was acting in a quasi-official capacity.[69]

Beza's reply to Hay work is a *response*, much like many of Beza's other polemical works (quote your opponent, then reply, section by section). Beza writes the reply to Hay prosaically, not scholastically. He eschews syllogisms and technical terms for fallacies. Similarly, Beza's disputation against the Lutheran Daniel Hoffman (1585) also never lays out its arguments in syllogistic form, and only rarely does it name fallacies. Beza's scholastic method in the latter treatise amounts to numbering some arguments, presenting some theses and isolating the *fundamentum* of each thesis. Thus, the method followed by Beza in both of these treatises matches his more humanist-driven interests in languages, rhetoric and original sources.[70]

In my judgment, Beza prefers to avoid writing in the scholastic style evidenced in such Protestant theologians as Jacob Schegk (1511–1587), Chandieu, Christian Amport (1540–1590) and Jean de Serres. That said, it should be kept in mind that Chandieu and Serres did not write all of their works in scholastic style, since they also wrote works of history and poetry, including some famous works such as Serres on the history of France and Chandieu's *Octonnaires de la vanité du monde*.

10.10 The Aftermath (1586)

The Savoyard blockade of Geneva did not ease during the months immediately following the publication of Beza's response to Hay. Rather, on 9 July 1586, the Savoyard blockade of grain was proclaimed from Chambéry, and it is likely that Genevans associated the Jesuits with some of these troubles. The collaboration of the Duke of Savoy with Jesuits was well-known, and rumors about the Jesuits' role in the assassination of Prince William of Orange of the Netherlands—true or not—were likewise well-known.[71] Moreover, the role of the Jesuits in a plot

---

68 HAY, J., *L'Antimoine, aux responses, que Th. de Beze faict a trente sept demandes de deux cents et six, proposees aux ministres d'Ecosse* (1588). The approval letter of certain Jesuit doctors is dated 15 September 1587. See ibid., a7v.

69 During his career, Beza occasionally used pseudonyms, including "Benedictus Passavantius" and "Nathanael Nesekius." See Benedictus Passavantius [BEZA, T.], *Epistola magistri Benedicti Passavanti responsiva ad commissionem sibi datum a verabili D. Petro Lyseto* (1553); Nathanael Nesekius [BEZA, T.], *Adversus sacramentariorum errorem pro vera Christi praesentia in coena Domini homiliae duae* (1574). For a brief description of the earlier of these two works, see MALLINSON, J. (2003), 86–87.

70 For an overview of the exchange between Hay and Beza, see MALLINSON, J. (2003), 89–92.

71 Beza to Gwalther, 24 March 1584, in CB 25:55; see also CB 25:247n.13.

of Mary, Queen of Scots, against the English Queen Elizabeth became public knowledge a few months later.[72] While the Genevans fought off open attacks at their city walls, suffered significant economic losses due to the trade embargo and openly wondered whether they would have food enough to get through the winter, the theologians fought the battle with their quills. That August, in fact, Beza did something rather uncharacteristic.

In August 1586, Beza discovered that Christian Amport, Jr., who was then studying at the Genevan Academy, had with him a manuscript written by his father, Christian Amport, Sr., who was a teacher in Bern. The manuscript was written in the form of a disputation against a Catholic priest named Sebastian Verro (1555–1614) of Fribourg and engaged him on the sufficiency and authority of Scripture in the church. Uncharacteristically, Beza gave the manuscript to the printer Eustache Vignon and the two men published it without Amport's permission. Beza provided a defense of his actions in a letter to the reader, dated 4 August 1586, claiming that Amport was very modest and the work was so valuable that it had to be published.[73] Verro was not a Jesuit, but he had translated Hay's *Demandes* into German, and this must have increased Beza's sense that Amport's manuscript needed to be published.

During the latter months of 1586 Beza was extremely busy: on 5 August he signed the epistolary preface to his reply to the Lutheran Daniel Hofmann, a work of about equal length to his reply to Hay. On 20 August he completed the dedicatory letter to his fellow pastors of Geneva that prefaced his published sermons on the first three chapters of the Song of Songs.[74] This publication was a longer-term work that Beza had in mind for some time and to which he devoted extensive attention.

Geneva's political and military situation continued to be grave. On 23 August 1586 Beza was concerned enough about the precious manuscript of his Greek-Latin New Testament that he sent it out of the city to Gryaneus in Basel for safe-keeping and possibly for printing. Beza was not certain that Robert Étienne could publish it in Geneva under the circumstances of the blockade.[75] By 29 October the Genevan Academy was closed, leaving only Beza and Antoine de

---

72 Beza to Johann Rudolph Stumpf, 29 October 1586, in CB 27:194. Other rumors would very soon implicate Jesuits in the death of the French King Henri III (1589), even though a Dominican had actually committed the murder. Some of their Society were banished in 1594 when a young man attempted to take Henri IV's life. HOLLIS, C. (1968), 30–31.

73 AMPORT, C., *Ad Sebastiani Verronis Friburgensium apud Helvetios Parochi ac Sacerdotis Iesuastri, quaestiones de Verbo Dei* (1586). See Beza to Christian Amport, 4 August 1586, in CB 27:127–128.

74 BEZA, T., *Sermons sur les trois premiers chapitres du cantique des cantiques, de Salomon* (1586b), a4r; Beza to the Pastors of Geneva, 20 August 1586, in CB 27:240.

75 Beza to [Grynaeus], 23 August 1586, in CB 27:162–165.

la Faye to perform teaching responsibilities. Beza chose to lecture on the Book of Job to help his students struggle through difficult questions of theodicy. In December the blockade had eased, and by the end of the month Beza requested the return of his New Testament manuscript.[76]

These events followed the publication against Hay. They made the atmosphere intense and increased the worries of the Genevans. But the concerns they had were of the same kind as prior to April 1586—they were now more intense, but not qualitatively different.

10.11   Why the brevity of Beza's Response to Hay?

Let us finally consider why Beza kept his reply to Hay rather short and straight-forward. This was, first, because Hay's treatise was not exceptionally learned, though some of his questions were difficult to answer. Hay had the advantage in this debate because of the simplicity of his questions and their sheer number—206 in total. Many of them were memorable and likely to connect with his readers. No reply as briefly written as the questions would satisfy readers. I do not doubt that Hay's demands were rather annoying if not infuriating to the Reformed theologians. It is possible that Beza's patience was exhausted as he worked out his responses to Hay's many questions.

We are on firmer ground, however, to remember that Beza was completing the publication of his sermons on the Canticles during this time. The epistolary preface that accompanied these thirty-one sermons on the Song of Songs was dated as 20 August 1586. The reformer believed that its publication would do much to advance the Reformed faith and expose the errors of the Jesuits, as he wrote to a correspondent already on 17 March 1585.[77] Indeed, these sermons contain extensive teaching about the marks of the true Christ, and the true church over against false Christs and the false church. Employing an allegorical interpretation of the Canticles, the reformer points out what he sees as the shortcomings, errors and even blasphemies of the Roman Church, with the Jesuits being singled out mainly for two things: abusing, polluting, usurping and profaning the name of Jesus by the title of their society, and assembling an unprecedented quantity of riches in forty short years.[78] Since Beza had preached these sermons well before the publication against Hay, he knew what he intended to publish. Their importance is also underlined by the

---

76 Beza to Grynaeus, 29 December 1586, in CB 27:218.

77 Beza to Dudith, 17 March 1585, in CB 26:62.

78 BEZA, T., *Sermons sur les trois premiers chapitres du cantique des cantiques* (1586b), 217, 233, 242, 401, 415, 444, 539, 580–582, 636.

speed—within the year—with which they were translated and published into Latin and English.

Another reason for Beza's brevity was that two fellow Reformed theologians had replied to Hay already, namely Jacques Pineton de Chambrun and Jean de Serres, as we have already noted. Between Chambrun and Beza, 57 of the 206 questions raised by Hay received a reasoned response in French. (Beza answered questions 1–37; Chambrun answered questions 131–150). In fact, Hay himself, in his rebuttal of 1588, suggested that Beza did not reply to all of his demands because Beza wanted his work to be read alongside the works of Serres and Pineton.[79] Hay probably was correct on this point.

In relation to the clandestine volumes of the *Doctrinae Iesuiticae* that were being published by Eustache Vignon in Geneva around the same time, we suggest that with the response to Hay, Beza published just enough material to show that Geneva recognized the threat of the Jesuits, but not too much, lest he arouse more Jesuit attention upon Geneva. This interpretation is supported by Beza's letter to Gwalther on 2 November 1583, where he expressed concern not to provoke the Jesuits in Lucerne and Fribourg. This would explain why the *Doctrinae Iesuiticae* was falsely-attributed to the city of La Rochelle so as to divert attention away from Geneva.

10.12 Conclusion

This chapter has attempted to set one of Beza's publications in its historical context, as far as the sources allow, and in connection with a recent discovery of six large volumes of collected anti-Jesuit treatises that were published in Geneva around the same time, though falsely attributed to La Rochelle. I have suggested that with respect to Beza's response to Hay, the visit of Antoine de Chandieu, who returned to Geneva for a short visit during his service as chaplain to Henri de Navarre, may have played an important role in moving Beza either to finish writing and publish or simply to publish what he had already completed. Whereas Beza had once pressured Chandieu to target the Jesuits as adversaries in his theological writings, it may well be that Chandieu also encouraged Beza to oppose Hay's *Demandes faictes aux Ministres d'Ecosse* in 1586.

---

79 HAY, J., *L'Antimoine* (1588), 6v.

Jill Fehleison

Chapter 11: Nemeses to the End

Theodore Beza and His Last Catholic Adversaries

During John Calvin's lifetime, the Reformed church was an evangelical one, sending pastors into France, training followers in Reformed doctrine, and establishing important networks with other Protestants throughout Europe. After Calvin, the approach of Geneva changed as it shifted from expansion to survival and faced challenges on multiple fronts. First, survival meant sustaining the city and the Reformed Church established there. While Geneva certainly maintained contact with its embattled brethren in France and elsewhere, Geneva did have important matters of its own. The approach I use builds on the works of other scholars, including William Naphy and S.K. Barker, who see the Reformed faith in both Geneva and France possessing more local and regional identities in the years after John Calvin's death and with the increased violent attacks on Protestantism.[1]

Geneva found itself in a precarious position in the closing decades of the sixteenth century for a variety of reasons. The events of the French civil wars left the Huguenots in a disastrous situation and left Geneva with fewer powerful friends in France. Geneva also faced increasing isolation from other Protestant cities, especially Berne, who had made a separate peace with the Duke of Savoy, Charles-Emmanuel I, and left its fellow Protestants to fend for themselves.[2] Geneva faced a resurgent Duke of Savoy with few allies. Facing challenges from spiritual, political and military fronts, Geneva and Calvin's successor, Theodore Beza, led a very different church. One notable shift was that by the 1580s there was a more level playing field in the area of polemics. Beza and other members of the Company of Pastors found themselves embroiled in confessional conflicts that at times led to lengthy published polemical debates and a few face-to-face exchanges. If one wanted something published to attack a religious adversary, a sympathetic press could be found. In the French-speaking world, Catholics favored Paris, Lyon and Bordeaux for quick publications; Geneva had a very healthy publishing industry of its own and had little trouble disseminating

---

1 NAPHY, W. (1994); BARKER, S.K. (2009).
2 The Treaty of Nyon of 1589 was signed between Berne and Savoy. See DUFOUR, A. (1958), 87–97.

materials to Protestants abroad for translation and further distribution.[3] Geneva entered the fray with its Catholic foes for a number of reasons. One key motive was to ensure that the city remained at the intellectual center of international Protestantism. Other prominent voices increasingly emerged, especially in the Netherlands and England. Additionally, Catholic publications, especially those by Jesuit polemicists, were widely distributed and offered real challenges to Reformed ideas and doctrine. In the 1540s, Calvin had battled his opponents in print, including Catholics, Anabaptists and those he deemed Nicodemites and Libertines.[4] By the 1590s, Beza faced such a wide variety of opponents during the last years of his life that he could not respond to them all.

Beza had tangled with Catholic adversaries in person and in print, including Jesuit John Hay in the 1580s. While the Reformed faith had solidified its place in Geneva, Beza, like Calvin, remained a steadfast opponent of any reconciliation with Catholicism during the 1590s, when the parameters of coexistence were continuing to evolve. This essay will examine Beza's view of and interaction with Protestants who converted to Catholicism, Catholic missionaries who challenged Geneva's influence in the region and Protestants who saw openings for reconciliation among Christians after years of unrest and religious violence. The final decade of his life proved to be challenging for Beza. The faith he had championed for decades as leader of the Company of Pastors found itself besieged in multiple ways and on multiple fronts. Using Beza's writings, his correspondence and the writings of those who challenged him, this essay will explore how Catholicism and religious compromise continued to bedevil Beza personally in new and unexpected ways.

11.1 Beza and his Catholic Opponents

Beza does not appear to have shared the irenic tendencies others possessed during the late Reformation. Despite his resistance to any confessional reconciliation, rumors of his own conversion to Catholicism plagued Beza the last years of his life. Donald Nugent asserted that "irenical ideal(s)" were still present in reformers of the sixteenth century, especially those that participated in councils and colloquies, and the tendency ran deep since it was "reinforced by the Renaissance stress upon the unity of the world."[5] Beza had himself participated in the Colloquy of Poissy in 1561, and his actions at this event were subject

---

3 For an overview of publishing for French language Reformation works, see HIGMAN, F. (1998), 110–118.

4 GORDON, B. (2009), 188, 193.

5 NUGENT, D. (1974), 4.

to scrutiny at the time, particularly his behavior in front of the Royal Family. Cardinal François de Tournon (1489–1562) ridiculed Beza's behavior, and he openly challenged and insulted Beza during his oration on the Lord's Supper.[6] The Catholics quickly circulated an anti-Beza pamphlet concerning his negative views on private baptism.[7] Meetings between opposing confessions were always fraught with peril, and both sides used accounts of such encounters for their own purposes. Was Beza more open to compromise or reconciliation earlier in his life? As Beza assumed his leadership role in Geneva, he retreated from these gatherings with religious opponents and focused more on challenging in print those that attacked him, Geneva, Calvin's legacy and the Reformed faith.

Because ecumenism did not win the day in late sixteenth-century Europe, historians tend to marginalize those who held views more accepting of reconciliation and toleration. Beza's rejection of any dialogue with those who wanted to find common ground is important to understanding the state of the late Reformation. While my primary focus is on Beza's religious opponents in the last decade of his life, one earlier episode is illustrative of the approach Calvin and Beza took to anyone whose views were seen as a threat to Geneva and the Reformed faith (particularly when they were put into print). Savoyard, Sebastian Castellio (1515–1563) faced the full wrath of Beza and Calvin; they tried to ruin him both personally and professionally after he condemned in writing the execution of Michael Servetus and accused Calvin of lacking charity, acting intolerant and being self-righteously dogmatic.[8] Castellio questioned the concept of heresy itself and believed in tolerating religious differences.[9] Beza published a response in Geneva to Castellio's *Concerning Heretics* in September 1554, and the leadership of Geneva pressured those in Basel who employed or supported Castellio to expel him from all positions. When Castellio died in 1563 he was facing yet another inquiry into his writings and beliefs seemingly instigated by supporters of Geneva.[10] The Company of Pastors used the scorched-earth policy against others, particularly Protestants, who advocated for any path that Reformed leadership viewed as deviating from its orthodoxy.

---

6 NUGENT, D. (1974), 93, 99–103.

7 During the Colloquy of Poissy, a Reformed minister from Metz, Jean Taffin, inquired of Beza whether an infant baptism done by a "personne privée" was valid. The exchange does not survive but some of it was reproduced in an anti-Calvinist pamphlet published by François de Beaucarie-Péguillon, Bishop of Metz, *Adversus impium Calvini ac Calvinianorum dogma de infantium in matrum uteris sanctificatione* (1567). See CB 3:275–278.

8 *De haereticis an sint persequendi & omnino quomodo sit com eis agendum* (Concerning Heretics) was anonymously published by Castellio in March 1554. *Contra labellum Calvini* (Against Calvin's Book) probably reached Geneva in manuscript form by June 1554. ZAGORIN, P. (2006), 102, 105–106, 116.

9 ZAGORIN, P. (2006), 112–113.

10 GUGGISBERG, H. (2003), 196–201.

In the 1590s, despite Geneva's best efforts, prominent members of the French Reformed faith either converted to Catholicism or embraced a very catholic view of Christendom seeking reconciliation among confessions. Two under discussion here both had close ties to King Henri IV. Both had lived through the French Civil Wars and spent time in captivity at the hands of the Catholic League, something neither Beza nor Calvin had faced safe behind the walls of Geneva, but the men received no sympathy from Geneva. Scott Manetsch noted that Beza and his colleagues likened those who converted to dogs returning to eat their own vomit.[11] Geneva also faced problems closer to home as Catholic missionary activities in the region bore fruit.[12] Two notable converts, Jean de Sponde (1557–1595) in France and Antoine de Saint Michel, Baron d'Avully (d. 1610) in Savoy are worth exploring because both produced significant print challenges to Geneva and Beza in particular.

11.2 Jean de Sponde: Late in Life Convert

Jean de Sponde was a great poet, a politician and a close advisor to Henri IV, who converted to Catholicism in 1593, the same year as the French king.[13] While Sponde was baptized Catholic, his family embraced the Protestant cause when Jean was a child. His father, Enécot, had important connections to the House of Navarre, serving as a secretary and advisor, laying the foundation for his son to follow him into serving the royal house. The young Jean found his education disrupted due to displacement and economic problems brought on his family by the French Civil Wars.[14] Jeanne d'Albret intervened personally to ensure that the gifted Jean could continue his education despite early struggles due to his family's frequent moves.[15] Arriving as a student in Geneva in 1579, Sponde moved on to Basel in 1580 and matriculated into the University.[16] Basel was a city more open to multiple ideas than Geneva, as illustrated by both Castellio and Paracelsus finding positions there. Alan Boase theorizes that while in Basel, Sponde may have drifted away from the strict Reformed ideas of Geneva, worked with friends on a money-making scheme and even dabbled in alchemy. Furthermore, Boase notes that despite Sponde's increasing

---

11 MANETSCH, S. (2000b), 273. This graphic image is an allusion to Prov 26:11.

12 Catholic conversions began with a mission established in 1594 when the Diocese of Geneva sent out Francis de Sales to preach in the towns in the duchy of Chablais that surrounded Geneva. For a full discussion see chapter 3 of FEHLEISON, J. (2010), 53–99.

13 He was lieutenant-governor of La Rochelle.

14 BOASE, A. (1977), 11–16.

15 BOASE, A. (1977), 14–15.

16 BOASE, A. (1977), 21–22.

involvement with the court of Navarre during the 1580s, Beza's letters to the court make no mention of Sponde.[17] Whatever offense Sponde committed that led to Beza's rebuke of him, he possessed a nimble mind that allowed him to adapt to a changing landscape. He owed much of his success to the support of the Navarre family, and his livelihood was increasingly connected to Henri.

Sponde was imprisoned multiple times by the Catholics between 1587 and 1593.[18] During these times, he had access to Catholic writings, and he had contact with the Bishop of Evreax, Jacques Davy Du Perron (1556–1618), who had also been raised Huguenot before his conversion to Catholicism. Perron was instrumental in the conversion of Henri IV.[19] While his motives were certainly complex, the Reformed church in France and Geneva condemned his abandonment of them. In the wake of Sponde's departure from the French Reformed Church, Beza accused him of gaining financial benefits in his conversion. In a letter to Johann Jakob Grynaeus, Professor of the New Testament in Basel, Beza noted that the king of Navarre had paid for Sponde's studies in the city so it was not surprising that he would follow the king to Catholicism.[20] Beza was also disturbed that Sponde published an account of his rationale for conversion.[21] In a short span of time, Sponde published three works associated with his embrace of the Catholic Church, with two explaining his reasons for converting to Catholicism and the other attacking Beza's recently published French version of *Traité des vrayes, essencielles et visibles marques de la vraye église catholique* (1592) that was dedicated to Henri IV.[22] This French version of Beza's *Marques de la vraye église* was an update of the original Latin one from 1579 and numbered less than seventy pages.[23] While Sponde faced anger from other Reformed leaders for abandoning his faith, it was his 800-page invective published posthumously first in Bordeaux and then in Paris that upset Beza the most. Sponde died before he completed his work, and its ultimate publication was overseen by the Catholic polemicist Florimond de Raemond.

17 BOASE, A. (1977), 46–47, 52.
18 BOASE, A. (1977), 52, 56, 71.
19 BOASE, A. (1977), 71.
20 Beza to [Johann Jakob] Grynaeus, 25 November/5 December 1594, in CB 35:166, 168, 168n.13.
21 Beza to Grynaeus, 25 November/5 December 1594, in CB 35:168.
22 Sponde's published accounts of his conversion were *Response d'un catholique apostolique romain au Protestant* (1593); *Declaration des Principaux Motifs, Qui ont Induict le feu sieur de Sponde conseiller et maître des requêtes du roi à s'unir à l'Eglise* (1595a); and his challenge to Beza was *Response du feu Sieur de Sponde au Traicté des Marques de l'Eglise, fait par Th. de Beze* (1595b).
23 BEZA, T., *Traité des vrayes, essencielles et visibles marques de la vraye église catholique* (1592c). There was also an English translation from the original Latin version, *A Discourse of the true and visible Marks of the Catholique Church* (1582a). See GEISENDORF, P.-F. (1967), 332.

Raemond claimed that Sponde stayed in Bordeaux working day and night on his challenge to Beza, which was more than his health would allow.[24] Even with 800 pages, Sponde did not address all of the critical topics, most notably his planned attacks on the Reformed interpretation of the Lord's Supper.[25] Sponde's attempt at dismantling Beza's work was similar in form to much of the polemical literature of the period. He offered a short statement from Beza and then provided a lengthy counterpoint. Like the Catholic polemicists of the period, Sponde highlighted the Catholic Church's links to antiquity and the early church fathers.[26] He also noted Beza's unwillingness to debate Catholic points of doctrine. According to Beza's biographer Paul Geisendorf, Sponde's attack hurt the aging theologian deeply because Beza viewed his *Marques de la vraye église catholique* as his grand masterpiece, but he did not have the strength to respond.[27] While Beza faced more opponents than he could handle alone, he still found the energy to respond personally either by letter or pamphlet to those he found too dangerous to ignore.

11.3   Jean de Serres: Dream of Reconciliation

Jean de Serres (1540–1598) lived a varied life as his career crisscrossed between Geneva, Lausanne and France. His brother Olivier was renowned for his work on soil science, and he brought silkworms to the Tuileries Gardens in Paris. Jean trained as a pastor under both Calvin and Beza as part of the first class in 1559 at the Academy of Geneva, residing in the city until 1572.[28] Even before his theological departure from Geneva, Serres faced controversy there, including the scrutiny of his marriage by the consistory and taking leave of a church without the Company's permission.[29] He served as a Reformed minister in several places, including Nîmes beginning in 1579, where he participated in the polemical debate with the Jesuit John Hay alongside Beza, writing at least

---

24 "il avoit un corps foible & debile mais un esprit fort & robuste," from Florimond de Raemond's letter to the reader at the beginning of SPONDE, J., *Response du feu Sieur de Sponde au Traicté des Marques de l'Eglise, fait par Th. de Beze*, 2.

25 The work ends mid-sentence followed by a note that Sponde had hoped to address all disputed points of faith, but his death prevented him from addressing the Eucharist. See SPONDE, J., *Response du feu Sieur de Sponde au Traicté* (1595), 817.

26 SPONDE, J., *Response du feu Sieur de Sponde au Traicté* (1595), 90–112.

27 GEISENDORF, P.-F. (1967), 389.

28 DARDIER, C. (1883), 296–298.

29 He also did not want to become minister in the city of Foncenay while the plague was active. DARDIER, C. (1883), 299–300, 309–310.

four anti-Jesuit works, three in Latin and one in French.[30] Serres and Beza maintained a correspondence over almost two decades, and Serres continued to coordinate with his co-religionists, approaching Geneva in November 1583 about publishing "a work against the Jesuits," presumably part of the debate with Hay.[31]

For more than two decades, Serres was a prolific defender of the Reformed faith through his histories and polemics, making his turn to a more ecumenical outlook more intriguing. This change in direction seems to have taken root during his service as a diplomat for the Huguenot side. He came to serve both Henri, Prince of Condé (1552–1588) and King Henri IV as a diplomat. He was captured by the Catholic League in July 1592 and held for almost nine months in brutal conditions.[32] In recounting his ordeal to Beza after his release, Serres referred to himself as a martyr without death.[33] Serres faced more personal hardship during the French Civil Wars than either Beza or Calvin, and like Castellio and Sponde, faced personal and professional attacks when his views strayed from those of Geneva. At the end of his life, Serres too searched for a path of reconciliation to end the violence of the period. His "Harmonie" was a call for common ground and potential reconciliation between the Reformed and Catholic Churches in order to bring peace to France; he circulated it in manuscript form as early as 1594, and both the Reformed Church of France and Geneva received copies.[34] A version of the manuscript was sent to Beza by a pastor from Basel in September 1594. In this brief treatise, Serres asserted that military arms had not brought people to God but had led to endless impious acts. No one was wiser or happier in their convictions of "a single truth." All Christians of France must come together in support of their king and recognize the beliefs they had in common rather than focus on the ones that divided them.[35] The Company of Pastors surely believed that even when not formally published, a work like this in circulation could be dangerous. Beza and Serres corresponded about this work and despite Serres personal relationship with

---

30 DARDIER, C. (1883), 314; see *Bilbiothèque de la Compagnie de Jésus*, vol. 4, 163–165 for full list of Serres's anti-Jesuit tracts.

31 *Correspondance de Théodore de Bèze* from the 1580s and 1590s contain periodic letters between the two men; The phrase "un ouvrages 'Contre les jesuites,'" appears in RCP 5:24. Note 126 incorrectly assumes that this is a new printing of Serres's *Commentaires*, but it is mentioned with another anti-Jesuit work by Lambert Daneau, making it clear that this is one of Serres responses to Hay.

32 Jean de Serres to Beza, 19/29 July 1593, in CB 34:200–201.

33 Jean de Serres to Beza, 19/29 July 1593, in CB 34:200.

34 "Avis de Jean de Serres sur la Réunion des Protestants et des Catholiques en France," in CB 35:208–217.

35 "Avis de Jean de Serres," in CB 35:208–210, 216–217.

the leader of the Company of Pastors, Beza's final letter to his former student in February 1598 was a lengthy condemnation of his writings, wondering if there were financial reasons for Serres's views and questioning his connection to the French Royal court. In Beza's view, Serres was a "moyenneur" whose desire to see the similarities in practices and beliefs among all Christians was a dangerous path. Beza reiterated the Reformed view that the Pope was the Antichrist and any variation from that belief was blasphemy.[36] Beza ordered Serres to present himself to the National Synod to be held in Montpellier in the spring of 1598, but he died before he could attend. Rumors spread that Serres had been poisoned. Despite his death, the Synod condemned Serres's work, and the Company of Pastors continued to discredit and suppress his writings, viewing any work that explored common ground to be dangerous to the survival of the Reformed Church.[37] Geneva and Beza emphasized the unique nature, in their eyes the true path to salvation, of the Reformed church. For Beza, like Calvin, the differences, not commonalities, were always key to the Reformed faith.

11.4   Antoine de Saint Michel, Baron d'Avully: Local Convert

While the weakening of the Reformed faith in France was of great concern for Geneva, a resurgent Catholicism was even closer to home. Missionary efforts from the Catholic diocese of Geneva, exiled in Annecy, made inroads into the towns surrounding Geneva beginning in 1594. Antoine de Saint Michel, Baron d'Avully was a regional elite who Francis de Sales converted in 1596, and he was a significant Catholic convert for a number of reasons. He was born a Protestant, and he maintained a residence in Geneva. He had served as a diplomat for the Reformed city during the war of 1589 with the Duke of Savoy.[38] De Sales convinced Avully to convert after a lengthy process of nearly nine months of meetings and correspondence with him, and he made his final absolution in Turin at the end of August 1596. Correspondence reveals that de Sales and Avully discussed various points of doctrine over the course of their interactions, including Saint Jerome's explanation of purgatory and the treasury of merit. It proved to be a family affair with Avully's daughter along with her maid preceding her father in their embrace of Catholicism in the spring of 1596.[39] His son Gabriel followed closely behind his father in October of the

---

36 Beza to Jean de Serres, 5/15 February 1598, in CB 39:12–24.

37 See the letters between the Company of Pastors and other Protestant churches during 1598 in CB 39:73–75, as well as Beza to Théophile Cassegrain, 9/19 December 1598, in CB 39:233–237.

38 DUFOUR, A. (2016), vii–viii.

39 F. de Sales to Antoine de Saint-Michel, seigneur d'Avully, 10 May 1596, in WSFS 11:198–199.

same year. In his abjuration, Gabriel stated that he had "sinned greatly" for following the "diverse heresies" of the Reformed faith. He sincerely and spontaneously acknowledged the real presence of the Eucharist and the invocation of the Saints.[40] Despite efforts, presumably from Geneva, to discredit Avully's conversion through rumors and gossip, he embraced his new confession.[41] De Sales wrote to the papal nuncio that Avully "has not lost a single occasion to provide a good example."[42] Avully became chief propagandist for the Catholic mission, composing multiple accounts to support the missionary activities in the region that highlighted Catholics successes and portrayed Protestant failures.[43]

Baron d'Avully entered the polemical arena with the vigor of a new convert with his *Response a La Lettre d'Un Gentilhomme Savoisien A un Gentil-Homme Lyonnois* (1598), published anonymously but widely accepted to have been written by the Baron, and it covered a number of topics related to Geneva. He noted the happy news of the conclusion of peace between Spain and France, and his hope that Catholics could now focus their energy on suppressing "Turks, infidels, and heretics."[44] He also reported on the recent pamphlet from Geneva attacking the rumors of Beza's conversion and death.[45] The Company of Pastors was deeply troubled by these rumors and decided to respond, with Antoine de la Faye taking the lead and composing an account that was published in both Latin and French in 1597.[46] The same year, la Faye would respond to Catholic placards distributed near Geneva that would lead to a written debate with de Sales over the image of the cross.[47] Since the false rumors about Beza had spread, a version of the refutation was also published in German and Dutch Protestant cities.[48] Avully wrote that he knew the rumors about Beza were untrue, but he also defended the Jesuits, saying they were too honorable to have spread such

---

40 Abjuration of Gabriel Avully, in WSFS 23:16–17.
41 F. de Sales to Jules-César Riccardi, papal nuncio in Turin, F. de Sales to Jules-César Riccardi, papal nuncio in Turin, September 1596 and 12 December 1596, in WSFS 11:202–205, 219–224.
42 F. de Sales to Jules-César Riccardi, papal nuncio in Turin, 23 April 1597, in WSFS 11:278.
43 Three works attributed to Avully are: *Lettre d'un Gentilhomme Savoisien a un Gentil-homme Lyonnois* (1598) reproduced in DUFOUR, A. (2016); *Copie de la lettre du seigneur d'Avully: Touchant la dispute des ministres avec le R.P Cherubin, prescheur de l'Ordre des Capucins* (1598); and *La Voluntaire Conversion de Pierre Petit, cy devant ministre de Genève, à nostre saincte foy et religion catholique, apostolique et romaine* (1598c), reproduced in VUARNET, E. (1913), 1–62.
44 AVULLY, G., *Lettre d'un Gentilhomme Savoisien* (2016), 3.
45 AVULLY, G., *Lettre d'un Gentilhomme Savoisien* (2016), 4.
46 Beza to Johann Stucki, 18/28 October 1597, in CB 38:173.
47 FEHLEISON, J. (2014), 257–274.
48 Beza to Johann Stucki, 18/28 October 1597, in CB 38:173. The cities were Hanau, Heidlberg, and Haarlem.

lies. Avully wondered if the author was a Lutheran who was both the enemy of Beza and the Jesuits and used the rumor in order to exact vengeance on both. Furthermore, Avully asserted that Catholics wanted Beza to have a long life so he could return to Catholicism.[49]

This published letter by Avully was primarily an account of the ongoing negotiations between Geneva and the Catholic missionaries for a public disputation of their respective faiths. This lengthy negotiation was in the wake of a brief debate between the Capuchin missionary Chérubin de Maurienne and Herman Lignaridus, a theology professor from Geneva who was a reluctant participant in the encounter between the two in nearby Thonon.[50] Avully offered a detailed narrative of the events surrounding the efforts to hold a more extensive debate, including the names of the individuals, Jean Corojod and Jacob Gradelle, from Geneva who corresponded with Chérubin without the knowledge of the full Company of Pastors and the City Council.[51] To prove that at least some in Geneva were supportive of the debate, Avully reproduced letters from those in Geneva involved in the negotiations.[52] Simon Goulart was most likely the minister of the Company of Pastors who knew about the negotiations with the Catholic missionaries.[53] Perhaps Goulart used the two men as go-betweens because he needed plausible deniability, since he probably lacked the support of Beza and other members of the Company of Pastors. Ultimately, Geneva chose not to continue the debate in person. The negotiations do reveal disagreements within the Company of Pastors on whether to engage or ignore their Catholic neighbors of the region.[54] With the quick publication of his "letter," Avully hoped to goad Geneva into some fuller response.

11.5 Theodore Beza and His Last Polemic

While the actions of Sponde and Serres upset Beza, he did not publish responses to either of them, but he did summon the energy to respond to Avully in print. What about Avully's writing proved too much to resist? Beza found it difficult to restrain himself from attacking Jesuits in print in large part because he blamed the Society for the campaign of misinformation against the Reformed faith and

---

49 AVULLY, G., *Lettre d'un Gentilhomme Savoisien* (2016), 14.
50 For a full narrative, see FEHLEISON, J. (2014), 80–89.
51 AVULLY, G., *Lettre d'un Gentilhomme Savoisien* (2016), 24.
52 AVULLY, G., *Lettre d'un Gentilhomme Savoisien* (2016), 25, 30–32.
53 JONES, L.C. (1916), 113, 123, 125.
54 *Pièces relatives à la Dispute entre le Counseil de Genève et le père Chérubin de Maurienne, capuchin* at the University of Geneva Library, MS FR 8, contains some of the correspondence about the negotiations between the two sides.

him.[55] In his *Sermons sur l'histoire de la passion*, published in 1592, Beza calls the Jesuits "serpent monks" who "wear robes in the name of Jesus to serve as flying buttresses for this unhappy siege of Babylon through apostasy."[56] The military imagery would have reaffirmed the image of the Jesuits as soldiers for Rome's mission in a conflict with Geneva. He accused them of being "forgers of a Christian philosophy" who revived Epicureanism and Atheism.[57] Perhaps Beza hoped he could strike a serious blow to the Jesuits, who were vulnerable in France after their expulsion in 1594.[58] Beza used his response not only to answer Avully, but also to challenge the Jesuits. Beza saw the Jesuits as dishonest in their faith, and he surely felt assaulted by what he viewed as personal attacks from its members.

For what would be his final polemic, *Response a La Lettre d'Un Gentilhomme Savoisien* (1598), Beza attempted to set the record straight, to discount rumors, to weigh in on religious disputes and to lay out his legacy. Beza wrote about himself in the third person since this response was anonymous, but since he uses very precise information to defend himself, there is little doubt he composed the piece. Beza wrote another anonymous pamphlet in 1586 against the Jesuit John Hay, so leaving his name off written work is not without precedent. Perhaps he preferred not to reveal his authorship on tracts that were primarily polemical rather than theological so as not to detract from his reputation as a scholar and theologian.

While Avully had spent most of his tract detailing the ongoing negotiations between the Catholic mission and Geneva, Beza used much of his ink accusing the Jesuits of the false rumors of his conversion and defending his moral character against the charges his enemies often leveled. Beza addressed Avully as the "gentleman of Savoy," accusing him of blasphemy for what he wrote about Beza.[59] The Genevan reformer seemed angry with Avully for defending the Jesuits and for concluding they were not the source of many of the rumors about the Reformed leader. Beza replied that "for some time Theodore Beza has been very well informed of the very impudent falsehoods sown against

---

55 BEZA, T., *Response a La Lettre d'Un Gentilhomme Savoisien, ne se nommant point* (1598c). My citations come from a copy of this work located at the Folger Shakespeare Library in Washington D.C. I also use the introduction and notes of the recent transcription by Alain Dufour.

56 BEZA, T., *Sermons sur l'histoire de la passion ... de nostre Seigneur Iésus Christ* (1592b), 247–248.

57 BEZA, T., *Sermons sur l'histoire de la passion* (1592b), 247–248.

58 NELSON, E. (2005), 114–117.

59 BEZA, T., *Response a La Lettre d'Un Gentilhomme Savoisien, ne se nommant point* (1598c), 8.

him throughout Christendom by these good fathers."[60] Beza offered a detailed analysis of why the rumors were false despite Avully agreeing with him.[61] This pamphlet was more about defending his reputation as leader of the Reformed faith than about responding to what Avully wrote. For Beza, the account of his conversion already had spread to Germany, the court of the Holy Roman Empire, France and Italy. Geneva must have had genuine concern that people might believe the story about Beza's conversion. After all, other prominent Protestants had recently embraced Catholicism.

Beza began by pointing out flaws in the account of the false rumor. As we all know, even unfounded rumors can be believed and revived, making Beza believe an additional rebuttal besides la Faye's was necessary in order to quell them again. He also wanted his version of the narrative to be the one circulating. He asserted that the report floating around Europe was "a letter purely of their invention." He then proceeded to deconstruct the account of his conversion to demonstrate how it could not possibly be true. According to Beza, there were two letters from Italy that recounted the rumors: one from Venice at the beginning of June 1597, which may have been the account the Company of Pastors addressed with their first response, but then he says another one from Florence appeared in February 1598.[62]

One Jesuit in particular, Clément Dupuy or Puteanus, was the object of Beza's displeasure, who he believed was the continuing source of the false stories about him.[63] Puteanus was Father Provincial of the Jesuits for the French Province from 1592–1597.[64] Alain Dufour noted that the Jesuit had been preaching in Dole in the fall of 1597 about Beza's alleged conversion and death.[65] Beza emphasized that the false accounts claim that Puteanus was Superior General of the Jesuits, when it was actually Claudio Aquaviva who served as the fifth Superior General of the Order from 1581–1615. Despite the errors in his biography, Beza believed that Puteanus was a real person who had recently preached at Nancy during Advent and Lent. He was a Jesuit from a good family of Paris, and according to the letters from Italy, he had been sent to Dole so that from there he could go on to Geneva "to preach to the people there, all freshly converted for the most part by Theodore Beza."[66] This Jesuit seemed to be a combination

---

60 "Il y a quelque temps que Theodore de Besze, tresbien informé des treimpudentes faussetés semees contre lui parmi toute la Chrestienté, par ces bons Peres." BEZA, T., *Response a La Lettre d'Un Gentilhomme Savoisien* (1598c), 4.

61 BEZA, T., *Response a La Lettre d'Un Gentilhomme Savoisien* (1598c), 11–12.

62 BEZA, T., *Response a La Lettre d'Un Gentilhomme Savoisien* (1598c), 11–12.

63 BEZA, T., *Response a La Lettre d'Un Gentilhomme Savoisien* (1598c), 13.

64 DUFOUR, A. (2016), 70n.4.

65 DUFOUR, A. (2016), 70n.4.

66 BEZA, T., *Response a La Lettre d'Un Gentilhomme Savoisien* (1598c), 13–14.

of fact and fiction. It is debatable whether Beza was more upset about the false accounts of his conversion or his death.

Beza relayed what he viewed as the true story of "bon Clemons," refuting numerous falsities in the account so as to demonstrate that his reported conversion could not possibly be true. Beza described as "ministral invention" that he, Beza, reportedly addressed the full Senate of Geneva. He argued that there was a Senate in Chambery, not in Geneva, "which is neither ancient, nor the new Rome, no more than Geneva." Despite Avully denying the account, Beza accused him of repeating rumors and, as a result, keeping them in fresh circulation.[67] This rumor did spread widely and of course would have arrived at different places at different times to be received by a fresh population as new. Its dissemination, though a bit slower, is not unlike modern day urban legends or internet hoaxes.

To further cast the Jesuit as the villain of his piece, Beza claimed that as the provincial father of Bordeaux, Puteanus had been involved in the Catholic League. General Aquaviva then sent Puteanus to Paris to be provincial father over the colleges of the region, including Rouen, Nevers, Eux, Verdun, Pont-à-Mousson and Bourges. Beza raised the renewed challenges against the Jesuits by the University of Paris because of their justifying the killing of a king. The Jesuits were banished and Puteanus retired to Pont-à-Mousson where there was a Jesuit university founded by the Cardinal of Lorraine in 1572. The university was a center for Jesuit polemicists during the last decades of the sixteenth century.[68] Puteanus then supposedly transferred to Dole so he could easily go to Geneva to preach to the people. In other words, in Beza's estimation, Puteanus is a Leaguer waiting in the wings for a chance to strike.

Beza ended his condemnation of the Jesuits and their false rumors by tying them to international intrigue through the Catholic League and to regicide through the attempted assassination of Henri IV in December 1594 by Jean Chastel, which led to the Jesuits' expulsion from much of France.[69] He concluded that Jesuits were dangerous enemies of "the church of God" who justified rebellion against rulers.[70] To reiterate this point, Beza noted the attempted assassination of Count Maurice of Nassau, whose father had been killed by a fanatical Catholic (Balthasar Gérard) who also had ties to Jesuits.[71] In a transition to his second subject, Beza linked the Jesuits to a new local adversary,

---

67 BEZA, T., *Response a La Lettre d'Un Gentilhomme Savoisien* (1598c), 16, 18.
68 John Hay was a professor of philosophy at Pont-à-Mousson for several years beginning in 1576. See HAY, J. (1901), *Catholic Tractactes of the Sixteenth Century 1573–1600* (1901), xxxvi.
69 BEZA, T., *Response a La Lettre d'Un Gentilhomme Savoisien* (1598c), 19.
70 BEZA, T., *Response a La Lettre d'Un Gentilhomme Savoisien* (1598c), 17.
71 BEZA, T., *Response a La Lettre d'Un Gentilhomme Savoisien* (1598c), 19.

the Capuchins, saying that they were together in their "falseness." The Jesuits and the Capuchins were both present in the duchy of Chablais supporting the missionary efforts there.

Beza turned to his second subject, which was the mission in Thonon and the efforts of the Capuchin Chérubin to engage the pastors of Geneva in a dispute.[72] As noted earlier, the majority of Avully's writing about the mission concerned the disputation and not the rumors of Beza's death and conversion. I have written about Chérubin's antagonism of the Company of Pastors over this public debate elsewhere.[73] Beza was unhappy that "two artisans" had negotiated with Chérubin in the name of the Company of Pastors, but most likely the two men had the support of some in the Company, just not from Beza.[74] The church in Geneva was under pressure to make a stand against the Catholic mission, and ultimately concluded print was better than in person, but Beza's response to Avully demonstrates that the issues were troubling for him.

In examining Avully and Beza's works side by side, there is a certain level of parallelism in their back and forth. Both men use similar imagery when describing their foes. Avully referred to "Turks, infidels, and heretics" and "pernicious locusts."[75] Beza said that monks, curés, canons and abbots go from country to country like a plague of locusts and take the harvests in the name of Jesus, which he described as "execrable sacrilege." He also accused Avully of "transforming the pastors of Geneva into pests" in the new Catholic's portrayal of Reformed preachers.[76] Beza mocked Catholic pilgrimages, claiming those who took part travelled from one idol to the next exercising meaningless rituals.[77] Both men employed the imagery of biblical plagues of insects in portraying the other side as pests in their accounts.

There is no tight organization to Beza's response, which supports the interpretation that it was written hastily and for the specific purpose of challenging the misinformation Beza believed to be floating around about him, the Company of Pastors and Geneva. This is not unlike the polemical response that Beza had written in 1586 in response to the Jesuit John Hay. In addition to the personal attacks, Beza took issue that Avully questioned that one of the ministers, presumably Antoine de la Faye, who had written the 1597 response to the rumors, had studied medicine. Avully had implied that de la Faye used medical skills for spiritual purposes. Beza said that if one had studied magic or exorcism as

---

72 BEZA, T., *Response a La Lettre d'Un Gentilhomme Savoisien* (1598c), 20.

73 FEHLEISON, J. (2010), 85–89.

74 BEZA, T., *Response a La Lettre d'Un Gentilhomme Savoisien* (1598c), 20–23.

75 AVULLY, G., *Lettre d'un Gentilhomme Savoisien* (2016), 3.

76 BEZA, T., *Response a La Lettre d'Un Gentilhomme Savoisien* (1598c), 28.

77 BEZA, T., *Response a La Lettre d'Un Gentilhomme Savoisien* (1598c), 29–30.

some popes, cardinals, bishops and other "Roman clergy do still today, that would be a serious crime." Beza goes on to point out that Saint Luke was also a doctor and that Juvenal had been both bishop of Narni and a doctor.[78] He reminded the "gentleman of Savoy" that the Reformed faith was based only on the canonical books of the Old and New Testament whereas the papacy created "a chaos of idolatry." Beza noted that reformers had refuted the decrees of the Council of Trent and that the Catholic reliance on Thomas Aquinas was suspect since he lived 1200 years after Jesus Christ.[79] Reformed writers often hurled the charges of idolatry at Catholics who attacked the Reformed church structure or leadership.

The third key subject Beza addressed was the personal attack on his character, and while he tried to maintain the anonymity of the piece in this section, the personal nature of the defense made it difficult.[80] Perhaps sensing that this would be his final contribution to the battle with his enemies, Beza defended aspects of his personal life and his character. Avully had referred to Beza in his letter as more of a mite than a man. Beza, not surprisingly, took offense to this insult and proceeded to recount his distinguished heritage and education, reminding the Savoy gentleman of his ancient and noble family from Burgundy and his excellent education.[81] Beza wanted to set the record straight and counter what he saw as the enduring misinformation offered in the biography of Jerome Bolsec (c. 1524–1584). The Jesuits often turned to Bolsec's salacious biographies for use in their polemical works.[82] Beza commented that Bolsec died in Annecy in a "miserable state for his conscience."[83] Irena Backus argued that Bolsec's biographies of both Calvin and Beza were really an attack on Beza more so than Calvin, but in tandem were meant "to destroy the image of Geneva as quickly and effectively as possible."[84] To defend against the attacks on his moral character, Beza addressed the criticism of his poetry by pointing out that they were "his first poems of his adolescence" with some inventions but nothing excessive and nothing compared to actions of Pope Alexander VI [Rodrigo Borgia].[85] The Genevan reformer claimed that some poetry attributed to him were forgeries.[86] Beza also tried to dispel rumors concerning his marriages. In some circles, Beza had been criticized for remarrying a much younger woman

78 BEZA, T., *Response a La Lettre d'Un Gentilhomme Savoisien* (1598c), 63.
79 BEZA, T., *Response a La Lettre d'Un Gentilhomme Savoisien* (1598c), 66–67.
80 BEZA. T., *Response a La Lettre d'Un Gentilhomme Savoisien* (1598c), 62.
81 BEZA, T., *Response a La Lettre d'Un Gentilhomme Savoisien* (1598c), 49.
82 Jesuit John Hay used them in his polemical debates with Beza, Serres and others in the 1580s.
83 Other sources say Jerome Bolsec died in Lyons.
84 BACKUS, I. (2008), 28.
85 BEZA, T., *Response a La Lettre d'Un Gentilhomme Savoisien* (1598c), 51–52.
86 BEZA, T., *Response a La Lettre d'Un Gentilhomme Savoisien* (1598c), 52.

at the age of 70, and Catholic critics tried to cast his late marriage as scandalous and inappropriate. He noted that his second wife was in her forties so not that young and passed child bearing age. He then proceeded to counter with criticism of Avully's "Roman Church" and its views of virginity and marriage. Beza wanted all aspects of his biography to be models for the Reformed faithful.

Beza wanted to be placed alongside the giants of the Reformation in Geneva of John Calvin, Pierre Viret and Guillaume Farel who were remembered for their contributions to the Reformed faith and not for their personal lives or rumors spread about them. Of course they had all been dead for more than 25 years so their legacies were left to others to craft. Since Beza was very much alive and still actively defending himself, he was reproached for his ambition.[87] Perhaps this is another reason he chose anonymity. He challenged this portrait of himself by reminding the reader that if he were so ambitious, why did he leave his country, parents and allies for a modest existence in Geneva?[88] In this short pamphlet, Beza revealed the struggles that he and Geneva faced at the end of the sixteenth century and the effort he made to control the narrative of himself, the Reformed faith and Geneva.

11.6 Conclusion

From its inception, Christianity has been an evangelical faith, making conversions a perpetual reality every time a new group emerged. Why did certain conversions worry the Reformed leadership in Geneva more than others at the end of the sixteenth century? Their social status and power of their pens in the cases of Sponde, Avully and Serres were a danger to the Reformed faith. Both Sponde and Serres had been reprimanded by Beza or the Company of Pastors or both in the 1580s, leading to Beza's predisposition to be critical of the two men's activities. Beza implied there were financial reasons for both men's move away from the Reformed faith and towards Henri IV of France. Both men had chosen different paths for their careers than the one through Geneva.

In the 1590s, Beza worried about his legacy and maintaining what he saw as the purity of doctrine in the Reformed Church. He witnessed the increasing political and religious isolation of Geneva and personally confronted attacks on his character as well as declining health. Geneva did not have the military might to be the aggressor in waging war, and the Company of Pastors could not defend itself in print against every attack, but the city's leaders still saw themselves as the center of the Reformed faith. Despite these setbacks, the compromise

---

87 BEZA, T., *Response a La Lettre d'Un Gentilhomme Savoisien* (1598c), 57–58.
88 BEZA, T., *Response a La Lettre d'Un Gentilhomme Savoisien* (1598c), 58–59.

envisioned by men like Jean de Serres was not an option. The religious landscape of France was dramatically different from that in Geneva. While Henri IV's conversion in 1593 was a major blow, the embrace of Catholicism by men like Sponde and Avully was especially troubling to Geneva as both men had been raised Protestant and both held positions of respect and influence in society, making their publications a real threat.

It is striking that Sponde, Serres and Avully all participated in diplomacy at some point in their lives while they were Protestant. Compromise is a critical part of any successful negotiation; perhaps all three of these men came to believe that conciliation was the only path for a return to peace and stability in France. It is easier to be uncompromising when you do not have to interact with those who hold different religious views. The isolation of Geneva (neither Calvin nor Beza ventured out of the city very often once established there) geographically and politically contributed to a very different outlook in comparison to those like Sponde, Serres and Avully who interacted with adversaries in an often fraught world. This willingness to compromise with or even embrace Catholicism made them some of Beza's final foes.

Part Five: Memories of Theodore Beza

Martin Klauber

Chapter 12: Michel Le Faucheur and Edme Aubertin

Seventeenth-Century Memories of Theodore Beza's Eucharistic Polemics

As one of the most significant early figures in the Reformation and as John Calvin's successor in Geneva, Theodore Beza helped lay the groundwork for much of Reformed theology that followed, especially in France during the late sixteenth and well into the seventeenth century. In his famous speech at the Colloquy of Poissy in 1561, he remarked:

> His [Christ's] body is as far removed from the bread and wine as the highest Heaven is from the earth, since, as to ourselves, we are on the earth, and the sacraments also; while, as to Him, His flesh is in Heaven, so glorified that his glory, as says St. Augustine, has not taken away from Him the nature, but only the infirmity of a true body.[1]

The best known part of this citation is the first part, but his mention of Augustine as an authority pointed to the importance of using patristic sources to support the Reformed position on the Eucharist. Beza's oration was so pointed that it drew the response of *blasphemavit* or blasphemy.[2]

Beza's views on the Eucharist were thus memorialized and he became an important resource for Reformed theologians who followed him well into the seventeenth century. After the close of the Wars of Religion in France, theological debates continued and, in some ways, supplanted armed conflict as Catholics and Protestants jockeyed for position; the Reformed for survival and the Catholics for dominance during the era of the Edict of Nantes from 1598–1685.

One of the most significant events in these Eucharistic debates was the celebrated Conference at Fontainebleau presided over by King Henri IV in 1600. This debate pitted the Roman Catholic bishop and future Cardinal Jacques-Davy Du Perron against the revered Huguenot hero, Philippe du Plessis-Mornay. The focus of the meeting had been to determine the accuracy of Mornay's 5,000 citations from the church fathers over the nature of the Eucharist, Mornay had claimed that transubstantiation had been a theological innovation, unknown in the early church. His use of patristic sources continued the trend that went

---

1 BAIRD, H. (1889), 1:519.
2 BAIRD, H. (1889), 1:519.

back to the earliest days of the Reformation. Although the early reformers, such as Beza, held to *sola scriptura*, they also believed that they had the testimony of the fathers to support them and to show that Protestant theology was not new but could trace its roots back to the New Testament era. Perron clearly defeated Mornay, who was accused of taking many of his citations out of context or truncating them.[3]

Mornay's defeat at Fontainebleau threatened this narrative, and some of his followers took up the pen to vindicate his honor. They were careful to do so in writing, however, as in the post-Tridentine era, most Reformed scholars shied away from public academic disputations for fear that they would come up short, which could lead to abjurations. Patrick Cabanel counts 166 confirmed conferences between 1593 and 1685. Many more of them were instigated by Roman Catholics (21%), especially Jesuits and Capuchins, than by Protestants (only 3%). The purpose, in many cases, was the targeting of Reformed believers for conversion to Roman Catholicism.[4]

One of the major centers for French Reformed thought, where the doctrine of the Eucharist loomed large was the large church outside of Paris in the town of Charenton. According to the Edict of Nantes, it was illegal for the Huguenots to worship within the city, so they constructed a massive "temple" at Charenton for Parisian Protestants who made the trek to the outskirts of the city. Some 15,000 Huguenots worshipped there regularly. This was a large church structure with two balconies that seated up to 4,000 people at a time. Membership included some of the most prominent noblemen and public officials in Paris, who helped to represent the cause of the Protestants in the royal court. Since the church was so massive, the congregation typically employed up to five pastors at any one time, most of them being not just pastors but scholars as well who published academic books, sermon series and polemic works on a number of topics. They were well-educated, having studied at the various Protestant academies training pastors such as Saumur, Montauban, Sedan, Nîmes and Geneva, and included some of the best scholars of the era. The local consistories and pastors themselves typically had extensive libraries and the church at Charenton was no exception, boasting up to 548 volumes acquired between 1626 and 1664.[5] The most important duties for the pastors was to preach and to administer the Lord's Supper. The sermons were central to the worship service and they were quite long, typically about an hour and twenty minutes. The Lord's Supper was

---

3 For more on this debate see KLAUBER, M. (2015), 45–72; WOLFE, M. (2009), 65–85; LALOT, J. (1889); HOLT, M. (2007), 65–85.

4 CABANEL, P. (2012), 408.

5 MCKEE, J. (2008), 260–261.

typically administered quarterly with the accompanying sermons lasting a bit longer, about an hour and forty-five minutes.[6]

These pastors included Pierre du Moulin (1568–1658), Jean Daillé (1594–1670), Jean Mestrezat (1592–1657), Ami Aubertin (1595–1652), Michel Le Faucheur (1585–1657), Charles Drelincourt (1595–1669) and later Jean Claude (1619–1687). Le Faucheur was probably the best orator in the group. All of these pastors displayed fond memories of their forbears in the faith, especially Calvin and Beza. This essay will look at how two of these ministers used Beza, in particular, as an authority on a number of topics, especially Eucharistic theology.

12.1 Michel Le Faucheur

The first pastor to be considered is Michel Le Faucheur, who was born in Geneva in 1585, where his Huguenot family had fled from France. His father, also named Michel Le Faucheur, was the son of a lawyer at the Parisian parlement and his mother Suzanne came from Dijon. The younger Michel was also the great-nephew of John Calvin's colleague, Nicholas des Gallars.

Le Faucheur was educated at the Academy of Geneva where he gained a mastery of Latin, Greek, Hebrew and Syriac, languages that would prove important to him in his study of the church fathers on the nature of the Eucharist. He also became acquainted with Beza. It is doubtful that he formally studied with Beza, seeing that the reformer had retired from lecturing at the Academy in January 1599, while Le Faucheur's name is inscribed in the *Livre du recteur* in March of the same year.[7] There is interesting but unconfirmed speculation reported by the nineteenth-century historian Charles Weiss that Le Faucheur displayed a similar oratorical accent to Beza.[8] So any influence that Beza may have had on the young Le Faucheur must have been informal and may have come in part from Beza's emphasis on the art of speaking well as displayed in his *On the Correct Pronunciation of the French Language*.[9]

Le Faucheur maintained a life-long friendship and correspondence with Beza's godson, Théodore Tronchin (1582–1657), who was also the son of Beza's adopted daughter Théodora Rocca. It is likely that the two had studied together at the Academy. In his letters to Tronchin, he made a couple of comments about Beza. In the first, he chided him for using the term "supralapsarian" to describe

---

6 CABANEL, P. (2012), 444.
7 LE FORT, C./REVILLIOD, M.G./FICK, I.G. (1860), 55.
8 WEISS, M. (1854), 1.64.
9 BEZA, T., *De Francicae linguae recta pronuntiatione* (1584); FARNUM, E. (1964), 25–26.

Beza, Junius and Polanus and lamented that he was scandalized that these "great men" would be given that label. However, although he said that he highly revered them, he disagreed with them on that subject.[10] The second mention of Beza came in a letter to Tronchin dated 3 June 1636, where Le Faucheur was discussing the views of the controversial theologian at the Reformed Academy of Saumur, Moïse Amyraut. The latter espoused a more moderate doctrine on the extent of the atonement known as hypothetical universalism, whereby he argued that Christ had died for the world, though it was only effective for the elect. Le Faucheur was a leading advocate of Amyraut and defended his views vigorously in his correspondence with Tronchin, who held the opposite view. Le Faucheur asserted that Amyraut had done a nice job answering the accusations of one of the leading French Reformed theologians of the era, Pierre du Moulin, who believed that Amyraut's views were dangerously similar to the universalism of the Arminians. Amyraut, Le Faucheur surmised, had responded to du Moulin "with all the respect that he could have used with M. Calvin and M. Beza."[11] Although Le Faucheur disagreed with Beza on the nature of the extent of the atonement, he still revered him and placed him in a class with Calvin himself.

Upon completing his studies at Geneva, Le Faucheur accepted a call to the pastorate at Annonay in the province of Vivarais in 1607 and distinguished himself so quickly that he was chosen as a delegate to the National Synod of Privas in 1612. With his outstanding oratorical skills, it did not take long for him to be sought out by more prestigious churches, and in 1612 he took a ministerial position at Montpelier, where he served for twenty years. He had been a frequent visitor since his sister lived there, and the position carried with it the opportunity to teach at the Reformed Academy.[12]

Le Faucheur served ably and was chosen as a representative to the National Synod of Alais in 1620, where the Canons of Dort were accepted as binding on the French Reformed churches. Unfortunately for Le Faucheur, the parlement of Toulouse passed an edict in 1623 forbidding foreign-born pastors from serving in their jurisdiction. As a result, he went to Paris in 1623 to plead his case at court and was granted permission to continue his ministry. In 1625, he was commissioned to go to Nîmes to encourage the Protestants to remain loyal to the king. His cooperation in this affair led Cardinal Richelieu to believe that Le Faucheur could be turned and so he sent him a gift of 10,000 francs during the Revolt of Monsieur in 1632, which ended with the arrest and execution of Henri

---

10 Le Faucheur to Tronchin, n.d. Archiv Tronchin, 27:204.
11 Le Faucheur to Tronchin, 3 June 1636, Archiv Tronchin, 27:206. See also FARNUM, E. (1964), 65–66.
12 CABANAC, P. (1901), 15–18.

II Duke de Montmorency. Le Faucheur expressed bewilderment about why the Cardinal would send him money and did not cooperate. Since he clearly either did not get the message or decided to decline the bribe, his suspension from preaching was reinstituted and remained in effect until he became pastor at Charenton.[13]

In 1626 Le Faucheur went to the National Synod of Castres, where he was encouraged to publish his refutation to Cardinal Du Perron's posthumously printed massive work on the Eucharist.[14] In 1631 he was elected moderator of the Second National Synod at Charenton. Eventually, he did accept a position on the pastoral staff at Charenton in 1636, strangely after encountering a Franciscan monk, who held an important position at Richelieu's Cabinet-Council, in an apothecary shop on the *rue Saint Jacques*. The monk, after asking who he was, encouraged him to preach at Charenton and promised that he would not be disturbed or arrested for doing so. Le Faucheur told his brother of the incident who, in turn, informed the elders at Charenton, and the next Sunday he was invited to preach. He continued his ministry there until his death in 1657.[15]

Le Faucheur first gained attention in Paris in 1609 while probably visiting his two brothers who lived there, and he was invited to preach three times at Charenton. His preaching was so well-delivered that luminaries such as the diarist Pierre L'Estoile, a Roman Catholic who was sympathetic to the Protestants, wrote in his diary that the sermon moved most of the congregation to tears, including M. de Sully. L'Estoile, ironically, was not even present at the sermon, but was recounting the praises of his friends and reported that "truly his wit and his learning far outstripped his years." As a Roman Catholic, it would have been virtually impossible to attend the service since, as he reported, "in Paris, so stupid and corrupt is everybody here—to go to a house of ill fame is for those of the Catholic persuasion more tolerable by far than to go to Charenton."[16]

Le Faucheur's best known work, *Traitté de l'action de l'orateur; ou de la Prononciation et de geste*, was not published until the year after his death by the founder of the Académie française, Valentin Conart. Some believed that Conart was the real author because, when it was translated into Latin by Melchior Schmidt in 1690, Conart was listed as the author. Le Faucheur was not recognized as the author until the end of the seventeenth century. In spite of the lack of initial credit for this prodigious book, it went through seven editions in French and one in Latin. It also went through three editions in English and had a great

---

13 CABANAC, P. (1901), 16–20.
14 QUICK, J. (1692), 2:289.
15 QUICK, J. (1692), 2:318.
16 FARNUM, E. (1964), 4–5.

impact on the so-called Elocution movement in England. His instruction on the public speaking skills of a lawyer and of a pastor served as a model for generations that followed.[17] He also published many of his sermons and a major treatise on the Lord's Supper, which was a direct refutation of Du Perron.

So, Le Faucheur served as one of the primary preachers at one of the most important Reformed churches in all of France and he was surrounded with colleagues of impressive abilities. What is interesting about this coterie of clergy at Charenton was that most of them composed a major treatise on the Lord's Supper and all of them were addressed, at least in part, directly against Du Perron, who wrote a major refutation of Mornay which was not published until 1622, after the Cardinal's death in 1618.[18] Le Faucheur displayed interest in writing a response to Du Perron in a letter to Tronchin dated 19 April 1623, where he wanted to know if anyone in Geneva was working on a response.[19]

Le Faucheur's text was his *Traitté de la Cene,* which was not published until 1635.[20] This is a massive and highly technical tome that took many years to complete and he discussed the work in his letters to Tronchin, noting that he had sent drafts of the work to the publisher, Pierre Chouet, at Geneva, for review. This treatise has gone relatively unnoticed throughout the years, but was well received in the seventeenth century. Its importance was eclipsed to some extent by a similar work written by Edme Aubertin. Le Faucheur received a draft of Aubertin's work and examined it as early as 1633 to see if there were any discrepancies. In a letter to Tronchin he stated that "we meet on many points, and thank God I have as yet encountered none on which we clash."[21] Although the vast majority of this work was devoted to the views of the church fathers on the nature of the Eucharist, Le Faucheur did, in several instances, invoke the authority of Beza to support his position that the early church never sanctioned the doctrine of transubstantiation.

First, in his discussion of Augustine's position on the subject, one had to determine whether figurative or literal language was being used. Ironically, this was the same issue that many biblical scholars faced when analyzing the biblical words of institution. Du Perron had argued that to prove that Augustine was using figurative language when discussing the nature of Christ's presence in the Eucharist, one would have to point to other places in Augustine's writings where he interpreted Scripture in a similar way. For example, in his discussion of Gen 2:9, the verse about the tree of life and the tree of the knowledge of good

---

17 GAILLET, L. (1994), 70–74.
18 DU PERRON, D., *Traité du Saint Sacrement de l'Eucharistie* (1622).
19 Le Faucheur to Tronchin, 19 April 1623, Archiv Tronchin, 27:159.
20 LE FAUCHEUR, M., *Traitté de la Cene* (1635).
21 Le Faucheur to Tronchin, 18 April 1633, Archiv Tronchin, 27:173.

and evil, Augustine noted that the passage possesses both literal and figurative aspects:

> What comes next, certainly, and the tree of life in the middle of Paradise and the tree of knowledge of discerning good and evil (Gen 2:9), calls for more careful consideration, to avoid its forcing us into allegory and having to say that these were not real trees, but that they signify something else under the name of tree. It is said about wisdom, after all, that she is the tree of life to all who embrace her (Prov 3:18). However, while there is an eternal Jerusalem in the heavens, there is also the city founded on earth by which that one is signified; and though Sarah and Hagar signified the two covenants, they were also nonetheless two women; and while Christ waters us with a spiritual stream through his suffering on the tree, he was also nonetheless the rock which poured out water to a thirsty people when struck with a wooden rod, about which it is said, now that rock was Christ (1 Cor 10:4). All these things stood for something other than what they were, but all the same they were themselves bodily realities. And when the narrator mentioned them he was not employing figurative language, but giving an explicit account of things which had a forward reference that was figurative.[22]

Du Perron argued that, for Augustine, the literal sense was of paramount importance, and when one uses that principle in discussing the words of institution, the proper exegesis should be governed by that rule. Du Perron called these types of interpretations *locutions figurées,* which he took to mean that the literal meaning should supersede the figurative. According to Le Faucheur, Augustine did admit that figurative language alone could be used, but only in passages where no literal interpretation was possible. Then, Du Perron brought Beza into the discussion in support of his position in his discussion of Prov 25:21-22, which states: "If your enemy is hungry, give him food to eat, and if he is thirsty, give him water to drink. For in so doing, you will heap burning coals on his head"; and Eccl 12:4 "Give to the godly man, but do not receive the sinner." Du Perron explained:

> There is not a single one of these passages which, besides the figurative expression which St. Augustine observes, that has a more basic, true, proper and real sense according to the letter such as the Proverbs as Beza confesses, the one of Ecclesiastes according to the ministers of Geneva and that of the gospel according to St. Augustine especially, according to their commentaries on this passage.[23]

Du Perron's effort to claim the support of Beza and his Genevan colleagues was a clever argument, but Le Faucheur would have none of it, responding that there was no question about how Beza and his associates interpreted these passages, which they did correctly. One must interpret each passage and each book of the

---

22 AUGUSTINE, *De Genesi ad litteram* (1982), 8.8.
23 DU PERRON, D., *Réfutation de toutes les objections* (1624), 121.

Bible on its own merits rather than impose an arbitrary rule from one passage on all of them. So, it is interesting that both Du Perron and Le Faucheur, in this case, used Beza as an authoritative figure, whose opinion carried significant authority in biblical and theological interpretation.[24]

A second instance where Le Faucheur invoked the authority of Beza was in the discussion of the patristic view of whether or not a communicant consumes the sacramental elements in the same way that one eats non-sacramental food. The key citation in this section came from Origen, in his discussion of Matt 15:17, where Christ said, "Don't you see that whatever enters the mouth goes into the stomach and then out of the body?" Origen agreed that even sacramental food is consumed in the same way as any other food, saying:

> Even the meat which has been sanctified through the Word of God and prayer, in accordance with the fact that it is material, goes into the belly and is cast out into the draught, but in respect of the prayer which comes upon it, according to the proportion of the faith, becomes a benefit and is a means of clear vision to the mind which looks to that which is beneficial, and it is not the material of the bread but the word which is said over it which is of advantage to him who eats it not unworthily of the Lord.[25]

This was a difficult passage for Du Perron to refute, and he did so based on the proper translation from the Greek, saying that Greek word ὑλικό and its cognates do not always mean *materia* in Latin. Le Faucheur countered by saying that the word clearly means *materia* and, furthermore, Erasmus in his edition of Origen's *Commentary on Matthew* confirmed it. After having failed in the argument based on an incorrect translation, Du Perron went on to point out that Origen was a confirmed heretic and both Calvin and Beza had even said so.[26] Le Faucheur did not contest the assessment of Origen by Calvin and Beza but argued that, although Origen had some strange and unorthodox ideas, he was by no means the only patristic figure who had such. Furthermore, many of the ancient Christian writers had very positive things to say about Origen, such as Basil the Great, Gregory of Nazianzus, Chrysostom or more recent Roman Catholic theologians such as Sixtus of Siena or Gilbert Génébrard who edited the works of Origen and dedicated them to the French King Charles IX.[27]

This whole section seems a bit torturous to read, but is typical of the wrangling between the two sides of this debate. What is interesting is Du Perron's coupling of both Calvin and Beza as authorities and then Le Faucheur's response where he defended them and then went to other Roman Catholic sources to turn the tables

---

24 LE FAUCHEUR, M., *Traitté de la Cene* (1635), 533.

25 ORIGIN, *Commentary on Matthew*, ANF 12:14.

26 DU PERRON, D., *Traité du Saint Sacrement* (1624), 217.

27 LE FAUCHEUR, M., *Traitté de la Cene* (1635), 567.

on his opponent. So, we have the Roman Catholics using Protestant authorities and then the Protestant countering by using Roman Catholic authorities as a means of argumentation.

Another instance where both Du Perron and Le Faucheur invoked Beza was in their discussion of Col 2:11-12, "In him you were also circumcised with a circumcision not performed by human hands. Your whole self, ruled by the flesh, was put off when you were circumcised by Christ, having been buried with him in baptism, in which you were also raised with him through your faith in the working of God, who raised him from the dead." Du Perron argued:

> St. Paul does not call in this passage circumcision sacramental baptism, nor does he call baptism, sacramental circumcision, but calls the thing figured by circumcision, sacramental in order to understand the suppression of sins of the flesh by the work of the Holy Spirit rather than by human power. He says this to support baptism, as the real figure of sacramental circumcision, as Beza himself recognized, admitting that St. Paul compares baptism with circumcision, as the truth coming out of the shadows.[28]

Le Faucheur was quick to reply that the thing signified by circumcision in this passage is clearly identified as baptism and the thing signified by baptism is circumcision. Therefore, he argued they must both be similar, one for the Old Testament and the other for the New Testament. The abolition of sin accomplished through circumcision in Old Testament time, would now be accomplished by baptism. Then Le Faucheur cited Beza, who agreed with this interpretation, when he argued in his discourse on this passage that circumcision was

> the seal of justification by faith of believers and, as a result, also of sanctification in the hearts of the righteous, but since the need for circumcision had been abrogated, we no longer need this external sign, since we now have another one, that is baptism. We now have a marker, a very efficacious seal through which we have the substance of circumcision in order to know the spiritual grace that it signifies and that he [Beza] says nothing of the sort that Du Perron attributes to him that circumcision had only been a shadow, a vain, empty, and naked sign.[29]

So, again, one sees in this exchange that both Du Perron and Le Faucheur were citing Beza as an authority to lend more credence to their respective interpretations of an important sacramental passage. Le Faucheur got the last word on the subject since he was responding to a posthumously published work, so it would be up to others to try to refute Le Faucheur.

The third section where Le Faucheur referred to Beza was the discussion of Heb 10:1, "The law is only a shadow of the good things that are coming." Du

---

28 DU PERRON, D., *Traité du Saint Sacrement* (1624), 99.
29 LE FAUCHEUR, M., *Traitté de la Cene* (1635), 625.

Perron interpreted this to mean that the law is different from the perfection that was to come. Then he cited Beza's use of the Syriac translation where it says, "For in the law there was a shadow of the good things to come; not the substance of the things themselves."[30] This time, in his response, Le Faucheur did not refer to Beza at all, but instead turned to Origen and Theodoret and then to Roman Catholic sources, Thomas Aquinas, Thomas Cajetan and Francisco Suárez. These authorities interpreted the passage to refer to things to come, the greater light of the gospel compared to the law. Le Faucheur contrasted the Old Testament sacraments as shadows that do reflect the truth of Christ but do so much more dimly than the sacraments of the New Testament and, ultimately, Christ himself. Here, he cited Col 2:16-17, "Therefore do not let anyone judge you by what you eat or drink, or with regard to a religious festival, a New Moon celebration or a Sabbath day. These are a shadow of the things that were to come; the reality, however, is found in Christ."[31]

The final citation of Beza comes in a section where Le Faucheur analyzed Cyril of Alexandria's *Commentary of St. John*. Du Perron focused on the section where Cyril argued that the communicant partakes of the body and blood of Christ corporeally and substantially. Here Le Faucheur cited some Roman Catholic sources to counter this argument, such as Robert Bellarmine, who said that Christ is in the Eucharist really and substantially but not corporeally. He focused here on the word "substantially," arguing that Calvin and Beza both agreed in the substantial but not the physical presence of Christ in the elements. He then cited the contemporary Gregory of Valencia, the Spanish theologian who taught at Ingolstadt from 1575–1597, and who had cited Calvin's view that Christ is united with the souls of believers in the Lord's Supper and is communicated to them substantially even though the body of Christ is present in heaven. Furthermore, Gregory pointed out that Beza agreed with this interpretation. So, when Cyril referred to a corporeal and substantial union, he was not referring to Christ's physical presence in the elements, but a true union with the communicant according to both his humanity and divinity.[32]

What is particularly striking about Le Faucheur's references to Beza is that he often was defending him against misinterpretation by his Roman Catholic opponents. A common tactic on both sides of the Eucharistic dispute was for the Protestants to cite Roman Catholic sources to support their own positions and vice versa. As a result, Le Faucheur was forced to protect such sources, such as Beza, from misuse. So, Beza served as both a positive source to support

---

30 DU PERRON, D., *Traité du Saint Sacrement* (1624), 422.
31 LE FAUCHEUR, M., *Traitté de la Cene* (1635), 629.
32 LE FAUCHEUR, M., *Traitté de la Cene* (1635), 675.

the Reformed position and also had to be protected from serving as a basis for
Roman Catholic polemics.

12.2   Edme Aubertin

Le Faucheur's colleague at Charenton, Edme Aubertin, shared his passion for
defending the Reformed position on the Eucharist as well as his admiration for
Theodore Beza. Aubertin pastored first at Chartres from 1621 to 1631 before
accepting the more prestigious post at Charenton, where he served until his
death in 1652.[33]

Aubertin was no stranger to controversy. He certainly aroused the suspicion
of royal officials when he referred to himself as a "ministre de l'Eglise" instead
of the required title of "minister de la religion prétendue reformé" or when
he referred to Cardinals Robert Bellamine and Du Perron as enemies of the
church. When he was on his deathbed, a *curé* was sent to offer him last rites
in the Roman Catholic faith, which would have been quite a public relations
coup. The family tried in vain to get the priest to leave but to no avail. Aubertin
finally refused extreme unction and died firmly in the Protestant faith.[34]

He is best known for his magisterial tome on the history of the Eucharist,
L'Eucharisitie de l'ancienne Eglise (1633), which cemented his reputation as one
of the best patristic scholars of his day.[35] As was the case with Le Faucheur,
Aubertin's work was a refutation of Du Perron. In fact, Aubertin published a
treatise in 1626, also responding to the cardinal, which focused on the views of
Augustine on the Lord's Supper entitled *Conformité de la créance de l'Église et
de S. Augustin.*[36]

Aubertin's *L'Eucharisitie* was accepted at the time as the definitive treatment
on the subject. The son of his colleague, Jean Daillé, praised it saying: "The great
and incomparable work *L'Eucharistie* has outlived all the attacks of the other
communion, not one of whom has ventured into open war with it, or, so to
speak, dared to meet it tête-à-tête."[37] Jean Claude, the pastor at Charenton who
engaged in a back and forth debate on the Eucharist with Jansenists Antoine
Arnauld and Pierre Nicole later in the century, acknowledged his indebtedness
to Aubertin's groundbreaking work and claimed that Aubertin had never been
and could never be refuted. Twentieth-century historian Remi Snoeks, who

---

33   On Aubertin, see KLAUBER, M. (2014), 205–215.
34   HAAG, 1:148–150.
35   AUBERTIN, E., *L'Eucharistie de l'ancienne Eglise* (1633).
36   AUBERTIN, E., *Conformité de la créance de l'Église* (1626).
37   FÉLICE, G. (1850), 353.

composed a major work on the seventeenth-century Eucharistic debates in France, referred to Aubertin's treatise as the most important of its kind in the entire era, serving as an essential source book for other Protestants who were debating sacramental theology. In other words, Aubertin's *L'Eucharistie* carried with it an aura of invincibility that would have required a monumental effort to try to refute it.[38]

It is not surprising, therefore, that Aubertin would use Beza as an important source for his work on the history of the Lord's Supper. In his *Conformité*, Aubertin cited Beza repeatedly on the crucial Eucharistic passage 1 Cor 11:23-24, "For I received from the Lord what I also passed on to you: that the Lord Jesus, on the night He was betrayed, took bread, and when He had given thanks, He broke it and said, 'This is my body, which is broken for you; do this in remembrance of me.'" Here Aubertin accused Roman Catholic interpreters of truncating a quotation from Berengar of Tours (999–1088) to make it seem like he supported the Real Presence. Then, Aubertin provided a more complete citation and then used a quotation from Beza's comments on these verses to support the interpretation that the breaking mentioned in verse 23 referred to Christ's body rather than to the bread because the Lord was saying that the body was broken for you rather than to you. If Christ had said the latter, it would have referred to the bread. Beza was saying that Jesus was pointing to the kind of death he would die. Aubertin went on to accuse Nicolas Coeffeteau, the Dominican polemicist who had written against Mornay, of misinterpreting Beza's comments. Aubertin explained: "This great man [Beza] explaining these words of our Lord as told by the Apostle to mean, 'this is my body which is broken for you' was saying clearly that this must appropriately refer to the body of the Son of God broken in pain on the cross for his love for us. M. Coeffeteau tears this passage out of context and applies it falsely to these words, 'the bread which we break, is it not the communion with the body of Christ?'"[39]

What one sees in this exchange is similar to the case of Le Faucheur. The Roman Catholic polemicist adopted Beza as a source for his position on the Eucharist. Aubertin only used Beza as a source in his response saying that Coeffeteau had misused Beza and had taken his views out of context. However, when he did refer to Beza, Aubertin extolled him as a "great man," thereby conferring on him the status of a foremost authority on the subject.

In his *L'Eucharistie*, Aubertin did refer to Beza in a few places. In the first instance, he cites Beza's interpretation of a canon of the Council of Nicea, where the translation was disputed. So, Du Perron alleged that the canon stated that one sees the lamb of God laying on the altar. At the Council, this section

---

38 SNOEKS, R. (1951), 133–134.
39 AUBERTIN, E., *Conformité de la créance de l'Église* (1626), 114–116.

referenced Heb 11:3, "By faith we understand that the universe was formed at God's command, so that what is seen was not made out of what was visible." Here, Aubertin referenced Beza and Calvin's interpretation of the biblical passage emphasizing the phrase "by faith."[40]

A second citation of Beza came in Aubertin's discussion of Gregory of Nyssa's *On the Baptism of Christ* where he said:

> Despise not, therefore, the Divine laver, nor think lightly of it, as a common thing, on account of the use of water. For the power that operates is mighty, and wonderful are the things that are wrought thereby. For this holy altar, too, by which I stand, is stone, ordinary in its nature, nowise different from the other slabs of stone that build our houses and adorn our pavements; but seeing that it was consecrated to the service of God, and received the benediction, it is a holy table, an altar undefiled, no longer touched by the hands of all, but of the priests alone, and that with reverence. The bread again is at first common bread, but when the sacramental action consecrates it, it is called, and becomes, the Body of Christ. So with the sacramental oil; so with the wine: though before the benediction they are of little value, each of them, after the sanctification bestowed by the Spirit, has its several operation.[41]

The question on this passage was whether or not the altar or the bread was transformed into something else when it was consecrated. Here, Aubertin concluded that since the altar remained an altar even after it had been blessed, so the bread remains bread after its consecration, agreeing with how Mornay interpreted it. Aubertin used Beza, as well as Aristotle and Guillaume Budé, here as authorities in his interpretation of the phrase ἑκάτερον αὐτῶν ἐνεργεῖ διαφόρως, translated "has its several operation" or "each one of them operates differently." Beza took the phase passively, meaning "each is made differently." Aubertin went on to compare the elements to the staff of Moses; when it was turned into the serpent, it remained in its substance a staff.[42] In this instance, Aubertin was relying on Beza as an expert linguist along with the famous humanist scholar Guillaume Budé.

The third reference to Beza came in Aubertin's section on Augustine and is a repetition of the argument that he made in his previous work *Conformité* on 1 Cor 11: 23-24. The difference in this citation is that Aubertin adds that Beza disagreed with some of the Greek and Latin commentators on the passage to support his own interpretation. Here Beza added considerable weight, and Aubertin relied upon his expertise over and against ancient and medieval exegetical studies.[43]

40 AUBERTIN, E., *L'Eucharistie de l'ancienne Eglise* (1633), 168.
41 GREGORY OF NYSSA, *On the Baptism of Christ*, NPNF 5:519.
42 AUBERTIN, E., *L'Eucharistie de l'ancienne Eglise* (1633), 245.
43 AUBERTIN, E., *L'Eucharistie de l'ancienne Eglise* (1633), 383–384.

The last citation of Beza came in Aubertin's discussion of Augustine's use of figurative language throughout his interpretation of biblical passages and is one of the same passages where Le Faucheur also cited Beza, Prov 25: 21-22. The reason that both cited Beza here was that Du Perron had done so. The interpretation is obvious that one is not being commanded to put literal coals on someone's head but to do such good work that they would be surprised or even shocked at the good deed. Beza certainly saw it that way as did Augustine. However, Aubertin went further to say that if Augustine interpreted a symbolic reference of a barbarous act in a figurative fashion, he would also do so when it came to an alleged literal eating and drinking of the Lord's body and blood.[44]

In this passage, the citation of Beza's interpretation of Proverbs really did not add anything substantial to Aubertin's overall argument except that he used Beza's name as an authoritative source. Beza's expertise as a biblical scholar and a linguist added depth and supporting documentation.

12.3 Conclusion

So, what can one conclude about Aubertin's overall use of Beza and how can his usage be compared to his colleague Le Faucheur? First of all, Aubertin's work on the Eucharist is more technical in its approach than Le Faucheur's, and that is likely why his work was more difficult to refute. As a result in part of Aubertin's work, much of issue of the history of Eucharistic interpretation fell somewhat dormant until later in the century when the Charenton pastor, Jean Claude, picked it up in his debates with the Jansenists, Antoine Arnauld and Pierre Nicole. Furthermore, Aubertin was relying more on Beza as a linguistic authority, while Le Faucheur was mainly trying to refute misuses of Beza's authority by his Roman Catholic opponents. Both men revered Beza as an important source for his expertise on the Eucharist and saw him as a "great man." Beza's reputation as an important pillar of the Reformed faith remained solid well into the seventeenth century. It would be interesting to see how later Reformed scholars such as Claude made use of Beza as well.

---

44 AUBERTIN, E., *L'Eucharistie de l'ancienne Eglise* (1633), 427.

Max Engammare

Chapter 13: Theodore Beza, Collector of Paintings

Unexpected Intellectual Commerce in the First Century of the Reformation[1]

As we honor Theodore Beza five hundred years after his birth in Vézelay on 24 June 1519, it is interesting to revisit (for the first time since the beginning of the eighteenth century) his personal collection of art, that is, his gallery of paintings, etchings, and medals, so as to understand its genesis and the frequent additions made to it. We know, in fact, that Beza kept several portraits in a room in his house on *rue des Chanoines*, two of which depicted himself, one as a young man and the other as an older man. It was a Catholic polemicist named Antoine de Saint-Michel, the Lord of Avully, who, at the end of a century filled with bitter renunciations and feigned conversions, first admonished Beza for this collection of portraits. After him, a whole cohort of Catholic polemicists were only too happy to go after a critic who did not appreciate their images. The Lord of Avully writes:

> Just as Beza blatantly demonstrates his ostentation and vanity in his writing, he makes an even greater spectacle of it in his home. In one particular room (*sallette*), in an effort to decorate it with beautiful and rare paintings, he added lifelike portraits of Calvin, Vermigli, Musculus, and others which he shows to household visitors as a testimony to these men's blessed memory. But lest one think that he forgot about himself, he had two different self-portraits made, one of him in his youthful self-importance, and the other at the age of seventy-eight, wearing a hat, the brim folded on both sides, so that no one would think he lost his ears. I do not find this curiosity a matter of his impertinence, as much as an indication of his vain compulsion to eternalize his memory, convinced that it will last longer in an image than in all his writings, which will soon serve as nothing more than waste paper for the apothecaries of Geneva, or for lighting a fire. But I find it unfortunate that he accuses us of being idolaters and pastorally rebukes us, saying that we abandon the creator and put our hope in the creature, because we keep in our bedrooms the image of the crucifix to remind us of our redemption, and that we can barely restrain our lust for evil as we cast our eyes on such an image. But let's leave Beza in his 'Bezan world' and all the misleading fabrications of his letter.[2]

---

1   We are grateful to Thomas Carlton, a doctoral student in French at the University of Alabama, for kindly making the initial translation of this essay.

2   BEZA, T., *Réponse au gentilhomme savoisien ne se nommant pas* (1598), preceded by [Antoine de Saint-Michel d'Avully] *Lettre d'un gentilhomme savoisien* (1598), in DUFOUR, A. (2016), 18.

The Lord of Avully was quite the contrarian, and his snide remarks were read with a smile, even in Geneva. He was spirited, certainly, but with a poor pictorial judgment. The polemicist confuses the intent behind secular portraits, such as those depicting Protestant pastors and theologians, with religious images such as a crucifix. Beza did not place his hope in the three Protestant authorities named by the Lord of Avully: neither in John Calvin; nor in Peter Martyr Vermigli, the former Italian abbot who became a reformer first in England and then in Zurich (the fledgling Geneva Academy bought his personal library in 1565); nor in Wolfgang Musculus. Rather, Beza remembers these reformers as he looks at their portraits, but without adding an ineffectual prayer to these dead reformers.

Because the dogmatic counterattack was key, Beza once again takes up the matter of the portraits at the end of his *Réponse au gentilhomme savoisien*, reproaching Avully for his lack of "civil honesty," since it was as a friend that Beza had invited him into his home and allowed him to see his portrait gallery. The pastor then explains the meaning of this collection:

> Is it so blameworthy that he [i.e. Beza] wished and wishes daily to refresh the blessed memory not only of these exceptional persons that you name, but also of some princes and great lords who bestowed on him this honor of knowing and loving him here on earth, before death (which is as precious before God and his angels as it is disgraceful to a world that was unworthy of them) took them to heaven? And as for his portrait, one that, in fact, was completed and given to him without request, when he sees himself painted in his youth and compares it with his old age of seventy-six years, is it so bad that he fondly remembers the amazing grace that God bestowed on him in such a dramatic change of appearance and life condition, and thanks him with a full heart? And is it blameworthy if one tells you that this vanity of seeing yourself in a painting has no more titillating effect than if you gaze upon your grey beard in the mirror?[3]

Beza concludes this passage by inviting the Lord of Avully to come and visit him again in person, so that he might verify for himself that Beza is still alive and Reformed, since the Jesuits had been spreading the rumor that Beza had died after converting to Roman Catholicism.

In this passage, Beza mentions his esteem for the princes and the lords that knew him; not those that *he* knew, but—switching the point of view—those that knew and loved *him*, and who were no longer alive. The *Icones* in 1580 already included engravings of sovereigns and lords, starting with the dedication to James VI of Scotland, but also Francis I and Georg von Anhalt. We know that Beza immediately thought about publishing a second volume, which he

---

Émile Doumergue did not fail to cite this passage in his *Iconographie calvinienne* (1909), 50 ff., as well as Beza's response to Avully's criticisms.

3 BEZA, T., *Réponse au gentilhomme savoisien*, in DUFOUR, A. (2016), 125 ff.

mentions in the preface in 1580, that would be "reserved for the Kings, Princes, Magistrates, and Governors of the Republic, nurturers of the Church, and for the valiant military leaders who spilled even their own blood to preserve the true Religion."[4] Beza's *sallette* already displayed such paintings, among which we find the portrait of Jeanne d'Albret, Queen of Navarre, and the portrait of Jan de Trocznow, surnamed Zizka (the One-Eyed), the Bohemian commander during the fifteenth-century Hussite War—to which we will return shortly. While viewing his paintings, Beza recalls the great figures of his century, and, in a certain manner, continues to converse with them, without any hint of spiritualism or praying to the dead.[5]

13.1 Theodore Beza

There is one date that disturbs this reconstruction: that of the second portrait of Beza. The Lord of Avully mentioned a precise date, seventy-eight years old. Now, we know of a certain painting, of mediocre craftsmanship (Illustration 1), where Beza does not appear in all his nobility and elegance, but on the contrary, exhibits something Avully points out: "the other at the age of seventy-eight, wearing a hat, the brim folded on both sides, so that no one would think he lost his ears." The Catholic critic could not have viewed this decidedly average portrait (painted in 1597) as anything but a mockery. On the other hand, Beza spoke of the painting of his seventy-sixth year (1595). Within the span of a few years, there had been essentially two new portraits of Theodore Beza created, one at seventy-six and one at seventy-eight years old. We know of many more authentic portraits of Beza than of Calvin. (Thus, for example, another portrait of Beza was executed in 1577, when he was fifty-eight years old.) It is true that the disciple lived much longer than the master. In the painting of him at age seventy-six (Illustration 2), the flaps of the hat are lowered down over the ears, creating an unhappy image, as if Beza were telling the viewer, via his covered ears, that he was becoming more and more deaf.[6] He was hardly preaching any longer due to this loss of hearing; we know from elsewhere that the morning of

---

4 BEZA, T., *Les vrais portraits* (1581), preface to James VI of Scotland, f° (***) iii r°.

5 On the creation of the portrait as a memory of death, starting with Pliny (*Historia Naturalis* XXXV, 15:43), see the work of STOICHITA, V. (2000), 11–20.

6 The portrait "THEOD. DE BEZE", reproduced in CB 36, facing page 1. This portrait is not the one that the Lord of Avully saw in the *sallette* of Beza's home on the *rue des Chanoines*. The legend explains "Beza in his 77th year" (Geneva, BGE, Centre d'iconographie genevoise; "Catalogue de la collection des portraits…" n. 291). It is not related to the portraits with inventory number 0008bis (copy of the time) and 0181 (later replica), both online on the CIG site.

12 December 1602, after the Escalade was decisively repelled, he was not the pastor who stood in the pulpit in St Pierre to preach. Is it possible that Theodore Beza had gotten rid of the self-portrait painted when he was seventy-eight years old, the portrait someone had given him, in order to replace it with the one we know in his majestic old age, painted two years prior?[7]

The first painting depicting Beza "in his youthful self-importance" (Illustration 3) is inscribed in the bottom-right "IN ETA 24," meaning between 24 June 1543 and 23 June 1544. It was no doubt made for him when he was in Paris, although neither his correspondence nor his *Poemeta* of 1548 mention this painting.[8] Nonetheless, we note that this period corresponds to the first manuscript collection of his *Poemata* completed at the beginning of 1544 and which belonged to his friend Germain Audebert in Orléans.[9] In these first poetic efforts, moreover, Beza shows an interest in statues, one of Venus (*De Veneris statua*) and another the gigantic and semi-legendary one of Jupiter (original since lost) by Phidias, the famous Greek architect and sculptor, "In imaginem Jovis Phidiaci,"[10] an image that could have been an engraving, a coin or a painting. If a portrait permits us to know a man or a woman, it also helps one to know oneself.

To come back to the *Lettre d'un gentilhomme savoisien*, the Lord of Avully's biting irony that the writings of Theodore Beza would soon serve as wrapping paper for pharmaceutical potions or as kindling for fire is in a certain respect prophetic, since the number of reprints of the pastor's poetic writings would quickly fall off after 1620s. Before that, the Latin annotations of the New Testament, his editions of *Poemata* (also in Latin) and other dogmatic works would keep the Genevan and European presses quite busy.[11]

---

7 The portrait given to the Bibliothèque publique et universitaire (BPU) in 1925 by Henry Tronchin, inventory number 0291, is visible at the URL http://www.ville-ge.ch/musinfo/bd/bge/cig/detail.php?type_search=simple&lang=fr&criteria=%22portrait+de+Th%C3%A9odore-de-B%C3%A8ze%22&terms=any&pos=7&id=24194 (search with quotations "portrait de Théodore-de-Bèze", found 28 August 2019). I do not believe that this portrait is the one that the Lord of Avully saw. The brim of the hat is lowered. On the other hand, the armaments of Theodore Beza are represented in the upper left corner, which the Lord of Avully could have mocked, although he too was a provincial noble.

8 The etching on the frontispiece of the *Poemata* of 1548, with Beza holding a laurel crown, could have used the painting of 1543–1544. We can presume that the 24 years were preceding the civil age of majority by one year (the Ordonnances de Blois in 1579 confirmed the age at 25 years). The following decade, Pierre Woeiriot notes 24 years in his superb etched self-portrait: "Petrus Woeiriot Lotaringus has faciebat eiconas cuius effigies haec est anno suae aetatis. 24."

9 See AUBERT, F./BOUSSARD, J./MEYLAN, H. (1954).

10 "Ut tali sese cognovit imagine pictum:/Tandem etiam geminus Juppiter, inquit, ero." AUBERT, F./BOUSSARD, J./MEYLAN, H. (1954), 12. This epigram will be reprised in BEZA, T., *Poemata* (1548), 57.

11 Consult GARDY, F. (1960).

Illustration 1:   Theodore Beza in 1597. Source: La Société de l'histoire du protestantisme français

The Lord of Avully speaks of five "lifelike portraits," not only engravings or medals, but five paintings: Calvin, Vermigli, Musculus, and the two of Beza that we have just uncovered. Returning to the first three, I will obviously refer to the 1580 *Icones* project of the pastor-poet, translated as soon as the ink was dry by Simon Goulart and published in French in 1581 as *Les vrais pourtraits*.

THEOD · DE BEZE~

Illustration 2: Theodore Beza at age 76, recently restored to its original form. Source: Bibliothèque de Genève

Illustration 3:   Theodore Beza in his youth. Source: Bibliothèque de Genève

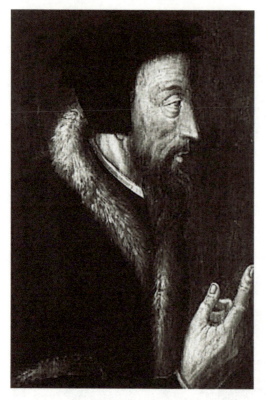

Illustration 4: John Calvin. Source: Bibliothèque de Genève

13.2 John Calvin

Calvin's last will and testament says nothing about the portrait that he possessed of himself in his old age (Illustration 4); it was simply a part of the belongings that had to be sold to satisfy the clauses in the will and the distribution of sums of money to various people.[12] One could speculate that Theodore Beza bought it, but it is more likely that Calvin gave it to him before his death. In any case, the portrait never left Geneva and Beza owned it.[13]

It is this portrait of the "old" Calvin that Beza used in the *Icones* of 1580 (Illustration 5). In 1909, this same portrait was still in the Tronchin collection. In 1932, it became the property of the Bibliothèque publique et universitaire

---

12 "C'est en somme tout le bien que Dieu m'a donné, selon que je l'ay peu taxer et estimer tant en livres qu'en meubles, vaisselle et tout le reste." In CO 20:301.

13 The portrait of Calvin in his younger years is an entirely different question.

Illustration 5:   John Calvin, in *Les vrais pourtraits* (1581). Credit: Max Engammare.

(painting 290),[14] being donated by Henry Tronchin in 1925, along with one of the old portraits of Beza (painting 291).[15]

13.3   Wolfgang Musculus

On 5 March 1578 Beza thanked Abraham Musculus, the son of Wolfgang, for sending several portraits (*imagines*), including the one of his father (Illustration

---

14 See BOUVIER, A. (1932), 171n.2. Geneva, BGE, Centre d'iconographie genevoise, "Catalogue de la collection des portraits…" n. 0290, online at the URL http://www.ville-ge.ch/musinfo/bd/bge/cig/detail.php?type_search=simple&lang=fr&criteria=%22portrait+de+Jean-Calvin%22&terms=any&page=1&pos=8&id=135919; referenced a second time on 28 August 2019 (it is necessary to include quotation marks on "portrait de Jean-Calvin" to find the portrait).
15 See Buyssens, D. (2002), 95n.20 (paintings 290 and 291).

Illustration 6: Wolfgang Musculus. Source: Bibliothèque de Genève

6).[16] This portrait still remains in the Genevan Iconography Center in the Bibliothèque de Genève (the unfortunate new name of the defunct Bibliothèque publique et universitaire—the BPU) and it is worth noting that the depiction in the *Icones* and the *Vrais pourtraits* is a mirrored copy of it, albeit engraved (Illustration 7). The portrait of Musculus was in fact obtained in 1724 along with nine other paintings, including the copy of the portrait of Bullinger, another of Melanchthon, and that of Beza's beloved teacher, Melchior Wolmar.

---

16 "magnam tibi gratiam habeo pro imaginibus tantorum virorum ad me missis." In Beza to Abraham Musculus, 5 March 1578, in CB 19:54. In the same letter, Beza also gives thanks for the excellent life of his father Wolfgang ("vita videlicet reverendi viri parentis tui diligenter et accurate scripta"). He again requested the pieces on Vadian, as he planned to introduce him in his *Icones* (which he, in fact, did).

Illustration 7: Wolfgang Musculus, in *Les vrais pourtraits* (1581). Credit: Max Engammare

The *Memoire des entrées* from the Library, dated 29 August 1724,[17] mentions that "The benefactor Louis Tronchin gifted the following portraits to the Library:

Portrait of Jeanne d'Albret, Queen of Navarre, Mother of Henri IV.[18]
Of Louis de Bourbon, Prince of Condé.

---

17 Cf. *Mémoire de tout ce qui est entrée dans la Bibliothèque depuis le 1. Juillet 1711, tant en achats qu'en dons ou autrem[ent] justqu'au 19 auost 1726* (BGE, Archives BPU Dd 3), 240–241. See also BOUVIER, A. (1932), 172n.6. I want to thank Nicolas Schätti who entrusted me with the documentation regarding the Bullinger painting sent by Gwalther to Beza—from the seminar led by Mademoiselle Rillet—which was an excellent starting point. Le Monumentum (BGE, Archives BPU Dd 6), p. 118 gives the list in Latin, specifying that Briquenaud was the Counselor to the Parlement of Paris.

18 I am not venturing into the discussion as to whether the only portrait preserved today in Geneva comes from the Beza-Tronchin collection (donated by Louis II Tronchin in 1724) or from the donation made three years later by J. B. Micheli Du Crest (1727), whose proof of origin is still held today (going back to the nineteenth century). See BOUVIER, A. (1933), 204n.96.

Of Louis Briquemaud, counselor to the parlement of [blank; "Paris" per the *Monumentum*]

Of Joannes Zizka Bohemus of Trocznow.[19] Superbiae simul et Avaritiae Clericorum Severus Ultor.

Of Henrich Bullinger[20]

Of Philipp Melanchthon

Report on both catalogues [the gifts and acquisitions] // p. 241

Portrait of Joachimus Vadianus 1551.

Of Thomas Cramner.

Of Wolfgang Musculus Duranus [= Dusanus per the *Monumentum*]

Of Melchior Wolmarus Willensis.

The secretary specifies further that "these ten portraits were in the hands of the late Louis Tronchin, Pastor and Professor of Theology, by bequest of his mother Theodora Rocca, daughter of the wife of Monsieur Beza, in whose presence she grew up, and among those portraits that Monsieur Beza's wife had gotten from her husband."

More than a century after the fact, Louis II Tronchin miscalculated by a generation, since Theodora was the grand-daughter (not the daughter) of Beza's second wife, though Tronchin did clarify that this list referred to the paintings that had belonged to Theodore Beza. The ten paintings from Theodore Beza's collection certainly never left the Tronchin family, as the second wife of Beza, Catherine del Piano, had a daughter from her first marriage, Anna Taruffo, called "Mademoiselle Beza," who married Jean-Baptiste Rocca. They had three daughters, the oldest of whom was named Theodora (1591–1674), who married the first Tronchin pastor and professor of theology, Theodore, who was also the Rector of the Academy.[21] Theodore Tronchin, in his will and testament dated 21 April 1657 (he died in November of the same year), favored Louis by bequeathing him his library, his manuscripts and (of particular interest to us) the collection *in toto* of paintings passed down from Theodore Beza.[22] When Louis I Tronchin died in 1705 (he was born in 1629), the recipient was surely the grandson Louis II, great-grandson of Theodore. According to Louis I's blessing upon the eight-year old Louis II in 1705, if the lad were to study theology, he

19 Jan Zizka de Trocznow (Bohemia) (c. 1360–1424) was a Hussite general who commanded the Taborites. See BOST, J.-A. (1884), 990ff. In the said manuscript, one could read it as *Bohemux*, but that makes no sense (the first letter of the ending was crossed out and the final s was inserted on top of a small dash). It is possibly in relation to the Latin quote "Vengeur rigoureux de l'orgueil et en même temps de l'avarice des clercs." In any case, this reference in 1724 allows one to recall the military feats of this forgotten Bohemian, who had been dead for more than three centuries.

20 See also BOUVIER, A. (1932), 172n.7 ("Don de Louis Tronchin, 1724").

21 See DUFOUR, A. (2009), 251n.14.

22 See FATIO, O. (2015), 133ff.

would then inherit "a silver basin and pitcher from Monsieur Beza, along with a gold medallion and a silver one from the synod of Dordrecht from his [great] grand-father."[23] At the same time, Louis II inherited the paintings that came from Theodore Beza's collection, whether in part or in whole I do not know, but in any case some important ones.

It should be remembered that Louis I Tronchin, who died in 1705, lived in the house on the *rue des Chanoines* where Calvin and then Beza both had lived.[24] The house was destroyed in 1706, after the death of Louis I Tronchin, in order to erect the magnificent building situated today at 11 *rue Calvin*, adjacent to the Buisson Hotel (1699–1700). For more than a century, the Beza collection never traveled farther than a *sallette*.

A few months before this donation, on 10 January 1724, the pastors Butini and Gallatin the Elder came to inform the Counsel that Louis Tronchin and Jean-François Pictet had just been accepted into the Venerable Company of the Genevan pastors. Louis Tronchin (born in 1697) had just turned twenty-four years of age, the minimum for becoming a pastor, but Pictet was only twenty-three.[25]

It was common practice for a new professor to offer a book to the library of the Academy,[26] but as for Louis II Tronchin, he wanted to donate a painting upon becoming a pastor—not just one painting, rather an entire collection of paintings. By doing this, he confirmed that he belonged to the family of Theodore Beza and Theodore Tronchin (personal merits aside, familial ties were reported when one was inducted into the Company of Pastors or into membership of the city counselors[27]). Nevertheless, Louis II Tronchin chose to hold back the portraits of Calvin and Beza, which were still in the Tronchin collection in Bessinges at the beginning of the twentieth century,[28] two of

---

23 FATIO, O. (2015), 1070.

24 FATIO, O. (2015), 38.

25 See Archives d'État de Genève (database ADHÉMAR consulted in July 2019 at the url: https://ge.ch/arvaegconsult/ws/consaeg/public/fiche/) *Registres du Conseil* 223 (1724), 29–31.

26 Personal communication from Barbara Roth, former conservator of the Department of Manuscripts of the BGE (Spring 2019).

27 "tant en considération de leur merite personnel, qu'à celle de messieurs leurs parents, dont les longs services, soit dans l'État, soit dans l'Église et l'Académie, sont parfaitement connus de ce Conseil." Having dismissed the pastors, along with the members of the Tronchin and Pictet families, the Counsel confirmed the admission of the two young applicants into the Venerable Company of Pastors, "tant en considération de leurs talens et de leur merite, que de leur famille." Archives d'État de Genève (database ADHÉMAR consulted in July 2019 at the url: https://ge.ch/arvaegconsult/ws/consaeg/public/fiche/) *Registres du Conseil* 223 (1724), p. 30.

28 See DOUMERGUE, É. (1909), 50ff.

which were donated to Geneva's Bibliothèque publique et universitaire by Henry Tronchin in 1925.[29]

One notes in the same *Memoire,* as well in the *Monumentum* of 1702, that at the beginning of the eighteenth century several other paintings from the sixteenth century had been donated by pastors, professors and counselors in Geneva. The donors were Jean Pictet (1702 and 1703),[30] Jérémie Pictet (1702 and 1703), Georges Louis d'Aubigné (1704),[31] Jean-Alphonse Turrettini (1705, 1711, 1720), Professor Gautier (1711),[32] François Mestrezat (1712,[33] 1714), Antoine Tronchin (1713),[34] Michel Léger (1719),[35] etc. By 17 May 1703, Louis I Tronchin had already given the portraits of the Coligny brothers.[36] On 8

---

29 See BUYSSENS, D. (2002), 95n.20 (paintings 290 and 291).

30 17 August: "Icones Lutheri, Zwinglii, Farelli, Vireti." See *Monumentum horum honoro positum Qui Vel libris editis, vel Manuscriptis Codicibus, vel Iconibus, vel Numismatibus, vel exquisita supellectile vel numerata pecunia, vel alio quopian doni genere, Bibliothecam Genevensem locupletarunt, Inde ab Anno praesertim MDCCII* (BGE, Archives BPU Dd 6), 19. Jean Pictet was a counselor in the Council of Two Hundred. Jean Pictet's family, being tied to the Tronchins, may have been able to inherit these old paintings that came from Beza's collection through the Tronchin heritage (with the exception of the Luther painting). See BOUVIER, A. (1932), 171n.1, 3, 4.

31 "Theod[ori] Agrippae d'Aubigné imaginem pictam." See *Monumentum horum honoro positum Qui Vel libris editis, vel Manuscriptis Codicibus, vel Iconibus, vel Numismatibus, vel exquisita supellectile vel numerata pecunia, vel alio quopian doni genere, Bibliothecam Genevensem locupletarunt, Inde ab Anno praesertim MDCCII* (BGE, Archives BPU Dd 6), 24.

32 "Le portrait de M. Michel Roset", chronicler of the sixteenth century, published multiple times, first published at the moment of the Escalade. See *Memoire de tout ce qui est entré dans la Bibliothèque depuis le 1. Juillet 1711, tant en achats qu'en dons ou autrem[ent] justqu'au 19 aoust 1726* (BGE, Archives BPU Dd 3), 4. Jean-Antoine Gautier was appointed as a young professor already in 1695. See BORGEAUD, C. (1900), 485. This portrait is on display today at the International Museum of the Reformation.

33 12 April: "L'ancien syndic Franç[ois] Mestrezat a donné le portrait de feu Monsieur le Professeur Mestrezat, son père. " See *Memoire de tout ce qui est entré dans la Bibliothèque depuis le 1. Juillet 1711*, 10. On April 15, it was Benjamin Micheli who made a donation to the library. "Le portrait de Joseph Scaliger." (ibid.) The same day, "On a remis à la Bibliothèque de la part de Mademoiselle Louyse Bonnet le portrait de S.A.S. Charles, Electeur Palatin" (ibid.). Donors become younger and younger, as on 18 July, M. Jean Sarrasin, student, donated the portrait of the King of France Louis XIV (ibid., 12). On 12 November 1712, M. Ami Buisson, Brigadier in the army of the King of France, donated the portrait of Calvin and of Beza in relief. (ibid.,15), etc. On 25 August 1713, M. Louys Simon Masson donated "Le portrait de Calvin gravé d'une manière particulière" (ibid., 21).

34 "Ledit jour [18 April 1713], M. le Conseiller Tronchin a donné le portrait de feu M. le Prof[esseur] Tronchin, son père" (ibid., 18).

35 See BOUVIER, A. (1932), 171–174n.1–21.

36 "Maii d. 17. D. Ludovicus Tronchinus, Civis Genevensis, in Ecclesia Genev. Verbi divini Minister, et in Academia s. Theologiae Professor, sequential dono dedit: Icones fratrum de Coligni, Gaspari, nempe Oedti, et Francisci. / Pentateuchum cum paraphrase Chaldaïca [...

June 1705, Charles de Bornimb (Karl von Bornimb or Pornimb), painter from Saint-Gallen, donated two portraits of Calvin and Beza that he had copied from those in the Beza-Tronchin collection.[37] In 1702, the library had moved to the great room of the College and there was now enough space to house these paintings.[38] Members of various patrician families also donated old portraits of forgotten Protestant celebrities.

Louis II Tronchin did not initiate a new practice in 1724; it was already established. In the century of the *philosophes*, these old paintings were no longer in style, and their commercial value nearly nothing, since quite often we are talking about copies—copies from the sixteenth century, to be sure—but copies of inferior quality.[39] In some cases, the donations could be akin to putting them in storage, for the double benefit of being a reminder of a donor's ties to a patrician family, and also to adorn the great room of the Library—or rather for its reserves, since the Library received far more than it could accommodate.

13.4   Peter Martyr Vermigli

In January 1578 (the letter is since lost), Beza asked Gwalther for the portraits of the Zurich reformers, for the latter responded on 3 February: "I will write to you several other things, when I send you also the portraits (*imagines depictas*) of Vermigli and of my friend Simler, as you asked of me."[40] Gwalther no doubt had these paintings copied for his Genevan correspondent and had already sent them to him by the end of the month, on 27 of February: "You are receiving both

---

et un autre Pentateuque]," in *Monumentum horum honoro positum Qui Vel libris editis, vel Manuscriptis Codicibus, vel Iconibus, vel Numismatibus, vel exquisita supellectile vel numerata pecunia, vel alio quopian doni genere, Bibliothecam Genevensem locupletarunt, Inde ab Anno praesertim MDCCII [...]* (BGE, Archives BPU Dd 6), 18.

37   "D. Carolus de Bornimb. Sangallensis, pictor, dono dedit Calvini et Bazae Imagines pictes," in *Monumentum horum honoro positum Qui Vel libris editis, vel Manuscriptis Codicibus, vel Iconibus, vel Numismatibus, vel exquisita supellectile vel numerata pecunia, vel alio quopian doni genere, Bibliothecam Genevensem locupletarunt, Inde ab Anno praesertim MDCCII* (BGE, Archives BPU Dd 6), 30. This painting is difficult to identify. See BUYSSENS, D. (2002), 96n.22. Even the Kunstmuseum of St. Gallen does not know the name Bornimb (exchange on 23 and 28 August 2019 with Matthias Wohlgemuth, conservator, and Roland Wäspe, director, whom I thank for their assistance).

38   See MONNOYEUR, P. (2002), 45–79; BUYSSENS, D. (2002), 92ff.

39   One can see similar paintings every day hanging on the walls of the Bonivard, such as the Jean Hus, which was in the *Icones / Vrais pourtraits* of Beza, made with fairly poor craftsmanship (copied etched via mirror, as was necessary).

40   "Plura alias, quando etiam D. Martyris et Simleri mei imagines depictas mittam, ut petebas." Gwalther to Beza, 3 February 1578, in CB 19:23.

the portraits (*effigies*) of Vermigli and of my friend Simler, the latter painted lifelike (*ad vivum expressam*), and the former of Vermigli as he was when first he came to Zurich."[41] Beza no doubt thanked him in a letter, sent in early March, but now lost.[42] Gwalther's remark (*quando primum ad nos venit*) is invaluable, because it indicates that the portrait of Vermigli depicted him in his prime during the summer of 1542, shortly after Vermigli had fled Italy and arrived in Zurich. He would come back there in 1556, but the first time was a brief visit before pushing onward to Strasbourg, where Martin Bucer offered him a post as a theology professor. Thus, we are not dealing with a copy of the portrait painted by Asper in 1560, when Vermigli was a second time at Zurich, then at the age of 60 (Illustration 8: *ANNO DOMINI MDLX / AETATIS LX*).

It is surprising that Beza would ask Gwalther for a portrait of Vermigli, when he already possessed a medallion of the Florentine theologian turned Zurich reformer (Illustration 9). Indeed, starting in the 1560s, Beza was searching for portraits for his collection and possibly for his *Icones* project that he was already beginning to plan. It was on 31 May 1563, when Heinrich Bullinger, the Zurich Antistes and successor of Zwingli, sent Beza an image (*icon*) of Vermigli, this very holy man of blessed memory ("Mitto hic D. Petri Martyris beatae memoriae viri sanctissimi iconem"). Vermigli had died in Zurich on 12 November 1562 while Beza was in France. Beza returned to Geneva on 5 May 1563, and now free to speak, wrote a long letter on 12 May to the pastors of Zurich which started with a eulogy for Vermigli. (Beza had learned of his death when he was in Strasbourg.)[43] This is certainly the commemorative medallion of Vermigli that Bullinger sent to Beza in his name and in the name of his colleagues in Zurich (*symmystae*).[44]

On 12 June 1562, Bullinger was writing Beza once again, impatient for not having yet received thanks for the portrait, which was a token of his affection ("Spero te, mi frater, jamjam accepisse nostras literas una cum symbolo amoris incluso"). On 1 July, Beza thanked Bullinger for his two letters and for the *imago* of Vermigli ("una cum Martyris nostri imagine").[45] *Icon* or *imago*, this was how Beza would come to call the medallion he had received.

41 "Accipies simul D. Petri Martyris et Simerli mei effigies, hanc quidem ad vivum expressam ut vix melius potuisse videtur, illam vero qualis Martyr fuit quando primum ad nos venit." Gwalther to Beza, 27 February 1578, in CB 19:42.

42 Gwalther to Beza, 26 March 1578, in CB 19:79n.1, 82. Gwalther also states in this letter that he will send the portrait of Conrad Gessner (*Gesneri imago*).

43 See Beza to the Pastors of Zurich, 12 March 1563, in CB 4:144.

44 See Bullinger to Beza, 31 March 1563, in CB 4:150 (and reproduction of the medallion facing the text).

45 See Beza to Bullinger, 1 July [1563], in CB 4:161.

Illustration 8: Peter Martyr Vermigli. Source: National Portrait Gallery of London

A portrait provides more details than a medallion, when one is engraving an in-quarto picture. In any case, one notices that the engraver of Vermigil's portrait in the *Icones* in 1580 did not reproduce a copy of the portrait by Hans Asper, but instead a copy similar to the Zurich medallion of 1562 that Bullinger had just sent to Beza (Illustration 10).

In addition to paintings in his *sallette*, Beza also had various medallions. Many people in the sixteenth century were partial to this medium; this was also true among Reformed Christians, who had their medals representing Calvin.[46] Thus, for example, on 20 December 1569, Simon Simonius, from Leipzig, wrote to Beza that a few days earlier he had sent him by way of travelers from Nuremberg a silver medallion that someone from Transylvania had given him (though we do not know who was represented on it).[47] Joachim Camerarius, the Younger, had asked Simonius to do this.

---

46 See CAMPAGNOLO, M. (2000), 103–113.
47 Simon Simonius to Beza, 20 December 1569, in CB 10:248.

Illustration 9: Medallion of Peter Martyr Vermigli. Source: Swiss National Museum

We find in the correspondence, especially in the second half of the 1570s, requests for portraits, thanks for portraits received, and the existence of a collection of paintings owned by the reformer. On 21 June 1570 Beza thanked his doctor friend Lorenz Dürnhoffer for the self-portrait that he had sent him ("de icone ad me transmissa"), a portrait that Beza did not include in his *Icones*,[48] since the volume only represented those who had died. At the end of the decade, however, on 16 December 1578, he thanked him again for his portrait.[49] Another one? On 3 December 1577, Beza asked his friend for a portrait of Joachim Camerarius, the Elder, who had died in 1574, a Lutheran humanist of blessed memory ("beatae memoriae"), who was close with his teacher and friend Melchior Wolmar, whose portrait is also present in the *Icones*.[50] On 25 March 1578

48 Beza to Dürnhoffer, 21 June 1570, in CB 11:199.
49 "Mi carissime frater, heri tuae mihi redditae sunt una cum imagine duplici [...] in altera candorem tuum intueor." Beza to Dürnhoffer, 16 December 1578, in CB 19:198.
50 Beza to Dürnhoffer, 3 December 1577, in CB 18:204. Beza repeated this urgent request in his letter to Dürnhoffer, 13 January 1578, in CB 19:2.

Illustration 10:   Peter Martyr Vermigli, in *Les vrais pourtraits* (1581). Credit: Max Engammare

Beza thanked Dürnhoffer for the anticipated shipment of etchings (*inprimis DD. Camerariis*) of both Joachim Camerarius the father and the son, and especially for the portrait (*pro [...] imagine*) of the father.[51] The requests and acknowledgements of receipt would almost always appear at the end of the letters, being more of a postscript. Gwalther and Dürnhoffer are the correspondents from whom he solicited the most. The former promised him the *imago* of Gessner on 26 March 1578;[52] from the latter, on 21 October 1578, Beza urgently requested several portraits (including those of Bucer, Capito and Fagius), calling his project *Libellum elogiorum*—"the booklet of eulogies"[53] The publication

---

51 Beza to Dürnhoffer, 25 March 1578, in CB 19:77.

52 "D. Gesneri imaginem ut accipias curabo." Se Beza to Dürnhoffer, 26 March 1578, in CB 19:80.

53 "Libellum elogiorum cogor ad tempus retinere domi, dum iconas ex variis locis emendico. Requiro inter caeteras veras Joannis Federici Saxonis Electoris et Philippi Landgravii, itemque Buceri, Capitonis et Fagii imagines, quas nancisci nulla dum ratione potui." Beza to Dürnhoffer, 20 October 1578, in CB 19:187.

of *Elogia,* illustrated by Paolo Giovio, the previous year in Basel (1577), had certainly influenced Beza, who briefly considered calling his *Icones, The Book of Eulogies* (*Libellum elogiorum*).

On 15 March 1576 Beza wrote to Johann Jakob Grynaeus, a Hellenist, to say that his family was not unfamiliar to him, since he had once dedicated a poem to his great-uncle Simon Grynaeus, although he had never met him during his lifetime.[54] (Simon Grynaeus, who was the scholarly editor of Livy's five books of *Histories* [published in 1531], had died in 1541.) Beza continued: "It seems to me that I can see his facial features in you; his portrait, which I look at every day, testifies to a gentle character."[55] Already in 1576 Beza possessed the portrait of the great Hellenist Simon Grynaeus (Illustration 11), whom Calvin had not only met but frequently visited and admired during his stay in Basel in 1535–1536. It was to Simon Grynaeus that Calvin dedicated his first Biblical commentary, that of the Epistle to the Romans, in 1540. Beza's remark that he looks at this portrait daily ("quotidie aspicio") indicates that the reformer's art gallery already existed and that the pastor-poet lived with his paintings and his etchings. He would stop in front of the portraits of his friends, not to pray for the dead, but so as to think about them, with friendship or admiration, the kind of familiar exchanges that death never takes away.

A few years later, in his dedication to James VI of Scotland in the *Icones,* dated 1 March 1580, Beza explains what he imagines in a painted or engraved portrait:

> Who, then, when we read books, can prevent us from hearing the perspective of good and knowledgeable persons who, after their passing, communicate so familiarly with us, just as by their true portraits we also profit from being able to look at and (in a manner of speaking) converse with these people whose presence was so honorable to us while they still lived? [...] I can say concerning myself that, in reading books of such individuals and especially when casting my eyes upon their effigies, I am deeply moved and made alive with holy thoughts as if I were still seeing them preaching, admonishing and correcting their listeners.[56]

We get the impression that Beza was referring to Calvin in the second part of this quotation; Beza probably looked at, and in a sense, conversed with his treasured life-like portrait Calvin. Since 1566, another portrait of Calvin had adorned the front matter of posthumous editions of the *Institutes of the Christian Religion,* and the *Recueil des opuscules.* This etching was by Pierre Woeiriot, dated 1566, and was no doubt commissioned by Beza (see Illustration 12).

---

54 "quem mini vivum videre non licuit." See Beza to Grynaeus, 15 March 1576, in CB 17:63.

55 Beza to Grynaeus, 15 March 1576, in CB 17:63.

56 Adapted from the translation of GOULART, S., *Les vrais pourtraits des hommes illustrés* (1581), f. (***) iiv-(***) iiir.

Illustration 11:   Simon Grynaeus, in *Les vrais pourtraits* (1581). Credit: Max Engammare

13.5   Some Tentative Conclusions

In a letter dated 7 February 1601, the tutor of the Moravian Count Zastrisell the Younger named Paludius—who had visited Theodore Beza at his home twice between 1596 and 1598, had exchanged epigrams with his host, had served as the go-between in the purchase of the old man's library, and had seen Beza's *sallette*—made mention of the ambassadors that the king of Persia had sent to Emperor Rodolphe II. Aware of Beza's interest in portraits, Paludius added: "I am sending you true-to-life portraits of them."[57] Unfortunately, the portraits painted of the Persian ambassadors were not preserved or identified. What is remarkable is that, twenty years after the publication of the *Icones*, people such as Paludius continued to send portraits to the old Theodore Beza, aware of his interests in them and of his portrait gallery. Both before the *Icones* project was completed—Theodore Beza had certainly come into possession

---

57 "Illorum tibi veras mitto effigies." Paludius to Beza, 7 February 1601, in CB 42:5n.9, 10.

Illustration 12: John Calvin. Source: H. Henry Meeter Center for Calvin Studies

of the Calvin painting in 1564—and even well after, the pastor-poet collected portraits, paintings, medallions and engravings. Beza had a relationship with portraits in the same way that others have a relationship with books. One finds the thoughts of an author in his work; Beza finds them in the portraits of people with whom he rubbed shoulders and whom he admired, and those who also admired and loved the collector himself. He said it plainly: he rereads writings and recalls sermons by looking at the portraits in his collection.

The *sallette* of Beza was not unique for its time. Cabinets and galleries proliferated in the sixteenth century, the Kunst- und Wunderkammer, or the *galleries of effigies*.[58] One of the most remarkable ones was that of Paolo Giovo (Paul Jove).[59] In a letter to his patron, Mario Equicola, in Mantua in 1521, Jove wrote

---

58 See, for example, HAENEL, Y. (2019), 121.

59 Cf. MÜNTZ, E. (1901), 249–343, read online 12 May 2019, https://www.persee.fr/docAsPDF/minf_0398-3609_1901_num_36_2_1578.pdf.

that he already possessed a collection of portraits of Dante, Petrarch and Boccaccio, Leonardo Bruni, Pontano, Alberti, Politien, Marsilio Ficino and Pico de La Mirandola.[60] Important people were solicited to contribute to the collection. It was at Como that Jove established his museum. That led to the publication of the *Elogia* in Florence in 1551, which had no engraved portraits, no more than the Italian translation did.[61] Jove died in December 1552. Pietro Pera in Basel published the first illustrated editions of the *Elogia* in 1575 and 1577 (both in-folio format). Perna had sent artists and engravers to reproduce the portraits from Jove's collection. We do not know if Beza owned this edition (which was not at that time in the library of Calvin's Academy), but the Savonarola found in the *Icones* (1580) was a reproduction from the one found in the *Elogia* of 1577 (as I will show elsewhere).[62]

These collections had their models, in particular in Varro and his *Imagines* or *Hebdomades*, which included seven hundred portraits of famous figures from Athens and Rome. Varro added a versified eulogy for each famous figure. However, we do not have the entirety of Varro's *Imagines*, merely a few scattered fragments. Petrarch brought together a collection of Roman coinage that he offered to Emperor Charles IV in 1354.[63] In the sixteenth century, these collections multiplied and were printed as well, as seen among Vasari and his most excellent painters (1550), and especially with the inclusion of versified eulogies and engraved portraits in 1568; Guillaume Rouillé's *Prontuario de le medaglie de più illustri e fulgenti huomini e donne* (1553), etc. The same enthusiasm is evident in literary works. For example, Gilles Corrozet includes in his *Blasons domestiques* (1539) a poem entitled "The Heraldry of the Cabinet" in which one reads: "Cabinet of Paintings full / and holding such beautiful images / of figures great and small."[64]

The reproach issued by the Roman Catholic camp against replacing venerated images of saints with portraits of reformers was nothing new. Already in 1535, Georg Wizel (1501–1573), who was a follower of Luther before returning to Catholicism—just as the Lord of Avully, who had recently renounced his Reformed faith—criticized Lutherans for multiplying portraits of Martin Luther

---

60 MÜNTZ, E. (1901), 257 and importantly n. 2.

61 MÜNTZ, E. (1901), 266. The twelve Visconti had been printed in Paris by Robert Étienne in 1549 (engraver Geoffrey Tory) and reprinted in 1552.

62 See CHAZALON, C. (2001), 1:30 ff. and illustrations 22a and 22b. (Illustration 22a is reserved for use from the *Elogia* [illustrated by Giovio] by the engraver for the *Icones*). I thank the author for having provided me a copy of his memoire from the end of 2001. See also DUFOUR, A. (1986), i–viii, and BORGEAUD, C. (1934), 11–36.

63 MÜNTZ, E. (1901), 252.

64 CORROZET, G. (1539), f. 30v or 31r.

and of his wife Katharina von Bora, a specialty of Lucas Cranach's workshop.[65] Beza's collection of paintings is also related to the development of portrait art within the Protestant sphere, Lutheran as well as Calvinist.[66]

After this detour into Beza's collection of paintings and the way he looks at them, we can return to the theology of the pastor; to his place in the world; to his love of neighbor; to his status as a creature living on this earth; to his faith founded on double predestination; and even to his incessant and tiresome attacks against the ubiquitarian Lutherans. His interest in portraits as a lasting exercise in poetry was part of his *ethos* as a Reformed humanist pastor—another way of understanding and living as a *pictura poesis*.

---

65 See WIRTH, J. (1984), 40ff, which cites the works of VON DÖLLINGER, I. (1848), 1:21ff. I thank Wirth for pointing me to Von Döllinger, apostle of the old Catholic church, after his holy rejection of papal infallibility.

66 See CHRISTIN, O./DESCHAMP, M. (2011), 195–219.

Bibliography

1. Archival materials

AEG database ADHÉMAR, at https://ge.ch/arvaegconsult/ws/consaeg/public/ fiche/.

AEG, Finances M, vol. 7v, 22, 36v.

AEG, Reg. Conseil 65 (1570), 147v.

AEG, Reg. Conseil 66 (1571–1572), fol. 4-4v, 11, 24.

Apologetic memoir of the Lausanne chapter and Firet, BPU, Archiv Tronchin vol. 7 and 64.

Archives Départmentales des Pyrénées-Atlantique. Menaud de Lexia, notaire de Pau, Registre E. 2001, 1570–1573.

Catalogue de la collection des portraits, Geneva, Centre d'iconographie genevoise, no. 0008bis, 0181, 0290, 0291.

Letters of Michael Le Faucheur, BPU, Archiv Tronchin vol. 27, fols. 159, 173, 204, 206.

Mémoire de tout ce qui est entré dans la Bibliothèque depuis le 1. Juillet 1711, tant en achats qu'en dons ou aturem[ent] jusqu'au 19 aoust 1726, BGE, Archiv BPU Dd3, p. 240ff.

Monumentum horum honori positum qui vel libris editis, vel manuscriptis codicibus, vel iconibus, vel numismatibus, vel exquisite supellectile vel numerata pecunia, vel alio quopian doni genere, Bibliothecam Genevensem locupletarunt, inde ab anno praesertim MDCCII, BGE, Archives BPU Dd 6, p. 118.

Pièces relatives à la Dispute entre le Conseil de Genève et le père Chérubin de Maurienne, capuchin, BPU, MS FR 8.

2. Reference Works

ARNDT, WILLIAM/WILBURG GINGRICH (1952), A Greek-English Lexicon of the New Testament and Other Early Christian Literature, 4th revised edition, Chicago, Ill.: University of Chicago.

BOST, JEAN-AUGUSTIN (1884), Dictionnaire d'histoire ecclésiastique, Paris and Geneva: Librairie Fischbacher.

CHAMBERS, BETTYE (1983), Bibliography of French Bibles, Geneva: Librairie Droz.

French Dictionary, College Edition Completely Revised for American English (1990), New York: Harper and Row.

GARDY, FRÉDÉRIC (1960), Bibliographie des oeuvres théologiques, littéraires, historiques et juridiques de Théodore de Bèze, THR 41, Geneva: Librairie Droz.

GILDERSLEEVE, BASIL (ed.) (1903), Gildersleeve's Latin Grammar, 3rd ed., London: Macmillan & Company.

GRIMM, CARL LUDWIG/JOSEPH HENRY THAYER (trans. and rev.) (2010), Greek-English Lexicon of the New Testament, being Grimm's Wilke's Clavis Novi Testamenti, Charleston, S.C.: Nabu Press.

HAAG, EUGÈNE/ÉMILE HAAG (1857), La France Protestante: ou vies des protestant français qui se sont fait un nom dans L'Histoire depuis les premiers temps de la reformation jusqu'à reconnaissance du principe de la liberté des cultes par l'Assemblé nationale, Paris: J. Cherbulier.

- (1886), La France Protestante, 2nd ed., Henri Bordier (ed.), Paris: Librairie Fischbacher.

HERZOG, J.J. (1896–1913), Encyklopädie für protestantische Theologie und Kirche, 24 vol., 3rd ed., Lepizig: J.C. Hinrichs.

LAMPE, G. W. H. (1961), A Patristic Greek Lexicon, Oxford: Clarendon Press.

LE FORT, CHARLES/GUSTAVE REVILLIOD/EDOUARD FICK (1860), Le Livre du recteur: Catalogue des Étudiants de l'Académie de Genève, Geneva: Jules-Guillaume Fick.

LIDDELL, HENRY/ROBERT SCOTT (1968), A Greek-English Lexicon, New Edition, Sir Henry Stuart Jones (ed.), Oxford: Clarendon Press.

SOMMERVOGEL, CARLOS (1893), Bibliothèque de la Compagnie de Jésus, 4 vol., Bruxelles: Oscar Schepens.

3. Works of Theodore Beza

- (1548), Poemata, Paris: Conrad Badius.

- (1554), De haereticis a civili Magistratu puniendis, Geneva: R. Étienne.

- (1555), Summa totius christianismi, sive descriptio et distributio causarum salutis electorum and exitii reproborum, ex sacris literis collecta, Geneva, n.p.

- (1556), Novum D. N. Iesu Christi testamentum, Latine iam olim a Veteri interprete, nunc dunuo a Theodoro Beza versum; cum eiusdem annotationibus, in quibus ratio interpretationis redditur, Geneva: R. Étienne.

- (1559a), Confession de la foi chrestienne, faite par Theodore de Besze, contenant la confirmation, d'icelle, et la refutation des superstitions contraires: Reveue et augmentee de nouveau par lui, avec un abregé d'icille, [Geneva:] Conrad Badius.

- (1559b), Novum D. N. Jesu Christi Testamentum, 1st ed., Basel: n.p.
- (1560), Confessio christianae fidei, Geneva: Jean Bonnefoy.
- (1561), An Oration made by Master Theodore de Beze, Minister of the word of God ... Tuesday the ix day of September, Edinburgh: Robert Lekprewik.
- (1562a), Ane answere made the fourth day [sic 24th] of septembre a thousand five hundredth syxtie & one, by Maister Theodore de Besza, Edinburgh: Robert Lekprewik.
- (1562b), The second Oration of Master Theodore de Beze Minister of the Holy gospel, made and pronounced at Poissy ... the XXVI day of September, London: John Tysdale.
- (1565a), A Briefe and Pithie Summe of Christian Faith made in Forme of a Confession, with a Confutation of all such Superstitious Errors, as are Contrarie Thereunto, R.F. (trans.), London: n.p.
- (1565b), Iesu Christi D. N. Novum testamentum, sive Novum foedus, 2nd ed., Geneva: H. Éstienne.
- (1569), Poematum editio secunda, Geneva: H. Éstienne.
- (1571), Ad Nicolae Selnecceri et Theologorum Ienensium calumnias brevis et necessaria Th. Bezae responsio, Geneva: Jean Crespin.
- (1572), Modesta et Christiana defensio ad D. Nicolae Selnecceri maledicam et virulentam responsionem, Geneva: Jean Crespin.
- (1573a), Apologia tertia ad Nicolae Selnecceri κοκκυσμούς, Geneva: E. Vignon.
- (1573b), Epistolarum Theologicarum Theodori Bezae Vezelii, Liber Unus, Geneva: E. Vignon.
- (1575a), Apologia modesta et Christiana ad Acta Conventus quindecim theologicorum Torgai nuper habiti, Geneva: E. Vignon.
- (1575b), A Briefe Declaration of the Chiefe Points of the Christian Religion in a Table, William Whittingham (trans.), London: n.p.
- (1576), Poemata, Geneva: H. Étienne.
- (1578), Ad repetitas Jacobi Andreae et Nicolai Selnecceri calumnias responsio, Geneva: E. Vignon.
- (1579a), Psalmorum Davidis et aliorum prophetarum libri quinque; argumentis et Latina paraphrasi illustrati ac etiam carminum genere Latine expressi, Geneva: E. Vignon.
- (1579b), De veris, et visibilibus ecclesiae catholicae notis, tractatio, Geneva: E. Vignon.
- (1580a), Icones, id est verae imagines virorum ... illustrium ... quibus adiectae sunt nonnulae picturae quas Emblemata vocant, Geneva: Jean de Laon.
- (1580b), Psalmorum sacrorum libri quinque, vario carminum genere Latine expressi, et argumentis, atque paraphrasis illustrati; secunda editio tum emendatior, tum actior quatuordecim canticis, Geneva, E. Vignon.

- (1581), Les vrais pourtraits, Simon Goulart (trans.), Geneva: Jean de Laon.
- (1582a), A Discourse of the true and visible Marks of the Catholique Church, London: n.p.
- (1582b), Iesu Christi D. N. Novum Testamentum, sive Novum Foedus, 3rd ed., Geneva: H. Étienne.
- (1582c), De Predestinationis doctrina et vero usu tractatio absolutissima. Ex Th. Bezae praelectionibus in nonum Epistolae ad Romanos caput a Raphaele Eglino Tigurino Theologiae studioso in schola Genevensi recens excepta, Geneva: E. Vignon.
- (1582d), Tractationes theologicae, vol. 1, Geneva: E. Vignon.
- (1584), De Francicae linguae recta pronuntiatione, Geneva: E. Vignon.
- (1585), The judgment of a most reverend and learned man from beyond the seas concerning a threefold order of bishops, London: [Thomas Wilcox].
- (1586a), Response aux Cinq Premieres et Principales Demandes de F. Jean Hay, Geneva: Jean le Preux.
- (1586b), Sermons sur les trois premiers chapitres du cantique des cantiques, de Salomon, [Geneva]: Jean le Preux.
- (1588), Ad acta Colloquii Montisbelgardensis Tubingae Edita, Theodori Bezae Responsionis, Pars Altera, Geneva: Jean le Preux.
- (1589a), A briefe and pithie Summe of Christian faith, Made in the Forme of a Confession, Robert Fyll (trans.), London: Roger Ward.
- (1589b), Iob Expounded by Theodore Beza, partly in manner of a Commentary, partly in manner of a Paraphrase, London: John Legatt.
- (1589c), Testamentum Novum, sive Novum Foedus, 4th ed., Geneva: H. Étienne.
- (1592a), Ad tractationem de ministrorum Evangelii gradibus ab H. Saravia … responsio, Geneva: Jean le Preux.
- (1592b), Sermons sur l'Histoire de la Passion et Sepulture de nostre Seigneur Iésus Christ, Geneva: Jean le Preux.
- (1592c), Traité des vrayes, essencielles et visibles marques de la vraye église catholique, Geneva: Jean le Preux.
- (1593a), Sacratiss. Psalmorum Davidis libri V; duplici poetica metaphrasi, altera e regione opposita, vario genere carminum Latine expressi, Geneva: Jean le Preux.
- (1593b), Sermons sur l'Histoire de la Resurrection de nostre Seigneur Jesus Christ, Geneva: Jean le Preux.
- (1597), Poemata varia, sylvae, elegiae, epitaphia, epigrammata, icones, emblemata, Cato Censorius, Geneva: H. Étienne.
- (1598a), Iesu Christi Domini nostri Novum Testamentum, sive Novum Foedus, cuius Graeco contextui respondent interpretationes duae: una, vetus; altera, Theodori Bezae; eiusdem Th. Bezae annotationes, Geneva: E. Vignon.

- (1598/1599b), Poemata varia, sylvae, elegiae, epitaphia, epigrammata, icones, emblemata, Cata Censorius, Geneva: H. Étienne and Jacob Stoer.
- (1598c), Response a La Lettre d'un Gentilhomme Savoisien, ne se nommant point, Geneva: M. Bergon.
- (1599), Abrahamus sacrificans: Traegaedia Gallice a Th. Beza iam olim edita, recens vero latine a Ioanne Iacomoto Barrensi conversa, Jean Jaquemot (trans.), Geneva: Jacob Stoer.
- (1603), Maister Beza's Houshold Prayers, London: Jonathan Barnes.
- (1883–1889), Histoire Ecclésiastique des Église Réformées au royaume de France, 3 vol., Paris: Fischbacher.
- (1954), Un premier recueil de poésies latines de Théodore de Bèze, Fernand Aubert/Jacques Boussard/Henri Meylan (ed.), Geneva: Société du Musée Historique de la Réformation.
- (1959), Response a la confession du feu duc Iean de Northumberlande, n'agueres decapité en Angleterre, facsimile ed., A. H. Chaubard (ed.), Paris: Presses Academiques.
- (1960–2017), Correspondance de Théodore de Bèze, Hippolyte Aubert et al. (ed.), 43 vol., Geneva: Librairie Droz.
- (1970), Du Droit des Magistrats, Robert Kingdon (ed.), Geneva: Librairie Droz.
- (1972), De Triplici Episcopatu (c. 1576), in: W. Nijenhuis (ed.), Ecclesia Reformata. Studies on the Reformation, Leiden: Brill.
- (1982), The Potter and the Clay: The Main Predestination Writings of Theodore Beza, Philip Holtrop (trans.), Grand Rapids, Mich.: Calvin College.
- (1986), Les vrais portraits des hommes illustrés, Geneva: Slatkine Reprints.
- (2007), A View from the Palatine: The Iuvenilia of Théodore de Bèze, Kirk Summers (ed. and trans.), Tempe, Ariz.: Arizona State University Press.
- (2009), Life of John Calvin, in: Henry Beveridge (ed. and trans.), John Calvin Tracts and Letters, vol. 1, Carlisle, Pa.: Banner of Truth Press.
- (2016), Réponse au gentilhomme savoisien ne se nommant pas précédée de [Antoine de Saint-Michel d'Avully] Lettre d'un gentilhomme savoisien 1598, Alain Dufour (ed.), Geneva: Librairie Droz.
BEZA, THEODORE/BUCHANAN GEORGE (1581), Psalmorum sacrorum Davidis libri quinque duplici poetica metaphrasis, altera alteri e regione opposite vario carminum genere Latine expressi, Morges: Jean le Preux.

4. Other Primary Sources

ALBA, MARTIAL, ET AL. (1854), Correspondance inédite des cinq étudiants martyrs brulés à Lyon en 1553, retrouvée dans la bibliothèque de Vadian, à St-Gall, et suivie d'un cantique attribué à Pierre Bergier, Geneva: Emile Beroud.

Albertus Magnus (1952), Alberti Magni . . . Opera Omnia. 19 vol., Münster in Westfalorum: Aschendorff.

Ambrosiaster (1516), Divi Ambrosii episcope Mediolanensis omnia, Basel: A. Petri.

ANDREAE, JAKOB (1977), Andreae and the Formula of Concord: Six Sermons on the Way to Lutheran Unity, Robert Kolb (trans.), St. Louis, Mo.: Concordia Publishing House.

- (1583), Apologia oder Verantwortung deß Christlichen Concordienbuchs: In welcher die wahre Christliche Lehre, so im ConcordiBuch verfasset, mit gutem Grunde heyliger Göttlicher Schrifft vertheydiget: Die Verkehrung aber und Calumnien, so von unruhigen Leuten wider gedachtes Christlich Buch im Druck außgesprenget, widerlegt warden, Heidelberg: Johann Spies.

- (2017), Lutheranism vs. Calvinism: The Classic Debate at the Colloquy of Montbéliard 1586, Clinton Armstrong (trans.), Jeffrey Mallinson (ed.), St. Louis, Mo.: Concordia.

[ANONYMOUS] [1553], The saying of John late Duke of Northumberland upon the scaffolde, at the tyme of his execution. The XXII of Auguste 1553, n.p.: n.p.

[ANONYMOUS] (1573), Epicedia illustria heroi Caspari Colignio Colignii Comiti, Castilionis Domino, magno Galliarum Thalassiarchae, Christianae veritatis fortissimo et religiosissimo pace belloque assertori, beato Christi martyri, variis linguis a docetis piisque poetis decantata, Geneva: Jean Durant.

Aquinas, Thomas (1852–73), Sancti Thomae Aquinatis doctoris angelici Opera Omnia, Parma: P. Fiaccadori.

- (2006), Summa Theologiae, vol. 45, Prophecy and Other Charisms, Roland Potter (trans.), Cambridge: Cambridge University Press.

AUBERTIN, EDME (1626), Conformité de la créance de l'Église et de S. Augustin sur le sacrament de l'Eucharistie, oppose à la refutation des cardinaux Du Perron, Bellarmin et autres, n.p.: n.p.

- (1633), L'Euchariste de l'ancienne Eglise ou traitté il est monstré quelle a esté, Durant les six premiers siècles depuis l'institution de l'eucharistie, la créance de l'Eglise touchant ce sacrament, Geneva: Pierre Aubert.

AUGUSTINE (1982), De Genesi ad litteram: The Literal Meaning of Genesis, John H. Taylor (trans.), Long Prairie: Newman Press.

AVULLY, G. (1598), Copie de la lettre du seigneur d'Avully: Touchant la dispute des ministres avec le R.P. Cherubin, prescheur de l'Ordre des Capucins, Lyon: n.p.

- (1913), La Voluntaire Conversion de Pierre Petit cy devant ministre de Genève, à nostre saincte foy et religion catholique, apostolique et romaine, in: Emile Vuarnet (ed.), Découverte d'une livre de 1598 relatif à la celebration des Quarante Heures de Thonon, Mémoires et Documents Publiés par l'Académie Chablaisienne 26, 1–62.

- (2016), Lettre d'un Gentilhomme Savoisien a un Gentil-homme Lyonnais, in: Alain Dufour (ed.), [Antoine de Saint-Michel d'Avully], Lettre d'un Gentil-homme Savoisien, Geneva: Librairie Droz.

BATMAN, STEVEN (1581), The Doome Warning All Men to the Judgment, London: Ralphe Nubery.

BIEL, GABRIEL (1968), Gabriel Biel's Defensorium Obedientiae Apostolicae et alia Documenta, Heiko Oberman (ed.), Cambridge, Mass.: The Belknap Press.

BONAVENTURE (1891–1902), Opera Omnia S. Bonaventurae, 10 vol., Quaracchi: Saint Bonaventure College Press.

The Book of Concord: The Confessions of the Evangelical Lutheran Church (2000), Robert Kolb/Timothy J. Wengert (ed.), Minneapolis, Minn.: Fortress Press.

BRAHE, TYCHO (1573), De nova stella, Copenhagen: Lorenz Benedict.

Brenz, Johannes (1588), In Epistolam, quam apostolus Paulus ad Romanos scripsit, commentariorum libri tres, Tübingen: Georgius Gruppenbachius.

Bucer, Martin (1523), Das ym selbs niemant, sondern anderen leben soll, und wie der mensch dahyn kummen moeg, Strasbourg: F. Schott.

- (1527), Epistola D. Pauli ad Ephesios, Strasbourg: J. Herwagen.

- (1530), Enarrationes perpetuæ in Sacra Quatuor Evangelia, recognitæ nuper [et] locis compluribus auctæ, Strasbourg: Georgius Ulricherus Andlanus.

BUCHANAN, GEORGE (1566), Psalmorum Davidis paraphrasis poetica . . . eiusdem Davidis Psalmi aliquot a Th. B. V. versi, Geneva: Henri and Robert Étienne.

Bugenhagen, Johannes (1524), Annotationes Ioan. Bugenhagii Pomerani in X. epistolas Pauli, scilicet, ad Ephesios, . . . Hebraeos, Strasbourg: J. Herwagen.

Bullinger, Heinrich (1532), De prophetae officio, et quomodo digne administrari posit, oratio, Zurich: C. Froschauer

- (1534), In priorem d. Pauli ad Corinthios epistolam, Heinrychi Bullingeri commentarius, Zurich: C. Froschauer.

- (1538), De scripturae sanctae authoritate . . . perfection, deque Episcoporum..., Libri duo, Zurich: C. Froschauer.

- (1557), In Apocalypsim conciones centum, Basel: Johannes Oporinus.

- (1575), Heinrychi Bullingeri Jeremias fidelissimus et laboriosissimus Dei Propheta ... concionibus CLXX, Zurich: C. Froschauer.

Calendar of State Papers, Foreign Series, of the Reign of Elizabeth, 1560–1561 (1865; reprint ed. 1966), Joseph Stevenson (ed.), Nendeln, Lichtenstein: Kraus Reprint.

Calendar of State Papers, Foreign Series, of the Reign of Elizabeth, 1562–1563 (1867; reprint ed. 1966), Joseph Stevenson (ed.), Nendeln, Lichtenstein: Kraus Reprint.

Calendar of State Papers, Foreign Series, of the Reign of Elizabeth 1560–1574 (1874; reprint ed. 1966), Allan James Crosby (ed.), Nendeln, Lichtenstein: Kraus Reprint.

CALVIN, JOHN (1541), Petit traicté de la sainte Cene de nostre Seigneur Jesus Christ. Auquel est demontré la vraye institution, profit et utilité d'icelle, Geneva: Michel Du Bois.

- (1549), Advertissement contre l'astrologie qu'on appellee iudiciaire, et autres curiositéz qui regnent aujour-d'huy aue monde, Geneva: Jean Girard.

- (1557), In Omnes Pauli Apostoli Epistolas Atque Etiam in Epistolam Ad Hebraeos Ioannis Calvini Commentarii, Geneva: I. Crispinus.

- (1564), Commentaires de M. Iehan Clavin, sur le livre de Josué. Avec une preface de Theodore de Beze, contenant en brief l'histoire de la vie et mort d'iceluy, Geneva: François Perrin.

- (1846), Commentaries on the Twelve Minor Prophets, vol. 2, "Joel, Amos, Obadiah," Edinburgh: Calvin Translation Society.

- (1960), Institutes of the Christian Religion, J.T. McNiell (ed.) and F. L. Battles (trans.), Philadelphia, Pa.: Westminster Press.

- (1985), Advertissement contre l'astrologie judiciare, Olivier Millet (ed.), Geneva: Librairie Droz.

CAMERARIUS THE ELDER, JOACHIM (1558), De eorum qui Cometae appellantur, nominibus, natura, caussis, significatione, Leipzig: Valentin Bapst's heirs.

- (1532), Norica sive de ostentis libri suo, Wittenberg: Georg Rhau.

- (1561), The History of Strange Wonders, London: R. Hall.

CAPITO, WOLFGANG (2009), The Correspondence of Wolfgang Capito, 2 vol., Erika Rummel (ed. and trans.), Toronto: University of Toronto Press.

CASTELLIO, SEBASTIAN (1551), Biblia, Basel: Johann Oporinus.

- (1571), Catechesis continens explicationem simplicem et brevem, Decalogi; Symboli Apostolici; Orationis Dominicae; Doctrinae de poenitentia et de sacramentis. Contextam ex corpore doctrinae Christianae, quod amplectuntur ac tuentur ecclesiae regionum Saxonicarum et Misnicarum ... edita in Academia Wittebergensi et accomodata ad usum scholarum puerilium, Wittenberg: Johann Schwertel.

CHANDIEU, ANTOINE DE, (1577), Sophismata F. Turriani Monachi ex eorum sodalitate qui sacrosancto Iesu nomine ad suae sectae inscriptionem abutuntur: Collecta ex eius libro De Ecclesia, & Ordinationibus Ministrorum Ecclesiae, adversus Capita disputationis, [Geneva]: Pierre de Saint-André.

- (1580a), Locus de Verbo Dei scripto, adversus humanas traditiones, theologice et scholastice tractatus, Morges: Jean le Preux.

- (1580b), Ad repetita F. Turriani Monachi Iesuitae sophismata de Ecclesia et ordinationibus Ministrorum ecclesiae, Responsio, Morges: Jean le Preux.

- (1581a), Centum flosculi Turrianicae disputationis ex utroque eius libro decerpti, et in Iesuitarum gratiam collecti, Morges: Jean le Preux.

- (1581b), Responsionis ad repetita F. Turriani … par altera, Morges: Jean le Preux.

- (1583), Index Elenktikos repetitionem & Tautologi Turriani ex Tertio eius libro quem dibiblon inscripsit, collectus, Morges: Jean le Preux.

CHARPENTIER, PIERRE (1572), Lettre de Pierre Charpentier, Jurisconsulte, addressée à François Portes, Candois, par laquelle il monstre que les persecutions des Eglises de France sont advenues, non par la faulte de ceux qui faisoient profession de la Religion, mais de ceux qui nourissoient les factions et conspirations qu'on appele la Cause, Strasbourg, n.p.

CHEMNITZ, MARTIN (1561), Repetitio sanae doctrinae ad vera praesentia corporis et sanguinis Domini in coena, Leipzig: E. Voegelin.

- (1570), Fundamenta sanae doctrinae de vera et substantiali praesentia, exhibitione, et sumptione corporis et sanguinis Domini in Coena, Jena: D. Ritzenhain.

- (1571a), Bedencken der Theologen zu Braunschweigk von dem newen Wittenbergischen Catechismo gestelletlder gantzen Christenheit zur Warnung ausgengen, Jena: D. Ritzenhain.

- (1571b), Wideholte Christliche Gemeine Confession und Erklerung, Wolfenbüttel: Konrad Horn.

- (1573), Epistola Gregorij Stammichij Pastoris Ecclesiae Hamburgensis, De tertia Apologia Bezae Monstrans Vervm Statum, et explicans praecipua capita huius controuersiae, Wolfenbüttel: Konrad Horn.

- (1578), De Duabus Naturis in Christo: De hypostatica earum vnione. De communicatione idiomatum, et de aliis quaestionibus inde dependentibus. Libellus ex Scripturae sententiis, & ex purioris antiquitatis testimoniis / iam denuo recognitus & retextus per Martinum Chemnicum D.; cum praefatione D. Nicolae Selneccer, Leipzig: Johannes Rhamba.

- (1591–1592), Epistola D. M. Chemnitii De Coena Domini. Ad Reverendum Et Clarissimum Virum, Dominum Timotheum Kirchnerum Doctorem & Superintendentem Ecclesiarum in Ducatu Brunsfuuicensi, in tertiam Apologiam Bezae, in: Loci Theologici Reverendi et Clarissimi Viri, D. Martini

Chemnitii, Sacrae Theologiae Doctoris, Atque Ecclesiae Brunsvicensis quondam Superintendentis fidelißimi. Quibvs et Loci Communes D. Philippi Melanthonis Perspicuè explicantur … Editi Nomini Haeredum, Opera Et studio Polycarpi Leiseri D. Successoris ipsius, Secunda Pars, Tertia Pars, Leyser: Frankfurt/Main.

- (1599), Locorum Theologicorum Reverendi Et Clarissimi Viri, Dn. Martini Chemnitii, S. Theologiae Doct. atque Ecclesiae Brunsuicensis quondam Superintendentis fidelissimi, Pars Prima. (-Tertia) Quibvs Et Loci Communes D. Philippi Melanchthonis perspicue explicantur, et quasi integrum Christianae doctrinae corpus Ecclesiae Dei syncere proponitur. Editio nova, emasculata & Indice aucta. Opera et studio Polycarpi Leyseri D., Polycarp Leyser (ed.), Frankfurt/Main: Zacharius Paltenius and Johann Spieß.

- (1610), Loci Theologici Reverendi Et Clarissimi Viri, Dn. Martini Chemnitii, Sacrae Theologiae Doctoris, atque Ecclesiae Brunsvicensis quondam Superintendentis fidelissimi: Quibus Et Loci Communes D. Phil. Melanchthonis Perspicue Explicantur, & quasi integrum Christianae doctrinae corpus, Ecclesiae Dei sincere proponitur / Editi opera & studio Polycarpi Leyseri D., Polycarp Leyser (ed.), vol. 3, Wittenberg: Clemns Berger and Zacharias Schülrer.

- (1971), The Two Natures of Christ, J.A.O. Preus (trans.), Saint Louis, Mo.: Concordia Publishing House.

- (1979), The Lord's Supper, St. Louis, Mo.: Concordia Publishing House.

- (2008–2018), Chemnitz's Works, 10 vol., Jacob Corzine/Matthew Carver/Kevin Walker (ed.), St. Louis, Mo.: Concordia Publishing House.

CHEMNITZ, MARTIN/MÖRLIN, JOACHIM (1571), Treuhertzige Warnung des Gottsgelerten frommen Dieners Christi zu Braunschweig Doctoris Martini Kemnitii. Wider den newen calvinischen catechismum der Theologen zu Wittenberg, Königsberg: Hans Daubmann.

CHEMNITZ, MARTIN, et al. (1580), Doctrinae Iesuitarum praecipua capita, A doctis quibusdam Theologis … retexta, solidis rationibus testimoniisque sancarum Scriptuarum & Doctorum veteris Ecclesiae confutata, [Geneva]: [Antoine Chuppin].

The Christian Book of Concord, or Symbolical Books of the Evangelical Lutheran Church; Comprising the Three Chief Symbols, the Unaltered Augsburg Confession, the Apology, the Articles of Smalcald, Luther's Smaller and Larger Catechisms, the Form of Concord, An Appendix, and Articles of Visitation; to Which is Prefixed an Historical Introduction; translated from the German (1851), New Market: Solomon D. Henkel and Bros.

COCHLAEUS, JOHANNES (1524), De Auctoritate Ecclesiae et Scripturae: libri 2 adversus Lutheranos, Strasbourg: 1524.

Concordia Triglotta: Die symbolischen Bücher der evangelisch-lutheranischen Kirchen, deutsch-lateinisch-english, als Denkmal der vierhundertjährigen Jubelfeier der Reformation, anno Domini 1917, herausgegeben auf Beschluß der evangelisch-lutherischen Synode von Missiouri, Ohio und andern Staaten (1921), Tübingen: Gruppenbach.

Concordia: Christliche widerholete einmütige Bekentnüs nachbenanter Churfürsten, Fürsten und Stende Augspurgischer Confession und derselben zu end des Buchs unterschribnen Theologen Lehre und Glaubens (1580), Tübingen: Gruppenbach.

Confessio fidei exhibita invictiss. Imp. Carolo V … anno MDXXX (1540), Wittenberg: Georg Rhau.

CORROZET, GILLES (1539), Blazons domestiques, Paris: Denis Janot.

CRESPIN, JEAN (1878), Des cinq escoliers sortis de Lausanne bruslez a Lyon, Geneva: Jules-Guillaume Fick.

Denis the Carthusian (1558), D. Dionysii Carthusiani insigne opus commentariorum in Psalmos omnes Davidicos, Cologne: Haeredes J. Quentelii & G. Calenium.

Die Debatte um die Wittenberger Abendmahlslehre und Christologie (1570–1574), in: Irene Dingel (ed.), Controversia et Confessio 8 (2008), Göttingen: Vandenhoeck & Ruprecht.

DU BARTAS, GUILLAUME DE SALLUSTE (1588), La Sepmaine ou Creations de monde, Simon Goulart (ed.), Geneva: J. Chouet.

DU PERRON, JACQUES-DAVY (1622), Traité du Saint Sacrement de l'Eucharistie, divisé en trois Livres, contenant la refutation du livre du Plessis Mornay, Paris: Antoine Étienne.

- (1624), Réfutation de toutes les objections tirées des passages de St-Augustin alléguez par les hérétiques contre le Sainct Sacrement de l'Eucharistie, Paris; A. Étienne.

ERASMUS, DESIDERIUS (1516), Novum Instrumentum Omne, Basel: J. Froben.

- (1522), Novum Testamentum omne, 3rd ed., Basel: J. Froben.

- (1535), Ecclesiastes: sive de ratione concionandi, Basel: J. Froben.

ESTIUS, GUILIELMUS (1841), Estius in Omnes Canonicas Apostolorum Epistolas, Paris: Mogunriae.

FOXE, JOHN (1583), Actes and Monuments, London: John Day.

- (1830), Fox's Book of Martyrs, or The Acts and Monuments of the Christian Church, John Malham (ed.), Philadelphia, Pa.: J. J. Woodward.

GOODMAN, CHRISTOPHER (1558), How Superior Powers Oght to be Obeyd of their Subjects, Geneva: J. Crespin.

GOULART, SIMON (1600–1628), Histoires admirables et memorables de nostre temps, 3 vol., Paris: Jean Houzé.

- (1607), Admirable and Memorable Histories Containing the Wonders of Our Times, London: George Eld.

Gregory the Great (1986), Homélies sur Ézéchiel, Charles Morel (tran.), Paris: Les Éditions du Cerf.

GREGORY OF NYSSA (2004), On the Baptism of Christ, in: Philip Schaff and Henry Wace (ed.), Nicene and Post-Nicene Fathers, Peabody, Mass.: Hendrickson.

Gwalther, RudolF (1566), In D. Pauli apostoli epistolam ad Romanos homiliae, Zurich: C. Froschauer.

- (1590), In Epistolam D. Pauli Apostoli ad Corinthios Priorem, Zurich: C. Froschauer.

HAY, JEAN (1580), Certaine Demandes Concerning the Christian Religion and Discipline, Proposed to the Ministers of The New Pretended Kirk of Scotland, Paris: Thomas Brumen.

- (1583), Demandes faictes aux Ministres d'Ecosse: Touchant la religion Chrestienne, Michel Coyssard (trans.), Lyon: Iean Pillehotte.

- (1588), L'Antimoine, aux responses que Th. de Beze faict a trente sept demandes de deux cents et six, proposees aux Ministres d'Ecosse, Tournon: Claude Michel.

Hoffman, Melchior (1526), Das XII. Capitel des propheten Danielis ausgelegt, ... christen nutzlich zu wissen, Stockholm: Königliche Druckerei.

HOTMAN, FRANÇOIS, (1573a), A true and plaine report of the furious outrages of Fraunce & the horrible and shameful slaughter of Chastillion the admirall, and diuers other noble and excellent men, and of the wicked and straunge murder of godlie persons, committed in many cities of Fraunce, without any respect of sorte, kinde, age, or degree, London: Bynneman.

- (1573b), Narratio de furoribus Gallicis, London: Bynneman.

Hugh of St. Cher (1977), Théorie de la prophétie et philosophie de la connaissance aux environs de 1230: La Contribution d'Hugues de Saint-Cher (Ms. Douai 434, Question 481), Jean-Pierre Torrell (ed.), Leuven: Spicilegium Sacrum Lovanense.

JAQUEMOT, JEAN (1591), Lyrica, Geneva: Jacob Stoer.

- (1597), Musae Neocomenses, Geneva: Matthieu Berjon.

- (1601), Variorum poematium liber, Lyon: Jean de Tournes.

Jerome (1977), Commentaire sur Saint Matthieu, Émile Bonnard (trans.), Paris: Sources chrétiennes.

JUNIUS, FRANCISCUS (1592), D.N. Iesu Christi Testamentum Novum, sive Foedus Novum, e Graeco archetype, Latino sermone redditum, Theodoro Beza interprete, et iam ultimo ab eo recognitum; cui ex adverso additur eiusdem Novi Testamentum ex vetustissima translatione Syra, Latina translatio Immanuelis Tremellii coniuncta notis ad linguae et rerum intelligentiam, 2nd ed., London: George Bishop, Ralph Newberry and Robert Baker.

KNOX, JOHN (1558), First Blast of the Trumpet Against the Monsterous Regiment of Women, Geneva: J. Poullain and A. Rebul.

Lambert of Avignon, François (1525), Praefatio in In Primum Duodecim Prophetarum, nempe, Oseam, Strasbourg: J. Herwagen.

- (1526), Commentarii de Prophetia, Eruditione et Linguis, Strasbourg: J. Herwagen.

LECT, JACQUES (1595), Poematum liber unus, Geneva: E. Vignon.

LE FAUCHEUR, MICHEL (1635), Traitté de la Cene du Seigneur: Où est monstré qu'il faut croire de la Nature & de l'Usage de ce S. Sacrement: ce qu'en ont enseigné les Saincts Peres és meilleurs Ages de l'Eglise, Geneva: Pierre Chouet.

LUTHER, MARTIN (1522), Das Newe Testament Deutzsch, Wittenberg: Melchior Lotter for Christian Döring and Lucas Cranach.

- (1883–), D. Martin Luthers Werke: Kritische Gesamtausgabe, K. Drescher et al. (ed.), Weimar: Verlag Hermann Böhlaus Nachfolger.

- (1995–), Luther's Works. American Edition, 58 vol. Jaroslav Pelikan/Helmut Lehmann/Christopher Boyd Brown (ed.), Philadelphia, Pa./St. Louis, Mo.: Fortress Press/Concordia Publishing House.

Melanchthon, PhilipP (1834–60), Corpus Reformatorum: Philippi Melanthonis opera quae supersunt omnia, 28 vol., Karl Bretschneider and Heinrich Bindseil (ed.), Halle: A. Schwetschke & Sons.

MELANCHTHON, PHILIP/LUTHER, MARTIN (1523), Von dem PapstEsel zu Rom vnd Münchkalbs zu Freyburg in Meyssen fundem, ain deüttung der zwu grewlichen figurn, Augsburg: Nadler.

MÖLLER, HEINRICH (1573–1574), Enarrationis Psalmorum Davidis, 3 vol., Wittenberg: Academy of Wittenberg.

MORELY, JEAN (1562), Traicté de la discipline & police chrestienne, Lyon: Jean de Tournes.

MUSCULUS, WOLFGANG (1550), In Epistolam Apostoli Pauli ad Romanos, Commentarii Per Vvolfgangum Musculum Duasanum, Basel: J. Herwagen.

- (1569), In Epistolas Apostoli Pauli ad Galatas, et Ephesios Commentarii, Basel: J. Herwagen.

Nicholas of Lyra (1483), Lyra Biblia Latina: Biblia Latina cum postillis Nicolai de Lyra et expositionibus Guillelmi Britonis in omnes prologos S. Hieronymi et additionibus Pauli Burgensis replicisque Matthiae Doering, Nuremberg: Anton Koberger.

OBSEQUENS, JULIUS (1552), Prodigiorum liber, ab urbe condita usque ad Augustum Caesarem, cuius tantum extabat fragmentum, nunc demum historiarum beneficio, per Conradium Lycosthenem Rubeaquensem, integritati suae restitutus; Polydori Vergilii Urbinatis de Prodigiis libri III; Ioachimi

Camerarii Paberg. De Ostentis libri II, Basel: J. Oporinus.

Oecolampadius, Iohannes (1526), In epistolam B. Pauli Apost. ad Rhomanos adnontationes a Ioanne Oecolampadio Basileae praelectae, & denuo recognitae, Basel: Andr. Cratandrum.

OLEVIANUS, GASPAR (1579), In epistolam D. Pauli Apostoli ad Romans notae, ex Gasparis Oleviani concionibus excerptae, & a Theodoro Beza editae: cum praefatione eiusdem Bezae, Geneva: E. Vignon.

ORIGEN (2004), Commentary on Matthew, in Allan Menzies (ed.), The Ante-Nicene Fathers, 10 vol., Peabody, MA: Hendrickson.

Patrologiae cursus completus, series Graeca (1857–99), 161 vol., Jacques Paul Migne (ed.), Paris: Garnier.

Patrologiae cursus completus, series latina (1844–1904), 221 vol., Jacques Paul Migne (ed.), Paris: Garnier.

Pelikan, Konrad (1539), In omnes apostolicas epistolas, Pauli, Petri, Iacobi, Ioannis et Iudae D. Chuonradi Pellicani, Zurich: Officina Froschoviana.

PERKINS, WILLIAM (1607), The arte of prophecying, or, A treatise concerning the sacred and onely true manner and methode of preachin, London: Felix Kyngston.

PEUCER, CASPAR (1553), De praecipuis divinationum generibus, Wittenberg, J. Crato.

PHLEGON OF TRALLES (1996), Book of Marvels, William Hansen (trans.), Exeter: University of Exeter Press.

- (2019), Fragmente der griechischen Historiker part IV, K.E. Shannon-Henderson (ed.), Leiden: Brill Jacoby Online, DOI: http://dx.doi.org/10.1163/1873-5363_jciv_a1667.

The Register of the Company of Pastors of Geneva in the Time of Calvin (1966), Philip Edgcumbe Hughes (trans.), Grand Rapids, Mich.: Eerdmans.

Registres de la Compagnie des Pasteurs de Genève (1962–2001), 13 vol., Jean-François Bergier/Robert Kingdon (ed.), Geneva: Librairie Droz.

RÜDINGER, ESROM (1571), Disputatio grammatica de interpretatione graecorum verborum Act. III: Ἰησοῦν Χριστὸν ὃν δεῖ οὐρανὸν μὲν δέξασθαι; complectens ἠθολογίαν responsionis, qua Collegium Theologicum Academiae Witebergensis uti posset ad chartam de his verbis superioribus diebus editam, cui nomen est praescriptum D. Nicolai Selncceri. Aucta & recognita, Wittenberg: Johann Schwertel.

SALES, FRANÇOIS DE (1892–1932), Oeuvres de Saint François de Sales, 26 vol., Annecy: J. Nierat.

SARAVIA, ADRIAN (1591), De diversis ministrorum Evangelii gradibus … ac perpetuo omnium Ecclesiarum usu confirmati, Frankfort: Iohannes Wechel.

- (1840), A Treatise on the Different Degrees of the Christian Priesthood, Oxford: John Henry Parker.

Savonarola, Girolamo (1996), Compendio di Rivelazioni; Trattato sul Governo della città di Firenze, Casale Monferrato: Piemme.

SELNECKER, NICOLAS (1570), Exegema collationis N. Selnecceri cum theologis Wittebergensibus 28 Juli anno 1570 Wittebergae institutae, Wolfenbüttel: Konrad Horn.

- (1571a), Ad D. Theodori Bezae calumnias, brevis et necessaria … responsio, continens invictam doctrinam de ascensione Christi ad coelos, de sessione Christi ad dexteram Dei Patris; de maiestate, gloria, et potentia Filii hominis; de Coena Domini, Wolfenbüttel: Konrad Horn.

- (1571b), De verbis Actorum 3, "Oportet Christum coelum accipere." Brevis et necessaria commonefactio, Wolfenbüttel: Konrad Horn.

- (1572), Responsio vera et Christiana ad Theodori Bezae falsam et minime Christianam . . . defensionem et censuram, Wolfenbüttel: Konrad Horn.

- (1573), Ad Theod. Bezae tergiversationem et criminationem tertiam, responsio et apologia tertia Nicolai Selnecerri, Wolfenbüttel: Konrad Horn.

SERRES, JEAN DE (1578), Platonis opera quae extant omnia, Geneva: H. Étienne.

- (1586), Quarti anti-Iesuitae, sive de vera verae Ecclesiae autoritate, adversus Ioannis Hayi monachi-Jesuitae commenta & conuicia, Responsionis posterior pars, in: Martin Chemnitz, et al., Doctrinae Iesuiticae Praecipua Capita, [Geneva]: [E. Vignon].

SIMLER, JOSIAS (1568), De aeterno Dei Filio, Zurich: C. Forschauer.

SPONDE, JEAN DE (1595), Declaration des Principaux Motifs, Qui on Induict le feu sieur de Sponde conseiller et maître des requêtes du roy à s'unir à l'Eglise, Bordeaux: S. Millanges.

- (1595), Response du feu Sieur de Sponde au Traicté des Marques de l'Eglise, fait par Th. de Beze, Bordeaux: S. Millanges.

SQUARCIALUPI, MARCELLO (1580), De cometa in universum atque in illo qui anno 1577, visus est, in: De cometis dissertationes novae, Basel: Leonard Ostenius.

THEOLOGICAL FACULTY OF WITTENBERG (1571), Christliche Fragstück von dem Unterschied der zweyen Artikel des apostolischen Glaubens Bekenntnis, dass Christus gen Himmel auffgefaren sey... gestellt durch die Theologen in der Universitet Wittenberg, Wittenberg: L. Schwenck.

URSINUS, ZACHARIAS (1563), Catechismus, oder christlicher Underricht, wie der in Kirchen und Schulen der Churfürstlichen Pfaltz getrieben wirdt, Heidelberg: Johann Mayer.

- (1852), The Commentary of Dr. Zacharias Ursinus on the Heidelberg Catechism, 2nd ed., G. W. Williard (trans.), Phillipsburg, NJ: Presbyterian and Reformed Publishing Company.

VERMIGLI, PETER MARTYR (1559), In epistolam S. Pauli Apostoli ad Romanos … commentarii doctissimi, Zurich: A. Gesner.

- (1560), In Epistolam S. Pauli Apostoli ad Rom. D. Petri Martyris … commentarii doctissimi, cum tractatione perutili rerum & locorum, qui ad eam epistolam pertinent, Basel: Petrum Pernam.

- (1566), Est regum libri Duo posteriors cum commentariis Petri Martyris Vermilii, Zurich: C. Froschauer.

- (1567), In duos libros Samuelis prophetæ qui uulgo priores libros Regum appellantur D. Petri Martyris Vermilii … Commentarii doctissimi, cum rerum & locorum plurimorum tractatione perutili. Zurich: C. Froschauer.

- (1568), In Epistolam S. Pauli Apostoli Ad Romanos D. Petri Martyris Vermilii Florentini … Tertia Editio, Basel: Perna.

- (1579a), In Primum librum Mosis, qui vulgo Genesis dicitur, commentarii doctissimi D. Petri Martyris, Vermilii Florentini, . . . nunc denuo in lucem editi, Zurich: C. Froschauer.

- (1579b), In Selectissimam D. Pauli Apostoli Primum ad Corinthios Epistolam Commentarii, Zurich: C. Froschauer.

- (2019), On Original Sin, Kirk Summers (trans. and ed.), Leesburg, Va.: The Davenant Institute.

VIRET, PIERRE (2012), Epistolae Petri Vireti: The Previously Unedited Letters and a Register of Pierre Viret's Correspondence, Michael W. Bruening (ed.), Geneva: Librairie Droz.

WHITGIFT, JOHN (1851–1854), The Works of John Whitgift, 3 vol., John Ayre (ed.), Cambridge: Cambridge University Press.

WIGAND, JOHANN/HESHUSEN, TILEMANN/COELESTIN, JOHANN FRIEDRICH/ KIRCHNER, TIMOTHEUS (1571), Warnung vor dem unreinen und sacramentarischen catechismo etlicher zu Wittenberg. Durch die Theologen zu Jena, Jena: Thomas Rebart.

WILLIAM OF AUXERRE (1500), Summa Aurea in quattuor Libros Sententiarum, Frankfurt: Minerva.

WOLLFHART, KONRAD (LYCOSTHENES) (1557), Prodigiorum ac ostentorum chronicon. Quae propter naturae ordinem, motum, et operationem, et in superioribus et his inferioribus mundi regionibus, ab exordio mundi usque ad haec nostra tempora, acciderunt. Quod portentorum genus non temere evenire solet, sed humano generi exhibitum, severitatem iramque Dei adversus scelera, atque magnas in mundo vicissitudinis portendit, Basel: Heinrich Petri.

ZANCHI, JEROME (2007), De religione Christiana fides/Confession of the Christian Religion, 2 vol., Luca Baschera/Christian Moser (ed.), Leiden: Brill.

ZELL, MATTHÄUS (1523), Christeliche Verantwortung, Strasbourg: Christliche Verantwortung.

The Zurich Letters, Comprising the Correspondence of Several English Bishops and Others with Some of the Helvetian Reformers during the Reign of Queen Elizabeth, 2nd series (1845), Hastings Robinson (ed.), Cambridge: The University Press.

Zwingli, Ulrich (1905–59), Sämtliche Werke, Emil Egli/Georg Finsler/Walther Köhler (ed.), Berlin: Schwetschke.

- (1984), Huldrych Zwingli: Writings, 2 vol., H. Wayne Pipkin/Edward Furcha (ed.), Allison Park, Pa.: The Pickwick Press.

5. Secondary Literature

ADAMS, EDWARD (2001), Calvin's View of Natural Knowledge of God, International Journal of Systematic Theology 3, 280–292.

Alphandéry, Paul (1932), Prophètes et ministère prophétique dans le Moyen Age latin, RHPR, 12, 334–359.

ANDERSON, MARTIN (1987), Evangelical Foundations: Religion in England, 1378–1683, New York: Peter Lang.

[ANONYMOUS] (1986), Le Psautier de Genève, 1562–1865: Images Commentées et Essai de Bibliographie, Geneva: Bibliothèque publique et universitaire.

ARMSTRONG, ELIZABETH (1954), Robert Étienne: Royal Printer, New York: Cambridge University Press.

AUBERT, FERNAND/BROUSSARD, JACQUES/MEYLAN, HENRI (1953), Un premier recueil de poésie latines de Théodore de Bèze, BHR 15, 257–294.

AUSTIN, KENNETH (2007), From Judaism to Calvinism: The Life and Writings of Immanuel Tremellius (c. 1510–1580), Aldershot, UK: Ashgate.

AUWERS, JEAN-MARIE (1995), Le Colloque international sur le *Codex Beza*, Revue théologique de Louvain 26.3, 405–412.

BACKUS, IRENA (1980), The Reformed Roots of the English New Testament. The Influence of Theodore Beza on the English New Testament, Allison Park, Pa.: The Pickwick Press.

- (1991), The Early Church in the Renaissance and Reformation, in: Ian Hazlett (ed.), Early Christianity: Origins and Evolution to AD 600, London: SPCK.

- (1998), The Church Fathers and the Canonicity of the Apocalypse in the Sixteenth Century: Erasmus, Frans Titelmans, and Theodore Beza, SCJ 29, 651–665.

- (2000), Calvin and the Greek Fathers, in: Robert Bast/Andrew Gos (ed.), Continuity and Change: The Harvest of Late-Medieval and Reformation History, Leiden: Brill, 253–276.

- (ed.) (2007), Théodore de Bèze, 1519–1605: Actes du Colloque de Genève (septembre 2005), Geneva: Librairie Droz.

- (2008), Roman Catholic Lives of Calvin from Bolsec to Richelieu: Why the Interest?, in: Randall C. Zachman (ed.) John Calvin and Roman Catholicism: Critique and Engagement, Then and Now, Grand Rapids, Mich.: Baker Academic.

- (2013), Life Writing in Reformation Europe: Lives of Reformers by Friends, Disciples and Foes, Aldershot, UK: Ashgate.

BACKUS, IRENA (ed.) (1997), The Reception of the Church Fathers in the West: From the Carolingians to the Maurists, 2 vol., New York: Brill.

BAIRD, HENRY M. (1889), History and Rise of the Huguenots in France, 2 vol., New York: Charles Scribner's Sons.

BAKER, J. WAYNE (1996), Erastianism, in: Hans Hillerbrand (ed.), Oxford Encyclopedia of the Reformation, Oxford: Oxford University Press, 2:59–61.

BALSERAK, JON (2010), "There will always be prophets"; Deuteronomy 18:14-22 and Calvin's Prophetic Awareness, in: Herman Selderhuis (ed.). Saint or Sinner? Papers from the International Conference on the Anniversary of John Calvin's 500th birthday, Tübingen: Mohr Siebeck, 85–112.

- (2011), Establishing the Remnant Church in France; Calvin's Lectures on the Minor Prophets, 1556–1559, Leiden: Brill.

- (2012), "We need Teachers today, not Prophets"; Peter Martyr Vermigli's Exposition of Prophecy, ARG 103, 148–172.

- (2014a), John Calvin as Sixteenth-Century Prophet, Oxford: Oxford University Press.

- (2014b), Peter Martyr Vermigli, History, and the Anabaptist Menace; Considering the Italian's Handling of Prophecy, RRR, 15.1, 17–32.

- (2017), Inventing the Prophet: Vermigli, Melanchthon, and Calvin on the Extraordinary Reformer, in: John Balserak/Jim West (ed.), Zwingli to Amyraut: Exploring the Growth of European Reformed Traditions, Göttingen: Vandenhoeck & Ruprecht, 123–136.

BANGERT, WILLIAM (1972), A History of the Society of Jesus, St. Louis, Mo.: Institute of Jesuit Sources.

BARKER, S.K. (2009), Protestantism, Poetry and Protest: The Vernacular Writings of Antoine de Chandieu (c. 1534–1591), Aldershot, UK: Ashgate.

BARNAUD, JEAN (ed.) (1911a), Pierre Viret; Sa vie et son oeuvre, Saint-Amans: G. Carayol.

- (1911b), Quelques lettres inédites de Viret, Saint-Amans: n.p.

BARNES, ROBIN (2015), Astrology and Reformation, Oxford: Oxford University Press.

BARTLETT, KENNETH (1996), Marian Exiles, in: Hans J. Hillerbrand (ed.), The Oxford Encyclopedia of the Reformation, New York: Oxford University Press, 3:8–10.

BATES, ALAN (2005), Emblematic Monsters: Unnatural Conceptions and Deformed Births in Early Modern Europe, New York: Dodopi.

BEARDEN, ELIZABETH (2019), Monstrous Kinds: Body, Space, and Narrative in Renaissance Representations of Disability, Ann Arbor, Mich.: University of Michigan Press.

BEDIER, JOSEPH (1928), La tradition manuscrite du Lai de l'ombre: Reflexions sur l'art d'éditer les anciens texts, Romania 54, 161–196.

BEEKE, JOEL (2003), Theodore Beza's Supralapsarian Predestination, Reformation and Revival 12.2, 69–84.

- (2017), Debated Issues in Sovereign Predestination: Early Lutheran Predestination, Calvinian Reprobation, and Variations in Genevan Lapsarianism, Göttingen: Vandenhoeck & Ruprecht.

BELL, CHARLES (1983), Was Calvin a Calvinist?, SJT 36:4, 535–540.

BENNETT, CHARLES (1900), The Stipulative Subjunctive in Latin, Transactions and Proceedings of the American Philological Association 31, 223–250.

BENTE, GERHARD FRIEDRICH (2005), The Crypto-Calvinist Controversy (1560–74: Articles VII and VIII), in: Paul McCain (ed.), Concordia: The Lutheran Confessions, A Reader's Edition of the Book of Concord, 2nd ed., St. Louis, Mo.: Concordia Publishing House.

BERTRAM, JOHANN GEORG/MÜLLER, SAMUEL ALBERT (1719), Das evangelische Lüngeburg: oder, Reformations- und Kirchen-Historie Der Alt-berühmten Stadt Lüngeburg, Braunschweig: Johann Georg Bertram.

BESSON, JEAN-ANTOINE (1759), Mémoires pour l'histoire ecclésiastique des dioceses de Genève, Tarantaise, Aoste, et Maurenne, et du décanat de Savoye, Nancy: Sebastien Henault.

BETTENSON, HENRY/MAUNDER, CHRIS (2011), Documents of the Christian Church, 4th edition, Oxford: Oxford University Press.

BIETENHOLZ, PETER (1971), Basle and France in the Sixteenth Century: The Basle Printers and Humanists in their Contacts with Francophone Culture, Geneva: Librairie Droz.

BITBOL-HESPÉRIÈS, ANNIE (2006), Monsters, Nature and Generation from the Renaissance to the Age of Reason: The Emergence of Medical Thought, in: Justin Smith (ed.), The Problem of Animal Generation in Modern Philosophy, Cambridge: Cambridge University Press, 47–62.

BOASE, ALAN (1977), Vie de Jean de Sponde, Geneva: Librairie Droz.

BOER, ERIK DE (2012), The Genevan School of the Prophets: The Congrégation of the Company of Pastors and Their Influence in 16th Century Europe, Geneva: Librairie Droz.

BOLLIGER, DANIEL (2004), Bullinger on Church Authority: The Transformation of the Prophetic Role in Christian Ministry. In Bruce Gordon/Emidio Campi (ed.), Architect of Reformation; An Introduction to Heinrich Bullinger, 1504–1575, Grand Rapids, Mich.: Baker Academic, 159–177.

BONNET, JULES (1870), Nouveaux récits du seizième siècle, Paris: Grassart.

- (1885), Récits du seizième siècle, 2nd series, Paris: Grassart.

BORGEAUD, CHARLES (1900), Histoire de l'Université de Genève: L'Academie de Calvin, 1559–1798, Geneva: Georg & Co.

- (1934), Le 'vraie portrait' de John Knox, BSHPF 83, 11–36.

BOUVIER, AUGUSTE (1932), Catalogue de la collection de portraits, bustes, miniatures et medallions de la Bibliothèque publique et universitaire, GENEVA 10, 170–180.

- (1933), Catalogue de la collection de portraits, bustes, miniatures et medallions de la Bibliothèque publique et universitaire (suite), GENEVA 11, 204.

BRAY, JOHN (1971), Theodore Beza's Doctrine of Predestination, Ph.D. Dissertation, Stanford University.

BRUENING, MICHAEL (2005), Calvinism's First Battleground: Conflict and Reform in the Pays de Vaud, 1528–1559, Dordrecht: Springer.

- (2006), "La nouvelle reformation de Lausanne": The Proposal by the Ministers of Lausanne on Ecclesiastical Discipline (June 1558), BHR 58, 21–50.

- (2008), Pierre Viret and Geneva, ARG 99, 175–197.

- (2012), Epistolae Petri Vireti: the Previously Unedited Letters and a Register of Pierre Viret's Correspondence, Geneva: Librairie Droz.

BRUENING, MICHAEL/CROUSAZ, KARINE (ed. and trans.) (2011), Les actes du synode de Lausanne (1538): Un rapport sur les résistances à la Réforme dans le Pays de Vaud, Revue Historique Vaudoise 119, 89–126.

BRUNNER, EMIL (1959), The Letter to the Romans, A Commentary, London: Lutterworth Press.

BÜSSER, FRITZ (1950), Calvins Urteil über sich Selbst, Zurich: Zwingli-Verlag.

- (1973), Huldrych Zwingli: Reformation als prophetischer Auftrag, Zurich: TVZ.

BÜSSER, FRITZ/SCHINDLER, ALFRED (1994), Die Prophezei: Humanismus und Reformation in Zürich: Ausgewählte Aufsätze und Vorträge, Bern: Peter Lang.

BUYSSENS, DANIELLE (2002), Le premier musée de publique, in: Danielle Buyssens/Thierry Dubois (ed.), La Bibliothèque étant un ornement publique, Réforme et embellissements de la Bibliothèque de Genève in 1702, Geneva, Georg Editeur, 91–131.

CABANAC, PAUL (1901), Un prédicateur protestant du XVIIe siècle: Michel Le Faucheur (1585–1675), Montauban: J. Granié.

CABANEL, PATRICK (2012), Histoire des protestants en France: XVIe-XXIe siècle, Paris: Fayard.

CAMERON, EUAN (ed.) (2016), The New Cambridge History of the Bible from 1450 to 1750, New York: Cambridge University Press.

CAMILLOCCI, DANIELLA (2014), Pédagogies en combat: Pierre Viret et les Jésuites à Lyon, in: Daniella Camillocci/Karine Crousaz (ed.), Pierre Viret et la diffusion de la réforme, Lausanne: Éditions Antipodes, 349–367.

CAMPI, EMIDIO (2007), Beza und Bullinger im Lichte ihrer Korrespondenz, in: Irena Backus (ed.), Théodore de Bèze (1519–1605), Actes du Colloque de Genève (septembre 2005), Geneva: Librairie Droz, 131–144.

CAMPAGNOLO, MATTEO (2000), Jean Calvin *ka hoi peri auton*. Choix de médailles et de quelques portraits à l'huile et graves, in: Olivier Reverdin (ed.), Homère chez Calvin, Figures de l'Hellenisme à Genève, Geneva: Librairie Droz, 103–113.

CARBONNIER-BURKARD, MARIANNE (2007), *L'Histoire Ecclésiastique des Églises Réformées* …: La construction Bèzienne d'un 'Corps d'histoire,' in: Irena Backus (ed.), Théodore de Bèze (1519–1605): Actes du Colloque de Genève (septembre 2005), Geneva: Librairie Droz.

CÉARD, JEAN (1996), La Nature et les Prodiges: L'insolite au XVIe siècle, Geneva: Librairie Droz.

CHALFANT, MAY (1921), The Modal Usage in Relative Qui Clauses in the Letters of Pliny, the Younger, M.A. Thesis, University of Chicago.

CHAZALON, CHRISTOPHE (2001), Les Icones de Théodore de Bèze. Etude d'une galerie idéale de portraits imprimée au temps des guerres de religion, PhD Dissertation, University of Geneva.

CHRISTIN, OLIVIER/DESCHAMP, MARION (2011), Une politique du portrait? L'héritage calvinien, ARG 102, 195–219.

CHUNG-KIM, ESTHER (2009), Use of the Fathers in the Eucharistic Debates between John Calvin and Joachim Westphal, Reformation 14.1, 101–125.

- (2011), Inventing Authority: The Use of the Church Fathers in Reformation Debates over the Eucharist, Waco, Tex.: Baylor University Press.

COFFEY, JOHN/LIM, PAUL C.H. (2008), The Cambridge Companion to Puritanism, Cambridge: Cambridge University Press.

COLLINSON, PATRICK (1990), The Elizabethan Puritan Movement, Oxford: Clarendon Press.

CONȚAC, EMANUEL (2017), Noul Testament de la Bălgrad și Reforma: Studiu istorico-filologic 1648, Iași, Romania: Editura Universității Alexandru Ioan Cuza.

COSTIL, PIERRE (1935), André Dudith, humaniste hongrois, 1533–1589, Paris: Les Belles Lettres.

COTTRET, BERNARD (1995), Calvin: Biographie, Paris: Éditions Jean-Claude Lattès.

CRAIG, JOHN (2008), The Growth of English Puritanism, in: John Coffey/Paul C. H. Lim (ed.), Cambridge: Cambridge University Press, 34–47.

CRAMER, LUCIEN (1958), La Seigneurie de Genève et la Maison de Savoie de 1559 à 1595, vol. 4, Geneva: A. Jullien.

CRISPINI, FRANCO (1983), La Storia dei Monstri dalla 'Cultura dei Prodigi' al 'Sapere Illuminista' (Prospettive di Ricerca), Rivista Critica di Storia della Filosofia 38, 387–408.

CROSS, CLAIRE (1966), The Puritan Earl. The Life of Henry Hastings Third Earl of Huntingdon, 1536–1595, London: MacMillan.

CROUSAZ, KARINE (2012), L'Académie de Lausanne entre Humanisme et Réforme (ca. 1537–1560), Leiden: Brill.

Crouzet, Denis (1990), Les Guerriers de Dieu: La Violence au temps des troubles de religion (vers 1525–vers 1610), 2 vol., Seyssel: Champ Vallon.

- (2000), Jean Calvin: vies parallèles, Paris: Fayard.

DANNER, DAN (1999), Pilgrimage to Puritanism: History and Theology of the Marian Exiles at Geneva, 1555–1560, New York: Peter Lang.

DARDIER, CHARLES (1883), Jean de Serres, sa vie et ses écrits, Paris: Extraits de la Revue historique.

DAWSON, JANE (1994), The Apocalyptic Thinking of the Marian Exiles, in: Michael Wilks (ed.), Prophecy and Eschatology, Studies in Church History, Oxford: Blackwell Publishers, 75–91.

- (2015), John Knox, New Haven, Conn.: Yale University Press.

DENIS, PHILIPPE (1992), "Viret et Morély: Les raisons d'un silence," BHR 54, 395–409.

DENT, C. M. (1983), Protestant Reformers in Elizabethan Oxford, Oxford: Oxford University Press.

DICKENS, A.G. (1976), The English Reformation, New York: Schocken Books.

DINGEL, IRENE (ed.) (2008), Die Debatte um die Wittenberger Abendmahlslehre und Christologie (1570–1574), Controversia et Confessio 8, Göttingen: Vandenhoeck & Ruprecht.

- (2010), Calvin in the Context of Lutheran Consolidation, RRR 12, 155–187.

DIXON, SCOTT C. (1999), Popular Astrology and Lutheran Propaganda in Reformation Germany, History 84, 403–418.

DONNELY, JOHN P. (ed. and trans.) (2006), Jesuit Writings of the Early Modern Period, 1540–1640, Indianapolis, Ind.: Hackett.

DORIGNY, JEAN (1716), La Vie du Pere Emond Auger, Lyon: Nicolas de Ville.

DOUMERGUE, ÉMILE (1909), Iconographie calvinienne, Lausanne: Georges Bridel.

- (1899–1917), Jean Calvin: Les hommes et les choses de son temps, 7 vol., Lausanne: Georges Bridel & Cie Éditeurs.

DUFAU, ARMAND DE/JAURGAIN, JEAN DE (1976), Armorial de Béarn 1697–1701, 3 vol. Réimpression de l'édition de Paris, 1889–1893, Marseille: Laffitte Reprints.

DU FRESNOY, NICOLAS LENGLET (1775), Histoire de Jeanne d'Arc, dite la Pucelle d'Orléans, Amsterdam: Compagnie.

DUKE, A.C. (ed.) (1992), Calvinism in Europe, 1540–1610: A Collection of Documents, Manchester, UK: Manchester University Press.

DUFOUR, ALAIN (1958), La guerre de 1589–1593, Geneva: A. Jullien.

- (2009), Théodore de Bèze: Poète et théologien, Cahiers d'Humanisme et Renaissance 78, Geneva: Librairie Droz.

ENGAMMARE, MAX (1997), Les Bibles genevoises en français au XVIe siècle: la destinée de la traduction d'Olivétan, in: Schwabe (ed.), La Bible en Suisse : origines et histoire, Basel: La Société biblique suisse, 177–189.

- (1998), Calvin: A Prophet without a Prophecy, in: John Leith/Robert Johnson (ed.), Calvin Studies IX; Papers Presented at the Ninth Colloquium on Calvin Studies, Davidson College, January 30–31, 1998, Davidson, N.C.: Davidson College, 88–107.

EPP, ELDON (2016), Critical Editions of the New Testament, in: Euan Cameron (ed.), The New Cambridge History of the Bible from 1450 to 1750, Cambridge: Cambridge University Press, 110–137.

FARNUM, EMILY (1964), Michel Le Faucheur and His Influence," PhD Dissertation, University of Wisconsin.

FATIO, OLIVIER (2015), Louis Tronchin. Une transition Calvinienne, Paris: Editions Classiques Garnier.

FEHLEISON, JILL (2010), Boundary of Faith: Catholics and Protestants in the Diocese of Geneva, Kirksville, Mo.: Truman State University Press.

- (2014), The Place of the Cross: The Pamphlet Battle between François de Sales and Antoine de Faye, in: Sarah Alyn Stacey (ed.), Political, Religious, and Social Conflict in the States of Savoy, 1400–1700, Bern: Peter Lang, 257–274.

FÉLICE, GUILLAUME DE (1850), Histoire des Protestants de France depuis l'origine de la Réformation jusqu'au temps present, Paris: Librairie protestante.

FELLAY, JEAN-BLAISE (1984), Théodore de Bèze exegete: Traduction et commentaire de l'Epitre aux Romains dans les *Annotationes in Novum Testamentum*, Ph.D. Dissertation, University of Geneva.

FOGELQVIST, INGVAR (1993), Apostasy and Reform in the Revelations of St. Birgitta, Stockholm: Almqvist & Wiksell International.

FRAENKEL, PETER (1961), Testimonia Patrum: The Function of Patristic Argument in the Theology of Melanchthon, Geneva: Librairie Droz.

- (1979), Beatus Rhenanus, Oecolampade, Théodore de Bèze et quelques-unes de leurs sources anciennes, BHR 41, 63–81.

FRERE, W.H./DOUGLAS, C.E. (ed.) (1954), Puritan Manifestoes. A study of the Origin of the Puritan Revolt. With a Reprint of the Admonition to the Parliament and Kindred Documents, 1572, London: Church Historical Society.

FREUD, SIGMUND (1938), The Basic Writings of Sigmund Freud, A.A. Brill (trans. and ed.), New York: Random House.

FRIEDMAN, JEROME (1993), The Battle of the Frogs and the Fairford's Fire: Miracles and the Pulp Press during the English Revolution, New York: St Martin's Press.

GÁBOR, ALMÁSI (2009), The Uses of Humanism: Johannes Sambucus (1531–1584) and André Dudith (1533–1589), and the Republic of Letters in East Central Europe, Leiden: Brill.

GAILLET, LYNÉE LEWIS (1994), Michel Le Faucheur (1585–1657), in: Michael G. Moran (ed.), Eighteenth-Century British and American Rhetorics and Rhetoricians: Critical Studies and Sources, Wesport, Conn.: Greenwood Press, 70–74.

GANOCZY, ALEXANDRE (1966), Le jeune Calvin: genèse et évolution de sa vocation réformatrice, Wiesbaden: Franz Steiner Verlag.

- (1969), La Bibliothèque de l'Académie de Calvin: Le Catalogue de 1572 et ses Enseignements, Geneva: Librairie Droz.

GARDY, FRÉDÉRIC (1946), Catalogue de la partie des Archives Tronchin acquise par la Société du Musée historique de la Réformation, Geneva: Librairie A. Jullien.

GARRETT, CHRISTIANA (1966), The Marian Exiles. A Study in the Origins of Elizabethan Puritanism, Cambridge: Cambridge University Press.

GAUTIER, JEAN-ANTOINE (1903), Histoire de Genève des Origines à l'année 1691, 8 vol., Geneva: Société Genérale d'Imprimerie.

GAZAIGNES, JEAN (1764–1765), Annales de la société de soi-disans Jésuites, 2 vol., Paris: n.p.

GEISDENDLORF, PAUL-F. (1949), Théodore de Bèze, Geneva: Labor et Fides.

GORDON, BRUCE (2009), Calvin, New Haven, Conn.: Yale University Press.

- (2012), "Christo testimonium reddunt omnes scripturae": Theodor Bibliander's Oration on Isaiah (1532) and Commentary on Nahum (1534), in: Bruce Gordon/Matthew McLean (ed.), Shaping the Bible in the Reformation; Books, Scholars and Their Readers in the Sixteenth Century, Leiden: Brill, 107–141.

- (2016), The Bible in Reformed thought, 1520–1750, in: Euan Cameron (ed.), The New Cambridge History of the Bible from 1450 to 1750, Cambridge: Cambridge University Press, 462–488.

- (2017), "For If We Are True Prophets": Huldrych Zwingli on Martin Luther, Reformation 22.2, 102–119.

GORDON, BRUCE/CAMERON, EUAN (2016), The Early Modern Latin Bible, in: Euan Cameron (ed.), The New Cambridge History of the Bible from 1450 to 1750, New York: Cambridge University Press, 187–216.

GOSSELIN, EDWARD (1976), David in Tempore Belli: Beza's David in the Service of the Huguenots, SCJ 7.2, 31–54.

GRAHAM, FRED (1996), Presbyterianism, in: Hans Hillerbrand (ed.), Oxford Encyclopedia of the Reformation, Oxford: Oxford University Press, 3:338–341.

GRANE, LEIF/SCHINDLER, ALFRED/WRIEDT, MARKUS (ed.) (1993), Auctoritas Patrum: zur Rezeption der Kirchenväter im 15 und 16 Jahrhundert, Mainz: Verlag Philipp von Zabern.

GRAVES, THOMAS (ed.) (1901), Catholic Tractates of the Sixteenth Century 1573–1600, Edinburgh: William Blackwood and Sons.

GREGORY, BRAD (2012a), Author's Reply, Church History 81.4, 939.

- (2012b), The Unintended Reformation: How a Religious Revolution Secularized Society, Cambridge, Mass.: The Belknap Press.

GRENDLER, PAUL (2017), The Jesuits and Italian Universities, 1548–1773, Washington D.C.: Catholic University of America Press.

GUGGISBERG, HANS (2003), Sebastian Castellio, 1515–1563: Humanist and Defender of Religious Toleration in a Confessional Age, Bruce Gordon (trans. and ed.), Aldershot, UK: Ashgate.

GUNNOE, CHARLES, (2010), Thomas Erastus and the Palatinate: A Renaissance Physician in the Second Reformation, Leiden: Brill.

GUNNOE, CHARLES/SHACKELFORD, JOLE (2009), Johannes Crato von Krafftheim (1519–1585): Imperial Physician, Irenicist, and Anti-Paracelsian, in: Marjorie E. Plummer/Robin Barnes (ed.), Ideas and Cultural Margins in Early Modern Germany, Burlington, Vt.: Ashgate, 201–216.

HABERKERN, PHILLIP (2016), Patron Saint and Prophet: Jan Hus in the Bohemian and German Reformations, Oxford: Oxford University Press.

HALL, BASIL (1966), Calvin Against the Calvinists, in G.E. Duffield (ed.), John Calvin, Appleford, Abingdon: Sutton Courtenay, 19–37.

HALL, DAVID (1990), Worlds of Wonder, Days of Judgment: Popular Religious Belief in Early New England, Cambridge, Mass.: Harvard University Press.

HAMILTON, ALASTAIR (2016), Early Modern Polyglot Bibles: Alcalá (1510–1520) to Brian Walton (1654–1658), in: Euan Cameron (ed.), The New Cambridge History of the Bible from 1450–1750, New York: Cambridge University Press, 17–36.

HART, D. G. (2013), Calvinism, A History, New Haven, Conn.: Yale University Press.

HELM, PAUL (1998), John Calvin, the Sensus Divinitatis, and the Noetic Effects of Sin, International Journal of Philosophy of Religion 43, 87–107.

- (2004), John Calvin's Ideas, Oxford: Oxford University Press.

HENNING, JÜRGENS (2008), 'Einleitung' to 'Torgauer Artikel', in: Irene Dingel (ed.), Debatte um die Wittenberger, Göttingen: Vandenhoeck & Ruprecht.

HERMINJARD, AIMÉ LOUIS (1866–1897), Correspondance des Réformateurs dans les pays de langue français, 9 vol., Geneva: H. Georg.

HERZIG, TAMAR (2008), Savonarola's Women: Visions and Reform in Renaissance Italy, Chicago, Ill.: University of Chicago.

HIGMAN, FRANCIS (1995), L'harmonia confessionum fide de 1581, in: Madelaine Fragonard/Michel Peronnet (ed.), Catechismes et confessions de foi, Montpellier: Le Centre d'histoire des réformes et du protestantisme de l'Université de Montpellier, 243–262.

- (1998), French-speaking regions, 1520–62, in: Jean-François Gilmont (ed.), The Reformation and the Book, Karin Maag (trans.), Aldershot, UK: Ashgate.

HOEKSEMA, HERMAN (2002), Righteous by Faith Alone: A Devotional Commentary on Romans, David J. Engelsma (ed.), Grandville, Mich.: Reformed Free Publishing Association.

HOITENGA, DANIEL (2003), The Noetic Effects of Sin: A Review Article, review of Stephen Moroney, The Noetic Effects of Sin: A Historical and Contemporary Explanation of How Sin Affects our Thinking, CTJ 38, 68–102.

HOLDER, R. WARD (2009), Calvin and Tradition: Tracing Expansion, Locating Development, Suggesting Authority, Toronto Journal of Theology 25.2, 215–225.

- (2017), The Reformers and Tradition: Seeing the Roots of the Problem, Religions 8.6, at https://doi.org/10.3390/rel8060105.

- (2020), Calvin in Context, New York: Cambridge University Press.

HOLLIS, CHRISTOPHER (1968), The Jesuits: A History, New York: Barnes & Nobles.

HOLT, MACK P. (1995), The French Wars of Religion, 1562–1629, Cambridge: Cambridge University Press.

- (2007), Divisions Within French Calvinism: Philippe Mornay and the Eucharist, in: Mack P. Holt (ed.), Adaptations of Calvinism in Reformation Europe: Essays in Honor of Brian G. Armstrong, St. Andrews: Ashgate, 65–85.

HOLTROP, PHILIP (1993), The Bolsec Controversy on Predestination from 1551 to 1555: The Statements of Jerome Bolsec, and the Responses of John Calvin, Theodore Beza, and Other Reformed Theologians, 2 vol., Lewiston, N.Y.: E. Mellen.

HUNDESHAGEN, KARL (1842), Die Conflikte des Zwinglianismus, des Luthertums und des Calvinismus in der Bernischen Landeskirche 1532–1558, Bern: C. A. Jenni.

JONES, GWILYM (1967), The Welsh Psalter of 1567, Journal of the Historical Society of the Church in Wales, 17, 56–61.

JONES, LEONARD CHESTER (1916), Simon Goulart sa vie et son oeuvre, 1543–1628, Geneva: Albert Kundig.

JORINK, ERIC (2010), Reading the Book of Nature in the Dutch Golden Age, 1575–1715, Leiden: Brill.

KAYE, HOWARD (1993), Why Freud Hated America, The Wilson Quarterly 17.2, 118–125.

KEENER, CRAIG (2009), Romans: A New Covenant Commentary, Cambridge: Lutterworth Press.

KINGDON, ROBERT (1961), Concerning Theodore Beza, BHR 23:2, 415–422.

- (1967), Geneva and the Consolidation of the French Protestant Movement, Madison, Wisc.: The University of Wisconsin Press.

- (ed.) (1974), Transition and Revolution: Problems and Issues of European Renaissance and Reformation History, Minneapolis, Minn.: Burgess, 1974.

KIRK, JAMES (1996), Scottish Books of Discipline, in: Hans Hillerbrand (ed.), Oxford Encyclopedia of the Reformation, Oxford: Oxford University Press, 4:31–33.

KLAUBER, MARTIN (2014), Edme Aubertin and the Eucharistic Debates in Seventeenth-Century France, in: Michael Parsons (ed.), Reformation Faith: Exegesis and Theology in the Protestant Reformations, Carlisle, UK: Paternoster Press, 205–215.

- (2015), Showdown at Fontainebleau: The Debate between Philippe Duplessis-Mornay (1549–1623) and Cardinal Jacques-Davy du Perron (1556–1618) on the Nature of the Eucharist, in: Amy Nelson Burnett/Kathleen M. Comerford/Karin Maag (ed.), Politics, Gender, and Belief: The Long-Term Impact of the Reformation, Geneva: Librairie Droz, 45–72.

KNAPPEN, M.M. (1966), Tudor Protestantism: a chapter in the history of idealism, Chicago, Ill.: University of Chicago.

KNECHT, ROBERT (2014), The French Wars of Religion 1562–1598, Oxford: Bloombury.

KOLB, ROBERT (1999), Martin Luther as Prophet, Teacher, and Hero; Images of the Reformer, 1520–1620, Grand Rapids, Mich.: Baker.

- (2012), The Critique of Melanchthon's Doctrine of the Lord's Supper by his 'Gnesio-Lutheran' Students, in: Irene Dingel/Robert Kolb/Nicole Kuropka/-Timothy Wengert (ed.), Philip Melanchthon: Theologian in Classroom, Confession, and Controversy, Göttingen: Vandenhoeck and Ruprecht, 236–262.

KRANS, JAN (2006), Beyond What Is Written: Erasmus and Beza as Conjectural Critics of the New Testament, Leiden: Brill.

KRISTELLER, PAUL (1979), Renaissance Thought and Its Sources, New York: Columbia University Press.

KRUMM, JOHN (1962), Continental Protestantism and Elizabethan Anglicanism (1570–1595), in: Franklin Littell (ed.), Reformatioin Studies. Essays in Honor of Roland H. Bainton, Richmond, Va.: John Knox Press, 129–144.

KRÜTLI, JOSEPH (1861), Die Eidgenössischen Abschiede aus dem Zeitraume von 1556 bis 1586, Bern: Rätzer.

KUSUKAWA, SACHIKO (1995), The Transformation of Natural Philosophy: The Case of Philip Melanchthon, Cambridge: Cambridge University Press.

LAKE, PETER (2004), Moderate Puritans and the Elizabethan Church, Cambridge: Cambridge University Press.

LALOT, J. A. (1889), Essai historique sur la conference tenue à Fontainebleau enter Duplessis Mornay et Duperron le 4 Mai 1600, Paris: n.p.

LANE, ANTHONY N.S. (1981), Calvin's Use of the Fathers and the Medievals, CTJ 16.2, 149–205.

- (1997), Calvin and the Fathers in Bondage and Liberation of the Will, in: Wilhelm H. Neuser/ Brian Armstrong (ed.), Calvinus Sincerioris Religionis Vindex: Calvin as Protector of the Purer Religion, Kirksville, Mo.: Sixteenth Century Journal Publishers, 67–96.

- (1999), John Calvin: Student of the Church Fathers, Edinburgh: T&T Clark.

- (2009), Anthropology, in Herman J. Selderhuis (ed.), The Calvin Handbook, English ed., Grand Rapids, Mich.: Eerdmans, 275–288.

LASSMAN, PETER/VELODY, IRVING/MARTINS, HERMINO (1989), Max Weber's "Science as a Vocation," London: Unwin Hyman.

LINDER, ROBERT D. (1964), The Political Ideas of Pierre Viret, Geneva: Librairie Droz.

LUDWIG, WALTHER (1997), Théodore de Bèze und Heinrich Rantzau über ihre Bücherliebe, Philologus 141, 141–144.

LUPHER, A. DAVID (2017), Greeks, Romans, and Pilgrims: Classical Receptions in Early New England, Leiden: Brill.

MACBAIN, BRUCE (1982), Prodigy and Expiation: A Study in Religion and Politics in Republican Rome, Brussels: Collection Latomus.

MAGER, INGE (1993), Die Konkordienformel im Fürstentum Braunschweig-Wolfenbüttel, Göttingen: Vandenhoeck & Ruprecht.

MALLINSON, JEFFREY (2000), Fides et Cognitio: The Direction of Religious Epistemology under Theodore Beza, Ph.D. Dissertation, Oxford University.

- (2003), Faith, Reason, and Revelation in Theodore Beza, 1519–1605, New York: Oxford University Press.

MANDELBROTE, SCOTT (2016), The Old Testament and its ancient versions in manuscript and print in the West, from c. 1480 to c. 1780," in: Euan Cameron (ed.), The New Cambridge History of the Bible, New York: Cambridge University Press, 82–109.

MANETSCH, SCOTT (2000a), Psalms Before Sonnets: Theodore Beza and the Studia Humanitatis, in: Robert Bast/Andrew Gow (ed.), Continuity and Change: The Harvest of Late-Medieval and Reformation History, Leiden: Brill, 400–416.

- (2000b), Theodore Beza and the Quest for Peace in France, 1572–1598, Leiden: Brill.

- (2003), A Mystery Solved? Maister Beza's Houshold Prayers, BHR 65.2, 275–288.
- (2006), The Journey Toward Geneva: Theodore Beza's Conversion, 1535–1548, in: David Foxgrover (ed.), Calvin, Beza and Later Calvinism: Papers Presented at the 15th Colloquium of the Calvin Studies Society, April 7–9, 2006, Grand Rapids, Mich.: Calvin Studies Society, 38–57.
- (2007), "The Most Despised Vocation Today"; Theodore Beza's Theology of Pastoral Ministry, in: Irena Backus (ed.), Théodore de Bèze (1519–1605), Actes du Colloque de Genève (septembre 2005), Geneva: Librairie Droz, 241–256.
- (2013), Calvin's Company of Pastors, Pastoral Care and the Emerging Reformed Church, 1536–1609, New York: Oxford University Press.
- (2014), Theodore Beza and the Crisis of Reformed Protestantism in France, in: Martin Klauber (ed.), The Theology of the French Reformed Church: From Henry IV to the Revocation of the Edict of Nantes, Grand Rapids, Mich.: Reformation Heritage Books, 24–56.
MARTIN, A. LYNN (1988). The Jesuit Mind: The Mentality of an Elite in Early Modern France, Ithaca, N.Y.: Cornell University Press.
MARTIN, CHARLES (1999), Les Protestants Anglais réfugiés à Genève au temps de Calvin, 1555–1560, Geneva: Librairie Droz.
MARUYAMA, TADATAKA (1978), The Ecclesiology of Theodore Beza. The Reform of the True Church, Geneva: Librairie Droz.
MATHESON, PETER (1995), Argula Von Grumbach: A Woman's Voice in the Reformation, Edinburgh: T&T Clark.
McGinn, Bernard (1985), The Calabrian Abbot: Joachim of Fiore in the History of Western Thought, New York: Macmillan Publishing Co.
MCKEE, ELSIE ANNE (1998), Katharina Schutz Zell; Volume One. The Life and Thought of a Sixteenth-Century Reformer - Volume Two. The Writings, A Critical Edition, 2 vol., Leiden: Brill.
MCKEE, JANE (2008), Books and Scholarship in the Correspondence of Charles Drelincourt, in: Phyllis Gaffney/Michael Brophy/May Gallagher (ed.), Reverberations: Staging Relations in France since 1500, Dublin: University College Dublin, 260–261.
MCNUTT, JENNIFER POWELL (2020), Calvin Legends: Hagiology and Demonology, in: R. Ward Holder (ed.), Calvin in Context, New York: Cambridge University Press, 383–392.
- (2014), Calvin Meets Voltaire: The Clergy of Geneva in the Age of Enlightenment, 1685–1798, Aldershot, UK: Ashgate.
MCNUTT, JENNIFER POWELL/LAUBER, DAVID (ed.) (2017), The People's Book: The Reformation and the Bible, Downers Grove, Ill.: IVP Academic.

MCPHEE, IAN (1979), Conserver or Transformer of Calvin's Theology? A Study of the Origins and Development of Theodore Beza's Thought, 1550–1570, Ph.D. Dissertation, Cambridge University.

MÉNAGER, DANIEL (1983), Théodore de Bèze, biographe de Calvin, BHR 45:2, 231–255.

MEYLAN, HENRI (1956), La bonne fontaine de Saint-Cergue, Revue Historique Vaudoise 64, 99–106.

- (1959), En marge de la correspondence de Théodore de Bèze: Un hérétique oublié, RTP 9.3, 177–181.

- (1976), La conversion de Bèze ou les longues hesitations d'un humaniste chrétien, in: Henri Meylan (ed.), D'Érasme à Théodore de Bèze, Geneva: Librairie Droz, 145–166.

- (1978), Pierre Viret et les Lausannois: Vingt années de lutes pour une discipline ecclésiastique, Mémoires de la Société pour l'Histoire du Droit et des Institutions des anciens pays bourgignons, comtois et romands 36, 15–23.

MILLER, PERRY (1954), The New England Mind: The Seventeenth Century, Cambridge, Mass.: Harvard University Press.

MILLET, OLIVIER (1998), Eloquence des prophètes bibliques et prédication inspirée: la 'prophétie' réformée au XVIe siècle, in: Prophètes et prophétie au XVIe siècle, Paris: Presses de l'Ecole Normale Supérieure, 65–82.

- (2011), Calvin's Self-Awareness as Author, in: Irena Backus/Philip Benedict (ed.), Calvin & His Influence, 1509–2009, Oxford: Oxford University Press, 84–101.

MONTER, E. WILLIAM (1967), Calvin's Geneva, New York: John Wiley & Sons.

- (1999), Judging the French Reformation: Heresy Trials by Sixteenth-Century Parlements, Cambridge, Mass.: Harvard University Press.

MOO, DOUGLAS (1996), The Epistle to the Romans, Grand Rapids, Mich.: Eerdmans Publishing Company.

MORGAN, D. DENSIL (2017), The Reformation and Vernacular Culture: Wales as a Case Study, in: Jennifer Powell McNutt/David Lauber (ed.), The People's Book: The Reformation and the Bible, Downers Grove, Ill: IVP Academic, 69–88.

MOSLEY, ADAM (2014), The History and Historiography of Early Modern Comets, in: Miguel Granada/Adam Mosley/Nicholas Jardine (ed.), Christoph Rothmann's Discourse on the Comet of 1585, Leiden: Brill, 282–325.

MULLER, RICHARD (1999), The Use and Abuse of a Document: Beza's *Tabula Praedestinationes*, the Bolsec Controversy, and the Origins of Reformed Orthodoxy, in: Carl R. Trueman/R.S. Clark (ed.), Protestant Scholasticism: Essays in Reassessment, Carlisle, U.K.: Paternoster, 33–61.

- (2005), The Placement of Predestination in Reformed Theology: Issue or Non-Issue?, CTJ 40, 184–210.

MÜNTZ, EUGÈNE (1901), La musée de portraits de Paul Jove. Contributions pour server à l'iconographie du Moyen Âge et de la Renaissance, in: Mémoires de l'Institut National de France, 36.2, 249–343.

NAPHY, WILLIAM (1994), Calvin and the consolidation of the Genevan Reformation, Manchester: Manchester University Press.

NELSON, ERIC (2005), The Jesuits and the Monarchy: Catholic Reform and Political Authority in France, 1590–1615, Aldershot, UK: Ashgate.

NEW, JOHN (1968), The Whitgift-Cartwright Controversy, ARG 59.2, 203–211.

NICOLLIER, BÉATRICE (2007), Le role de Bèze dans le maintien et le rayonnement de l'Académie de Genève, in: Irena Backus (ed.), Théodore de Bèze (1519–1605), Actes de Colloque de Genève (septembre 2005), Geneva: Librairie Droz, 41–54.

NIJENHUIS, W. (1972), Ecclesia Reformata. Studies on the Reformation, Leiden: Brill.

- (1980), Adrianus Saravia (c. 1532–1613), Dutch Calvinist, first Reformed defender of the English episcopal Church order on the basis of the ius divinum, Leiden: Brill.

NUGENT, DONALD (1970), Ecumenism in the Age of Reformation: The Colloquy of Poissy, Cambridge, Mass.: Harvard University Press.

OBERMAN, HEIKO (1998), Calvin and Farel: The Dynamics of Legitimation in Early Calvinism," JEMH 2, 32–60.

- (1999), Hus and Luther: Prophets of a Radical Reformation, in: C. Pater/R. Peterson (ed.), The Contentious Triangle: Church, State, and University, Kirksville, Mo.: Truman State University Press, 135–167.

OLSON, JEANNINE (1989), Calvin and Social Welfare: Deacons and the Bourse française, Selinsgrove, Pa.: Susquehanna University Press.

- (2001), The Family, Second Marriage, and Death of Nicolas Des Gallars within the Context of His Life and Work: Evidence from the Notarial Records in Paris and in Pau, BHR 63.1, 75–79.

- (2007), Nicolas Des Gallars and the Colloquy of Poissy: The Neglected Participation of a Pastor of the London Stranger Church in an Ecumenical Council, Proceedings of the Huguenot Society 28.5, 664–683.

- (2009), An English Window on the Huguenot Struggle for Recognition: Nicolas Des Gallars and the Colloquy of Poissy, Toronto Journal of Theology 25.2, 227–238.

- (2012), The Mission to France: Nicolas Des Gallars' Interaction with John Calvin, Gaspard de Coligny, and Edmund Grindal, Bishop of London, in: Herman Selderhuis (ed.), Calvinus clarissimus theologus: Papers of the Tenth International Congress on Calvin Research, Göttingen: Vandenhoeck &

Ruprecht, 344–357.

- (2015), The Flight from France of Nicolas Des Gallars: Archival Discoveries on His Interlude in Geneva (1568–1571) and the *Histoire ecclésiastique des Eglises reformées au Royaume de France*, BHR 77.3, 573–604.
- (2016), A Struggle against Democracy in Reformed Churches: Beza and Nicolas Des Gallars Collaborate against John Morély, in: Herman Selderhuis/Arnold Huijgen (ed), Calvinus Pastor Ecclesiae: Papers of the Eleventh International Congress on Calvin Research, Göttingen: Vandenhoeck & Ruprecht, 409–21.
- (2017), A Dowry, Will, and Blended Family of Calvin's Geneva Put Anne Colladon to the Test, JEMC 4.1, 63–89.
- (2018), The Quest for Anonymity: Laurent de Normandie, His Colporteurs, and the Expansion of Reformed Communities through Worship, in: Barbara Pitkin (ed.), Semper Reformanda: John Calvin, Worship, and Reformed Traditions, Göttingen: Vandenhoeck & Ruprecht, 33–35.
- (2020), Freed by Grace and Politics: Calvinism Realized in Béarn: Pierre Viret, Nicolas Des Gallars, and Queen Jeanne d'Albret, in: Karin Maag/Albert Huijgen (ed.), Calvinus frater in Domino, Papers of the Twelfth International Congress on Calvin Research, Göttingen: Vandenhoeck & Ruprecht, 323–335.
OPITZ, PETER (2007), Von prophetischer Existenz zur Prophetie als Pädagogik; Zu Bullingers Lehre vom munus propheticum, in: Emidio Campi/Peter Opitz (ed.) Heinrich Bullinger; Life – Thought – Influence; Zurich, Aug. 25–29, 2004 International Congress on Heinrich Bullinger (1504–1575), 2 vol., Zurich: TVZ, 2: 493–513.
- (2017), Ulrich Zwingli; Prophet, Ketzer, Pionier des Protestantismus, Zurich: TVS.
OSBORNE, GRANT (2017), Romans: Verse by Verse, Bellingham, Wash.: Lexham Press.
PAK, G. SUJIN (2012), Rethinking Prophecy: The Functions of Prophecy in the Writings of Argula von Grumbach and Martin Luther, RRR 14.2, 151–169.
- (2018), The Reformation of Prophecy: Early Modern Interpretations of the Prophet and Old Testament Prophecy, New York: Oxford University Press.
PARK, KATHARINE/DASTON, LORRAINE (1981), Unnatural Conceptions: The Study of Monsters in Sixteenth- and Seventeenth-Century France and England, Past and Present 92, 20–54.
PARKER, D.C. (1992), *Codex Bezae*: An early Christian manuscript and its text, Cambridge: Cambridge University Press.
- (2009), Manuscripts, Texts, Theology: Collected Papers 1997–2007, Berlin: De Gruyter.
PELIKAN, JAROSLAV (1996), The Reformation of the Bible: The Bible of the Reformation, New Haven, Conn.: Yale University Press.

PETER, RODOLPHE (1971), Introduction to John Calvin's Sermons sur les livres de Jérémie et des Lamentations, Rodolphe Peter (ed.), Neukirchen: Neukirchner.

PETER, RODOLPHE/GILMONT, JEAN-FRANÇOIS (1991–2000), Bibliotheca Calviniana. Les œuvres de Jean Calvin publiées au XVIe siècle, 3 vol., Geneva: Librairie Droz.

PETER, RODOLPHE/ROTT, JEAN (1972), Les lettres à Jean Calvin de la Collection Sarrau, Paris: Presses Universitaires de France.

PETERSON, RODNEY (1991), Bullinger's Prophets of the 'Restitutio', in: Mark S. Burrows/ Paul Rorem (ed.), Biblical Hermeneutics in Historical Perspective, Grand Rapids, Mich.: Eerdmans, 245–260.

- (1993), Preaching in the Last Days: the Theme of the 'Two Witnesses' in the 16th and 17th Centuries, New York: Oxford University Press.

PETTEGREE, ANDREW (1986), Foreign Protestant Communities in Sixteenth-Century London, Oxford: Clarendon Press.

PETTEGREE, ANDREW/WALSBY, MALCOLM/WILKINSON, ALEXANDER (ed.) (2007), French Vernacular Books, 2 vol., Leiden: Brill.

PIDOUX, PIERRE (1962), Le Psautier Huguenot, vol. 2, Basel: Edition Baerenreiter.

POT, OLIVIER (ed.) (2013), Simon Goulart, Un Pasteur aux Intérêts Vastes comme le Monde, Geneva: Librairie Droz.

POTTER, MARY (1983), Jean Calvin, 'A Warning against Judiciary Astrology and Other Prevalent Curiosities', CTJ 18, 157–189.

PREUSS, HANS (1933), Martin Luther. Der Prophet, Gütersloh: C. Bertelsmann.

PREUSS, J.A.O. II (1994), The Second Martin: The Life and Theology of Martin Chemnitz, St. Louis, Mo.: Concordia Publishing House.

PROBES, CHRISTINE MCCALL (1974), Calvin on Astrology, WTJ 37, 24–33.

QUICK, JOHN (1692), Synodicon in Gallia Reformata, or, the Acts, Decisions, Decrees, and Canons of thouse famous National Councils of the Reformed Churches in France, 2 vol., London: T. Parkhurst.

RAITT, JILL (1972), The Eucharistic Theology of Theodore Beza: Development of the Reformed Doctrine, Chambersburg, Pa.: American Academy of Religion.

- (ed.) (1981), Shapers of Religious Traditions in Germany, Switzerland and Poland, 1560–1600, New Haven, Conn.: Yale University Press.

- (1993), The Colloquy of Montbéliard: Religion and Politics in the Sixteenth Century, New York: Oxford University Press.

Reeves, Marjorie (1969), The Influence of Prophecy in the Later Middle Ages: A Study in Joachimism, Oxford: Oxford University Press.

REID, W. STANFORD, Calvin and the Founding of the Academy of Geneva, in: Richard Gamble (ed.), Calvin's Work in Geneva, vol. 3, New York: Garland Press, 2–9.

Repression, Suppression, and Conscious Awareness (2010), American Psychological Association, 27.2, 164–181.

RHYS, HOWARD (1961), The Epistle to the Romans, New York: McMillan Company.

RICHAT, ABRAHAM/VULLIEMIN, LOUIS (1727), Histoire de la Réforme de la Suisse, où l'on voit tout ce qui s'est passé de plus remarquable depuis l'an 1516 jusqu'en l'an 1556 dans les Églises des XIII. Cantons et des États confédérez qui composent avec eux L. Corps Helvetique, 6 vol, Geneva: n.p.

RODOCANACHI, E. (1896), Une Protectrice de la Réforme en Italie et en France, Renée de France, Duchesse de Ferrara, Paris: Paul Ollendorff.

ROTT, JEAN (1993), Jean Morély (ca. 1524–ca. 1594) et l'utopes d'une démocratie dans l'Église, Geneva: Librairie Droz.

ROYSTER, DMITRI (2008), St. Paul's Epistle to the Romans: A Pastoral Commentary, Crestwood, New York: St. Vladimir's Seminary Press.

SANTSCHI, CATHERINE (2007), Théodore de Bèze et les Bernois, in: Irena Backus (ed.), Théodore de Bèze (1519–1605): Actes du Colloque de Genève (septembre 2005), Geneva: Librairie Droz, 113–130.

SCHICKLER, F. DE (1892), Les Églises du Refuge en Angleterre, 3 vol., Paris: Fischbacher.

SCHREINER, SUSAN (2009), Creation and Providence, in: Herman J. Selderhuis (ed.), The Calvin Handbook, English ed., Grand Rapids, Mich.: Eerdmans, 267–275.

SCHULZE, MANFRED (2001), Martin Luther and the Church Fathers, in: Irena Backus (ed.), Reception of the Church Fathers in the West from the Carolingians to the Maurists, Leiden: Brill, 573–626.

SCRIBNER, ROBERT W. (1981), For the Sake of Simple Folk: Popular Propaganda for the German Reformation, Cambridge: Cambridge University Press.

SCRIVENER, FREDERICK (ed.) (2015), *Bezae Codex Cantabrigiensis*, Cambridge Library Collection, Cambridge: Cambridge University Press.

SHANNON-HENDERSON, K.E. (2019), Phlegon of Tralles (1667), Fragmente der griechischen Historiker Part IV and Brill Jacoby Online, Leiden: Brill, DOI: http: //dx.doi.org/10.1163/1873-5363_jciv_a1667.

SHEETS, R. A. (2012), Pierre Viret: The Angel of the Reformation, Tallahassee, Fl.: Zurich Publishing.

SKALNIK, JAMES (2002), Ramus and Reform: University and Church at the End of the Renaissance, Kirksville, Mo.: Truman State University.

SNOEKS, REMI (1951), L'argument de tradition dans la controverse eucharistique entre catholiques et réformés français au XVIIe siècle, Louvain: Publications Universitaires de Louvain.

SOERGEL, PHILIP (2012), Miracles and the Protestant Imagination: The Evangelical Wonderbook in Reformation Germany, Oxford: Oxford University Press.

SPEELMAN, HERMAN (2014), Calvin and the Independence of the Church, Albert Gootjes (trans.), Göttingen: Vandenhoeck & Ruprecht.

STEINMETZ, DAVID (1971), Reformers in the Wings: From Geiler von Kaysersberg to Theodore Beza, Philadelphia, Pa.: Fortress Press.

- (1991), Calvin and the Natural Knowledge of God, in: Heiko Oberman/Frank James (ed.), Via Augustini: Augustine in the Later Middle Ages, Renaissance, and Reformation, Essays in Honor of Damasus Trapp, O.S.A., Leiden: Brill, 142–156.

- (1995), Calvin in Context, New York: Oxford University Press.

- (ed.) (1999), Die Patristik in der Bibelexegese des 16. Jahrhunderts, Wiesbaden: Harrassowitz Verlag.

- (2001), Reformers in the Wings: From Geiler von Kaysersberg to Theodore Beza, 2nd ed., New York: Oxford University Press.

STOICHITA, VICTOR (2000), Brève histoire de l'ombre, Geneva: Librairie Droz.

STRYPE, JOHN (1718), The Life and Acts of the Most Reverend Father in God, 4 vol., London: T. Horne.

SUMMERS, KIRK (1991), Theodore Beza's Classical Library and Christian Humanism, ARG 82, 193–207.

- (2001), A View from the Palatine: The *Juvenilia* of Théodore de Bèze, Tempe, Ariz.: Arizona State University.

- (2018), Morality after Calvin: Theodore Beza's Christian Censor and Reformed Ethics, Oxford: Oxford University Press.

- (2018), Reformation Humanism: Reading the Classics in the New Theology, RRR 20.2, 134–154.

- (2020), Theodore Beza's 'Bare-Breasted Religion.' Liturgical Mystery and the English Vestments Controversy, in: Arnold Huijgen/Karin Maag (ed.), Calvinus frater in Domino. Papers of the Twelfth International Congress on Calvin Research, Göttingen: Vandenhoeck & Ruprecht, 337–351.

TATLOCK, JOHN (1914), Some Medieval Cases of Blood-Rain, Classical Philology 9, 442–447.

TAYLOR, CHARLES (2007), A Secular Age, Cambridge, Mass.: The Belknap Press.

THOMAS, G. MICHAEL (2000), Constructing and Clarifying the Doctrine of Predestination: Theodore Beza's Letters During, and in the Wake of, the

Bolsec Controversy (1551–1555), RRR 4, 7–28.

THOMPSON, NICHOLAS (2005), Eucharistic Sacrifice and Patristic Tradition in the Theology of Martin Bucer, 1534–1546, Boston, Mass.: Brill.

TIMMERMAN, DANIËL (2015), Heinrich Bullinger on Prophecy and the Prophetic Office (1523–1538), Göttingen: Vandenhoeck & Ruprecht.

VAN DEN BERG, MACHIEL (2006), Friends of Calvin, Reinder Bruinsma (trans.), Grand Rapids, Mich.: Eerdmans.

VAN RAALTE, THEODORE (2012), "Noster Theophilus": The Fictitious 'Printer' Whose Anti-Jesuit Volumes Issued from Various Presses in Geneva Between 1580 and 1589, BHR 74:3,569–591.

- (2018), Antoine de Chandieu: The Silver Horn of Geneva's Reformed Triumvirate, New York: Oxford University Press.

VISSER, ARNOUD (2011), Reading Augustine in the Reformation: The Flexibility of Intellectual Authority in Europe, 1500–1620, New York: Oxford University Press.

Voaden, Rosalynn (1999), God's Word, Women's Voices: The Discernment of Spirits in the Writing of Late-Medieval Women Visionaries, Rochester, NY: Boydell & Brewer.

VUARNET, EMILE (1913), Découverte d'une livre de 1598 relatif à la celebration des Quarante Heures de Thonon, Mémoires et Documents publiés par l'Académie Chablaisienne 26, 1–62.

VUILLEUMIER, HENRI (1927–33), Histoire de l'Église Réformée du Pays de Vaud sous le régime bernois, 4 vol., Lausanne: Éditions La Concorde.

WEBER, MAX (1989), The Protestant Ethic and the Spirit of Capitalism, Talcott Parsons (trans.), London: Unwin Hyman.

WEBSTER, RICHARD (1595), Why Freud was Wrong: Sin, Science, and Psychoanalysis, New York: HarperCollins.

WEISS, M. CHARLES (1854), History of the French Protestant Refugees: From the Revocation of the Edict of Nantes Until our Own Days, 2 vol., Henry W. Herbert (trans.), New York: Stringer & Townsend.

WENGERT, TIMOTHY J. (2012), Philip Melanchthon's 1557 Lecture on Colossians 3:1-2: Christology as Context for the Controversy over the Lord's Supper, in: Irene Dingel (ed.), Philip Melanchthon: Theologian in Classroom, Confession, and Controversy, Göttingen: Vandenhoeck and Ruprecht, 209–235.

WILSON, DUDLEY (1993), Signs and Portents: Monstrous Births from the Middle Ages to the Age of Enlightenment, London: Routledge.

WIRTH, JEAN (1848), La Réforme luthérienne et l'art, in: Jacques Marx/Michèle Mat (ed.), Luther mythe et réalité, Bruxelles, 1:21.

WOLFE, MICHAEL (2009), Exegesis and Public Performance: Controversialist Debate and Politics at the Conference at Fontainebleau (1600), in: Alison Forrestal/Eric Nelson (ed.), Politics and Religion in Early Bourbon France,

New York: Palgrave Macmillan, 65–85.

WRIGHT, JONATHAN (2005), The Jesuits: Missions, Myths, and Histories, London: Harper Perrenial.

WRIGHT, SHAWN (2004), Our Sovereign Refuge: The Pastoral Theology of Theodore Beza, Eugene, Ore: Wipf and Stock.

ZABADOS, BÉLA (1982), Freud, Self-Knowledge and Psychoanalysis, Canadian Journal of Philosophy 12.4, 691–707.

ZAGORIN, PERA (2006), How the Idea of Religious Toleration Came to the West, Princeton, N.J.: Princeton University Press.

Index

A

Aaron   216, 217
Abraham   159, 172, 212, 255
Adam   28, 147, 212, 229
adiaphora   105–109, 116, 122, 130, 133, 135
Admonition Controversy   113, 119, 125
Admonition to the Parliament   113, 114
Affair of the Placards   78
Albret, Jeanne d'   50, 89, 92, 95, 286, 319, 327
Albret, Queen Jeanne d'   170, 175
Ambrosiaster   207
Amport, Christian, Sr.   280
Amyraut, Moïse   306
Anabaptists   206, 209, 215, 284
analogy of faith   189
Andreae, Jakob   22, 180, 198, 233, 277
Anhalt, Georg von   318
Antichrist   18, 41, 42, 75, 118, 119, 128, 216, 290
Antitrinitarians   25, 215
Apostles' Creed   179
Aquinas, Thomas   207, 208, 297, 312
Aristotle   20, 21, 23, 24, 32, 33, 36, 143, 188, 315
Arius   180
ascension   177–181, 183, 184, 186, 187, 192–195, 197, 198, 201, 271, 303
astrologers   258
atheism   20, 249, 252, 293
Aubertin, Edme   305, 308, 313–316
Auger, Émond   271, 272, 277

Augsburg Confession   121, 179, 201
Augustine   15, 124, 131, 186, 190, 207, 212, 214, 221–223, 225, 228–238, 303, 308, 309, 313, 315, 316
Avully, Antoine de Saint Michel, Baron d'   286, 290–299, 317–321, 339

B

Bacon, Ann   119, 120, 134, 164
baptism   64, 105, 107, 115, 215, 277, 285, 311
Barnes, John   16
Bartas, Guillaume du   254
Barth, Karl   141, 147, 152, 155
Basel   37, 47, 79, 123, 249, 252, 253, 263, 269, 273, 274, 280, 285–287, 289, 336, 339
Basil the Great   310
Baume, Pierre de la   268, 271
Béarn   76, 92, 94, 175
Bellamine, Cardinal Robert   313
Bérauld, François   72
Bern   57–63, 69–71, 73, 75, 110, 160, 230, 274, 280
Béroald, Matthieu   89
Bertram, Corneille Bonaventure   169
Beza, Theodore
 – *Abraham Sacrifiant*   24, 160, 172
 – *Ad Acta Colloquii Montisbelgardensis*   223, 232, 233
 – *Ad acta Colloquii Montisbelgardensis Tubingae Edita*   223, 228

– *Ad calumnias brevis et necessaria responsio* 191
– *Ad Nicolai Selnecceri et Theologorum Ienensium calumnias* 182, 193–195
– *Apologia modesta et Christiana ad Acta Conventus quindecim theologicorum Torgae nuper habiti* 41
– *Apologia tertia* 191, 192
– as chaplain of Louis de Bourbon 102
– as chaplain of Navarre 86, 101, 266, 282
– as pastor 51
– birth 13, 77, 317
– *Chrestiennes meditations* 120
– *Commentary on Job* 124
– *Confessio Christianae fidei* 13, 107
– *Confessio christianae fidei* 238
– *Confession de la foi chrétienne* 119, 132
– *Confession de la foy Chrestienne* 111
– correspondents 38
– *De peste* 119
– *De Praedestinationis Doctrina* 232
– *De Triplici Episcopatu* 113, 116–119, 126, 129, 131, 133, 136
– *De veris et visibilis ecclesiae catholicae notis* 214–216
– dedication of NT *Annotationes* to Elizabeth I 103, 105
– *Emblemata* 14, 28, 244
– *Epistolae Theologicae* 109, 110, 113, 116, 119, 132
– *Epistolae theologicae* 35, 38
– false rumors of his conversion to Catholicism 284, 287

– fretting over his poetry 47
– friendships 30
– *Histoire Ecclésiastique* 57, 59, 70, 73, 74
– *Histoire ecclésiastique* 91, 92
– Houshold Prayers 17, 24
– humanism 13, 14, 23–26, 29, 47, 48, 52–54, 74, 79, 159, 161, 165, 221, 224, 252, 279, 315, 334, 340
– *Icones* 15, 28, 48, 101, 244, 245, 318, 321, 324, 326, 330–334, 336, 337, 339
– *La vie de Calvin* 119, 158, 205
– lectures on the Book of Job 281
– *Les vrais pourtraits* 18, 321, 325, 327, 335–337
– *Modesta et Christiana defensio* 184, 185, 190–194, 201
– New Testament annotations 14, 19, 23, 49, 50, 104, 106, 125, 132, 134, 139, 162–164, 166, 174, 182–184, 208, 214, 225, 228, 234–238, 256, 320
– on Greek philosophers 16, 20
– on pastoral qualifications 52
– *On the Correct Pronunciation of the French Language* 305
– *Petit catéchisme* 119
– *Poemata* 14, 24, 26–28, 125, 241, 244, 246, 247, 260, 320
– Psalms 40–42, 46, 48, 49, 119
– *Quaestiones et responsiones* 119
– *Response a la confession du feu duc Iean de Northumberland* 99
– *Response a La Lettre d'Un Gentilhomme Savoisien* 291, 293–298, 317, 318
– *Response aux cinq premiere et principals demandes de F. Iean*

Hay 214, 217, 218, 227, 228, 263–265, 269, 280

- *Response aux cinq premieres et principales demandes de F. Iean Hay* 214, 217, 218, 264, 271, 278, 279, 281
- *Right of Magistrates* 75
- *Saincts cantiques recueillis tant du Vieil que du Nouveau Testament* 134
- second wife Catherine del Piano 328
- *Sermons sur le Cantique of Cantiques* 52, 267, 280, 281
- *Sermons sur l'histoire de la passion* 52, 214, 215, 217, 293
- *Sermons sur l'histoire de la resurrection* 52, 53, 215, 216, 227
- *Summa Totius Christianismi* 230, 231
- *Tabula Praedestinationis* 100, 119, 158, 225, 230, 232, 234, 235
- *The judgment of a most reverend and learned man from beyond the seas concerning a threefold order of bishops* 117
- *Tractationes Theologicae* 228
- *Tractationes theologicae* 20, 21, 112, 230
- *Traité des vrayes, essencielles et visibles marques de la vraye église catholique* 287, 288
- use of harbor motif 14–16, 18, 28, 29, 53, 54, 105, 152

blasphemy 21, 181, 198, 276, 290, 293, 303

Bodley, John 100

Bolsec, Jerome 59, 70, 74, 158, 229–232, 236, 297

Book of Concord (1580) 121, 180, 198, 199

Bourbon, Louis de, Prince of Condé 86, 102, 103, 112, 136, 327

Bourse française 95

Bradford, William 174

Brenz, Johannes 148, 187, 208

Brunner, Emil 147, 155

Bucer, Martin 115, 148, 159, 172, 213, 218, 226, 332, 335

Buchanan, George 40, 45–48

Budé, Guillaume 315

Budé, Louis 80, 93, 162

Bugenhagen, Johann 148, 208

Bullinger, Heinrich 14, 31–40, 63, 71, 73, 75, 93, 94, 97–99, 105, 106, 109–113, 120, 127, 148, 159, 205, 218, 225, 229, 241, 248, 252, 273, 326–328, 332, 333

C

Cajetan, Thomas 148, 185, 312

Calvin, John 13, 14, 19, 28, 29, 54, 58, 63, 64, 73, 75, 78–85, 87, 90, 93–95, 100–103, 106, 115, 119, 120, 132, 140, 141, 143, 144, 147, 148, 151, 152, 154, 157–160, 162, 165, 167–174, 179, 184, 196, 201, 205, 206, 209–211, 213–219, 222, 226, 227, 229–232, 238, 242, 251, 257, 258, 264, 268–271, 276, 278, 283–286, 288–290, 297–299, 303, 305, 306, 310, 312, 315, 317–319, 321, 324, 325, 329–331, 333, 336, 338, 339

Cambridge 111, 114, 120, 125, 161–165

Camerarius, Joachim, the Elder 32, 47, 253–255, 334, 335

Camerarius, Joachim, the Younger 47, 333

Canons of Dort 306

Capito, Wolfgang 209, 335

Capuchins   277, 292, 296, 304
Cardinal of Lorraine   84, 248, 295
Cartwright, Thomas   111, 113–116,
   122, 125, 135, 164
Casimir, Jean   15, 16
Castellio, Sebastian   74, 162, 168,
   173, 184, 200, 285, 286, 289
Castol, Jean   117, 126, 128, 130, 134
Catherine de Medici   84, 85, 99
Cecil, Sir William   101–103, 112,
   116, 120, 122–124, 128, 132, 133,
   135, 164
ceremonies   104, 106–109, 122,
   130–133, 135
Chambéry   269, 272, 273, 279
Chambrun, Jacques Pineton de   267,
   276, 282
Chandieu, Antoine de   124, 130,
   132, 263, 265, 266, 270, 273–279,
   282
Charlemagne   171
Charles IX, King of France   32, 85,
   310
Charles V, Emperor   246, 247
Charpentier, Pierre   31, 32
Chemnitz, Martin   177–183, 191,
   195–200
Christ
   – real presence of in the Lord's
      Supper   178, 200, 312
   – sitting at the right hand of the
      Father   17, 178, 181, 185–187,
      190–192, 194
Chrysostom, St. John   144, 171, 186,
   194, 222, 226, 228, 271, 310
Church of England   104, 110, 125,
   126, 131, 133
Cicero   26, 30, 33, 193, 224, 228
circumcision   107, 311
Codex Bezae   159, 161–165
Codex Claromontanus   161

Coligny, Gaspard de   84, 85, 87, 89,
   92, 102, 259
Colladon, Nicolas   93, 158
Colloquy of Poissy   84, 86, 94, 99,
   101, 102, 226, 265, 269, 270, 284,
   285, 303
Company of Pastors   79
Company of Pastors, Geneva   33, 78,
   82, 83, 88, 89, 92, 95, 109, 116, 121,
   135, 157, 160, 168–170, 283–285,
   289–292, 294, 296, 298, 329
Complutensian Polyglot   160, 164
Conart, Valentin   307
Confession of Augsburg   84
confessionalization   168, 177
Consensus Tigurinus   70
Consistory   19
Constantinople   165
Cop, Nicolas   79
Council of Nicea   314
Council of Trent   112, 121, 123, 134,
   158, 161, 297, 304
Coverdale, Miles   100, 108, 109
Cramner, Thomas   328
Cranmer, Thomas   98, 101, 171, 174
Crespin, Jean   159, 162, 167, 175,
   241, 242, 245, 250
Crypto-Calvinists   41, 43, 177,
   198–200, 253
   – 1571 *Catechism*   177, 179–181,
      183, 197, 200
Cyril of Alexandria   312

D

Damascus, John of   186
Daneau, Lambert   132, 289
David, King   40, 43, 44, 123, 173,
   255, 259, 264
de l'Hôpital, Michel   84
Denosse, Claudine   80

discipline 34–36, 38, 57, 63, 64,
69–71, 73, 76, 89, 100, 104–106,
109–111, 113, 114, 116, 118, 121,
125–127, 129, 130, 132–135, 216,
219, 254
divine revelation 155, 207
Doctrinae Iesuiticae 266, 267, 275,
276, 278, 282
Drake, Sir Francis 121, 123
Dudith, André 20, 26, 27, 42, 45, 46,
110, 259, 263, 281
Dudley, John, Duke of Northumberland 98, 99
Dupuy, Clément 294, 295
Dürnhoffer, Lorenz 17, 18, 22, 23,
41–43, 46, 47, 120, 191, 196, 200,
201, 248, 249, 278, 334, 335

E
Eck, Johann 185
ecumenism 285
Edict of Nantes 163, 303, 304
Edward VI, King of England 98,
103
election 229, 233, 235, 236
Elizabeth I, Queen of England 20,
97–99, 101–106, 108–110, 112, 113,
116, 120–125, 131–136, 163, 175,
280
– upset with Geneva 101, 104
Emmanuel, Charles, Duke of Savoy
121, 266, 283
England's Reformation 97
Enoch 212
Epicureanism 116, 293
episcopal office 97, 105, 108, 110,
112–114, 116–119, 126, 128, 129,
131–134, 217, 268
Erasmus, Desiderius 140–142, 145,
148, 154, 160, 166, 183, 185, 192,
208, 222, 235, 237, 238, 310

Erastus, Thomas 127–131, 255, 259
Estius, Guilielmus 208
Étienne, Henri 163, 166, 168
Étienne, Robert 40, 160–168, 273,
280, 339
Eucharist
– See Lord's Supper 37
excommunication 34, 110, 114, 118,
127
extraordinary vocation 218

F
Fabricius, Constantin 121, 169, 170
fall of mankind 27, 28, 147, 229,
236
fall, noetic effects of 28, 140, 141,
144, 147–149, 151–153
Farel, Guillaume 79, 80, 94, 99, 108,
109, 162, 210, 268, 269, 298
Faucheur, Michel Le 305–314, 316
Faye, Antoine de la 135, 265, 281,
291, 294, 296
Field, John 113–115, 126, 129
Fontaine, Étienne de la 89, 122, 126,
134, 172
Fontainebleau, Conference at 303,
304
Formula of Concord 21, 22, 177,
178, 181, 185, 191, 195, 198–200
Francis I 82, 162, 246, 247, 318
Frankfurt Book Fair 169
French Geneva Bible 159, 167, 169,
170, 172, 173, 175
Freud, Sigmund 141, 150, 151, 154
Freudian, Sigmund 147, 151, 152,
154
Fribourg 264, 266, 269, 273, 274,
276, 280, 282

G

Gallars, Nicolas Des   77–96, 305
Gasgneux, Jean le   33
Gaurico, Luca   253
Geneston, Mathieu de   78, 79
Genevan Academy   13, 24, 33, 54,
  80, 83, 100, 111, 119, 160, 164, 169,
  224, 228, 229, 265, 267, 280, 288,
  305, 318, 328, 329, 339
Gentile, Valentino   16
Gilpin, John   111, 135
Giovio, Paolo   336, 339
Glamis, Lord   117, 118, 126
glorification   194, 195
Gnesio-Lutherans   41–43, 177, 178,
  181, 184, 185, 187, 191, 192, 198,
  200, 201
Goliath   123
Goodman, Christopher   100, 105,
  106, 122
Goulart, Simon   254, 292, 321
Greek Philosophers   29
Gregory of Nazianzus   310
Gregory of Nyssa   315
Gregory the Great   207, 208
Grindal, Edmund   87, 91, 106–108,
  112, 113, 115, 116, 126, 132, 135
Grumbach, Argula von   205
Grynaeus, Johann Jakob   47, 123,
  124, 126, 127, 249, 256, 259, 263,
  273, 277, 278, 280, 281, 287, 336,
  337
Guillaume IV of Hesse, The Land-
  grave   195, 201
Guise, Francis de, Duke   103, 170,
  277
Gwalther, Rudolf   15, 22, 23, 31, 34,
  37, 39, 42, 47, 50, 109, 113, 120,
  121, 126, 208, 249, 251, 273, 279,
  282, 327, 331, 332, 335

H

Hardesheim, Christopher   39, 46, 47,
  121
Harmonia confessionum fidei   121
Hastings, Henry   43, 45, 48, 119, 134
Hay, John   217, 227, 228, 263–267,
  270, 271, 273–282, 284, 288, 289,
  293, 295–297
Henri II, Duke de Montmorency
  307
Henri III   251, 277, 280
Henri IV, King of France   175, 280,
  286, 287, 289, 295, 298, 299, 303,
  327
Henri, King of Navarre   50, 88, 89,
  124, 136, 266, 277, 282, 287
Henri, Prince of Condé   289
Henry II   82
Hexaglot   165
Hoffman, Daniel   279
Holy Spirit   44, 123, 171, 184, 197,
  198, 209, 215, 311
Hooper, John   98, 101
Hotman, François   37
Huguenots   17, 31, 33, 84, 86, 102,
  103, 124, 136, 169, 170, 173, 248,
  254, 259, 270–272, 277, 283, 287,
  289, 303–305
humanism   225
Humphrey, Laurence   100, 108, 109
Hus, Jan   205, 216, 331
hypostatic union   194, 195

I

idolatry   110, 147, 210, 211, 297

J

James VI, King of Scotland   15, 45,
  48, 118, 120, 318, 319, 336
Jansenists   313, 316
Jaquemot, Jean   24–26, 169

Jena, University of 180, 200
Jerome 59, 131, 140, 141, 145, 171, 185, 207, 222, 225, 226, 228, 229, 290, 297
Jesuit 123, 217, 227, 263–277, 279, 280, 282, 284, 288, 289, 293–297
Jesuits 127, 201, 251, 263, 265, 267, 269–282, 289, 291–295, 297, 304, 318
Junius, Franciscus 164, 169, 194, 306
Justinian 171

K

Kirchner, Timothy 196, 198, 199
Knox, John 100, 101, 104–106, 116, 122, 205, 209, 218, 264
– *First Blast of the Trumpet* 101, 104
Krafftheim, Johannes Crato von 15, 19, 33, 53, 54, 250, 257

L

Lanfranc of Bec 208
Lasco, Johannes à 98
Latimer, Hugh 101
Laurent de Normandie 78–80, 93, 159
Lausanne 57, 58, 60–64, 69–76, 80, 81, 98, 100, 160, 205, 229, 230, 241, 274, 288
Lavater, Ludwig 273
Lawson, James 15
Lect, Jacques 26, 124, 130
Leyser, Polycarp 196
Libertinism 284
Lombard, Peter 208, 225
London 16, 37, 83, 84, 86, 87, 101, 103, 106, 108, 111–114, 116, 119, 122, 124, 126–128, 130, 132, 134, 136, 147, 254, 333

Lord's Supper 21, 42, 51, 53, 61, 63–65, 70, 71, 74, 78, 81, 84, 105–107, 110, 158, 177–184, 186–190, 192, 195, 196, 198–201, 269, 277, 285, 288, 291, 303–305, 307, 308, 312–314, 316, 366
– Christ's real presence in 42, 178, 183, 184, 186, 188, 190, 198, 291, 312, 314
Luther, Martin 13, 148, 157, 172, 177–183, 185, 188, 189, 192, 193, 197, 200, 201, 205, 212, 218, 222, 250, 253, 330, 339
Lutherans 21, 22, 40–43, 84, 121, 148, 177–185, 187–189, 191, 192, 194–196, 198–201, 218, 233, 250, 263, 267, 277, 279, 280, 292, 334, 339, 340
L'Estoile, Pierre 307
Lycosthenes 252, 253, 255
Lyon 117, 161, 162, 241, 242, 244, 245, 255, 264, 269, 271, 272, 283
Lyon, John 117, 118

M

Macard, Jean 82
Maçon, Robert Le 89, 122
Malliet, Jean 122
Marburg Colloquy 178, 179, 189
Marburg, Colloquy of 178, 179, 188, 189
Marian Exiles 100, 166
Marot, Clement 172, 264
martyrs 29, 32, 37, 99, 103, 110, 194, 241, 242, 244–246, 250, 254, 255, 258
Mary I, Queen of England 97, 98, 100, 101, 103, 105, 122, 124
Mary Stuart 112
Mary, mother of Jesus 192
Mary, Queen of Scots 280

Mayflower   174
Melanchthon, Philipp   20, 41, 148, 178–180, 196, 200, 212, 222, 226, 250, 253, 326, 328
Melville, Andrew   111, 117, 126
Methuen, Paul   264
Mildmay, Walter   20, 21, 23, 111, 112
Mohammed   180, 190
Möller, Heinrich   15, 20, 41
monergism vs synergism   231
Montbéliard   232, 277
Montpellier   290
Morély, Jean   34–36, 75, 88, 89, 94, 95, 219
Mornay, Philippe du Plessis-   15, 277, 303, 304, 308, 314, 315
Moses   212, 213, 216, 315
Moulin, Pierre du   305, 306
Musculus, Wolfgang   143, 145, 146, 148, 213, 277, 317, 318, 321, 325–328

N
Navarre, House of   286
Nérac   83
Nestorius   180
Nicodemism   210, 284
Nîmes   34, 87, 94, 267, 274–276, 288, 304, 306
Noah   17, 212, 250
Noue, François de la   250

O
Obsequens, Julius   252, 253
Oecolampadius, Johannes   148, 178, 208, 214, 218
Olevianus, Caspar   127, 143, 146–148, 208, 258, 259
Oporinus, Johannes   252
Origen   226, 310, 312

Orléans   13, 78, 79, 87–92, 103, 157, 320
orthodoxy   21, 22, 27, 30, 41, 232, 237, 285

P
Palmer, Sir Thomas   99
Paludius   15, 337
Paris   30, 32, 33, 35, 77, 79–84, 157, 159, 162, 168, 228, 246, 247, 251, 263, 283, 287, 288, 294, 295, 304, 306, 307, 320, 327, 328, 339
Parker, Matthew   104, 105, 161, 162, 164
Pays de Vaud   58, 63, 69, 70, 74, 76
Pelagianism   223
Pelikan, Konrad   148, 208, 252
Pentecost   216, 256
Perkins, William   206
Perron, Cardinal Jacques-Davy Du Perron   287, 303, 304, 307–314, 316
Perrot, Charles   169
Peucer, Gaspard   41, 179, 252
Pezel, Christoph   179
Philippists   41, 179–181
Phoenix   243–245
Pilgrims   174
Pinelli, Luca   263
Pius V, Pope   112
plague   51, 87, 268, 288, 296
Plato   27–29, 143, 193
Polanus, Amandus   306
Polycarp   196, 245
polyglot Bibles   160, 166, 173
Porto, Francesco   31, 32
Possevino, Antonio   272
Prayer Book   113, 114, 125, 174
prayers to the dead   319
predestination   58, 61, 63, 70, 158, 223, 228–231, 233–235, 277, 340

presbyterian polity   97, 100, 108, 110, 113, 114, 117–119, 126–129, 131, 132, 134–136
Preux, Jean le   46, 276, 278
prophecy   27, 29, 33, 34, 36, 205–214, 216–219, 255, 256, 259, 320
Prugner, Nocolaus   209
Psalms   20, 40–48, 102, 162, 172–175, 210, 245, 255, 264
Puritan   87, 97, 104, 108–113, 115, 116, 119, 122, 125, 126, 129, 130, 132, 164
Puritans   104, 108, 111, 114, 115, 119, 125, 128–130, 132, 134, 164

R
Ramus, Pierre   21, 31–38, 40
Regius, Theophilus   266, 267
reprobation   230, 233, 235
resurrection   52, 53, 215, 216, 244
Richelieu, Cardinal   306, 307
Ridley, Nicholas   101
Rihel, Josias   46
Rosier, Hugues Sureau, called du   88–90
Rotan, Jean-Baptiste   169
Rüdinger, Esrom   44, 182, 200

S
sacramentarian disputes   41, 187, 190
Sacramentarians   181, 187, 190, 196, 198, 199
Sales, France de   286, 290, 291
Sampson, Thomas   100, 108–111, 135
Sandys, Edwyn   113, 114
Saravia, Adrian   97, 117, 127–131, 133, 134, 217
Savanarola, Girolamo   205

Savoy   14, 121, 122, 124, 125, 130, 135, 136, 265, 266, 268, 272, 276, 277, 279, 283, 285, 286, 290, 293, 297
Saxony   41, 44, 180
Schegk, Jacob   279
Schlüsselberger, Gabriel   248, 249
Scholasticism   20–23, 158, 232, 275, 279
Schwenckfeld, Kaspar   178
Second Admonition to Parliament   114
Selnecker, Nicholas   22, 177, 178, 180, 182–195, 198, 200, 201
Serres, Jean de   27, 28, 263, 265, 267, 273, 275, 276, 278, 279, 282, 288–290, 292, 297–299
Servetus, Michael   285
Simler, Josias   25, 26, 39, 331, 332
sola scriptura   304
Spanish Armada   121, 123, 124
Sponde, Jean de   286–289, 292, 298, 299
St. Bartholomew's Day Massacre   31, 37, 93, 121, 159, 170, 248, 259
Stafford, William   100
Stammich, Georg   196
studia humanitatis
  – see humanism   224
Stumpf, Johannes   123, 273, 280
superstitions   106, 107, 110, 147
Sutcliffe, Matthew   97, 127, 129, 131, 133
Synod of La Rochelle   34, 92, 170
synod of Nîmes   36
Syriac version   164, 166, 171, 185, 186, 193, 194, 305, 312

T
textus receptus   166
Thalmann, Benedict   43, 44

Theodoret 208, 312
Thirty-Nine Articles 125
Thretius, Christoph 26, 44
Throckmorton, Sir Nicholas 101–103
Tillet, Louis du 210
Torgau Articles 40, 41, 180, 181, 200
Torres, Francisco 263, 274, 275
Tournon 265, 269–273, 275, 285
Toussain, Daniel 22, 201
transubstantiation 303, 308
Travers, Walter 111, 114–116, 122, 126, 129, 135
Treaty of Hampton Court 102
Treaty of Nemours 276, 277
Tremellius, Immanuel 164, 166, 169, 194
Tronchin Family 57–59, 61, 63, 64, 71–74, 165, 305, 306, 308, 320, 324, 325, 327–331
Tronchin, Théodore 305
Turks 253, 291, 296

U
ubiquitarianism 187
Ubiquitarians 20, 263
University of Orléans 78, 79
Ursinus, Zacharias 132, 146, 177

V
Van Til, Thomas 51
Vergil 48, 245
Vermigli, Peter Martyr 71, 73, 85, 98, 115, 143, 145–148, 152, 189, 205, 206, 212–214, 217–219, 226, 228, 245, 257, 269, 317, 318, 321, 331–335
Vestments Controversy 97, 104–106, 109, 110, 112, 132, 135
Vézelay 13, 77, 317

Vignon, Eustache 266, 267, 280, 282
Villiers, Pierre Loiseleur de 16
Viret, Pierre 57, 58, 60, 62–65, 69–73, 75, 76, 80, 81, 83, 92, 94, 95, 108, 109, 160, 205, 242, 269, 271, 272, 298
vocation 30, 47, 89, 211, 218, 219
vocations
– extraordinary 215, 217
Vossius, Isaac 48, 49
Vulgate 139–142, 145, 154, 161, 162, 165, 183, 185, 235

W
Walsingham, Francis 121, 122
Wars of Religion 86, 87, 91, 102, 103, 112, 162, 169, 266, 277, 283, 303
Weber, Max 251
Whitgift, John 114–117, 124–135
– *The Defence of the Answer to the Admonition* 115
Whittingham, William 100, 111, 174
Wiburn, Perceval 100, 108, 109, 111, 135
Wilcox, Thomas 113–115
William of Orange, Prince 279
William of St. Thierry 207
Wingfield, Anthony 120, 165
Wittenberg 20, 41, 44, 177, 179–183, 195, 196, 200, 253
Wittenberg theologians 177, 180
Wittgenstein, Ludwig 129, 169
Wolffhart, Konrad 252
Wolmar, Melchior 13, 14, 19, 23, 30, 78, 80, 157, 224, 225, 237, 326, 334
Words of Institution 196
Wyclif, John 216

Y

Young, Peter   15, 42, 45, 47

Z

Zanchi, Girolamo   22
Zastrisell the Elder   14–16, 19, 50
Zastrisell the Younger   16, 337
Zastrisell, Georges Sigismond de   25
Zébédée, André   59, 61, 70, 74
Zell, Katharina Schütz   205

Zell, Matthew   209, 218
Zurich   14, 22, 25, 31, 32, 34–39, 47, 97, 98, 100, 101, 105, 108, 109, 111, 113, 189, 259, 266, 273, 274, 318, 331–333
Zwingli   70, 180
Zwingli, Huldrych   31, 148, 178, 188, 205, 206, 209, 211, 212, 218, 219, 226, 332
Zwinglians   196

Notes on Contributors

Jon Balserak is Senior Lecturer at the University of Bristol (England)

Michael Bruening is Associate Professor of History at Missouri Science and Technology University

Molly Buffington Lackey is a doctoral candidate at St. Louis University

Max Engammare is an independent scholar and the senior editor of Librairie Droz (Geneva)

Jill Fehleison is Professor of History at Quinnipiac University

Eunjin Kim is a doctoral candidate at Duke University

Martin Klauber is Affiliate Professor at Trinity Evangelical Divinity School

Scott Manetsch is Professor of Church History and the History of Christian Thought at Trinity Evangelical Divinity School

David Noe is Professor of Classics at Calvin University

Jeannine Olson is Professor of History at Rhode Island College

Jennifer Powell McNutt is Associate Professor in Biblical and Theological Studies at Wheaton College

Kirk Summers is Professor of Classics at the University of Alabama

Theodore Van Raalte is Professor of Ecclesiology at Canadian Reformed Theological Seminary